MORE THAN WORDS

MORE THAN WORDS

Readings in Transport, Communication and the History of Postal Communication

Edited by John Willis

MERCURY SERIES
CANADIAN POSTAL MUSEUM PAPER 5
CANADIAN MUSEUM OF CIVILIZATION

Published by the
Canadian Museum of Civilization Corporation
100 Laurier Street
P.O. Box 3100, Station B
Gatineau, Quebec J8X 4H2

Manager, Publishing: Deborah Brownrigg
Coordinator, Publishing: Rosemary Nugent
Editors: Wendy McPeake, Pierre Cantin
Mercury Series Design: Hangar 13
Production Artist: RLDesign
Printer: Delta Printing
Front cover photograph: A Canadian airman from 430 Squadron writes a letter in wartime England (detail). Painted in 1943 by official war artist Eric Aldwinckle. Beaverbrook Collection of War Art, ©Canadian War Museum, AN19710261–1300
Back cover photographs: Top: Postcard dated November 6, 1928, sent from Val Morin to Montréal (Private Collection) *Bottom:* Kenneth Edgard Clayton-Kennedy writes a letter to loved ones at home in Canada (Canadian War Museum, 19900346–32)

Library and Archives Canada Cataloguing in Publication

More than words : readings in transport, communication and the history of postal communication / John Anthony Willis, editor.

(Mercury series)
(Paper / Canadian Postal Museum 5)
Includes bibliographical references.
Includes abstract in French.

ISBN 978-0-660-19696-1
Cat. no.: NM28-1/5E

1. Postal service—History.
2. Communication and traffic—History.
3. Letter writing—History.
I. Willis, John, 1954–
II. Canadian Museum of Civilization
III. Canadian Postal Museum
IV. Title: Readings in transport, communication and the history of postal communication.
V. Series.
I. Series: Paper (Canadian Postal Museum) no. 5

HE6055.M67 2007   383'.49   C2007-980032-7

Object of the Mercury Series
This series is designed to permit the rapid dissemination of information pertaining to the disciplines in which the Canadian Museum of Civilization Corporation is active. Considered an important reference by the scientific community, the Mercury Series comprises over 400 specialized publications on Canada's history and prehistory. Due to its specialized audience, the series consists largely of monographs published in the language of the author. In the interest of making information available quickly, normal production procedures have been abbreviated. As a result, grammatical and typographical errors may occur. Your indulgence is requested.

But de la collection Mercure
La collection Mercure vise à diffuser rapidement le résultat de travaux dans les disciplines qui relèvent des sphères d'activités du Musée canadien des civilisations. Considérée comme un apport important dans la communauté scientifique, la collection Mercure présente plus de 400 publications spécialisées portant sur l'héritage canadien préhistorique et historique. Comme la collection s'adresse à un publique spécialisé, celle-ci est constituée essentiellement de monographies publiées dans la langue des auteurs. Pour assurer la prompte distribution des exemplaires imprimés, les étapes de l'édition ont été abrégées. En conséquence, certaines coquilles ou fautes de grammaire peuvent subsister: c'est pourquoi nous réclamons votre indulgence.

How to Obtain Mercury Series Titles

E-mail: publications@civilization.ca
Web: cyberboutique.civilization.ca
Telephone: 1 819 776-8387 or, toll-free in North America only, 1 800 555-5621
Mail: Mail Order Services
              Canadian Museum of Civilization
              100 Laurier Street
              P.O. Box 3100, Station B
              Gatineau, Quebec J8X 4H2

Comment se procurer les titres parus dans la collection Mercure

Courriel :   publications@civilisations.ca
Web :   cyberboutique.civilisations.ca
Téléphone :   1 819 776-8387 ou sans frais, en Amérique du Nord seulement, 1 800 555-5621
Poste :   Service des commandes postales
              Musée canadien des civilisations
              100, rue Laurier
              C.P. 3100, succursale B
              Gatineau (Québec) J8X 4H2

Canadä

TABLE OF CONTENTS
TABLE DES MATIÈRES

List of Figures/Liste des illustrations ix
Preface/Préface 1

Introduction/Introduction
John Willis 3

PART ONE: The Post
PREMIÈRE PARTIE : Le système postal

**1 : Le réseau de communications postales durant le régime français :
Le réseau officiel**
Bernard Allaire 19

**2: "Agitators of the Worst Type": Riot and Occupation at the
Vancouver Post Office, 1938**
Duncan Stacey 35

3: One Hundred Years of Postal Processing in Canada
Krista Cooke 53

4: September 11, 2001: Collecting and Exhibiting a National Tragedy
Nancy A. Pope 71

**5: Testing the Boundaries of Postal Enterprise in the U.S. Free-market
Economy, 1880–1920**
Richard Kielbowicz 85

**6: The History and Geography of the Post Office on Prince Edward
Island, 1870–1914**
John Willis 101

PART TWO: Epistolary Practice and Culture
DEUXIÈME PARTIE : Pratiques et culture épistolaires

**7 : Une industrie de la plume d'oie : les pennes de la Compagnie de
la Baie d'Hudson**
Bianca Gendreau 127

8 : Sous le sceau du secret – Correspondance chiffrée en Nouvelle-France pendant la guerre de Sept Ans
Nicole Castéran 141

9 : S'écrire au XIXe siècle en France – Histoire d'une acculturation
Cecile Dauphin-Memeteau et Danièle Poublan. 159

10: "From a Fine Pen Much Art and Fancy Flows": Letter Writing and Gentility in Early New England
Sheila McIntyre 173

PART THREE: People and Their Letters
TROISIÈME PARTIE : Les gens et leurs missives

11: The Immigrant Experience and the Creation of a Transatlantic Epistolary Space: A Case Study
Yves Frenette and Gabriele Scardellato 189

12 : La vie familiale d'un administrateur colonial : Herman Witsius Ryland
Lorraine Gadoury 203

13 : Liaisons épistolaires illégitimes entre l'abbé Casgrain et l'Irlandaise Kate E. Godley
Manon Brunet 215

14 : Correspondance d'un immigrant français au Canada au début du XXe siècle
Marguerite Sauriol. 233

15: Wartime Correspondence: Living, Loving, and Leaving through Letters During the Two World Wars
Liz Turcotte 251

16: A Timeless Experience? Perceptions of Two Educated German Immigrants to the United States, 1863 to 1996
Susanne C. Knoblauch. 267

PART FOUR: Communication and Transport
QUATRIÈME PARTIE : Communications et moyens de transport

17: Instructions from Terra Nova: Aspects of Communication in the Sixteenth-Century Fishery
Brad Loewen 285

18 : La filière morutière normano-bretonne : Capitaines et habitants pêcheurs de l'île Scatarie (1714–1754)
Jean-Pierre Chrestien 299

19: A Distant Shore: Steamer Mail to and from Gold-Rush California
Marianne Babal 321

20: "A Living, Moving Pageant": The CBC's Coverage of the Royal Tour of 1939
Mary Vipond 335

21 : Transporter le Canada à l'étranger : Les militaires canadiens à travers le monde, de 1945 à 1975
Jean Martin 351

Epilogue
Meg Ausman 363

LIST OF FIGURES
LISTE DES ILLUSTRATIONS

Introduction

Figure 1   "Votre correspondant attend", Écrivez
Your correspondant awaits you: Write now 8

PART ONE

Figure 1.1   La côte maritime entre Rochefort et La Rochelle 21
Figure 1.2   La côte maritime de l'estuaire de la Seine 22
Figure 1.3   Schéma des principaux ports d'arrivée des correspondances officielles en
provenance du Canada 23

Figure 2.1   Main Post Office at Hastings and Granville Streets, Vancouver, 1935 36
Figure 2.2   Protesters sleeping inside the post office 40
Figure 2.3   Evacuation of sit-down strikers from the Post Office, June 19, 1938 43

Figure 3.1   Post office clerks in the sorting area of the Toronto post office, ca 1913 56
Figure 3.2   Advertisement of the publicity campaign to promote public usage of
the postal code 61
Figure 3.3   A bold reminder that automation had a negative impact on labour
relations 62
Figure 3.4   Poster published by Canada Post showing the route taken by a letter in
a modern postal plant 64

Figure 4.1   U.S. postal hand cancellation stamp from the Church Street post office,
New York City, New York 75
Figure 4.2   U.S. letter carrier Emma Thornton examining her sorting table unit at
the National Postal Museum 78
Figure 4.3   Sorting table unit recovered from the Church Street post office, New York
City, New York 79

Figure 5.1   Cartoon that appeared just weeks after the start of parcel post in
the U.S. 91

Figure 6.1   Post offices on Prince Edward Island, 1880 109
Figure 6.2   Post offices in the neighbourhood of Cavendish 110
Figure 6.3   Village of Campbellton on the east coast of P.E.I., 1880 113
Figure 6.4   Plan of Tignish, 1880 116
Figure 6.5   Post offices in Lot 1, 1880 118

PART TWO

Figure 7.1   Carte d'affaires de Christopher Henry Edwards, vers 1760   128

Figure 8.1   Lettre chiffrée de Vaudreuil au ministre de la Marine   147
Figure 8.2   Section de la table chiffrante du code du ministère de la Guerre entre
Montcalm et le ministre d'Argenson (1757)   148

Figure 9.1   Lithographie de Gavarni parue dans le journal humoristique *Le Charivari*,
le 11 septembre 1837   165

Figure 10.1 John Fearing's copybook   175
Figure 10.2 John Fearing's copybook   177
Figure 10.3 John Fearing's copybook   179

PART THREE

Figure 11.1 Picture from Bennedsen's Danish passport, April 12, 1956.   190
Figure 11.2 The new and old homes of Danish Immigrant Christian Bennedsen   191
Figure 11.3 Aerogramme destined for Denmark, July 1, 1954   195

Figure 12.1 Portrait de Herman Witsius Ryland   205
Figure 12.2 Armoiries de George H. Ryland   207

Figure 13.1 Lady Kate E. Godley, Montréal (Québec), 1864   216
Figure 13.2 Le Villa Bagatelle, sise en marge de Spencer Wood   220

Figure 14.1 Brochure de promotion de l'Ouest canadien, en 1900   235
Figure 14.2 Carte des environs de Red Deer, vers 1909   238

Figure 15.1 Kenneth Edgard Clayton-Kennedy, who served in the RCAF during
World War One, finds a quiet spot to write a letter   252
Figure 15.2 Sketch based on a photograph of Margaret Edith Alston Rutherford
Scythes from a scrapbook kept by Freddie Scythes   261

Figure 16.1 Diagram of family and friends corresponding with Carl or mentioned
in his letters   272
Figure 16.2 *Racism*, collage by Gauri Vengurlekar, Architect, Santa Fe, New Mexico   277
Figure 16.3 *Fast Food*, collage by Gauri Vengurlekar, Architect, Santa Fe, New Mexico   279

PART FOUR

Figure 17.1 The transatlantic fishery in the 16th century 288

Figure 18.1 *Le Canada, ou Nouvelle France*, par Nicolas Sanson d'Abbeville, 1656 303
Figure 18.2 Détail montrant l'île *Scatarie* avec le Cap-Breton, Terre-Neuve et le golfe
Saint-Laurent 303
Figure 18.3 Plan ou toisé de la grave de l'île Pontchartrain, vers 1714 305
Figure 18.4 L'île Scatarie et l'île *La Tremblade* (Hay Island) 306
Figure 18.5 Les habitants de l'île Scatarie et leurs familles (1716-1753) 307
Figure 18.6 Pêcheurs, chaloupes et bateaux de pêche à l'île Scatarie (1716-1753) 310
Figure 18.7 Navires forains de pêche ou de commerce à Scatarie (1716-1753) 312

Figure 19.1 Early communications routes to the Pacific prior to 1869 323
Figure 19.2 "Arrival of a Steamship," from *The Annals of San Francisco*, published
in 1855 324
Figure 19.3 Letter addressed to Major General Ethan Allen Hitchcock in New York 327
Figure 19.4 Letter delivered to Stockton California by Reynolds & Co.'s Express 328

Figure 20.1 King George VI delivers a radio broadcast on Empire Day, May 24, 1939 336
Figure 20.2 Eaton's Catalogue, Fall/Winter 1927–1928, cover 342

Figure 21.1 Les grands déploiements militaires canadiens entre 1950 et 1970 352
Figure 21.2 L'avion long-courrier Yukon, construit spécialement pour les Forces
canadiennes 355

Epilogue
Figure 1 Stamp commemorating Mercury, winged messenger of the gods, 1930 368

PREFACE
PRÉFACE

Walking has long for me been an enjoyable mode of reflection. Enjoyment has become necessity since my acquisition of a black lab named Rocket. We follow an itinerary that leads through a wooded stretch and skirts the perimeter of a golf course before doubling back to our original entrance into the bush. We have a little routine. Rocket strays behind, I tap the side of my thigh and call his name, or whistle, and he comes running, bolting well in advance. He then becomes the leader, sniffing snow tracks and what-have-you, grasping at any interesting looking branch or piece of information. My control over the dog, who throughout is off his leash, is relative. Obedience is entirely based upon his consent. Any sense of discipline is cast to the wind when an intruder appears: a hiker and/or another dog. Then I become peripheral to the exchange that follows a course set by the two that Konrad Lorenz would have far less trouble understanding than I do. In hot pursuit of his impulses, Rocket pushes on ahead with or without me, although I usually succeed in drawing him back once the excitement of a close encounter is over.

For humans as for dogs, the desire to communicate is integral to our being. Elle est incontournable, voire-même implacable la communication, mais elle est aussi source d'émerveillement. We look at the stars, consider the lilies, with the ultimate purpose of telling someone about what we have discerned. The eyes alone are engaged first, but not for long, once the tongue rolls over and the telling begins. Ce livre est donc œuvre de communication qui relate… la communication.

I would like to thank my supervisors, Francine Brousseau and Chantal Amyot for their ongoing support, Deborah Brownrigg of CMC Publishing for shepherding production along; Marguerite Sauriol for invaluable assistance, and Wendy McPeake and Pierre Cantin for their careful editing of the manuscript. And, to all the authors who worked so very hard to get their texts in and collaborated so professionally with the editing team, Merci! The black-and-white pen sketches distributed here and there about the book are the work of artist Madelaine Lachance. Her wings will help carry the message, "au chant de l'alouette." This work is dedicated to Sylvie, Vanessa, Dave and Chuck; to my mother who did everything with a passion, and my father whose memory still moves this beating heart.

John Willis
Fall 2006

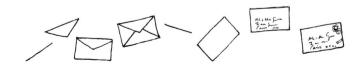

INTRODUCTION[1]

John Willis, Historian, Canadian Postal Museum, Canadian Museum of Civilization

In 1991, I began working at the Canadian Postal Museum, and a year later I became a historian there. Shortly after I started, I met with a colleague from a history department, who, upon learning of my appointment, queried me in a doubtful tone: "Postal history, what is postal history?" While for some, a job is a justification in and of itself, it does seem some answer is in order. The present book is one part of an inevitably protracted answer to this question.

In 1997, the Canadian Postal Museum published its second work on the history of the post since it was integrated to the Canadian Museum of Civilization. (The first had examined the history of the railway mail service in Canada.[2]) The second work, by Jane Harrison, focused on the colonial mails in Canada, primarily in New France and Upper Canada and Lower Canada, up to 1820.[3] The thrust of Harrison's work was the reconstruction of the post as a medium of communication by rereading old collections of public and private correspondence and piecing together the elements that might allow us to better understand the operation of the post at this point in time. The work, eventually followed by a doctoral thesis, was meticulous and groundbreaking for it allowed readers to perceive the operation of what was largely a system of informal arrangements.[4] There was no formal postal system at the time of New France, and the informal system of interpersonal conveyance of mail outside the postal system was still quite popular during the early years of the British regime. One might be well-advised to describe this communication in terms of myriad postal networks rather than a single postal system at least during the era of New France. Striking indeed was the personal investment of a colonial letter writer in the conveyance of his or her mail.

In 1999, two postal history sessions were organized at the annual meeting of the Canadian Historical Association. One focused on letters: epistolary and material culture. The other session examined the postal system and its early manifestations in the Red River area, the functional and iconic role of the post, and mid–nineteenth century reform. It was clear that two streams of work were emerging in the field. One stream examined the post as institution or service, with its enabling legislation, workforce, social impact,

3

etc. The other approached the subject through the art and culture of letter writing and correspondence exchange.

Initially, the Museum focused on the postal service, particularly the rural postal service. A research report was prepared for an exhibit, a revised version of which was eventually published as *Country Post: Rural Postal Service in Canada, 1880 to 1945.*[5] During the late nineteenth and early twentieth centuries, the Post Office department functioned as a government institution providing a wide variety of services, but it was also shaped by the manner in which it was used by the Canadian rural public. The Canadian rural postal experience was a "top-down" and "bottom-up" affair: The government was in charge of the system, yet the system was responsive to the needs of the average citizen.

Scholars focusing on the same time period used the postal vantage point to address other questions. Philippe Garvie examined postal data as a means of studying centrality (metropolitanism) in New Brunswick.[6] The central focus of communication in New Brunswick was not located in the most populous city of the province, but was situated along a more diffuse axis running between Saint John and Shédiac through Moncton. Grégoire Teyssier studied the role of the postal service in the emergence of the daily press in Quebec during the late nineteenth century.[7] The post was a *sine qua non* of distribution in the newspaper business, responsible for, in some instances, up to 80 per cent of circulation, although, in 1911, there were regions—rural and peripheral (the Gaspésie among them)—that were still relatively untouched by postal service. Furthermore, publishers began turning to private messenger systems to distribute an increasing percentage of their newspapers, especially during 1880 to 1910.[8]

Brian Osborne has written a good deal on the history of the postal service, including the rural postal service.[9] He has published his research in numerous articles and opened up the field considerably; the geographic approach to a system predicated on transport and spatial networking has been especially helpful. The central argument laid out in "Lowering the Walls of Oblivion" is persuasive:

> The development of a mass postal system [in Canada from 1850 to 1911] constituted a revolution in communications. First and foremost it facilitated private interpersonal communications as well as making messages from a greater variety of organizational sources more accessible. Easily accessible postal communications were thus widely perceived by more and more individuals and organizations to be a necessary public amenity of everyday life...[10]

The modern, dependable system of postal delivery made the travails caused by geographic separation—especially acute for migrants—more bearable, for those living far apart could correspond with one another on a regular basis. Commercial and cultural commodities—newspapers, department store catalogues, and mail-order commercial ephemera of all kinds—flowed through the postal networks with greater ease.[11] Recent work further substantiates the contribution of the post to retailing and the making of the modern Canadian industrial economy.[12]

To reiterate, the thrust of Osborne and Pike is that the postal service alone was responsible for a revolution in communication in Canada during the late nineteenth and early twentieth centuries. Their assumption is that once the provinces of British North America, including the province of Canada, obtained control of their domestic post, these became powerful tools of development in the hands of a new elite hungry for power, railways, and territory. This is a far-from-banal conclusion based on a far-from-banal line of scholarly enquiry. It forces us to recognize the major role of the post in transforming Canadian society. Regrettably, the average Canadian history textbook is no place to look for information on this subject, although scholars from other countries have addressed the theme head on.[13] Thus, the need for this publication, which is intended, in part, as a further means to drive home Osborne's message.

The Epistolary Approach

A second scholarly line of enquiry that has marked Canadian postal historiography is the epistolary approach to the writing of letters. Two French historians, Cécile Dauphin and Danièle Poublan, effectively expanded the core of their scholarly interests from the postal service proper to the entire epistolary world of letters. The transition commenced with their contributions to Chartier's *La Correspondance*, which features, *inter alia*, studies of the French postal system in 1847 and a hilarious discussion of letter writing textbooks, replete with striking male and female stereotypes, studies of letters, and the representation of letter writing.[14] The transition climaxed with the appearance of *Ces bonnes lettres*, in which the long and fascinating methodological introduction looks at the circumstances of play acting and conviviality surrounding the *pacte épistolaire*.[15]

In Canada, the epistolary approach has benefited greatly from research conducted into "intimate writings" by literary historians. The published papers of a colloquium held at the Université du Québec à Trois Rivières in 1992 contain a number of interdisciplinary contributions pertaining to one aspect or another of correspondence.[16] Benoit Melançon, literary historian and Diderot specialist, has emphasized the materiality of a letter—as opposed to a specimen of email, for example—and the remarkable emotional engagement that ensues when correspondents exchange letters, and sometimes vows, by mail.[17] Letters may arrive smelling of perfume or stuffed with photographs of the beach last summer. A letter's enclosures might be so disappointing that the recipient wants to tear them up. A printed email doesn't usually evoke such senses, although certain keyboards have been known to take a solid thumping.

Postal service and interpersonal communication are the two pools of historiography from which *More than Words* derives. Together they constitute a broad field of historical enquiry. The field, which is international in scope as this book testifies, will hopefully contribute to a renewal of the conceptual approach to communication.[18] In the world of the post, scholars are looking at the post as institution and as interpersonal phenomenon.[19] They are looking at people as well as power relationships. In so doing, they are gradually constructing a new interpretative framework through which to understand this facet of what is a much larger world: the universe of communication. At the same time, within the overall field of communication, some scholars have begun to overhaul certain traditional conceptual assumptions. As a result, we have a better understanding of what makes us modern and what makes us tick as Canadians and as citizens of the world. The discussion begins with Harold Innis.

Communication: More than Words

Harold Innis, first a student of economic history, developed a proficiency in communication history toward the end of his career. Innis made sweeping, grandiloquent statements—the likes of which I have no intention of disputing here—on the role of communications or certain communication media. One statement examines the bias of communication:

> Large-scale political organizations such as empires must be considered from the standpoint of two dimensions, those of space and time, and persist by overcoming the bias of media which overemphasize either dimension. They have tended to flourish under conditions in which civilization reflects the influence of more than one medium and in which the bias of one medium toward decentralization is offset by the bias of another medium towards centralization.[20]

Certain media were more emphatic by virtue of their spatial impact. Others resonated more fully in time. Durable media—parchment, clay, stone—allowed for an accumulation of power over time and a decentralization of power in space. Meanwhile, the much lighter or more portable papyrus and paper favoured the centralization of power within imperial units of considerable aerial extent.[21] In Innis's view, Canada, beginning with the French regime, implicitly represented a particular form of spatial bias based on the expanding capacity of paper and stone. The paper allowed for the transmission of orders, the stone was quarried and mortared to help build the fortifications, which, along with gunpowder, arranged for the execution of the orders.

Innis's generalization, elaborated originally with ancient history in mind, applies all too well to New France: "The written word signed, sealed and swiftly transmitted was essential to military power and the extension of government. Small communities were written into large states and states were consolidated into empire."[22] Canada was a creation of French power; the British, of course, followed suit with their own imperial mechanisms and traditions. The French power, Innis might have been thinking, was the measure of successful communication. Or, put another way, communication was necessary for power to obtain and incorporate into a single unit the St. Lawrence Valley, the *pays d'en haut*, and the southwest beyond, not to mention Louisiana and the French West Indies.

Kenneth Banks takes this assumption a step further in his study of communication and the French empire in the eighteenth century. He looks at how communication enabled the spread and maintenance of formal imperial ties in three colonial settings: Canada, Louisiana, and *les iles du vent* (Gaudeloupe and Martinique).[23] The reader is treated to a broad and rewarding discussion of the means of transport and influence within and to each of these jurisdictions. The comparative perspective is especially refreshing. The sensitivity to Carey's double-barrelled concept of communication—transmission and ritual dimensions—is present in the introduction and throughout.[24] However, the overall focus on state power and communication as two sides of the same coin is frustrating because there is more to communication than subservience.

Banks may have been looking to apply Headrick's comment that "information was the lifeblood of European imperialism" in the eighteenth and nineteenth centuries.[25] Yet, in his conclusion, he enumerates all the factors that made the communication of imperial power in the French Atlantic less efficient than it should have been. Of these factors, one is struck by the impression that the French imperial state was not in control of communication. In most cases, the key problem was to ensure the cooperation of people to make imperial communications work: Dispatches had to be transported great distances by someone—not necessarily French from France—through the interior of the continent. The state experienced great difficulty in communicating with and obtaining the deference and cooperation of the popular classes whether the issue was symbolic or practical. With respect to the merchants: "[T]he state could not do without the extensive contacts and information gathering provided by merchants and their ships."[26] Finally, within each of the colonies, there were concurrent systems of patron-client networks and information systems.

This scenario provides a history of communication as expression of power, in which the imperial order offered a disappointing performance. In counterpoint, as a Canadian or *canadien*, one might be tempted to celebrate colonial insubordination to imperial imperatives as integral to our North American birthright. It bears pointing out as well that there was much more communication going on in the French Atlantic world than between *fonctionnaires* and officers of the king. I will return to this issue below. Third and finally, Banks may have been expecting too much in terms of control than the type of state he was studying was then capable of. His conclusions should be tested, first, against a comparison of communication and postal communication between Britain and the thirteen colonies during the pre-revolutionary seventeenth and eighteenth centuries.[27] Second, careful study of the British imperial factor in the development of Canadian postal communication after the conquest of 1763 would be a most welcome course of study.[28] The British took some initiatives of capital importance, among them, the introduction of a postal service (in 1763) under the administration of a Deputy Postmaster General and the award of a mail contract for transatlantic steam-powered vessels to Samuel Cunard in 1839.[29] But, they also became entrapped in a tug of war with colonial assemblies in which, in the latter's view, imperial involvement became synonymous with imperial meddling as gradually the provinces achieved some measure of self (or responsible) government.[30]

James Beniger is as fascinated by the functional correlation between power and communication as Innis and Banks. Indeed, the relationship between the two forms the core of his interpretation of the transformation of our modern Western society since the late industrial era. This transformation he calls the Control Revolution.

Grappling with the consequences of late twentieth century developments in computer microchips and digitization, Beniger strives to get at the roots of our modern information society. Rather than view it as an unforeseen development, Beniger prefers to envisage the information society as the consequence and not the cause of a longer process, or Control Revolution, that has played out for 100 years or more. Specifically, the Control

Figure 1 "Votre correspondant attend : Écrivez!" Your correspondant awaits you: write now, the message says. During the post-war period, the Canadian Post Office was soliciting more business. The tradition of writing and sending letters, is as old as the country.
Library and Archives Canada, Records of the Post Office, RG 3, vol. 2223 file 4-8-4, vol. 3 (1948–53).

Revolution is a response to a crisis in social control wrought by the great transformation of industrialization.[31] Industrialization effectively swept away agencies of control and information that were especially important at the local level, i.e., the entire range of media associated with face-to-face relationships. For a time, there ensued a relative vacuum, but gradually during the mid- and late-nineteenth century a mechanism was set in place that allowed the re-merger of the twin agencies of power and communication. The process involved change along three lines: the development of bureaucracy; the introduction of new transport and communication infrastructures; and, the advent of system-wide communication, i.e., the mass media.[32]

Developments in all three fields are systematic. Information processing is conveyed throughout the social fabric. Communication has a necessary feedback component that informs the powers that be of the relative success or failure of their enterprises. The corollary to Beniger's time-specific concept of the Control Revolution is that the ability of a society to maintain control is predicated on the development of information technologies. Among these technologies are the agencies making up the new infrastructure: the railway, the telegraph, the post. These, along with other agencies, allow for a more efficient flow of information and control, as well as a more effective distribution of goods and services. The world becomes smaller as information travels faster and more regularly. Information—power—is increasingly centralized and there is less need to rely on a delegated representative whose responsibility is to make decisions in situ according to his or her own view.

Borrowing from the idiom of Innis, there doesn't seem to be any bias, discrepancy, or dysfunctionality in the operation of communication. The cords of communication—increasingly digital in this modern age—bind us ever closer to some vague but influential nexus of power.

The Beniger view has the inherent virtue of encouraging us to present any approach to communication in a continuum of historical evolution. Different mechanisms apply according to the context. The stay-at-home Italian merchants of the fourteenth and fifteenth centuries had to rely on the eyes, ears, and initiative of a commission merchant in situ in accordance with a distributed control structure.[33] In the nineteenth century, a more centralized control structure was taking shape. The transatlantic mails allowed foreign partners to keep a closer eye on one another; commercial newspapers gave plantation owners in the American south the opportunity to verify the economic situation with their own eyes; manufacturers tested foreign markets with new product lines. In each case, an intermediary or delegated (i.e., distributed) instance of the control structure has been removed.[34]

Beniger's view of communication is that it is defined by its functional relationship to the rest of society; there is no sign of a contest. As disciples of the humanities, historians of communication might prefer to take a different tack, for communication can have a subversive dimension. Our modern cities are awash in words: billboards comporting scriptographic messages encouraging us to buy this, drink that, or imagine what lies beneath the low-cut blouse. We live, to borrow Fritzche's expression, in a word city. And not a few of us, like early twentieth-century Berliners, are enthralled by, if not addicted to, our daily newspaper.[35] A German philosopher wryly observed that newspapers served as a substitute for early morning prayers.[36] But, other messages are broadcast literally or figuratively on the flip side of the billboards and elsewhere. Graffiti colours the underpinnings and overhangs of our highways. A host of activities, illicit or private, obtain on any average day, as people, especially young people, stare and/or talk into their cell phones. None of this communication emanates from a central approved source. Nor does a call centre exist with the ability to listen in on all that is being said. Gerald Friesen proposes a more nuanced view of the evolution of communication and power in Canada during the late nineteenth and early twentieth centuries. He argues persuasively that the rise of the capitalist print mode of communication in late nineteenth-century Canada did indeed fashion an imagined Canadian community. Yet, at the same time, it sowed the seeds of a countervailing popular momentum that manifested itself in the realm of communication and politics. The mass media, personified by the large urban dailies, emerged as the appendage of the new urban-industrial way of life. So strong was the transformation that it sent shock waves through the emerging Canadian socio-economy. The waves elicited a popular response.[37]

Within the confines of the press, a separate local world emerged, predicated on a weekly or monthly press with a more narrow, intense, ethnic, religious, or geographic focus. Dissenting values were herein expressed and communicated.[38] A wide reform movement emerged during the first half of the twentieth century embodied by trade unionism, the social gospel movement, farm movements, and various cultural travellers, for example, the Canadian Broadcasting Corporation and the National Film Board. The movement sustained and became an oppositional constituency and, in turn, became the foundation for the Canadian socialist movement. The entire movement, its ancestors, and *aboutissements* were one vast exercise by which the common people, in an ongoing grassroots cultural response, rebuilt the economic and political fabric of the country. Friesen's implicit view is that historians viewing the advent of mass media *sui generis* as a process without contest are missing half of the story.

Communication in its rapport with power, according to Friesen, operates from top to bottom and from bottom to top. It is a complicated, interactive business. Nothing advances in one direction without attracting some concurrent, competing, or contradictory force. The postal historian regrets only that Friesen was unable to invoke the mail as part and parcel of the popular versus capitalist ebb and flow. For, as sure as the mails supported the business and sales of Timothy Eaton, Robert Simpson Limited, and Dupuis Frères, so did they provide for the conduct of trade union business and the articulation and promotion of socialism.

In terms of cause, communication is a two-way street. It is also a broad band of phenomena, carrying in its sweep the spoken as well as the written word. Communication among humans is a social experience and it is, Robert Darnton states, germane to every form of human society: "I would argue that every age was an age of information, each in its own way, and that communication systems have always shaped events."[39] Each society develops its own ways of hunting for and gathering information. Darnton develops his argument with respect to Paris in the eighteenth century during the years leading up to the Revolution, where the press was not much developed but word most surely got around.

Words spread from gatherings of people beneath the tree of Cracovie in the gardens of the Palais Royal on the right bank. They were carried by itinerant raconteurs who regaled an interested café audience with bits of information on scraps of papers with the latest news of impending taxes or the king's sex life, a favourite subject of Parisians; one popular verse in honour of Mme de Pompadour was titled "*Qu'une batarde de Catin.*"[40] The same raconteurs might have traded scraps of information among themselves. The unlucky ones, if caught by the police and taken to the Bastille, might have had to empty their pockets.

In Paris, royal anecdotes might have done the rounds of court gossip before finding their way into the general rumour mill (*bruits publics*) of the city; thereafter they appeared in one of many news sheets, before eventually, but not invariably, appearing in a *libellé*, or scandalous book. One author of a controversial *roman à clef*—a novel with covert meanings in which one has to use a key to unlock the double entendres—a mere chamber maid, astounded the police when they came to arrest her.[41] Where, they asked, did she get all her information? Why, from what the people were saying in public, she replied. There could be no better illustration of the ease with which *les bruits* move between the spoken and written worlds.

Three propositions vis-à-vis the history of communication complete Darnton's discussion.[42] First, oral and written worlds of communication are not separate but rather operate in tandem. Second, it is difficult, nay pointless, to establish whether or not a message begins its life in someone's mouth or on a writing desk; what matters is the degree of amplification. Does the message resonate and how so? Third, elite and popular cultures are not separate. In the fluid world of communication that constitutes the huge fishbowl of Paris, the two crossed paths and rubbed shoulders constantly. The dynamic world of communication depicted here is no mere sideshow of antiquarian interest. For, according to Darnton, the various agencies of communication, once knitted together, brought about the collapse of the *ancien régime*, so thoroughly did they undermine the legitimacy and reputation of the monarchy.[43]

The world of communication depicted in this volume is primarily a written one. This should not, however, allow us to forget the broad dynamic world to which it belongs, for words once spoken can spin with remarkable velocity into and out of letters, newspapers, and into and out of and back again from the audience. Jane Kamensky reminds us that colonial New Englanders were diligent listeners with excellent memories: Their writings and written statements were suffused with talk.[44] Talk and writing are part of a common communications infrastructure, an infrastructure, Richard John reminds us, that is responsible for both processing information and its transmission or movement over space.[45] Men and women are given to taking the time to consider or mull over the news in the presence of one or more other human beings. Roberston Davies reminds us that gossip, "is the cud of life which they [two Victorian characters in this instance] chew and re-chew with unfailing relish."[46]

Today, talk and text messaging are at times indistinguishable, not because it must be so, but because we want it to be so. McLuhan was fond of telling us that the medium is the message. His central mistake was in assuming that one prevalent medium operated at a time; equally erroneous was the assumption that media superseded one another.[47] Moreover, he assumed we could become the victims of machines, "prisoners of our own device." Men and women are not always victims and they don't communicate with just one device. They are both too clever and too stupid for that kind of simplistic, submissive, and linear behaviour. They are unreliable by definition. The selections below provide ample food for thought in this respect.

This book is organized in four sections. Part one consists of contributions dealing with the systemic and symbolic import of the Post Office, from the era of New France to the year 2001. Bernard Allaire's *reseau officiel* shows how the French crown's mail was shunted back and forth across the Atlantic. A key factor in making the exchange possible was the community of *fonctionnaires* in the various official French ports who were personally familiar with French America. Addressing a more recent period, Krista Cooke offers a summary of postal mechanization consisting of three separate historical phases or generations since 1900. Strictly speaking, she argues, mechanization did not begin during the 1970s. Duncan Stacey takes us to the scene of the workers' riot and occupation of the main downtown Vancouver post office in 1938. The post office became a target for highly organized left-wing action on behalf of the unemployed workers. Yet, the incident, which filled the columns of the Vancouver newspapers at the time, received, at best, passing mention in the RCMP's annual report.

Articles by Pope on September 11, by Kielbowicz on the relationship between the post office and the private communication sector in the U.S., where powerful corporate interests sought to contain the institutional thrust of the post office, and by Willis on the postal service in Prince Edward Island, a single predominantly rural region, round out the discussion of postal service. To be sure, the authors focus on departmental history, but it is a service with a human face, belonging to strikers and policemen, to lobbyists and officials, or to survivors pictured beside the vestiges of the post office who just happened to be in the wrong place, beside the World Trade Center, at the wrong time, on the morning of September 11, 2001.

Parts two and three are more epistolary in focus. In part two, Sheila McIntyre explores the correlation between, and cultivation of, letter writing and gentility in early New England. In polite society, the important thing is not what you say but how you say it. Dauphin and Poublan glean what they can of the depiction of letter writing in sundry pictorial and popular media in nineteenth-century France. Castéran analyzes the codes and covert practices behind the exchange of secret mail during the height of the Seven Years' War while spies lurked in the wings. The French and English conducted a covert war of intrigue that was consistent with the best practices of the Cold War. Gendreau invites us to take another look at the Hudson Bay Company (HBC) in the late eighteenth and nineteenth centuries. The HBC embarked on a little studied policy of the harvesting and commercialization of goose quills. These sold well in the English market especially among the thoroughbred classes.

In part three, People and Their Letters, we are introduced to six types of people. Four came to Canada as immigrants. Frenette and Scadellato delve into the life of the late Christian Bennedsen who came here in 1951 and, despite inauspicious beginnings, had a good life. He left all his letters to the Canadian Postal Museum. Herman Witsius Ryland came to Lower Canada with Lord Dorchester in 1793, but one gets the impression from Lorraine Gadoury's analysis that he rather regretted it. Strange that a man could inhabit so beautiful a region as Quebec with a house outside the town of Beauport and access to some of the most powerful men in the colony, yet appear so melancholy toward the end of his life. A French immigrant, Pierre Gilibert, as Marguerite Sauriol relates, settled in Alberta in 1905 but eventually decided to return home; we are not exactly sure why. His letters offer an unusual if quantitatively modest francophone perspective on the Canadian West. Liz Turcotte read letters of Canadian soldiers serving in the two World Wars. Susie Knoblauch, herself a German immigrant to the U.S., rediscovered the letters of her great-great Uncle Carl written after he moved to New York City in 1863.

In each and every case, there is a personal story that fits into a more general tableau. The immigrants tried to make a go of it in the New World. Exceptionally, Susanne Knoblauch is well suited to comment on her own ancestor's experience for she lived through a similar transition. The soldiers on or behind the front line kept their wits about them by writing home. As the war drew on, they found ways to kill time instead of Germans. One soldier reconstituted a complete if composite human skeleton, there being no want of materiel at hand in 1917. Manon Brunet pieced together a story about an illicit and discrete relationship between a French-Canadian literary figure (Abbé Casgrain) and the wife of a visiting Protestant British official. The warmth of feeling in the letters is unmistakable. These and others remind us that old letters are a treasure trove of human experience. They remind us of the things that matter most, for life in these letters is lived close to the grain of day-to-day existence.

The fourth and final section is Communication and Transport. For this section, Mary Vipond was invited to submit a piece on Canadian radio history, namely the coverage of the 1939 Royal Tour of King George VI and Queen Elizabeth. The royal tour and pageant was pitched as a major event. My own father kept a special newspaper supplement on the tour in his bedroom dresser at the cottage for nearly thirty years. The tour and especially the coverage were nothing if not an exercise in public relations management and planning with radio occupying centre stage as Canadian, British, and American broadcasters sought to sell the royal couple. The Second World War was just around the corner and events to further ally the three countries were very much in demand.

Radio became a central infrastructure of communication in the twentieth century. The movement of information and people during our early colonial history relied on other types of transport infrastructure, yet they were effective. This is amply demonstrated in Loewen's piece on sixteenth century Terra Nova. Information circulated through networks of entrepreneurial sailors, port officers, insurance agents, and merchants from Labrador and the Grand Banks all the way to the Basque coast and the southwest of France. Scatarie was an island off the southeastern coast of Isle Royale (Cape Breton). The community of sailors, captains, and fishermen was not lacking in entrepreneurial strategy as they strived to get their catch to market. Not a few powerful women were involved. Men jealous of each other's social status battled. The story reminds us that in the human pursuit of fortune there has never been such a thing as a straight utilitarian line. Emotions and extra-economic considerations always come into play.

The transport of mail and thousands of would-be millionaires halfway across the world around the Horn or through the Isthmus of Panama was a laborious affair even in 1849, the year of the California Gold Rush. This did not diminish the import of Steamer Day, when, according to Marianne Babal, mails arriving aboard incoming steamships were heralded by semaphore telegraph messages and canon blasts. Everyone rushed down to the docks of San Francisco to meet the mail. Less laborious was the challenge of carrying materiel, arms, and provisions overseas by jet for Canadian troops serving in UN peacekeeping missions during the 1950s, 1960s, and 1970s. The challenge was considerably different from that of the Second World War, for this was a professional army performing the nation's peacekeeping obligations, not a mass of civilians in uniform for the duration of a single grand conflict. These men, Jean Martin reminds us, needed mail but much else as well: radio and telephone connections to talk with family or to listen to the Grey Cup, movies, newspapers, and, of course, their favourite beer. A piece of Canada invariably travels with Canadian detachments serving on UN overseas missions: This requires transmission and transport capacity so the soldiers can process the news and the mess fare.

The colleagues contributing pieces to this book offer a number of vantage points from which to consider postal communication and transport history. They look at systems of communication (radio and the post) and at epistolary norm, control, secrecy, and material culture. They look at people who wrote themselves all over the page, now engaging, now avoiding the norms, now recounting some experiences and dissimulating others, ever the artful dodgers. They examine the not infrequently entwined circumstances of communication and transport, laborious back in 1849 when compared to jet propelled peacekeepers, but nonetheless essential inasmuch as they are the infrastructure through which we have kept in touch with each other and with home since the arrival of the very first Basque ships in Terra Nova in the sixteenth century.

In sum, what is postal history? It is the study of an ability and a willingness to keep in touch, primarily in writing. It is an exploration into a past system of communication and culture of interpersonal messaging involving material elements of quill, quire, and ink. It charts the buildup of vast modern economic, social, and political networks. The postal system becomes a sophisticated means of handling the mail on an industrial scale and is, therefore, a dutiful servant, facilitator, and catalyst of the modern state and the modern corporation, which have shaped our lives in the twentieth century. It is an exercise in which the sense of self is gained through an exchange with others, irrespective of the increased scale of social experience. The discovery is shared at both the sending and receiving ends. The epistolary entourage or primary interacting group of correspondents is made and remade with each exchange of letters. Postal communication engages all the calculating abilities of men and women anxious to ensure they are making the right investment, whether the object is a piece of whale blubber off the coast of Labrador (It's August and we have caught this much so far. What is it worth and do we get the catch insured?) or a handful of gold mined somewhere inland from San Francisco that may have travelled through the hands of a "daughter of fortune."

Historically, the post has facilitated communication. As such, it belongs to the universe of communication that operates on many levels at once. It cannot be subsumed in some category of political economy, much less in one separate department of government. Communication, by post and any other media, is rooted in a historical context, but owing to the relative autonomy or unpredictability of its human practitioners it may have means and a mind of its own. Communication is the lifeblood of our species. It is the first thing we do upon our entry into this world and may very well be the last. It is not something to be taken lightly, and, as historians, we ignore it at our empirical peril. I leave it to my fellow authors to further convince the reader.

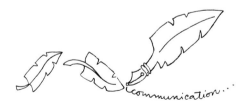

Notes

1. My thanks to Christian Pedersen of the Denmark PTT Museum and Professor Richard John of the University of Illinois at Chicago for their judicious remarks on a previous draft of this introduction.
2. Susan McLeod O'Reilly, *On Track: The Railway Mail Service in Canada* (Gatineau (Hull): Canadian Postal Museum/Canadian Museum of Civilization and Canada Post Corporation, 1992).

3. Jane Harrison, *Until Next Year: Letter Writing and the Mail in the Canadas, 1640–1830* (Gatineau (Hull) and Waterloo: Canadian Museum of Civilization and Wilfrid Laurier University Press, 1997).

4. Jane Harrison, "The Intercourse of Letters: Transatlantic Correspondence in Early Canada, 1640–1812" (Ph.D. Thesis (History), University of Toronto, 2000).

5. Chantal Amyot and John Willis, *Country Post: Rural Postal Service in Canada, 1880 to 1945*, CPM Mercury no. 1 (Gatineau: Canadian Museum of Civilization, 2004).

6. See P. Garvie, "Le réseau postal et son rôle dans l'articulation du système urbain au Nouveau-Brunswick, entre 1870 et 1909," *Acadiensis* 24, no. 2 (Spring 1995): 113.

7. Grégoire Teyssier, "La distribution postale de la presse périodique québécoise, 1851–1911" (Thèse de maîtrise (Information et Communication), Université Laval, 1996).

8. Ibid., pp. 139.

9. See, in particular, the four-part series by B. S. Osborne and R. Pike, "The Postal Service and Canadian Social History," which appeared in the *Postal History Society of Canada Journal* no. 35 (1983): 37–42; no. 41 (1985): 11–14; no. 42 (1985): 21–26; no. 44 (1986): 13–44.

10. B. S. Osborne and R. Pike, "Lowering the Walls of Oblivion: The Revolution in Postal Communications in Central Canada, 1851–1911, *Canadian Papers in Rural History*, vol. 4 (Gananoque: Langdale Press, 1984), pp. 201.

11. Ibid., pp. 220–221.

12. See the virtual exhibition "Before E-commerce: A History of Canadian Mail-order Catalogues" at www.civilization.ca/cpm/catalog/. See also John Willis, "The Mail Order Catalogue: An Achievement in Mass Distribution and Labour" in *Les territoires de l'entreprise/ The Territories of Business,* eds S. Bellavance and Pierre Lanthier, Collection Géographie Historique (Québec: Presses de l'Université Laval, 2004), pp. 173–199.

13. Richard John, *Spreading the News: The American Postal System from Franklin to Morse* (Cambridge, Mass.: Harvard University Press, 1995). The history textbooks of many other countries have chosen to ignore postal history. Part of the problem has been the propensity for writers of postal history not to engage directly their respective national historiographies. They have remained outside the academic mainstream, as has, to some extent their subject. My thanks to Christian Pedersen for this reminder.

14. R. Chartier, dir., *La correspondance: Les usages de la lettre au XIXe siècle* (Paris: Fayard, 1991). See, in particular, chapter 1, C. Dauphin et al, "L'enquête postale de 1847," pp. 21–119; chapter 4, "Les manuels épistolaires au XIXe siècle," pp. 209–272.

15. C. Dauphin et al., *Ces bonnes lettres: Une correspondance familiale au 19e siècle* (Paris: Bibliothèque Albin Michel, 1995). See "Une correspondance familiale," pp. 29–194.

16. M. Brunet et S. Gagnon, *Discours et pratique de l'intime* (Québec: Institut québécois de recherche sur la culture, 1993).

17. B. Melançon, *Sevigne@Internet: Remarques sur le courrier électronique et la lettre* (Montréal: Fides, 1996).

18. Two interesting works from other countries are Muriel Le Roux, dir., *Histoire de la poste: De l'administration à l'entreprise* (Paris: Éditions Rue d'Ulm/Presses de l'École normale supérieur, 2002), and R. R. John, *Spreading the News: The American Postal System from Franklin to Morse* (Cambridge, Mass.: Harvard University Press, 1995).

19. David Gerber, "The Immigrant Letter between Positivism and Populism: The Uses of Immigrant Personal Correspondence in 20th Century American Scholarship," *Journal of American Ethnic History* 16, no. 4 (Summer 1997): 3–34.

20. Harold Innis, *Empire and Communications* (Oxford: Clarendon Press, 1972), pp. 7.

21. Harold Innis, "Media in Ancient Empires," in *Communication in History: Technology, Culture, Society*, eds D. Crowley and P. Heyer (White Plains, N.Y., Longman 1995), pp. 29–37.

22. Ibid., pp. 7.

23. Kenneth Banks, *Chasing Empire across the Sea: Communications and the State in the French Atlantic, 1713–1763* (Montréal: McGill-Queen's University Press, 2002).

24. Ibid., pp. 11; see also chapter 4, "State Ceremonies and Local Agendas."

25. Ibid., pp. 11.

26. Ibid., pp. 219.

27. I. K. Steele, *The English Atlantic, 1675–1740: An Exploration of Communication and Community*, (New York, Oxford University Press, 1986.)

28. One starting point would be the old study by William Smith, *The History of the Post Office in British North America, 1639–1870* (Cambridge, Mass.: University Press, 1920).

29. J. C. Arnell, *Atlantic Mails: A History of the Mail Service between Great Britain and Canada to 1889* (Ottawa: National Postal Museum of Canada, 1980), pp. 93ff.

30. J. Willis, "The Canadian Colonial Posts: Epistolary Continuity, Postal Transformation," in *Canada 1849: A Selection of Papers Given at the University of Edinburgh Centre for Canadian Studies Annual Conference, May 1999*, eds D. Pollard and G. Martin (Edinburgh: University of Edinburgh Press, 2001), pp. 224–254.

31. James Beniger, "The Control Revolution," in *Communication in History: Technology, Culture, Society*, pp. 311, 317.

32. Ibid., pp. 311–312.

33. James Beniger, *The Control Revolution* (Cambridge, Mass.: Harvard University Press, 1986) pp. 126–127.

34. Ibid.. p. 167. The Beniger view assumes that the Control Revolution was invented by the advent of the mass media in the late nineteenth and early twentieth centuries. The Danish postal historian, Christian Pedersen, cautions that we should not underestimate the relationship between power and communication in *ancien régime* societies. Postal officials were directly involved in developing the handwritten press (as participants or publishers) for they had privileged access to information even if this brought them to open the mail illegally in search of newsworthy items. As well, postal clerks dutifully censored the press on behalf of their king and royal bureaucracy. On the latter topic, see Christian Pedersen, "Postal Espionage in 18th-century Denmark," forthcoming in "Actes du colloque: Les réseaux postaux en Europe du 18ᵉ au 21ᵉ siècle, Paris, 10–12 juin 2004."

35. Peter Fritzsche, *Reading Berlin 1900* (Cambridge, Mass.: Harvard University Press, 1996).

36. Hegel as quoted in Gerald Friesen, *Citizens and Nation: An Essay on History, Communication and Canada* (Toronto: University of Toronto Press, 2000), pp. 147.

37. G. Friesen, *Citizens and Nation: 2000*, chapter 6, "Literate Communication and Political Resistance," pp. 139–163.

38. Ibid., pp. 150.

39. Robert Darnton, "The News in Paris: An Early Information Society," in *George Washington's False Teeth*, ed. R. Darnton (New York: W.W. Norton, 2003), pp. 25.

40. Ibid., pp. 53–55.

41. Ibid., pp. 49–53.

42. Ibid., pp. 67–68.

43. Ibid., pp. 75.

44. Jane Kamensky, *Governing the Tongue: The Politics of Speech in Early New England* (New York: Oxford University Press, 1997), pp. 14.

45. Richard John, "American Historians and the Concept of the Communications Revolution," in *Information Acumen: The Understanding and Use of Knowledge in Modern Business*, ed. Lisa Bud-Frierman (London: Routledge and Kegan Paul, 1994), p. 105.

46. Robertson Davies, *Murther and Walking Spirits* (Toronto: McClelland and Stewart, 1991), pp. 210.

47. The point is made in John Seely Brown and Paul Duguid, *The Social Life of Information* (Boston: Harvard Business School Press, 2000). Our thanks to R. John for this reference.

PART ONE:
THE POST

PREMIÈRE PARTIE :
LE SYSTÈME POSTAL

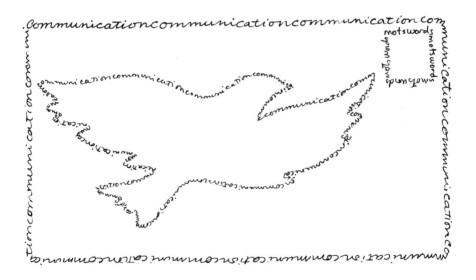

LE RÉSEAU DE COMMUNICATIONS POSTALES DURANT LE RÉGIME FRANÇAIS

Le réseau officiel

1

Bernard Allaire, historien canadien en France

Résumé

Sous l'Ancien Régime, la correspondance officielle à destination ou en provenance des colonies se distingue des autres types de courrier (lettres personnelles, documents commerciaux…) par ses modalités de circulation, c'est-à-dire ses mécanismes d'expédition parallèles et souvent indépendants du réseau postal public, les mesures de sécurité plus poussées mises en cause (valises et sacs scellés, lettres cryptées) et un suivi postal plus serré – liste des objets de correspondance, enregistrement des départs, des porteurs, accusés de réception notifiés, etc. Bien qu'elles soient écrasantes et déficientes, les modalités d'acheminement qui entourent ce type de courrier ont pour but de restreindre et de cloisonner, au maximum, la correspondance aux seules personnes autorisées. La pérennité de la colonie dépend grandement de ce protocole qui, d'un côté, réduit au minimum le risque d'espionnage par une puissance étrangère et, de l'autre, évite les affrontements entre les groupes dont les intérêts (politiques, religieux, marchands…) divergent au sein des implantations outre-mer.

Abstract

During the Ancien Régime period, official correspondence sent to or coming from the colonies can be distinguished from other types of mails (personal mails or commercial letters) by their methods of circulation. They had their parallel dispatching mechanisms often independent from the public postal network, employed more systematic safety measures (specific bags and sealed chests, encrypted letters), and a tighter postal follow-up (listing of correspondence recording of departures and carriers, notification of delivery, etc). Although burdensome and defective, a system for this type of mail aimed to restrict and to partition as much as possible, the correspondence to the only authorized readers.

The existence of the colony depended largely on this protocol which, on the one hand, reduced to a minimum the risk of espionage by foreign powers and, on the other hand, avoided confrontations between the numerous political, religious or commercial factions that had divergent interests within overseas establishments.

Introduction

La correspondance étatique, sous l'Ancien Régime, était un courrier nécessaire, entre autres, au bon fonctionnement de l'administration de la colonie. Elle servait à transmettre, outre-Atlantique, les décisions du pouvoir royal en matière politique et militaire, civile et religieuse. Ces envois étaient délibérément séparés des lettres commerciales ou personnelles traversant l'océan. Cette correspondance officielle se démarque non seulement par son caractère confidentiel, mais aussi sa dimension stratégique, aspect qui fait en sorte qu'elle circule, lorsque cela est possible, par des réseaux plus surveillés. Il existait donc en quelque sorte un système de traçabilité, plus ou moins efficace selon les périodes, permettant de suivre et de sécuriser les acheminements dans les limites des contraintes de l'époque. Nous allons donc, dans les pages qui suivent, faire porter notre regard sur les parcours empruntés, les points de chute, les modes de chargement, le profil des porteurs, leurs protocoles de sécurisation, bref, toutes les caractéristiques particulières de cette correspondance officielle.

Si l'histoire coloniale française en Nouvelle-France débute sous Henri IV et se structure sous Louis XIII, ce n'est que sous le règne de Louis XIV que se met réellement en place un suivi administratif serré de la correspondance coloniale officielle. Pour observer la montée et les transformations progressives des modalités de ce type de courrier, nous avons travaillé à partir de deux fonds bien connus, conservés par les Archives nationales de France, mais jamais exploités jusqu'à présent dans une telle optique : les archives des Colonies et, dans une moindre mesure, les archives de la Marine. Ces collections contiennent des dizaines de milliers de lettres, dont près de 30 000 concernant le Canada[1].

Le calendrier annuel de la correspondance officielle

L'expédition de la correspondance officielle est réglée sur la navigation saisonnière reliant le Canada à la France. Cette expédition cesse complètement de décembre à mars, en raison des glaces qui rendent périlleuse la navigation par le Saint-Laurent. Il s'agit d'une situation que les autorités contournent par des expéditions à travers l'Acadie, dès le 17e siècle, et dont elles s'affranchissent au siècle suivant, après la construction de Louisbourg, à l'île Royale, sur l'Atlantique, libre de glace, d'où l'on pourra faire parvenir le courrier à Québec par l'intérieur.

L'essentiel des départs de la France pour le Canada s'effectue de mars à juillet, tandis que ceux du Canada à destination de la France se font de mai à novembre. Tout ceci implique donc que les lettres officielles soient prêtes à partir à des périodes précises de l'année, au risque de devoir attendre, en cas de retard, à l'année suivante. L'essentiel du travail en France débute donc en hiver, lorsque les administrateurs de la colonie canadienne bouclent la majorité de leurs dossiers en vitesse à l'automne. Vu de Québec, le calendrier administratif est en effet totalement différent. L'analyse de la correspondance en provenance du Canada, à son arrivée en France, met en évidence une période d'activité intense durant les mois de septembre, octobre et novembre, période où plus de la moitié de toute la correspondance est rédigée. Le principal problème qui accable le gouverneur et l'intendant, à Québec, est ce court délai dont ils disposent entre l'arrivée de la correspondance officielle venue de France et le départ des derniers navires de cette ville. Durant la saison estivale, ils prennent connaissance des réponses à leurs requêtes de l'année précédente, puis essaient, tant bien que mal, d'appliquer les ordres qui figurent dans les dépêches du roi ou du ministre, avant le départ des vaisseaux. Si la majorité du courrier requiert une certaine attention des administrateurs, une part notable de ces envois est constituée de mémoires et de lettres qui ne demandent qu'à être approuvés par le roi, le ministre ou par les administrateurs de la colonie et renvoyés aussitôt à l'expéditeur, amplifiant ainsi le volume réel de la correspondance écrite qui voyage de part et d'autre de l'Atlantique.

Les itinéraires de sortie et d'arrivée de la correspondance canadienne

Après avoir identifié le calendrier de cette correspondance, nous avons étudié les lieux matériels par où elle transitait. Ils sont relativement faciles à identifier à partir des sources. À ce titre, ce sont les ports complémentaires de Rochefort et de La Rochelle qui demeurent les portes de sortie et de retour préférentielles pour les sacs de courrier officiel, et ce, pour plusieurs raisons évidentes aux acteurs de l'époque. Bien que la Charente n'ait pas un tirant d'eau important, le site de Rochefort présentait plusieurs avantages, entre autres, celui d'être à l'abri, à l'intérieur des terres, tout en étant proche de la mer, avec un mouillage en profondeur à la sortie de la rivière, face à l'île d'Aix[2]. Si les vaisseaux du roi sont choisis en priorité pour le transport du courrier, les autres navires marchands qui attendent à cet

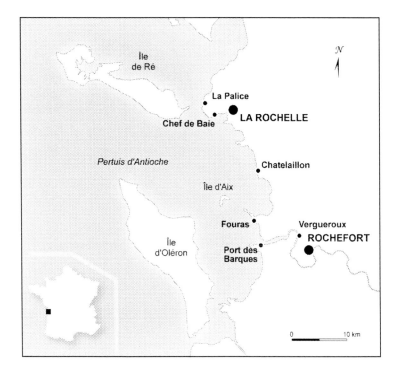

Figure 1.1 La côte maritime entre Rochefort et La Rochelle.
Carte d'Andrée Héroux.

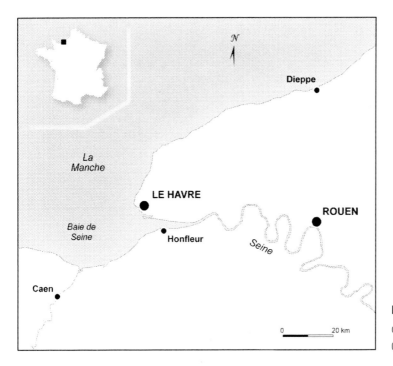

Figure 1.2 La côte maritime de l'estuaire de la Seine.
Carte d'Andrée Héroux.

endroit représentent un potentiel d'expédition auquel on fait souvent appel, d'autant plus que ce sont ces derniers qui transportent l'essentiel des denrées et des marchandises vers les colonies. Les navires marchands s'avèrent particulièrement utiles lorsqu'ils sont les premiers à pouvoir prendre la mer ou que les vaisseaux du roi sont déjà partis et qu'il y reste des articles de correspondance supplémentaires à expédier[3].

L'autre raison faisant de Rochefort un port d'embarquement privilégié pour le Canada est la proximité de La Rochelle, ville incontournable pour se rendre à Québec, mais également le principal port d'entrée des marchandises du Canada, où siègent plusieurs compagnies qui gèrent le commerce des fourrures. Ainsi les villes de La Rochelle et de Rochefort vivent-elles en symbiose. Les vaisseaux du roi et les contingents de Rochefort servent de protection au commerce et aux navires de La Rochelle.

L'estuaire de la Seine sert, dans une moindre mesure, de lieu d'expédition et de retour du courrier au 18e siècle, avec quelques autres ports qui entretiennent des liens avec le Canada, mais sans jamais réellement nuire à la prépondérance de l'axe Rochefort-La Rochelle. Ici encore, les conditions propices aux expéditions de courrier sont rassemblées. S'il n'y a pas d'arsenal militaire d'envergure à proximité, ni de vaisseaux du roi en grand nombre, il y a par contre une concentration de navires marchands similaire à ce que l'on peut observer dans le pertuis d'Antioche. Le triangle formé par Le Havre-de-Grâce, Honfleur et Caen est une véritable rade pour les navires des villes de la région qui s'y regroupent pour partir en convoi pour le Canada, l'île Royale, Terre-Neuve, les Antilles, etc.

Ce potentiel de navigation, situé dans l'estuaire de la Seine, est favorisé à plusieurs points de vue : entre autres, par une proximité des autorités royales regroupées dans la région parisienne; par l'intensité des échanges commerciaux des marchands de Rouen et

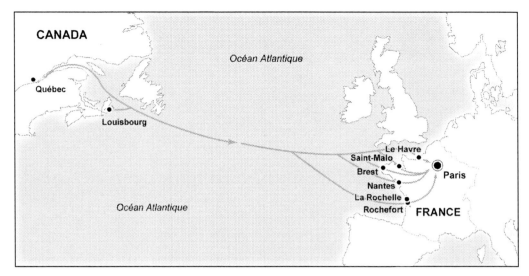

Figure 1.3 Schéma des principaux ports d'arrivée des correspondances officielles en provenance du Canada.

du Havre avec le Canada et par la présence d'installations portuaires importantes (Rouen, Le Havre, Honfleur, etc.) pour les Français souhaitant y émigrer. Si l'essentiel du courrier officiel est acheminé de ces deux régions, nous trouvons quelques rares cas d'embarquement du courrier à Brest, ainsi qu'au port de Marseille, pour un cas exceptionnel d'expédition de lettres à Louisbourg, en 1731[4], mais plus souvent Nantes, utilisé pour rallier Québec et l'île Royale[5]. Il n'en demeure pas moins que les volumes de courrier ne sont pas similaires. Dans les meilleures années, les quantités atteignent rarement les 250 lettres officielles expédiées de France et dépassent parfois les 500 articles de courrier reçus des colonies nord-américaines. Ce qui équivaut à dire que, pour chaque lettre expédiée au Canada par les autorités parisiennes, il leur en revient deux. Il s'agit d'une tendance que l'on constate dès le 17e siècle et qui perdure par la suite[6].

Les ports par lesquels la correspondance arrive du Canada, en France, sont plus difficiles à identifier, mais ils sont toujours situés de façon à rejoindre le plus rapidement la capitale. Ce courrier transitait par La Rochelle, Rochefort et l'estuaire de la Seine, mais également par un nombre varié de villes de la côte atlantique française. À côté de ces grands axes, qui servent de base de relâche à une majorité de navires, il existe quelques autres ports qui ont le profil suffisant pour servir de point de chute pour le retour du courrier officiel en provenance du Canada. Parmi ceux-ci se trouvent la ville de Brest, sur la pointe bretonne, et Lorient[7], où les convois de navires viennent souvent terminer leur traversée de l'Atlantique sous l'escorte des vaisseaux du roi. Ce recours fréquent aux navires marchands, par les gouverneurs et intendants du Canada et de Louisbourg, fait en sorte que des ports de financement des flottes qui fréquentent Terre-Neuve ou les Antilles, tels que Nantes[8] ou Saint-Malo[9], deviennent, à cette époque, des points d'arrivée notables du courrier officiel, et ce, bien qu'elles entretiennent des liens plus intenses avec les établissements coloniaux français de la côte atlantique (Terre-Neuve, le Labrador[10], l'Acadie ou l'île Royale[11]) qu'avec Québec. Les envois de courrier qui arrivent dans ces ports atteignent souvent, par la suite, l'intendance la plus proche, qui les achemine vers les autorités parisiennes.

Le rôle des postes et messageries en France

On aurait pu croire que des lettres dont dépend le sort de la colonie canadienne devaient faire nécessairement l'objet de transports spéciaux mais, comme l'attestent plusieurs sources, il n'en était rien. La plus grande partie de la correspondance empruntait tout simplement le réseau de distribution des postes et des messageries de France. Seules quelques lettres hautement stratégiques étaient parfois transportées de Versailles à Rochefort par des officiers qui, souvent, s'embarquaient eux-mêmes pour le Canada. Il existait bien, sous Louis XIII (1601-1643), un corps de messagers royaux appelés « chevaucheurs de cabinet », chargés de transporter la correspondance officielle mais, face au coût de leur entretien, on limita leur nombre au minimum et leurs interventions, aux seules dépêches royales ayant un caractère urgent, important ou secret. Les expéditions de courrier ne s'effectuant pas à tous les jours, il arrivait aussi que l'on dépêche en vitesse un cavalier pour rattraper le postier déjà parti sur les routes ou que l'on fournisse une escorte durant des périodes de conflits ou pour traverser des régions difficiles[12]. Cet abandon relatif d'un service spécifique de poste pour la correspondance officielle a donné l'occasion au surintendant des Postes et Messageries de France d'ériger un système de transport et de relais pouvant assurer un acheminement sûr et rapide. Cette prise en charge du courrier officiel n'a pu se faire qu'après la mise en place de divers mécanismes de sécurisation des expéditions pour compenser cette situation apparemment délicate.

Les paquets officiels insérés dans les malles des postiers étaient emballés et scellés mais, pour simplifier leur identification, il existait un timbre « Paquet du roi » que l'on estampillait et que l'on contresignait. À l'époque de la Régence (1715-1723), le courrier à destination du Canada expédié via Rochefort pouvait porter également les cachets « Lettre du conseil de Marine » ou « Paquet du roi », pour éviter qu'il ne se retrouve avec les lettres ordinaires durant le trajet. Les vols et la destruction d'articles de courrier n'étaient pas fréquents, mais survenaient parfois durant les guerres ou lorsque le courrier était de passage dans les régions éloignées. Un incident de ce genre arrive en 1685 : le commis du bureau de la poste de Dompierre, près de La Rochelle, constate, à l'arrivée du courrier, que les paquets du roi ont été ouverts; leurs sceaux, brisés; des lettres et des arrêts du conseil, décachetés, et les dépêches du roi, mélangées aux lettres ordinaires[13]. Ces incidents ne touchent néanmoins qu'une partie infime des lettres qui circulent sur les routes de France à cette époque et la correspondance atteignait, la plupart du temps, sa destination sans problème.

Le rôle des intendances de province

Bien que ces expéditions et réceptions de courrier officiel entre les ports français et la capitale semblent régulières et faciles, elles ne peuvent se concrétiser sans le concours de certains acteurs qui s'occupent de la correspondance à un endroit ou à un autre du réseau. Les maillons importants de cette chaîne de distribution sont constitués par les intendants et leurs personnels subalternes qui veillent aux modalités d'acheminement et au bon fonctionnement du protocole des livraisons. L'intendant est en effet le personnage idéal pour coordonner ce type d'activités : il est le représentant du roi en province, son lieu de travail est un point de chute relativement sécurisé, il a une formation administrative souvent très vaste; son mandat s'étend à la justice, à la police, à l'administration civile et aux finances. De plus, en tant que responsable des aspects matériels de la navigation vers les colonies, il a le pouvoir d'accélérer ou de retarder l'embarquement du courrier et le départ des navires.

Les exemples d'intendants qui acheminent du courrier officiel, au départ ou à l'arrivée, sont relativement nombreux. Leurs actions sont identifiables par des lettres de confirmation écrites au ministre de la Marine, des quittances d'embarquement de sacs de courrier ou des documents divers. Hormis les administrateurs de Rochefort et de la généralité de La Rochelle, les sources signalent les interventions, au Havre, des intendants Bochart de Champigny (en 1704 et en 1706), Michel Bégon (en 1734) ou de Mathieu D'Herchigny de Clieu (en 1738). Si, au 18e siècle, le bureau de l'intendant est devenu le principal point de chute du courrier allant dans les deux sens, celui-ci n'agit pas seul. Il est entouré par les officiers de plume que sont les commissaires de Marine, les commissaires ordonnateurs, les commissaires aux classes, les écrivains, les contrôleurs de la Marine, les gardes-magasins et autres, autant de gens qui l'aident ou qui le remplacent en son absence[14].

Cette présence importante des officiers de plume sur le terrain s'explique par le fait que les commissaires s'occupent souvent des aspects matériels de l'acheminement au nom de l'intendant, mais également parce que plusieurs ports français ne disposent pas d'intendance en bonne et due forme[15]. Certaines intendances ont des fonctions plus importantes, car leur ville est très liée avec le Canada sur le plan maritime – arsenaux militaires, ports d'armement pour Terre-Neuve, port d'émigration, etc. On retrouve souvent, dans ces villes, du personnel ayant déjà travaillé au Canada dans l'administration ou l'armée. Cette interaction permanente entre les statuts coloniaux et métropolitains fait en sorte de créer des réseaux personnalisés par lesquels sont transmis les ordres et la correspondance. C'est dans les principaux ports d'arrivée, mais surtout dans les villes de Rochefort, de La Rochelle et du Havre-de-Grâce, que se concentre le personnel administratif ou militaire ayant fait une partie de sa carrière au Canada. Les postes clés d'intendant de Rochefort et du Havre sont détenus, à plusieurs reprises, au 18e siècle, par d'anciens intendants canadiens ou leurs proches parents. Le cas de François de Beauharnois de la Chaussaye de Beauville est très représentatif. Frère du futur gouverneur général de la Nouvelle-France, il débute comme commissaire de Marine avant d'être nommé intendant au Canada, de 1702 à 1705. Il obtiendra le poste d'intendant de Rochefort et de la généralité de La Rochelle, cinq années plus tard (1710), poste qu'il conservera jusqu'en 1738.

Il va sans dire qu'il est bien au courant des dossiers canadiens. La situation est similaire du côté de l'estuaire de la Seine. Ici encore, des intendants viennent y poursuivre leur carrière après un séjour au Canada. C'est le cas de Jean Bochart de Champigny, sieur de Noroy et de Verneuil, qui devient intendant au Havre en 1702, après son retour de Nouvelle-France, et qui le sera jusqu'en 1720, et de Michel Bégon de la Picardière, nommé au même poste, en 1726, dans les mêmes circonstances, poste qu'il conservera jusqu'en

1736. Bégon était bien intégré dans ce milieu d'autant plus que son père (bien connu pour ses liens avec la botanique) avait été intendant de Rochefort, de 1688 à 1710[16]. Champigny est certainement l'un des plus intéressés à conserver des liens avec le Canada. Il cherche à s'entendre avec l'intendant de Rochefort (Bégon père) pour établir de bonnes relations avec Le Havre dans l'approvisionnement du Canada[17]. Le dernier exemple en ce domaine nous vient de Gilles Hocquart, intendant au Canada, pendant plus de 19 ans, nommé intendant à Brest, à son retour de la colonie, en 1748, où il demeure en poste jusqu'en 1764.

À côté de ces grands personnages issus du monde des gouverneurs et des intendants, nous avons une quantité de commissaires, de contrôleurs et d'officiers de tous genres qui, à un moment ou à un autre, ont travaillé au Canada et ont acquis une connaissance utile des mécanismes de fonctionnement des relations avec la colonie. C'est justement parce qu'ils sont au courant des conditions qui prévalent chez leurs correspondants canadiens que ces officiers[18] sont affectés à des postes reliés au Canada à leur retour en France. C'est le cas du commissaire de marine Pierre Belamy, déjà évoqué plus haut, qui s'occupe de recevoir, à La Rochelle, le courrier en provenance du Canada, ou celui du commissaire Jean-Baptiste Sully, qui assure même l'intérim d'intendant au Canada avant de revenir travailler au Havre. Le rôle de ces intendants et de ces officiers ayant un cursus canadien en France ne se limite pas à l'acheminement du courrier au départ et à l'arrivée. Ceux-ci servent à l'occasion de conseillers au roi et au ministre de la Marine pour des affaires concernant la colonie. Ils sont souvent appelés à donner leur avis sur des questions ou à rédiger des mémoires sur des sujets qui requièrent leurs compétences.

Le protocole d'expédition et de réception

S'il y a des similitudes entre les différents types de courrier qui traversent l'Atlantique, c'est sur le plan des modalités d'expédition et de réception que la correspondance officielle se démarque. Contrairement aux lettres personnelles ou commerciales, dont le transport ne repose souvent que sur des ententes orales avec les capitaines, le courrier officiel fait l'objet de soins particuliers et d'un suivi postal plus serré – liste des objets de correspondance, enregistrement des départs, des porteurs, accusés de réception, etc. Ces lettres, qui contiennent souvent des informations de la plus haute importance, requièrent un traitement particulier (enveloppes cachetées, sacs scellés, paquets ficelés, textes cryptés, etc.) qui a pour but de restreindre et de cloisonner au maximum la correspondance aux seules personnes autorisées. La pérennité de la colonie dépend grandement de ce protocole d'expédition qui, d'un côté, essaie de réduire au minimum le risque d'espionnage par une puissance étrangère et, de l'autre, évite les affrontements entre les groupes dont les intérêts (politiques, religieux, marchands, etc.) divergent au sein des implantations outre-mer[19].

Les mesures de sécurité supplémentaires : cryptage et traçabilité des envois

Pour les situations les plus délicates, on fait parfois appel au cryptage du courrier officiel, procédé qui demeure le moyen ultime d'assurer que le contenu de la correspondance ne tombera pas entre les mains de personnes non autorisées. Les textes faisant l'objet d'un tel traitement au sein de la correspondance officielle contiennent principalement des renseignements d'ordre militaire[20]. Il existe plusieurs niveaux de cryptages dont les codes sont changés périodiquement. Les plus communs servent aux intendants et aux officiers, et font souvent l'objet de circulaires internes[21]. En général, les tables de décodage de telles lettres sont remises, en mains propres, aux administrateurs et aux officiers militaires concernés, mais il arrive que l'on en expédie par le courrier. Les lettres cryptées représentent un très petit nombre des documents de la correspondance officielle. Elles s'accroissent logiquement en période de guerre, lorsque les risques d'interception se multiplient. Si les lettres cryptées ont l'avantage de rendre leur contenu inaccessible aux lecteurs externes, elles alourdissent par contre le processus de transmission de l'information qui requiert un encodage à la source et un décodage à l'arrivée. Il existe souvent des secrétaires chiffreurs affectés à cette tâche, mais la réussite du processus peut parfois être mise en péril par des problèmes techniques liés aux tables d'encodage qui ne sont pas à jour. (Voir aussi le chapitre 8 du présent ouvrage.)

Les lettres partent de Paris ou de Versailles dans des paquets ou des emballages scellés, marqués de tampons, paraphés de signatures officielles, et voyagent vers les ports d'embarquement dans des malles séparées où l'on évite tout mélange avec le courrier ordinaire. Ces mesures de sécurité ne sont cependant pas suffisantes, car d'autres épreuves peuvent empêcher le courrier de se rendre à destination à diverses étapes de l'acheminement. Ce peut être lors du transit des sacs au bureau de l'intendant, lors du chargement et du déchargement des paquets dans les chaloupes ou en rade, à bord des vaisseaux, au départ et à l'arrivée. Comme mesures de sécurité supplémentaires, les sacs de correspondance officielle sont accompagnés d'une liste des lettres et des pièces annexes qui s'y trouvent, ce qui permet de vérifier si toutes les pièces du courrier sont parvenues à destination[22]. Finalement, les accusés de réception, que l'on trouve en début de la plupart des lettres, confirment à l'expéditeur que toutes les pièces de courrier sont arrivées, voire qu'aucune autre n'y a été insérée.

Le procès verbal d'embarquement

Pour éviter une rupture de l'acheminement, les porteurs et les réceptionnaires de courrier doivent produire divers documents qui attestent du transit des sacs ou des paquets, et qui débouche sur une véritable traçabilité des envois. Le document le plus fréquemment trouvé dans les sources est le procès verbal d'embarquement du courrier, souvent dressé en quatre exemplaires[23] par un administrateur de la Marine et destiné au commandant d'un vaisseau du roi en partance pour le Canada. Cette attestation confirme au ministre l'arrivée de ses lettres au port et leur chargement à bord d'un navire. Cette opération est le plus souvent effectuée par un commissaire de la Marine envoyé par l'intendant, en présence d'un deuxième témoin, souvent un commissaire de port. Cette déclaration ne produit que très rarement l'inventaire des pièces contenues dans l'envoi, mais précise par contre les destinataires, les lieux et les conditions d'embarquement ainsi que la personne à qui sont confiés les sacs – les officiers subalternes du vaisseau, en l'absence du commandant. Non seulement ces procès-verbaux témoignent-ils d'une volonté de rendre compte, en haut lieu, du cheminement des sacs, mais encore peuvent-ils être utiles aux officiers d'un navire qui transporte des sacs à déposer dans différents ports.

Nous pouvons bien identifier certains navires qui reviennent à chaque année du Canada avec du courrier[24], mais il n'y en a pas, en tant que tels, qui sont affectés exclusivement à cette tâche, car tous les vaisseaux du roi transportent un minimum de lettres ou d'instructions officielles. Cette opération s'effectue dans le cadre de l'embarquement des autres marchandises à bord des navires (l'artillerie, les munitions, les vivres, les passagers, etc.), mais implique plus concrètement le commandant du vaisseau.

Les porteurs et transporteurs maritimes

Nous avons évoqué les méthodes utilisées pour contrer les risques de perte ou d'ouverture du courrier officiel durant son trajet terrestre, mais comment pouvait-on augmenter d'un cran la sécurité de la correspondance et en assurer la surveillance, une fois que les lettres se trouvaient à bord ? Cette ultime protection était confiée à un porteur qui faisait la traversée avec les paquets de la Cour. Ce dernier pouvait monter à bord des vaisseaux du roi ou des navires marchands, s'arrêter dans un port ou se rendre jusqu'à la Cour. Bref, plusieurs cas de figures étaient envisageables. Les sources font référence à des quantités substantielles d'objets de correspondance à transporter : 59 paquets de lettres dans un cas; 42 dans un autre[25]. Il s'agit d'envois volumineux, qui ne pouvaient pas tenir dans les bras d'une seule personne et qui devaient être nécessairement placés dans une malle ou des fûts. Nous avons parfois la description physique des contenants (boîtes, coffres, caisses, emballage, etc.) dans lesquels était remisé le courrier[26]. Lorsque nous parlons de porteurs, il ne s'agit donc pas d'une personne en possession d'une simple enveloppe sous le bras, mais bien du responsable du transport du sac ou des malles contenant les paquets de documents de correspondance officielle.

Parmi les profils clairement identifiés dans les sources, nous pouvons distinguer une différence entre les envois effectués de France et ceux du Canada. Sur 19 exemples retrouvés de remises de courrier au départ de la France pour le Canada, 10 concernent des militaires (6 commandants, 3 officiers de troupe, un capitaine de brûlot) et les neuf autres sont reliés à des capitaines de navires marchands se rendant dans la colonie. Ces chiffres sont, bien sûr, trompeurs puisqu'il ne s'agit pas des envois annuels par les vaisseaux du roi, mais plutôt des cas de remises exceptionnelles à des vaisseaux et à des navires que l'on va trouver en rade au large. Ces remises laissent cependant entrevoir que, dans ce genre de situation, on fait confiance aux capitaines de navires marchands dans un cas sur deux.

Le profil est différent du côté des expéditions au départ du Canada pour la France mais, là encore, nous devons composer avec l'état des sources qui sont beaucoup plus loquaces à ce sujet. Sur 57 cas de remises de courrier effectuées au Canada à destination de la France, 30 concernent des officiers des troupes de la Marine (4 capitaines, 3 lieutenants et 23 officiers); cinq autres, des officiers de vaisseaux du roi (2 commandants et 3 enseignes de vaisseaux); deux autres, des officiers de plume (un procureur du roi et un commissaire ordonnateur); un cas met en cause un intendant et 18 cas touchent des civils (17 maîtres de navires et un marchand). Tout ceci montre un recours plus systématique aux officiers militaires (de Marine ou d'infanterie), qui sont impliqués dans près de 70 % des envois.

Ces quantités recouvrent cependant de longues périodes et des situations différentes, tels certains cas d'officiers militaires s'embarquant à bord de vaisseaux marchands avec les paquets destinés à la Cour. Il n'en demeure pas moins que ces statistiques des départs du Canada sont probablement plus représentatives des proportions de transports par des civils et des militaires que les données trouvées sur les départs de la France, dispersées dans plusieurs séries d'archives et, au total, peu nombreuses.

En ce qui concerne les capitaines de navires marchands, les sources laissent clairement voir un recours plus fréquent à leurs services à partir des années 1720, c'est-à-dire lorsque la quantité de documents de la correspondance officielle augmente de façon considérable et que les destinations coloniales se multiplient. L'augmentation du volume de la correspondance officielle est reliée à la croissance de la population canadienne dans son ensemble et à la large place prise par l'État français dans le processus décisionnel de ses colonies en général. L'augmentation des recours aux navires marchands repose aussi sur l'accroissement de la navigation triangulaire avec les îles d'Amérique française, qui connaissent également une hausse fulgurante au 18e siècle. Le rôle des navires marchands n'est donc plus seulement complémentaire. Si les autorités font souvent appel à eux après le départ des vaisseaux du roi, ils sont aussi employés à cette tâche dès le printemps, parfois vers des destinations non desservies par les grosses unités militaires qui, souvent, ne s'arrêtent qu'à l'île Royale et à Québec[27]. Par contre, si l'on fait confiance aux capitaines de navires marchands pour l'acheminement du courrier officiel, leur rôle de porteurs s'arrête aux ports. En effet, ils ne se rendent jamais à la Cour et rarement chez l'intendant, mais se contentent de remettre le courrier aux officiers de Marine du port d'arrivée.

Au premier rang de ceux auxquels on a confié la tâche de transporter la correspondance d'État se trouvent, bien sûr, les gouverneurs et les intendants, dont certains font la traversée à plusieurs reprises durant leur mandat. Les sources font mention de Champigny, lors de son retour en France[28], et de Michel Bégon[29], mais il est probable qu'ils en transportent tous un minimum lorsqu'ils traversent l'Atlantique. Ces hommes ont non seulement une place d'honneur dans les vaisseaux du roi, mais ils y ont de plus un droit de 10 à 20 tonneaux de fret[30] durant leur mandat. Si ce fret ne concerne pas le courrier officiel, il permet, le cas échéant, de prendre en charge d'éventuels paquets de la part d'amis.

Dans un sens comme dans l'autre, l'officier militaire (noble) de la Marine émerge comme principal convoyeur durant la traversée ou comme porteur des lettres du Canada jusqu'à la Cour. Bien que certains acteurs jouent ce rôle à plusieurs reprises[31], il n'y a toutefois pas de « postiers » proprement dit, car cette tâche était confiée à différentes personnes d'une année à l'autre. En fait, les officiers de Marine sont les porteurs idéaux pour la correspondance officielle. Le transport d'enveloppes cachetées fait partie de leur quotidien. Leurs ordres d'affectation se trouvent dans des enveloppes scellées, qu'ils décachètent en mer pour connaître leur destination. Tous les gradés sont soumis à la règle du silence et formés au respect des consignes de sécurité. C'est aussi parce que la correspondance officielle est chargée à bord des vaisseaux du roi qu'on les choisit. Lorsqu'ils sont plusieurs à s'embarquer, on opte pour la préséance traditionnelle qui consiste à choisir, à grade égal, le plus âgé des officiers d'une compagnie d'infanterie ou de garde de la Marine[32]. Les officiers n'étaient pas rétribués pour ce service qui s'effectuait dans le cadre de leur mission, mais ils pouvaient être remboursés pour leurs déplacements en France pour y livrer de la correspondance de la Cour.

Il est finalement probable que des modalités différentes étaient appliquées à la correspondance à expédier de part et d'autre de l'Atlantique et que, rendu au 18e siècle, une grande quantité de pièces administratives relativement communes étaient acheminées par les navires marchands, alors que les objets de courrier les plus sensibles contenant des informations stratégiques ou d'importance traversaient à bord des vaisseaux du roi, sous la vigilance d'un officier porteur affecté à cette tâche. Cette répartition rationnelle des envois avait l'avantage de limiter les pertes, entre autres, en cas de naufrage ou d'avarie du seul navire transporteur, mais aussi lorsque des pièces de courrier étaient jetées à la mer, suite à l'approche d'un navire ennemi[33]. Par ailleurs, on ne lançait pas tout le courrier à la mer et, la plupart du temps, les porteurs recevaient des consignes précises à ce sujet de la part du ministre ou de l'intendant. C'est principalement la correspondance officielle contenant des informations d'ordre militaire qui faisait l'objet d'un tel traitement : tous les envois mentionnant la présence de troupes, de flottes, d'affectations, de projets d'attaques militaires, mais aussi ceux qui renfermaient les codes de cryptage des lettres[34], les signaux de navigation sur le Saint-Laurent et d'entrée dans les ports coloniaux[35] devaient être systématiquement détruits ou jetés à la mer en cas d'abordage par un navire ennemi.

Conclusion

De tous les types de courrier qui traversent l'Atlantique à l'époque coloniale, c'est sans conteste la correspondance officielle qui dispose de la meilleure structure d'acheminement. Si elles ne sont pas les plus importantes en terme de quantités, les dépêches officielles font par contre l'objet d'une attention particulière qui se reflète dans les sources consultées et qui nous permet de suivre leur parcours à la trace, leurs points de chute, leur transfert à bord des navires, leur mode de rangement, etc. Reste que ces lettres n'ont pas toutes le même statut et il existe ainsi plusieurs niveaux de sécurité, allant de la circulaire générale, distribuée à tous les intendants, jusqu'à la lettre cryptée, contenant des informations militaires, à remettre en main propre au gouverneur.

Mis à part les modalités d'acheminement, l'autre dimension que les sources permettent d'entrevoir, c'est l'encadrement humain de ces expéditions de courrier. À la lecture des archives, on se rend compte que la correspondance officielle est loin de circuler dans un univers impersonnel. Durant son acheminement, elle passe entre les mains de gens qui se connaissent et qui oeuvrent au sein des mêmes institutions (les postes et les messageries, l'intendance, la Marine, etc.), mais elle transite également entre les mains de personnes qui sont au courant des conditions de correspondance avec le Canada ou dans d'autres colonies pour y avoir déjà travaillé à titre d'intendant, de commissaire, d'officier, etc.

La structuration de cette correspondance officielle vers les colonies se fait en parallèle et à la même époque de la monopolisation progressive du courrier national par la Ferme des postes et messageries de France, et elle s'intègre dans une politique de centralisation étatique et d'unification de toutes les administrations coloniales à Versailles. Les défauts d'une telle structure sont nombreux et évidents : la complexité de l'appareil administratif et les lourdeurs bureaucratiques qui ralentissent le processus décisionnel. La mise en œuvre de toutes les politiques coloniales oblige à préparer les dépêches des mois à l'avance. Pour les autorités de la métropole, cette centralisation administrative a par contre l'avantage de pouvoir assurer une politique cohérente à l'intérieur de l'empire (que ce soit aux Antilles ou au Canada) et d'avoir un certain contrôle sur les élites et les populations coloniales tout en étant à l'écoute de leurs besoins. L'étude de la correspondance officielle traduit ainsi l'esprit qui anime les différentes composantes de l'État français tout en demeurant un rouage essentiel de son fonctionnement. Les différences que l'on peut constater en comparant ces modalités avec celles de l'empire anglais reflètent ainsi deux conceptions différentes de l'État et de ses rapports avec son empire colonial. Plus concrètement, cette politique de contrôle et de centralisation de la correspondance coloniale a sans nul doute aidé les Français à se maintenir en Amérique du Nord et à faire face, avec très peu de moyens, aux treize colonies qui, en dépit de leur énorme poids démographique, n'ont pas eu, avant le milieu du 18e siècle, la cohérence politique et militaire nécessaire pour entamer une conquête du Canada.

Notes

1. Les recherches ont porté sur les séries « Correspondance au départ »; « Correspondance à l'arrivée »; les « Lettres reçues à la Cour » et diverses autres séries des fonds de la Marine et des Colonies, conservés aux Archives nationales de France (ANF.
2. Voir Archives nationales de France, fonds des Colonies [ANF, Colonies], C11a-113, f. 225 (20 juillet 1707).
3. Cette suprématie du pertuis d'Antioche sur le plan des liens maritimes avec le Canada est particulièrement visible dans le corpus des documents de la correspondance au départ, où il existe des registres d'ordres spécifiques pour les ports de Rochefort et de La Rochelle, situation qui n'existe pas pour les autres ports.
4. Voir ANF, Marine B3-345, f. 207r-v (7 juin 1731).
5. Voir Expédition de courrier de Nantes au Canada, dans ANF, fonds de la Marine B3-350, f. 242 (7 juin 1732) ou à Louisbourg, dans Marine B3-369, f. 209-210 (5 mars 1735).
6. Lire Bernard Allaire, « Histoire de la poste maritime France-Canada, volume 3 : la correspondance officielle (1630-1765) », Musée canadien de la poste, Rapport de recherche, 2004, p. 6-10.
7. Siège de la Compagnie des Indes, Port-Louis attire une partie de la navigation et des arrivages du courrier officiel pour la cour. Ces arrivées se font parfois directement dans les ports voisins de Concarneau ou Belle-Île. Voir ANF, Marine B3-385, f. 200 (2 décembre 1738); Marine B3-415, f. 251 (16 décembre 1743); B3-477, f. 311 (19 novembre 1749) ou Colonies C11a-12, f. 312-314.
8. Voir Arrivées de paquets de Québec, dans ANF, Marine B3-257, f. 560-561v (18 juillet 1719).
9. Voir Transmission des paquets pour la Cour arrivés du Canada à Saint-Malo, dans ANF Marine B3-112, f. 426-429 (1701). Voir le même dossier, dans Marine B3-169, f. 162-166v (1709).

10. Voir Arrivée d'un paquet de lettres du Labrador à Saint-Malo, dans ANF, Marine B3-415, f. 84 (21 octobre 1743).

11. Voir Arrivée de paquets de l'île Royale à Nantes dans ANF, Marine B3-270, f. 311-313v (4 novembre 1721); Marine B3-280, f. 430 (8 décembre 1722); Marine B3-344, f. 333 (4 août 1731); Marine B3-380, f. 347 (1 mars 1737); Marine B3-380-380, f. 449 (28 décembre 1737). Le topo est identique pour le cas d'une arrivée de paquets à Cherbourg en provenance de l'île Royale : voir Marine B3-368, f. 365 (17 juin 1735).

12. Lire, à ce sujet, Eugène Vaillé, *Histoire générale des postes françaises*, Paris, PUF, 1950, vol. 4, p. 117.

13. L'incident se termine par l'emprisonnement du transporteur du courrier. Voir Bibliothèque nationale de France [BNF], Département des manuscrits, Nouvelles acquisitions françaises, n° 21331, fol. 56-64 (26 janvier 1685).

14. C'est le cas, par exemple, à Nantes, avec les commissaires et contrôleurs Duguay (en 1693), Crémont (1693), Marias (1719), Bigot de la Mothe (1721 et 1722), Renault (1728), D'Abbadie (1731), Dionis (1732, 1735 et 1737); à Saint-Malo, avec les commissaires Le Bigot de Gastines (1697), Saint-Sulpice (1701), Lempereur (1709, 1711 et 1714), Marin (1718) et Guillot (1743); à Port-Louis, avec le contrôleur La Touche (1738) et les commissaires Clairambault (1743) et La Ferrière de Vincelles (1743); à Marseille, avec le commissaire Poncet (1731); à Cherbourg, avec Jean-Baptiste Tixier de Saint-Prix (1735); à Concarneau, avec le commissaire aux classes Paubert (1749) et à Dunkerque, avec La Haye d'Anglemont (1738).

15. Hormis les arsenaux militaires (Brest, Rochefort, Toulon), qui ont des intendants attitrés, la France est divisée en plusieurs intendances qui couvrent de larges provinces. En l'absence d'intendant dans certaines villes importantes (Nantes ou Saint-Malo, par exemple, qui relèvent de l'intendance de Bretagne), ce sont des commissaires ordonnateurs, des contrôleurs de la Marine ou des capitaines de port qui s'acquittent des tâches administratives. Lire Charles Godard, *Les pouvoirs des intendants sous Louis XIV particulièrement dans les pays d'élections de 1661 à 1715*, Paris, Champion, 1974; Anette Smedley-Weill, *Les intendants de Louis XIV*, Paris, Fayard, 1995; Charles Tranchant, *Les intendants et commissaires royaux en Poitou d'Henri IV à Louis XIV*, Paris, Imprimerie nationale, 1906.

16. Voir « Michel Bégon », dans Michel Vergé-Franceschi, *Dictionnaire d'histoire maritime*, Paris, Laffont, 2002, vol. 1, p. 193, et Michel Sardet, *Le jardin botanique de Rochefort et les grandes expéditions maritimes*, Le Croit vif, 2000.

17. Voir ANF, Colonies C11a-20, f. 180 (1702).

18. Il est à noter que certains d'entre eux deviennent plus tard des intendants.

19. Au sujet de la dimension politique de la correspondance de l'administration française, lire Kenneth J. Banks, *Chasing Empire Across the Sea: Communication and the State in French Atlantic 1713-1763*, Montréal / Kingston, McGill / Queen's University Press, 2002.

20. Voir l'exemple décrypté de Beauharnois dans ANF, Colonies C11a-61-f. 230r.

21. Voir la circulaire aux intendants du 23 janvier 1674 pour l'acheminement des chiffres et leur conservation, cité dans Vaillé, *op. cit.*, vol. 4, p. 124.

22. Voir exemple de ces précautions, dans ANF, Colonies, C11a-6, f. 161r (novembre 1683) et 320r (octobre 1684).

23. Voir embarquement de paquets sur le vaisseau du roi *Le Héros,* dans ANF, Colonies C11a-113, f. 226r (20 juillet 1707).

24. Tel que *Le Chameau,* par exemple, qui aurait probablement continué ses tournées annuelles de livraisons s'il n'avait pas fait naufrage. Deux malles qui servaient peut-être à remiser le courrier furent néanmoins retirées de l'épave. Voir ANF, Colonies C11a-51, f. 501-503 (1729).

25. Voir ANF, Colonies C11a-54, f. 227 (20 octobre 1731).

26. Il existe quelques mentions de « caisses contenant les paquets de la Cour » ou de certains documents déposés dans des « boites en fer blanc » avant d'être mis dans des sacs scellés. Voir, par exemple, ANF, Colonies C11a-49, f. 403 (22 octobre 1727).
27. Voir le courrier donné à un navire marchand de Nantes, dans ANF, Marine B3-323, f. 187 (29 avril 1728).
28. Voir ANF, Marine B3-112, f. 426-429 (1701).
29. Voir ANF, Colonies C11a-51, f. 169 (1729).
30. Voir ANF, Colonies C11a-46, fol. 206 (1724).
31. Liénard de Beaujeu porte le courrier officiel à trois reprises alors qu'Aubert de la Chesnaye le fait deux fois.
32. C'est ce qui se passe en 1721, lorsque l'on remet les paquets pour la Cour au sieur de Saint-Martin, le plus ancien capitaine de compagnie, ou à Jean-Charles Darnaud, qui prend sa retraite à la fin de son service militaire au Canada, en 1746, et qui rapporte en France les paquets de la Cour. Voir ANF, Colonies C11a-85, f. 242 (9 novembre 1746).
33. Voir ANF, Colonies C11a-31, f. 190 (15 janvier 1710).

"AGITATORS OF THE WORST TYPE"

2

The 1938 Riot and Occupation of the Vancouver Post Office

Duncan Stacey, Industrial Historian, Richmond, B.C.

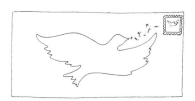

Abstract

The Depression of the 1930s wracked the entire nation and all levels of government that tried to cope with its challenges. In Vancouver, B.C., one such challenge was the Post Office Riot of 1938. The city's main Post Office represented a powerful symbol for those working on both sides of the barricades. In this article, new information on the Riot, long unknown and unavailable, is presented for the first time.

Résumé

La crise des années 1930 a été catastrophique pour l'ensemble du pays et tous les paliers de gouvernement qui ont essayé de régler les problèmes qu'elle a suscités. À Vancouver (C.-B.), l'un de ces problèmes a été l'émeute qui a eu lieu au bureau de poste en 1938. Le principal bureau de poste de la ville était un puissant symbole pour ceux qui se trouvaient des deux côtés des barricades. Dans cet article, de nouvelles informations sur l'émeute, longtemps ignorées et impossibles à trouver, sont présentées pour la première fois.

> "An historical understanding is what I am after, not agreement, approval or sympathy."
>
> Eric Hobsbawm, *Interesting Times*

Introduction[1]

In the 1930s, British Columbia had become a mecca for Canada's single unemployed men. Times were tough and the winter weather was more clement on the West Coast. By the fall of 1931, the province was awash with so many transients that Vancouver's chief of police advised the federal government to pull men from all westbound trains

Figure 2.1 Main Post Office at Hastings and Granville Streets, Vancouver, 1935. Photograph by Dunn and Rundle. City of Vancouver Archives Bu P 53.

and place them in special holding camps along the Alberta–British Columbia boundary.[2] That British Columbia subsequently became the epicentre of relief camp unrest is hardly surprising. The province had the largest number of men from all over Canada in the largest number of work camps. From the beginning of the federal relief program, British Columbia had more work camps than the three Prairie provinces combined.[3]

By the end of the decade, more than any other city in Canada, Vancouver had been scarred by the Depression. In the spring of 1938, the B.C. government reduced its loans to municipalities, arguing that single, able-bodied men should be able to support themselves during the summer months. At about the same time, around 1,600 men from the Prairies, who, at the request of the federal government, had been admitted to provincial forestry projects during the winter months, were offered free transportation out of the province. Rejecting the offer, the men began to march on Vancouver in late April. On May 10, George S. Pearson, the provincial minister of labour, announced that no relief would be offered to unemployed men from the Prairies. This announcement resulted in the June 1938 occupation by the single unemployed of the Vancouver Post Office, the Vancouver Art Gallery, and Hotel Georgia, as a means of drawing public attention to their plight.

The choice to occupy the Vancouver Art Gallery and the Vancouver Post Office was based on the belief that the buildings represented the powers that were the cause of their unemployment and distress: the Vancouver municipal government and the federal government, respectively. (The Post Office would linger as a powerful negative symbol for labour leaders. Two decades later, in the midst of a recession, a mass meeting was organized outside the new Vancouver Post Office to protest the federal government's inaction on the unemployment issue. The demonstration also served to commemorate the 20-year anniversary of the events of 1938.)

This article examines the events leading up to and including the occupation of the Vancouver Post Office in June 1938, an event that climaxed with the forceful eviction of the protesters and a full-scale riot outside the Post Office in the downtown district. If it can be said that the 1930s was the high point of street action by unemployed Canadians from coast to coast, it is also true that these confrontations produced their own specific blend of protest in B.C. Various regional and institutional rivalries and socio-political tensions simmered beneath the surface of West Coast life. I propose to explore these tensions to better understand the events of the Post Office riot and the objectives of the combatants. The Post Office is less the raison d'être of this article than the stage upon which conflicts originating elsewhere were played out. I begin with the events of 1935, when the planning for the 1938 Post Office occupation may have begun.

The Events of 1935

The Vancouver Post Office occupation and riot of 1938 is rooted in previous disturbances led by unemployed relief camp workers in Vancouver and throughout the West earlier in the 1930s. The disturbances were the Vancouver Relief Camp Strike of 1935 that led to the On-to-Ottawa Trek and culminated in the Regina Riot in the same year.

In 1935, men from the relief camps, who had been organized by the Communist Party through the Relief Camp Workers Union of the Workers Unity League, headed to

Vancouver from around the province to start the first major relief camp workers' strike.[4] The strikers demanded work and wages of 50 cents per hour, abolition of military control of the camps, recognition of camp committees, and other improvements. The turmoil of 1935 included a serious riot at Vancouver's Hudson's Bay department store on Granville Street and culminated in the mayor of Vancouver reading the Riot Act. The demonstrators were eventually prevailed upon to return peacefully to their headquarters.[5]

On June 3, 1935, the On-to-Ottawa Trek was initiated with the objective of raising the issues of work and wages with the federal cabinet. The trek was halted halfway across the country in Regina, where two cabinet members met with the trekkers. However, the trekkers' demands were not considered. Later, in Ottawa, a second meeting between Trek leader Arthur Evans and prime minister R. B. Bennett also terminated without consideration of their demands. The result is known in Canadian history as the Regina Riot, in which more than 100 strikers were injured or arrested. Charles Miller, a city detective, died; a dozen other policemen were seriously hurt.[6]

Following the Regina Riot, the relief camp (or "slave camp"[7]) system established by Bennett's Conservative administration, the limitations and hardships of which did so much to bring about the violent On-to-Ottawa Trek, was abolished when Liberal leader Mackenzie King came to power in 1935. The camps were reorganized and relief workers were paid fifteen dollars a month over and above board and lodging.

Three years later in 1938, the leaders of the 1935 Ottawa trek organized a sit-in in Vancouver of unemployed and relief camp workers. Ernest Cumber, the leader of the 1935 demonstrations was in the forefront, keeping a promise made in July 1935, after the failure of the camp workers' Vancouver demonstrations: "The return to the camps is not the end of the struggle. This is not a defeat, it is a strategic retreat."[8] Two other protagonists of the 1938 events in Vancouver were also involved in the 1935 Regina Riot. Steve Brodie, who sat on the Regina trekkers' strike committee, was to become the leader of the 1938 Vancouver Post Office occupation.[9] He was well known to another key player, Superintendent C. H. Hill of the RCMP. Hill had been on the force in 1935, and, in 1938, he was the officer in charge of clearing the sit-in participants from the Vancouver Post Office in 1938. It appears there was no love lost between these two adversaries.

Public Opinion

After 1935, conditions for the unemployed in British Columbia improved somewhat for nearly two years. Employment rose until November 1937 and then fell rapidly until April 1938.[10] In addition to the worsening employment situation, some relief camps in British Columbia were closed, and welfare budgets in municipalities were cut back. In the face of a mass migration of single unemployed men to Vancouver, reaching six thousand in May of 1938,[11] public opinion was becoming volatile. Ordinary citizens expressed their concern to Colonel W. Foster, Vancouver's chief of police:

> I want to express my admiration for your sympathetic and sensible treatment of the unemployed boys. It is a terrible situation for the unfortunate men, and also for the citizens of Vancouver to have to face, with a hopeless outlook, unless every one will

act with these men to force the Dominion to try to solve the work problem, which be done if we had a sincere man like president Roosevelt ... P.S. Remember we all respect you and your force, and the stand you are taking may steady the other police bodies (B.C & N Mounted) to be kind and humane like yourself, no bloodshed of innocent starving boys who might be our own sons. Don't let them forget that these are hungry British boys who want what they have a right to want—food and work. You could lead those men by kindness and understanding. Forgive me, but I feel so deeply about all this, I have boys of my own.[12]

Foster replied: "Dear Madam: Thank you very much for your kind letter regarding the unemployed situation, and I certainly hope a speedy and satisfactory solution will be found for what is a very difficult problem."[13] Foster's response was a restrained one. It was a measure of the weight of public opinion in favour of the unemployed and perhaps as well of his personal inclinations.

Evidence that the general populace of Vancouver and British Columbia was highly sympathetic to the unemployed can be found in the period immediately following the riot when emotions were still running high. On June 20, Thomas Dufferin Pattullo, the premier of British Columbia, sent an urgent message to Ottawa stating: "A considerable body of public opinion in sympathy with men" and "I cannot too strongly emphasize the seriousness of the situation here. There is a great deal of disaffection in the public mind; in fact, there are evidences of insubordination in the public services in the city of Vancouver which are very untoward..."[14] On June 22, Patullo wrote a private memo to Ian Mackenzie, then minister of national defense: "There is no doubt that the public at large has had a great deal of sympathy for these men and even although they discountenance the extreme measures taken in the recent episode [Post Office Riot] in Vancouver, they nonetheless feel that the situation [unemployment] is not being adequately met."[15] Patullo added that he would appreciate the minister of national defense reading his letter to all the members of the government as the time for definite action had come. As of July 6, 1938, Pattullo was still referring to public sympathy toward the unemployed: "The movement now in Victoria is a form of insurrection and the more dangerous because the insurrectionists are receiving the sympathy of large numbers of well meaning people, including representatives of the churches."[16]

West Coast public opinion was remarkably sympathetic to the province's unemployed, which was not necessarily the case elsewhere in the country. The divergence would add a twist of regional resentment to the situation. For example, in 1935, the mayor of Ottawa wired Vancouver's mayor concerning Vancouver's unemployment problem: "You ought to be fair-minded enough to see that your troubles should not be forced on other communities. Ottawa as a city has absolutely nothing to do with a national problem and as far as I am concerned, I shall refuse to deal with such a question."[17] The Vancouver mayor, who was looking perhaps for increased relief monies from the rest of the country, including the federal government, responded: "Vancouver has suffered enough and you ought to be willing to bear your share of the national grief that the depression caused. Most of these men came from Eastern Canada and ought to return there."[18] The problem of the unemployed was something of a political football to be kicked back and forth across the country, not unfamiliar political behaviour in Canada.

The coup de grace of regional insult was delivered by Conservative senator Rt. Hon. Arthur Meighen on June 9 while the occupation was in full progress. Meighen dismissed the contention of the unemployed demonstrators that Vancouver was an outcast colony. In his view, if the government bent its neck to the jobless, the result would be awful to contemplate.[19] Meighen's comments resonated through the B.C. press, which depicted this conservative view in suggestive and negative terms: "Vancouver Is 'Outcast Colony' to Ottawa" and "Government [B.C.] 'Bends Its Neck' to Jobless and Result is 'Awful to Contemplate.'"[20]

The Occupation

From the outset, the demonstrators made every effort to behave in a respectable fashion. On May 20, 1,600 single, unemployed men formed into orderly brigades, each with one group leader for every ten men, and marched into and occupied the Vancouver Art Gallery, the Vancouver Post Office and the Hotel Georgia. The men were not an unorganized subversive rabble. The move had been eight months in the planning. One of the men later asserted that the occupations were planned as early as 1930.[21] According to Steve Brodie, a leader of the 1938 occupation of the Post Office and the 1935 Regina Riot: "[W]e had committees for everything. You couldn't slice a loaf of bread into five bologna sandwiches without appointing a committee to see it was done according to plan. Discipline was an absolute must."[22]

The protesters were unemployed, but organized and self-reliant. They were not front

Figure 2.2 Protesters sleeping inside the post office, their shoes and boots lining the service wickets.

Vancouver Public Library, Special Collections Division, Photo number 13340.

men of some ulterior force within the political left. Accusations at the time that the Post Office demonstrators were Communist-led are not supported by the police records. It is of interest that on May 28, 1938, three weeks prior to the eviction at the Post Office, Inspector Fish of the RCMP reported to the Vancouver police that R. W. Campbell, a representative of the Post Office demonstrators, met Malcolm Bruce of the Communist Party. Fish was of the opinion that "the communist party are not directing the unemployed movement and consequently the communist party know little of the plans of the unemployed."[23]

A strong sense of organization was integral to this independent movement, which knew when to attack and when to quit. After ten days, the Hotel Georgia group of 300 protesters withdrew on the promise the city would pay $500 in temporary relief.[24] That left the occupiers in the Post Office and Art Gallery, neither of whom was prepared to leave. A showdown with authorities would eventually ensue but not before the expression of a few more gusts of popular support. A large group of women hurriedly gathered at the Post Office on May 25, when it was rumoured that the protesters were to be evicted; however, they disbanded after being assured that the rumours were unfounded. By May 27, several organizations had begun a campaign to feed the jobless occupying the two buildings, and prepared for a prolonged siege. The Church of England resolved that each parish church in Vancouver and district take a collection for the men. Over the weekend of May 29, many members of the Sixth Avenue Pentecostal Tabernacle held a hymn fest in the Post Office.[25]

In light of enormous public support, the demonstrators began publishing their own newspaper, the *Post Office Gazette*, which offered their view of events and political economy. The publication no doubt irked authorities on both the West Coast and in Ottawa, but there was no consensus as to whether or when the protesters should be removed. Thus far, the protesters had not interfered with postal business inside the building. And, while Vancouver civic authorities were not in sympathy with the tactics employed by the demonstrators, they were not prepared to remove the men from the Post Office unless requested to do so by the federal government as the building fell under federal jurisdiction.

The police monitored events inside the Post Office, more or less. On May 28, Inspector Fish of the RCMP identified Ernest Cumber and Steve Brodie as leaders of the action. He also noted that:

[A] large number of the original group which occupied the Post Office have quit, being replaced by older men mostly of the bohunk (Ukrainian) bum type. In this connection I am advised from another source that a number of those now in the Post Office were previously to be found in the East end gambling clubs, my informant being under the impression that these men are not in the Post Office to take advantage of the issues of tobacco, etc.[26]

For the time being, the police were consigned to make disparaging remarks about the protesters, but they were not unaware of the goings-on inside the building. This would become evident when, a few weeks later, matters came to a head.

The Evictions

On June 17, acting postmaster general J. C. Elliott delivered a telegram via the RCMP to the mayor of Vancouver, requesting that the demonstrators vacate the Post Office: "We feel the existing situation should not be permitted longer to continue."[27] The justification by Ottawa for clearing the Post Office was "the protracted illegal occupation of the Post Office in Vancouver, which is represented as an increasing nuisance to those who make proper use of this building and as a menace through possible contagion to health of the occupants and to others...,"[28] so wrote the acting postmaster general who, incidentally, was not objecting to interruption of the postal service as the mail did continue to go through.

On June 18, the demand to remove the sit-ins came from both the postal authorities and Art Gallery trustees, who requested immediate police action to clear the buildings: "[F]our weeks having elapsed since these premises were first entered, the situation both in regard to defiance of authority, intimidation of citizens, health, and menace to the public has become such that the authorities request immediate police action."[29]

The evacuation of the Post Office began at 5 a.m. on June 19. Although the postmaster general had asked that "the appropriate authorities of the city of Vancouver take such steps as deemed necessary to have this Federal building vacated,"[30] on June 18, Police chief Foster and the RCMP agreed that the RCMP would handle the situation inside the Post Office and the city police would manage the outside; part of the city force would clear the Art Gallery at the same time.[31]

Police chief Foster issued orders for the evacuation of the Post Office at 11 p.m. on June 18 saying: "If it is necessary to use force, the necessary personnel will be provided by the Royal Canadian Mounted Police under Assistant Commissioner Hill."[32] Foster's confidential instructions accompanying the orders for the evacuation (and copied to the RCMP) state:

> In executing orders handed you herewith every effort must be made to avoid injury to persons or damage to property and the orders have been framed, particularly in regard to the time given for voluntary evacuation with this end in view, but should a situation arise where after due warning as laid down in orders, there is deliberate defiance of authority then there must not be any hesitation in taking the necessary steps to maintain law and order.[33]

The Vancouver police evacuated the Art Gallery with no property damage or personal injury. However, the evacuation at the Post Office resulted in considerable damage to the building. In addition, in the ensuing riot outside the building, five city policemen were injured, two of them badly; twenty-four arrests were made for riotous conduct on the

Figure 2.3 Evacuation of sit-down strikers from the Post Office on the morning of June 19, 1938.
Vancouver Public Library, Special Collections Division, Photo number 1276.

streets. Three of the evicted protesters were hospitalized, none of whom were seriously injured. Twenty-eight others suffered minor injuries. Steve Brodie was beaten.

There is no doubt that the demonstrators in the Post Office were given ample warning to leave the building peacefully. At 5 a.m. and again at 5:20 and at 5:30, the strikers were warned by the RCMP to leave the building or face eviction by force.[34] On June 19, Vancouver's police chief wrote to the minister of defense: "In each building an extension of the time was given hoping that there would be a peaceful exit."[35]

The demonstrators in the Post Office were not tear-gassed until 5:40 a.m., fifty-five minutes after the RCMP riot squad had entered the building and forty minutes after the first eviction notice was read. According to an RCMP memo, in the event of force having to be used, the use of tear gas was agreed upon by both the RCMP and the city police as the most humane manner of evicting the men rather than manhandling them.[36] The discussion of the advantages of using tear gas is well documented in the historic record and may explain, in part, why there was no violence in the eviction of the demonstrators at the Art Gallery compared to the Post Office.

In the Art Gallery, the ceilings were much lower than in the Post Office, so the tear gas disabled the demonstrators far more quickly.[37] As well, the decision of Chief Foster to include Harold Winch, a CCF member of the provincial legislature who was highly supportive of the demonstrators, at the police reading of the eviction notice at the Art Gallery no doubt helped defuse the situation. A secret RCMP memo dated June 20, 1938, stated that Winch led the demonstrators out of trouble to the Ukrainian Farmers Labour Temple on East Pender Street after the eviction of the Art Gallery, where they were joined by the strikers from the Post Office. Winch addressed both groups of demonstrators.[38] His ability to handle the demonstrators was proven again at 2 p.m. (after the Post Office riot) when 3000 demonstrators assembled in front of the Vancouver police station demanding the release of the arrested protestors. Mr. Winch addressed the crowd, after which they left peacefully. In the Post Office eviction records no evidence was found of the federal government and/or police recruiting the support of persons sympathetic to the demonstrators in the eviction, an action which might have helped calm the situation. One wonders if, politically speaking, the federal government was not too far away from the situation to grasp the need to arrive at a compromise.

Understanding the Eviction at the Post Office

Two questions should be asked concerning the eviction. Why did the police wait so long? And, why was there violence at and around the Post Office, when a similar protest group was peacefully removed from the Vancouver Art Gallery?

Consider first the issue of the timing of the eviction. The police were waiting for public support of the demonstrators to dwindle and for the number of demonstrators to fall off as divisions arose within their ranks. The RCMP and Vancouver city police kept a daily count of the men in the occupied building. Between 11:30 a.m. on June 6 and 4 p.m. on June 7, the number of men in the Post Office dropped from 525 to 204. On June 11, the RCMP addressed a confidential report to authorities in Ottawa stating that there were 331 men in the Post Office and that their leaders were doing their best to hold them together.[39] The day before the eviction, another secret memo written by RCMP Superintendent Hill described the situation inside the Post Office and the Art Gallery: "It will be noted that no outward change is apparent in the situation. The strength of the demonstrators appears to be slowly decreasing, and dissension is rife within their ranks."[40]

The Post Office riot and the beating of Steve Brodie cannot be explained merely as a result of the gradual disaffection and dwindling in the ranks of the protesters. The answer lies elsewhere. Virtually all RCMP documents concerning the occupation and eviction of the unemployed demonstrators bear the heading, "Possible On-to-Ottawa Trek – 1938." There is, however, no mention of an On-to-Ottawa Trek in any of the Vancouver police records reviewed for this article. Even after the eviction and riot of June 19, 1938, RCMP Superintendent Hill still addressed his letters to his superiors in Ottawa "Re: Possible On-to-Ottawa Trek, unemployed demonstrations, Vancouver, B.C." It thus appears that the RCMP's objective was not only to evict the demonstrators, but, more important, to stop another On-to-Ottawa Trek. The fear here was not of apprehended insurrection (as in the October crisis of 1970) but of apprehended, politically motivated migration, all too reminiscent in the eyes of the RCMP of the events of 1935.

This obsession with another On-to-Ottawa Trek was, under the circumstances, strange. As early as June 7, Steve Brodie addressed the men in the Post Office, suggesting that they transfer their efforts to Victoria, as apparently no headway was being made with the federal government. The police were informed of this speech. Why did Superintendent Hill not inform his superiors in Ottawa of this fact? Prior to June 7, the demonstrators had intended to move on Ottawa to present their grievances. However, in a secret letter sent to the RCMP commissioner in Ottawa it was confirmed by RCMP officer J. K. Barnes that the demonstrators intended to carry their protest to Victoria, not Ottawa: "Trekking to Ottawa presented many difficulties which did not seem surmountable, but trekking to Victoria is a comparatively easy matter."[41]

This letter was forwarded to the RCMP Commissioner in Ottawa by Superintendent Hill, commander of "E" Division, who must have known that no On-to-Ottawa Trek was in the offing as of June 13. In fact, it was known to the RCMP in Vancouver on June 12 and to the federal minister of justice on June 16 that "Certain business men in Vancouver are said to be attempting to secretly raise a fund to transport demonstrators to Victoria so as to avoid possible damage to their stores in the event of the unemployed being forcibly ejected from the Art Gallery and Post Office building."[42]

On June 15, Detective Corporal Barnes again reported to Superintendent Hill that on June 14 Brodie planned "to send a delegation of 100 men to Victoria this weekend. [Brodie] also spoke to the gathering, stating that arrangements had been made in Victoria to find the men should they be successful in arranging transportation from here [Vancouver] to that point."[43] It is obvious that, by June 14, Superintendent Hill, the chief RCMP officer in B.C., and the federal minister of justice knew that the possibility of an On-to-Ottawa Trek was highly unlikely. Yet, Superintendent Hill, a veteran of the 1935 On-to-Ottawa Trek and subsequent Regina Riot, was still fearful that history could repeat itself. Perhaps he wanted to crush another such occurrence in the bud. While no evidence was found in the RCMP documents of orders from Hill or his superiors to this effect, it is possible that if such did exist, they were removed under the Access to Information Act.

The attempt to stop another On-to-Ottawa Trek by preemptive intimidation was accomplished in part by beating up Post Office demonstration leader, Steve Brodie. Although Brodie's beating helped stop another trek, it backfired because it reinforced public sympathy for the demonstrators, even after the eviction riot. Brodie's beating was delivered by undercover Vancouver Police officers outside the Post Office, not by the RCMP. Although the RCMP admit that "Mr. Brodie ... was the last to leave and had to be 'manhandled' out of the building, outside he was clubbed by city plainclothes men, and RCMP Sergeant Cronkhite stood over him to try and protect him as he appeared in pretty bad shape."[44] In fact, no serious injuries were inflicted on the strikers during the eviction from the Post Office. All thirty-two injuries to demonstrators and the five city police occurred in the riot that followed the eviction.[45]

In our view, the explanation for the outbreak of violence at the Post Office and not at the Art Gallery is twofold. The first factor has to do with the different architecture and design of the two buildings. Tear gas took far longer to be effective in the Post Office because of the height of the ceilings (higher than in the Art Gallery) and the decision of the demonstrators to break the windows for fresh air. At the Art Gallery, only one shot of tear gas was used, no windows were broken, and twenty minutes after the use of the gas the demonstrators left peacefully. Many of the demonstrators who were disoriented by the gas were assisted by city police. However, at the Post Office evacuation, a second canister of tear gas was used after the demonstrators smashed every window. Unlike at the Art Gallery, some occupants resisted and had to be forcibly removed.[46]

Twenty-five minutes before the riot in the Post Office, the demonstrators made their intentions known. At 5:15 a.m., RCMP Inspector Radcliffe "was notified personally by the officer commanding, C. H. Hill, that the men, through their leader, one Steve Brodie, had requested to be arrested in the Post Office, and that there was apparently no intention on their part of leaving the building in an orderly manner."[47]

From the police point of view, both federal and municipal, the last thing they wanted to do was arrest Brodie. This would give the demonstrators their day in court, which would probably have further increased public sympathy for their cause. This proposition is made because even after the riot in the Post Office and Brodie's beating, Brodie was never arrested or charged.

Another riddle remains to be solved: Although Steve Brodie was beaten by officers of the Vancouver police department, not the RCMP, he was more supportive of the Vancouver police chief. After the beating, he was quoted as saying "He [Chief Foster] has treated us pretty decently all along. The boys all appreciated the way he handled things at the Art Gallery. I wished he'd been in charge of the Post Office." Brodie also expressed regret for any injury or inconvenience caused to Post Office officials.[48] It is conceivable that Brodie's support of the Vancouver police and federal Post Office officials was based on the fact that he did not want to lose local public sympathy for the unemployed demonstrators. As well, the animosity directed towards the RCMP may have been the result of bad blood between himself and Superintendent Hill that may have dated back three or more years. This proposition is informed by a consultation of the written historical record and an interview with a Vancouver police officer, who was involved in clearing the Vancouver Art Gallery. Our informant admitted that the Vancouver police were generally quite sympathetic to the demonstrators. The information seems to dovetail with comments made by the B.C. premier to the prime minister a day after the Post Office riot; "[T]here is evidence of insubordination in the public services in the City of Vancouver which are very untoward."[49]

Conclusion

Upon close inspection of the remaining RCMP records concerning the events in Vancouver on June 19, 1938—for which some of the material has been withheld in accordance with the Freedom of Information Act—it becomes clear that the two police forces involved, although working together, had different objectives. Unlike the RCMP reports, the city police records make no mention of a possible On-to-Ottawa Trek. The job of the city police was merely to clear the demonstrators from the occupied buildings with the least disturbance, thereby preventing an increase in public sympathy for the demonstrators' cause. Moreover, there is no doubt there was sympathy for the demonstrators both within the city police and the provincial police forces.

Two members of the British Columbia provincial police recalled their frustration vis-à-vis the single unemployed whom they had to police during the dirty thirties:

> For years, we kept those poor unemployed men on the move, counted their numbers, over and over again. The freights had many more people riding on them than any passenger trains did then. Men would come into a place like Kamloops and would hop off outside of town, either to disappear into the jungle or drift through town, probably stopping at a couple of houses to see if they could chop wood in exchange for a sandwich. Then on the other side of town, they would catch a freight on the way out. They had insufficient food and skimpy clothes which did not keep them warm. So many people with nowhere to go. Most were patient, stoic, polite.[50]

A senior officer summarized the hopelessness of the unemployed and his own sadness at their plight:

> Sometimes there might be fifty people camped in the underbrush, other times, two hundred and fifty. They lived in shacks made out of old boards, flattened tin cans, cardboard. Hard to tell numbers. They moved about frequently, hoping to get even a day or two of work. Men looked gaunt, unwell from months of living in damp and cold with barely enough food to keep them alive. Many of them were young high school graduates who had grown up during the golden twenties, while others were veterans in their prime who couldn't believe that, after a youth spent in French trenches, this was now happening to them.[51]

Another reason for the sympathy towards the unemployed by the provincial police could be that they would have to live alongside many of these people for years to come, while RCMP officers could be transferred to another province. This sympathy was not evident in the RCMP records and may account for the demonstrators being supportive of the provincial police actions and not those of the RCMP.

The city police were also sympathetic to the cause and dignity of the unemployed. For this they and their leadership had their own good practical reasons. The Vancouver police chief had made a deal with the leaders of the demonstrators: "If your boys don't beat mine, mine won't beat yours. I must use tear gas, but it will be mild gas."[52] Such an agreement might be considered unorthodox or subversive. However, considering the sensitive situation and the police chief's conservative background, his action should probably be more appropriately labelled "practical." There is no doubt that Chief Foster defused a serious situation with the least possible violence, as he had done before in the riot of 1935. A commander of the 52nd Battalion in World War One, Foster was accustomed to dealing with men in extreme situations. Elected Dominion President of the Canadian Legion, a veteran's association, in February of 1938, he belonged to a group that displayed considerable concern at the plight of B.C.'s single unemployed, some of whom were veterans.[53] By virtue of his ties to the Legion and his assessment of the confrontation, Foster was led to exercise police action with restraint.

Such was not the case with the RCMP. Records show that at least some RCMP officers involved in the eviction were manifestly unsympathetic to the demonstrators and their political supporters. Inspector E. W. Radcliffe wrote: "[T]here were approximately 350 single employed [sic] in the Post Office at the time and from my personal observations of these men I have no hesitation in stating that a considerable percentage of them are agitators of the worst type."[54] Interestingly, similar comments about the demonstrators do not exist in the city police records. Perhaps those officers on the day-to-day city beat could not afford the luxury of openly indulging their negative feelings?

Of CCF and provincial politician Harold Winch, well-known supporter of the single unemployed, who demanded at a mass meeting in Vancouver on June 13 that "the citizenry support these single men's 'splendid attempt' to force the Government to realize its responsibilities," an RCMP officer wrote: "Winch was particularly vitriolic and urged everyone to stand behind the 'movement' with not only money and moral support, but by using their fists if necessary."[55] Chief Foster, on the other hand, was quite prepared to commandeer Mr. Winch in the clearing of the Art Gallery. Winch was "delivered" to the scene of the Art Gallery by two Vancouver police detectives just before the city riot police entered the building. This shows that Chief Foster better understood the mood of the demonstrators and the general public than his RCMP counterpart. Clearly, RCMP Superintendent Hill succeeded in his mission of clearing the Post Office, but his men's "manhandling" of the demonstrators, albeit much of it due to the demonstrators' resolve, no doubt paved the way for the ensuing riot.

I also firmly believe that had the RCMP recruited supporters of the demonstrators in the eviction as did the city police, there is a good chance there would have been less violence or none as was the case with the Art Gallery eviction. Is it possible Hill let his personal feelings towards Steve Brodie due to their previous meeting three years earlier during the Regina riot cloud his judgement? Or was he merely following orders from his superiors in Ottawa?

A final comment serves to further illustrate the more restrained behaviour of the city police force throughout this entire affair. Brodie's attitude towards the police and his beating by the police are initially confusing when one considers that, unlike the RCMP, the city police were highly unionized and had been since 1918. Their general sympathy would have been with fellow members of the labour movement. Based on private interviews, there is no doubt the Vancouver police were highly sympathetic to Brodie's cause and that of the unemployed in general. The beating enabled the demonstrators to gain further public support for their cause and this, I believe, is the reason Brodie was so supportive of the Vancouver police rather than the RCMP. Even though he realized that an RCMP officer had stopped the beating, there is no doubt the demonstrators hated the RCMP because they represented the federal government, the government they blamed for the unemployment situation as did most British Columbians.

The day after the Post Office riot, Chief Foster sent a notice by registered mail to all the leaders of the demonstrators, warning them against future assemblies:

[N]o further congregations of a similar nature will be permitted. It is the duty of the authorities to disperse unlawful assemblies and riots and to use whatever force may be necessary for that purpose. Citizens are warned to avoid such assemblies, and all are notified that any gatherings of a similar nature will be dealt with under the section of the criminal code defining riots and unlawful assemblies.[56]

By sending the leaders the warning in a letter, rather than packing them in a paddy wagon and hauling them down to headquarters, Foster's action shows that the Vancouver police leadership had far greater respect for the unemployed demonstrators than their counterparts on the federal police force, who took no such action. Even though Brodie's beating was conducted by the Vancouver police and stopped by a member of the RCMP, the Vancouver Labour Council unanimously condemned not the city police but the RCMP and the Dominion government for their total lack of sympathy in handling the situation:

[I]t was resolved unanimously that whereas the peace, order and good government of the city of Vancouver was violently disrupted Sunday morning, June 1938, by the ruthless actions of the officers acting on behalf of the dominion of Canada … this council condemned in their strongest possible language the actions of the dominion government for total lack of sympathy in handling this problem.[57]

The strength of regional resentment in B.C. was such that it recast the distribution of good cop and bad cop in the interpretation of events that followed the riot. Moreover, the bad blood between this left-wing movement and the RCMP created a dynamic of its own. The lack of sympathy for the unemployed demonstrators is well documented in the RCMP files. The protesters were no friends of the Mounties. The riot was probably sparked by the RCMP's refusal to arrest the demonstrators. Instead, they chose to manhandle the protesters inside the Post Office with riding crops, not billy clubs as has been stated. No city police were present during the exchange, which became rather vicious. To defend themselves, the demonstrators tore off the Post Office's brass wickets to use as clubs. One Vancouver police officer stationed outside the building stated: "Thank god for us there were not enough wickets to go around."[58] Fortunately, not all the lock boxes were taken up in arms; they are now in the collection of the Canadian Postal Museum. What a story they could tell.

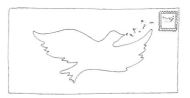

Notes

1. This work is dedicated to Colonel William W. Foster and Steve Brodie: Colonel Foster for his ability at riot control and to both men for their humanity and sympathy towards Canada's single unemployed during the Great Depression. I wish to thank Larry Proke, retired RCMP, and Jack Norris Harrison and Early Roy Tabbut, retired Vancouver City policemen, for their interviews and comments. As well as special thanks to Len McCann for his editorial assistance and for helping to keep me focused, no easy task.

2. Bill Waiser, *All Hell Can't Stop Us: The On-to-Ottawa Trek and Regina Riot* (Calgary: Fifth House, 2003), p. 27.

3. Ibid., p. 42.

4. Stuart Jamieson, "Times of Trouble: Labour Unrest and Industrial Conflict in Canada, 1900–66," in *Task Force on Labour Relations*, Study No. 22 (Ottawa: 1968), pp. 242-43.

5. Jamieson, "Times of Trouble," p. 244.

6. Jamieson, "Times of Trouble," p. 247.

7. Jamieson, "Times of Trouble," p. 267.

8. City of Vancouver Archives, Vancouver Police Records, 75-F-2, file 2. Vancouver Police Communist Activities Branch re Relief Camp Workers, August 10, 1935.

9. Jean Evans Sheilds and Ben Swankey, *Work and Wages: A Semi-documentary Account of the Life and Times of Arthur H. (Slim) Evans* (Vancouver: Granville Press Ltd, 1977), p. 291.

10. Canada, *The Labour Gazette* 38, no. 8 (August 1938): 902.

11. Jamieson, "Times of Trouble," p. 267.

12. City of Vancouver Archives, Vancouver Police Records, 75-F-2, file 27. Letter to Colonel W. Foster, Chief of Police, Vancouver, from Maisie Armytage-Moore, no date. The letter refers to the B.C. Provincial Police and the North West Mounted Police.

13. City of Vancouver Archives, Vancouver Police Records, 75-F-2, file 27. Letter to Maisie Armytage-Moore from Colonel W. Foster, Chief of Police, Vancouver, May 24, 1938.

14. British Columbia Archives and Records Service (hereinafter BCARS), Pattullo Papers, letter to Mackenzie King from T. Pattullo, June 25, 1938, add. mss 3, vol. 75, file 6, p. 43.

15. BCARS, Pattullo Papers, letter to Ian Mackenzie from T. Pattullo, June 22, 1938, vol. 75, file 6, p. 32.

16. BCARS, Pattullo Papers, letter to Mackenzie King from T. Pattullo, July 6, 1938, vol. 75, file 6, p. 50.

17. *Vancouver Sun*, June 6, 1935, p. 1.

18. Ibid.

19. Not all senators shared his view. Senator Dandurand of Quebec remarked: "It [Vancouver] is just as much a part of Canada as Ontario or the city of Ottawa. The Post Office of Vancouver is the Post Office of the people of Canada and the government is the trustee of that office." *Vancouver Province*, June 9, 1938, p.1.

20. *Vancouver Province*, June 9, 1938, p. 1.

21. *Vancouver Province*, June 20, 1938, p. 13.

22. Sheilds and Swankey, *Work and Wages*, p.106.

23. City of Vancouver Archives, Vancouver Police Records, 75-F-2, file 2. Vancouver Police re Relief Project Workers Union, May 28, 1938.

24. Ibid.

25. Not all religious organizations were sympathetic toward the demonstrators. The Abbott House Association, "a Christian home for men," was spying on the men they sheltered and reporting to the Vancouver Police on the plans and movements of the unemployed. They paid special interest to the demonstrators' leaders Robert (Red) Jackson and Steve Brodie. City of Vancouver Archives, Vancouver Police Records, 75-F-2, file 12. The Public record supplies no instance of the Roman Catholic Church providing succour to the strikers. In 1933 on

August 19, the British Columbia Catholic church condemned the moderate Socialist Regina Manifesto of the Cooperative Commonwealth Federation. However, it is likely that during the events of 1938, church members and perhaps some clergy in Vancouver quietly provided humanitarian support.

26. City of Vancouver Archives, Vancouver Police Records 75-F-2, file 27. Reported in a letter to his worship Mayor G. C. Miller (Vancouver) from Chief Constable, May 31 1938; note based on information from the RCMP.

27. Library and Archives Canada, CSIS, RG 146, vol. 4705, part 4, RCMP file H-V-3, vol. 5, pp. 25 and 26. Unemployed Demonstrations 1930s, B.C., correspondence from June 10, 1938 to June 19, 1938 inclusive. Telegram to mayor of Vancouver from acting postmaster general.

28. Ibid., p. 25.

29. City of Vancouver Archives, Vancouver Police Records, 75-F-2, file 24. Confidential instructions to accompany orders for the evacuation of Post Office and Art Gallery, Vancouver, B.C., July 18, 1938, from Vancouver Police Chief Constable.

30. Library and Archives Canada, CSIS RG 146, vol. 4705, part 4, RCMP file H.V.-3, vol. 5, p. 27. Telegram to Officer in Charge (OC) "E" Division, RCMP Vancouver from Postmaster General via S. T. Wood, June 17, 1938.

31. Library and Archives Canada, CSIS RG 146, vol. 4705, part 4, RCMP file H-V-3, vol. 5, p. 2. Telegram to Commissioner, RCMP, Ottawa, from C.H. Hill, June 19, 1938.

32. City of Vancouver Archives, Vancouver Police Records 75-F-2, file 24. Orders for the evacuation of the Post Office, June 18, 1938, from Vancouver Police Chief Constable.

33. Sheilds and Swankey, *Work and Wages*, p. 106.

34. Library and Archives Canada, CSIS RG 146, vol. 4705, part 5, RCMP file H-V-3, vol. 6, p. 75. Letter to Officer in Charge "E" Division RCMP Vancouver from RCMP Inspector E. W. Radcliffe re occupation of Vancouver Post Office by single unemployed. June 20, 1938.

35. City of Vancouver Archives, Vancouver Police Records, 75-F-2, file 28. Night letter to Ian Mckenzie, Minister of Defense, Ottawa, from W. W. Foster.

36. Library and Archives Canada, CSIS RG 146, vol. 4705, part 5, RCMP file H-V-3, vol. 6, p. 75. Secret letter to RCMP Commissioner in Ottawa from Superintendent C. H. Hill, Commanding "E" Division re possible On-to-Ottawa Trek, June 20, 1938.

37. Library and Archives Canada, CSIS RG 146, vol. 4705, part 6, RCMP file H-V-3, vol. 6, p. 85. Letter re possible On-to-Ottawa Trek, June 20, 1938, Division "E," removed by Access to Information Act.

38. Ibid.

39. City of Vancouver Archives, Vancouver Police Records, 75-F-2, file 28. Notice, June 20, 1938, by W.W. Foster, Single Unemployed Relief Workers Union.

40. Library and Archives Canada, CSIS RG 146, vol. 4705, part 4, RCMP file H-V-3, vol. 5, pp. 9, 10. Secret letter from C. H. Hill, June 18, 1938.

41. Library and Archives Canada, CSIS RG 146, vol. 4705, part 4, RCMP file H-V-3, vol. 4, p. 55. Letter re possible On-to-Ottawa Trek 1938 to RCMP Commissioner, Ottawa, June 13, 1938, by D/Cpl J. K. Barnes, forwarded by Supt. C. H. Hill.

42. Ibid.

43. Ibid.

44. Library and Archives Canada, CSIS RG 146, vol. 4705, part 5, RCMP file H-V03, vol. 5, p.3. Secret letter to Officer Commanding RCMP "E" Division from G. W. Fish, Inspector in charge, C.I.B. Vancouver, June 20, 1938.

45. Library and Archives Canada, CSIS RG 146, vol. 4705, part 4, RCMP file H-V-3, vol. 5, p. 4. Unemployed Demonstrations 1930s, B.C., correspondance from June 10, 1938 to June 19, 1938 inclusive. Telegram to mayor of Vancouver from Acting Postmaster General.

46. Library and Archives Canada, CSIS, RG 146, vol. 4705, part 5, RCMP file H-V-3, vol. 5, p. 76. Letter to officer commanding RCMP "E" Division re occupation of Vancouver Post Office by single unemployed from Inspector E. W. Radcliffe, June 20, 1938.

47. Ibid., p. 75.

48. *Vancouver Province*, June 20, 1938, p. 6.

49. BCARS, add. mss 3, Pattullo Papers, vol. 75, file 6, p. 43. Letter to Prime Minister Mackenzie King from T. Pattullo, June 25, 1938. See reference in footnote 14.

50. Lynne Stonier-Newman, *Policing a Pioneer Province: The B.C. Provincial Police, 1858–1950* (Vancouver: Harbour Publishing, 1991).

51. Ibid, p. 173.

52. Private interview with John A. McDonald, grandson of Chief W. W. Foster.

53. See *The Zone*, newsletter of the Vancouver Zone Council of the Canadian Legion, June 1938, p. 5, 7. See also *The Zone*, March 1938, front page.

54. Library and Archives Canada, CSIS, RG 146, vol. 4705, part 5, RCMP file H-V-3, vol. 5. Letter to C. H. Hill from Inspector E. W. Radcliffe, June 20, 1938, p. 76.

55. Library and Archives Canada, CSIS, RG 146, vol. 4705, part 4, RCMP file H-V-3, vol. 4, p. 54. Letter to RCMP Commissioner, Ottawa, from C. H. Hill, June 13, 1938.

56. City of Vancouver Archives, Vancouver Police Records, 75-F-2, file 28. Notice by W.W. Foster, Single Unemployed Relief Workers Union, June 20, 1938.

57. Minutes of Vancouver, New Westminster and District Trades and Labour Council, June 21, 1938, p.1.

58. Interview with Earl Roy Tabbut, July 31, 2003.

ONE HUNDRED YEARS OF POSTAL PROCESSING IN CANADA

3

Krista Cooke, Assistant Curator, Archaeology and History Division,
Canadian Museum of Civilization

Abstract

The development of Canada's postal system has been characterized by a drive for efficiency and technological innovation. From a labour-intensive manual process requiring hundreds of clerks, postal processing has become highly mechanized, run almost entirely by digital technology. The first generation of Canadian post offices, built shortly after Confederation, were designed largely as symbols of federalism. Postal processing depended more on manpower than on mechanized technology. Between 1920 and 1965, the Post Office department underwent major changes. Skyrocketing mail volume and increasing urbanization ensured processing bottlenecks while the federal government placed new importance on revenue generation and postal efficiency. New "postal factories" saw numerous technological advances that influenced the speed and efficiency of postal processing, including several experimental sorting machines. During the late 1960s, a national postal code was introduced. As a result, revolutionary new technology that allowed for fully automated mail sorting transformed postal processing. Without the technological advancements made over the course of these three eras of postal processing, achieving current mail volume would have been impossible.[1]

Résumé

Le développement du système postal canadien a été caractérisé par l'accent mis sur l'efficacité et l'innovation technologique. Au départ, les processus manuels exigeant une main-d'œuvre nombreuse constituée de centaines d'employés, le traitement des envois postaux s'est depuis fortement mécanisé, jusqu'à être presque entièrement effectué par technologie numérique. Les bureaux de poste canadiens de la première génération, construits peu après la Confédération, étaient principalement conçus comme des symboles du fédéralisme. Le traitement du courrier, très peu mécanisé, se faisait principalement à la main. De 1920 à 1965, la Société canadienne des postes a connu de nombreux changements. L'augmentation en flèche du volume du courrier et la croissance de l'urbanisation ont provoqué des ralentissements dans le traitement, alors que le gouvernement fédéral accordait une importance accrue à la production de recettes et à la productivité. Les nouvelles « usines postales » ont bénéficié de nombreuses avancées technologiques, notamment de plusieurs types de machines à trier expérimentales, qui ont eu une incidence sur la rapidité et l'efficacité du traitement des objets postaux. La fin des années soixante a vu l'instauration du code postal national. Suite à cela, une nouvelle technologie révolutionnaire permettant le tri entièrement automatisé du courrier en a transformé le traitement. Sans les avancées technologiques de ces trois époques du traitement du courrier, il aurait été impossible de traiter le volume de courrier actuel.

First Generation City Post Offices, ca 1900

Shortly after Confederation in 1867, Canada's new national government undertook the construction of a series of impressive public buildings in an effort to promote the new Dominion. By centralizing mail processing in urban centres, the Post Office department began to phase out the previous generation of independently managed post offices spread haphazardly across the landscape and, instead, created a highly visible national postal network. In addition to serving as symbols of the Dominion, prosperity, and permanence in the fledgling nation's city centres, these elaborate edifices helped transform postal processing operations.[2]

The new post offices were carefully designed to match the division of labour, maximize productivity, and take full advantage of current technology. First generation city post offices were a highly staffed environment, with sometimes more than 200 postal clerks working around the clock to process mail. Unlike smaller post offices, where postmasters could sometimes afford to close service wickets to sort letters, moving Canada's mail was now a non-stop task. At the end of the nineteenth century, long before widespread post office automation, the challenge faced by postal employees was enormous—letters, catalogues, packages, and newspapers were all, for the most part, processed by hand.

For their day, first generation city post offices were models of efficiency. Each stage of postal processing was studied intensively for cost and time saving methods. Mail treatment was a well researched process; information was available from postal administrations around the world. In particular, the U.S. postal department served as one of the primary models for the Canadian system. In the new urban post office, processing efficiency was founded on the clear division of labour into six steps: receiving, facing, separation, cancelling, sorting, and bundling. Understanding these six phases of mail processing, as well as the technological advancements that changed them over time, is crucial to understanding the subsequent evolution of Canadian mail processing in the twentieth century.[3]

The first of the six steps in postal processing involved the reception of large canvas mailbags, which employees hauled from arriving wagons, trucks, or train cars into the reception area of the post office, usually through the basement loading docks. There, clerks tabulated the bags on a "Mail Bags Received" sheet and then emptied them onto long receiving tables. Coloured mailbags designated the type of mail: Registered letters, newspapers, and parcel post received different treatment from the rest of the mail, as did packets of "through mail," which were placed into outgoing mailbags awaiting pickup.

The reception area was one of the first places where the Post Office department tested early automation concepts. The earliest mechanical aids in Canadian post offices were based on early experiments done in England, where, as early as 1846, the London post office introduced elevators to lift men and bags of mail to upper floors. The Montréal Place d'Armes post office included numerous conveyors and lifts, and exemplified the drive for efficiency and innovation in Canada's first generation post offices.[4]

Following reception, clerks "faced up" regular mail items, including postcards, letters, cards, and bills. Using tables divided lengthwise with a long, raised shelf running down the centre, "collectors" and "stampers" worked across from each other. The collectors sorted letter mail so the postage stamp and address were located in the same place on each item and then placed the mail onto the shelf that divided them from the stampers. The collectors were also responsible for removing any mail that was too large, irregularly shaped, or insufficiently stamped. These items were then taken to a separate location for other clerks to process.

The stampers were responsible for cancelling each piece of mail. Until the introduction of Canada's first cancelling machine in Montréal in 1896, each individual item was cancelled by hand. The stampers used hand-held cancellation hammers to obliterate the postage stamps and to mark each piece of mail with an accurate time and date. Mail arriving from other post offices, railway mail trains, or city branch stations was already cancelled and needed only a new "back stamp" to indicate the time the item passed through that particular post office. A specially assigned clerk made the rounds every thirty minutes to change the time on every hammer and record changes in a special ledger.

Many efforts were made to improve the efficiency of this stage in postal processing and the resulting cancelling machine was a revolutionary first step towards post office automation. A facing clerk fed letters into the machine, where in one brief instant each stamp was cancelled and every letter postmarked. Initially powered either by foot pedal or by steam engine, the electric cancelling machines introduced in the 1890s demonstrated the potential of postal mechanization. Before the advent of cancelling machines, a quick clerk could barely process 1,800 letters per hour whereas new machines could each handle up to 30,000 to 40,000 letters per hour.

Following cancellation was sorting, the most labour-intensive step in mail processing. The first stage of sorting, the "primary sort," divided mail into rough categories by its next destination: railway mail service, rural mail, local mail delivery, and outside mail by province or country. All sorting was done by hand and was time consuming. It was a daunting task in the evening, when most of the day's mail arrived in bulk at the post office. Clerks, standing in front of huge sorting cases, read the bottom address line of each piece of mail and flipped individual items into one-foot square [92 cm^2] "pigeon holes" labelled with the name of each location. One amazed author described the process, noting that "the letters fly through the air like the flakes of an April snowstorm, and it seems impossible that the clerks can read the inscriptions, so swiftly do they do their

Figure 3.1 Post office clerks in the sorting area of the Toronto post office, ca 1913.
City of Toronto Archives, Fonds 1244, Item 123.

work."[5] Every few minutes, junior clerks would remove mail from the rapidly filling pigeonholes. Some mail was bundled and removed to external destinations. Only the mail that was to remain in the city where the post office was located would be forwarded on to the next stage in the sorting process. This "secondary sort" further divided the mail and was even more challenging for clerks as the pigeonholes on these sorting cases were smaller and the names of ever changing destinations and letter carrier routes had to be constantly memorized and revised. Three or four clerks might work together on a larger case, walking back and forth and throwing mail into the holes from a few metres away. Experienced clerks averaged an astonishing 50 to 55 letters per minute, almost one per second.

Technological advancements at the reception and cancelling stations were matched by experimentation with new sorting methods. The specific problem of sorting had long drawn the attention of postal administrators: The reason it took so many rounds of hand sorting to direct a letter to its final destination was partly because each sorting case could only accommodate enough pigeon holes to do a partial sort. The notion of building a larger manual sorting case was problematic because the reach of each clerk restricted the size of the sorting case: If cases were too large, then the extra walking and reaching would eliminate the time saved by these enlarged cases. During the 1870s, experimental circular sorting cases were built into the new Montréal and Halifax post offices with the hope they would increase productivity. The *Halifax Daily Reporter and Times* excitedly reported in 1871:

Nothing has been left undone in the new office to save unnecessary labour, and to render the internal economy of the establishment perfect ... The distributing Clerk stands inside the distributing circle, and as the letters are conveyed to it ... he can easily, and without moving from his position, distribute them into their proper receptacles with the greatest ease and facility ... This is considered the most complete labour-saving arrangement in the whole office, as one clerk can do as much work as three could under the ordinary or old system.[6]

After sorting came the last processing stage. All mail was bundled into batches, tied together and placed into the appropriate mailbag for distribution. Tying the perfect bundle was a skill requiring much attention so as to avoid any lost or improperly directed mail. Once tied, the bundles were then "pouched" or thrown into mailbags destined for various points outside the post office. Some of the letters remained in the post office to be distributed by letter carriers on their delivery routes. These letters required one "final sort" before distribution, for which the letter carriers themselves were responsible. During this final sort letter carriers put the mail in order according to the distribution route and took note of any changes of addresses, incorrectly addressed mail, registered letters, and any other irregular mail.

The staff required to manage Canada's growing mail volume during this era was substantial. With only one or two steps having been successfully mechanized, mail processing required vast amounts of time, skill, labour, and money. Increasing administrative focus on cost savings and the efficient division of labour led directly to automation research during the second generation of Canadian post offices.

Second Generation Postal Processing: The Postal Factory, 1920–1965

The era of the postal factory was characterized by significant change and a drive for automated processing solutions. By 1920, the Post Office department was more concerned with cost efficiency than symbolic nation building. At the same time, overwhelming mail volume and suburbanization were placing increasing pressure on the postal system. What with old-style processing requiring up to twenty-one different steps per letter and mail volume increasing incrementally each year, it was rapidly becoming impossible to maintain a manual system. The Post Office department had to evolve to fit a new model: the automated postal factory. In 1959, the postmaster general stated, "[I]n the postal service it is perfectly apparent that increased mechanization—automation—can be the only answer to the problem of coping with an ever growing volume of mail."[7] During the era of the postal factory many innovative processing technologies were introduced. It was not until the post-Second-World-War era, however, that mechanized sorting technology became the focus of research and experimentation in Canada. Three failed experimental sorting machines introduced during this period were the basis for future fully automated postal processing.[8]

The second generation Canadian post offices were industrial buildings built specifically to house mail sorting operations, rather than to serve as public postal outlets. Located close to railway stations serving major Canadian cities, these post offices were built with automation and the scientific management of mail processing in mind. The plain exteriors of the new postal facilities were designed to accommodate the industrial layout required within, as opposed to the grandiose first generation urban post offices that had been conceived as impressive public buildings first and post offices second. First generation post offices were now outdated and overcrowded. The postal factory industrial-scale layout and elaborate division of labour were seen as a way to improve both efficiency and working conditions.[9] While the new postal terminals did not replace entirely the first generation post offices, serving instead as regional distribution centres, their construction signalled the eventual passing of the era of the elaborate downtown post office: genteel and symbolic of Canadian Confederation, but less and less practical.

Montréal's Peel Street postal terminal, begun in 1928, epitomized the factory concept characteristic of Canada's second generation urban post offices. Peel Street was similar in many respects to other postal factories built across the country in large cities like Toronto and Vancouver. With the exception of a small, first-floor postal outlet, the entire building was devoted to mail processing on a mass scale. The new postal terminal was a multi-storied, industrial-style building with an open plan interior located just outside the downtown area adjacent to several rail lines. Peel Street was built with six stories, each of which served a specific purpose in the new mail processing system.

Mail arrived at the basement loading docks, generally in the late afternoon, and was hoisted up to the fifth floor to be emptied. Once mailbags were emptied and a rough sort conducted, the different types of mail were sent to various locations throughout the building by chutes and conveyors. The third floor held the international mail, metropolitan mail was on the second floor, and parcels were sorted on the first floor. Regular letter mail was processed on the fourth floor. Most of the work took place during the evening, from five p.m. to midnight. Groups of eight clerks, clustered around facing tables, prepared the letter mail for the cancelling machines. Conveyors ran quickly and constantly beneath each facing table and transported letters into the cancelling machines. Facing clerks perfected the art of tossing individual letters, stamp down and left, into small one-inch [2.5-centimetre] slots on the conveyors. One clerk oversaw the cancelling machines, while another carried the letter mail to the preliminary sorting stations, where all sorting was done by hand. In the early morning hours, after being sorted, bundled, and bagged, mail was sent back to the basement for transportation by truck or train to its next destination.[10]

The era of the postal factory was marked by experimentation in mechanized postal processing. Conveyor driven transportation was one area that saw much development during this period and the widespread use of internal conveyor systems characterized the new postal factories. There were over eight kilometres of conveyor belts in the new Peel Street post office building.[11] Whereas previously most mail being moved from station to station within the post office had been pushed in "mail trucks" or carried in baskets, now conveyors moved mail quickly around the post office. Conveyors reduced walking for clerks, minimized collisions, and ensured faster emptying of pigeonholes. Innovations in external mail transportation were also introduced during this period. In 1959, Vancouver's main post office inaugurated its "tunnel conveyor system," a half-a-kilometre-long tunnel designed to transport mail between the main post office and the CPR station. These developments in internal and external mail transportation were essential to the postal factory concept, speeding mail from process to process.

Sorting, the most time-consuming element of mail processing, remained the area that was least mechanized. Despite the introduction of dozens of experimental machines designed to speed mail processing, sorting was left virtually unmodified in Canada until the years following the Second World War, when overwhelming wartime volume spurred interest in postal automation. Automated bag emptying machines, mechanized facing tables, and business postage meters used to process bulk mail before its arrival at the post office were just a few of the postal machines developed during this period. Fundamentally, however, the mail processing system could not be substantially altered without changes to the sorting stage. Mail could only be delivered as fast as it was sorted, and skyrocketing mail volume and increasing suburbanization ensured processing bottlenecks. In accordance with the manual system, sorting clerks were required to memorize all the individual routes within their postal region, the names of thousands of city post office lock-box holders, or unending lists of street addresses. Memorization skills were taken very seriously and sorting clerks faced regular examinations with a mandatory passing grade of 85 per cent. Growing suburbanization made sorting an increasingly difficult task, especially in cities like Toronto, where, in 1956, there were 10,000 postal sub-sections. It was simply impossible for sorters to constantly memorize and revise the huge volume of information required in mail distribution and postal administrators feared "an ultimate breakdown."[12]

During the 1950s, the Post Office department began to focus on sorting, the crux of the processing problem, and introduced three experimental sorting machines. Although there had been sorting technology experiments in development as early as the 1920s, none of the machines were efficient enough to be officially adopted by the Canadian postal service. In the 1930s, despite the establishment of a "Postal Engineering Unit" assigned to the task of advancing postal automation and improving working conditions, experimentation slowed during the Great Depression and the Second World War. Finally, in the years following the war, the first prototype sorting machines were introduced. The three mechanical sorting experiments developed during the postal factory era were significant. Although all three machines were eventually scrapped, they held the keys to the fully automated postal processing system of the 1970s.[13]

The first of the three machines was the Transorma Automatic Letter Sorting Machine, introduced in Peterborough, Ontario, in 1955. Based on similar Transorma machines used in the Netherlands and Great Britain since the early 1930s, it was the first machine of its type in the world. The Transorma attracted hoards of onlookers to the new Peterborough post office grand opening and was billed in newspapers as "revolutionary" and "the most efficient [equipment] the twentieth century has yet produced."[14] The machine worked on the same principles as manual sorting, but extended each clerk's reach using a combination of keypads and conveyor belts. A press release issued at the Peterborough grand opening read: "[T]he sorting clerk need never touch the letters, yet his 'reach' is extended to 300 separate receptacles by the use of this machine, or three times what is possible by manual sortation."[15] Nicknamed the "Iron Postman," the Transorma was unable to process several common sizes of envelopes and its use was limited to a small percentage of incoming mail. Despite the initial excitement by the Canadian postal administration, the Transorma was never implemented nationally and was removed from service in Peterborough in 1963.

Another machine developed and tested in Ottawa during the 1950s was the Levy postal sorting machine. Unlike the Transorma, which relied on the sorter's ability to memorize distribution routes, the Levy machine used a system of basic postal coding.[16] Based on the concept of coding and marking letters and using the first computers ever employed for postal purposes, the Levy sortation machine processed letter mail at a rate of 36,000 letters per hour with a marginal error rate. The machine was groundbreaking because of its reliance on a solid-state transistor system that was incrementally faster and smaller and consumed much less energy than older vacuum-tube operating systems. Despite excited reviews from worldwide postal administrations during a 1957 international postal conference in Ottawa, changes in government and postal administrators, cost overruns, and missed deadlines interrupted the machine's development and the project never progressed past the testing stage. The Post Office noted that the machine was not cost effective and that efficiency "suffered from a lack of a public postal code."[17] As a result the prototype, a unique Canadian invention that served as inspiration for future generations of Canadian electronics and worldwide postal mechanization systems, was shelved.

The third experimental machine, the SEFCAN, or Automatic Segregator, Stacker, Facer Canceller, stimulated much discussion among postal administrators and engineers. Special phosphorescent "tagged" postage stamps were the basis for the new sorting machine introduced in Winnipeg in 1964. The SEFCAN automatically separated local and out-of-town mail by using two different types of tagged stamps: one phosphorescent stripe for local city mail and two stripes for out-of-town mail. SEFCAN, the first machine of its kind in North America and one of only four in the world, was slated for use nationwide if successful in Winnipeg. Unfortunately, like the Transorma and Levy machine before it, the SEFCAN was not as efficient as the Post Office department expected. SEFCAN's multi-stage processing machinery, based on conveyors and revolving drums, successfully mechanized all processing stages leading up to sorting but was only capable of a very basic pre-sort.

Although none of these machines was able to overcome the multitude of challenges in the mechanization of postal sorting, these early experiments showed considerable potential. Each had specific strengths that were built upon in the next generation of processing equipment. The Transorma and Levy machines' keypad-directed sorting, Levy's innovative computer system and basic postal coding, and the SEFCAN's first attempt at full post office automation all influenced the future development of fully automated postal processing equipment. However, it was not until a nationwide coding system was introduced that mechanized sorting could become cost effective and suitable for national implementation.

Third Generation Postal Processing: Postal Coding and Full Post Office Mechanization, 1969 to the Present

With over three decades of intense mechanization research behind it, the Post Office realized that the key to efficient sorting was the postal code. For full automation to function properly, a universal coding system was needed, whereby each Canadian address could be reduced to a code. This code, printed on each letter in a format that could be understood by processing machines, was to become "the backbone of the postal system."[18] Following the success of a pilot postal code program in 1971, full post office automation was gradually introduced across Canada. A new generation of processing equipment handled mail from the loading docks through to the final sorting stages prior to delivery. The equipment was installed in fully automated plants and this new technology and the postal code that supported it became the basis for today's postal system.

Third generation Canadian post offices were based on the concept of a fully automated processing system. The physical location and interior layout of second generation post offices, once considered so innovative, were now outdated. By the mid–1960s, the majority of Canada's post offices required massive renovations to be brought up to standard in preparation for full post office automation. Most postal factories like Montréal's Peel Street post office had been located adjacent to railway stations for ease of transporting mail. However, the increasing expense of railway travel and a newly established web of highways and airports, as well as the ever increasing volume of mail ensured the collapse of the Railway Mail Service and made the location of these older urban post offices obsolete. In order to house Canada's increasingly mechanized postal service efficiently, a series of industrial warehouses, designed specifically for systematic mechanized processing, was constructed. These new, expansive buildings located outside the costly downtown cores of Canada's cities were called MAPPs, or Major Postal Plants. Their dimensions and layout well suited the automated plant concept, allowing vast amounts of space to accommodate the new machinery and conveyor belts. One such plant, the Toronto South Central Letter Processing Plant, was designed in 1968 to relieve congestion in downtown Toronto postal facilities and was promoted as a way to improve working conditions for employees.[19]

While the Post Office department built MAPPs to house new processing equipment, research was underway to develop the coding system that would work in tandem with

Figure 3.2 Advertisement of the nationwide publicity campaign used by the Post Office department during the early 1970s to promote public usage of the postal code.

Canadian Postal Museum/ Canadian Museum of Civilization, 1990.18.19.2.

Figure 3.3 This sticker serves as a bold reminder that automation had a negative impact on labour relations between the Post Office department and its employees.

Canadian Union of Postal Workers / Syndicat des travailleurs et travailleuses des postes.

the equipment. In 1969, the Division of Coding and Mechanization was created to develop a plan for the future development of Canadian postal processing. The first step in developing a postal code system was research. The Canadian postal administration had years of experience collaborating with worldwide postal administrations on mechanization issues. Several coding systems already in effect in different parts of the world served as examples for Canadian researchers. Germany, the United States, Great Britain, and Japan all used unique coding systems, but eventually an alphanumeric system was selected for the Canadian postal code. Loosely based on the British postal code, the code allowed for precision down to the level of a single dwelling. Postal codes were always written in the same way—ANA NAN (Alpha/Numeric)—and each letter and number designated a specific area, moving from a vast territory, such as a province, down to a very specific point (building, rural post office box, or important corporation). The first three characters represented the regional locator and the second set of characters the local locator or specific address.

In October 1970, Ottawa was selected for the postal code pilot program. The advertising, internal training, and implementation of the pilot program were highly successful and soon the Post Office department focused on coding addresses province by province. The success of the postal code program depended entirely on convincing the Canadian public to use it on every piece of mail and so an intensive advertising campaign accompanied the Ottawa pilot program. As a result of the national publicity, public usage of the postal code took place twice as fast in Manitoba than it had in Ottawa. The system was not without problems and at times Canada's postal code usage lagged behind other coding nations. However, the potential for full postal automation was undeniable and the coding and mechanization program continued.[20]

Mechanization research also proceeded rapidly during the early 1970s as a part of the postal administration's automation plan. After an extended period of comparative research, the Division of Coding and Mechanization reported that a variety of automated sorting machines were already in use in several other countries. The main stumbling block for the efficient functioning of these machines was their inability to read addresses correctly. In Belgium, government bulk mail used printed address labels, and postal machines were calibrated to read only that specific type of label. All public mail was still sorted by hand. During the 1960s, the United States was experimenting with an automated system, but all addresses had to be printed according to very strict specifications in order to pass through their prototype machines. Although instructive, the American and Belgian experience was impractical and required refinement from the Canadian point of view. Of considerable relevance to Canada's mechanization research was the work undertaken by the Japanese postal administration. Japan was unquestionably the most advanced nation in postal mechanization, with their use of Optical Character Readers (OCRs). For several years, they had been experimenting with machines that could read envelopes coded with precisely located handwritten or printed postal codes.

The success of the postal code pilot program convinced engineers that it was possible for Canada to mechanize letter sorting nationwide, a world first. In May 1972, the Post Office department put out tenders for a fully automated processing system, including an OCR designed specifically to meet Canadian postal needs. The selected OCR would have to be able to read 80 per cent of the various fonts used on printed or typed postal codes. Hand addressed mail was not considered a problem: A very small proportion of letters were addressed by hand and the cost of developing a machine to read them was prohibitive. Of that initial 80 per cent, the machine had to read the code correctly, translate it, print a corresponding barcode on each letter, and complete a preliminary sort, all at a success rate of 60 per cent. This meant that 48 per cent of all typed or printed mail had to be successfully sorted by the new OCR machines. Eventually, a contract was awarded to a company that designed and produced Canada's first fully automated processing system based on Japanese technology. The result was a series of four machines designed to work together to take incoming mail from the entrance of a postal plant through to the exit. As opposed to older automated equipment that mechanized individual steps in mail processing, this first generation of full-system automated equipment joined each process together mechanically.[21]

In the new MAPPs, mail could now be processed by machine from start to finish. Although a small percentage of mail was treated by hand (incompletely addressed, outsized and problem items), the vast majority of Canada's mail was automatically processed. Mailbags arriving at the loading dock were placed on conveyors leading to the reception area. There, an attendant input the type of mailbag into a computer that then sorted the bags into different categories as they passed by. Once hydraulic machines had emptied the bags onto conveyor belts, employees culled the mail by selecting awkwardly shaped parcels or letters for separate processing. The mail then passed through an artificial eye, where it was faced up by moving belts and, if correctly stamped and sized, obliterated by an automated canceller called the Culler Facer Canceller (CFC). The mail was then fed

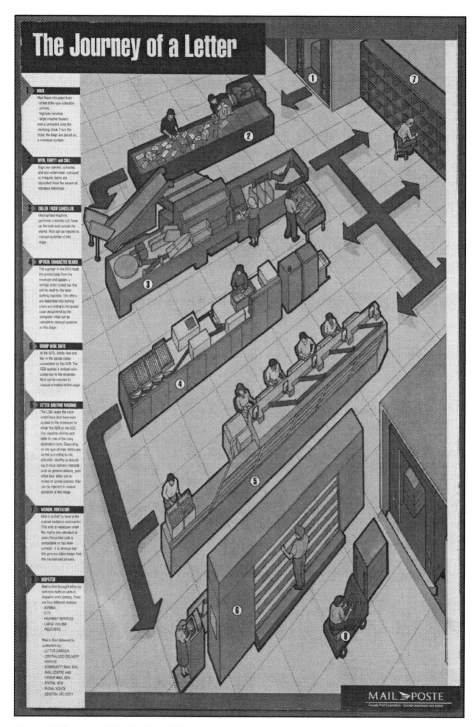

Figure 3.4 Poster published by Canada Post showing the route taken by a letter in a modern postal plant. Note the OCR, GDS, CFC, and LSM, all the component parts of the first generation of automated mail processing machines, ca 1980.

Canada Post.

into plastic holding trays where it awaited further processing. An OCR read all printed postal codes and a corresponding bar code was sprayed onto each envelope. In addition to transforming each letter's postal code to a distinctive phosphorescent orange bar code, the OCR began a rough sort by destination and redirected letters whose postal codes were handwritten, illegible, or incorrect. These rejected letters arrived at the Group Desk Suite (GDS), where they received individual attention by postal employees who hand typed the postal code into a computer keyboard to assist with the bar-coding process. The OCR processed up to 32,000 letters per hour, a far cry from the performance of the fastest mail clerk decades before. The last stage of mail processing was the final sort where the last machine, the Letter Sorting Machine (LSM), read the bar codes imprinted by the OCR and GDS and sorted each letter by its final destination.

This fully automated system was highly efficient and marked the transformation of Canada's postal processing from a labour-intensive, hand processing system to a modern digital environment. The same 1,000 letters that now cost four dollars to process by machine had once cost a staggering forty dollars to hand sort. By 1974, Ottawa's Alta Vista plant alone had forty-eight coding desk (GDS) systems and four OCR machines.[22] Eventually, nine fully automated postal plants were opened across Canada, anchored by the South Central Letter Processing Plant in Toronto. Although it was a radical transformation, mechanization was soon integral to the functioning of the Canadian postal system. Only a few years after the first OCRs were introduced in Ottawa, over half of all letters mailed in Canada were being processed mechanically.

Today, the post office has expanded further the automated processing technology introduced in the early 1970s. New conveyor scanners direct mail into "lettertainers" that are coded and delivered to the correct area of the plant. In the early 1990s, a one-billion-dollar National Control Centre was built to monitor the nation's mail at Canada Post headquarters in Ottawa. Individual packages, trucks, and employees can be traced and, in case of emergencies, such as inclement weather or power black outs, mail can be redirected for processing at alternate locations to ensure that delivery is not delayed. Most recently, a new type of OCR has been added to Canadian mail processing plants. Installed nearly thirty years after the first OCRs, the Remote Computer Reader (RCR) was introduced in 2000. The RCR gives the original OCR machines the ability to read handwritten addresses, varied fonts, illegible bar codes, and even letters without postal codes. As a result of the introduction of the RCR, the need for manual processing has been reduced by over 70 per cent.[23]

Conclusion

Postal automation has become a priority of the Canadian Post Office department in the years since the first dominion post offices were built immediately following Confederation. First generation city post offices equipped with conveyor belts, circular sorting cases, and electric-powered cancelling machines evolved into the production-line postal factories of the 1930s. With skyrocketing mail volume and growing suburbanization in the years following the Second World War, research centred on automated sorting technology as a way to forestall the breakdown of the old manual processing system. Three revolutionary sorting machines tested during the 1950s provided clues for the development of fully automated processing technology. In the early 1970s, a technological revolution in postal processing accompanied the successful introduction of the postal code. Today's fully automated postal processing systems are due, in large part, to the success of postal coding during the 1970s.

With the advent of the twenty-first century, there is a demand for newer, faster, and more efficient machines and sorting technology. The new computer age has magnified rather than diminished the utility of the postal service. Consider, for example, the new wave of direct mail advertising, bulk mail, and the growing population (240,000 new addresses were created in 2003 alone).[24] Although some predicted that the advent of email would reduce Canada Post's workload, today's mail volume remains staggering. Amazingly, the same volume of mail was processed each day in 1995 as came through the postal system during the first year of the Dominion Post Office department in 1868. Without modern sorting methods resulting from the technological advancements of the last fifty years, this ever increasing mail volume would have been impossible to manage.[25] Canada's postal system is superbly equipped to handle increased demand. The question is, will that demand continue to grow?

Notes

1. Postal processing technology has been a topic of interest at the Canadian Postal Museum, where I formerly worked, for many years. Dozens of internal research papers, articles, and oral history projects produced by curator Bianca Gendreau and postal historian John Willis have contributed to the history of Canadian mail processing and are the basis for this article.

2. For descriptions of post office operations at the end of the nineteenth century, see: Bianca Gendreau and John Willis, "Peu de machines mais beaucoup d'hommes," *Philatélie Québec*, March 1995; Janet Wright, *Crown Assets: The Architecture of the Department of Public Works 1867–1967* (Toronto: University of Toronto Press, 1997); Chantal Amyot, Bianca Gendreau, and John Willis, *Special Delivery: Canada's Postal Heritage* (Gatineau and Fredericton: Canadian Museum of Civilization and Gooselane Editions, 2000); Post Office Department, *Annual Reports* [1870-1915] (available at Library and Archives Canada); Ken Desson, *Three Hundred Years of Postal Communication: A Brief History of Postal Technology in Canada* (Ottawa: Canada Post Corporation, 1992).

3. Much of the descriptive information about the six stages in mail processing was found in E. Mayo, "Post Office Work and Methods," *The Outlook*, October 3, 1903, pp. 298–310. Despite being an American source, it is a very complete description of postal processing and is representative of methods used in Canada's large urban post offices. For other resources describing early postal procedures see: Post Office Department, *City Post Office Procedure* (Ottawa: Post Office Department, 1934) (available at Library and Archives Canada); *Scientific American*, January 25, 1890; United Postal Union, *Mechanical Handling of the Mails in Large Sorting Offices* (Joint publication of Britain, Netherlands, and Swiss Postal Administrations,

1951); Library and Archives Canada, RG3, vol. 596, file 502–524: letter dated December 1, 1875; *The Novascotian*, April 13, 1846; Ken Barlow, *Canadian Machine Cancellations* (booklet; Vancouver: n.p., n.d.); L. Brown, Apropos Planning, *Interpreting Postal Technology at the National Postal Museum* (Unpublished Report, May 2, 1994).

4.   Library and Archives Canada, RG3, vol. 596, file 502-524: letter dated December 1, 1875.

5.   Mayo, "Post Office Work and Methods," p. 300.

6.   *Halifax Daily Reporter and Times*, December 9, 1871, p. 2, col. 34. For more information about the evolution of sorting technology during this period see J. J. M. L. Marchand, *Modernization of Postal Services* (Netherlands: De Boekerij, 1945); Library and Archives Canada, RG3, series 5, vol. 596: correspondence from the Chief Inspector, January 1875.

7.   The postmaster general was quoted at the Ontario Branch Conference of the Canadian Postmasters Association, October 6, 1959, in *The Postmark*, December 1959, p. 6. Mail volume increased rapidly, particularly in the years following the Second World War. According to the Canadian Postal Museum website, *A Chronology of Canadian Postal History*, 1971: The Postal Code (http://www.civilization.ca/cpm/chrono/index_e.html), in 1950, 1.3 billion mail items passed through the Canadian postal system and, by 1966, volume was up to 49 billion letters. As a result, between 1957 and 1966, the number of postal staff increased from 30,000 to 44,000.

8.   For more information about the era of the postal factory see Ian Lee, "The Canadian Postal System: Origins, Growth and Decay of the State Postal Function, 1765–1981" (PhD thesis, Carleton University, 1989); Post Office Department, *Annual Report* and Postmaster Generals' *Annual Reports* [1915–1960]; Library and Archives Canada, RG3 vol. 1165, 1910–1913 Scrapbook; *The Mail Bag*, January 14, 1953; *Speeding up Your Business: Toronto Post Office*, 1922 (film); François Legault, Canada Post Communications Department, conversation March 2005; Canada Post, Manuel des employés, 1978. See also Speeches by J. G. Fultz, Director of Operational Systems Division, Canada Canadian Post Office Department, 1976–1977, in particular, his speech of April 21, 1977, "The Implications of Coding and Mechanization." In addition, see United Postal Union, *Mechanical Handling of the Mails in Large Sorting Offices*, a joint publication of Britain, Netherlands and Swiss Postal Administrations, 1951, sections 1, p. 3; Wright, Crown Assets, pp. 167–168; Desson, *Three Hundred Years of Postal Communication*, pp. 7–12; Marchand, *Modernization of Postal Services*.

9.   Horrific working conditions often accompanied overcrowding. Hundreds of bodies, dozens of loud machines, uneven temperatures, fuming gas lanterns, and long hours of walking and lifting heavy loads made big city post offices difficult places to work in. *The Outlook* reported that the New York City post office had the worst working conditions in the whole of the United States (Mayo, "Post Office Work and Methods," pp. 298–310). For more information about post office working conditions, see *Annual Report 1897* (Ottawa: Canadian Post Office Department, 1897); *The Mail Bag*, 1940–1965; *Vancouver Postal Club Magazine*, January 1955; Marchand, *Modernization of Postal Services*; Post Office Department, *Deputy Postmaster General Report, 1929–1930*, p. 7; Canada Post Office Department, *Mechanical Equipment in Canadian Post Offices* (Ottawa: Canada Post Office Department, 1955). Automation was often promoted as a way to improve working conditions. In fact, the mechanization of postal processing resulted in labour relations problems for the Post Office department. Reduced productivity, work stoppages, strikes, poor morale, and a tarnished reputation for efficient service plagued the Post Office from the mid-1960s through the early 1980s. For more information about automation and labour, see *The Postmark*, December 1959, p. 6; Lee, "The Canadian Postal System," pp. 373–385; Thomas Hillman, *The Post Office in Canada* (Calgary: Auxano Philatelic, 2003), pp.106–107; Canada Post Office Department, *A Blueprint for Change* (Ottawa: Canada Post Office Department, 1969); Rosemary Speirs, "Most Mail Sorters Work as Automated Centre

Opens in Scarborough," *Toronto Star*, July 8, 1975, p. B1; "Union Ignored, Mail Sorters Working at New Site," *Globe and Mail*, July 1975.

10. Guy Pinard, *Montréal: son histoire, son architecture* (Montréal: Éditions du Méridien, 1992); Bianca Gendreau and John Willis, "Derrière les murs d'un centre de tri historique," *Cap Aux Diamants* no. 46 (Summer 1996); Gerard Chartrand (employee of the Peel post office from 1946 to 1959) in interview, January 23, 1996; Wright, *Crown Assets*, p.167; *Mail Bag* (November 1960): 4; *The Postmark* (May 1959); Marchand, *Modernization of Postal Services*.

11. Guy Pinard, *Montréal*, p.338.

12. Levy, M. "The Electronic Aspects of the Canadian Sorting of Mail" in *Proceedings of the National Electrical Conference*, February 1955, p. 545; Ted Paul and John Vardalas, "Canada Post's First Electronic Mail Sorter," *CIPS Review* (July/August 1987); *Scientific American*, January 25, 1890; Library and Archives Canada, RG3, vol. 2608, file 1 1917–1937: Canadian Post Office Department Chief Superintendent, October 26, 1929; *Maclean's*, May 1, 1927, p.18.

13. For discussions of the three experimental sorting machines, see Bianca Gendreau, "Acquisition Proposal: Optical Character Reader" (Unpublished report; Gatineau: Canadian Postal Museum, 2002); Douglas Crawford, "A Unique Type of Postal Marking from Peterborough, Ontario," *Canadian Philatelist* (January/February 1974): 27, 29; Honourable Alcied Coté, Postmaster General, Unpublished speech, June 27, 1955, in Canadian Postal Museum research files; *The Postmark*, September 1955, February 1964, and September/October 1977, p. 9; *Financial Post*, January 17, 1959; Sally Tunnicliff, "Letter Sorting Mechanization in Canada," *Machine Cancel Forum* no. 51 (July 1978); J. G. Fultz, *Coding and Mechanization: 52 Months Later* (Ottawa: Canada Post, 1974), p. 1; Hillman, *The Post Office in Canada*, p. 106; Fred Inglis, "Licking the Stamp Problem" (Unpublished report; Gatineau: Canadian Postal Museum, n.d.); Paul and Vardalas, "Canada's First Electronic Mail Sorter"; Lee, "The Canadian Postal System," p. 289; Desson, *Three Hundred years of Postal Communication*, p.12; M. Levy, "The Electronic Aspects of the Canadian Sorting of Mail," in *Proceedings of the National Electrical Conference*, February 1955; "New Stamps Make Letters Self Sorting," Canadian Postal Museum research files, n.d.

14. *Financial Post*, January 17, 1959, front page; *Peterborough Examiner*, June 28, 1955, centre section.

15. Alcide Coté, Postmaster General, "Federal Building to Be Opened at Peterborough," press release, June 27, 1955.

16. The coding system used by the Levy machine was called "extract coding." Extract coding required machine operators to draw key information from the letter's address (for example, the first four letters of each street and town and the first letter of each province) and transform that information into a code, which was then marked onto letters and "read" electronically during sorting. This coding style was impractical and was eventually replaced by the national postal code system in the 1970s. Levy, "The Electronic Aspects of the Canadian Sorting of Mail," p. 547.

17. J. G. Fultz, Speech, Canada Post Seminar, Southeast Asia, Spring 1978, p. 2.

18. *Performance*, May 4, 1988.

19. *Central Post Magazine* 1, no. 1 (May 8, 1972); Wayne Edison Fuller, *The American Mail: Enlarger of the Common Life* (Chicago: University of Chicago Press, 1972), pp. 334–35; Susan McLeod–O'Reilly, *On Track: The Railway Mail Service in Canada* (Gatineau: Canadian Museum of Civilization, 1992), pp. 19–34; Lee, "The Canadian Postal System," p. 290. For further discussion about working conditions in post offices, see footnote 8.

20. For more information about the postal coding process see United States Postal Service, *History of the United States Postal Service, 1775–1993* (Washington, D.C.: United States Postal Service, 1993), p. 103; Martin Daunton, *Royal Mail: The Post Office since 1840* (London: n.p., 1985),

pp. 345–346; Fultz, *Coding and Mechanization; Performance*, May 4, 1988. At the Canadian Postal Museum website, see *A Chronology of Canadian Postal History*, 1971: The Postal Code: Postal unions openly criticized the postal code system and this, combined with the Canadian public's resistance to change, hampered the implementation of the postal code system.

21. For a complete description of fully automated postal processing in Canada, see Fultz, *Coding and Mechanization*; Gary Stix, "Zip Code Breakers," *Scientific American*, February 1993, p. 102; Canada Post, *Manuel des Employees*, 1978; Bianca Gendreau, "Acquisition Proposal for the OCR"; Desson, *Three Hundred Years of Postal Communication*, p. 345.

22. Fultz, *Coding and Mechanization*, p. 41.

23. For more on modern processing technology see *The Postmark*, December 2003, p. 21; *Performance*, July/August 1994; *Ottawa Citizen*, October 27, 1993, section E; Henri-Pierre Penel, "Quand les ordinateurs lisent vos lettres," *Sciences et Vie*, August 1988, pp. 94–95.

24. François Legault, Canada Post Communications Department, conversation March 2005.

25. François Legault, Canada Post Communications Department, conversation March 2005; Desson, *Three Hundred Years of Postal Communication*, pp. 1, 7.

SEPTEMBER 11, 2001

Collecting and Exhibiting a National Tragedy

Nancy A. Pope, Historian, National Postal Museum, Smithsonian Institution, Washington, D.C.

Abstract

On Thursday, October 4, 2001, the U.S. National Postal Museum (NPM) began collecting objects related to the September 11, 2001, attacks. Museum staff had engaged in extended, often emotional, debates over the collection of 9/11 objects prior to this trip. After the final decision to collect had been made, the real difficulties began. The staff had to determine which items would be sought and work with postal and other government authorities to access the site. Most important, NPM staff had to insure not only the preservation of selected objects, but avoidance of contaminants.

The National Postal Museum's involvement in object collection at the 9/11 Ground Zero site was limited to items from, or representing, the Church Street station post office. The post office, located across the street from the World Trade Center (WTC), served the local neighbourhood, including the WTC buildings. The Museum sought these objects in response to its mission to collect, preserve, and display the history of the U.S. Postal Service.

Résumé

Le jeudi 4 octobre 2001, le National Postal Museum (NPM) des États-Unis a commencé à recueillir des objets relatifs aux attentats du 11 septembre 2001. Le personnel du musée s'est livré à des débats intensifs, et souvent plein d'émotions, sur la collecte d'objets du 11 septembre avant ce voyage. C'est une fois prise la décision finale de recueillir des objets que les véritables difficultés ont commencé. Le personnel devait déterminer quels objets rechercher et travailler avec l'administration des postes et d'autres autorités gouvernementales pour avoir accès au site. Plus important encore, le personnel du NPM devait veiller non seulement à la préservation des objets choisis, mais à éviter les contaminants.

L'implication du National Postal Museum, dans la cueillette d'objets sur l'emplacement de Ground Zero, se limitait à ceux qui avaient été expédiés du bureau de poste de la Church Street Station ou qui le concernaient. Le bureau de poste, situé de l'autre côté de la rue, en face du World Trade Center, desservait le voisinage, dont les deux tours. Le musée désirait obtenir ces articles dans le cadre de son mandat qui est de colliger, de préserver et de présenter des éléments de l'histoire du U.S. Postal Service.

Introduction

On Tuesday morning, September 11, 2001, staff at the National Postal Museum gathered at the television in the guards' lounge to watch reports of the attacks. We listened nervously to ominous warnings of a fourth plane possibly heading for Washington, D.C. The Museum sits a scant three blocks from a prime target, the U.S. Capitol. Futile efforts to reach friends and family in New York City or the Pentagon did nothing to ease the collective tension. Staff trickled out throughout the day, finding their way home alongside other shocked workers. By late afternoon, most of our staff members had joined the rest of the nation watching and waiting at home.

Over the next few days the thought of object collection crept into our collective discussions of the attacks. The National Postal Museum (NPM) is small in comparison to other Smithsonian Institution museums. In the fall of 2001, there were only two people in the Museum's curatorial department, me and Jeffrey Brodie. Our debate over the appropriateness versus the need to collect items from the site was echoed among NPM staff and in other museums. The focus of our talks was the large New York City post office on Church Street, which was located next to, and served, the World Trade Center complex.

In the end, the National Postal Museum obtained a number of objects from the Church Street post office. Each was chosen for its relevance to the day of the attack or its importance to the work of this post office within the community. These items are significant additions to our collection. Some were placed on display in the fall of 2003 as part of an exhibit devoted to the dangers faced by U.S. postal workers past and present.[1]

On Thursday, October 4, 2001, Jeff Brodie travelled to the Church Street post office in New York City to collect objects for the Museum. This post office served the 10007 Zip code for the surrounding neighbourhood and processed and delivered mail to the entire World Trade Center, which was represented by its own Zip code, 10048.

The Church Street post office is located at the corner of Church and Vesey streets. It faced World Trade Center building number 7 to the west and buildings 5 and 6 of the complex to the south-southwest. Building number 7 collapsed the afternoon of September 11. Building numbers 5 and 6 sustained critical damage and were later demolished. The Church Street post office sustained significant damage from the debris of the fallen buildings and the force of the explosion. Firefighters fought the fires in nearby World Trade Center buildings from the post office adding water damage to the building's interior. The post office remained structurally intact, although many of its windows were either blown out or shattered and debris was scattered atop and throughout the building.

This paper outlines internal National Postal Museum debate over object collection and the resulting efforts to secure objects related to the mission of the Museum from that site. The incomprehensible level of tragedy and subsequent issues of object contamination added unprecedented layers of emotionalism and concern to the collecting and preservation decision-making process.

Should We Collect?

A full NPM staff meeting was called in the week after the attacks, following our informal, and occasionally heated, curatorial discussions. Approximately twenty staffers from all areas of the Museum debated the options for collecting and exhibiting materials from the Church Street post office. I stood (mistakenly now I believe) firmly on the side of not collecting anything from the site. There were several reasons for my reluctance, rooted in the emotional turmoil of the time. I was unable to set aside the mental image of the site as a graveyard, a place that we had no business disturbing, not even for historic collection. Mine was not the only voice of hesitation in the Museum. Staff opinion was also mixed regarding an appropriate time (if any) for exhibiting collected materials. As with the curators, general staff opinion was mixed regarding collecting materials and the appropriate time to mount the items on public display. Those who urged collection viewed it as a focused goal, documenting the work of the U.S. Postal Service itself, not an emotionally morbid collecting frenzy.

Many staff members focused primarily on the tragedy and people involved for various reasons (including those who knew someone among the killed and missing) and not the big picture of viewing and documenting the role of the U.S. Postal Service in this national tragedy. We considered it unthinkable that the Museum would disrupt the site for any reason. Staffers who were able to see past the disaster and incorporate the Museum's mission into their thinking recognized that we needed to be at Church Street, locating and documenting this history.

The only area of agreement reached by all staff was that, regardless of object collection, the Museum should seek to obtain oral histories from clerks and carriers who were working at the Church Street post office that day. Following hours of often impassioned debate, a final decision was made to collect items from inside the post office.

At this time, mid-September 2001, our collecting debate remained an internal one. Although there were brief discussions with other museum personnel both inside and outside the institution, these were all informal, short discussions. Staff inside the Smithsonian's National Museum of American History faced the same tough decisions. As James Gardner explained in *Collecting a National Tragedy*, "While some staff argued that the Museum should move cautiously to avoid appearing self-serving in a time of national crisis, most recognized that the public would expect us to gather artifacts related to the terrorist attacks. If we didn't collect, we would have to be prepared to explain why."[2]

The possibility of outside pressure and second guessing over NPM's role in documenting the tragedy was not as demanding as that of American History's. Thankfully, no postal employees had been injured or killed in the attacks. Although the Church Street post office received significant damage that day, it was collateral damage; the building had not been attacked. Viewed this way, our need to collect was not as vital as that of the Smithsonian's National Museum of American History or New York City museums such as the Museum of the City of New York and the New York Historical Society.

Although the pressure of collecting for the national public was not an overwhelming factor in discussions, the pressure of time unquestionably was. Work at the site, as well as the exposure to the elements, were constant reminders that decisions and actions had to be made quickly. Although the post office remained standing, interior damage (from debris blown into the building by the fallen towers to water damage from firefighting operations set up to fight the fires in World Trade building number 7) was significant. We had no way of knowing what materials the Postal Service would mark as unsalvageable and consign to destruction prior to our travelling to the site. With that in mind, object selection decisions took on the appearance of a "wish list" discussion.

Why the National Postal Museum?

For those unfamiliar with the National Postal Museum or who may think the Museum is limited to philatelic display, the answer would be difficult to discern. The National Postal Museum's mission directs us to collect, preserve, and display the history of the U.S. Postal Service. The U.S. postal system has a historic role in connecting individuals, government, and business. Just as the NPM relates the history and development of those connections, we also document incidents and times at which those bonds are threatened or broken.[3] Individuals, businesses, and organizations of the World Trade Center complex were part of the Church Street neighbourhood. Carriers, clerks, and a myriad of other postal workers serviced the complex. World Trade Center residents were part of the national and international system of mail that connects individuals, government, and businesses. When that connection was destroyed, when an entire Zip code disappeared in a single day, the National Postal Museum had a duty to examine, record, and interpret the loss.

What to Collect?

A general list of items to be selected was determined by discussion prior to the trip. Although still reticent to gather materials from the site, I had become convinced that some collecting was needed to ensure an accurate preservation of this history. When discussing possible collection options we started with a variety of items that can be found in city post offices, and then began to consider specific items that would fit into one of two categories: first, the object's relevance to the day of the attack, second, the object's relevance to the work of the Church Street post office in its community.

Two objects already in the Museum's collection gave us some direction. These consisted of two hand cancelling stamps from the USS *Oklahoma*, sunk at Pearl Harbor during the December 7, 1941 attack. Both carry the date Dec 6, 1941.[4] The emotional effect of these two objects is still felt today. Their significant impact is heightened by the visual manifestation of the date.

Even before it become apparent that the attacks on the World Trade Center and Pentagon were becoming known by the date, September 11, we realized that it would be important to collect artifacts that displayed the date. For a post office, this meant hand

Figure 4.1 U.S. postal hand cancellation stamp from the Church Street post office, New York City, New York.

National Postal Museum, Smithsonian Institution.

cancellation and marking stamps, such as the one retrieved from the USS *Oklahoma*. These items were put on the top of our target list.

In our discussion over objects that represented the role of the post office in its community we agreed to look for items that carried the World Trade Center Zip code (10048). Finally, we discussed the representation of postal employees in their community through the gathering of iconic objects such as mailboxes and mailbags. While these discussions prepared our curator with some items to locate during his collecting trip, we would not know what else he would locate until he arrived at Ground Zero.[5]

Ground Zero, October 2001

In the wake of the attacks, curators and other museum staff in New York City met to discuss object collection and display. The meeting held on October 4, 2001, was co-sponsored by the National Museum of American History and the Museum of the City of New York and was a critical first step in helping America's museums step into this uneasy collecting realm. The meeting brought together historians representing over 30 institutions, including historical societies and museums from New York, New Jersey, Pennsylvania, and Washington, D.C.

Attendants agreed that their organizations would not engage in competitive collecting and that they would work together to help document and interpret the events of 9/11. NPM curatorial staff member, Jeff Brodie, was accompanied to the New York City meeting by Miguel Bretos, Acting Director of the Museum.

Brodie's trip to New York City that week was not only to attend the meeting, but to ascertain the condition of objects in the Church Street post office and arrange for their donation to the Museum. The early October visit was organized through the efforts of the U.S. Postal Inspection Service. The Inspection Service had offices in the building and had been actively involved in securing the Church Street mail after the attack. Without their assistance, our staff would not have been able to access the site.

While at the Church Street post office, Brodie tagged a number of items for NPM collection. Most of the smaller items, from cancellation devices to mailbags, were set aside to be sent to the Museum through the U.S. mail. Larger items were examined and remained at Church Street until decontamination and transportation could be arranged.[6]

Brodie returned to the Museum with a few cancellation and marking stamps, which had been wrapped in plastic for protection.

The Church Street Post Office

The Church Street post office and federal building, completed in 1935, was the responsibility of Lewis A. Simon, the supervising architect of the Treasury from 1933 to 1939 who oversaw its design. While this sturdy, New Deal-era building was not destroyed, significant damage resulted from the attack and subsequent collapse of the twin towers. Windows were blown out, dust and debris covered floor after floor of the building. A remnant of one of the airplanes and other debris landed on top of the building. The damage was compounded by water and other wreckage resulting from the day-long fight by firefighters to hold back fires in nearby World Trade Center buildings. On the afternoon of the 11th, the last collateral damage was sustained when building number 7 collapsed.

In addition to mail processing services, Church Street was the home office for a number of postal inspectors, postal police officers, and support staff as well as for employees of the U.S. Postal Service's New York City crime lab. Postal inspectors hurried into the streets to offer assistance to civilians and local police officers injured in the attack and helped to evacuate the area as glass and debris fell from the sky.

The Church Street post office was one of four New York post offices closed after the attack. The others were able to reopen within the following week. The Peck Slip post office at 1 Peck Slip was the first to reopen, followed by the Bowling Green post office at 25 Broadway and the Wall Street post office at 73 Pine Street. The three were up and running by September 21, ten days following the attack.

That Tuesday morning, September 11, the Church Street postal employees were busy at work inside the building. The first hours of a letter carrier's day is spent "casing" or organizing the day's mail deliveries. The World Trade Center carriers usually began their rounds inside the buildings at 10 a.m., so when the airplanes struck, the U.S. Postal Service employees were still at work inside the post office. No one in the Church Street building was hurt that morning, as the building had been successfully evacuated by the time the south tower (building number 2) collapsed.[7]

Although the Church Street post office could not be used after the attack, mail was still arriving, and workers were needed to process it. The Church Street employees were detailed out to different work locations on September 12. Delivery and customer service employees were reassigned to the Farley Post office building on 33rd Street, about six kilometres north. Processing staff were told to report to the nearby Morgan processing centre three blocks away. In just two days, the Church street employees set up a functioning version of their old office on the ground floor of the Farley building. Clerks dusted off old surplus metal mailboxes and used them to hold mail for the almost 4,000 post office boxes that sat remarkably undamaged, but inaccessible, at Church Street.

The ten carriers whose daily rounds had been in the corridors of the World Trade Center complex began sorting the mail that was still arriving into bins. The carriers continued to process mail for the approximately 16,000 addresses that made up the twin towers. Among the envelopes they handled were pieces addressed to hundreds of individuals who had been killed, people known to the carriers for years. In the first weeks following the attack, carriers spoke of the steady depression of sorting mail for those who would never retrieve it.

Over 80,000 delivery points were initially affected when delivery service was suspended below 14th street in Manhattan for days following the attack. Thirty thousand delivery points remained affected even after most of the post offices reopened. Carriers who began to return to their old routes had trouble reaching some homes as the police and National Guard moved barricades and switched street closings. At the beginning of each day, carriers did not know whether or not they would be allowed into certain areas.

After the attack, patrons of the Church Street post office travelled to the Farley Building for their mail. For the first two weeks, patrons stood in long lines, which were set up outside the Farley building, designated by Zip codes, to get their mail. The block-long lines finally eased as post offices reopened and carriers began to reach more of the formerly cordoned-off areas. The Church Street post office finally reopened on August 2, 2004. However, the employees process significantly less mail than before. As of late 2004, the building was receiving approximately 200,000 pieces of mail daily, roughly one quarter of the pre-9/11 amount.[8]

U.S. Postal Service Response to 9/11

The U.S. Postal Service faced a series of daunting challenges after the 9/11 attacks. Mail left at the Church Street post office that Tuesday was retrieved by U.S. postal inspectors, aided by the National Guard and local police. The mail was moved by truck to the main post office at the Farley building at 33rd street for processing. At the same time, the Postal Service's ability to move the mail across the country had also been dealt a serious blow.

As postal officials tried to determine the extent of the damage to Church Street and nearby post offices they learned that the Federal Aviation Administration had halted all flight operations at U.S. airports, bringing commercial aviation to a grinding halt. Up to a quarter of the 650 million pieces of mail carried per day by the Postal Service at that time was carried by air. Postal officials scrambled to keep the mail moving until the airports reopened and commercial aviation could continue. Amtrak added additional train cars to carry people and mail. USPS also contracted with 6,000 private trucking companies to move tons of stranded mail.

U.S. commercial and private airplanes remained grounded until Thursday, September 13. USPS-owned airplanes were finally operating again at near capacity the next day. But, the issue of mail on passenger flights remained problematic. The Federal Aviation Administration had banned both mail and cargo from the passenger flights. By Tuesday, September 18, the Postal Service was finally permitted to move letters and small flats on commercial airplanes.

In the weeks following the attacks, the USPS and its employees strove to get the mail moving to as many of the affected New York City addresses as possible. As Vincent Sombrotto, head of the National Association of Letter Carriers noted, "[T]here's nothing that's more normal than seeing a letter carrier come and deliver mail. That's just a signature of normalcy in our society. And for that [the public was] thankful."[9]

Outside of New York City, postal inspectors also worked with FBI agents to collect evidence at the crash site at the Pentagon.[10] In Pennsylvania, a team of inspectors from the Pittsburgh area reported to the crash site of United Airlines flight 93 at Somerset County to assist in securing the site and any mail present. Among the items retrieved was a battered and torn section of a plastic mail container. This was later acquired by the National Postal Museum.

The Postal Inspection Service provided significant investigative assistance and support to the FBI, Federal Aviation Administration, and emergency management agencies across the nation over the next months. Postal inspectors helped track down a number of post-attack scams and confidence schemes. These included individuals raising money for victim's families and pocketing the proceeds. The chief postal inspector reported: "Postal inspectors will aggressively pursue those con artists. And we are offering some advice to the American public on how to make sure their donations go where they are intended."[11]

Ground Zero, November 2001

In early November 2001, Jeff Brodie was accompanied by the Postal Museum's conservation specialist, Linda Edquist, to the Church Street post office to select additional items for the collection. Edquist recalls the scene at Ground Zero that November as very eerie. Although much clean up had been done within the post office, "everything still had its layer of dust."[12] A critical issue facing those working at the site was the type and level of contaminants present. According to an advisory memo co-authored by Kathryn Makos of the Smithsonian's Office of Safety and Environmental Management (OSEM) and Monona Rossol, President of the Arts, Crafts and Theater Safety Association, dust and debris at the Ground Zero site was unlike any encountered in the past. The smoke from the fire alone contained "products of incomplete combustion of plastic computers, miles of vinyl coated

Figure 4.2 U.S. letter carrier Emma Thornton examining her sorting table unit at the National Postal Museum. National Postal Museum, Smithsonian Institution.

wiring, acres of flammable carpet, tons of office furniture, reservoirs of hydraulic oil and other fuels including some contaminated with polychlorinated biphenyls (PCBs)."[13]

The variety and enormity of the dust contamination was an ongoing concern. Makos and Rossol advised caution for a variety of potential health risks, including "asbestos (cancer, lung disease), fibreglass (skin, eye, and respiratory irritant, suspect carcinogen), cement and drywall dust (respiratory irritant, caustic, contains silica dust which can cause serious lung disease and cancer), organic particulates from burning plastic such as polyvinyl chloride, PCBs, dioxins and other polynuclear aromatic hydrocarbons, and metals such as lead, copper, iron oxide, and cadmium."[14]

Contamination on this scale (diversity of contaminants, geographic level of contamination) and of this intensity (the Ground Zero fire was the longest burning commercial building fire in U.S. history) led to widespread confusion over safety procedures. This was true especially in the first weeks after the attacks, as rescue parties frantically dug into the ruins. By November, the organizations working the Ground Zero sites had begun to follow a wide range of decontamination protection rules. The worker safety challenge was enormous and complex. Dust contamination levels varied not only from block to block, but also day to day, as recovery and demolition work continued.

By this time, the Smithsonian's National Museum of American History was actively involved in locating items for preservation from the site. Conservation staff from both museums spent hours in discussions with OSEM staff prior to Brodie's and Edquist's trip. Prepared guidelines advised that the site be treated as a hazardous materials location, but little was known of the level of harmful materials. The Postal Museum was, in Edquist's

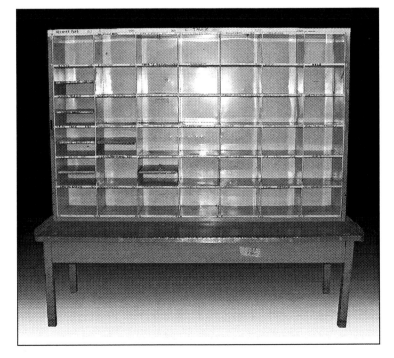

Figure 4.3 Sorting table unit recovered from the Church Street post office, New York City, New York. The sorting holes are marked with the names of companies located on floors 77 through 110 of tower 1.

National Postal Museum, Smithsonian Institution.

words, "the guinea pig"[15] in assessing the site and helping to determine successful reactions to dealing with the site's possibly deadly contaminants.

NPM access to Ground Zero still required the assistance of the U.S. Postal Inspection Service in November. By then, building number 7 had been cleared away. The post office's roof had been cleared off and was being decontaminated. While Edquist and Brodie were clothed head to toe in decontamination suits (unlike Brodie's October trip to the site, during which he wore no protection at all), they were accompanied in some instances by individuals simply dressed in work clothes, and at others by workers dressed in varied levels of decontamination protection gear.[16]

The entire site was well secured. Nothing was allowed to be taken out of the post office unless it had been decontaminated. Inside, one floor had been cleared of debris and was being used for decontamination work. After decontamination, items were shrink-wrapped and set aside for removal. Among the larger items NPM staff hoped to collect was a postal sorting unit. These familiar tables topped by pigeon-holes are easily recognizable postal artifacts. The sorting units are used by letter carriers to "case," or sort, their mail before making the day's deliveries.

Unbeknownst to Brodie and Edquist, I had been working with New York City postal officials to arrange a video-taped oral interview with letter carrier Emma Thornton. Thornton had worked out of the Church Street post office for over 20 years. Her route, 24D, covered floors 77 through 110 of the north tower (number 1). Among her patrons were over 70 businesses and organizations, including Windows on the World restaurant and Cantor Fitzgerald Securities. A long-time New Yorker, Thornton told us that "Every time I think about it, tears come to my eyes. A lot of my friends didn't make it."[17] Thornton cherished little victories in the months following the attacks, such as the times survivors came to retrieve waiting mail. Sadly, those happy reunions were few.

By sheer coincidence, Edquist and Brodie selected the sorting unit used by Emma Thornton at Church Street.[18] In the end, we were able to bring Thornton to the Museum, where she participated in an oral history project while being filmed in front of her sorting table.

Decontamination

Site contamination issues eventually became object contamination issues. Dust at the site contained asbestos and silicates, both threats in their own way to object collection and preservation work. The chrysotile fibre form of asbestos used widely in building construction when the towers were built is a known carcinogen and hazardous to the lungs. In a study done in the weeks following the attack, the Occupational Safety and Health Administration (OSHA) found settled dust containing as much as five per cent asbestos fibre. More dangerous to the preservation of the objects themselves was the presence of silicates such as synthetic vitreous fibres (SVA), also known as fibreglass. The siliceous dust is hazardous to the lungs and hard and sharp enough to scratch metal surfaces.

The content and hazard level of the debris and dust was an ongoing source of debate. Since the fall of 2001, news stories have highlighted health problems experienced by rescue workers and others who spent long amounts of time at Ground Zero or surrounding areas. An exact determination of contaminants varied greatly depending on day, weather, and site location. Since an analysis of every area was unrealistic, Edquist labelled the entire working site and object dust and debris as hazardous.

All of the objects were covered to varying degrees with dust and debris from the collapse of the towers. When Edquist accompanied Brodie on his second trip to the Church Street post office, it was to assist with the removal of as much of the debris as possible from the items prior to transportation. To complete their task, they were fitted and certified for half-mask air respirators with particulate cartridge filters, disposable full body suits, and disposable barrier gloves for hazardous material handling. They also arranged for the use of a High Efficiency Particulate Adsorption (HEPA) vacuum.[19]

Inside the post office, our team covered their working area with plastic sheeting. Each object had its own needs. They lightly misted the mailbox to prevent accumulated dust from becoming airborne and spreading. Larger debris was scooped into bags for hazard waste disposal and the remaining dust vacuumed with the HEPA unit. Finally, the surfaces were gently wiped with a solution of water and a drop of surfactant.[20] The area was then cleaned, and all cleaning and protection materials (including coveralls, gloves, filters for the respirator, and vacuum bag) collected for hazardous waste disposal. The mailbox was shrink-wrapped and shipped to the Smithsonian in Washington for final decontamination work.

The Anthrax Curve

While NPM staff were dealing with the large Church Street objects, the story of the smaller pieces was not yet over. On October 6, 2001, two seemingly innocuous letters travelled through Washington, D.C.'s Brentwood mailing centre. Addressed to U.S. Senators Daschle and Leahy, the letters contained anthrax in a fine-powder form. As the letters passed through the mail sorting equipment, especially the optical character reader, they were squeezed between other letters. The pressure caused some of the spores to be released into the facility. The Postal Service shut down the Brentwood mail facility on October 21, 2001, after two postal workers were sickened and killed from anthrax inhalation.

Among the millions of stranded and possibly contaminated mail left in the building were the two boxes of objects from New York City's Church Street post office bound for NPM. The boxes contained several objects that had been set aside at Church Street by Brodie during his October trip to the site. Postal inspectors had agreed to mail these items to the Museum. By a quirk of fate and timing, the boxes had just reached the Brentwood mail facility in Washington, D.C., when the building was closed down and sealed shut.

By the time these items reached the Museum (following the reclamation and decontamination of Brentwood), they had become part of a second tragic story from the fall of 2001. The boxes were labelled with information regarding their stay in Brentwood and subsequent decontamination. Now part of another piece of postal history, the boxes themselves were placed into the Museum's collection.

Decontamination at the Smithsonian Institution

While significant decontamination work had been done on-site in New York City, problem objects remained. Among those were hand stamps retrieved by Brodie during the October trip to the Church Street post office and the items mailed to the Museum during the Anthrax attacks.[21] These hand stamps had been brought back to the Museum by Brodie in a simple plastic bag.

Discussions over potential contamination issues with 9/11 objects at the Smithsonian Institution was jump-started by Brodie's plastic bag of hand stamps. There they were segregated, wrapped, and prepared for decontamination by Smithsonian experts. This work was done at the Smithsonian's Garber facility. Each piece was carefully examined and tested for asbestos, mercury, and PCBs before work began. Once conservators knew what they were working with, the decontamination treatments began. The processing work took about three months, after which all the objects were returned to the Postal Museum.

In the Line of Duty

In early October 2003, two years after the first 9/11 objects had been brought into the Postal Museum, the main section of Emma Thornton's sorting unit went on display as part of the Museum's exhibit, "In the Line of Duty." Also on display in this portion of the exhibit were the U.S. Postal Service collection mailbox that had been retrieved from the front of the Church Street post office, a mail cart used in World Trade Center building number 6, and one of the retrieved hand stamps. The hand stamp legend reads simply, "Church Street, NYC, Sept 11, 2001."

When interviewed by a *New York Times* reporter shortly after the meeting on October 4, 2001, in New York City, Jan S. Ramirez, then Director of the New York Historical Society's museum, articulated the danger of waiting to collect items documenting the 9/11 tragedy. "These materials will disappear," she argued, "if we don't try and collect them now."[22]

Ramirez's words are significant for those charged with identifying and preserving artifacts that document our world. A challenge for curators and historians documenting human tragedy is to find a way to do so without being overcome by the emotional toll of that tragedy. Yet, they must remain sensitive to the moment in order to recognize those artifacts that will best interpret the tragedy for future generations.

The search for balance is not new. It was underway in the months following the April 19, 1995, bombing of the Alfred P. Murrah Federal building in Oklahoma City, Oklahoma, which killed 168 men, women and children. The Archives Subcommittee task force was responsible for identifying and preserving documents and bombing artifacts and created six areas in which to collect: 1) the history of the site; 2) the rescue and recovery efforts; 3) public and media response; 4) resulting changes that could prevent similar acts in the future; 5) the investigations and trails; and 6) the memorial process.[23]

Discussions over documenting the bombing through objects included not only items recovered from the building, but also personal memorials and mementos left by the public at the fence surrounding the bombing site. These items are part of the collections of the

Oklahoma City National Memorial Museum. In 1984, park rangers of the National Park Service began collecting personal items left at the Vietnam War Memorial in Washington, D.C. Artifacts from this collection, numbering over 70,000, have been successfully displayed around the country.

Curators and historians faced with determining what to collect from the 9/11 attacks certainly had these examples to learn from. Positive public reaction to the collection and display of artifacts recovered from the Oklahoma City bombing site and those collected from the Vietnam War Memorial helped guide and inform 9/11 collection discussions.

Positive public reaction to the display of objects documenting 9/11 in the National Museum of American History[24] and the National Postal Museum's "In the Line of Duty" exhibit has shown that the public wanted, even needed, the public display and acknowledgement of the tragedy.

The determination of curators and historians to work toward collecting representative objects in the days and weeks following the attacks ensured the preservation of these items and the people and histories that they represent. The exhibition of 9/11 artifacts continues to offer visitors a way to channel their emotions and thoughts. As Mark Schaming, Director of Exhibitions and Public Programs at the New York State Museum in Albany, New York, noted, "People need to be in the presence of these objects."[25]

Notes

1. "In the Line of Duty" opened October 2003. The online exhibit can be found at http://postalmuseum.si.edu/duty.
2. James B. Gardner, "Collecting a National Tragedy," *Museum News*, March/April, 2002.
3. Items from the Civil War, national disasters, and other incidents of communication "disconnection" are among these kinds of objects in the Museum's collection.
4. The ship's post office had not opened on the Sunday of the attack. The date reflected the previous day's work.
5. Jeff Brodie made the preliminary trip to the site. Although I had been convinced that some collecting should be done, I could not bring myself to travel to the site on that trip nor on the second one in November.
6. Among the larger items collected by the Museum are a letter carrier's sorting unit and postal cart. Museum staff also obtained a mail collection box from outside the post office and a brass "Cutler-style" mail collection box from the Marriott Hotel.
7. 8:45 a.m. (EST): American Airlines flight 11 crashes into the north tower of the World Trade Center.
   9:03 a.m.: United Airlines flight 175 crashes into the south tower of the World Trade Center.
   9:40 a.m.: The FAA halts all flight operations at U.S. airports.
   9:43 a.m.: American Airlines flight 77 crashes into the Pentagon.
   10:05 a.m.: The south tower of the World Trade Center collapses.

10:10 a.m.: United Airlines flight 93 crashes in Somerset County, Pennsylvania, southeast of Pittsburgh.

10:28 a.m.: The World Trade Center's north tower collapses.

8. David D. Dunlap, "A Return to Sending," *The New York Times*, August 19, 2004.

9. Vincent Sombrotto, President, National Association of Letter Carriers, Speech in front of the Church Street post office in New York City, September 25, 2001.

10. Postal inspectors' presence at the Pentagon site was related to the presence of mail on American Airlines flight 77, the airplane that crashed into the Pentagon.

11. Kenneth C. Weaver, Chief U.S. Postal Inspector, "Testimony before the Senate Subcommittee on International Security, Proliferation and Federal Services," September 20, 2001.

12. Linda Edquist, Interview, Washington, D.C., December 9, 2004.

13. Monona Rossol, President, Arts, Crafts and Theater Safety, and Kathryn Makos, Certified Industrial Hygenist, Smithsonian Institution Office of Safety and Environmental Management, "World Trade Center Dust: Safe Work Practices for Conservators," memorandum, December 6, 2001.

14. Ibid.

15. Linda Edquist, Interview, Washington, D.C., December 9, 2004.

16. During Brodie's October trip to the site, neither he, nor anyone else wore much protective gear. Some of the inspectors and workers at the area wore, or carried, breathing masks, but contamination concerns had not yet registered with most at the site. The chief worry at the time was dust inhalation.

17. Emma Thornton, Interview, November 16, 2002.

18. Edquist later revealed that she had selected Thornton's unit because she thought that the piece, with its easily recognizable organizational names, would make a powerful exhibit object.

19. HEPA filters were first designed by the Atomic Energy Commission in the Second World War for trapping plutonium particles. Regular vacuums release small particulate matter they are sucking into the machine back out of the exhaust, trapping only larger particles (10 microns and above). A HEPA vacuum seals the contaminants being sucked into the machine, capturing approximately 99 per cent of particles 0.3 microns or larger. They are made from a media such as fibreglass, bonded together by a synthetic resin and the construction is so tight that almost all the tiny particulate up to .3 microns gets trapped permanently in the filter.

20. A suffcant is a molecule that, when added to a liquid at low concentration, changes the properties of that liquid at a surface or interface.

21. While the boxes from the Brentwood postal facility had been irradiated to eliminate any danger from anthrax, the objects inside remained tightly sealed as they had been sent from Church Street in October. No decontamination was done of the pieces prior to mailing.

22. Glenn Collins, "Historians Weigh Attack's Impact on New York City," *The New York Times*, October 6, 2001, pp. A13, A15.

23. Carol Brown, "Out of the Rubble: Building a Contemporary History Archive—The Oklahoma City National Memorial Archives" *Perspectives* (American Historical Association), October 1999, Exhibitions and Interpretive Programs column.

24. The National Museum of American History exhibit, "September 11: Bearing Witness to History," is now a travelling exhibit. The Museum maintains an online version of the exhibit at http://americanhistory.si.edu/september11/. The online exhibit continues to offer visitors the opportunity to record their 9/11 related stories through an online archive.

25. David W. Dunlap, "Oh, the Stories These Mute Pieces Could Tell," *The New York Times*, March 31, 2004, section G, p. 1.

TESTING THE BOUNDARIES OF POSTAL ENTERPRISE IN THE U.S. FREE-MARKET ECONOMY, 1880–1920

5

Richard Kielbowicz, Associate Professor, Department of Communication, University of Washington

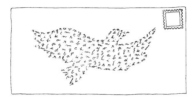

Abstract

Any reasonable reading of the U.S. Constitution's postal clause empowered the federal government to establish an institution that transmitted information and some goods. When the Post Office considered launching ambitious new services, however, many of these initiatives triggered debates about the proper relationship between government and the private sector. Few disagreed that the postal service should facilitate communication and commerce, but at what point did facilitation become unwanted intrusion into a largely free-market economy? This essay sketches the debates about the boundaries of postal enterprise. It focuses on three key initiatives, widely discussed between 1880 and 1920, in which opponents argued that government would overstep the proper boundaries of postal enterprise and intrude into the precincts of the private sector. Specifically, it examines the controversies surrounding efforts to establish postal savings, parcel post, and a postal telegraph and telephone service.

Résumé

Toute interprétation raisonnable de la clause concernant les postes dans la Constitution américaine permet au gouvernement fédéral de mettre sur pied une institution acheminant de l'information et certains biens. Toutefois, lorsque le service des postes a songé à offrir de nouveaux services ambitieux, beaucoup de ces initiatives ont provoqué des débats sur le rapport approprié qui devait exister entre l'État et le secteur privé. Rares étaient ceux qui n'admettaient pas que le service postal devait faciliter les communications et le commerce, mais à quel moment cela devenait-il une intrusion indésirable au sein d'une économie qui est surtout une économie de marché ? Cet essai aborde les débats sur les limites de l'entreprise postale. Il s'intéresse particulièrement à trois initiatives essentielles qui ont fait couler beaucoup d'encre entre 1880 et 1920, et à propos desquelles leurs opposants soutenaient que le gouvernement outrepasserait les justes limites de l'entreprise postale et empiéterait sur le terrain du secteur privé. Il s'attarde spécifiquement sur les controverses soulevées par les efforts pour instaurer des caisses d'épargne, des services d'envoi de colis ainsi que des services de télégraphe et de téléphone dans les bureaux de poste.

Introduction

The boundaries of postal enterprise were tested more vigorously by the Populists and Progressives from 1880 to 1920 than at any other time in American history. Their notions of political economy offered the best developed rationale for an aggressively innovative Post Office. The Populists, a coalition of rural interests that emerged in the 1880s, worked to redress some of the excesses of large-scale industrialization that were transforming the United States. For the most part, Populists sought an "active, neutral state," according to Norman Pollack. Government regulation of or participation in key sectors of the economy—transportation, communication, and banking—would preserve competitive opportunities for private firms regardless of their size. Without state action in these basic services, Populists feared, capitalism degenerated into monopoly when firms parlayed transportation, communication, or banking advantages into anti-competitive positions. Formal American economic thought at the time, heavily influenced by German theorists, had much in common with the Populists' pragmatic notions of the activist state.[1]

Early in the twentieth century, Progressives—a force in both major parties—carried much of the Populist agenda forward, but with a more urban, cosmopolitan flavour. Progressives accepted many Populist precepts, especially as they applied to public utilities, including some aspects of communication. Progressives also strengthened claims for government-run enterprises by championing "scientific management," shorthand for reducing the influence of partisanship while incorporating businesslike principles in the administration of public affairs. When Progressives sought authority to support public enterprise, the Constitution's commerce clause furnished some hope but proved more helpful in regulating private-sector activities than in initiating public-sector ones. Instead, enthusiasts for government enterprise embraced the postal clause. Citing that authority, Populists and Progressives spoke of postal savings, a postal express (i.e., parcel post), and a postal telegraph and telephone all in the same breath. The first two objectives were attained by 1912.

The debates surrounding all three measures tested the boundaries of postal enterprise and thus illuminate a major, although largely overlooked, chapter in the history of American political economy. The campaigns to establish postal savings, parcel post, and a postal wired communication system thus deserve attention by more than postal historians. Principles of American political economy remained far from settled during the early 1900s, and the efforts to draw the boundaries of postal enterprise figured centrally in the larger process of contesting, refining, and validating principles about the role of the state, especially federal bureaucracies. In short, these debates over postal initiatives did not so much apply established rules of political economy as they helped create the principles themselves.

Postal Savings Banks

The financial panic of 1873, which brought the collapse of three leading securities firms and a ten-day closure of the New York Stock Exchange, prompted the postmaster general to recommend a postal savings system. But, the ramifications of this proposal for American political economy were clear to his successor who observed: "[T]he time has come when a resolute effort should be made to determine how far the Post Office department can properly go in its efforts to accommodate the public, without trespassing unwarrantably upon the sphere of private enterprise." Nevertheless, postal officials and Populists kept the idea alive during the late 1800s.[2]

Populists saw a savings system as a logical extension of the Post Office department's responsibilities. Postal banks, they asserted, would encourage thrift among immigrants, the working class, and rural inhabitants. Furthermore, they would promote economic stability by bringing unused money into the economy, thereby providing capital for business growth, and by helping to stop the flow of U.S. dollars to other countries. The banks would also protect vulnerable people against "swindlers, unsafe deposits and unwise investments, and at the same time increase the investors' loyalty to the government by giving them a stake in a stable economy."[3] Finally, all of this could be accomplished with "no new organ of government." As one advocate argued:

> The post-office, of all institutions, seems to be the best adapted to carry the influence of the savings banks to every fireside. The most pervasive, the best understood, and the most familiar institution of any civilized country is the post office. And likewise in every rural community the most widely known individual is the postmaster, and in every urban community the most familiar individual is the letter carrier. ... Thus, he is peculiarly qualified to serve the savings bank, which requires not only facilities but missionaries.[4]

Proponents tried to defuse the opposition by claiming that postal savings banks would not compete against commercial banks because people interested in depositing money at their post office would not be the same people investing in private institutions. One study, for example, reported that many Americans, especially in the South and the West, lived hundreds of miles from private savings banks.[5]

Opponents nonetheless insisted that a postal savings system would indeed intrude upon private enterprise and would suffer from mismanagement. Bankers aggressively—and for many years successfully—lobbied against federal legislation to enact such a system. They worried that their customers would close their banking accounts and redeposit the money in government protected postal accounts.[6]

The establishment of postal savings banks around the world, especially in the United Kingdom (1861) and Canada (1868), heartened the movement in the United States. At the request of Congress, U.S. consuls investigated postal savings banks in their respective countries. The postmaster general also sent a postal expert to Canada to determine why the Canadian system worked so well.[7]

It took, however, the 1907 financial panic with the accompanying collapse of numerous banks to prod Congress to enact the 1910 postal savings law. President Theodore Roosevelt and postmaster general George von L. Meyer urged Congress to authorize a postal savings system to help restore Americans' faith in the virtue and security of systematic savings. This theme—the moral value of thrift—also influenced the operations of Canada's postal savings system. The major American political parties endorsed the idea in their party platforms and, when William H. Taft assumed the presidency in 1909, he made postal savings banks one of his top legislative priorities. Postmaster general Frank H. Hitchcock reiterated the benefits long claimed for postal savings: It would serve people who lived far from private banks, provide security for savings, aggregate capital for businesses to reinvest, and accomplish all of this without unduly competing with private banks.[8]

Despite Hitchcock's reassurance, banking interests continued aggressively to oppose any legislation that would establish a competing financial institution within the government. Acknowledging the banking industry's concerns, policymakers structured the legislation to minimize direct competition with private banks. Specifically, they set the interest rate payable to depositors at two per cent, half of what private banks could offer. This was the lowest interest rate of any postal savings system in the world, even though the private American banks were paying the highest interest rates on deposits. Congress also initially set the maximum account balance at $500, and specified that the money the local postal bank collected from depositors should be redeposited in solvent local banks, if available. This served a dual purpose: It kept the government from controlling the funds and also aggregated small deposits for the private banking system. Although the American Bankers Association committed one million dollars to block the legislation, it finally conceded that the creation of voluntary postal savings banks was inevitable and certainly preferable to legislative action to guarantee bank deposits, another proposed remedy stemming from the panic of 1907.[9]

Effective January 1, 1911, the postal savings system "was established as an experiment in a new field of public benefits."[10] It immediately attracted deposits from rural and immigrant groups and especially flourished during the Depression of the 1930s, when many lost confidence in private banks. Postal savings peaked in 1947 with 4,196,517 depositors and a balance of $3,392,773,461. By the 1960s, postal administrators agreed that federal insurance of private savings accounts and the nearly universal access to banks had rendered postal savings superfluous. In 1966, Congress voted to discontinue the service.[11]

Parcel Post

Seemingly uncontroversial today, parcel post originally marked a dramatic departure in public-sector initiatives: It put the federal government in direct competition with well-established package-delivery firms. Government, of course, had long influenced business operations through contracts, grants, subsidies, and tariffs. Congress, however, had repeatedly resisted calls for government ownership of key industries. Parcel post legislation stopped short of appropriating private firms, but proponents and opponents both acknowledged that it redefined the accepted domain of postal activity.[12]

Parcel post formed the capstone in a postal communication and transportation system that already promoted marketing on a national scale. When Congress halved second-class postage to one cent a pound in 1885, advertisement-filled popular magazines poured out of major cities. Mailings of periodicals rose twenty times faster than the population between 1880 and 1920. Fast mail trains rushed big-city dailies to readers in the hinterlands; in 1894, Chicago papers dispatched more than twenty tonnes each day. The inauguration of Rural Free Delivery in the late 1890s brought city newspapers and national magazines directly to farmers' lanes. Mail-order retailers could now reach most of the nation with ads, and modest letter postage allowed reader-consumers to respond with orders. Yet, at the outset of the twentieth century, Congress still prohibited the postal delivery of the commercial fruits of all this communication—parcels.[13]

Before the inauguration of parcel post on January 1, 1913, the Post Office accepted no package weighing more than four pounds [1.8 kilograms] and only then at the steep rate of 1 cent an ounce [28 grams]. Without a parcel post, mail-order customers typically paid to have their packages shipped by railroad freight or express. (Express companies were the chief small-package delivery service.) Americans began to question why the Post Office failed to carry parcels at a competitive rate. At a minimum, parcel post could deliver to the twenty million Americans who lived outside express companies' service areas. And, lower postage rates would further open the countryside to urban merchandisers or, viewed from the customer's vantage point, allow rural residents to choose from the offerings of a modern consumer society. Parcel post advocates testified that reputable mail-order firms offered a wider choice of goods at cheaper prices than any small-town store. "[T]he assertion of the local merchant that the parcel post will destroy or injure his business is an admission that he can not sell as cheaply as the mail-order house," a representative of farm groups told Congress. "This, in effect, is a demand that the farmer pay him a premium or bounty in order that he may continue to conduct business by antiquated methods and be protected from the progressive spirit of modern merchandising and twentieth-century methods."[14]

Much of the campaign for parcel post turned on beliefs about the ability of the Post Office department to manage new tasks. Could the department assume a private-sector function and operate it along businesslike lines? The size, complexity, and reach of the Post Office had earned it accolades as "the greatest business concern in the world." In this view, the department possessed the requisite expertise to successfully manage a parcel delivery business. Many postal officials believed that adding parcel post made good business sense because it capitalized on the department's unrivaled nationwide infrastructure.[15] They repeatedly observed that all other industrial nations had a parcel post. "[P]arcels post is a success wherever it is in operation" around the world, postmaster general John Wanamaker proclaimed, blaming the "four great express companies"—Adams, American, United States, and Wells Fargo—for blocking it in the United States. As owner of one of the nation's leading department stores and a pioneer in using the mails for marketing, Wanamaker might have benefited from parcel post, but his interest in expanding the realm of postal enterprise was genuine. Wanamaker also noted that foreign governments and international postal congresses had asked the United States to provide parcel post on the same terms as other industrial nations to facilitate cross-border package exchanges.[16]

The Progressives' penchant for investigations, data, and publicity kept package-delivery firms under a public microscope. A report by the Interstate Commerce Commission (ICC), which regulated railroads and related industries, basically corroborated what the pro-parcel post muckrakers had been telling magazine readers for several years: Package-delivery companies double charged and over charged, refused to tell customers about free delivery areas beyond rail depots, sent shipments by circuitous routes to inflate costs, discriminated among customers, and more. The commission blamed most problems on the complexity of the system and rate schedules. "There are some thirty-five thousand express stations in the United States. To separately state the rates from each one of these stations to each of the others requires the statement of over 600,000,000 rates." The commission's own rate experts, let alone ordinary express agents, could hardly find the correct rates. Journalists and Progressive lawmakers, however, pointed to collusion among express companies, and between railroads and express firms, as the root of the problem.[17]

Despite such findings, Congress declined to hold hearings on parcel post until 1910. Private carriers exerted considerable influence over lawmakers such as house speaker Joseph Cannon and key senators. A month after Cannon was ousted from the speakership in March 1910, the House convened its first hearings on the subject and held another round in June 1911. The Senate provided the most extensive public forum, running from November 1911 to April 1912, producing a hearing record that filled 1,290 printed pages. These two years of hearings fueled a wide-ranging discussion in newspapers, popular magazines, agricultural journals, trade publications, and pamphlets.[18]

By 1912, the Republican, Democratic, and Progressive Parties, and their presidential candidates, had all endorsed parcel post; socialists subsumed it among more radical proposals. Accordingly, at least twenty parcel post bills were introduced in Congress and referred to the post office committee. As the parcel post debate crested, Congress considered four options: (1) leave the parcel delivery business entirely to private-sector competition; (2) subject private carriers to stricter regulation by the Interstate Commerce Commission; (3) launch a postal package-delivery service to compete with the private sector; or (4) invoke the Constitution's postal clause to establish an outright public monopoly.[19]

Much of the attack on the proposal moved beyond the practicality of parcel post to matters of political economy. Letters, petitions, pamphlets, articles, and testimony warned against government intrusions into the realm of private enterprise, either as a monopolist or as a competitor. At a minimum, parcel post overstepped the traditional bounds of government activity, transforming an information utility, the Post Office department, into a transportation common carrier. At its worst, parcel post represented federal paternalism and even socialism. The principal opposition, the 300-member American League of Associations, invoked John Stuart Mill on the dangers of extending government power and Adam Smith and David Ricardo on the correct principles of political economy. The widespread adoption of parcel post in other countries suggested how alien it was

LASHT TO THE POST.

Figure 5.1 This cartoon, which appeared just weeks after the start of parcel post in the U.S., correctly suggested that the government's package-delivery service would compete effectively with similar private-sector operations, *Literary Digest* 46 (February 15, 1913): 331.

University of Washington Libraries.

to American political economy, they argued. An essay in the *Journal of Political Economy* identified features of the Post Office that distinguished it from for-profit businesses and concluded "that the Postal Department as now organized and operated would be utterly unable to compete with express companies upon purely a business basis."[20]

Finally, parcel post opponents invoked the slippery-slope argument: The arguments in favour of parcel post applied "to the telegraph and telephone and would inevitably precipitate the Government into the control of other large public utilities," a wholesaler told Congress.[21] This was not mere hyperbole. After all, many parcel post advocates had vowed to use parcel post as a step toward placing functionally related communication and transportation facilities under postal control, just as had been done in many other countries. Recognizing the strong sentiment for parcel post, opponents instead urged stronger regulation. "Would it not be better for the Government to undertake to regulate and guide commercial enterprises rather than to try to own them?" asked a representative of the National Retail Hardware Association.[22]

At the other extreme were proponents of the fourth option—a government monopoly over parcel delivery. Some believed that the Constitution's postal clause provided sufficient basis to acquire the express companies and operate them under the Post Office department. Many viewed government acquisition of the express industry as a realistic goal considering the relatively small capital investment involved (express firms relied heavily on railroads' organization and equipment). Postmaster general Frank H. Hitchcock gave Congress a pragmatic reason for a government parcel-delivery monopoly: Without one, the expresses would skim off the lucrative business, leaving revenue-losing routes to the department. The Post Office already had the unprofitable business—delivering parcels under four pounds [1.8 kilograms] to sparsely settled parts of the country. A full-fledged parcel post would develop profitable routes that compensated for the unprofitable ones found in any system promising universal service. Parcel post, in sum, would improve the department's finances.[23]

The successful option—a government delivery service that competed with private firms—was crafted mainly by Senate post office committee chairman Jonathan Bourne. He had embraced parcel post as part of his 1906 campaign platform and, once on the post office committee, vigorously sought information from all quarters. He gathered details about the workings of foreign parcel post and obtained data from the ICC on the U.S. express industry. Behind the scenes, he coordinated his parcel post campaign with lobbyists and journalists; publicly, Bourne contributed articles to popular magazines and muckraking journals.[24]

Bourne believed that public-private competition in the package delivery business would maximize service and minimize rates. The most likely outcome, he predicted, was "decreased cost to the public whenever the Government can operate as cheaply and efficiently as a private individual." Outright government ownership "tends toward paternalism and bureaucracy," Bourne argued, though he held it out as "a dernier resort, where regulation has been demonstrated to be a failure."[25] Others who supported postal competition with private expresses invariably applauded its value in making "express companies come to a just price in sending articles."[26] President William H. Taft endorsed parcel post even though Bourne headed the National Progressive Republican League, a group working to find another presidential candidate for the 1912 elections.[27]

As passed, the law raised the fourth-class weight limit to 11 pounds [5 kilograms], the Universal Postal Union's standard, and charged postage according to distance. Furthermore, the law suggested that rates needed to be adjusted when necessary to cover costs. These three provisions—a strict weight limit, zoned postage, and rates tied to costs—constrained the Post Office department's ability to compete with private carriers. Nonetheless, parcel post initially reached twenty million people outside the service areas of private express companies and early tests comparing the two showed that the government service generally was faster.[28]

Before leaving office, president Taft's postmaster general recommended that his successor cut rates and raise weights. He did. Woodrow Wilson appointed as postmaster general Albert S. Burleson, a member of Congress from Texas who, though conservative on social issues, subscribed to most of the old Populist agenda on government enterprise. Within a year, Burleson had cut rates for all zones, most sharply for the first two, a radius of 240 kilometres, and dramatically increased the weight limit. He also admitted books over four pounds [1.8 kilograms] to the mail as parcels, a goal long sought by the nation's librarians that Congress had just as long ignored. To stimulate use of parcel post, Burleson, acting under power given him by Congress, also authorized two accessory services. Collect-on-Delivery (COD), inaugurated in 1913, provided a measure of certainty in transactions between parcel mailers and recipients who usually did not know each other. Insurance on parcel shipments was also provided for a fee.[29]

Parcel post, plus stepped-up ICC regulation, undercut the express companies. The securities of the four largest carriers—Adams, American, United States, and Wells Fargo, all highly overvalued in the minds of many—dropped $32 million one month after government entered the field. Within a year, the express companies stopped competing with parcel post in many small towns. When the government took over operation of the railroads during the First World War, the express companies consolidated their operations in a unified service, the American Railway Express Co. The railroads reverted to private management in 1920, but the Railway Express Co. continued, becoming the Railway Express Agency in 1929.[30]

Postalizing the Telegraph and Telephone

With the passage of postal savings and parcel post, it seemed to many but a short step to postal telegraph and telephone. Informed commentators proclaimed congressional enactment of a postal telecommunications system a near certainty. Except for the United States and Canada, virtually every nation regarded the telegraph and telephone as natural extensions of the state's mail monopoly and operated them under a postal ministry.[31]

The idea of placing telecommunication in the hands of the U.S. Post Office dated from the very beginning of telegraphy. Most people associated with the first American telegraph line, built in 1844 with federal funds and operated by the Post Office, viewed it as a natural extension of the state's postal power. The decision to remove the Post Office from telegraphy stemmed mostly from circumstances of the moment rather than fundamental objections to the principle. After a period of wildcat competition, private telegraph firms increasingly cooperated and absorbed one another. In 1866, the year that Western Union acquired its two major rivals, the United States Telegraph Company and the American Telegraph Company, Congress passed a law with the potential to restructure the telegraph industry. The legislation provided for the government to purchase any company that accepted privileges from the government to use public rights of way. The purchase price would be set by a five-person committee jointly selected by the government and industry. Looming in the background, the 1866 law heartened advocates of post office innovation. The nationalization of the British telegraph in 1869 also invigorated the U.S. campaign for a postal telegraph. British experience was frequently invoked in the American debate, both because it provided a precedent for nationalizing an established industry and because of the relative congruence of the two nations' values.[32]

In the late 1800s, agrarian groups joined the Post Office department's efforts to secure a postal telegraph. Western Union's own operations and rhetoric suggested that competition in telegraphy wasted resources and yielded inferior service. And yet, competition was the touchstone of private-sector enterprises. Agrarian groups thus popularized the view of telegraphy and later the telephone as natural monopolies. Furthermore, telecommunications had become a strategic input for other sectors of the economy: finance, commerce, transportation, and more. But, in private hands, a monopolistic telegraph company could use its power to restrict competition in industries dependent on the information it transmitted. Western Union earned a reputation, partly derived from the machinations of key stockholders such as Jay Gould and Cornelius Vanderbilt, of using its control over the transmission of information to stifle competition in finance, transportation, and other sectors of the economy. Thus, agrarian groups could plausibly argue that a telegraph operated by the Post Office department would preserve competition in industries dependent on the electrical transmission of information. The Post Office department drew on its international connections to amass data on the operation of postal telegraphs in other countries. The findings provided ammunition for postal officials and others who pressed their case in Congress.[33]

The issue crested after the 1912 election brought progressive Democrat Woodrow Wilson to the presidency. In 1913, postmaster general Albert S. Burleson, representative David J. Lewis, and members of post office committees in Congress began working on legislation to buy the nation's telegraph and telephone lines and turn them over to the Post Office department. President Wilson reportedly concurred but backed away when AT&T agreed to divest its telegraph holdings.[34] Burleson, Lewis and others, however, pushed ahead. Lewis worked tirelessly to publicize the case for putting telecommunications under Post Office control. In December 1913, for instance, he filled seventy-two columns of the *Congressional Record* with data about postal telegraphy and telephony around the world, evidence that pointed toward the merit of government systems.[35]

AT&T responded with a broad and sophisticated campaign designed to build a bulwark against any further expansion of postal enterprise. The most potent weapon in this campaign was a loose-leaf service, *Brief of Arguments against Public Ownership*. Started around 1913, the information service supplied opinion leaders with hundreds of documents that challenged government enterprise generally and postal innovations in particular. Each item arrived complete with instructions on how to file it according to type of utility (railroads, postal, telecommunications, energy), country (more than a dozen), and the nature of the argument.[36]

The *Brief* conceded that some government regulation of private utilities was healthy. But, it then provided "general arguments against public ownership," including the "inapplicability of foreign precedents." The heart of the brief asserted that government ownership harmed the public in a variety of ways: It interfered with the "primary function of government," "increased opportunities for political corruption and abuses," exerted "undue political influence" by expanding the civil service, and produced an "undemocratic tendency toward centralization, militarism and bureaucracy." Furthermore, public ownership destroyed "individual initiative." It hurt public finance by encouraging false accounting, fixing rates according to political pressure, and taxing members of the public who did not use the service. Consumers would suffer from "poor service," "arbitrary treatment" by government employees, "high rates," and a stodgy bureaucracy's reluctance to adopt the latest innovations. Ordinary consumers would suffer discrimination in rates set to favour those with political influence.[37]

AT&T gathered evidence for each of these arguments for its campaign against postal telecommunications. The evidence ranged from short news items published in the United States and abroad to lengthy excerpts from U.S. and foreign government reports. The smallest and silliest evidence against government-owned telecommunications was not overlooked. For instance, item No. 107, Index No. D1 (arguments about government systems' poor service), filed under "COUNTRY: Germany" and "UTILITY: Telephones" came from the *New York Times* Marconi Transatlantic Wireless Telegraph datelined Berlin: A witness, testifying at hearings on the telephone, "asserted that ... Government telephone girls had been permitted by the Inspectors to utilize one of the big exchanges for the reception of their fiancés." Another "amusement of the girls of this exchange was to look up all the subscribers having the same name, to connect all of them, ring them all up, and laugh loudly at the result." The lesson for Americans contemplating the postalization of telecommunication was clear: Employees of government-owned telephone systems rendered poor service. Most of the items in the *Brief* were much more substantial, but all were intended for wide circulation in the campaign against postal telecommunication.[38]

The Lewis plan for the postalization of telecommunication died when Democrats who had originally backed it decided that new powers granted the ICC to regulate the telegraph and telephone provided sufficient reform for the time being. But, just when it appeared that the campaign for postalization of the wires had stumbled in the arenas of public opinion and policymaking, the outbreak of the First World War gave the Post Office department a last opportunity to prove its administrative capability. In December 1917, Congress subjected railroads to government control as a wartime measure and several months later put the Post Office department in charge of the nation's wire communications. Postmaster general Burleson's goal of converting the Post Office department into a department of Communication seemingly had been realized except for the name change.[39]

Because the authorizing legislation required government to pay equitable compensation to the telecommunication companies, Burleson was forced to raise phone rates and institute service charges. Wages rose rapidly with wartime labour shortages, and strikes by workers further undermined the Post Office's management. In such a situation, "the public could see no advantage in government operation." Congress returned wires to private control after one year, much faster than the railroads, because the experience had been so bad. Some congressional postmortem analyses tried to show that Burleson's management—not public control per se—was the problem. Regardless, the campaign for a postal telegraph and telephone was dead.[40]

Conclusion

Adam Smith, no friend of government involvement in the economy, offered a surprisingly charitable view of postal enterprise. "The post office is … perhaps the only successful mercantile project which has been successfully managed by, I believe, every sort of government," he wrote in *The Wealth of Nations*. But, Smith and many of his contemporaries viewed the Post Office as a revenue-generating government unit.[41] The U.S. Post Office, in contrast, operated with a public service mandate whose ambiguous mission meant that it continually struggled to find its proper place in American political economy. Why, for instance, did the Post Office win approval to offer banking and package-delivery services while being rebuffed in its efforts to enter the field of telecommunication?

The Post Office and its allies advanced several reasons to justify innovations in postal enterprise. First, initiatives such as postal savings and parcel post allowed the department to capitalize on its nationwide infrastructure; this applied a widely accepted business principle to the management of a public agency. Second, the Post Office could provide banking services and delivery packages where private sector firms found it unprofitable to do so; the department, in a sense, provided a social safety net as part of its universal service obligation. A third reason to launch new postal services was to compete with private firms and thereby force them to act more efficiently; this was frequently offered as a justification for parcel post.

When Congress did authorize new postal services, it explicitly circumscribed them to limit competition with private firms. Parcel post's rates and size-weight limits were initially designed to keep the Post Office from undercutting private carriers. Furthermore, the Interstate Commerce Commission, which regulated the private carriers, also had to approve changes in the Post Office's service. And Congress mandated that parcel post break even; if it incurred a deficit, rates had to be raised. Still, the administrative latitude that lawmakers gave the postmaster general allowed the department to liberalize terms of the service and turn parcel post into a formidable competitor with private express firms. Congress likewise, and more successfully, constrained postal savings banks. By capping interest rates and the maximum deposit, Congress minimized competition with private institutions.

The successful campaigns for postal savings banks and parcel post galvanized those who opposed further postal enterprise. AT&T redoubled its efforts to derail a postal telegraph and telephone by popularizing arguments against federal enterprise generally and postal innovation in particular. AT&T messages in popular media and policymaking forums asserted that most new government services violated accepted tenets of American political economy. Another common theme disparaged the administrative ability of the Post Office department. Carefully disseminated throughout the nation, such arguments infused the campaigns of those who opposed postal enterprise and government initiatives in realms beyond communication. Not until the Great Depression, when a catastrophic economic crisis called into question the prevailing tenets of American political economy, did the prospects for government enterprise brighten.

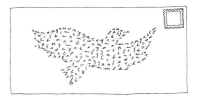

Notes

1. Norman Pollack, *The Humane Economy: Populism, Capitalism and Democracy* (New Brunswick: Rutgers University Press, 1990), pp. 136, 163; Morton Keller, *Affairs of State: Public Life in Late Nineteenth Century America* (Cambridge: Belknap Press of Harvard University Press, 1977), pp. 375, 429–430, 571.
2. Quoted in Carl H. Scheele, *A Short History of the Mail Service* (Washington, D.C.: Smithsonian Institution Press, 1970), p. 99.
3. Wayne E. Fuller, *The American Mail: Enlarger of the Common Life* (Chicago: University of Chicago Press, 1972), pp. 178–180, quote at p. 179.
4. James Henry Hamilton, *Savings and Savings Institutions* (New York: Macmillan, 1902), quotes at pp. 306 and 300–301.
5. Edwin W. Kemmerer, *Postal Savings: An Historical and Critical Study of the Postal Savings Bank System of the United States* (Princeton: Princeton University Press, 1917), pp. 10–13.
6. Kemmerer, *Postal Savings*, pp. 1, 12; Edwin W. Kemmerer, "The United States Postal Savings Bank," *Political Science Quarterly* 26, no. 3 (1911): 462–65. For a convenient guide to much of the contemporary literature, see Library of Congress, *List of Books, [and] References to Periodicals, Relating to Postal Savings Banks* (Washington, D.C.: Government Printing Office, 1908).
7. National Monetary Commission, *Notes on the Postal Savings-Bank Systems of the Leading Countries*, Sen. Doc. No. 658, 61st Cong. 3d Sess. (Washington, D.C.: Government Printing Office, 1910), pp. 59–128; "Postal Service Extension: What Postal Savings Banks and a Cheap and Efficient Parcel Post Would Mean to the Farmer and Wage-Earner," *Craftsman* 14 (September 1908): 587–94.
8. Kemmerer, *Postal Savings*, p. 5; Kemmerer, "The United States Postal Bank," p. 464; 1909 *Post Office Dept. Annual Report*, pp. 17–19 [hereafter cited as *Annual Report*]. The American experience with postal savings can be productively compared with the Canadian system. See

Chantal Amyot and John Willis, *Country Post: Rural Postal Service in Canada, 1880 to 1945* (Gatineau, Quebec: Canadian Museum of Civilization, 2003), pp. 138–46.

9.   Jean Reith Schroedel and Bruce Snyder, "People's Banking: The Promise Betrayed?" *Studies in American Political Development* 9 (Spring 1994): 181–93. For the law, see Act of June 25, 1910, p. 36, U.S. Statutes at Large, pp. 814–19.

10. Clyde Kelly, *United States Postal Policy* (New York: D. Appleton, 1932), p. 182.

11. 1915 *Annual Report* 30; *Congressional Record*, 89th Cong., 2d Sess. p. 5595 (March 14, 1966); 1966 *Annual Report*, p. ix.

12. The best overview of parcel post's origins and impact is Wayne E. Fuller, *RFD: The Changing Face of Rural America* (Bloomington: Indiana University Press, 1964), pp. 199–233. For an examination of parcel post's implications for government-business relations, see Richard B. Kielbowicz, "Government Goes into Business: Parcel Post in the Nation's Political Economy, 1880–1915," *Studies in American Political Development* 8 (Spring 1994): 150–72.

13. Richard B. Kielbowicz, "Postal Subsidies for the Press and the Business of Mass Culture, 1880–1920," *Business History Review* 64 (Autumn 1990): 451–88.

14. *Parcel Post: Hearings Before the Subcommittee on Parcel Post of the Senate Committee on Post Offices and Post Roads*, 62nd Cong., 2d Sess., pp. 851–75, quote at p. 860 (1911–1912) (testimony of George P. Hampton representing the Farmers' National Committee on Postal Reform) [hereafter cited as 1912 Senate Hearings]. See also *Parcel Post: Hearings Before the House Committee on the Post Office and Post Roads*, 61st Cong., 2d Sess., pp. 58–59 (1910) (testimony of T. C. Atkinson representing the National Grange) [hereafter cited as 1910 House Hearings]; Richard B. Kielbowicz, "Rural Ambivalence toward Mass Society: Evidence from the U.S. Parcel Post Debates," *Rural History* 5 (Spring 1994): 81–102.

15. Postmaster General Charles E. Smith, *Greatest Business Organization in the World: The United States Postal Service* (N.p.: n.p., 1899), p. 3; "A National Opportunity—A Business Postal Department," *World's Work* 19 (March 1910): 12643-44; 1912 *Senate Hearings* 202 (testimony of Postmaster General Hitchcock).

16. 1891 *Annual Report* 7, 113, quote at p. 114; 1890 *Annual Report*, pp. 7–8.

17. *In re* Express Rates, Practices, Accounts, and Revenues, 24 ICC, pp. 380–541, quote at p. 413 (1912). For one example of the journalistic attack on railroad-express ties, see Frederick F. Ingram, "The Parcels Post," *Twentieth Century Magazine* 3 (March 1911): 514–22.

18. John B. Walker, "The People versus the Express Companies," *Pearson's Magazine* 24 (July 1910): 56–60, advertising section pp. 28–30; *Parcels Post: Hearings Before Subcomm. No. 4 of the House Comm. on the Post Office and Post Roads*, 62nd Cong., 1st Sess. (1911) [hereafter cited as 1911 House Hearings]; 1912 Senate Hearings. A bibliography suggesting the scope of the debate is Hermann Henry Bernard Meyer, comp., *Select List of References on Parcels Post* (Washington, D.C.: Government Printing Office, 1911).

19. For parties' platform statements, see Arthur M. Schlesinger, Jr., ed., *History of U.S. Political Parties*, vol. 3 (New York: Chelsea House Publishers, 1973), pp. 1845, 2488, and 2594. For congressional deliberations, see discussions in the House of Representatives at 48 *Cong. Rec.*, pp. 5641–52, pp. 11749-61, and appendix pp. 107–109, 137–57, 156–57, 194–95, 254–55, 583–86, 669, 742–45, 918–20 (1912); and in the Senate at 48 *Cong. Rec.*, pp. 9448-65, pp. 11673-77, and appendix pp. 128–30, 254–55, 669–75 (1912).

20. 42 *Cong. Rec.* 2846 (March 3, 1908) (remarks of Rep. Smith of Calif.); 1912 *Senate Hearings*, pp. 541–88, esp. pp. 543, 563, 572 (testimony of E. B. Moon of the ALA); Don C. Seitz, "The Post-Office: An Obstructive Monopoly," *World's Work* 21 (February 1911): 13978–13986; Albert N. Merritt, "Shall the Scope of Governmental Functions Be Enlarged So as to Include the Express Business?" *Journal of Political Economy* 16 (July 1908): 417–435.

21. 1912 *Senate Hearings*, pp. 461–75, quote at p. 467 (testimony of Harry B. French, president of Smith, Kline & French Co.).

22. 1911 *House Hearings*, pp. 290–97, quote at p. 293 (testimony of W. P. Bogardus).

23. 1911 *House Hearings*, pp. 246–65 (testimony of James L. Cowles for the Postal Progress League); John Brisben Walker, "The Aid which the Post-Office Department Might Render to Commerce," *Cosmopolitan* 36 (February 1904): third unnumbered page following p. 378; "The Enormous Profits of the Express Companies," *Mail Order Journal* 13 (December 1909): 30; 1912 *Senate Hearings*, pp. 191–241.

24. Memorandum from J. W. Slack, assistant to the Senate Post Office committee, to Bourne, Aug. 15, 1911, Box 33, folder 10; drafts of speeches on parcel post, Box 33, folder 7, Jonathan Bourne Papers, University of Oregon Library; *Parcel Post in Foreign Countries* (1912) (committee print prepared under Bourne's direction).

25. *Parcels Post: Report Submitted to the Subcommittee on Parcel Post of the Senate Committee on Post Offices and Post Roads* (Washington, D.C.: Government Printing Office, 1912), p. 12. See also 1912 *Senate Hearings*, p. 235 (remarks of Sen. Bourne).

26. R. W. Lynn, Agency, Iowa, to Sen. William B. Allison, Dec. 30, 1908, file S60A-J110 Senate Records, Record Group 46, National Archives.

27. John M. Stahl, Farmers National Congress, to Bourne, June 10, 1912, Box 28, file 1, Bourne Papers. Stahl's letter quotes president Taft: "You can count on my giving the bill every assistance in my power."

28. Fuller, RFD, p. 230; 1912 *Annual Report*, pp. 7–8.

29. Adrian N. Anderson, "Albert Sidney Burleson: A Southern Politician in the Progressive Era" (Ph.D. dissertation, Texas Tech, 1967), pp. 166–77; Daniel C. Roper, "Fundamental Principles of Parcel-Post Administration," *Journal of Political Economy* 22 (June 1914): 526–35.

30. Editorial from the *Syracuse Post–Standard*, Feb. 8, 1913, attached to letter from Bourne to the paper's editor, Feb. 10, 1913, Box 28, file 1, Bourne Papers; Anderson, "Albert Sidney Burleson," p. 175; T. W. van Metre, *Transportation in the United States* (Chicago: Foundation Press, 1939), pp. 166–67.

31. Lindsay Rogers, *The Postal Power of Congress: A Study in Constitutional Expansion* (Baltimore: Johns Hopkins University Press, 1916), pp. 156–57.

32. Richard John, "The Politics of Innovation," *Daedalus* 127, no. 4 (1998): 198; Lester G. Lindley, "The Constitution Faces Technology: The Relationship of the National Government to the Telegraph, 1866–1884" (Ph.D. dissertation, Rice University, 1971), pp. 41–83.

33. Nathaniel P. Hill, *Speeches and Papers on the Silver, Postal Telegraph and Other Economic Questions* (Colorado Springs: Gazette Printing Co., 1890), pp. 167–98. A convenient summary of statements on postal telecommunication by postmasters general can be found in Senate Document No. 399, 63d Cong., 2d Sess., pp. 22–30 (1914). One historian has recently documented how control of the telegraph companies was used to manipulate information to gain investment advantages. See Richard White, "Information, Markets, and Corruption: Transcontinental Railroads in the Gilded Age," *Journal of American History* 90 (June 2003): 19–43.

34. In an April 4, 1913, letter to Burleson, president Wilson wrote, "For a long time I have thought that the government ought to own the telegraph lines of the country and combine the telegraph with the post office. How have you been thinking in this matter?" Burleson Papers, Box 6, Library of Congress.

35. *Cong. Rec.*, 63d Cong., 2d Sess., pp. 1377–1412 (1913); Thomas D. Masterson, "David J. Lewis of Maryland: Formative and Progressive Years, 1869–1917" (Ph.D. dissertation, Georgetown University, 1976), pp. 403–28; David Lewis, *The Postalization of the Telephone and Telegraph* (Washington: Government Printing Office, 1914).

36. American Telephone and Telegraph Co., Commercial Engineer's Office, comp., *Brief of Arguments against Public Ownership* (New York: n.d., ca 1913–14).

37. All quotes from "Index" in ibid. (capitalization altered slightly).

38. Ibid., item no. 107.

39. Masterson, "David J. Lewis," pp. 403–28.

40. Richard W. Howard, "The Work of Albert Sidney Burleson as Postmaster General" (M.A. thesis, University of Texas-Austin, 1938), pp. 85–95, quote at p. 91; Robert B. Horwitz, *Irony of Regulatory Reform: The Deregulation of American Telecommunications* (New York: Oxford University Press, 1989), pp. 101–102.

41. Adam Smith, *An Inquiry into the Nature and Causes of the Wealth of Nations* (1776; reprint Chicago: Encyclopedia Britannica, 1952), p. 358. This passage appeared in a chapter on sources of government revenue; furthermore, England at that time operated the Royal Posts as a revenue-generating agency.

THE HISTORY AND GEOGRAPHY OF THE POST OFFICE ON PRINCE EDWARD ISLAND, 1870–1914[1]

6

John Willis, Historian, Canadian Postal Museum, Canadian Museum of Civilization

Abstract

Prince Edward Island is an interesting field in which to develop a more detailed understanding of the history of the rural postal service in Canada, particularly with respect to its unfolding and change in time and space from the 1870s to 1914. This article looks at some of the main features characterizing the postal system on the Island: the ice boats, the capital city of Charlottetown, the post office, and the railway. The locational patterns of the rural postal service in Campbellton and Tignish are then examined. Each case provides a perspective for a better understanding of how the post office was embedded in the rural socio-economy. For smaller communities, the post office acted in conjunction with church and school. In the case of slightly larger agglomerations, economic factors of need for or location of post offices come to the fore. Finally, a discussion of Tignish and vicinity depicts a key transformation of rural postal service, which, in our view, has a bearing on the larger transformation of relationships between town and country.

Résumé

L'Île-du-Prince-Édouard est un milieu intéressant pour acquérir une connaissance plus détaillée de l'histoire de la poste rurale au Canada, particulièrement en ce qui concerne son déroulement et sa métamorphose dans le temps et l'espace des années 1870 à 1914. Cet article examine quelques-unes des caractéristiques principales du système postal dans l'île : les bateaux à glace, la capitale, Charlottetown, le bureau de poste et le chemin de fer. Est ensuite abordée la structure des emplacements du service postal rural à Campbellton et à Tignish. Chaque cas permet de mieux comprendre l'imbrication du bureau de poste dans la société et l'économie rurales. Dans le cas des petites localités, l'action du bureau de poste était liée à celle de l'église et de l'école. Dans celui des localités un peu plus grandes,

des facteurs économiques liés à la nécessité d'un bureau de poste et à l'emplacement de celui-ci jouaient un rôle important. Enfin, un examen du cas de Tignish et des environs décrit une transformation importante du service postal rural, laquelle, à notre avis, a eu une incidence sur la transformation, plus générale, des relations entre ville et campagne.

Introduction

Prince Edward Island is an interesting slice of rural Canada. As an island with a predominantly rural population accounting for 75 per cent or more of the total population between 1871 and 1951, it is, to some extent, a laboratory of convenience.[2] Ostensibly its limits are clearly delineated in space, for while its outer limits follow the contours of beach and bluff, the surrounding sea is also part of its geography. Just below the waterline, the sea provides a harvest of mussels and oysters. Lobster traps are set out in the bays. And still further out at sea are navigation routes leading to other fish, other coastlines, and other destinies. This study examines one facet of P.E.I. history and geography, that is, postal communication from 1870 to 1914, with a view to furthering our knowledge of the Island province, a predominantly rural society, and the evolution of the Canadian rural postal system.

Postal communication was embedded within rural society of P.E.I. in particular ways according to time and place. The nature of the experience was not uniform; it varied according to a place's size and/or its function in the overall ensemble. Put another way—with all due respect to Gertrude Stein—it could not be said that a post office is a post office is a post office. There were substantive differences of degree. One need only look at the matter from the point of view of those doing the work to better understand the discrepancy between a simple and straightforward experience in a hamlet post office and a more labour-intensive situation in a substantial premises distributing mail to ten or more post offices.

Our purpose here is to unroll the postal map of a particular region with a view to reconstituting the elements of the rural postal service in P.E.I. A previous and more general study of rural postal service in Canada allowed us to sketch broadly the elements of the rural postal service—railway mail service, ancillary mail transport routes, post offices, and postmasters. This, in turn, fit into an analysis depicting the regional framework—the urban hierarchy, town-country linkage—that structured the Canadian countryside. The study of the postal system became an exercise in verifying the genesis of centrality on the Canadian rural landscape during the late nineteenth and early twentieth centuries.[3] The result was rather long on geography and short on history in terms of the nature of the rural postal service. A discussion of postal service in P.E.I. serves to highlight the transformation of this postal service over time during this period. This "small" place will, in turn, allow us to return to the overall Canadian context, rural and postal, and ask of it, some "big" questions.[4]

The postal experience evolved over time. The railway represented a strong factor of change in terms of post office locations throughout the province. Another factor was the introduction by the Post Office department, beginning in 1908, of Rural Mail Delivery (RMD), which resulted in a substantial reduction in the number of post offices. Yet, an impoverishment of communication did not ensue. Rural residents still received their mail and read it. It was the relationship to the post office—a physical entity in space—that changed in accordance with the transformation between small-town Main Street and the rural countryside. During the early twentieth century, a new kind of town-country relationship emerged in Canada. The transformation is quite visible within the rural postal system and nowhere more so than in Prince Edward Island.

To some extent, post offices and postal service rose and fell in accordance with corporate or departmental fiat. Yet, the balance of initiative did not lie entirely with the railway companies, politicians, and postal authorities. Grumbling and petitions, if not demands, not infrequently originated from the ranks, if not the lower ranks, of P.E.I. rural society. The game of give-and-take could involve down-to-earth common sense. It might also have flowed from a sharp sense of identity. The people of Lower Cardigan (Lot 54) wanted their post office to be known as Newport because there was already a Cardigan Bridge post office nearby and mail was sent there by mistake.[5] Who other than the locals would know about such things? The petitioners of Kildare Station (Lot 2) wished to change the name of their post office to Saint-Louis. The community was located near the nucleus of the Island's French-speaking, Acadian population, so the name Kildare—a place near Dublin, Ireland—probably meant nothing to them.[6]

The study is based on period maps, notably, Meacham's *Illustrated Historical Atlas of the Province of P.E.I.* (1880)[7]; province-wide directories for 1871 and 1881; two collections in the P.E.I. Provincial Archives and Records Office: a Journal of the ice-boat service across the Capes and the papers of the Summerside post office;[8] and, Douglas Murray's highly useful *The Post Office on Prince Edward Island*.[9] The lion's share of the data is from the Inspectors' Reports in the Post Office archives. The superb documentation provides a poignant feel for the texture of postal history as well as for interpersonal relations in rural communities.

Three main elements of the Island postal system will be looked at first: on-off island winter transportation, the central postal terminus of the province at Charlottetown, and the railway. Part two explores how the postal system was embedded in the rural geography of P.E.I., in certain simple, as well as other, more complex, situations, as well as the partial removal and transformation of rural postal service.

The Postal System of Prince Edward Island

No man an island, says the poet, each a part of the continent.[10] Prince Edward Island was very much a part of the continent. Islanders had no wish to sever themselves from the rest of the Canadian Dominion, nor could they help but be informed when the news arrived by telegraph in a flash. The Island was connected to the North American and transatlantic cable service of the New York and Newfoundland Telegraph Company beginning in the late 1860s. The telegraph was not perfect. In 1871, the cable was found "cut, a short distance from the Island," the explanation, according to the *Charlottetown Herald*, "that some schooner's anchor fouled with the cable and the crew, [and] to get out of it cut the cable with an axe."[11] In the following decade, the telegraph cable was repaired and extended inland throughout the Island.

Apart from the telegraph, news and people travelled more slowly on and off the Island throughout the year. Fortunately, the Islanders received their news steadily, unlike the citizens of the nearby gulf islands of Anticosti and Madeleine, who were almost completely isolated from civilization in mid-winter when the ships stopped calling at their frozen harbours.[12] In 1832, winter service to the mainland consisted of a steamer connection between Charlottetown and Pictou, Nova Scotia.[13] The vessels working this route were frequently trapped in the ice, a source of bitter frustration to Islanders anxious to get freight and mail on and off the Island. Another option was to convey bags of mail aboard amphibious iceboats across the Northumberland Strait. Mail weighed less than freight and was conducive to such handling. Although the iceboat was vulnerable in some respects, it was central to overcoming the threat of winter isolation.

The Iceboats

Iceboats crossed the Northumberland Strait as early as the 1770s. After the start of the nineteenth century, the main route likely ran from Wood Islands, near the southeastern tip of the Island, to the mainland in Nova Scotia. Beginning in 1828, mail and passengers travelled on a monthly basis between Cape Tormentine, New Brunswick, and Cape Traverse, P.E.I., across a 14-kilometre stretch of water. When P.E.I. entered Confederation in 1873, the iceboat service was transferred to the Post Office department. During the late 1880s, the provincial government waged an aggressive campaign to improve winter communication facilities. Provincial MPs issued threats of secession if the situation did not improve, and the premier took his case all the way to London in 1886.[14] The belated response of the federal government was to transfer responsibility for the iceboats to the Marine department. New safety standards were introduced, among them the obligation for boats to travel in fleets of at least three vessels in case something unexpected occurred.[15]

Outfitted with sails, the Northumberland ice boats were primitive affairs with wooden hulls shod with an iron keel. Iron bars were attached to both sides of the boat. When necessary, the men fastened their belts or harnesses to the bars on the sides and dragged the vessel over an icy patch. It was easier to make a crossing when the prevailing surface was entirely iced over or clear, but this was far from the norm. The ice along the shore, called board ice, made for laborious progress at either end of the trip. Meanwhile, the middle of the channel was susceptible to the unpredictable movement of sea ice that swept down from the Gulf of St. Lawrence on short notice, forcing crews, passengers, and mail to wind their way through the ice or sit out inclement weather on the frozen surface of the Strait. In extreme cases, crews lay stranded on a sheet of ice for days on end before they could make a run for the shoreline.[16]

The Journal of the iceboats offers a day-to-day glimpse of how the service was conducted. Journal entries for the late 1880s indicate that the season began sometime in January and wound up during the second half of April, sometimes as late as the 5th of May. There were two crews, one in Cape Traverse, the other at Cape Tormentine. The boats started out from their respective ports, probably passing each other midstream. On occasion, one crew made it to the other side while the other did not. This happened five times during the winter of 1887. On four other occasions during the same year, neither side was able to make the crossing, the climate being the main culprit. On February 11, 1887, the Journal reports "wind northeast and snow"; there was no crossing either way that day. The next day there was no crossing: "wind northwest very cold and blowing and drifting." February 25, yet again no crossing: "wind northwest too hard to cross, blowing a gale." And, finally, on March 12, "wind northeast blowing hard with squalls of snow;" there was no crossing either way.

Wind, snow, and ice conspired to make work on the iceboats difficult. Interruption in service invariably signified an increase in the workload. For example, when the boats were unable to cross on a Saturday, they would try the following day, even though, officially, the boats were not supposed to carry mail on Sunday. Allowing the mail to lie over and accumulate might make the backlog of mail on a Monday too heavy to handle. The mail was like the tide: It had a mind and momentum of its own.

The exchange of mails between the two Capes involved coordination on both sides of the Strait. On the New Brunswick side, mail bound for P.E.I. was sorted by railway mail clerks in a New Brunswick and Prince Edward Island Railway mail car that was parked on the tracks outside of Sackville.[17] Then it was taken to Tormentine for the trip over to P.E.I. During the early 1880s, once the mail reached the Island, it was conveyed between Cape Traverse and Summerside and/or Charlottetown by special horse-drawn teams.[18] Later on during the decade, a branch line of the P.E.I. Railway was extended down to Cape Traverse so the bags could be taken off the boats and loaded directly onto a railway mail car. The combination of primitive and mechanized technologies of transport is striking. Here, as elsewhere in Canada, there simply was no other way to move things around.

The winter iceboat mail service kept the people of P.E.I. alive and in touch with the rest of the world and thus infused with what one newspaper called, "the progressive spirit of the age."[19] In the late nineteenth-century era of big cities and railways and technological transformation, it was remarkable to see these Canadians turn to a relatively "primitive" mode of transport to keep the mail stream flowing. The iceboats were an expediency that allowed Islanders to adhere to the dictum of the age: "Communication oblige." Other expedients and other agencies also contributed to the flow of mail.

Charlottetown, the Capital City

During the late nineteenth century, prior to and following Confederation, Charlottetown served as the capital of Prince Edward Island and was the Island's premier central place. With a population of 9,000 to 13,000 between the 1870s and 1931, the city was a considerable cut above smaller centres such as Summerside and Georgetown, whose populations for the same period hovered between 3,600 and 3,700 in the former case and just under 1,000 for the latter.[20] The ceremonial heart of the capital was Queen Square, where the five key institutions of the provincial establishment were aligned: St. Paul's Anglican Church, the law courts, the colonial building (Legislature), the market hall, and the post office and customs house.

The post office was completed by the colonial government in 1871, at a cost of $60,000. It burned down in the winter of 1884. Mr. Kennedy, a Richmond street confectioner, was setting out rat poison in his store late one night when his kerosene lamp fell and some highly flammable tissue paper was ignited. The fire spread throughout the nearby quarter engulfing the post office in a few short hours. The post office and postal savings bank were moved temporarily to the building formerly occupied by the Bank of Prince Edward Island. Construction on a new post office commenced in 1885, and, by 1887, the new building housing both the post office and the Dominion Savings Bank—proudly described in the *Charlottetown Herald* as the finest in the Maritimes—was finally opened.[21] A symbol of dignity, the building was lit by powerful arc lamps encased in alabaster globes and was decorated for ceremonial occasions such as the death of Queen Victoria in 1901.[22]

In 1888, fourteen employees worked at the Charlottetown post office, including a temporary clerk, eleven third class clerks, one second class clerk, and the postmaster, who was also assistant inspector for the P.E.I. division.[23] The pre-eminent postal personalities on the Island were the Charlottetown postmaster and the division postal inspector. The authority of the inspector and his assistant was not unqualified. His superiors in Ottawa— the postmaster general and deputy postmaster general—called many of the shots. The inspector's authority was also limited by the direct line of communication between the postmaster general and the backbenchers of his party. Ultimately, the inspector had to deal directly with the Islanders, who had their own opinions as to how the post office should be run.

Charlottetown performed certain postal functions for the entire Island. Around 1895, foreign mails were forwarded by steamer via Charlottetown and Summerside.[24] It is likely that a good portion of the incoming and outgoing provincial mail travelled via the Charlottetown post office. This might account, in part, for the much higher volume of postal revenues at Charlottetown—close to $26,000 in 1911—compared with those at a small-town post office like Tignish, roughly $1,000 for the same year. Village post offices, such as Cavendish, might bring in less than $90 per annum.[25]

The central role of the Charlottetown post office was paralleled by the role of the town as a focal point of communication on the Island. In 1871, seven weeklies were sent out to the rest of the province from there. A daily stage ran between Charlottetown and Summerside.[26] Traditionally, in colonial times and up to the mid-nineteenth century, mail and traffic circulated outwards, or in the reverse direction, along the province's main postal roads east, west, and south of Charlottetown, thus reinforcing the town's entrepot function.[27] For perhaps a century, the web of spatial relationships into which postal relations originally fit was spun gradually from the Charlottetown core. Then came the railway.

The Railway

Railway fever began agitating the political waters of Prince Edward Island during the 1860s. The *Charlottetown Herald* urged the people and politicians of the province to fight for a railway between Summerside and Charlottetown.[28] Other communities, not to mention real estate speculators, were gripped by railway enthusiasm, among them Georgetown, Souris, and Alberton. Eventually, in 1871, a line was laid out across the province from Alberton in the west to Georgetown in the east. The following year, the line was extended north of Alberton to Tignish and east of Georgetown to Souris, covering the breadth of the Island and more.[29]

Completed in about 1875, the railway was remarkable because of the generous amount of track used in the layout. The agreement with the contractor placed a ceiling on costs per mile [1.6 kilometre], but not on total mileage. As a result, the builders, according to A. H. Clark, "were thus encouraged to wind the railway about in the most serpentine fashion to avoid as many hills or estuaries as possible."[30] There was lots of track—147 miles [237 kilometres] of it for an island only 193 kilometres wide—and there were 65 railway stations, on average, one every five kilometres. It seems that the P.E.I. Railway was conceived as a public service railroad rather than a strictly commercial venture.

The railway was omnipresent. The entire province, with the exception of the protrusion due southeast from Charlottetown (Lots 62 and 64), lay within twenty kilometres of the line. Also significant was the introduction of Railway Mail Service in May–June 1875. Two travelling post offices carried the mail from coast to coast. During the 1880s, two to three railway mail clerks sorted the mail on the train.[31] With its twice-daily service, the railway became the backbone of the postal service and introduced a new geography to the distribution of mail throughout the province. In so doing, it encountered, and possibly altered, the older pattern of postal distribution predicated on the centrality of Charlottetown and the movement of the mail and communication outwards from the capital.

The impact of the railway was as follows. First, it was responsible for the establishment of new post offices along the railway line. Six such examples were found.[32] Second, existing post offices and other services were moved to the vicinity of the rail line. For example, an agglomeration emerged to the west of the old Cape Traverse post office following the construction of the railway branch line in 1885. The newer Cape Traverse community had a railway station, two hotels, two stores, and several workshops. Ottawa was informed in 1887 that the stationmaster was willing to fulfill the duties of postmaster for free. The offer was indicative of the synergy between railway and postal service.[33]

Generally speaking, mail distribution and delivery tended to flow from the post offices and trains stations along the P.E.I. Railway toward the outlying rural communities. The impact was twofold. On the one hand, post offices situated along the rail line might, by mere virtue of their location, be ranked or endeavour to rank themselves above the others. Mount Stewart petitioned the postmaster general in 1892 for an upgrade in its status from post office to money order office on the grounds it was situated on the railway and distributed mail to two other offices.[34] On the other hand, mail distribution was rerouted to or from a station post office. In the case of Wellington, the station post office simply put the older, village post office out of business and became a distribution post office in its own right. The brand new post office of St. Lawrence (Lot 3) received its mail from Alma Railway Station; the mail probably travelled five kilometres along the Centreline Road.[35] The multiplication of the number of railway stations along the line may have served to further funnel the flow of mail via post offices with direct access to the railway.

The impact of the railway was potentially far greater as it reached deep into Island rural society. Whole villages or clusters of craft shops and general stores and mills grew up along the railway, as did the postal service. Drawing all manner of activity in its wake, the railway possibly transformed the distribution of industries and agglomerations, not to mention communication throughout the Island. At the same time, one must remember that the railway was not working from a clean slate, postal, economic, social, or otherwise. The new had to come to terms with the old, an interface not unfamiliar to historians.

Locational Patterns

The accompanying map makes clear a number of patterns. Around 1880, some areas had more post offices than others: All of Queen's county and the area south of Georgetown appear to have been well-favoured. There were few post offices in the mid-section of King's County to the northwest of Georgetown; the western fringe of the Island, beginning from Lot 10 onwards, also seems to have had sparse post office accommodation. In each case, the data is consistent with the distribution of population, at least for 1871.[36]

Two other trends are evident. They are not contradictory but they present a challenge for the historian. There is, first, a definite alignment of post offices the length of the railway. Not surprisingly the three most important urban centres of the province—Summerside, Charlottetown and Georgetown—are all situated along the rail line. At the same time, each had direct access to a harbour with potential links to the mainland, other P.E.I. ports, and the entire Gulf of St. Lawrence region. One could argue that the intersection between railway and shipping helped establish the centrality of each of these towns.

Careful scrutiny of the map shows another pattern: a strong incidence of post offices at crossroads locations, with no railway in sight. The very existence of these post offices suggests that, although the railway had an impact on the distribution of post offices throughout the Island, it was not the cause of the elimination of all the older post offices, which had been established for reasons that continued to exist after the advent of the railway. The post office was a basic community service. In the case of Cavendish and other small communities, it was as much a part of village life as church and school.

Cavendish

Situated on the north side of P.E.I. in lot 23 on the Gulf side of the Island, Cavendish was a small community of about 200 people around 1871. The topography of grassy dunes set the northern limit of the community. The strong gusts of winter wind off the Gulf of St. Lawrence would have been enough to keep any person away from the shore if not in doors, at least at certain times of the year. The centre of the community was located at the intersection of a road running east and west, known as Cavendish Road, and another one running north and south, also known as Cavendish Road! The institutional nucleus of Cavendish consisted of the Presbyterian and the Baptist Church, a schoolhouse, and the post office. The occupational profile of Cavendish was not complex: Most people were farmers, but there was a blacksmith, a shoemaker (1871), and, as of 1881, a Presbyterian and Baptist clergyman. There was a mill owner and dealer, Alexander Simpson; but,

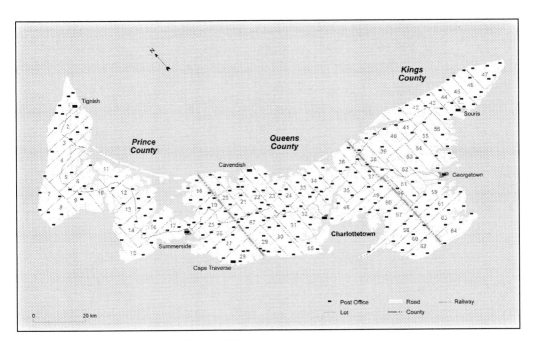

Figure 6.1 Post offices on Prince Edward Island, 1880.

Map by Andrée Héroux, using Meacham Atlas.

the people of Cavendish probably shopped at one of the stores in the nearby village of Stanley.[37]

There were five main clans in Cavendish: the Simpsons, the Robertsons, the Macneills, the Grahams, and the Clarks. They accounted for twenty-two (65 per cent) of all heads of household in the 1871 directory. A handful of families, therefore, accounted for the lion's share of social experience in this tightly knit rural community. Long-time resident Maud Montgomery summed it up well when, in describing the links between three of these families, she made the point: "[They] had inter-married to such an extent, that it was necessary to be born or bred in Cavendish in order to know whom it was safe to criticize."[38] Perhaps it was best to be from Cavendish to know whom it was safe to marry?

In 1870, Alexander Macneill was appointed postmaster of Cavendish. His uncle, Daniel Macneill, had been postmaster before him. Evidently there was something of a postal tradition in the family. Alexander was postmaster for twenty-eight years. Following his death he was succeeded by his widow, Lucy Woolner Macneill (1898 to 1911). In turn, she left the job to John Franklin Macneill, probably a relative, until the post office was closed in 1913 due to the introduction of Rural Mail Delivery.[39] In effect, the Macneills presided over the post office continuously for about 80 years. Annual revenue at the post office was not spectacular: Revenues amounted to about $41 a year in 1880, $49 in 1895. In 1911, the figure rose to $89 per annum.

Around 1880, mail arrived only three days a week. But, there were other things to do at the post office, which functioned like a village water hole:

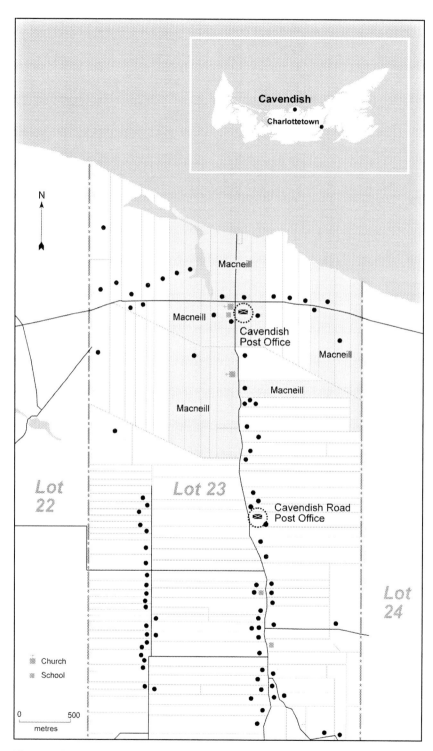

Figure 6.2 Post offices in the neighbourhood of Cavendish.

Map by Andrée Héroux, using Meacham Atlas.

Hardly anyone would ever come to the house if we had not had the post office. As it was, in the evenings, especially the winter evenings, the neighbours would come in for the mail and stay to talk politics and news with grandfather and each other around the old kitchen. Occasionally a boy friend, who would never have dared to come otherwise, ventured to linger for an hour or so and chat to me.[40]

The post office left a firm impression upon Alexander Macneill's granddaughter, Lucy Maud Montgomery, novelist and creator of Anne of Green Gables. When her grandfather died in 1898, Maud went to live with her widowed grandmother. As her grandmother was getting on and as Maud was assistant postmistress, she was effectively in charge of postal matters. There were some disadvantages to the work. There was so much coming and going in connection with the post office that, on occasion, Maud had to move to the kitchen if she wished not to be distracted in her writing.[41] But, there were also benefits. Lucy wrote long texts on the back of official post office letter bills, which measured a metre in length, courtesy of the Post Office department.[42] Another advantage was that Maud could send manuscripts to various Canadian and American publishers without having to share bad news with the rest of the village. She alone put the submissions in the mail; she alone opened the envelopes with the publishers' replies.

Maud eventually left Cavendish in 1911, but this country world stayed with her wherever she went and in everything she wrote. Church and school were important to the aspiring author. For a time, Maud worked as a schoolteacher, which she was trained for at a college in Charlottetown.[43] She played the organ at the nearby Presbyterian church where she met her eventual husband, the Reverend Ewan MacDonald.[44] Church and school were implacable vestments of community in Cavendish. They were integral to rural life and the making of the rural postal service throughout P.E.I.

Church and School: Post Office Location

Cavendish highlights the postal experience of a community with a simplified institutional and socio-economic structure. The post office usually emerged at a location of some transport convenience in conjunction with a church, a school, or both, the presence of which were perceived by postal officials and the petitioning public alike as factors in favour of the establishment of a post office in a particular place. A petition drawn up in 1894 asked for a post office near the Presbyterian Church in Belfast (Lot 58).[45] Another spot near the centre of Lot 15 was considered a good place for a post office because it had a church. The inspector was not deterred from making a favourable recommendation in this case, despite the absence of a bona fide village.

The presence of a church was reason enough to establish a post office. Schools were also cited in petitions and inspectors' reports as an even stronger reason for establishing a post office. In reply to a petition from the inhabitants of Baldwin's Road (Lot 51), the postal inspector recommended the post office be established near the local schoolhouse.[46] Other petitions came from communities whose sole public building was a district school house.[47] Why the emphasis on schoolhouses? Perhaps the answer lies in the convenience of pick up and delivery such cohabitation implied. After school, children could be relied on to fetch the mail and carry it home. Maybe they took something to be mailed in the morning?

The correlation between school and post office may have reflected a deeper sense of community-territorial identity beyond considerations of convenience. The petitioners of New Dominion (Lot 65) requested a new post office for their community and asked that the neighbouring post office of Fairview be moved three kilometres east to accommodate them. This exercise in postal reshuffling was entirely logical because it would leave each of the four local school districts with a post office.[48]

Church and school were by no means the sole rationale of post office location in rural neighbourhoods. Trade was another factor. About sixteen kilometres from Charlottetown, the nearest post office to James Howell's Creek (Lot 30) was a little over five kilometres away in Bonshaw, but the people of Howell's Creek preferred to go to New Haven next door in lot 31, also just over five kilometres away, because that is where their trade took them.[49] In this instance, the requirements of business and the post were collapsed into a single habit of travel. Economics thus forged postal habits among public and postal officials.

In the petitions and the inspectors' reports, economic equipment received repeated mention. Winsloe Station was a good site for a post office because it combined a general store and carriage and blacksmith shops with a church and school. The application for a post office at Baltic (Lot 18) was recommended by the inspector as it had a school, mill, and starch factory. Similarly, Mull (Lot 16) had a tailor, a forge, and as many as ten private houses. Generally speaking, the standard acceptable market for a local post office ranged from as few as twelve to sixteen families up to thirty families who would benefit from the improved postal service. Petitioners and postal inspectors were committed to the notion that the diversity of economic and cultural activities made for an especially suitable site for a post office. The degree of commitment was even more pronounced in the larger rural agglomerations.

Campbellton: The Economy and the Postal Service

The village of Campellton was located on the western shore of P.E.I., population 150 in 1870. The plan below illustrates the range of pursuits in which the local population was engaged. Near the intersection of O'Halloran Road and Dock Road were a forge, cooper shop, and shoemaker. Near the boundary of Lots 4 and 7 there was a saw and shingle mill, both probably powered by water. The heart of the community was situated at the junction of O'Halloran Road and the road to Miminegash. Here, within easy walking distance, were a carriage shop, Presbyterian Church and cemetery, a school, and a post office, probably in the store. Out on the shore were the fishing stages, a limekiln, a series of buildings—probably for processing fish or the upkeep of boats—and the lobster factories. Campbellton served as a microcosm of the kind of "secondary" activity one is liable to encounter in a rural P.E.I. village agglomeration. No doubt there was nothing but farmland beyond the village limits.

Campbellton was not located along the railway. The mail was probably brought in from Bloomfield Station, six kilometres away on the P.E.I. Railway. Campbellton was, however, well-served by roads that converged there, among them Dock Road, O'Halloran Road, and Palmer Road (the road to Miminegash). The nearest post office down the coast was eight kilometres away at Cape Wolfe; the nearest up the coast was eleven to thirteen kilometres away at Miminegash. It was likely, therefore, that residents all around travelled to Campbellton to transact their postal business. At the same time, they could transact whatever other business they might have at the village saw mill, shoemaker, and store, and/or to attend church. The village likely exercised a magnetic pull on the surrounding area, a phenomenon that had emerged prior to the railway era. A map dating from the 1860s shows a similar but more modest cluster of mills, shops, and stores at these same crossroads.[50]

Economic Rationale

Prince Edward Island post office records contain poignant examples of the economic and industrial rationale behind the establishment of new post offices and the maintenance of older ones. Agents of the economy wielded powerful arguments and spoke with authority. In a petition to the Post Office department, the Reid Brothers, owners of the North Tryon Woollen Mills, stressed the importance of keeping the post office near their mill, which was responsible for half of the business at the local post office.[51] North Tryon also boasted a telegraph office, carriage and shoe factories, blacksmith, two stores, and a tailor. The petition contained 110 signatures. Furthermore, the Reids reminded the assistant postal

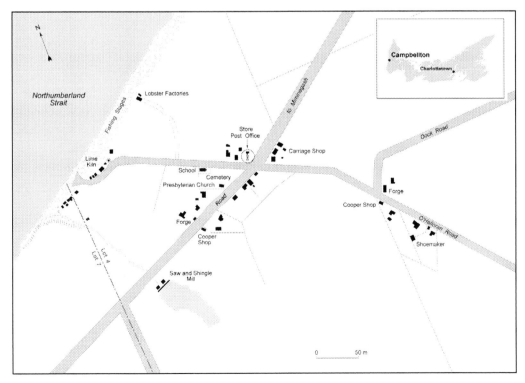

Figure 6.3 Village of Campbellton on the east coast of P.E.I., 1880.

Map by Andrée Héroux, using Meacham Atlas.

inspector that the area around North Tryon had voted for two Conservative government candidates in the previous Dominion election. The owners had used their influence on their employees to sway voters to the Tory side. The assistant postal inspector wisely recommended accepting the petition of the woollen mill owners.[52]

Typically for a maritime province, fishing was an important business in late nineteenth-century Prince Edward Island. It generated postal traffic and postal attention. In 1894, the assistant postal inspector reported that Campbell's Cove (Lot 47) was a resort and shelter for fishing boats and 70 to 90 fishermen would benefit from a post office at this location.[53] The inspector's report also mentions that there was considerable fishing activity at North St. Eleanor's (Lot 17), St. Chrysostome (Lot 15), and Miminegash (Lot 2). Also at Miminegash was significant lobster and mackerel fishing around 1889. Lobster was of capital importance to the rural economy of P.E.I. during the 1880s and 1890s and was responsible for 59 per cent of the value of fish production by 1904.[54] The factories—many of which were in fact sheds—appeared all along the coastline, and their presence was often invoked in inspector's reports as a good reason for establishing a post office. In Chelton, for example, there were four lobster factories near the site recommended for a post office in 1895.

The list of examples of the correlation between lobster fisheries and postal service is lengthy. The post office had certain expectations of the economy upon which it based its decision to develop services. In turn, the economy had certain requirements of the postal service. Somewhere in the inspectors' reports one gets a sense of the discriminating experience of growth in the rural P.E.I. economy.

A Cut Above the Others

In postal and economic terms, some communities were more successful and more important than others. Cardigan Bridge, a village of some 400 inhabitants on the P.E.I. Railway, had considerable mercantile, manufacturing, and fishing business. A direct connection to the Railway Mail Service was probably responsible for the village's special status as a distribution office: Mail was forwarded from this station to ten other post offices. In 1894, a request was put to the postmaster general to upgrade the post office to a money order office and savings bank.[55] Cardigan Bridge was in the process of becoming a cut above the other rural settlements in the immediate vicinity.

In 1891, there were five money order offices/post office savings banks in P.E.I., one each in Alberton, Georgetown, Kensington, Summerside, and Tignish. Each was a local centre in its own right; each was located astride the railway. Georgetown was graced with a new customs building and post office in 1909. According to *The Watchman*, the structure was to feature hot-water heating and first-class plumbing.[56]

Kensington first petitioned the postal authorities for a money order office in 1885. The assistant inspector's report describes it as a "thriving village" involved in a considerable amount of trade.[57] There were five tailors, five retail stores, four grist and sawmills, etc. It was also a central point for receiving goods and shipping produce and ranked third or fourth in the province in railway traffic. Six roads converged at Kensington carrying a daily stream of traffic in and out of the town; the post office distributed mail to ten other post offices. Around 1901, the Kensington post office was enlarged and included improvements such as 73 accommodation boxes—the names of the individual patrons were written on the sides of the boxes—and new wickets and letterboxes.[58]

Summerside was both a railway and port hub. A post office savings bank was established here sometime after 1885. Working out of the new Dominion Building in 1887, the postmaster was a busy man.[59] He and his clerk sorted the mail for forty different post offices in addition their own. On a daily basis, they made up the mail exchanged with the provincial capital of Charlottetown–Summerside. They also forwarded the mail for eleven other post offices located, for the most part, in the western part of the island. Mail was distributed three times a week to eleven offices and twice a week to eighteen others. Given the workload, it is not surprising the postmaster wished to receive compensation. Interestingly, he did a heavy trade in postage stamps. Town bankers and merchants continuously received large quantities of stamps from the country villages in lieu of cash remittances, usually for one dollar or less. Postage stamps served as a kind of paper currency. One could find no better metaphor for the marriage between the post office and exchange activities at the ground level of the rural economy.

Tignish: Postal Service in a Rail Town

To some extent, the postal pecking order in P.E.I. was predicated on the province's spatial hierarchy of trade linkage and town–country relations. Ultimately, in its decision to locate here and expand or reduce service there, the Post Office served the economy. However, as the twentieth century progressed, the department introduced policy criteria that helped reshape the geography of postal service. The implementation of Rural Mail Delivery reinforced the extant trend of differentiation, by which some postal places were more important than others. The discussion begins with Tignish.

Tignish began as a small village with a population of 150 in 1871. By the turn of the century (1901), the total had risen to about 600 people, a fourfold increase.[60] The accompanying 1880 plan of the village introduces some of the key elements of Tignish's socio-economy and shows some of the reasons for the growth in population.

The population was Acadian with such names as Gaudet, Chiasson, and Gallant. The Notre Dame Convent, the Roman Catholic parish church and presbytery, the cemetery, and the school occupied much of the northern part of Tignish. Further south on Chapel Road were the stores, one of which belonged to village notable Edward Hackett, merchant, accountant, and MP in the House of Commons (1878–1887).[61]

Across the lane from Hackett's warehouse and store were the warehouses, coal depot, train station, etc. of the P.E.I. Railway, for which Tignish served as the western terminus. The post office was just south of the railway station in the general store of postmaster Sylvan Perry. Around 1880, the mail was brought in daily.[62] Across from the store and the post office lay fifty enticingly empty urban building lots, all waiting for a buyer and a builder. The future beckoned.

No slumbering country village, Tignish became a going concern. The town filled up with homes and businesses, so much so that, in the great fire of 1896, 62 buildings burned to the ground, taking a hotel, round house, carriage factory, post office, and a host

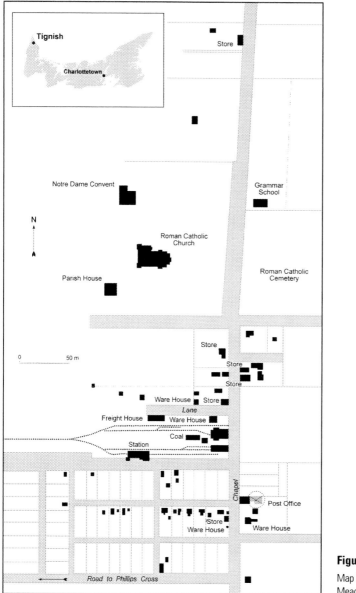

Figure 6.4 Plan of Tignish, 1880.

Map by Andrée Héroux, using Meacham Atlas.

of other warehouses, stores, and homes.[63] Fourteen families were left homeless. The fire all but obliterated the stillborn rail town. Yet, the community picked itself up and rose from the ashes.

Tignish was a forward looking place. The telephone line, installed in about 1894, would, a decade later, allow subscribers to converse long distance with parties in Charlottetown. Tignish had its own newspaper, *L'Impartial*, published by schoolteacher Gilbert Buote and his son François-Joseph, from 1893 to 1915. A French paper that spoke up for Acadian interests, *L'Impartial* is a useful source of information on the railway and postal service in Tignish, matters that were much interrelated.

The newspaper reported on mundane events—such as the new coat of paint applied to the railway station a year after it was rebuilt—as well as significant ones. Twice yearly, in summer and winter, the railway schedule was adjusted. The introduction of twice-daily service to Charlottetown in 1902 was an important development; it promised to speed up the mails although delays could occur, winter being the main culprit. Just before Christmas 1893, the mail remained in the Tignish post office for three days before it was taken out. A snowstorm stopped the mail train at O'Leary station; there was no mail that day in 1896. On another occasion, the people of Tignish had to travel to the next-to-last stop down the line at Harper Station to fetch their mail trapped aboard a snowbound train.[64]

From 1895 to 1910, the post office in Tignish changed locations no fewer than six times. The decision to build a new post office and customs building put an end to the shuffling. The idea was first put forward in the spring of 1910, and, in summer, the local MP came to inspect the terrain and thereby offer his political benediction. He was accompanied by the government's inspector of public buildings. It all looked so official. The terrain was surveyed in August, but, strangely, the whole project disappeared from the public view. Finally in June 1911, a contract was awarded to a Summerside contractor and building plans were sent down from Ottawa; the following year the new building was open for business.[65]

In stature, the building in Tignish stood head and shoulders above the other post offices in Lot 1, for it served as a distribution office, a money order office, and a postal savings bank. Even before the advent of the post office and customs building in 1912, far more postal business was transacted in Tignish (roughly $1,000) than in any of the surrounding county post offices, where perhaps $20 in revenue was earned in a single year. The accompanying map shows the location of the five post offices in Lot 1. Most or all of them received their mail via Tignish. The country post offices were small and vulnerable, especially when political manoeuvres took place, a case in point being the chain reaction of postal politics in Peterville and vicinity.

Peterville lay to the west of Tignish. The post office was established in 1876. Twenty years later, it was thought the area could support two post offices instead of one. So, shortly before the general election of 1896, the Conservative government appointed a postmaster a few hundred metres down Peters Road at Léoville. The idea was to put the Peterville postmaster, a well-known Liberal, out of business. Following the Liberal victory in the election, the Léoville post office was moved just over half a kilometre, probably to the south; that took care of one Conservative postmaster. The local MP then suggested that the Palmerston Road post office next door in Lot 2 be moved, presumably to ensure the two were not too close together. This might potentially dispose of another conservative postmaster. Meanwhile, the original Liberal post office of Peterville, which had in the interval been forced to close, was reopened in 1898. Here, then, was a possible third opening for a would-be Liberal postmaster.[66]

When necessary, political surgery made a deep incision in the postal network of the P.E.I. countryside. Yet, far worse was in store for these small-time post offices. Out of nine post offices in Lot 1, by 1918, only one remained: Tignish.[67] Three closed in 1913

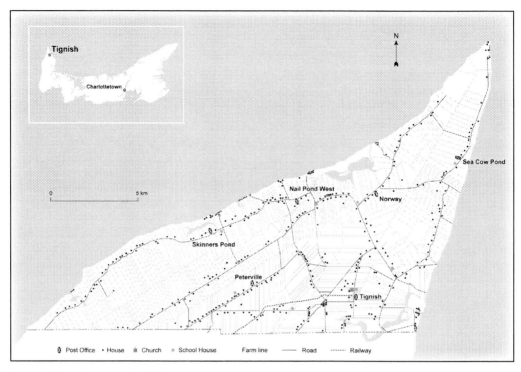

Figure 6.5 Post offices in Lot 1, 1880.
Map by Andrée Héroux, using Meacham Atlas.

and two others in 1915 and in 1918. The system of Rural Mail Delivery was progressively taking over from the network of tiny country post offices. An entire way of doing country postal and political business was about to disappear.

Rural Mail Delivery was first introduced in Canada in 1908, but was not implemented in the Tignish area until the spring of 1914 when a route was opened between Tignish, Skinners Pond, and Nail Pond West (L'Étang des Clous).[68] Thereafter, the rural mail system, whereby mail was delivered by couriers from a central post office to mailboxes strung out along the various concession roads, spread to the entire territory of Lot 1. As a result, there was no need for a post office outside Tignish. The railway brought the mail in and out of the area, while the Tignish postmaster and staff did the sorting and the couriers the delivery and pick up. Tignish was not only the biggest post office around, it was the only one. The substantial increase in revenues, from about $1,000 in 1911 to $2,800 ten years later, demonstrates the windfall effect of the town's monopoly of the postal business. It is possible that the concentration of postal facilities in fewer centres occurred across Canada and P.E.I. The policy was likely part of a transformation in the ways in which town and country interacted.

Conclusion

The postal service in P.E.I. was ubiquitous, inescapable, and much relied upon. It brought newspapers and letters from kith and kin, so many of whom had moved away to earn a living somewhere else.[69] Whether in the relatively streamlined institutional setting of a hamlet such as Cavendish or in a more elaborate village–small-town setting, the post office blended into the rural landscape. Where there was merely a store, a school, and perhaps a church, there was invariably a post office, usually at or near the intersection of two or more country roads. Where the landscape was marked by mills and factories and perhaps dozens of houses clustered together, one might also find a post office. The social and political clout of the mill masters ensured postal services would be provided. Finally, in the larger towns, Summerside, for example, the postal facilities were more elaborate, in keeping with the centrality of such a place, which performed specific communication and trade functions for the surrounding rural communities.

The postal system was not static for it came with built-in dynamic variables. The discussion of Tignish shows some of the personal, ethnic, and political contingencies in the development of the rural postal service. In the medium- and long-run, larger factors of change affected the postal makeup of P.E.I. In effect, the railway polarized social, economic, and, therefore, postal activity along certain axes on the Island. It helped refine the hierarchy of spatial relationships, which, as it turned out, were destined to have no small impact on the course of postal affairs. The reorganization of rural space, instigated by the railway in conjunction with the Post Office department's implementation of Rural Mail Delivery, produced a spatial pattern consisting of larger agglomerations with substantial postal accommodations and smaller ones with essentially no postal accommodation, with the exception of the rural mail carrier. The overall statistics of the province show that the number of post offices rose from 180 in 1873 to 456 in 1911, but the subsequent decline from 246 in 1921 to 117 in 1931 and a mere 41 in 1989 was precipitous.

The railway and rural mail delivery introduced a strict sense of hierarchy to the conduct of postal relations in space. It is likely that the hierarchy was part of a general re-ordering of relations between town and country in P.E.I., as elsewhere in Canada. The post office was, is, a pillar of Main Street, rural Canada. It is part of a complex of social, cultural, and economic activities that constitute the drawing power of a small-town Main Street vis-à-vis its surrounding rural districts.

The rural district and the small town merged to form an enlarged common trade zone, characterized by automobile transport and the institution of Saturday shopping.[70] The automobile allowed for an increase in the trading radius from 8 to 11 kilometres to as much as 40 to 56 kilometres.[71] In any small Canadian town, the building of movie theatres, pool halls, beer parlours, and other Main Street retail and leisure places had a lot to do with the preferences and needs of the country clientele. Wetherell's study of small-town Alberta shows how communities vied with one another for the country family's business, for not only could farmers go to town more often in their cars, they could choose which towns to visit.[72] Walking or driving down Main Street, the farmer and his wife called in at a store, or a bar, or perhaps a cheap café. As they spent, they bought into an urban culture, with its small talk, cheesecakes, and movie stars. The standards for this culture might be set thousands of kilometres away, but one did not have to be on St. Catherine

Street (or Yonge Street in Toronto) to think like the people on St. Catherine Street. The cultural symbols and the habits of consumption were effectively spread from one end of the country to the other via Main Street, a linear shopping and social experience punctuated by greetings from people whom you know you could or could not trust.

Among these people was the incumbent at the local post office. The postal system contributed to the making of Main Street for it helped bring country people to Main Street. More importantly, however, as a facilitator disseminating letters, the press, and the mail-order catalogue, the postal system taught them what to expect and what to ask for when they got there. This is the rural and small-town universe—itself a changing world—that is currently disappearing before our very eyes, as our economy gets caught up in the wave of "wallmartization."

Curious and interesting indeed this laboratory of Prince Edward Island, I am convinced the Island has much more to teach us.

Notes

1. I would like to thank Andrew Horrall, Doug Murray, David Keenlyside, Peter Rider, and Xavier Gélinas for their collaboration in reading and commenting upon a previous version of this article. A previous draft was delivered as a paper to the Atlantic Studies Conference at the Université de Moncton in 1996.
2. Andrew Hill Clark, *Three Centuries an Island: A Historical Geography of Settlement and Agriculture in Prince Edward Island, Canada* (Toronto: University of Toronto Press, 1959).
3. Chantal Amyot and John Willis, *Country Post: Rural Postal Service in Canada, 1880 to 1945*, Canadian Postal Museum Mercury no. 1 (Gatineau: Canadian Museum of Civilization, 2003)
4. The terminology is from a work by Anita and Darrett B. Rutman, *Small Worlds, Large Questions: Explorations in Early American Social History, 1600–1850* (Charlottesville and London: University Press of Virginia, 1994).
5. At the time, there was no box-to-box rural mail delivery (RMD); one had to go to the nearest post office to fetch the mail. See Library and Archives Canada, Post Office Archives, RG-3 D-3 (hereafter LAC), Postal Inspector's Reports: Charlottetown, reel C-7264, vol. 32, file no. 315/1884: Inhabitants of Lower Cardigan to the Postmaster General, July 5, 1884.
6. LAC, reel C-7265, vol. 32, file no.1893/974: Joseph O. Arsenault (Senator) to Postmaster General, April 11, 1896.
7. *Illustrated Historical Atlas of the Province of Prince Edward Island* (J. H. Meacham and Company Publishers, 1880; facsimile, Belleville, Ontario: Mika Publishing, 1989). All five figures or maps featured in this article are based on the Meacham Atlas.
8. Prince Edward Island Public Archives and Records Office, accession 2561/2: Journal of Winter Mail Service. For Summerside, see accessions 2654 and 2593.
9. G. Douglas Murray, *The Post Office on Prince Edward Island, 1787–1990* (Bridgetown, N.S.: Mailman Publishing, 1990).

10. The complete quote is from John Donne: "No man is an island, entire of itself; every man is a piece of the continent, a part of the main. If a clod be washed away by the sea, Europe is the less, as well as if promontory were, as well as if a manor of thy friend's or of thine own were. Any man's death diminishes me, because I am involved in mankind; and therefore never send to know for whom the bell tolls; it tolls for thee," John Donne, Meditation XVII. Thanks to Peter Rider for the quote.

11. *Charlottetown Herald*, May 3, 1871, p. 2.

12. Winter isolation was not overcome until the advent of winter airmail service between Moncton and Charlottetown in 1928. The service became year-round in 1935. See Library and Archives Canada, RG-3, vol. 2300, file no. 12-1-25: Memorandum to Acting Postmaster General, March 2, 1938. See also the historical summary in Memo to the Postmaster General, April 23, 1941.

13. Clark, *Three Centuries an Island*, p. 143.

14. Mary Cullen, "The Transportation Issue, 1873–1973" in F.W.P. Bolger, *Canada's Smallest Province: A History of P.E.I.* (Charlottetown: Prince Edward Island Commission, 1973), pp. 238–242.

15. P.E.I. Provincial Archives and Records Office, accession no. 2561, item no. 2: Journal of Winter Mail Service, Cape Traverse. See also Harry Bruce, *Lifeline: The Story of the Atlantic Ferries and Coastal Boats* (Toronto: Macmillan of Canada, 1977), p. 114.

16. See examples in Bruce, *Lifeline*, pp. 113–116.

17. Sackville was located along the Intercolonial Railway, the main railway mail line through the Maritimes.

18. LAC, reel C-7264, vol. 32, file no. 1883/252: Assistant Postal Inspector to Postmaster General, August 21, 1883.

19. *Charlottetown Herald*, March 29, 1893, p. 3

20. Data from the published version of the *Census of Canada*, 1890–1891, 1961.

21. *Charlottetown Herald*, February 23, 1887, p. 3 and August 26, 1855, p. 3.

22. *Charlottetown Herald,* January 30, 1901, p. 3. See also LAC, reel C-7265, vol. 33, file no. 1897/589: Correspondence of 1897 between P.E.I. Full Electric Co. and P.E.I. Electric Co., Report to Postmaster General, September 14, 1897.

23. *Annual Report of the Postmaster General for the Year ending 30 June 1888.*

24. *Charlottetown Herald*, May 15, 1895, p. 3.

25. Data from the *Annual Report of the Postmaster General for 1911.*

26. *Prince Edward Island Directory for 1871.*

27. Clark, *Three Centuries an Island*, p. 117.

28. *Charlottetown Herald*, January 10, 1866, p.2.

29. On the P.E.I. Railway, see F. W. P. Bolger, "Railways and the Dénouement" in Bolger, *Canada's Smallest Province*, p. 199 ff. See also Clark, *Three Centuries an Island*, pp. 138–143.

30. Clark, *Three Centuries an Island*, p. 140.

31. See *Annual Report of the Postmaster General* during the 1880s as well as *Annual Report of the Postmaster General for the Year Ending June 30, 1875*, and *Annual Report of the Postmaster General for the Year Ending June 30, 1876*. Our thanks to D. Murray for helping us with the dates.

32. The six cases are West Devon (Lot 10), Coleman (Lot 9), Conway Station (Lot 11), Bloomfield Station (Lot 5), Richmond Station (Lot 14), and Suffolk Station (Lot 34). References to the establishment of these post offices can be found in the postal inspectors' reports, LAC (RG-3D-3), for various dates and file numbers, and in Murray, *The Post Office on Prince Edward Island*.

33. LAC, reel C-7264, vol. 32, file no. 1887/280: Assistant Postal Inspector to Postmaster General, May 10, 1887.

34. LAC, reel C-7265, vol. 32, file no. 1892/928: Assistant Postal Inspector to Postmaster General, November 21, 1892. The ranking of post offices according to their importance is a complex matter for the late nineteenth and early twentieth centuries. To simplify, one could say that there were at least three types of post office in rural Canada during this period, in order of importance: the savings banks post offices, i.e., those with savings bank facilities; the money order offices, i.e., those empowered to issue and reimburse money orders; and the regular post offices, i.e., those with no special banking or money order facilities. Availability of telegraph communication may have somehow contributed to this hierarchy.

35. LAC, reel C-7265, vol. 33, file no. 1895/221: Report to the Postmaster General from Assistant Post Office Inspector Brecken, March 18, 1895; and, for Wellington, LAC, reel C-7264, file no. 1883/249: Assistant Postal Inspector to Postmaster General, August 7, 1883.

36. This was not entirely the case for 1891 in Prince County. See "The Land Transformed 1800–1891," in *Historical Atlas of Canada*, ed. R. L. Gentilcore, vol. 2 (Toronto: University of Toronto Press, 1993), plate 29.

37. W. E. Barry, "The Geography of Anne of Green Gables," in Wendy E. Barry et al., *The Annotated Anne of Green Gables by L. M. Montgomery* (New York: Oxford University Press, 1997), p. 416. See also *Lovell's Directory for Prince Edward Island 1871*.

38. L. M. Montgomery, *The Alpine Path: The Story of My Career* (1917; reprint, Toronto: Fitzhenry, 1975), p. 18.

39. The neighbouring post office of Cavendish Road suffered the same fate in 1913. See the database of postmasters and post offices at www.collectionscanada.ca/archivianet.

40. M. Rubio and E. Waterston, eds, *Selected Journals of Lucy Maud Montgomery*, vol. 2 (Toronto: Oxford University Press, 1987), entry for May 4, 1920, p. 377.

41. Ibid., vol. 1, entry for January 12, 1908, p. 334.

42. Montgomery, *The Alpine Path*, p. 53.

43. Maud came in sixth place in the teacher certificate examinations. See *The Watchman*, June 28, 1894, p. 1.

44. Mary Rubio and E. Waterston, *Writing a Life: L. M. Montgomery: Biography of the Author of Anne of Green Gables* (Toronto: ECW Press, 1995), p. 40.

45. LAC (RG-3D-3), reel C-7265, vol. 33, file no. 1894/124: Petition to Postmaster General from Belfast residents, April 11, 1894.

46. Ibid., file no. 1882/63: Assistant Postal Inspector to Postmaster General, February 18, 1882.

47. For example, communities of Piusville and Acadia, LAC (RG-3D-3), reel no. C-7264, vol. 32, file no.1882/132: Assistant Postal Inspector to Postmaster General, August 24, 1882, and file no.1888/439: Assistant Postal Inspector to Postmaster General, October 29, 1888.

48. Ibid., file no. 1895/204: Report to Postmaster General from Assistant Postal Inspector, February 7, 1895.

49. Ibid., file no. 1884/360: Letter from James Howell's Creek, July 6, 1885.

50. Library and Archives Canada, National Map Collection, NMC-10863 1/6.3: D. J. Lake, Topographical Map of Prince Edward Island in the Gulf of St. Lawrence, Saint John, N.B., 1863.

51. LAC, reel C-7264, vol. 32, file no. 1883/283: Various correspondence dated October 24, 1883.

52. Ibid., Letter to Assistant Postal Inspector from Reid Bros., October 24, 1883, and Assistant Postal Inspector to Postmaster General, October 24, 1883.

53. LAC, reel C-7265, vol. 33, file no. 1894/159: Assistant Postal Inspector to Postmaster General, August 9, 1894.

54. Clark, *Three Centuries an Island*, p. 148, and L. D. McCann, "The 1890s: Fragmentation and the New Social Order," in *The Atlantic Provinces in Confederation*, eds E. R. Forbes and D.

Muise (Toronto: University of Toronto Press, 1993), p. 137. Georges Arsenault, *The Island Acadians 1720–1980* (Charlottetown: Ragweed, 1999), p. 148.

55. LAC, reel C-7265, vol. 33, file no. 1894/123: Assistant Postal Inspector to Postmaster General, May 11, 1894.

56. *The Watchman*, October 1, 1909, p. 3.

57. LAC, reel C-7264, vol. 32, file no. 1885/120: Assistant Postal Inspector to Postmaster General, September 21, 1885.

58. *Charlottetown Herald*, January 2, 1901, p. 3.

59. P.E.I. Provincial Archives and Records Office, accession no. 2564, item 218: Correspondence, Summerside postmaster H. C. Green to Postmaster General of Canada: January 11, 1887.

60. The latter data are from the 1901 manuscript census. The 1901 census also contains information on the population of Tignish Road, Tignish Shore, and Tignish Corner. If these hamlets are included, the grand total rises to 751. Since 1956, when published population data first became available, the population of Tignish has hovered between 900 and 1000.

61. Hackett's term of office in Parliament was interrupted from 1887 to 1896. During this interval, he worked as a fisheries Inspector. In 1896, he was re-elected only to lose his seat the following year. He finally returned to Parliament in 1900. See J. K. Johnson, ed., *The Canadian Directory for Parliament, 1867–1967* (Ottawa, 1968), pp. 249–250.

62. Tear's *P.E.I. Directory for 1880–1881*. Perry was of Acadian origin and spoke French. Both of his successors, Francis Gallant (1995–1905) and Buote (1905–1909), were Acadian. Following Perry's departure, *L'Impartial* asked publicly if the government was willing to respect the town's French-speaking majority, as it had at Shediac, N.B., where a French-Canadian postmaster had been appointed. An English-language paper replied nastily that French was not necessary for this job, as all the business was done in English. I expect that Acadians throughout the Maritimes faced this kind of hostility. See *The Watchman*, November 29, 1894, p. 2, and *L'Impartial*, May 9, 1895.

63. *L'Impartial*, September 3, 1896. The *Charlottetown Herald*, reporting on the same fire (September 2), offered the hypothesis that the fire broke out in Mr. Kinch's carriage factory as a result of his little daughter setting fire to some shavings. The shavings ignited the carriage shop, which, in turn, set the rest of the village ablaze. In our research, we encountered six rural P.E.I. post offices that burned to the ground: Millview, Southport, Elmsdale, Little Sands, O'Leary, and O'Leary Station. The postmaster of O'Leary lost everything to a fire in 1908, with the exception of the money and registered letters that he had (wisely) taken home with him (*The Watchman*, March 18, 1908, p. 3). In 1889, his counterpart at O'Leary Station lost his books, two registered letters, a dozen ordinary letters, and $26 in stamps, as well as the proceeds from the sale of stamps. His first instinct was to resign and leave immediately for the U.S., but he later changed his mind. See LAC, reel C-7264, vol. 32, file no. 1889/541: Assistant Postal Inspector to Postmaster General, September 30, 1889.

64. Ibid., March 21, 1895, December 12, 1893, and March 19, 1896.

65. *L'Impartial*, various dates from April 26, 1910 to June 13, 1911. See also *The Watchman*, June 9, 1911, p. 3. The delay in the onset of construction (between 1910 and 1911) can be attributed to the electoral timetable of the Liberal government as the resurrection of the project in June came just three months prior to the general election of September 1911.

66. This paragraph is based on LAC, reel C-7624, vol. 33, file no. 1897/571: Assistant Postal Inspector to Postmaster General July 6, 1897. See also file no. 1898/608: S. F. Perry to Minister Marine and Fisheries, January 3, 1898.

67. Murray, *The Post Office on Prince Edward Island*, p. 55.

68. *L'Impartial*, April 7, 1914, p. 2.

69. During the 1860s, the curves of immigration and emigration crossed one another. Immigration plummeted, while emigration rose steadily. The Boston area would attract many Islanders (Clark, *Three Centuries an Island*, p. 121).

70. On the concept of the trade zone, see Charles J. Galpin, *Rural Life* (New York: Century, 1918).

71. Clark, *Three Centuries an Island*, p. 142.

72. See D. G. Wetherell, *Town Life: Main Street and the Evolution of Small-town Alberta, 1880–1947* (Edmonton: University of Alberta Press, 1995), p. 221.

PART TWO:
EPISTOLARY PRACTICE
AND CULTURE

DEUXIÈME PARTIE :
PRATIQUES ET CULTURE
ÉPISTOLAIRES

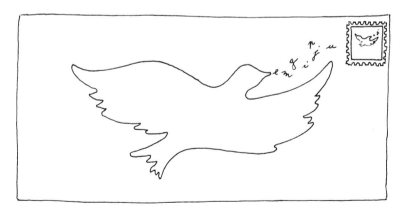

UNE INDUSTRIE DE LA PLUME D'OIE

7

Les pennes de la Compagnie de la Baie d'Hudson

Bianca Gendreau, Conservatrice, Musée canadien de la poste, Musée canadien des civilisations

Résumé

La plume d'oie est l'instrument principal de l'épistolier et elle règne sur le monde de l'écriture pendant de nombreux siècles. Elle constitue un marché très lucratif. La Compagnie de la Baie d'Hudson fait commerce des pennes dès le début de ses activités et celles-ci bénéficient d'une réputation d'articles de grande qualité. Le succès des pennes de la CBH repose sur leur durabilité et une technique de préparation soignée, considérée comme un art. Ces plumes d'oie ont longtemps occupé l'avant-scène chez les grands marchands d'instruments d'écriture.

Abstract

Goose feathers were once the principal instrument of letter writers within the world of correspondence for many centuries. The market for goose feathers was a highly lucrative one. The Hudson's Bay Company (HBC) traded in feathers from its earliest days, and benefitted from a reputation for supplying feathers of high quality. The success of HBC's quill market lay in the durability of its product and careful preparation, which was considered an art in itself. For a considerable time, HBC goose feathers would remain highly sought-after by the great merchants of writing instruments.

Introduction

Les plumes d'oies dominèrent le monde de l'écriture durant plus de 1000 ans. Elles demeureront l'instrument d'écriture de prédilection jusqu'au milieu du XIXe siècle. La demande pour cet instrument fut en effet très forte. Uniquement pour la ville de Londres, on en importa une impressionnante quantité. Ainsi, en 1834, un papetier londonien a pu préparer, à lui seul, plus de six millions de ces plumes avant qu'elles ne soient prêtes à être vendues[1].

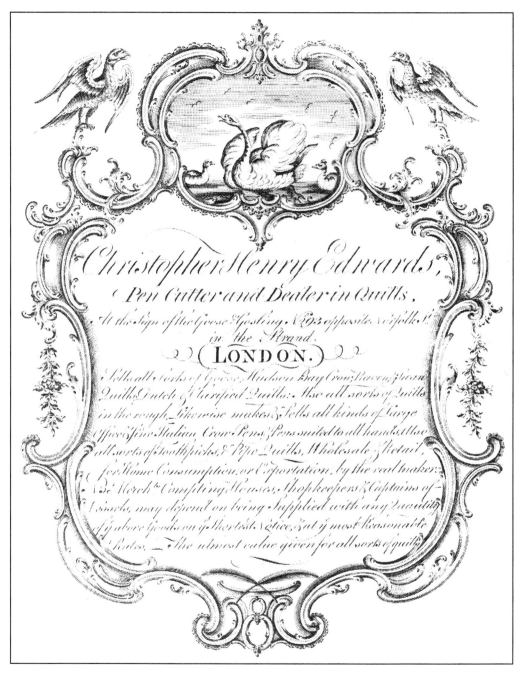

Figure 7.1 Carte d'affaires de Christopher Henry Edwards, vers 1760.

Cet article portera sur l'industrie de la plume d'oie transformée et mise en vente par la Compagnie de la Baie d'Hudson (CBH)[2]. Notre recherche combine une démarche historique qui repose sur de nombreuses sources primaires et une étude de la culture matérielle. Une étude de journaux personnels, de rapports provenant des postes de traite et d'instructions venant de Londres nous permettra de voir comment se déroulaient la chasse aux oies et la transformation des pennes en plumes à écrire. Nous verrons ensuite les particularités des plumes d'oie de la CBH et leurs conditions de vente.

Vivre de la plume

On peut retracer l'utilisation de la plume d'oie grâce aux enluminures ou aux gravures conservées à travers les siècles. Parmi les plus anciennes représentations d'un écrivain tenant dans ses mains une plume d'oie, il y a celle de saint Jean l'Évangéliste, gravée sur une plaque anglo-saxonne en or, retrouvée en 1978 à Brandon, dans le Suffolk, en Angleterre, et datant du IXe siècle[3]. Un autre exemple est celui que l'on trouve dans la bible de Worms, en Allemagne, ouvrage qui remonte à 1148[4]. On y voit clairement les outils d'écriture du copiste. Une de ses enluminures nous montre saint Jérôme écrivant une lettre à Paulinus. Il tient dans sa main droite une plume d'oie et, dans l'autre, un petit couteau servant à affûter la plume.

La plume d'oie, bien que peu dispendieuse et facile à obtenir, occasionnait bien des ennuis. Le besoin de constamment en réparer ou en modifier la pointe, le fait que celle-ci se brisait ou s'effritait rapidement, l'obligation de constamment retremper l'instrument dans l'encre, sont sans cesse mentionnés dans les lettres et la correspondance des épistoliers.

Dès le XVIe siècle, on expérimente les premières pointes de plumes en métal. Le chroniqueur anglais Samuel Pepys écrit, dans son journal, le 5 août 1663, à quel point on désire un nouveau type de plume.

> This evening came a letter about business from Mr. Coventry, and with it the silver pen he promised me to carry inke in, which is very necessary[5].

Pendant cette période d'expérimentation, la plume de métal souffre de deux problèmes : le manque de flexibilité et la corrosion. Il faudra véritablement attendre le milieu du XIXe siècle pour que la plume d'oie cède sa place à la plume de métal. Le développement de celle-ci et son utilisation généralisée sur une période d'uniquement cinquante ans sont remarquables lorsqu'on pense au long règne de la plume d'oie.

Le règne absolutiste de la plume d'oie exige un approvisionnement constant du marché. Certains épistoliers prolifiques, entre autres, l'ancien président américain Thomas Jefferson, préfèrent avoir leur propre élevage d'oies et s'en servir pour fabriquer leurs plumes. Auteur prolifique, il avait besoin d'avoir sous la main la matière première nécessaire, car il entretenait des échanges épistolaires avec de nombreuses personnalités de son époque. Au cours de sa vie, Jefferson aurait reçu 26 000 lettres et 16 000 des lettres écrites de sa main sont conservées aux archives de Monticello, à Charlottesville, en Virginie. On y trouve des missives affectueuses envoyées à sa famille; d'autres, plus élaborées, adressées à des hommes politiques de son époque. Le matin, selon sa routine, Jefferson s'installait pour une longue période d'écriture, « from sun-rise to one or two o'clock », remarquait-il, « I am drudging at the writing table ». Il écrivit à John Adams qu'il souffrait « under the persecution of letters, of which every mail brings a fresh load », calculant qu'il avait reçu, durant l'année 1820, 1 267 lettres, « many of them requiring answers of elaborate research, and all to be answered with due attention and consideration[6] ».

Le 26 décembre 1808, dans une lettre à sa fille, Cornelia Jefferson Randolph, Jefferson souligne les multiples usages d'une oie :

> I congratulate you, my dear Cornelia, on having acquired the valuable art of writing. How delightful to be enabled by it to converse with an absent friend as if present ! […] I rejoice that you have learnt to write, for another reason; for as that is done with a goose-quill, you now know the value of a goose, and of course you will assist Ellen in taking care of the half-dozen very fine gray geese which I shall send by Davy[7].

Il est certain que bon nombre de personnes ne sont pas en mesure de maîtriser l'art de préparer leurs propres plumes, aussi préfèrent-elles les acheter pré-taillées et vendues en paquets.

La compagnie de la Baie d'Hudson a, dès le début de ses activités de traite des fourrures, fait commerce de plumes d'oie. Une requête de Londres au responsable de Fort York, datée du 17 juin 1693 et demandant d'envoyer des plumes d'oies, témoigne de l'importance croissante accordée à cet instrument :

> We now recommend againe to you the sending home of what feathers you can gett as are fit for beds & to keep the Goose feathers apart they being a very good commodity in England this warr time. We hope you may the next yeare make a beginning & send us half a dozen Baggs we meane only such as are fitt for beds except you find the Goose Quills to be fitt for pens & if so returne as many as you can thereof likewise we refer the Gratuety to be given to those of the factory that gott the Feathers to the Discretion of the Councill but those brought by the Indians theres noe reason we should allow any thing for them because they are bought of the Indians & we hope you may procure quantityes[8].

Un empire diversifié

La Compagnie de la Baie d'Hudson est bien connue pour son commerce de traite des fourrures, en particulier le castor, mais les appels à la diversification de ses activités n'en sont pas moins fréquents. Cela est très clairement mentionné par Edwin Ernest Rich dans *The History of the Hudson's Bay Company, 1760-1870*[9], lorsqu'il affirme que le comité de Londres exerce des pressions sur le gouverneur John Nixon pour que celui-ci trouve une alternative au castor. Londres demande donc d'envoyer d'autres types de fourrures et des plumes. Dans un autre document, ses directives sont précises[10] : on y mentionne que la traite des fourrures axée uniquement sur le castor est précaire et assujettie à la guerre et à la chute des prix de la peau de cet animal. Londres insiste sur le besoin de diversification et perçoit rapidement le potentiel offert par le commerce des plumes.

> … you find the goose quills to be fitt for pens and if soe returne as many as you can …[11]

La correspondance entre Londres et les divers postes de traite est abondante et les échanges, fort détaillés. Il est clair que Londres n'est pas uniquement intéressé aux résultats, mais désire aussi connaître les motivations qui entourent la prise de décision et les facteurs susceptibles de contribuer à la baisse ou à l'accroissement des ventes de certains produits. Par exemple, dans une lettre du 22 août 1722, Joseph Myatt, de Fort Albany, explique l'impact du climat sur la traite des fourrures. Il y mentionne la rudesse du climat hivernal et précise que les abondantes chutes de neige ont eu un effet négatif sur le nombre de fourrures échangées. Il ajoute que tous les efforts ont été entrepris pour encourager la chasse de diverses espèces, car il reconnaît la valeur des petites fourrures[12].

Dans la correspondance entre Londres et les postes de traite, les références aux plumes se font plus nombreuses. Dans une lettre datée de Fort York, le 23 août 1723, Thomas McCliesh[13] décrit au gouverneur le cargo qu'il envoie à Londres. Il répond aussi à la requête de la métropole avisant la CBH de ne pas troquer les plumes d'oies, car celles-ci s'avéraient une source de revenus de plus en plus importants[14]. Cette stratégie de diversification va donc permettre au commerce des plumes de s'épanouir. Aussi, dès le XVIIIe siècle, la valeur marchande des plumes d'oie est-elle reconnue. Tout se mesure en « Beaver » puisqu'il s'agit de la commodité de traite principale. Un rapport des ventes effectuées entre 1738 et 1748 fait état de la production obtenue durant cette période[15]. Le nombre de plumes d'oie envoyées à Londres est significatif :

18 900, en 1746;

12 000, en 1747;

43 000, en 1748.

Les pennes valaient plus cher à certains postes qu'à d'autres. On remarque clairement les fluctuations de ce commerce dans les journaux de York Factory et de Fort Albany, au cours de la période antérieure à 1783. Deux milles pennes valaient un castor à York Factory et à Severn House, tandis qu'à Fort Albany, cinq cents suffisaient.

Le commerce des oies et des plumes et des pennes atteindra son plein développement au XIXe siècle[16]. Cette volonté de diversification demeure une préocupation de Londres, tout au long du siècle[17]. On constate, à la lecture des minutes des réunions du comité de Londres, que la CBH subissait à l'époque les répercussions des guerres napoléoniennes. Dans une lettre écrite en 1808 au trésorier, et dans laquelle on demandait un délai dans les activités d'importation, la CBH indique[18] « the difficulties the company labours under on account of the nonexportation of their furs to the Continent[19] ». Pourtant, la réaction de la Compagnie vis-à-vis de la situation en Europe n'était pas de diminuer la quantité de fourrures exportées en Angleterre, mais plutôt d'en changer la composition.

The committee resolved that every exertion should be used to promote as much as possible, the importation of those articles which meet a ready sale for home consumption[20].

Un autre exemple, plus tardif, celui des postes de traite de Little Whale River et de Great Whale River, fait état des quantités et de la variété des marchandises de traite obtenues pour la période 1814-1815 et précise que le volume était quelque peu supérieur à celle de 1813-1814.

The trade consisted of bear, beaver, fox, marten, mink, musquas [...], otter, wolf, and wolverene skins, plus castoreum feathers and quills[21].

La chasse aux oies

Il est clair, suite à la lecture de nombreux journaux de postes de traite et de livres de compte, que le commerce des plumes d'oie était fort rentable, donc, florissant à Londres. Par contre, que sait-on des moyens employés par les postes de traite pour obtenir les plumes ? Les meilleures sources d'informations sur ce sujet demeurent les récits de naturalistes ou d'ornithologues[22]. Les données accumulées par des employés des postes de traite et envoyées à Londres procurent aussi une mine supplémentaire de renseignements sur la faune et la flore.

Il faut savoir que les comptoirs de la CBH dépendaient fortement de la chasse aux oies et autres oiseaux de rivage pour le ravitaillement des hivernants et des équipages des navires qui retournaient à Londres. Au printemps surtout, mais aussi à l'automne, on embauchait donc des Cris de la baie d'Hudson pour chasser les oies. Des spécialistes entreprirent des recherches dans le but de comprendre quelles étaient les habitudes de vie et de migration des espèces d'oiseaux qu'on retrouvait en Amérique du Nord[23]. L'un d'eux, George Barnston, fera part de ses découvertes lors d'une conférence donnée à la Montreal Natural History Society, en 1851. Il y souligne comment le cygne et surtout les oies étaient des sources de nourriture très appréciées par les peuples autochtones vivant près de la baie d'Hudson. Il y rapporte de quelle façon les habitants du poste de traite de Fort Vancouver s'approvisionnaient :

Before Oregon was settled by the Americans, The Hudson's Bay Company post of Fort Vancouver used to be supplied by Indian hunters with grey geese, large and small, as well as with occasional swans and white gesse, and this at times so liberally, that a day's rations twice a week could be furnished to an establishment of 30 to 40 men [...] This game formed our best rations...[24]

Joseph Cohen, responsable du poste de York Factory, en 1798, note que les vivres frais dont ils dépendent, canards et autres oiseaux aquatiques, sont tués par des Autochtones[25].

Il ne semble pas y avoir d'unanimité chez les historiens sur le fait que les Cris se seraient mis à chasse les oiseaux après l'arrivée des Européens et auraient utilisé le fruit de leur chasse comme monnaie d'échange ou, comme certains chercheurs l'affirment, que cette pratique aurait existé avant la période de contact. Victor Lytwyn affirme que diverses circonstances, entre autres, la présence d'établissements commerciaux et la possibilité de se procurer des armes à feu, firent en sorte que les Cris privilégièrent cette proie comme ressources alimentaires et commerciales[26]. Les commentaires provenant de commerçants de la CBH abondent dans le même sens. Andrew Graham observe que les Cris capturaient une grande quantité d'outardes pendant la mue estivale en les assommant[27]. Il donne des informations sur les types d'oiseaux fréquentant les terres de la CBH de même que la saison durant laquelle ils étaient chassés et de quelle façon ils l'étaient. L'oie du Canada arrivait sur les terres en mai et pondait au début de juin. Elle était chassée en grande quantité par les Autochtones à l'emploi des postes de traite. Graham décrit les diverses espèces d'oies de même que les méthodes de conservation de certaines espèces qui servaient de nourriture pour l'hiver[28]. D'après Michael Payne, de Fort York, les Cris fournissaient une main-d'œuvre nombreuse et, par leurs prises, assuraient le ravitaillement de la population. On leur confiait également le transport du courrier entre les forts[29].

L'arrivée des premières oies et la débâcle du printemps étaient des événements importants du cycle annuel des postes de la CBH et fréquemment signalés dans leurs journaux. Les conditions climatiques se retrouvent souvent mentionnées dans les documents de la CBH. Ainsi, William Falconer, gérant du poste de Severn House, attribue l'arrivée tardive des oies, au printemps 1784, à l'absence de vents d'ouest[30]. À la lecture des nombreuses pièces de correspondance entre Londres et les postes de traite, on comprend bien que la Compagnie veuille faire progresser le commerce des oies. Par exemple, le nombre moyen de pennes échangées annuellement à Fort Albany grimpe de 53 600, dans les années 1770, à plus de 90 000 au cours de la première décennie du XIXe siècle. Pendant la même période, les recettes produites par les plumes passent de 1 480 livres à 1 820 livres.

La préparation des plumes avant leur expédition

Des directives émanant du comité de Londres sur le tri et l'empaquetage des pennes étaient acheminées aux postes de traite. Un message, envoyé de Londres, le 26 mai 1721, à Henry Kelsey, à Fort York, indique très précisément les démarches à suivre dans le prélèvement des plumes.

> Whereas wee have mentioned the Sanding [sending] of goose Quills, wee would have you observe The following directions Viz, Take Six Quills out of Every Wing from The Pinion at Theird ful Length with all the Feathers on, and 8 Quills out of each wing of A Swan all Tyed up hard in Bundles of 120 Each[31].

Dans le journal de Fort Moose, on décrit au jour le jour les activités des hommes qui travaillent au poste de traite. On constate, à la lecture du document, que le tri et l'emballage des pennes ne constituent pas des tâches négligeables et qu'on y consacre de longues heures[32]. Edward Clouston, par exemple, est assigné, durant trois jours consécutifs, en juin 1785, au tri des plumes. C'était une étape importante, car le prix d'une plume à écrire dépendait de sa qualité. La production de juin devait être imposante car, en juillet 1785, le journal rapporte que plusieurs hommes sont affectés à attacher les plumes par paquet. Ce qui semble varier, c'est le nombre de plumes par paquet. Au cours des années, mais surtout lorsque la vente des plumes se fait par des papetiers, il y a une fluctuation constante du nombre de plumes constituant un paquet.

Les plumes demeurent une source de revenu importante et Londres continue d'envoyer ses instructions à leur sujet. Dans une lettre du 24 mai 1821, Londres fait un rapport sur l'arrivée de marchandises diverses et le point 11 est consacré aux plumes reçues :

> More care should be taken in assorting the goose quills than has hitherto been the case: four samples are sent you no. 1 to 4 and the quills should be separated according to these samples, and tied up in bundles of 100 each. The swan quills should not be cut as been the case latterly, this reduces their value more than half they should be shiped in the full lenght as they are pluck'd from the swan wing[33].

Qu'est-ce qui fait la qualité d'une plume ?

La qualité d'une plume dépend de sa position dans l'aile de l'oiseau. Idéalement la plume d'oie est choisie parmi les cinq premières rémiges de l'oiseau[34]. Ces plumes se retrouvent sur la surface portante de l'aile du volatile.

La première plume est appelée « pinion », c'est celle qui se trouve à l'extrémité de l'aileron. Plutôt courte, elle se distingue par la dureté de son corps. Les plumes exposées au vent sont étroites. Celles-là sont particulièrement appréciées de ceux qui aiment écrire d'une main fine. Au cours des années, elles sont de plus en plus appréciées et leur prix de vente connaîtra une importante croissance. La deuxième plume est appelée la « seconde », en raison de sa position. Elle est plus longue de corps que la « pinion » et plus souple. On la reconnaît également à la forme de son plumage. La plume suivante est aussi appelée la « deuxième », mais son corps est plus large que les autres. Ces premières plumes sont considérées les meilleures pour l'écriture. Les autres sont nommées « troisièmes », mais sont en réalité la quatrième et la cinquième. Elles se distinguent des deuxièmes pour n'avoir pas ou peu de courbe à l'extrémité du plumage. Le corps de ces plumes est sensiblement aussi long, mais n'est pas aussi large ni aussi robuste. Elles demeurent d'excellentes plumes à écrire et peuvent être considérées, par certains, comme les meilleures car, étant plus minces, elles peuvent être plus faciles à préparer. Cependant, elles durent moins longtemps. Les autres plumes sont appelées « flags » et « feathers ». Il s'agit des sixième et septième. Le plumage des « flags » est plus large de chaque côté et leur corps, plus étroit. Les plumes qui sont situées près de l'extrémité de l'aile sont les « feathers ». Elles sont petites et minces. Une fois transformées en plumes, elles se vendent bon marché.

Un deuxième élément qui témoigne de la qualité d'une plume est la technique employée dans sa préparation. La méthode classique pour ce faire s'appelle la technique du « hollandage », ou « dutching », en anglais. Cette technique d'apprêt viendrait de Hollande[35]. La plume est d'abord humidifiée afin de lui redonner son élasticité, puis elle est chauffée. Une fois chaude, la plume redevient maniable et elle est nettoyée à l'aide d'un crochet qui en débarrasse le tube des matières graisseuses. Les plumes de la Compagnie de la Baie d'Hudson étaient préparées selon cette méthode. Le *Manitoba Free Press*, de Winnipeg, aurait envoyé à ses lecteurs, à l'occasion de Noël 1904, un livret accompagné d'une plume d'oie[36]. Le feuillet indique qu'il s'agit probablement d'une plume provenant d'une oie sauvage chassée sur les berges de la baie d'Hudson, près de York Factory. Une deuxième méthode, plus simple, voulait que la plume subisse d'abord un trempage pour l'humidifier, puis un séchage dans des cendres chaudes ou du sable chaud. Cette opération permettait de débarrasser le tube de la plume des matières graisseuses qui empêche l'encre de s'y fixer et de s'écouler librement. La dernière étape, similaire aux deux méthodes de préparation, consistait à polir la plume à l'aide d'une peau de poisson. Même parfaitement apprêtée, la plume devait ensuite être taillée. Là aussi, il s'agissait d'un art véritable.

Les plumes peuvent être vendues taillées ou non taillées, selon la préférence de l'acheteur. La taille des plumes devient une véritable industrie et cela est bien apparent si l'on en juge par le nombre de papetiers qui font la promotion de ce service dans les annuaires commerciaux. Pourtant, cette habilité pouvait être développée par l'épistolier qui désirait tailler sa propre plume et, pour cela, il pouvait utiliser les manuels sur l'art d'écrire.

Dans un but à la fois technique et pédagogique apparaissent, en italien, les premiers traités sur l'art d'écrire. Ils donnent des conseils sur la taille de la plume et la préparation de l'encre. Parmi les plus connus, l'œuvre de Giovanni Battista Palatino, *Libro nuovo d'imparare a scrivere*, paru en 1540, et le manuel du père Augustino da Siena, *Opere nella quale si insegna a scrivere varie sorti de lettere*, qui est publié en 1565[37]. Ces ouvrages étaient essentiels pour quiconque devait préparer lui-même sa plume. Certains manuels contiennent même des illustrations. *The Universal Penman*, publié en 1743[38], nous montre une vignette sur laquelle un maître apprend à son élève comment tenir une plume, la tailler et écrire. Le *Pigot and Co. National Commercial Directory*, de 1834, annonce, pour Sheffield, dans le Yorkshire, une catégorie intitulée « Pen and pocket knife manufacturers ». On y dénombre 294 commerçants. Certains indiquent qu'ils vendent également des ciseaux et autres types de couteaux. Leur nombre élevé témoigne bien de leur nécessité auprès de la population. La préparation et la taille des plumes est un art et plusieurs gagnent leur vie à pratiquer cette activité. Pride affirme qu'il faut de nombreuses années de pratique avant d'acquérir l'expérience nécessaire pour tailler une bonne plume à écrire[39]. Avant d'arriver dans les mains de l'épistolier, une plume passe entre celles de six ou sept personnes. Cette manipulation requérait une grande expérience et une habilité certaine.

Lorsque l'épistolier se sert d'une plume d'oie, deux outils lui sont essentiels : le taille-plume, ou canivet, et le grattoir. En effet, les pennes s'usant très vite, leur bec a constamment besoin d'être retaillé. Le taille-plume était une sorte de petit canif tranchant, nécessaire pour continuer à entretenir la pointe de sa plume. Les enluminures nous montrent très bien le scribe tenant d'une main la plume et, de l'autre, le taille-plume. Toutefois, leur rendu artistique est très différent des exemples qui ont survécu et qui sont maintenant conservés dans des collections muséales ou privées. Évidemment, le taille-plume pouvait être décoré et le manche, incrusté de pierreries ou de pierres semi-précieuses, tel l'ivoire ou l'argent, selon la richesse de son propriétaire. Une des premières descriptions et illustrations du taille-plume est donnée par Palatino[40]. Avec les siècles, cet outil évolue et la lame pourra se replier dans le manche[41].

La préparation et l'entretien de la plume sont des tâches difficiles à maîtriser et surtout répétitives. On verra donc apparaître un taille-plumes mécanique qui prépare la pointe de la plume en une seule opération. Ce petit instrument, qui atteint 6 centimètres de hauteur, avait une ouverture dans laquelle on déposait la pointe de la plume. On appuyait ensuite sur un levier qui permettait de trancher la pointe à l'entrée voulue. Un exemple très décoratif, en laiton, datant des années 1725-1750 est conservé au Victoria & Albert Museum de Londres[42]. Le deuxième instrument de l'épistolier, le grattoir, est lui aussi un petit couteau. Les épistoliers qui faisaient des erreurs les biffaient ou encore pouvaient les effacer en utilisant un grattoir. Il avait une lame en forme de feuille bien aiguisée pour gratter la surface du papier.

Le succès des plumes de la Compagnie de la Baie d'Hudson

Au XVIIIe et au XIXe siècles, l'Europe s'approvisionnait en plumes en Norvège, en Irlande, en Suède et en Russie, mais c'étaient celles de la Compagnie de la Baie d'Hudson qui étaient réputées pour leur durabilité et leur qualité. Une publicité de la firme Sir Joseph Causton & Sons, de Londres, précise que les plumes de la CBH sont utilisées par des juristes et des membres du Parlement. Dès les années 1760, une autre publicité, celle-ci de Christopher Henry Edwards, « Pen Cutter and Dealer in Quills », en fait la promotion[43]. Pride, un spécialiste de la taille de plumes, affirme que les plumes d'oies de la CBH sont celles des meilleurs plumassiers pour écrire.

> The geese of Hudson's Bay produce the best quills, they are distingued from others by a black feather and stem; and the barrels of the large Hudson's Bay quills have a thick tint. These pens are very elastic, very durable, and in very respect very valuable[44].

Une publicité de *A. Hayes & Co. Pen-Cutters & Quill-Dressers*, de Liverpool[45], abonde dans le même sens. La mention spécifique de la CBH dans la provenance des plumes témoigne de l'importance que l'on accordait à ces plumes. Hayes indique :

> A.H. & Co. respectfully acquaint their friends and stationers in general, that they have regularly ready for sale a large and elegant assortment of superior dressed Hambro, Hudson's Bay, and English quills and pens …[46]

À elle seule, selon Pride, l'Angleterre utilisait à l'époque neuf millions de plumes d'oie. On distinguait les plumes venant d'Angleterre et d'Irlande et celles d'Europe par l'appellation « plumes d'oie de Hambourg », car cette ville était un important port où s'écoulaient beaucoup des marchandises européennes. Pride soutient que l'usage d'une plume doit être la première considération lors de son achat. Les plus chères ne sont pas destinées à toutes les mains. Certains épistoliers écrivent délicatement et ne pèsent pas trop sur leur plume alors que d'autres ne se soucient aucunement de l'apparence de leur écriture. Quelques-uns préconisent la rapidité et ne veulent pas retailler leur plume fréquemment. Dans ces cas, une plume au corps plus large est nécessaire. Toutefois, ce type de plume s'avèrera plus dispendieux.

Les plumes étaient triées selon leur taille, puis attachées par des fils de coton coloré. La couleur du lien en indiquait la qualité et le prix. Le prix de vente des plumes est basé sur leur niveau de qualité, spécifié par des rubans colorés : rose, rose et vert, rose et mauve, rose, mauve et jaune. La qualité était évaluée par gradation, et cela pouvait aller jusqu'à 19 niveaux. Cela n'empêchait pas certains commerçants peu scrupuleux de dissimuler des plumes de mauvaises qualités à l'intérieur des fagots. Le prix varie entre 12 et 16 shillings, mais il pouvait parfois atteindre les 20 shillings pour 100 plumes[47]. Mais les plumes de la CBH ne se classent aucunement dans cette catégorie. Leur coût varie d'une guinée à 30 shillings, le paquet de 100. D'après Pride, la grande qualité des plumes de la Compagnie justifie leur prix exorbitant quand on les compare aux autres vendues sur le marché. Il reconnaît toutefois que le monopole détenu par la compagnie laisse peu de latitude quant à leur prix de vente. Il mentionne que leur durabilité justifie leur prix et qu'à la longue elles reviennent malgré tout à un prix sensiblement égale à celui des autres plumes.

Le commerce des plumes était pris en charge par des papetiers que l'on connaît sous le nom de « stationers ». Ces papetiers vendent non seulement des instruments d'écriture, des plumes, du papier à lettres et des cartes de visite, mais également des livres. Les plumes pouvaient également être vendues dans des commerces spécialisés dans la préparation des plumes à écrire, tels que les « Quill & Pen Manufacturers ». Dans l'annuaire Pigot de 1822, on compte, uniquement pour la ville de Londres, 27 commerçants inscrits sous cette rubrique[48].

Les plumes sont vendues dans des boîtiers décoratifs, pratique qui semble avoir été de plus en plus populaire dans le dernier quart du XIXe siècle. Certains exhibent le nom du manufacturier tandis que d'autres sont anonymes. Un superbe exemple d'emballage est celui de la Watkin's & McCombie's, qui annonce des plumes de la CBH, « Genuine Hudson's Bay Pens », vers 1880. Le boîtier en carton est richement décoré. L'inscription annonce fièrement : « Patronized by her Majesty the Queen ». Un autre boîtier, qui n'indique aucun nom de marchand, annonce encore des plumes de la CBH : « Genuine Hudson's Bay Quill Pen's Hand Cut ».

Les plumes d'oies de la CBH ont donc constitué un marché très prisé dans le monde des instruments d'écriture. Elles étaient reconnues pour leur qualité et elles étaient vendues chez des marchands réputés. Cette recherche nous a fait découvrir le marché européen de ces plumes. Nous n'avons malheureusement pas trouvé d'informations qui nous permettent de découvrir si ces plumes étaient également vendues en Amérique du Nord. D'après un inventaire des volumes publiés par les libraires et les papetiers de Montréal et de Toronto conservé dans les collections de Bibliothèque et Archives du Canada, nous n'avons pas trouvé de référence aux plumes de la CBH[49]. À ce stade de nos recherches, nous ne croyons pas que ces plumes aient été vendues par des marchands canadiens, car l'identification de leur provenance était l'une des marques de reconnaissance de leur qualité.

Notes

1. *The Saturday Magazine*, No. 355, 13 January 1838, p. 16.
2. Nous aimerions remercier Nicole Castéran pour son travail de repérage de documents relatifs aux plumes produites par la Compagnie de la Baie d'Hudson ainsi que notre collègue au Musée canadien de la poste, John Willis. Toutes les citations sont retranscrites sans modifications.
3. Brandon plaque, The British Museum, M & ME 1978,11-1,1, Department of Medieval and Modern Europe (study collection).
4. Collection de la British Library, f.1v.
5. *The Diary of Samuel Pepys*. A new and complete transcription edited by Robert Latham and William Matthews, volume IV, 1663, Berkeley, University of California, 1971.
6. *The Domestic Life of Thomas Jefferson*, compiled from family letters and reminiscences, published for the Thomas Jefferson Memorial Foundation by the University of Virginia, Charlottesville, 1978, p. 380-381.
7. *The Domestic Life of Thomas Jefferson, op. cit.*, p. 319-320.
8. Headquarters Records, HBCA, PAM, A.6/2 fo. 77.
9. The Publications of the Hudson's Bay Record Society, vol. 1, London, 1958, p. 109. Cité dans Edwin Ernest Rich. *The history of the Hudson's Bay Company, 1670-1870*, London, Hudson's Bay Record Society, 2 volumes, 1958-59.
10. *Hudson's Bay Copy Book of Letters. Commissions Instructions Outward, 1688-1696*, London, The Hudson's Bay Record Society, publié sous la direction de E. E. Rich, 1957.
11. Ibid.
12. *Letters from Hudson Bay 1703-1740*, London, The Hudson's Bay Record Society, 1965.
13. Il serait la personne responsable à Fort York à partir de 1722.
14. *Letters from Hudson Bay 1703-1740, op. cit.*, Lettre 20.
15. *Cumberland House Journals and Inland Journal 1775-1779*, London, The Hudson's Bay Record Society, 1951.
16. Victor Lytwyn, « Pleinement conscients de leur propre importance, les Cris des basses terres de la Baie d'Hudson et la chasse aux oies », dans *Recherches amérindiennes au Québec*, 1994, 24(3), p. 61.
17. Voir, à ce sujet, un feuillet publié par la CBH vers 1817, intitulé *Directions for Curing and Preserving Swan Skins*, PAM, HBCA A.63/22, fo.3 (N13516).
18. *The North American Fur Trade 1804-1821, A Study in the Life-Cycle of a Duopoly.*
19. Bibliothèque et Archives Canada, MG20, HBC Archives, Minute Book, MG20A1, 1808.
20. *London Correspondance Outward, Official,* HBC MG20A6.
21. B.372/d/2, fo.18; B.372/d/1, p. 25, The Hudson's Bay Record Society, 1963.
22. Voir, à ce sujet, Harry G. Lumsden. " The pre-settlement breeding distribution of trumpeter, *cygnus buccinator* and tundra swans in Eastern Canada ", *The Canadian Field-Naturalist*, octobre-décembre 1984.
23. Vol. VI, October 1861, No. 5. Article XXIV, " Recollections of the Swans and Geese of Hudson's Bay ", by George Barnston, of the Hon. Hudson's Bay Company, conférence reproduite dans *The Canadian Naturalist and Geologist*, Montréal, 1861.
24. Ibid., p. 339.
25. B.239/a/101, 25 juillet 1798, f. 42.
26. Lytwyn. *Op. cit.*, p. 54.
27. *Andrew Graham's obserfations on Hudson's Bay 1767-1791*, The Hudson's Bay Record Society, 1969, p. 41.
28. Ibid.
29. *The most respectable place in the territory. Everyday life in Hudson's Bay Company Service York Factory, 1788-1870*. Ottawa, National Historic Parks and Sites, Canadian Parks Services, Environnement Canada, " Studies in archeology, architecture and history ", 1989.

30. Post Records, B.198/a/29, 15 mai 1784, f. 32d.

31. HBCA, PAM, A.6/4 fo. 50.

32. *Moose Fort Journals 1783-85*, ed. by E. E. Rich, London, The Hudson's Bay Record Society, 1954, p. 246.

33. A.6/19, fos.119-20, *Minutes of Council Northern Department of Rupert Land, 1821-1831*, Toronto, The Champlain Society for the Hudson's Bay Record Society, 1940.

34. B. Pride. *The Art of Pen-Cutting, Comprising an history of the invention and first use of pens*, London, 1812, p. 14.

35. Dans *The Art of Pen-Cutting*, Pride mentionne que cette méthode remonte aux années 1760.

36. *A quill from a Canada wild goose*, Manitoba Free Press, Winnipeg, 1904, 16 pages. Numéro spécial remis au bureau de la Manitoba Free Press, Winnipeg, Noël 1904.

37. Augustino Da Siena, réimpression de l'édition de 1568 par Alfred Fairbank, publié par David R. Godine, Boston, 1975.

38. *The Universal Penman, engraved by George Bickman, London, 1743*, réimpression de Dover Publications, New York, 1941.

39. Pride. *Op. cit.*, p. 20.

40. L'œuvre de Palatino est comprise dans *Three Classics of Italian Caligraphy. An Unbridged Reissue of the Writing Books of Arrighi, Tagliente and Palatino*, édition préparée par Oscar Ogg, New York, Dover Publications Inc., 1953, p. 239.

41. *Inventaire général des monuments et des richesses artistiques de la France, principes d'analyse scientifique, objets civils domestiques, vocabulaire*, Paris, Imprimerie nationale, 1984, p. 542.

42. Quill pen cutter, M.418-1936.

43. Carte d'affaires, British Museum, Head Collection.

44. *The Art of Pen-Cutting, op. cit.*, p. 11.

45. Publicité parue dans l'annuaire *Pigot & Co. London and provinces new commercial directory*, Manchester, 1822.

46. Ibid., note 45.

47. *The Art of Pen-Cutting, op. cit.*, p. 13.

48. *Pigot and Co., op. cit.*

49. Voici les plus anciens pour les villes de Montréal et de Toronto : Thomas Doige. *An alphabetical list of merchants, traders and housekeepers residing in Montreal*, Montreal, printed by James Lane, 1819; *The city of Toronto and the Home District commercial directory and register with almanach and calendar for 1837; being first after leap-year, and the eight year of the reign of His Majesty King William the Fourth*, [compiled] by Geo. Walton, Toronto U.C., printed by T. Dalton and W. J. Coates, 1837.

SOUS LE SCEAU DU SECRET– CORRESPONDANCE CHIFFRÉE EN NOUVELLE-FRANCE PENDANT LA GUERRE DE SEPT ANS

8

Nicole Castéran

Résumé

Depuis la plus haute antiquité, l'homme employa les écritures secrètes pour exercer son pouvoir dans ses diverses sphères d'activités, qu'il s'agit de politique, de guerre, de commerce, de religion, de science ou même d'amour. En France, le cryptage de la correspondance officielle connut son heure de gloire sous le règne de Louis XIV et, à un moindre degré, sous celui de Louis XV. Pendant les périodes de guerre, et elles furent nombreuses, les autorités métropolitaines choisissaient de « chiffrer » leur correspondance avec leurs représentants coloniaux pour éviter que les renseignements stratégiques ne parvinssent à la connaissance de l'ennemi.

Un corpus de lettres chiffrées et des codes provenant des archives françaises du ministère de la Marine et des Colonies et de celui de la Guerre permettent de pénétrer le mode de transmission des renseignements secrets officiels en Nouvelle-France pendant la guerre de Sept Ans. Pourquoi chiffrait-on ? À qui accordait-on le privilège d'une correspondance chiffrée ? Quels types de codes utilisait-on et que chiffrait-on ? Voilà autant de questions auxquelles cet article tentera de répondre.

Abstract

From antiquity, humankind has used secret writing to maintain power in various spheres of activity such as war, commerce, religion, science—and even love. In France, the encryption of official correspondence first came to prominence during the reign of Louis XIV and, to a lesser degree, the reign of Louis XV. In times of war—and there were many during both reigns—France's metropolitan authorities chose to encrypt correspondence with their colonial representatives, in order to keep strategic information from falling into the hands of the enemy.

A body of encrypted letters and codes from the archives of France's ministry of the marine and the colonies and the minstry of war have enabled us to see how official secrets were transmitted in New France during the Seven Years War. Why was encryption used? Who was entitled to encrypted communications? What kinds of codes were used, and what was encoded? These are just some of the questions this article attempts to answer.

Introduction

Les lettres chiffrées représentent un aspect tout à fait passionnant des échanges épistolaires. Elles constituent aussi un champ de recherche très vaste, les écritures secrètes ayant servi au cours des âges aux chefs d'État et aux diplomates, mais aussi aux amants, aux adeptes de sociétés secrètes, aux scientifiques et aux commerçants. C'est aussi un objet d'étude relativement peu défriché[1] en raison même du mystère qui l'entoure et de la rareté des sources.

En temps de guerre, « le secret est l'âme de toute entreprise », devisait Napoléon[2]. Il est de fait que le secret constitue une arme redoutable, et parfois même décisive : sans secret point de surprise. Une cinquantaine de pièces provenant des archives françaises du ministère de la Marine et des Colonies et de celui de la Guerre[3] permettent de pénétrer le mode de transmission des renseignements secrets officiels en Nouvelle-France pendant la guerre de Sept Ans (1754-1760). Pourquoi chiffrait-on ? À qui accordait-on le privilège d'une correspondance chiffrée ? Quels types de codes utilisait-on et que chiffrait-on ? Voilà autant de questions auxquelles cet article apportera quelques éléments de réponse. Au préalable, il convient toutefois de tracer les origines de cette pratique en Europe, et surtout en France.

La petite histoire de la cryptographie

Depuis des temps immémoriaux, l'homme a usé du secret dans ses diverses sphères d'activités. L'écriture elle-même ne fut-elle pas, à ses origines, une forme de communication à l'adresse exclusive d'un cercle restreint d'initiés ? Au fil du temps, cependant, le secret de ces signes finit par s'éventer et on dut imaginer d'autres moyens pour préserver la confidentialité des messages. Ainsi naquit la cryptographie, technique qui consiste à brouiller l'écriture de façon à rendre le message inintelligible aux personnes qui n'en sont pas les destinataires. Les méthodes de brouillage se classent en deux grandes catégories : la transposition et la substitution. La transposition consiste à bouleverser l'ordre des lettres, mais à en conserver la valeur. L'écriture en dents de scie en est un exemple : il suffit d'écrire le message en disposant une lettre sur une ligne; la suivante, sur une autre ligne. La substitution consiste à modifier la valeur des lettres tout en préservant leur ordre – par exemple, « mot » devient NPU avec un alphabet de substitution décalé d'un rang[4]. C'est ce deuxième procédé qui retiendra ici l'attention.

L'antiquité fournit de nombreux exemples de cryptage par substitution. Le plus ancien cryptogramme connu remonte au XVIe siècle avant J.-C. Il cache non pas un secret d'État mais, plus prosaïquement, la recette de vernis d'un potier mésopotamien. Au Ier siècle avant J.-C., César employait un alphabet décalé de trois rangs : *Alea jacta est* devenant ainsi DOHD MDFWD HVW[5]. Dans l'occident médiéval, la généralisation de l'analphabétisme, le cloisonnement des royaumes et la difficulté des transports ne favorisèrent guère les écritures secrètes, qui tombèrent dans l'oubli. Cependant, sur le pourtour méridional de la Méditerranée et au Proche-Orient se développait une brillante civilisation arabe, où s'épanouit la cryptographie. La contribution exceptionnelle des Arabes réside dans l'invention de la *cryptanalyse* ou *décryptement*, c'est-à-dire la science qui consiste à découvrir le texte clair sans posséder le code[6].

À la renaissance, les cités italiennes reprirent le flambeau. La prospérité dont jouissait la péninsule au XVe siècle suscita le renouveau des arts et des sciences. Véritable mosaïque de cités-États rivales, l'Italie était le théâtre de sombres complots et d'intenses tractations diplomatiques qui remirent à l'honneur les écritures secrètes. Cet art se répandit dans les États européens voisins au XVIe siècle et explosa littéralement aux XVIIe et XVIIIe siècles. À cette époque, la plupart des chancelleries d'Europe utilisaient un procédé de substitution monoalphabétique amélioré, mis en place pendant la renaissance par un dénommé Lavinde. Il s'agissait d'un immense répertoire, appelé nomenclateur, qui comprenait un alphabet de substitution (où chaque lettre au clair est représentée par un signe) et une liste de codes pour certains mots. Ce procédé domina en Occident pendant 450 ans, parce qu'il alliait un grand degré de sécurité à une relative facilité d'emploi.

En France, c'est à Antoine Rossignol et, dans une moindre mesure, à son fils Bonaventure, que l'on doit l'établissement du chiffre français, qui brilla en Europe au XVIIe siècle, se transmit au siècle suivant et perdura même, par certains aspects, jusqu'au XXe siècle. De par sa nature secrète, ce service n'a pas conservé d'archives, de sorte que l'on doit se contenter d'informations éparses[7]. Nous savons que Rossignol avait mis au point une méthode de chiffrement par substitution extrêmement poussée et sûre pour l'époque. Ce mathématicien originaire d'Albi avait perfectionné le système élaboré par Lavinde. Il avait en effet dressé un nomenclateur où des nombres[8] (on en comptait plusieurs centaines) pouvaient représenter une lettre, un groupe de lettres ou un mot entier. Certains étaient des nuls, c'est-à-dire qu'ils ne représentaient rien, leur rôle étant de déconcerter les décrypteurs. Pour la même raison, il eut l'idée de créer des répertoires désordonnés, c'est-à-dire que les nombres composant la partie chiffrée étaient choisis au hasard, ce qui nécessitait deux tables : l'une, rangée par ordre alphabétique, servait à chiffrer; l'autre, par ordre numérique, servait à déchiffrer. C'est ce type de table qui était en usage pendant la guerre de Sept Ans.

Sous la dynastie des Rossignol, deux types de chiffres avaient cours[9]. 1) Les « grands chiffres », qui comportaient près de 600 groupes, servaient au roi et à ses ministres pour communiquer avec les commandants en chef des armées. Aucune de ces tables ne subsista dans les archives et il fallut attendre la fin du XIXe siècle pour qu'un décrypteur parvînt à percer le secret du « Grand Chiffre de Louis XIV » et à en reconstituer le répertoire. 2) Les « petits chiffres », moins étoffés avec leurs quelque 370 groupes, étaient destinés à la correspondance avec les gouverneurs et les intendants. Ils étaient modifiés tous les trois ans. Les détenteurs avaient pour consigne de renvoyer au bureau central les tables désuètes afin qu'elles y fussent brûlées et de conserver celles qu'ils utilisaient en sûreté[10]. Ils ne devaient, sous aucun prétexte, les transporter avec eux lors de leurs déplacements. Après la disparition des Rossignol, au XVIIIe siècle, le chiffre français perdit de sa splendeur.

À cette époque, Louis XV se livrait à des indiscrétions notoires sur les correspondances diplomatiques, voire sur celles des particuliers. Son Cabinet noir, ou Bureau du Dedans, comme on l'appelait aussi, réunissait une poignée de mystérieux spécialistes triés sur le volet, qui s'affairaient, dans le secret le plus strict, à briser et à contrefaire les sceaux, et à décrypter, à traduire et à copier des missives[11]. On continuait donc de chiffrer et de décrypter plus que jamais, mais sans apporter d'amélioration notable au système établi au siècle précédent[12]. On se laissait même déclasser par les autres puissances, comme le soulignait en 1758 le marquis d'Argenson (frère du ministre de la Guerre, dont il sera question plus loin) : « J'ai appris que la correspondance des Ministres étrangers devient de plus en plus difficile à pénétrer par le Cabinet. Les Anglais chiffrent avec une si grande recherche que l'on ne peut les lire. Le Roi de Sardaigne met aux lettres de ses ministres un sceau qu'il applique lui-même. Il le met avec une presse en sorte qu'on ne peut décacheter et refermer les paquets sans que cela paraisse. On ne le tente même plus[13]. »

L'Angleterre du XVIIe siècle avait aussi son « Rossignol » en la personne de John Wallis. Reconnu comme le plus grand mathématicien anglais avant Newton, cet ecclésiastique était aussi un décrypteur de génie. Charles II se l'attacha en le nommant aumônier du roi. Au siècle suivant, c'est la dynastie des Willes qui régna sur la *Decyphering Branch* avec un succès remarquable. Le cabinet noir le plus redouté d'Europe demeurait cependant celui de Vienne. Aucun chiffre, en quelque langue que ce fût, ne résistait longtemps à son armada de décrypteurs et de traducteurs. Les autorités autrichiennes poussaient même l'effronterie jusqu'à vendre à d'autres États les versions au clair des correspondances diplomatiques interceptées[14].

Puis la révolution française et le vent de liberté qui se mit à souffler sur toutes les monarchies européennes eurent raison des cabinets noirs, lesquels fermèrent leurs portes les uns après les autres, du moins officiellement. La cryptographie entama un long déclin. Elle ne se raviva réellement qu'à la fin du XIXe siècle sous l'impulsion des nouveaux moyens de communication qu'étaient le télégraphe et, au siècle suivant, la radio pour resplendir à nouveau au cours de la Première, mais surtout de la Seconde Guerre mondiale[15].

La nécessité de chiffrer

«Les intérêts des Anglais opposez aux nostres, et les piques qu'il y a entre les marchands et les nostres, demandent, Monseigneur, que vous ayez la bonté de m'envoyer un chiffre pour vous pouvoir rendre compte plus librement de toutes choses sur les intérêts du pays[16].» Cette demande du gouverneur de la Nouvelle-France, Denonville, au ministre Seignelay date de 1686, année de la déclaration de la guerre de la Ligue d'Augsbourg. En 1734, alors que couvait déjà la guerre de Succession d'Autriche, Beauharnois expliquait à son ministre, dans une missive partiellement chiffrée : « Je continuerai de me servir du chiffre dans les affaires de conséquence de manière que nos voisins ne puissent connaître nos forces, ni l'état de cette colonie[17]. » Voilà confirmé ce que l'on pouvait aisément supposer : les autorités françaises, de part et d'autre de l'Atlantique, chiffraient leur correspondance lorsque la tension montait entre elles et les Anglais. La guerre de Sept Ans, qui fut l'ultime combat entre les deux puissances pour la possession du Canada, nous a laissé un riche corpus de cette correspondance secrète.

Déclenchée par une escarmouche dans la vallée de la Belle-Rivière (Ohio), en 1754, cette guerre[18] dégénéra, deux ans plus tard, en un conflit de grande ampleur opposant la France, l'Autriche et la Russie à l'Angleterre et à la Prusse. L'Amérique septentrionale en constituait l'un des principaux enjeux. Sur le théâtre américain, les hostilités durèrent de 1754 à 1760. Si les Anglais avaient la maîtrise incontestée des mers et l'avantage du nombre, les Français détenaient une carte maîtresse : leur alliance avec de nombreuses tribus amérindiennes. Ils ne se firent pas faute d'utiliser cette arme redoutable pour tenir en échec un ennemi autrement plus puissant qu'eux. Les raids commandés que les Amérindiens effectuaient dans les établissements anglais, de la Virginie à la Nouvelle-Écosse, terrorisaient les populations et même l'armée britannique. Comme en plaisantait volontiers le gouverneur Duquesne en 1754, « dix chevelures levées arrêteroient une armée anglaise[19] ».

Toutefois, leur chance se tarit à partir de 1758. Sous la houlette du ministre britannique William Pitt, les Anglais, excédés par les humiliantes défaites qu'avaient essuyées leurs généraux, de 1755 à 1757, décidèrent de mettre en œuvre tous les moyens à leur disposition pour s'emparer du Canada. Pour leur part, les autorités françaises se laissèrent convaincre par Berryer, le nouveau ministre de la Marine et des Colonies, d'abandonner à son sort la lointaine Nouvelle-France, qui coûterait toujours plus qu'elle ne rapporterait. En 1758, Bougainville, qui venait réclamer à Berryer des secours pour le Canada, obtint pour toute réponse « qu'on ne cherchait point à sauver les écuries quand le feu était à la maison[20] ». Les Français se trouvèrent ainsi privés de vivres et de secours. N'étant plus en mesure de procurer aux Amérindiens les articles de traite propres à entretenir leur amitié, ils virent leur réseau d'alliances se désagréger en peu de temps. Leur défaite devenait inéluctable. Cela n'échappa guère à Vaudreuil, qui faisait le constat suivant en novembre 1758 : « D'ailleurs, telle est notre situation, la bataille perdue entraîne la perte de la colonie, la bataille gagnée ne fait que la différer[21]. »

Le parti que surent tirer les Anglais de leur suprématie maritime en entravant la communication entre la France et ses colonies eut de lourdes conséquences sur la transmission de la correspondance officielle. Avant même la déclaration de guerre, la formidable armada britannique se livra à des actes d'intimidation, voire à des attaques ostensibles, sur des navires français. Pendant l'été 1755, le capitaine de la *Geneviève* se plaignit par exemple, à son arrivée à Nantes, du fait que cinq vaisseaux anglais « l'ont visité et [ont] décacheté plusieurs lettres [et] qu'ils en ont gardé trois[22] ». À la même époque, l'amiral anglais Boscawen captura l'*Alcide* et le *Lis*, qui faisaient partie de l'escadre française chargée du transport de troupes au Canada. C'est alors que des papiers secrets transportés sur l'*Alcide* tombèrent aux mains des Anglais, grâce aux bons soins de l'espion français Thomas Pichon dont nous reparlerons plus loin[23].

Les prises se multiplièrent après 1756, date de la déclaration de guerre officielle. « Les Anglais ont jusqu'à présent pris la moitié des vaisseaux destinés à ce continent. Encore s'ils rendaient les lettres[24] », confiait, en 1757, Bougainville à sa mère. L'année suivante, Doreil avisait son ministre qu'il attendait toujours 24 des 36 navires partis de Bordeaux. Ce commissaire ordonnateur des guerres exprimait avec justesse l'inégalité des forces en présence : « La mer est couverte de corsaires Anglois et nous n'en avons pas un seul. Ces

Corsaires sont soutenus par des vaisseaux de guerre, et à peine donne-t'on une frégate pour escorte à douze de nos marchands[25]. » Étant donné la situation, on multipliait les précautions. Vaudreuil expliquait au ministre : « J'ai donné ordre au capitaine de faire route la plus convenable pour éviter l'ennemi et gagner le premier port de France et au cas où il ne peut éviter d'être pris de jeter nos dépêches et celles des particuliers à la mer[26]. »

Malgré l'infériorité de leur flotte, les Français n'en réussirent pas moins quelques coups d'éclat. En 1759, par exemple, ils saisirent des papiers hautement stratégiques : « Il vient de m'être remis un paquet qui a été trouvé sur une prise angloise revenant de la Nouvelle York : j'y ai vu un projet d'attaque par le haut du fleuve dressé par le Sr Montresor, Lieutenant Colonel Ingénieur en chef au département de New York et approuvé par le Général Amherst. Je me hâte de vous en faire passer une copie et je vous en ferai passer d'autres par d'autres occasions afin que vous soyés informé des raisons de l'Ennemi[27] », écrivait le ministre à Vaudreuil. Enfin, on ne peut passer sous silence l'aventure rocambolesque du commandant du *Machault*, chargé, en 1760, de transporter les paquets de la Cour au Canada. Voyageant de conserve avec cinq navires marchands à destination de Québec, cette frégate captura un bâtiment britannique dans le golfe. Les lettres saisies les informèrent qu'une escadre anglaise les avait devancés dans le fleuve. Pour éviter de se jeter dans la gueule du loup, ils se replièrent à la baie des Chaleurs. De là, ils envoyèrent un fantassin livrer les lettres de la Cour à Québec. Ils attendirent pendant plusieurs semaines l'arrivée des réponses, puis remirent le cap vers la France. Peu après leur départ, ils furent arraisonnés et capturés par des vaisseaux anglais, mais le commandant du *Machault* parvint *in extremis* à s'enfuir sur une goélette acadienne et à apporter les dépêches du Canada à Versailles[28]. Aussi heureuse qu'inespérée, cette issue n'en souligne pas moins les innombrables périls qu'encouraient les vaisseaux français pendant la guerre de Sept Ans et la nécessité, pour les ministres et leurs représentants coloniaux, de crypter leur correspondance.

La complaisance du chiffre

Le corpus de documents étudié a permis de reconstituer, dans ses grandes lignes, le réseau des correspondants détenant un code ou, comme on le disait alors, jouissant de la « complaisance du chiffre », pendant la guerre de Sept Ans. Il existait en réalité deux réseaux officiels : celui du ministère de la Marine et des Colonies et celui du ministère de la Guerre, chacun disposant d'un bureau du chiffre apparemment indépendant, qui élaborait ses propres nomenclateurs et les distribuait à ses représentants coloniaux de haut rang.

Les quatre ministres de la Marine qui se succédèrent de 1754 à 1760 – Machault, Mauras, Massiac et Berryer – entretinrent une correspondance chiffrée avec le gouverneur de la Nouvelle-France Duquesne[29], puis avec Vaudreuil, qui le remplaça en 1755. Comme le commandait la prudence, les répertoires étaient fréquemment changés. En 1756, le ministre écrivait à Vaudreuil : « Je vous envoie, Monsieur, un chiffre que j'ay fait faire pour vous[30]. » On lui en fit parvenir un nouveau en 1757. Dans son accusé de réception, Vaudreuil fit la remarque suivante qui trahissait son ignorance des principes élémentaires de sécurité : « Je n'ai, Monseigneur, reçu le chiffre que dans votre première. Si vous

Figure 8.1 Lettre chiffrée de Vaudreuil au ministre de la Marine. À son arrivée au ministère, la lettre passait d'abord chez le déchiffreur, qui inscrivait en marge le texte au clair. Elle était ensuite remise au premier commis, qui la résumait à l'intention du ministre. À remarquer, les mots en clair apparaissant dans le texte chiffré (« duplicata » à la 4e ligne), procédé expéditif qui contrevenait aux règles de sécurité.

France, Centre des Archives d'Outre-Mer, AOM. COL C11A, 104, fol. 79.

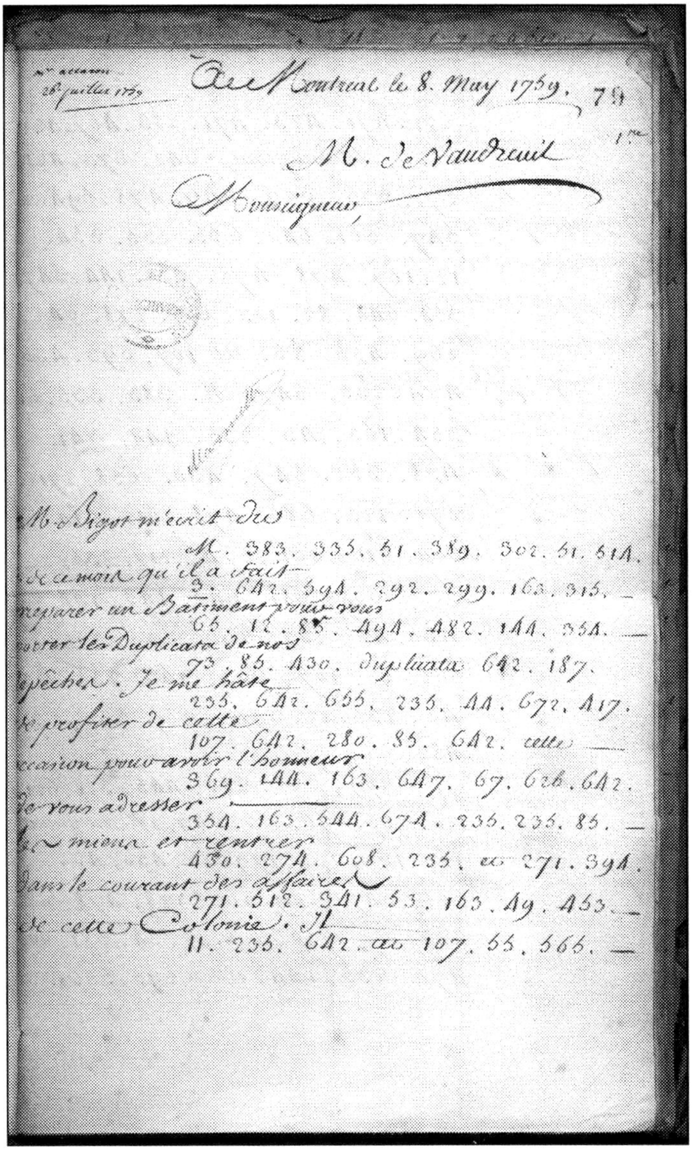
Au Montreal le 8. May 1759. 79

M. de Vaudreuil

Monseigneur,

M. Bigot m'écrit du
M. 383. 335. 61. 389. 302. 61. 614.
ce mois qu'il a fait
3. 642. 594. 292. 299. 163. 315.
préparer un Batiment pour vous
65. 12. 85. 494. 482. 144. 354.
porter les Duplicata de nos
73. 85. 430. duplicata 642. 187.
dépêches. Je me hâte
235. 642. 655. 236. 44. 672. 417.
de profiter de cette
107. 642. 280. 85. 642. celle
occasion pour avoir l'honneur
369. 144. 163. 647. 67. 626. 642.
de vous adresser
354. 163. 544. 674. 236. 235. 85.
le mieux et rentrer
430. 274. 608. 235. et 271. 394.
dans le courant des affaires
271. 512. 341. 53. 163. 49. 455.
de cette Colonie. Il
11. 236. 642. et 107. 55. 566.

me l'avez envoyé par duplicata il ne m'est point parvenu[31]. » On n'envoyait jamais de nomenclateurs par duplicata, leur perte entraînant automatiquement leur nullité. Le gouverneur de l'Isle Royale, Drucourt, correspondait également en chiffre avec le ministre[32]. Il ne semble cependant pas que M. Bigot, intendant de la Nouvelle-France, ni M. Prévost, commissaire ordonnateur à Louisbourg, aient eu ce privilège, malgré le rôle de premier plan que jouaient ces deux personnages dans l'administration coloniale. En tout cas, rien ne l'indique dans les fonds étudiés, où les seules lettres chiffrées à leur intention sont conjointes avec le gouverneur. En revanche, le commandant des troupes de terre au Canada (Dieskau, en 1755; Montcalm, de 1755 à 1759; Lévis, de 1759 à 1760), relevant pourtant du ministère de la Guerre, détenait un code de la Marine. Il pouvait ainsi

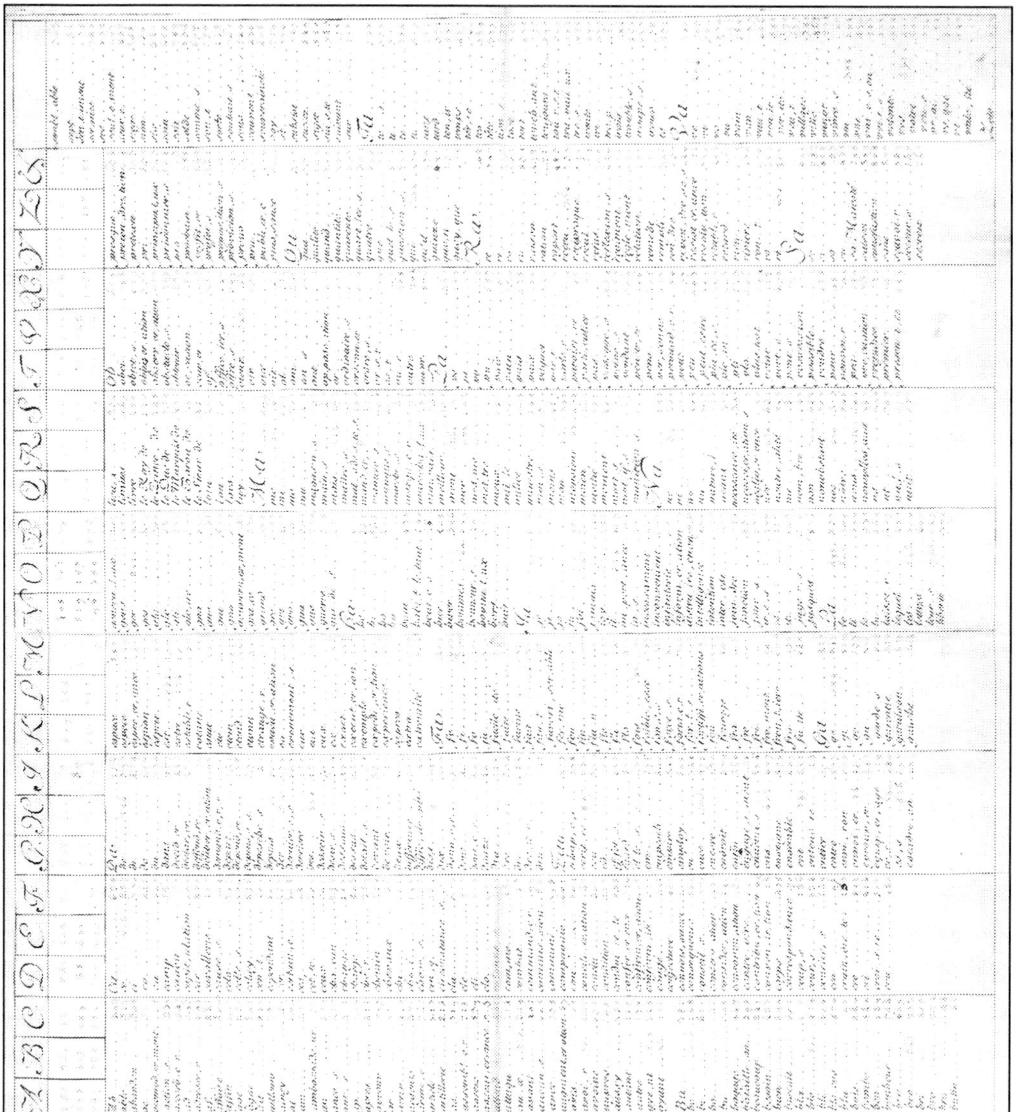

Figure 8.2 Section de la table chiffrante du code du ministère de la Guerre entre Montcalm et le ministre d'Argenson (1757), imprimée sur feuille cartonnée (42 x 51cm).

Bibliothèque et Archives Canada, MG18 K8, vol. 2, pt1, p. 229.

rendre compte au ministre de la Marine de ses opérations militaires. Nous n'avons trouvé aucun document à cet effet concernant le baron de Dieskau, mais le marquis de Montcalm reçut plusieurs nomenclateurs de ce ministère, différents de ceux de Vaudreuil. En 1757, Moras lui écrivait : « Vous trouverez ci-joint, Monsieur, un nouveau chiffre dont vous vous servirez à l'avenir pour les détails particuliers que vous pourrez avoir à me confier, et vous aurez agréable de me renvoyer celui qui vous a été remis l'année dernière[33]. » Ici encore le renvoi du répertoire au bureau central, où l'on aurait dû en principe le détruire, est conforme aux précautions mises en place au siècle précédent par Rossignol.

Berryer prit les rênes de la Marine et des Colonies en novembre 1758 avec la ferme intention de mettre fin à la corruption qui rongeait l'administration coloniale. Très mal disposé à l'égard des administrateurs du Canada, il subordonna Vaudreuil à Montcalm et ne laissa à Bigot aucun doute sur ce qu'il pensait de ses dépenses excessives. Ancien lieutenant de police, Berryer encourageait la délation et dépêcha même un espion en 1759 : sous le couvert de fonctions administratives, Querdisien de Trémais avait en effet pour mission de procurer au ministre les preuves irréfutables des malversations commises par l'intendant Bigot et ses affidés[34]. Il communiquait avec Berryer au moyen d'un chiffre particulier[35]. Enfin, ajoutons à ces correspondants du ministère de la Marine, le comte Dubois de la Motte, chef de l'escadre envoyée, en 1757, à la défense de Louisbourg, qui reçut une lettre chiffrée du ministre[36].

Durant cette période troublée, plusieurs personnages se suivirent également à la tête du ministère de la Guerre : le comte d'Argenson, le marquis de Paulmy (neveu du premier) et le maréchal de Belleisle. À ce ministère, on dotait d'un chiffre le commandant de l'armée de terre au Canada et le commissaire ordonnateur (Doreil, de 1755 à 1759, puis Bernier). Les codes utilisés par Dieskau, Montcalm et Doreil subsistent dans les archives de la Guerre. Conçus selon un même modèle mais tous distincts, ils étaient plus élaborés que ceux de la Marine. On les changeait, semble-t-il, moins souvent. Doreil, par exemple, utilisa le même chiffre durant toute la durée de son séjour. « Il m'avoit été remis en partant de la Cour un chiffre commun avec le M. le Comte d'Argenson dont je me suis servi avec ma correspondance avec ce ministre et avec M. le marquis de Paulmy. Je m'en sers avec le Maréchal de Belleisle et je vais m'en servir avec vous, Monsieur, parce ce que je suis persuadé qu'il est au bureau de M. de Fumeron[37] [fonctionnaire chargé de la correspondance avec le Canada] », explique Doreil à M. de Cremille, adjoint du ministre Belleisle.

En marge de ces réseaux officiels s'opéraient des échanges secrets de lettres destinés à échapper aux rouages du ministère et, peut-être même, aux effractions des correspondances perpétrées par le Cabinet noir. Ainsi Doreil possédait-il un chiffre particulier avec M. de Paulmy, que celui-ci lui avait fait remettre à Brest en 1755 – Paulmy était alors adjoint au ministre de la Guerre pour les affaires du Canada. En 1757, alors que Paulmy devint lui-même ministre, il proposa à Montcalm : « J'espère que vous voudrez bien indépendamment de votre relation ordinaire avec le ministre de la Guerre, en avoir avec moi une personnelle et secrète; mon oncle [le ministre précédent, le comte d'Argenson] m'a remis une adresse et un petit chiffre qui vous servira pour cet effet. » Il faut dire qu'à cette époque tous – même, et peut-être surtout, ceux qui se trouvaient dans l'entourage du roi – se méfiaient de Jannel, homme de confiance du monarque et chef tout-puissant du Cabinet noir, de 1752 à 1768. De par ses fonctions occultes et l'ascendant qu'il exerçait sur le roi et sa maîtresse, Mme de Pompadour, ce personnage ténébreux « tenait à vrai dire dans ses mains la faveur, la fortune, l'existence des plus grands[38] ». Le comte d'Argenson, qui cumulait les fonctions de ministre de la Guerre et de surintendant des Postes, en fit d'ailleurs les frais : il tomba en disgrâce en 1757, à la suite d'une manœuvre du Sr Jannel[39].

Pendant la guerre de Sept Ans, le réseau de correspondance secrète « officiel » était donc le suivant : d'une part, le ministre de la Marine communiquait régulièrement sous le couvert d'un chiffre avec le gouverneur général de la Nouvelle-France, le gouverneur de Louisbourg et le commandant des troupes de terre; d'autre part, le ministre de la Guerre correspondait avec le commandant des troupes de terre et le commissaire ordonnateur des guerres. Ainsi donc quatre personnes seulement disposaient d'un chiffre du ministère de la Marine ou du ministère de la Guerre, ou des deux dans le cas du commandant des troupes de terre. Pour des motifs évidents de sécurité, on accordait ce privilège à un nombre très restreint de personnes. Même l'ingénieur en chef, M. de Pontleroy, devait passer par Doreil, Montcalm ou Vaudreuil pour faire chiffrer ses mémoires à l'intention des ministres[40].

Les types de codes

Nous avons trouvé[41] sept codes appartenant à Montcalm, à Vaudreuil, à Doreil et à Dieskau, que nous pouvons classer en trois catégories : les codes du ministère de la Marine, les codes du ministère de la Guerre et un code particulier. Il s'agit, dans tous les cas, de nomenclateurs issus du système mis au point par Rossignol, un siècle auparavant.

Nous disposons de deux nomenclateurs de la Marine[42] : celui de Vaudreuil de 1757 et celui de Montcalm de 1758. Dans le fonds du chevalier de Lévis, il existe un deuxième exemplaire du code de Montcalm de 1758, probablement l'exemplaire de Montcalm lui-même, dont s'est certainement servi Lévis quand il a pris sa place. Ces deux nomenclateurs comptent 700 groupes. La table chiffrante comprend trois parties : un alphabet de 25 cases (il y manque la lettre « w »); un répertoire alphabétique de groupes de lettres et de mots; une liste de noms propres. On a constitué les nomenclateurs de Vaudreuil et de Montcalm à partir d'un même modèle (même alphabet et même répertoire), mais on les a personnalisés en donnant à chacun d'eux des codes (nombres de substitution) différents. Ayant à composer des nomenclateurs pour divers correspondants, les secrétaires du chiffre se servaient donc d'une table chiffrante modèle qu'ils avaient élaborée en fonction des besoins de leur ministère. Pour chaque correspondant, ils attribuaient des codes distincts, choisis au hasard : on peut aisément les imaginer puisant à l'aveuglette dans une boîte contenant des jetons numérotés de 1 à 700 et inscrire l'un à la suite de l'autre, sur leur table chiffrante, les numéros tirés. Une fois ce travail effectué, il était facile de composer la table déchiffrante : sur une table déjà préparée, il suffisait de consigner, vis-à-vis les nombres de 1 à 700, disposés en colonnes, la lettre ou groupe de lettres correspondant. Seule la liste des noms propres variait selon le correspondant auquel on destinait la table. Ainsi, la liste de Vaudreuil compte 36 groupes, dont plusieurs noms de tribus puisqu'il incombait au gouverneur de négocier avec les Amérindiens, tandis que celle de Montcalm n'en contenait que 21.

Dans le fonds du ministère de la Guerre se trouvent les codes de Doreil (1755), de Dieskau (1755) et de Montcalm (1756). Les préposés au chiffre de ce ministère disposaient aussi de tables modèles, qu'il leur suffisait de remplir pour confectionner les nomenclateurs de chacun de leur correspondant. Contrairement aux tables modèles du ministère de la Marine, qui étaient recopiées à la main à chaque fois, celles de la Guerre étaient imprimées; on peut d'ailleurs y lire la mention « Gravées par M^{tre} d^e Vincent ». Ces nomenclateurs comportent 900 groupes. Ils se divisent en trois parties. 1) Un alphabet de 25 cases, qui diffère légèrement de celui de la Marine. 2) Une liste de 70 noms propres fréquemment utilisés (personnes, bataillons, régions d'Amérique du Nord, îles, cours d'eau, villes, peuples); dressée à l'intention des correspondants d'Amérique du Nord, cette liste était manuscrite; les noms propres ne figurant pas dans cette liste étaient simplement écrits avec les codes de l'alphabet ou du répertoire. 3) Un répertoire de 770 syllabes ou mots. On y remarque quelques particularités par rapport aux nomenclateurs de la Marine : on attribue un même code à plusieurs mots ayant la même racine, le contexte de la phrase indiquant lequel choisir lors du déchiffrement (par exemple, les mots *favori, favoriser, favorable* correspondent au nombre 6 dans le nomenclateur de Montcalm); on affecte aussi un même code pour un mot au singulier et au pluriel, alors que dans les tables de la Marine, le chiffreur devait indiquer la marque du pluriel par un code distinct; on donne deux codes différents à certains mots ou groupes de lettres utilisés fréquemment (par exemple, dans le nomenclateur de Doreil, le mot *comme* est rendu par 829 et 345); enfin, on inclut des nombres nuls ainsi que des nombres qui ont pour rôle d'annuler celui qui les précède.

À côté des nomenclateurs élaborés par les fonctionnaires de la Marine et par ceux de la Guerre circulaient des « chiffres particuliers »; nous l'avons vu, par exemple, entre Montcalm et Paulmy. Le fonds du maréchal de Lévis nous livre le code qu'employa Bougainville en 1759 pour rendre compte à Montcalm de sa mission à la Cour. Son supérieur l'avait en effet dépêché en France pour qu'il plaide sa cause dans la querelle qui l'opposait à Vaudreuil. Inspiré du nomenclateur de la Guerre, dont il est, de fait, une version abrégée et simplifiée, ce petit chiffre manuscrit est ordonné, c'est-à-dire qu'il ne présente qu'une seule table servant à la fois à chiffrer et à déchiffrer : aux groupes de lettres ou mots classés par ordre alphabétique correspondent les nombres rangés par ordre numérique. On y trouve également une longue liste de noms propres (personnages de la Cour et du Canada, pays, peuples, toponymes), une liste de noms de charges et une autre intitulée « Mots omis [?]», ainsi que des chiffres nuls et des chiffres annulant celui qui précède. Montcalm aurait-il lui-même forgé ce petit code pour l'occasion ou s'agit-il du fameux « petit chiffre » que M. de Paulmy lui avait discrètement remis ? Il nous est impossible de le dire. Chose certaine, Bougainville le jugeait infrangible, puisqu'il exprimait en ces termes ses impressions : « Le Roi nul, madame la marquise toute-puissante…[43] »

Les chiffreurs et les déchiffreurs

Le cryptage des correspondances posait un dilemme : d'une part, l'opération de chiffrement et de déchiffrement était dévoreuse de temps; d'autre part, les règles élémentaires de sécurité interdisaient d'affecter un grand nombre de personnes à cette tâche.

On le sait, des personnages comme Vaudreuil, Montcalm et Doreil héritaient, de par leurs fonctions, d'une lourde correspondance. Montcalm se plaignait régulièrement d'être « exactement accablé d'écriture[44] ». En novembre 1757, il confiait à Lévis : « J'achève cette lettre qui a été interrompue ce matin par des ennuyeux oisifs qui trouvaient fort extraordinaire que je ne fusse pas visible ayant eu à écrire par triplicata : neuf lettres à Paulmy, avec divers mémoires, dix au Moras, soixante-quinze au moins par duplicata à des particuliers[45]. » S'ils disposaient de secrétaires pour les soulager, ils n'en consacraient pas moins de longues heures à dicter ou à rédiger de leur main de nombreuses missives. Nous savons que Doreil et Montcalm chiffraient eux-mêmes[46], mais ils ne pouvaient suffire à la tâche. Même si nous n'en avons trouvé aucune preuve dans les documents, il ne fait aucun doute qu'au moins leur premier secrétaire participait au chiffrement et au déchiffrement des dépêches de la Cour.

De mauvaises langues firent courir le bruit que Vaudreuil « ne faisait ni ne dictait aucune lettre », préférant s'en remettre totalement à André Grasset de Saint-Laurent, son secrétaire principal. Ce dernier, tout comme d'ailleurs le premier secrétaire de l'intendant Bigot, Joseph Brassard Deschenaux, fut condamné pour vol et concussion lors du procès de Bigot[47]. En revanche, Marcel, le premier secrétaire de Montcalm, et La Rochette, celui de Doreil, jouissaient d'une réputation irréprochable et de la confiance absolue de leur maître[48]. La question de la probité des secrétaires qui, comme leur titre l'indique, sont « soumis à la loi du secret[49] », se posait avec encore plus d'acuité lorsqu'il s'agissait de leur confier des codes et des secrets d'État, dont le dévoilement à l'ennemi eût été lourd de conséquence.

À ce propos, les conseils de François de Callières, diplomate, puis secrétaire « à la plume[50] » du cabinet de Louis XIV, de 1701 à 1708, sont instructifs. Dans son traité intitulé *De la manière de négocier avec les souverains*, il met en garde le négociateur contre un secrétaire infidèle : « s'il le prend débauché, fripon ou indiscret, il s'expose à de grands inconvénients[51] ». L'inconvénient suprême étant la trahison. On rapporte l'histoire d'un copiste d'ambassadeur français qui termina au bout d'une corde pour avoir vendu le chiffre de son maître[52]. La Nouvelle-France possède aussi son secrétaire espion en la personne de Thomas Pichon, venu à Louisbourg en 1751 en qualité de secrétaire du gouverneur, le comte de Raymond. Dès 1753, son maître le soupçonna de fournir des renseignements aux Anglais. Faute de preuves, on l'envoya à Beauséjour en tant que commis. Une fois sur place, il proposa sa plume, qu'il avait belle, au commandant du fort, un illettré répondant au nom de Vergor[53], ainsi qu'à l'abbé Le Loutre, lequel orchestrait l'action des Amérindiens et des Acadiens contre les Anglais de Nouvelle-Écosse. Pendant plusieurs mois, Pichon fit profiter l'ennemi des renseignements hautement confidentiels qu'il recueillait ainsi. Nous n'avons trouvé nulle mention de lettres chiffrées, mais il est vraisemblable que Pichon ait eu accès aux codes et aux lettres chiffrées lorsqu'il était secrétaire du gouverneur de Louisbourg. Après la prise du fort, le « traître de Beauséjour » passa en Angleterre, se convertit au protestantisme et, gratifié d'une pension à vie pour ses bons et déloyaux services, finit ses jours sur l'île de Jersey, en compagnie de Britanniques francophones, puisqu'il n'apprit jamais la langue de Shakespeare[54].

Chiffrer ou ne pas chiffrer

Le manque de temps et de personnel incitait à la parcimonie. Souvent, on se contentait de chiffrer partiellement les missives. Vivement critiqué, ce procédé expéditif ouvrait en effet une brèche par laquelle un éventuel décrypteur pouvait s'insinuer pour reconstituer la clef du chiffre[55]. Les renseignements que l'on estimait dignes d'être chiffrés étaient évidemment ceux que l'on souhaitait soustraire à la connaissance de l'ennemi : tout ce qui concernait l'état de la colonie (les fortifications, les effectifs, les munitions, les vivres, les demandes de secours, le moral des troupes et de la population, les négociations avec les tribus amérindiennes), les ordres et les directives de la Cour, les mouvements et projets connus de l'ennemi, les plans d'attaque ou de retraite, le recours à des espions, les signaux de reconnaissance pour les bateaux et même les désaccords entre Vaudreuil et Montcalm. En revanche, les demandes de promotion, omniprésentes dans la correspondance avec la Cour, apparaissaient généralement en clair, puisqu'elles n'avaient aucune incidence sur le cours des opérations.

Qu'en était-il des communications internes ? Les officiers recouraient-ils, sur le territoire de la Nouvelle-France, à une forme d'écriture secrète pour se transmettre les ordres et les informations stratégiques ? La collection des manuscrits du maréchal de Lévis, publiée par les bons soins de Henri-Raymond Casgrain, fourmille de renseignements sur la circulation interne des ordres et des renseignements durant la guerre de Sept Ans. Ces documents révèlent d'abord une communication permanente et intense entre les divers postes avancés (Belle-Rivière, Grands-Lacs, haut et bas Saint-Laurent, lac Champlain) et les centres de décision qu'étaient Québec et Montréal[56]. En août 1759, un capitaine des troupes de terre expliquait la raison d'être de ce système : « L'objet principal est d'assurer la communication entre les parties, de faire travailler au poste de Jacques Cartier pour empêcher les ennemis de s'en emparer, [de] nous instruire de tous les mouvements, d'assurer la marche de nos convois [et de] nous donner avis de tout ce qui viendra à sa connaissance, observant pour la promptitude de mettre sur les paquets *affaires du roy de poste en poste* et cette consigne sera commune à tous les commandants qui auront des avis à nous faire passer ou nos ordres[57]. » Pour organisé qu'il fût, le système de transport des dépêches, par Amérindiens interposés, n'en était pas moins vulnérable aux interceptions de l'ennemi, M. Péan en témoigne : « J'ai eu tant d'inquiétude pour la lettre que je vous avais écrite par le canot pris, que je vous prie de trouver bon que je ne m'explique pas davantage. Il pourrait arriver le même accident et nous sommes dans des circonstances à cacher nos mouvements à l'ennemi[58]. » Pourtant, nous n'avons trouvé, dans l'abondante littérature parcourue, aucune allusion à l'usage d'une quelconque forme d'écriture cryptée pour la correspondance interne. Pour obvier aux dangers d'interception, l'on se contentait, semble-t-il, d'expédients. On parlait à mots couverts : « Il faudrait faire un grand appareil afin de tromper l'ennemi d'une façon ou d'une autre. Je ne vous écris pas plus intelligemment[59]. » On jetait les lettres en cas d'attaque : « Communiquez, je vous prie cette lettre à

M. de Vaudreuil; je ne multiplie point le papier, car si le convoi étoit pris, il lui serait plus facile de détruire une seule lettre[60]. » Ou encore on donnait les ordres secrets oralement. Si l'on en croit ce témoignage de Bigot concernant deux prisonniers anglais, l'ennemi ne procédait pas autrement : « Vous pensez bien que les instructions secrètes de M. Amherst n'ont été données que verbalement à ces officiers[61]. » Plusieurs facteurs s'opposaient à l'usage de chiffre. D'abord, le trop grand nombre d'interlocuteurs : de nombreux codes auraient circulé, ce qui aurait multiplié les risques d'interception par l'ennemi et les occasions de trahison. En effet, les gens qui savaient prendre le vent ne manquaient pas en ces dernières années de la Nouvelle-France et les officiers se plaignaient « d'être entourés d'espions[62] ». Ensuite, le maniement des procédés de chiffrage et de déchiffrage s'adressait à des gens instruits, ce qui n'était pas le cas, loin s'en faut, de tous les commandants de poste. Nous en avons un bel exemple avec Vergor, ce militaire analphabète qui vint combattre au Canada après la chute de Beauséjour et y assumer le commandement de plusieurs postes, notamment celui de l'Anse-aux-Foulons, une certaine nuit du 12 au 13 septembre 1759[63]. Par ailleurs, le cryptage des correspondances, qui exigeait beaucoup de temps et d'attention, se prêtait mal à l'activité vibrionnante et aux conditions souvent spartiates des camps militaires.

Conclusion

Pendant la guerre de Sept Ans, la maîtrise quasi absolue qu'exerçaient les Anglais sur la mer rendait indispensable le cryptage des correspondances stratégiques entre la Cour de France et ses représentants coloniaux. Même s'ils n'excellaient plus comme sous le règne des Rossignol, les services du chiffre français disposaient tout de même, en ce milieu du XVIIIᵉ siècle, d'une infrastructure bien rôdée et de procédés bien établis. Le réseau officiel de correspondance secrète avec la colonie était le suivant : les gouverneurs de la Nouvelle-France et de Louisbourg, et le commandant des troupes de terre écrivaient au moyen d'un chiffre au ministre de la Marine et des Colonies; ce même commandant et le commissaire ordonnateur des guerres échangeaient avec le ministre de la Guerre. Sur la scène des hostilités, où les dangers d'interception étaient pourtant immenses, il ne semble pas qu'on ait eu recours à l'écriture chiffrée, tout simplement parce que ce mode de communication aurait occasionné plus de problèmes qu'il n'en aurait résolus. À côté de ces échanges chiffrés ayant pour but de déjouer l'ennemi existait une correspondance secrète visant à se prémunir contre d'éventuelles effractions commises par des clans rivaux au sein même de la Cour de France.

Si ce premier travail de défrichage a permis de comprendre un peu mieux le fonctionnement, la raison d'être et les limites du système de correspondance chiffrée, son principal intérêt réside ailleurs. Il pointe en effet vers plusieurs champs de recherche. Il conviendrait, par exemple, de s'intéresser aux lettres chiffrées échangées au cours d'autres périodes troublées que connut la Nouvelle-France. Une incursion dans les correspondances privées ne manquerait pas non plus de livrer quelque secret. Enfin, on pourrait porter le regard sur des périodes plus récentes, notamment les deux dernières guerres mondiales, où le cryptage fut remis à l'honneur.

Notes

1. Citons quelques études sur le sujet : Bernard Allaire. « Le décodage de la correspondance chiffrée des diplomates espagnols au XVIe siècle », dans Albert Pierre (dir.), *Correspondre jadis et naguère*, Paris, Éd. du CTHS, 1997, pp. 207-218; Henry Biaudet. « Un chiffre diplomatique du XVIe siècle », dans *Annales de l'Académie des sciences de Finlande*, volume BII4, Helsinki, 1910, pp. 1-19; Liisi Karttunen. « Chiffres diplomatiques des nonces de Pologne », dans *Annales de l'Académie des sciences de Finlande*, volume BII5, Helsinki, 1910, pp. 1-31; Monts de Savasse. « Les chiffres de la correspondance diplomatique des ambassadeurs d'Henri IV, en l'année 1590 », dans Albert Pierre, *op. cit*, pp. 220-222.
2. Edmond Lerville. *Les Cahiers secrets de la cryptographie*, Monaco, Éditions du Rocher, 1972, p. 17.
3. Le corpus des documents à l'étude provient des fonds suivants (microfilms des originaux consultés aux Archives nationales du Canada – ANC) : 1) Fonds des colonies (MG1), C11A (Correspondance générale Canada), C11B (Correspondance générale Isle Royale), série B (Lettres envoyées); 2) Fonds du ministère de la Guerre (MG4).
4. Lerville. *Op. cit.*, pp. 12-17.
5. David Khan. *La guerre des codes secrets*, Paris, InterÉditions, 1980, pp. 1-3.
6. À ne pas confondre avec le déchiffrement, qui consiste à rétablir le texte au clair à l'aide de la clef.
7. Eugène Vaillé. *Le Cabinet noir*, Paris, PUF, 1950, pp. 46-106; Lerville. *Op. cit*, pp. 65-74.
8. Ne pas confondre *chiffre* et *nombre*. Le chiffre est le caractère numérique servant à désigner un nombre. Ainsi, les dix chiffres (0, 1, 2, 3, 4, ... 9) permettent de représenter une infinité de nombres.
9. Lerville. *Op. cit.*, pp. 72-74.
10. Vaillé. *Op. cit.*, p. 73.
11. *Ibid.*, p. 99-101.
12. André Muller. *Les écritures secrètes. Le Chiffre*, Paris, PUF, « Que sais-je », n° 116, 1971.
13. Vaillé. *Op. cit.*, pp. 157-158.
14. Khan. *Op. cit.*, pp. 51-57.
15. *Ibid.*, pp. 58-59.
16. ANC, MG1 C11A, F 8, fol. 16v.
17. ANC, MG1 C11A, F 61, fol. 313 (10 octobre 1734).
18. Guy Frégault. *Histoire de la Nouvelle-France*, tome IX, *La guerre de la conquête*, Montréal, Fides, 1955; Gilles Harvard et Cécile Vidal. *Histoire de l'Amérique française*, Paris, Flammarion, pp. 414-454.
19. ANC, Fonds Thomas-Pichon, MG18F12, vol. 1, fol. 304.
20. Louis-Antoine de Bougainville. *Écrits sur le Canada*, Sillery, Septentrion, 2003, p. 349.
21. ANC, MG1 C11A, F 103, fol. 293v.
22. ANC, MG1 B F304, vol. 101, fol. 207.
23. Frégault. *Le Grand Marquis*, Montréal, Fides, 1952, pp. 15-17.
24. De Bougainville. *Op cit.*, p. 382 (Lettre à Mme Hérault de Séchelle, 20 septembre 1757).
25. Antoine Roy. « Les lettres de Doreil », *Rapport de l'archiviste de la province de Québec pour 1944-1945*, [s. l.], Redempti Paradis, 1945, p. 134 (Québec, 16 juin 1758).
26. ANC, MG1 C11A, F101, fol 110.
27. ANC, MG1 B F313, vol. 109, fol. 390 (Lettre du ministre à Vaudreuil, Versailles, 4 avril 1759).

28. Frégault. *Histoire…*, *op. cit.*, pp. 371-372.

29. ANC, MG1 B, F304, vol. 101, fol. 144 (17 février 1755).

30. ANC, MG1 B, F307, vol. 104, fol. 153 (non datée, mais probablement avril 1756, d'après la place de cette note).

31. ANC, MG1 C11A, F101, fol. 105 (22 septembre 1756).

32. ANC, MG1 C11B, F151, vol. 22, fol. 114-115 (3 août 1740) et F166, vol. 37, fol. 25-26 (22 octobre 1757); ces lettres sont écrites à partir d'un code distinct de ceux de Vaudreuil ou de Montcalm.

33. H[enri]-R[aymond] Casgrain. *Lettres de la cour de Versailles au baron de Dieskau, au marquis de Montcalm et au chevalier de Lévis*, Québec, Demers, 1890, p. 71.

34. Frégault. *François Bigot. Administrateur français*, IHAF, 1948, t. 2, pp. 250-253.

35. ANC, MG1 C11A, vol. 104, fol. 342-345.

36. ANC, MG1 B, F308, vol. 105, fol. 248-249.

37. Roy. *Op. cit.*, p. 146 (Québec, 30 juillet 1758).

38. Vaillé. *Op. cit.*, p. 169.

39. Ibid., pp. 163-164.

40. Roy. *Op. cit.*, p. 140 (Québec, 28 juillet 1758). Voir aussi ANC, MG1 C11a, F103, fol. 399 et 401 et F104, fol. 360-361.

41. Ces codes ont été trouvés dans trois fonds : Fonds du ministère de la Marine, MG1 CIIA, F 408; Fonds du ministère de la Guerre, MG4 B1 série A4, microfilm 730; Fonds du chevalier de Lévis, MG18 K8, microfilm C 929.

42. ANC, MG1 C11A, F408, non paginé, dernières pages de la bobine.

43. Lettre chiffrée de Bougainville à Montcalm, Blaye (18 mars 1758). Version déchiffrée dans Casgrain. *Lettres de la Cour de Versailles*, Québec, Demers, 1890, p. 105.

44. Casgrain. *Lettre du marquis de Montcalm au chevalier de Lévis*, Québec, Demers, 1894, p. 69 (Québec, 24 octobre 1757).

45. Ibid., p. 69.

46. Casgrain. *Lettres de Bourlamaque au maréchal de Lévis*, Québec, Demers, 1891, p. 302 (Lettre de Montcalm à Bourlamaque, Montréal, 22 mars 1759); Roy. *Op. cit.*, pp. 70-71 (Montréal, 30 octobre 1755).

47. P[ierre]-G[eorges] Roy. « Les secrétaires des gouverneurs et des intendants de la Nouvelle-France », *BRH*, vol. XLI, janvier 1935, n° 1, p. 91 et 105.

48. À preuve, les nombreuses marques d'intérêt de leurs maîtres pour leur avancement : P.-G. Roy. *Op. cit.*, pp. 105-106; A. Roy. *Op. cit.*, p. 96 (Montréal, 3 novembre 1756).

49. Yves-Henri Bonello. *Le secret*, Paris, PUF, « Que sais-je », n° 3244, 1998, p. 75.

50. Le secrétaire à la plume était capable « d'imiter si exactement l'écriture du roi qu'elle ne se puisse distinguer de celle que la plume contrefait (définition de Saint-Simon, citée dans François de Callières, *De la manière de négocier avec les souverains*, éd. critique d'Alain Pekar Lempereur, Genève, Librairie Droz S.A., 2002, p. 59).

51. De Callières. *Op. cit.*, p. 151.

52. Camille-Georges Picavet. *La diplomatie française au temps de Louis XIV*, Paris, Félix Alcan, 1930, p. 41.

53. Pichon ne calomniait pas Vergor quand il affirmait que ce dernier pouvait tout juste signer son nom. À preuve, cette note écrite de « Bocegour » : « Je neux vous sanpeche pas da gette toute la cargeson au si bien que le vingt et audevis. » Comprendre : je ne vous empêche pas d'acheter toute la cargaison aussi bien le vin et eau-de-vie (cité dans Bernard Pothier, « Vergor », *Dictionnaire biographique du Canada*).

54. Sur Pichon : John Clarence Wesbster. *Thomas Pichon, "the spy of Beauséjour" : An Account of his Career in Europe and America*, Sackville, N.-B., Public Archives of Nova Scotia, 1937, 161 p.; T. A. Crowley. « Thomas Pichon », *Dictionnaire biographique du Canada*, version électronique

– http://www.biographi.ca/FR/index.html.; George F. G. Stanley. *New France : The Last Phase, 1744-1760,* Toronto, McClelland and Stewart, 1968, pp. 115-117; ANC, MG18-F12, Fonds Thomas-Pichon, surnommé Thomas Tyrell.

55. La lettre de Vaudreuil du 16 février 1758 en fournit une bonne illustration : par exemple, « les cinq nations », avec *nations* en clair et le reste, en langage chiffré. Connaissant le contexte, le décrypteur devinera aisément que le mot *nations* peut être précédé de *cinq.*

56. *Lettres du chevalier de Lévis concernant la guerre du Canada* (1756-1760), Montréal, Beauchemin, 1889, 473 p.; *Lettres de M. de Bourlamaque au maréchal de Lévis,* Québec, Demers, 1891, 367 p.; *Lettres de l'intendant Bigot au chevalier de Lévis,* Québec, L.-J. Demers, 1895, 110 p.; *Lettres de divers particuliers au chevalier de Lévis,* Québec, Demers, 1895, 248 p.

57. ANC, MG3 III-25AP, liasse VII, no 1-29 (Fonds de Blau).

58. Casgrain. *Lettres de divers particuliers…, op. cit.,* p. 77 (Lettre de Péan à Lévis, Montréal, 25 juillet [1757]).

59. Ibid., p. 77.

60. Ibid., p. 146 (Isle aux Noix, 22 août 1760, 3 h de l'après-midi).

61. Casgrain. *Lettres de l'intendant Bigot…, op. cit.,* p. 49.

62. *Id. Lettres de Bourlamaque…, op. cit.,* p. 97 (Sorel, 17 août 1760).

63. Pothier, « Vergor », *op. cit.*

S'ÉCRIRE AU XIXᴱ SIÈCLE EN FRANCE

Histoire d'une acculturation

Cécile Dauphin, Danièle Poublan, École des hautes études en sciences sociales

Résumé

L'enquête postale de 1847 donne une photographie inégalitaire de l'entrée en écriture de la société française, en termes de compétences, d'usages et de fonctions. Quelques décennies plus tard, la guerre de 1914-1918 révèle les capacités scripturaires de toute une population. Les traces conservées de ces moments exceptionnels montrent que les gens de toutes conditions ont effectivement intégré les normes épistolaires tout en les réinterprétant.

Au-delà du constat chiffré se pose la question du contenu et de la diffusion de la culture épistolaire, dont cet article aborde quelques aspects. D'une part, l'écriture des lettres, qui associe le lien social et la subjectivité, décline un ensemble d'arguments qui sont essentiels pour entrer en communication, pour produire et prolonger une correspondance. La rhétorique du temps et de l'espace s'impose comme une trame discrète et efficace. D'autre part, le développement des médias, diffusant textes, images et musiques, offre une place de choix à l'imaginaire de la lettre, représentée dans sa matérialité et ses effets régulateurs ou subversifs. L'exemple d'une gravure de Gavarni et celui de la chanson populaire suggèrent que les représentations épistolaires faisant cohabiter stéréotypes et satire sociale, bons sentiments et transgressions deviennent une composante majeure de la culture du XIXᵉ siècle.

Abstract

The postal enquiry of 1847 outlined the uneven state of writing within French society at the time as far as level of skill, usage, and function were concerned. Some decades later, the First World War (1914–1918) would tell quite a different story, revealing the highly developed writing abilities of an entire population. The writings, which have been preserved from this exceptional time show that people from all walks of life had effectively adopted high standards of letter writing, while also reinterpreting these standards for personal use.

Beyond the bare statistics, numerous questions arise regarding the actual content and dissemination of this letter-writing culture—some of which are covered in this article. On the one hand, the writing of letters—which brings people together through social ties and common interests—leads to a range of ideas essential to communication, as well as the production and maintenance of a shared correspondence. The rhetoric of certain times and places thus becomes a discreet but effective framework. On the other hand, the development of media capable of disseminating texts, images, and music can lend letter writing an even greater importance and weight, as represented in both the physicality of a letter and the effects it can have on the reader. Using examples such as an engraving by Gavarni and a popular song, this article also suggests that letters can make strange bedfellows of stereotypes and social satire, and shows how sentiments, both honourable and less so, would become major components of nineteenth-century culture.

Introduction

Les séparations familiales qui vont de pair avec l'accélération de la mobilité géographique au XIXe siècle multiplient les occasions d'écrire. Que le mouvement s'effectue du hameau vers la ville proche, de la province vers Paris ou du vieux continent vers le Canada, les lettres qui circulent alors ne sont pas sans parenté. Au-delà de la diversité des situations et de l'ampleur des échanges apparaissent des formes spécifiques d'une époque et d'une société. Les lettres ont alors en commun un certain nombre de caractères qui manifestent la prégnance d'une culture épistolaire partagée. Nous proposons, dans cet article, d'en signaler des indices significatifs : dans les statistiques postales, les ressorts rhétoriques mis en œuvre par les épistoliers et les moyens de grande diffusion.

Constat chiffré

Dans les années 1840, les Français s'écrivent peu. Ils prennent la plume, avec parcimonie, pour traiter de leurs affaires lointaines plus que pour s'épancher et exprimer des sentiments intimes. Les vingt-cinq volumes de la correspondance de George Sand rassemblée par Georges Lubin[1] sont exemplaires d'une pratique réservée aux milieux aisés et éduqués. « Les uns reçoivent beaucoup de courrier, beaucoup d'autres peu, et le plus grand nombre point »; « la majorité des habitants ne reçoivent aucune lettre », note la distributrice du bureau postal de Villevocance (Ardèche) en 1847. Elle commente ainsi, pour son arrondissement postal, les résultats de l'enquête lancée par l'administration. Comme chaque responsable de bureau, pendant deux semaines, elle a relevé le nombre des lettres, tant expédiées que reçues, et minutieusement comptabilisé tous les objets postaux qui ont circulé dans chacune des communes rurales de son secteur[2]. Finalement 30 000 communes ont été auscultées. L'épistolier ordinaire de ces communes rurales ne reçoit pas deux lettres par an et ne parvient pas à en écrire une dans l'année. Or, les villes, exclues de l'enquête, restent, par leurs activités et la plus forte proportion d'alphabétisés, les grandes productrices de courrier. En effet, si on tient compte des lettres que leurs activités génèrent, les valeurs croissent sensiblement tout en restant faibles : pour la France entière, en 1847, les 130 millions de lettres échangées donnent une moyenne de 3,3 lettres annuelles par Français.

L'enquête de 1847 questionne les usages sociaux et les pratiques de la correspondance. Au-delà du constat de la rareté des échanges, elle délimite l'aire d'utilisation et l'économie du courrier. La lettre est le média des distances moyennes : localement, à l'intérieur du canton, la transmission orale supplante l'écrit; pour le lointain, au-delà de cent kilomètres, les échanges se raréfient, freinés par les frais de port qui sont alors prohibitifs avant l'instauration du timbre, en 1849. Malgré l'émiettement des données recueillies, et les effets aléatoires dans les très petites localités, la cohérence géographique des indicateurs souligne le caractère socialement et économiquement marqué du geste épistolaire. Les flux de lettres sont très denses autour des centres urbains – autour de la capitale en particulier; ils irriguent les régions animées d'une vie économique et commerciale intense à laquelle l'infrastructure postale a su s'adapter. En revanche, les mouvements postaux se perdent sur les confins les plus isolés et s'étiolent dans les régions rurales qui peinent à se dégager des formes autarciques de consommation et de communication orale.

Cinquante ans plus tard, à la fin du XIXᵉ siècle, l'économie épistolaire n'a pas été notablement modifiée : les affaires restent les vecteurs les plus actifs des échanges. Si le nombre moyen de lettres par habitant atteint alors 19[3], la lettre d'un parent remise par le facteur reste alors pour beaucoup un moment rare à la campagne. Il faut le drame de la guerre qui touche toutes les familles à partir de 1914, la séparation qui s'éternise, l'angoisse, le danger et la mort omniprésents, pour que tout un peuple, « comme pris d'une soudaine et irrépressible boulimie de mots, se lance dans l'aventure épistolaire[4] ». Dès le début de la guerre, les autorités prennent conscience de l'importance inédite des échanges entre les soldats et les familles. Constatant – en termes convenus – qu'il n'est pas « de meilleur réconfort, pour ceux qui chaque jour font le sacrifice de leur vie, que la réception et la lecture des lettres, des simples mais admirables lettres écrites par de vieux parents, par des femmes courageuses, par des enfants[5] », la Poste aux Armées est réorganisée pour assurer la transmission du flot des lettres qui bénéficient, entre le front et l'arrière, de la franchise. La guerre révèle les capacités scripturaires de la population française. Les traces conservées de ces moments exceptionnels montrent que la société a effectivement intégré les normes épistolaires tout en les réinterprétant.

Culture épistolaire

Dans l'immense océan du courrier échangé, et qui ne cesse d'enfler au cours du XIXᵉ siècle en France, subsistent quelques îlots de lettres ordinaires, à l'ombre des « grandes » correspondances d'écrivains ou personnages « historiques ». Correspondances familiales au long court (comme celles des Chotard-Lioret[6], des Limperani[7] ou des Duméril-Mertzdorff-Froissart[8]), pointillés des lettres d'émigrés (du Béarn, de Pologne, d'Alsace[9]), lettres de soldats happé par les événements (les guerres en fournissent un lot poignant[10]), échanges amoureux jalousement enfouis et parfois exhumés par les descendants (comme le cas d'Ursin et Ernestine, ou d'Auguste et Eugénie[11]), ou collections de cartes et de marques postales (constituées par les musées de la poste[12]), ces quelques exemples illustrent les particularités d'un vaste gisement encore peu exploré. Chacun de ces vestiges évoque les multiples manières, parfois dérisoires mais toujours inventives, de déjouer les contraintes du temps et de l'espace qui séparent les gens. Des écarts se lisent dans les entrées en matière ou les formules finales, dans la place accordée aux commissions ou dans les débordements en marge ou en lignes croisées. Certaines lettres affichent la solennité et l'effort alors que d'autres misent sur la spontanéité ou sur le négligé. Les formes d'énonciation peuvent être tenues pour un marqueur social mais, au-delà de leur diversité, aucune lettre n'échappe à la fonction symbolique de l'échange épistolaire : combler l'absence, rompre le silence, rassurer les siens, tisser des liens.

Ce rapide tour d'horizon pose la question de la constitution et de la diffusion d'une culture épistolaire au XIXᵉ siècle : à savoir, d'une part, l'ensemble, historiquement construit, de références textuelles et de techniques qui permettent d'écrire des lettres en suivant les règles adéquates; d'autre part, les modes de participation des acteurs sociaux à ces ressources, selon leurs compétences et leur statut. « Dans une histoire culturelle redéfinie comme le lieu où s'articulent pratiques et représentations, le geste épistolaire est un geste privilégié. Libre et codifiée, intime et publique, tendue entre secret et sociabilité, la lettre, mieux qu'aucune autre expression, associe le lien social et la subjectivité[13]. » Reste à comprendre comment se nouent ensemble le répertoire d'énoncés et d'émotions dicibles et recevables dans l'échange épistolaire, et les usages que font les personnes et les groupes sociaux de ces motifs, les reformulant ou les déplaçant. Les institutions (la poste, l'école), les discours (manuels épistolaires, critiques littéraires) défendent leurs raisons – économiques, politiques, techniques, littéraires –, construisent leurs réseaux – instances d'incitation et de contrôle –, mais, seuls, ils ne nous disent pas grand-chose des imaginaires qui unissent entre elles un certain nombre de représentations pour donner sens à des gestes et à des pratiques.

Dans la lecture des corpus de lettres érodés par le temps se profile une configuration d'arguments qui sont essentiels pour entrer en communication, bâtir un texte, multiplier et faire durer les échanges. La culture est d'abord affaire de technique. Le retrait dans un lieu, l'installation à la table ou à l'écritoire, la délimitation de la page blanche, la prise de la plume (sans parler de sa taille), le tracé des mots sont autant d'opérations nécessaires. Mais non suffisantes. Parmi d'autres, le témoignage du jeune Toinou, fils de paysans auvergnats, est de ce point de vue exemplaire : « Tous les mois, je devais écrire sur une page extraite d'un cahier à un sou la lettre de ma mère à mon père. Je m'installais sur un coin de la grande table et rédigeais le préambule suivant les termes invariables : 'Cher époux, Je t'écris ces deux mots de lettre pour te faire savoir de nos nouvelles et pour en recevoir des tiennes…' Je relisais à haute voix ce texte que ma mère approuvait de hochements de tête admiratifs […] ' Dis-lui que c'est un feignant et un goulant ' […] J'hésitais devant la rédaction de telles choses… Je prétendais que l'écriture ne permettait pas l'emploi de termes semblables ou alors la lettre ne serait pas une lettre. Après avoir discuté pendant tout un après-midi de dimanche, nous arrivions peu avant l'heure de la soupe à quelque conclusion fort adoucie[14]. » Cette mise en scène ne caractérise pas seulement l'écriture laborieuse et ponctuelle. La tenue habituelle d'une correspondance, comme dans la famille Mertzdorff[15], s'appuie aussi largement sur la rhétorique du décor comme composante de l'échange épistolaire : « Je t'écris dans le petit salon, à la lumière de la lampe, assis à ma place sur le canapé. » – « Je vous écris sur mes genoux dans la chambre de Marie pendant qu'on leur fait une dictée. » Rares sont les lettres qui n'évoquent pas, d'une façon ou d'une autre, le lieu où elles sont produites – et aussi lues et conservées.

D'un point de vue externe, l'écriture est conditionnée par un ensemble d'éléments spatiaux qui distinguent et séparent un espace spécifique dans le va-et-vient quotidien. Le choix d'un lieu et d'instruments appropriés conditionne le déroulement même de l'acte d'écriture. De façon interne, la mise en récit du rituel de l'écriture, du décor, de l'entourage et de son intervention, dans un jeu subtil d'effets de proximité et de séparation, contribue à fabriquer un imaginaire partagé par les correspondants, jalonné de lieux communs. Ainsi les représentations spatiales qui circulent, et se répètent de lettre en lettre, balisent l'écriture familiale comme autant de signes de reconnaissance, comme autant de mots de passe. Elles expriment le rapport au monde d'un groupe social donné, dans un contexte particulier.

Le poids des conditions matérielles ne se limite pas aux contraintes spatiales. L'inscription réciproque du temps dans la lettre, et de la lettre dans le temps, donne aussi lieu à de multiples modalités d'expression qui épousent les préoccupations d'un milieu et d'une époque. Ainsi les propos sur le « bon » rythme des échanges, les mentions sur les lettres reçues, expédiées, attendues, annoncées, promises…, les références aux marqueurs du temps comme la cloche ou l'horloge, la mise en scène de l'arrivée et du départ du courrier, le regard porté sur le temps passé à tracer les mots, tous ces motifs scandent et nourrissent l'écriture des lettres. Ils expriment la tension entre la conception d'un temps plein, intériorisé comme une morale de l'organisation des faits et gestes (tributaire du temps social dominant au XIXe siècle, qui impose la valeur travail[16]), et l'expérience plus personnelle de la durée dans sa dimension psychologique dont l'énonciation attie la conscience. Dans un contexte d'accélération du mouvement (transports, acheminement postal), la tenue d'une correspondance, dans ses multiples façons, rhétoriques et pratiques, d'anticiper, de rattraper, de synchroniser les moments de rencontre par lettres interposées, dispose des jalons dans la course du temps. Selon le sexe, le statut social et les itinéraires individuels (la correspondance au long court ne produisant pas les mêmes modes de ritualisation que les lettres de soldats pendant la guerre, par exemple), les motifs peuvent varier, mais esquissent une sorte d'archéologie du quotidien : déposés au fil de la plume et décrivant des objets, des lieux, des gestes, des activités, ils renvoient à l'expérience universelle du temps qui érode et use dans la souffrance et la vieillesse; en conservant les traces de ces instants éphémères inscrits dans les lettres, les familles développent des pratiques spécifiques en rapport avec la mémoire et avec le patrimoine.

Face aux aléas de l'existence, le travail d'écriture épistolaire, qu'il se pratique dans la quotidienneté domestique ou l'urgence des tranchées, permet d'exprimer des affects, de faire vivre et survivre, de cultiver et de partager un rapport spécifique au monde. Quels que soient les supports de communication (de la carte au papier, de la lettre au téléphone et au courriel), les catégories de temps et d'espace forment inextricablement la trame des échanges. Les manières si diverses de « braconner » (au sens où l'entend Michel de Certeau) dans le champ de l'épistolaire, finissent par constituer « un répertoire de performances, donnant à voir la capacité d'un groupe social, en un temps et un lieu donnés, à s'affirmer collectivement en arrachant d'autres conditions d'existence que celles qu'il subit[17] ».

Inégalement partagée, mais présente dans l'imaginaire, la culture épistolaire emprunte différentes pistes pour se diffuser. On peut ici en suggérer deux, à titre exploratoire : la gravure et la chanson.

Une gravure de Gavarni[18], exemple de métissage

Un ouvrage plusieurs fois réédité dans la deuxième moitié du XIXe siècle[19], *Masques et visages*, propose, dans l'un de ses chapitres, des « modèles » de lettres. Comme le reste du volume, ce chapitre est constitué de légendes de gravures de Gavarni; il n'est illustré que de minuscules vignettes sur bois (un ou deux centimètres de côté) attribuées à un jeune graveur, Godefroy-Durand[20]. Le livre veut plaire et amuser : « ce n'est pas précisément un manuel de style épistolaire que Gavarni a voulu donner dans ce recueil ; personne ne s'y trompera », prévient l'introduction. Cependant le point de vue satirique n'exclut pas le souci réaliste et les lettres se veulent « vraies dans le fond et dans la forme ». Copie de lettres originales[21] ou inventions de Gavarni, qu'importe ! ce sont des textes que l'on imprime et réimprime, qui font sourire et que l'on commente, des modèles ou des contre-modèles qui circulent, que l'on imite ou dont on se moque.

Sans surprise, la plupart des extraits évoquent des histoires d'amour – comme la musique populaire aujourd'hui : « Je fini en mouillant de mes larmes la main et la plume qui ont tracé ces caractère qui sont pour ainsi dire dicté par Lamour » ou « J'ai ta lettre chérie, ô mon Ernest ! je la presse sur mon cœur et la couvre de mes baisers… »[22]. La dernière lettre évoque, elle, l'amour conjugal – l'amour familial plutôt. Il se traduit ainsi, style et orthographe compris : « …Ma siere epouse je vous fait bien mes complimens a vous ynsi que ma petite je fais bien dé complimens a mes oncles etantes éa toutes anfans je fait vien de compliments a ma mere éa tou mes frères je fait vien des complimens a notre merene je fait bien de compl…[23] »

Gavarni, qui recherche « l'expression la plus saisissante et la plus vraie des mœurs[24] », donne le cachet de naïveté attendue par l'accumulation de fautes d'orthographe, l'absence de ponctuation et par des mots écrits comme les prononcent les provinciaux (*siere* pour chère, *ynsi* pour ainsi). L'écriture populaire se marque également par le style répétitif et la proximité, voire la confusion avec l'oralité, la rencontre réelle, la conversation. La critique est récurrente et ces traits sont épinglés dans une autre lettre du recueil, où les sentiments sont dits plutôt qu'écrits et s'expriment sous la forme unique du ressassement de la peine éprouvée : « Ma siere amie vous me dites que vous a ves été malade sela me fait biem de la pene vous me dites que quan j'ai quite lostre Jeoure sela vous faist vien de la pene ma que sela vous fas pas de la pene[25]. »

Dans la lettre à l'épouse, Gavarni insiste sur l'un des stéréotypes de la lettre « populaire » : son caractère familial, qui bannit la relation interpersonnelle et intime des épistoliers au profit d'une mise en relation large de tout le réseau familial. Les commissions qui consistent à transmettre des affections à chacun et dont les manuels déconseillent l'usage[26] sont en fait une pratique courante bien au-delà des milieux peu alphabétisés moqués ici : tous les corpus de lettres familiales du XIXe siècle, du jardinier à l'industriel, de l'ouvrière au professeur, en témoignent. Ce serait donc la lourdeur de la forme plus que le compliment lui-même qui serait dénoncé.

Figure 9.1 Lithographie de Gavarni parue dans le journal humoristique *Le Charivari*, le 11 septembre 1837, et tirée d'une série de dessins intitulée « La Boîte aux lettres », illustrant la vie parisienne sous le règne de Louis-Philippe. Le personnage attablé, qui écrit à sa famille, est un porteur d'eau auvergnat venu à Paris y « gagner sa vie ».
Musée de La Poste, Collections historiques, Paris, M1009.

Les lettres reproduites dans *Masques et visages* ne représentent qu'un moment éditorial dans une suite de publications commencées dans les années 1830, et qu'une partie tronquée des publications originales. En effet, au départ, Gavarni donne à Caboche, Grégoire et Cie, imprimeurs, des planches lithographiées qui se composent chacune d'un dessin surmontant le texte manuscrit d'une lettre. La lettre à l'épouse est ainsi tracée d'une écriture irrégulière au-dessous d'un dessin qui représente l'épistolier en pleine action : un homme assis sur un banc devant une table, la plume à la main, en train d'écrire la lettre reproduite. Le texte et la représentation de l'épistolier coïncident. Tous les deux insistent sur le côté « populaire » de la scène. Gavarni le dénonçait par le style, l'orthographe; le thème du message, il le montre à travers le décor. Le scripteur est un porteur d'eau en tenue de travail (on devine le crochet pour les seaux pendu à sa bretelle); il a fait halte dans une taverne aux murs graffités; à l'arrière-plan, d'autres consommateurs se serrent autour du poêle. Gavarni accumule, dans cette image, les poncifs que ses contemporains épinglent[27] : l'auteur de la lettre est un porteur d'eau à la tenue vestimentaire et à l'équipement conventionnels; il marque son attachement à l'Auvergne, où il est né, et aux traditions familiales; il reste en retrait des autres Parisiens qu'il côtoie pourtant, et même la bouteille sur la table de l'estaminet, repoussée pour placer la feuille de papier, ne remet pas en question sa légendaire sobriété.

Peut-être un deuxième niveau dans l'intention satirique (et moins critique qu'il n'y paraît au premier regard) est-il perceptible, aussi bien dans la peinture du décor que dans la lettre familiale. Les contemporains voient, dans le mariage, le moyen le plus efficace pour maintenir l'ouvrier « dans ses généreuses résolutions de travail et de bonne conduite[28] ». Le travailleur de Gavarni, père de famille appliqué, ne saurait se confondre avec les individus dont « l'effrayant pêle-mêle » inquiète la bourgeoisie, cette « classe dangereuse » et redoutée, qui menace le rêve d'harmonie sociale : les signes qu'il trace sur le papier le prouvent. La culture épistolaire véhiculerait ici des valeurs morales – tout comme les signes tracés au mur recèleraient une valeur esthétique. Les graffitis font office de marqueur social et confirment le caractère populaire du lieu d'écriture; mais, à l'époque, cette forme d'expression retient l'attention bienveillante des artistes romantiques et apparaît à certains comme une inscription naïve mais forte, dans l'espace public, d'aspirations politiques ou personnelles[29]. De la même façon que la lettre (re)produite par Gavarni souligne toute la distance qui sépare une écriture maladroite de la « belle » lettre que les lecteurs instruits sauraient, eux, envoyer, les graffitis du décor peuvent se lire en contrepoint d'un art pictural plus noble; cependant les productions populaires (écrites ou dessinées), moquées mais pas disqualifiées, suggèrent un enrichissement mutuel possible. Cette source de sincérité, de naturel, de spontanéité viendrait revivifier des pratiques figées, faire évoluer des modèles usés. L'acculturation ne passe-t-elle pas par les emprunts réciproques et le métissage ?

Ces lithographies touchent un large public. Lorsque Charles Philipon, directeur du *Charivari*, séduit par le succès de la première série de Gavarni qu'il vient de publier (*Fourberies de femmes en matière de sentiments*), lui en demande une autre, l'artiste reprend une douzaine d'anciennes planches, en ajoute de nouvelles et compose la série de la *Boîte aux lettres*, publiée pleine page dans le journal entre 1837 et 1839. La lettre du provincial à sa famille paraît le 11 septembre 1837. Ensuite, la série de la *Boîte aux lettres* est tirée à part, en noir et blanc ou en couleur, et vendue en feuilles ou en albums. Les publications de *Masques et visages* semblent paradoxales aujourd'hui, car les lithographies de Gavarni ont survécu beaucoup plus que ses textes, et plus qu'eux sont maintenant appréciées. Mais textes seuls ou textes et images n'ont cessé de nourrir l'imaginaire épistolaire des Français au XIXe siècle.

L'imaginaire de la lettre dans la chanson

Territoire des folkloristes et des musicologues, les chansons ont peu retenu l'attention des historiens[30]. Miroirs ou mirages en suspension dans l'air du temps, elles sont une source à la fois évidente et ignorée. Machines « ressassantes », où s'épanouissent et triomphent les stéréotypes, reliées au continent des arts et des rêves par des fils invisibles, elles croisent aussi les événements historiques[31] et reflètent la vie quotidienne, personnelle et intime. Elles appartiennent aux « figures majeures de l'idéologie » pointées par Roland Barthes. Des sensibilités collectives comme des desseins politiques, elles ne peuvent vraiment se soustraire.

L'abondance et le foisonnement peuvent former obstacle à une approche raisonnée et systématique. On peut cependant tenter d'ouvrir quelques pistes de réflexion sur la rencontre et les imbrications de la chanson avec l'imaginaire de la lettre. Les chansons présentent une parenté frappante avec l'art épistolaire dont elles tirent des effets à la fois poétiques et réalistes. La continuité dans le temps et les formes propres à ces deux genres offrent un socle particulièrement riche de représentations qui s'efforcent de donner sens à l'expérience humaine. Les chansons, comme les lettres, prennent racines et se déploient dans le mouvement, la circulation, la transmission, la sociabilité. Comme les textes épistolaires, elles tirent efficacité de leur extrême porosité aux marmonnements ordinaires, comme aux épopées ou aux événements historiques. Elles nourrissent, au-delà des temps et des lieux, un discours poétique sur une expérience collective. Berceuses qui font dormir, marches qui font marcher, complaintes qui font pleurer ou couplets qui font rire ne prétendent pas plus que les lettres « ordinaires », qui nourrissent le courrier quotidien et tissent la cohésion sociale, construire un savoir ou tenir un discours savant sur le monde; toutes ces bribes d'expressions naissent de la souffrance et de la joie, du souci et de l'inquiétude de gens qui savent ce qu'est avoir froid ou le mal d'amour, aller à la guerre ou s'éloigner des siens, le plaisir de recevoir des nouvelles et de partager mots et ritournelles.

La transmission orale des chansons marque cependant un écart avec le processus d'écriture mis en œuvre dans les lettres : d'un côté, l'économie scripturaire suppose un espace spécifique, celui de la page, limitée et fermée, la production d'un texte, adressé et signé, et la fonction performative de formules et d'énoncés; d'un autre s'élabore une œuvre collective, au sens vague du terme, dans son histoire, sa fonction et ses usages, mêlant les accents, retravaillée par la mémoire infidèle et créatrice comme la plus sage complice du poète; à travers rythmes et mélodies, elle s'incruste dans les têtes mieux que les mots qui les ont fait naître. Ces différences cependant n'érigent pas de frontières claires et étanches entre l'oral et l'écrit, entre la mémoire et les objets, entre les pratiques populaires et lettrées. Il est remarquable que les recueils de chansons, comme les ouvrages de modèles de lettres, se multiplient dès l'avènement de l'imprimerie et, avec elle, l'idée du florilège. L'entrée en édition, même sur feuilles volantes, a pour effet de sélectionner, de fixer, mais aussi de censurer.

Le goût pour la chanson « populaire » trouve, au XIXe siècle, un terreau particulièrement favorable. C'est l'ère des caveaux et des goguettes[32]. Les auteurs se mettent à publier leurs propres recueils – Désaugiers, Béranger, Debraux… Dans la sphère littéraire, un Gérard de Nerval s'efforce de sensibiliser le public aux chansons « anciennes » quelque peu oubliées[33]. C'est dans le milieu scolaire que s'invente la chanson enfantine, parallèlement à la littérature pour la jeunesse, portée par l'idée de l'instruction publique et de protection de l'enfance. La chanson va s'écrire et se noter dans les manuels scolaires, se présenter au programme du certificat d'études, ou devenir, en de beaux albums aux teintes pastel, le symbole de la bonne éducation. Mais la chanson pour enfants est le fait des adultes : on l'édulcore pour la rendre enfantine; dès 1880, on met l'instruction civique en rimes et en mesures à quatre temps[34]. La politique n'est pas en reste quand la chanson devient patriotique et revancharde après la défaite de 1870 puis, insouciante et fraternelle, avec les colonies de vacances ou les camps de mouvements de jeunesse au XXe siècle.

Les chansons, pourtant agiles et vivaces, en se coulant dans le moule éditorial et scolaire, se trouvent saisies par des modes de régulation autant que de transmission. Elles donnent prise, de façon plus tangible, aux idéaux politiques qui visent à entretenir une vision nostalgique du bon vieux temps, à assagir le peuple en le distrayant et à former des citoyens en les édifiant. En marge de la « grande » musique et de la poésie, les chansons subissent en quelque sorte le même sort que l'art épistolaire lorsqu'il est réduit à des codes et à des formules par les « secrétaires » ou recueils des plus belles lettres et des meilleurs auteurs. Mais dans le même mouvement se développe de nouvelles formes de médiation et de réception; à travers la diversité des lieux et des instances de contrôle se croisent et sont manipulés les imaginaires des grâces et des misères de la vie, des amours et des séparations, des plaisirs et des guerres, des séductions et des tromperies.

Le répertoire établi par Patrice Coirault (1875-1959), dans la première moitié du XXe siècle, offre le panorama le plus riche et le plus utile pour observer la présence du thème de la lettre dans la chanson populaire française. Au cours de son enquête pour inventorier l'ensemble des chansons, les motifs et les variantes, le folkloriste musicologue a dressé plus de deux mille fiches[35]. Sous la rubrique « lettre », le corpus décline les traits dominants d'un imaginaire épistolaire dominé par les tribulations de l'amour : la fille écrit au curé, aux parents, au gouverneur… pour obtenir le mariage ou pour annoncer qu'elle est partie avec son amant, l'amant promet d'écrire, l'absence de lettres est signe de rupture, le soldat en campagne ou prisonnier ne peut écrire, la lettre annonce que l'amant est mort ou va mourir, ou encore que la fille-soldat délaisse son amant pour s'engager dans l'armée.

Dans le kaléidoscope des situations de séparation des amants, des promesses, trahisons, ruptures ou retrouvailles, le jardin et les oiseaux jouent un rôle spécifique : ils figurent l'espace et le moment de la rencontre. L'instant de la cueillette prélude à un message amoureux. Le nom des fleurs varie, leur nombre est souvent fixé à trois. Toutefois, lorsque survient le rossignol, la caille ou l'alouette, se posant sur la main ou sur le sein de la belle, se joue le moment crucial de la révélation du message d'amour... ou de la trahison. La fontaine, la feuillée, le rossignol et le chagrin d'amour font partie du cadre traditionnel des chansons de toile qui remontent au XIIe siècle : ces airs chantent les femmes qui travaillent la toile (fileuses, tisseuses...), leurs espoirs et leurs chagrins. Ainsi « À la claire fontaine », le chant du rossignol avive le regret d'avoir trop vite refusé (ou accordé) le bouton de rose symbolique. Dans l'attente amoureuse, l'oiseau messager abolit les distances, se fait complice des amants pour déjouer le contrôle social, dévoile les secrets ou les ruses, décrypte les signes (ne serait-ce que « trois mots en latin »), et, tirant la morale de l'histoire, attise la querelle entre les sexes (« les garçons ne valent rien » et « les filles encore bien moins »).

Dans le répertoire des chansons populaires, qu'on écrive ou reçoive une lettre, l'objet reste évanescent au regard du message et du drame en train de se jouer. Il est pourtant significatif que la plus populaire des chansons, « Au clair de la lune », évoque l'histoire simple d'une sérénade qui manque de tourner court, faute de plume et de chandelle pour écrire. La métaphore de la plume empruntée pour dire la médiation entre les amants circule d'ailleurs dans la « grande » musique comme dans le répertoire populaire. Un opéra comique de Longuet, en 1870, portant le même titre, développe le scénario de la séduction par le recours au refrain le plus éprouvé du répertoire populaire. Au-delà de la trame relativement fixe d'un héros, d'une requête à adresser par écrit, des obstacles à surmonter et du dénouement galant, « Au clair de la lune » attire l'attention sur la place de l'écrit dans les scènes les plus ordinaires de la vie sociale, sur les conditions matérielles de la transmission du message, sur la difficulté à produire un texte et sur la croyance en son efficacité.

Dans la chanson comme dans la lettre, la voix, qu'elle porte la musique ou la parole, fait lien entre l'intime et le social, entre l'expression singulière et l'imaginaire collectif. La voix est lecture, chant, cri, rire. Que la musique enchante les mots ou que « la plume magique, inlassablement, mélodieusement, réenchante le monde[36] », quand on a affaire à la « lettre chantée », la confusion devient exemplaire. Présente dans la musique au moins depuis Monteverdi, avec la *Lettera Amorosa*, largement utilisée par l'opéra comme ressort dramatique (connaissant une fortune aussi prospère que dans la littérature romanesque), la lettre chantée rencontre, au XIXe siècle, l'environnement technique, social et culturel favorable à sa floraison[37]. Bien des auteurs compositeurs empruntent la forme épistolaire (adresse, signature, ton de l'épanchement et de la confidence) pour porter la critique sociale d'une bourgeoisie désinvolte et hypocrite, pour exploiter la veine inépuisable des bons sentiments ou le topos du conscrit désargenté et fêtard qui mendie quelques sous à ses parents. C'est encore un cadre idéal pour exacerber les sentiments patriotiques ou inversement, antimilitaristes, pour signifier des reproches ou faire acte de repentance. Les innovations techniques contribuent aussi à la diffusion et au succès des chansons : illustrations qui ornent certaines partitions, invention du cylindre de cire[38], puis du disque pressé.

Conclusion

L'historien qui s'interroge sur le développement des pratiques épistolaires ne peut se contenter d'approches statistiques ou institutionnelles. Son champ d'investigation s'étend à l'imaginaire qui se nourrit et se joue des hiérarchies sociales, des relations complexes entre les sexes, du mouvement des humeurs et des sentiments. En particulier, les formes imbriquées de la lettre et de la chanson, de la lettre et de l'image, proposent une sorte de répertoire des affects modelés par la situation de séparation et le désir de communiquer et de partager. Leur production massive au XIXᵉ siècle contribue à multiplier les modèles et les possibilités d'appropriation d'une culture épistolaire historiquement située.

Notes

1. Georges Lubin. *George Sand. Correspondance, 1812-1876*, Paris, Garnier/Bordas, 25 volumes, 1964-1991.
2. Les précisions demandées concernent non seulement d'autres données postales (journaux, colis, etc.), mais aussi des renseignements sur l'infrastructure postale, les lieux-dits, l'habitat et l'économie locale. Cécile Dauphin, Pierrette Lebrun-Pézerat et Danièle Poublan. « L'enquête postale de 1847 », dans *La correspondance* (Roger Chartier, dir., Paris, Fayard, 1991), présentent cette enquête menée dans plus de 30 000 communes : les intentions de l'administration, la description des formulaires, les conditions des relevés, la synthèse des résultats et l'analyse de leur signification culturelle et économique.
3. À la même date, en 1897, la moyenne, au Canada, est de 31.
4. Gérard Baconnier, André Minet et Louis Soler. *La plume au fusil. Les poilus du Midi à travers leur correspondance*, Toulouse, Privat, 1985, p. 17.
5. Intervention du rapporteur de la commission parlementaire des Postes et Télégraphes chargée de l'étude du fonctionnement de la Poste aux Armées (1915), citée par Maurice Ferrier. *La Poste aux Armées*, [s.l.], éditions Sun, 1975, p. 110.
6. Caroline Chotard-Lioret. « La socialité familiale en province : une correspondance privée entre 1870 et 1920 », thèse de 3ᵉ cycle, Paris 5, 1983; et « Correspondre en 1900, le plus public des actes privés », *Ethnologie française*, XV, 1985, pp. 63-72.
7. Chantal Savreux. *Clementine Limperani. Une correspondance familiale corse au XIXᵉ siècle*, Toulouse, Maxence Fabiani, 1999.
8. Dauphin, Lebrun-Pézerat et Poublan. *Ces bonnes lettres. Une correspondance familiale au XIXᵉ siècle*, Paris, Albin Michel, 1995.
9. Ariane Bruneton-Governari, Jacques Staes (éd.). *Cher père et tendre mère... Lettres de Béarnais en Amérique du Sud*, Biarritz, J. et D., 1995; Kula Witold. « Lettres d'Amérique, 1890-1891. L'émigration des paysans polonais vue par eux-mêmes », *Revue de la Bibliothèque nationale*,

n°50, 1993, pp. 48-57; Camille Maire. *Lettres d'Amérique. Des émigrants d'Alsace et de Lorraine écrivent au pays, 1802-1892*, Metz, Serpenoise, 1992.

10. Parmi de nombreux titres : Jean-Pierre Guéno. *Paroles de poilus. Lettres de la Grande Guerre*, Paris, Tallandier, 2003.

11. Mireille Bossis. *Ursin et Ernestine. La parole des muets de l'histoire*, Paris, Desclée de Brouwer, 1998; Danièle Poublan. « Les lettres font-elles les sentiments ? S'écrire avant le mariage au milieu du XIXe siècle », *Séduction et sociétés*, Cécile Dauphin et Arlette Farge (dir.), Paris, Seuil, 2001, pp. 141-182.

12. Poublan. « Affaires et passions. Des lettres parisiennes au milieu du XIXe siècle », *La correspondance, op. cit.*

13. Roger Chartier. *La correspondance, op. cit.*, pp. 9-10.

14. Antoine Sylvère. *Toinou, le cri d'un enfant auvergnat*, Paris, Plon, 1980, pp. 153-154.

15. *Ces bonnes lettres, op. cit.*

16. Alain Corbin. « L'arithmétique des jours au XIXe siècle », *Le Temps, le Désir et l'Horreur*, Paris, Aubier, 1991, pp. 9-22 ; Roger Sue. *Temps et ordre social*, Paris, PUF, 1994.

17. Charles Tilly, cité par Arlette Farge. *Histoire des femmes*, t. III, Paris, Plon, 1991, p. 482.

18. Gavarni (1804-1866) a saisi la société parisienne de son époque – celle de Balzac et de Daumier – dans ses dessins. Ses lithographies ont illustré de nombreux journaux, dont le *Charivari*, de Philipon, livres et recueils.

19. Gavarni. *Masques et visages*, Paris, Paulin et Lechevalier, 1857, *in-18* publié de son vivant; Gavarni. *Masques et visages*, préface de Hippolyte de Villemessant et H. Rochefort, notice par Jules Claretie, Paris, Librairie du *Figaro*, 1868, *in-8°*, 352 p. De Villemessant est le directeur du journal le *Figaro*; Gavarni. *Masques et visages*, notice par Sainte-Beuve, Paris, C. Lévy, 1886, *in-fol.*

20. Paul Charbon. *Gavarni. La boîte aux lettres*, Schirmeck, Jean-Pierre Guys, 1982, p. 198.

21. Les Goncourt racontent dans leur *Journal* (1852) que Gavarni aurait acheté, au poids, chez un épicier, des lettres qui auraient servi de légendes à ses lithographies.

22. *Masques et visages, op. cit.*, 1868, pp. 326 et 328.

23. Ibid., p. 332.

24. Rochefort. *Ibid.*, p. 9.

25. Ibid., p. 331.

26. Cécile Dauphin. *Prête-moi ta plume. Les manuels épistolaires au XIXe siècle*, Paris, Kimé, 2000, p. 156.

27. Joseph Mainzer. « Le Porteur d'eau », *Les Français peints par eux-mêmes*, Paris, Curmer, 1840-1842, t. 4, pp. 225-233.

28. M. J. Brisset. « L'ouvrier de Paris », *Les Français peints par eux-mêmes*, t. 5, p. 371.

29. Xavier Barral i Altet. *Dictionnaire critique d'iconographie occidentale*, Rennes, Presses universitaires de Rennes, 2003, p. 427.

30. Claude Duneton. *Histoire de la chanson française*, t. 2, *1780 à 1860*, Paris, Seuil, 1998; Martine David et Anne-Marie Delrieu. *Aux sources des chansons populaires. Petite histoire des chansons les plus connues*, Paris, Belin, 1984; Id. *Refrains d'enfance, histoire de 60 chansons populaires*, préface de Claude Roy, Paris, Herscher, 1988. Il faut souligner l'intérêt qui semble poindre avec l'exposition de la BNF en 2004, « Souvenirs, souvenirs… cent ans de chanson française », et autour d'un colloque intitulé « La chanson face à l'histoire », centré sur le XXe siècle.

31. La relation au politique a en effet retenu l'attention des historiens.

32. Sociétés chantantes ouvrières qui fleurissent au début de la Restauration.

33. Gérard de Nerval. *Chansons et légendes du Valois*, 1854.

34. Arrêté fixant le programme de l'enseignement du chant dans les écoles primaires, 1883, programme de Jules Ferry. L'éveil musical consiste à utiliser le rythme pour guider les pas des

écoliers, et les paroles de chansons bien choisies pour forger la conscience du futur citoyen : *ouvrage* rime avec *courage*; *vacances,* avec *récompenses*; *laïque,* avec *République,* etc.

35. Patrice Coirault. *Répertoire des chansons françaises de tradition orale*, ouvrage révisé et complété par Georges Delarue, Yvette Fédoroff et Simone Wallon, t. I : *La poésie et l'amour*; t. II : *La vie sociale et militaire*, Paris, BNF, 1996. Il est prévu de publier un troisième volume.

36. Annie Paradis. *Mozart, l'opéra réenchanté,* Paris, Fayard, 1999, p. 361.

37. Paul Charbon. « La lettre et la chanson », *La lettre dans tous ses états*, sous la direction de Jean Lerat, Schirmeck, Jean-Pierre Gyss, 2001, pp. 55-72.

38. Le Musée canadien des civilisations dispose de tels cylindres dans sa collection. Ils furent utilisés pour l'enregistrement de chansons folkloriques.

"FROM A FINE PEN MUCH ART AND FANCY FLOWS"

Letter Writing and Gentility in Early New England

Sheila McIntyre, State University of New York at Potsdam

Abstract

This article investigates how penmanship instruction and letter writing manuals worked to instill gentility in early colonial New England. Handwriting instruction shaped personal correspondence, as oral, scribal, and print traditions collided in the seventeenth-century world of communications. Seventeenth-century copybooks, seventeenth- and eighteenth-century letters, and printed manuals from both England and New England illustrate the impact that print forms had on scribal communication. While penmanship instruction understandably requires endless repetition and actively works to stifle creative variation in favour of regularity and predictability, we might expect personal correspondence to reflect the unique experiences of the writer. Was this intimate connection compromised when a letter's contents were heavily scripted? We might wonder if something was lost when letters become more about performance than about communication. But, the dichotomy of communication versus performance is misleading. For many letter writers, especially privileged correspondents, performance and communication were not mutually exclusive. The 1676 copybook of twelve-year-old John Fearing of Hingham, Massachusetts, serves as a window on the complex relationship between scribal instruction, letter writing, and gentility.

Résumé

Cet article examine comment les manuels enseignant l'art de l'écriture et de la rédaction des lettres ont inculqué la distinction dans la Nouvelle-Angleterre coloniale. L'enseignement de la calligraphie a influé sur la correspondance personnelle, alors que les traditions orales, de l'écrit et de l'imprimé entraient en conflit les unes avec les autres dans le monde des communications du XVIIᵉ siècle. Les cahiers d'écriture du XVIIᵉ siècle, les lettres des XVIIᵉ et XVIIIᵉ siècles et les manuels imprimés en Angleterre et en Nouvelle-Angleterre témoignent de l'incidence que les formes de l'écriture ont eue sur les communications écrites. Si l'enseignement de l'écriture exige naturellement une inlassable répétition et cherche à réprimer les variations fantaisistes en faveur de la régularité et de la prévisibilité, nous pourrions nous attendre à ce que la correspondance personnelle reflète l'expérience propre de son auteur. Est-ce que cet aspect intime se perdait lorsque le contenu d'une lettre était calligraphié selon les règles ? Il y a lieu de se demander si quelque chose s'est perdu lorsque la rédaction des lettres est devenue davantage une performance qu'un moyen de communiquer. Mais la dichotomie communications–performance est trompeuse. Pour beaucoup de personnes qui écrivaient des lettres, tout particulièrement des classes privilégiées, la performance et la communication ne s'excluaient pas l'une l'autre. Le cahier d'écriture datant de 1676 de John Fearing, de Hingham (Massachusetts), âgé de douze ans, montre la relation complexe entre l'enseignement de l'écriture, la rédaction des lettres et la distinction.

Introduction

John Fearing liked to doodle in his penmanship book, embellishing letters with curlicues and dramatic flourishes. Beginning in 1686, when Fearing was twelve years old, he copied words and numbers onto sewn pages that he entitled, "John Fearing His Book."[1] The book's sewn pages include Bible verses, rules of arithmetic, didactic poems, secular proverbs, and sample correspondence—both letters that had been sent, and ones that probably never would be. Some practice lines were repeated more than a dozen times to perfect the young man's handwriting and, most important, his signature. Drawing his pen, carefully filled with homemade ink, across the sewn pages of his copybook, young Fearing repeated his name again and again, practising the soft up curve of the capital "J" and the gentle dual-curve of the cap on his capital "F." Fearing was writing his young self onto the pages as he wrote his name, reminding himself and any readers that John Fearing's character was sewn into the pages of "John Fearing His Book."

The verses that Fearing copied reinforced the link between his handwriting and his developing character. According to his own set line, his writing must possess three graces. First, conformity: "All Letters even at heads and feet must stand/ And bend one way Exactly in each hand." Second, regularity: "Nothing to Writing is a greater Grace/ Than Clearnes true proportion and due Space." Third, restrained action: "Precious Lights poized hands fair Writing doth require/By which one skilfull man makes thousands to admire." Some of the verses reflect his Christian education: "Who would not flie fr help to such a one as can make water wine & bread of stone?" and, more ominously, "Sin's worse then hell it diggd that horrid pitt: 'tis sin that casts poor siners into it." Others prepared him for a life of business, or neatly summed up the obligations of a young man in a Christian commonwealth on the edges of the British Empire: "Honour all men, love the brotherhood, fear God, Honour the King." Reiterating these phrases again and again not only perfected his penmanship, but reminded him of his place in society. As another copy line stated, "Let us not soar too high nor sink too low/ But every one his proper Station know." Fearing was evidently expected to write well to satisfy more than his future business associates; as he was learning, others would judge him by his hand.

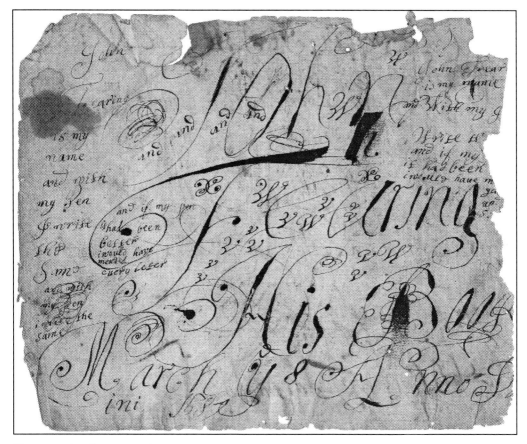

Figure 10.1 John Fearing's copybook.
Massachusetts Historical Society, Boston, Mass.

John Fearing was the eldest son of Israel Fearing, a prominent cooper in Hingham, Massachusetts. Fearing's grandfather, John, had immigrated to New England from Cambridge, England, in 1638 with his employer, Matthew Hawke. Although he emigrated as Hawke's servant, Fearing quickly acquired land and status, serving as selectman, constable, and deacon of First Church, Hingham. When he died in 1665, Fearing's grandfather left his family more than £334, as well as a large homestead, several additional farms, houses, meadows, and woodlots.[2] His sons, Israel and John, shared this inherited land and wealth with their sisters, Mary and Sarah, and widowed mother, Margaret. Israel Fearing (1644–1693) married Elizabeth Wilder in 1673, and had two sons, John and Israel, and two daughters, Elizabeth and Margaret. Young John (1674–1752) did not follow his father by becoming a cooper; instead, he eventually became a prominent and prosperous weaver. Like his grandfather, John served in public office as constable and selectman. The Hawke and Fearing families remained connected as young John married Matthew Hawke's granddaughter, Margaret, in 1708. While the Fearings were not among the extremely wealthy families of Boston or Salem, they are ranked among the important merchant families of Hingham, and would be considered privileged. John was expected to become a successful artisan and possibly a merchant[3] just as his father was and his grandfather had been.

Along with copying verses and practising arithmetic, Fearing copied sample letters into his book, thereby learning the epistolary forms expected of a merchant's son in a busy colonial seaport.[4] The letters include not only the expected sample business letters, for example, "A servants Letter to his master," but also letters to his "Loving and Kind Cousin," his "Deare and Loving Father," and his "Deare Mother." While penmanship instruction understandably requires endless repetition and actively works to stifle creative variation in favour of regularity and predictability, we might expect personal correspondence instead to reflect the unique experiences of the writer, or at least allow for a more impulsive approach to writing. How could Fearing learn how to write to his own mother by copying letters written by another son to a different mother? Rewriting the sample letters gave the young man scripts to follow; his creativity was clearly less important than his correctness, even when composing personal letters. Fearing's copybook even included lists of acceptable salutations and closings, because, as he copied, "it is an easie matter for to Frame or indict any Letter, if you know but how to begin or end it handsomely." For example, acceptable closings included, "with my best respects, and good wishes"; "and I account it my happyness to be reckoned in the number of your Friends"; "Fear not to commit your busyness unto me, since you know there is not anything that I can deny unto you"; "I will study to obey your commands in aney thing wherein I may serve you." This arsenal of openings and closings almost suggests that what lay in between florid hellos and goodbyes was unimportant.

Fearing's copybook is a rich representation of how penmanship instruction worked to instill gentility in early colonial New England. While gentility in the seventeenth-century colonies is difficult to define, historian Richard Bushman has suggested that "the genteel person was a set of aspects, almost a checklist of desirable traits and abilities."[5] The "courtesy-book" world that Bushman explores in the early American colonies, sought to "create refined and worthy hearts and minds" that embraced three standards of conduct: "respect for rank, bodily restraint, and regard for feelings."[6] Acceptable letters necessarily showcased all three. Handwriting instruction, a growing field in the early colonies, shaped personal correspondence, as the oral, scribal, and print traditions collided in the seventeenth-century world of communications. Just as Fearing's ABCs were intended to reflect conformity, regularity, and restrained action, his speech and his personal letters were also expected to adhere to scripts that marked his position in colonial culture. As he wrote in his copybook, "Courteous Behaviour and prudent Communication are/ most becoming Ornaments to a young man with/ which he may best be furnished by timely Education/ and the vertuous Example of his parents and Governours."

Literacy scholars have argued that as print became increasingly widespread in the seventeenth and eighteenth centuries, handwriting was all the more valued for personal communication because it was viewed as an extension of the writer's own body. Print was impersonal, even "duplicitous," while script was, by definition, personal, corporeal, and presumably authentic.[7] Reading handwritten letters allowed the reader to envision the writer in the act of writing, as a personal letter connected distantly settled people for

Figure 10.2 John Fearing's copybook.
Massachusetts Historical Society, Boston, Mass.

at least the time it took to write the letter and to read it. Was this intimate connection compromised when a letter's contents were heavily scripted? We might wonder if something was lost when letters become more about performance than about communication. But, the dichotomy of communication versus performance is misleading. For many letter writers, especially privileged correspondents, performance and communication were not mutually exclusive.[8] In fact, because letters served as the writer's representative, adhering to standards became increasingly important. Writing was expected to present the self to the reader, and writers wanted to present the appropriate self. As Fearing's copybook highlights, meeting expectations was sometimes more important than expressing passion, conveying thoughts, or even sharing news.

An understanding of letters begins with an understanding of penmanship. John Fearing worked to master a seventeenth-century hand that schoolchildren today still struggle to learn. Originating in fifteenth-century Italy, the humanist or italic hand had replaced the gothic and secretary hands by the mid-seventeenth century in most Anglo-American contexts.[9] Fearing composed his copybook under someone's tutelage, as the book contains at least two distinct hands. The short verses about handwriting and the other secular and religious verses scattered throughout the copybook appear in a manner common to both printed and handwritten copybook manuals. The line was written across the top, usually by an exemplary hand, and then repeated many times below by the student. It is hard to tell who "set the copy" in Fearing's book. While the hand on the top line is more mature and practised than Fearing's own, it seems less refined than one might expect from a penmanship instructor.

Beginning in 1636, penmanship instructors offered their services privately to students in Boston, and the town established its first writing school in 1667.[10] While the first colonial penmanship manual did not appear until 1748, copybooks imported from England provided writing students with appropriate instruction from the beginning of settlement. For example, the 1700 inventory from Michael Perry's Bookshop in Boston included Tobias Ellis's *English School*, John Hill's *Young Secretary's Guide*, 100 copies of the *Epitome of English Orthography* (printed in Boston), as well as 21 blank copybooks.[11] Many copybooks were designed for boys (and some girls) who were preparing for a mercantile life, and usually included bookkeeping materials, tables, weights and measures, sample bills of exchange or credit, and maxims of proper conduct in business.[12]

Literacy scholars agree that children did not learn to read and write simultaneously, nor did students learn to read handwriting at the same time they learned to read print. Rather, acquiring full literacy was a multi-level process: Mothers generally taught their children to read print, and fathers taught their children scribal literacy.[13] Many printed primers mirrored this progression, as in a page from William Mather's *Young Man's Companion* (1681). On the first page entitled, "A Primmer for Children/Letters for Reading," Mather constructed columns. The first contained an unadorned upright, linear, "print-form" letter, the second column featured an italic script, and the third, a traditional ornate gothic print.[14] John Fearing may have learned to write from his own father, from a private tutor or itinerant writing master, from classes at a writing school, or from copying from the dozens of English penmanship manuals that appeared in colonial Boston's bookstalls. Given his rather advanced age of twelve, the copybooks probably do not represent his first attempts at writing, but rather his efforts to refine his penmanship and to practise his epistolary skills.[15]

Although Fearing's book contains several pages in Latin, Fearing was being groomed for the mercantile life, not for college. According to historian Tamara Thornton, by 1684, students in public schools in Boston were divided between Harvard-bound boys who focused on the classical languages they would need to become Protestant ministers, and merchants-in-training who entered writing schools.[16] A mercantile education traditionally stressed clear penmanship, grammar, mathematics, bookkeeping, navigation, astronomy, and some legal forms. Would-be merchants could also purchase self-instruction manuals, which covered a dizzying array of subjects and taught the skills necessary to succeed in business: Mather's *Young Man's Companion* (1681) ran to more than 400 pages of useful information. Rather than elite or genteel display, these manuals stressed useful and practical knowledge to young businessmen, although some manuals included lists of proper titles of address and some Latin phrases, such as John Hill's *Young Secretary's Guide*

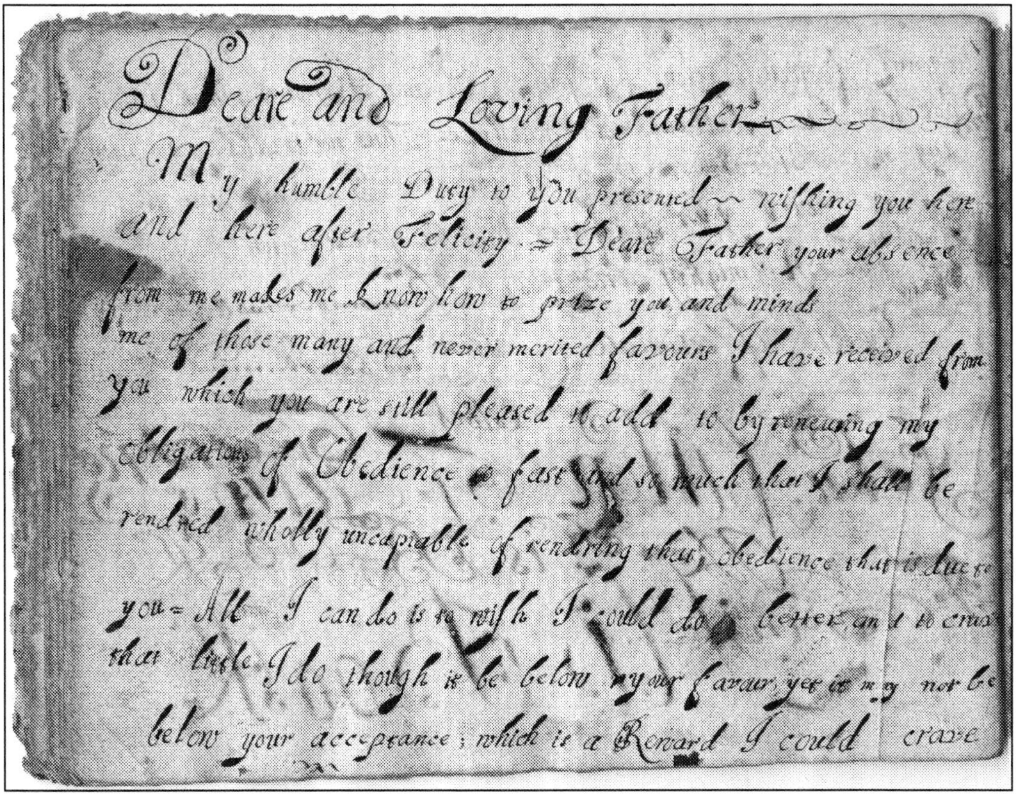
Deare and Loving Father
My humble Duty to you presented wishing you here and here after Felicity = Deare Father your absence from me makes me Know how to prize you and minds me of those many and never merited favours I have received from you which you are still pleased to add to by reneuing my obligations of Obedience so fast and so much that I shall be rendred wholly uncapable of rendring that Obedience that is due to you = All I can do is to wish I could do better and to crave that little I do though it be below your favour yet it may not be below your acceptance; which is a Reward I could crave

Figure 10.3 John Fearing's copybook.
Massachusetts Historical Society, Boston, Mass.

or a Speedy Help to Learning (1687, 7th edition, 1696). So, while Fearing rehearsed some Latin in his copybook, he was clearly bound for the counting house, as some of the verses in his copybook indicate: "A Scholar doth these three Rudiements de sign/ Grammer Arithmetick and Writing fine/ Attaining Grammer Rules we speake true Sence/ Concord in Words did first from her commence/ Arithmetick the Art of Numbring shows/ From a fine Pen much Art and Fancy flows." The art and fancy appear in Fearing's doodles. The extra designs that adorn his compositions not only mark his interest in the aesthetics of his words, but were also an excellent way for a young writer to practise manipulating the loaded nib of a pen.[17] Smudges and smears of ink suggested that the writer lacked skill, indulged in laziness, or cared little for his correspondents. As the *School of Good Manners* reminded its young pupils in its "Alphabet of Useful Copies": "Keep thy Books without Blot, thy Cloaths without Spot."[18]

Many of the published writing manuals—divided roughly into three types: secretaries, penmanship books, and epistolary guides—contain sample letters. Fearing's own handwritten version is no different. His book features two kinds of correspondence: letters that bear his own signature, presumably composed following a manual or sample letters, and copies of letters apparently sent by young men living in London in the 1670s and 1680s, and rewritten into Fearing's copybook by his writing teacher. A close reading of two of these sample letters indicate the impact that epistolary models could have on personal communication.

According to his copybook, Fearing wrote the following letter to his mother, Elizabeth Wilder Fearing (1652–1731), in Hingham:

> Deare Mother
> My humble Duty to you presented Wishing and earnestly Desiring the fruition of your Health encrease of serrene Happines here and your eternal Joy, Comfort and Felicity hereafter Having obtained some small skill in the Art of Writing I could do no less in manifestation of my Duty than to communicate to you the knowledge of my Welfare by my own hand of which I earnestly entreat yoor Acceptation which if I obtaine the knowledge thereof by a word or two from your self would be his great satisfaction and Encouragement who desires every way to manifest himself
> John Fearing   February ye 24
> dated at Hingham   Anno Domini 1687

John Fearing probably never sent this letter to his mother, although the letter may have been a practice copy for one he did send. But, what does the letter actually say? Aside from wishing her "eternal Joy, Comfort and Felicity," assuring her of his welfare, and requesting return correspondence, Fearing used the letter simply to display his newly acquired skills in the "Art of Writing."

Another sample letter from a son to his mother in Fearing's book "set the copy" for Fearing's own letter, just as the proverbs and verses set the copy for the penmanship sections of his book. Matthew Atkinson, a scholar in London, probably unknowingly provided the template for Fearing's composition:

> another Letter of a scholar unto his parents
> Honoured Father and Mother
> your kindness call for my dutiful acknowledgment; I wish I could better answer your Love to me, and your cost upon me; The encrease of my Learning is by me endeavoured, and in some measure pressed after. I hope I shall have the constant assistance of your prayers for the accomplishment thereof; in the confidence of which, I humble take my Leave, and rest,
> your dutiful son,   London, Feb 28
> Mat Atkinson   1683

Like Fearing's, Atkinson's letter simply thanks his parents for their kindnesses, reassures them that he is diligently pursuing his studies, and requests their prayers. The letters in Fearing's copybook echo those found in letter writing manuals. Consider, for example, "A Letter from a Son at School to his Mother" in John Hill's *The Young Secretary's Guide*:

A Letter from a Son at School to his Mother.

Ever-honoured Mother,

I Think my self duty bound to send you these Lines, as indeed I frequently ought to do, that I may put you in mind of my Duty, and the just Acknowledgments I make of your Love and tender Care over me; but especially, that I may, at the return of the Bearer, be informed of your Health and Welfare, in which, I must confess, all my Joy and Happiness on this side Heaven consists, as publickly owning, that, next to God, I owe my Life and Felicity to you, and in your Happiness can only rejoyce; for the continuation of which, my Prayers shall at no time be wanting, nor my Endeavours to perform whatever your Commands shall enjoin me as far as it lies in my power; And so I take leave to subscribe my self, Your most obedient and dutiful Son,

A.P.

The probably fictional A.P. writes to his mother out of a sense of duty, to acknowledge her love and care, to enquire after her health, and to pledge his concern for her. But, he tells her little else.[19]

While these things are certainly important both for a son to express and a mother to read, what is left out of both the printed and handwritten letters is notable. Compare, for example, this 1699 letter[20] sent by another young student, Theophilus Cotton, to his mother, Joanna:

camb.
Sept. 12: 1699:

honred mother.

Last Thirsday <Saturday>[21] night a message came to me, from Brother Cushing, who was att boston, Desiring me for to meet ym att Mistike, next morn about seven of ye clock, – wherupon I did accordingly; yy went <and and did> away about 9 of ye clock, and made account to get home yt day, I cant tell whether yy did, but I have heard yt Sarah is very ill sense. &c. this day Uncle Mather was here, and sent for me up In ye Library, and gave me a Letter for you, wrin he said he advised you <to goe> to goe to Carolina. he gave me hardness of heart, <and> which you have, and also a good deall of good councill. I desire yt I may get good by it. Here is no news att all, only Last week Governour Usher made a feast for my Lord (att Mistike) and for ye councell In wch was 15 sorte of victuals. I conclude, and Remaine your dutifull son (being past 11 clock att night).

Theophilus Cotton

I would Intreat you If you had any paper to send me some for I have but one sheet in ye world and I would have you send word whether, or when you Intend to goe to Carolina. and whether you have any business for me to doe for you. In getting any thing for you.

Like Fearing (if only in the practised world of his copybook) and Atkinson, Cotton was away from home at school and heavily indebted to his parents for their financial and emotional support. But, Cotton's letter sounds nothing like the other two. It omits both florid greeting and closing, and focuses on news: a trip from Cambridge to Mystic, Connecticut; a difficult meeting with his uncle, the powerful Boston minister, Increase Mather; some letters he received, sent, and transported; and a feast he attended featuring 15 different kinds of food. He also requests writing paper and promises to help his mother prepare for an upcoming trip to Carolina (which she never took) to join her husband, the exiled minister, John Cotton, Jr. of Plymouth, who was accused of adultery. Cotton's letter serves well as a paper messenger, informing his mother of all kinds of news, and even allowing her to envision his life, both the actions he took, and the setting in which he wrote the letter—by candlelight, after 11 o'clock at night. The loosely constructed, newsy letter contains none of the florid language suggested by the letter writing manuals that set the copy for Fearing's copybook.

So, how then do the epistolary forms found in letter writing manuals fit with the real world of letter exchange? It is both unfair and merely obvious to conclude that "real" letters are more complex, more interesting, and even more trustworthy than sample letters. It is not enough to simply suggest that historians distinguish between prescriptive and descriptive literature when trying to understand the nature of personal correspondence. Since no letters that John Fearing wrote outside the pages of his copybook remain, we cannot know whether he followed the forms he copied as a twelve-year-old. (Perhaps he did not.) But, epistolary forms often set the copy for personal letters in colonial New England as stilted salutations and melodramatic apologies for a host of writing deficiencies increasingly filled the lines of "real" letters in the late seventeenth and early eighteenth centuries.

Consider this baroque opening from a letter that young Belcher Noyes wrote to his mother in 1732: "Its from a sence of my Duty & the Respect due to you, that induces me to take pen in hand, & improve this opportunity of Giveing you some Testimony of the same, tho at ye same time, I trust the News of my Welfare will be no ways disagreeable to you. I flatter myself, Madm, that I have some small share in your good wishes for my prosperity, which is further encouragement to this freedom, as well as to convince you of my duty."[22] The letter informs his mother, who lived in Boston, of his safe arrival in North Carolina nearly three months earlier, but it contains no other information.

Apologies for the very act of writing also became increasingly common in upper-class correspondence by the mid-eighteenth century, as coy self-deprecating asides take up the space once devoted to news in personal letters.[23] In 1750, Anna Green admits that "to have so agreeable & obliging a friend to converse with & communicate my thoughts to would be an inexpressible satisfaction, an unknown Pleasure, a vast Delight," but she then apologizes: "you have thousands of better ways than thinking of me to employ your thoughts." She even closes her letter by somewhat disingenuously begging her correspondent's forgiveness for writing at all: "but I'm writing on not considering whose time I am taking up but tis my darling employment, & to you my agreeable

Correspondent, so you must excuse me & I will conclude."[24] Anna's letter informs her correspondent of very little, at least in its content.

The increasing prevalence of florid apologies for style, form, process, and content suggest that letters are serving different ends by the later decades of the eighteenth century, especially for elite writers settled in cosmopolitan areas who enjoyed privileged access to news and information. Letters become a prime vehicle for the display of gentility, in addition to, and eventually instead of, a vital source of information. The arrival of colonial newspapers also began to affect the tone and content of personal letters. Newspapers did not replace letters. Even after the proliferation of newspapers by mid-century, letters remained a primary means of a certain kind of information diffusion.[25] While local and family news filled letters, and many correspondents relied on personal communications—oral and scribal—to remain informed, the newspapers began to challenge the role letters once played as the primary source of information. Once colonial newspapers began offering a clear accounting of local, colonial, and international events in the 1730s and 1740s, letters continued to supplement and analyze that news, and letters also carried the personal and local news about which newspapers were understandably silent. But, newspapers assumed the responsibility of sharing the details of the event itself.

So, what is Fearing practising when he copies sample letters? He has been sharing information with his mother orally since he could speak and does not need a manual to communicate news to her, especially since he is probably living at home when he is writing in his book. What he is practising is **form**; as he wrote in his copybook, "It is an easie matter for to Frame or indict any Letter, if you only know but how to begin it or end it handsomely." If Fearing's letters do not share news, then what do they share? The form of Fearing's letter tells his mother many things about her son: that he was well, learning, maturing. While the letter contains little content, the sight of his letter illustrates much about Fearing as a young man. The form **is** the communication.

Returning letters to the oral-scribal-print context highlights the symbolic role of letter exchange in colonial New England. Letters straddled the liminal space between oral conversation and printed text. They were meant to represent face-to-face communication, which correspondents always claimed they would prefer, for people who are separated by distance. As John Hill wrote in the preface to his letter-writing manual: "Letters, whose Influences effectually create the same Effects, and right Understanding, as if the Sender or Writer were present; and are agreed upon by all Hands, to be the maintainers of Love."[26] But, letters are not exactly like conversation. They are more akin to seeing someone at a distance, to hearing someone without being able to respond directly and immediately to the voice. Both writer and reader call the other to mind each time the writer creates and the reader re-reads the letter; many letters describe the writer's setting—Theophilus Cotton's candlelight, for example—in an effort to transport the reader. And, more importantly, where conversation is fleeting, a letter is a written record of feelings, events, and opinions that is dangerously open to interpretation and misinterpretation—both intended and unintended—by readers.

Conclusion

Concerns for the security of letter exchange, as well as fears that their words might be misunderstood, led many letter writers to censor their own writing. Saying "nothing" was better than saying the wrong thing. Returning to the sample letters above offers a useful parallel: Theophilus Cotton's letter is effectively a handwritten oral conversation, while the nearly indistinguishable letters of Matthew Atkinson and John Fearing recall the reproducibility of printed texts and, in fact, sound very much like the printed version of a "son's letter to his mother." Even as handwriting was valued as more trustworthy for personal communication because it was thought to be an extension of the self, scribal texts are still written records that are dangerously permanent. Letter writing manuals and sample letters provided safe expressions that appropriately shared a writer's general intentions, without risking offence. Fearing was not learning how to write, he was learning how to copy the acceptable forms that mark him as an up-and-coming member of colonial society. His letters would serve as a kind of social currency. Maintaining a letter writing style that showcased the same graces as his penmanship—conformity, regularity, restrained action—best equipped John Fearing to join the ranks of genteel colonists by allowing him to practise his letters by rote and thus to choose the self he presented.

Notes

1. All quotations from the Fearing copybook are from John Fearing Notebooks, 1687–1688, Spaulding–Fearing Papers, Massachusetts Historical Society.
2. "Will of John Fearing," *New England Historic Genealogical Record* 13 (1859): 331–332; James Savage, *Genealogical Dictionary of the First Settlers of New England*, 4 vols (Boston, 1860–1862), vol. 2, pp. 150, 380–381; vol. 4, pp. 549–550.
3. Richard Bushman suggests that by the end of the eighteenth century in America, "smaller merchants and professionals, ordinary well-off farmers, successful artisans, school teachers, minor government officials, clerks, shopkeepers, industrial entrepreneurs, and managers" constituted a "middle class." In Fearing's context, I suspect there was little class difference between smaller merchants and successful artisans. Bushman, *The Refinement of America: Persons, Houses, Cities* (New York: Alfred Knopf, 1992), p. xiii.
4. Scholars have studied letter writing in early America beginning with Richard Brown's path-breaking *Knowledge is Power: The Diffusion of Information in Early America, 1700–1865* (New York: Oxford University Press, 1989). Elisabeth Nichols examines letter writing and letter reading in the early Republic, "How Long It Appears since I've Made You a Writing Visit: Writing and Reading Letters in the Early Republic" (Paper presented at the Organization of American Historians Conference, April 1998); Elisabeth Nichols, "Pray Don't Tell Anybody that I Write Politics: Letter-writing in the Early Republic," (Ph.D. Dissertation, University of New Hampshire, 1997). See also Konstantin Dierks, "The Feminization of Letter Writing in Early America, 1750–1800" (Paper presented at the Institute for Early American History and Culture Conference, May–June 1996); Dierks, "Let Me Chat a Little: Letter Writing in Rhode Island before the Revolution," *Rhode Island History* 53 (1995): 120–133; Dierks,

"Letter Writing, Gender, and Class in America, 1750–1800" (Ph.D. Dissertation, Brown University, 1999); William Merrill Decker, *Epistolary Practices: Letter-writing in America before Telecommunications* (Chapel Hill: University of North Carolina Press, 1998). Scholars interested in epistolarity have traditionally focused on epistolary fiction: *Writing the Female Voice: Essays on Epistolary Literature*, ed. Elizabeth Goldsmith (Boston: Northeastern University Press, 1989); Janet Gurkin Altman, *Epistolarity: Approaches to a Form* (Columbus: Ohio State University Press, 1982); Elizabeth Heckendorn Cook, *Epistolary Bodies: Gender and Genre in the Eighteenth Century Republic of Letters* (Stanford: Stanford University Press, 1996).

5. Bushman, *Refinement of America*, p. 63.

6. Bushman, *Refinement of America*, pp. 60, 38.

7. "If print entailed self-negation, then by contrast script would entail the explicit presentation of the self. The printed page might be 'void of all character,' but the handwritten one would present the self to its readers," Tamara Plakins Thornton, *Handwriting in America: A Cultural History* (New Haven: Yale University Press, 1996), pp. 4, 27–33. See also David Shields, *Oracles of Empire: Poetry, Politics, and Commerce in British America, 1690–1750* (Chicago: University of Chicago Press, 1990); *Civil Tongues & Polite Letters in British America* (Chapel Hill: University of North Carolina Press, 1997); and Michael Warner, *Letters of the Republic: Publication and the Public Sphere in Eighteenth-century America* (Cambridge: Harvard University Press, 1990).

8. For the connection between letter writing and the rise of gentility, see Thornton, *Handwriting in America*, pp. 2–41; Shields, *Civil Tongues & Polite Letters*; Bushman, *Refinement of America*; Warner, *Letters of the Republic*; Joan Gunderson, "Kith and Kin: Women's Networks in Colonial Virginia," in *The Devil's Lane: Sex and Race in the Early South*, eds Catherine Clinton and Michele Gillespie (New York: Oxford University Press, 1997).

9. The italic hand had three variations: "[T]he upright form which is more akin to printing became known as the roman hand because of its classical antecedents; the sloping, cursive form as the italic proper; and a round, matter-of-fact form as the round hand," Laetitia Yeandle, "The Evolution of Handwriting in the English-speaking Colonies of America," *The American Archivist* 43 (Summer 1980): 294–311.

10. E. Jennifer Monaghan, "Readers Writing: The Curriculum of the Writing Schools of Eighteenth Century Boston," *Visible Language* 21 (Spring 1987): 170; S. Michael Halloran, "From Rhetoric to Composition: The Teaching of Writing in America to 1900," in *A Short History of Writing Instruction: From Ancient Greece to Twentieth-century America* (Davis, CA: University of California Press, 1990). Janet Gurkin Altman offers a comparative approach in "Political Ideology in the Letter Manual (France, England, New England)," *Studies in Eighteenth Century Culture* 18 (1988): 105–22; Altman, "Teaching the 'People' to Write: The Formation of a Popular Civic Identity in the French Letter Manual," *Studies in Eighteenth Century Culture* 22 (1992): 147–73.

11. Tobias Ellis, *The English School*, Early English Books #1330:9 (London: John Darby, 1680); John Hill, *Young Secretary's Guide, or, a Speedy Help to Learning*, Early English Books #187:17 (London: H. Rhodes, 1696); *Epitome of English Orthography*, Evans #782 (Boston: B. Green, 1697). For Perry's inventory, see *John Denton's Letters from New England*, Publications of the Prince Society (Boston: T .R. Marvin & Son, 1867), pp. 314–319.

12. Thornton discusses writing masters, manuals, and female students in *Handwriting in America*, pp. 7–8.

13. For some discussion of who could write in the colonial period and why, see Thornton, *Handwriting in America*, pp. 4–23; Linda Auwers, "Reading the Marks of the Past: Exploring Female Literacy in Colonial Windsor, Connecticut," *Historical Methods* 13 (Fall 1980): 204–214; Ross W. Beales, "Studying Literacy at the Community Level: A Research Note," *Journal of Interdisciplinary History* 9 (1978): 93–102. David Hall suggests that literacy "involved different combinations" of skills, and that most colonial New Englanders could read and more could

write than historians generally suggest, in *Worlds of Wonder, Days of Judgment: Popular Religious Belief in Early New England* (New York: Alfred Knopf, 1989), pp. 31–38. For some discussion of increases in female literacy during the eighteenth century, see Gloria Main, "An Inquiry into When and Why Women Learned to Write in Colonial New England," *Journal of Social History* 24 (1991); E. Jennifer Monaghan, "Literacy Instruction and Gender in Colonial New England," in *Reading in America: Literature and Social History*, ed. Cathy Davidson (Baltimore: Johns Hopkins University Press, 1989), pp. 53–80; Joel Perlmann and Dennis Shirley, "When Did New England Women Acquire Literacy?" *William and Mary Quarterly* 48 (1991): 50–67; Brian Street, *Literacy in Theory and Practice* (Cambridge: Cambridge University Press, 1984). For some comparative perspectives, see Keith Thomas, "The Meaning of Literacy in Early Modern England," in *The Written Word: Literacy in Transition*, ed. Gerd Baumann (Oxford: Oxford University Press, 1986); David Cressy, *Literacy and the Social Order: Reading and Writing in Tudor and Stuart England* (Cambridge: Cambridge University Press, 1980).

14. William Mather, *A Very Useful Manual, or the Young Man's Companion*, Early English Books #1597:13 (London: T. Snowden, 1681), p. 1.

15. Margaret Spufford suggests that children in seventeenth-century England began to learn to write at age seven or eight in "First Steps in Literacy: The Reading and Writing Experiences of the Humblest Seventeenth-century Spiritual Autobiographers," in *Literacy and Social Development in the West: A Reader*, ed. Harvey Graff (Cambridge: Cambridge University Press, 1981), pp. 125–150. Ray Nash argues that "the colonial American writing school, public or private, ordinarily took boys from about seven years of age," "American Writing Masters and Copybooks," Publications of the Colonial Society of Massachusetts, *Transactions* 42 (1952—56): 352.

16. Thornton, p. 9.

17. Laetitia Yeandle, "The Evolution of Handwriting in the English-speaking Colonies of America," *The American Archivist* 43 (Summer 1980): 299; Nash, "American Writing Masters," p. 359.

18. Eleazar Moodey, *School of Good Manners, Composed for the Help of Parents in Teaching Their Children How to Carry It in Their Places during Their Minority* (New London, 1715 (no known copy); Evans 1778, 12553 (Boston: T&J Fleet, 1772). Moodey also included reminders that letters were private, reflecting an increasing distance from the seventeenth-century tradition of wide letter sharing. He told his young readers, "Touch not, nor look upon the Books or Writings of any one, unless the Owner invite or desire thee," and "Come not near when another reads a Letter or any other Paper," *School of Good Manners*, p. 16.

19. Hill, "A Letter from a Son at School to his Mother," *The Young Secretary's Guide*, p. 85.

20. Theophilus Cotton (Cambridge) to Joanna Rosseter Cotton (Sandwich), September 12, 1699, Miscellaneous Bound Collection, Massachusetts Historical Society.

21. The words between carets indicate words the letter writer scratched out.

22. Belcher Noyes (N. Carolina) to Katherine Noyes (Boston), February 19, 1732, Jeffries Family Papers, vol. 11, Massachusetts Historical Society.

23. Elisabeth Nichols suggests that late eighteenth-century apologies "beseech the reader to participate in the process of composing a letter, to join with the author in the struggle to reconcile vocabulary with sentiment, to help hurriedly fulfill a duty, or to engage in the process of letting thoughts evolve as ink flows onto paper," "How Long it Appears," p. 6. See also Bushman, *Refinement in America*, pp. 90–96.

24. Anna Green (Boston) to Sarah Kent (Newbury), July 10, 1750, Norton Family Papers, Massachusetts Historical Society.

25. Charles Clark argues that newspapers were supplemental to a thriving oral and scribal culture, which continued to spread news long after newspapers began publishing in the colonies, *The Public Prints: The Newspaper in Anglo-American Culture, 1665–1740* (New York: Oxford University Press, 1994). But, letters also began to reflect the presence of newspapers, changing in both in content and in style.

PART THREE: PEOPLE AND THEIR LETTERS

TROISIÈME PARTIE : LES GENS ET LEURS MISSIVES

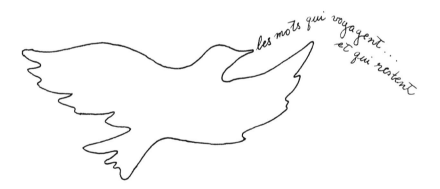

les mots qui voyagent... et qui restent

THE IMMIGRANT EXPERIENCE AND THE CREATION OF A TRANSATLANTIC EPISTOLARY SPACE

A Case Study[1]

Yves Frenette, Glendon College, York University, and Gabriele Scardellato, University of Toronto

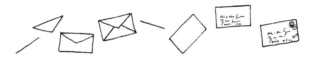

Abstract

Christian Bennedsen came to Canada from Denmark in the fall of 1951. He settled in Ontario where he began working on a farm and in several small towns and cities before moving to Toronto. He ended up staying in Canada. Bennedsen kept all the letters received from and sent to friends and relatives back home in Denmark between 1951 and 1998, a total of 700 or more documents. His correspondence constitutes an excellent opportunity to inquire into the construction of cultural space and immigrant identity. Discussion of the forty-year stream of correspondence is balanced with an oral history inquiry, conducted with the collaboration of Mr. Bennedsen.

Résumé

Christian Bennedsen a quitté le Danemark pour le Canada à l'automne de 1951. Il s'est établi en Ontario, où il a commencé a travailler dans un ferme et plusieurs petites villes et localités avant de déménager à Toronto. Il est finalement resté au Canada. Bennedsen a conservé toutes les lettres de ses amis et parents demeurés au Danemark, qu'il a reçues d'eux entre 1951 et 1998, au total plus de 700 documents. Sa correspondance constitue une merveilleuse occasion d'explorer la construction de l'espace culturel et de l'identité des immigrants. L'étude de cette correspondance, qui s'étend sur quarante années, est accompagnée d'une enquête d'histoire orale effectuée en collaboration avec M. Bennedsen.

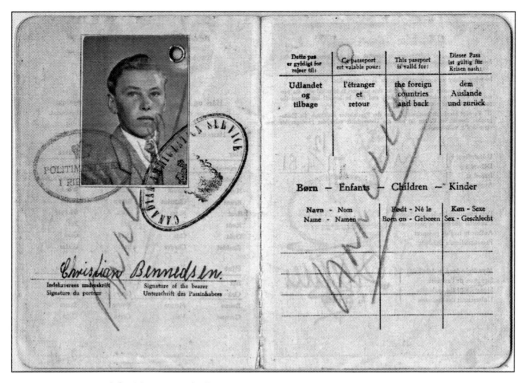

Figure 11.1 Bennedsen's Danish passport, April 12, 1956.

Christian Bennedsen Collection, Personal Documents, Passports, P45-7.1.4, Canadian Postal Museum/
Canadian Museum of Civilization Archives.

Introduction

In November 1951, motivated by the desire to improve his economic situation and by dreams of adventure, Christian Bennedsen, a 21-year-old Dane from the hamlet of Spandet, Denmark, 40 kilometres north of the German border, boarded the SS *Oslofjorden* bound for America. His father was a farm labourer, who later became a butcher and businessman but never achieved financial success. Bennedsen himself began working in the fields at the age of six, when he was hired out to a neighbouring farmer. At seven, he moved out of his family home, boarding with the farmers for whom he worked, while still attending school.

His childhood friend, Eric Skov, had already migrated to Canada, and, in 1948, Eric's cousin, Jens, began to speculate about the possibility of emigrating there with Bennedsen. In part, the attraction was produced by the advertising campaign carried out by the Canadian National Railway (CNR). Half a century later, Bennedsen remembered vividly looking at posters of Canadian prairie landscapes depicting endless wheat fields under a brilliant sun and the promise of endless acreage, enormous farm machinery, and so forth. While Jens was able to sail for North America in May 1951, Bennedsen was delayed due to the arrival of his notice of conscription for service in the Danish army. This was eventually deferred, and, on November 8, 1951, at the CNR Colonization department's offices in Copenhagen, he signed an Agricultural Labourer's Agreement

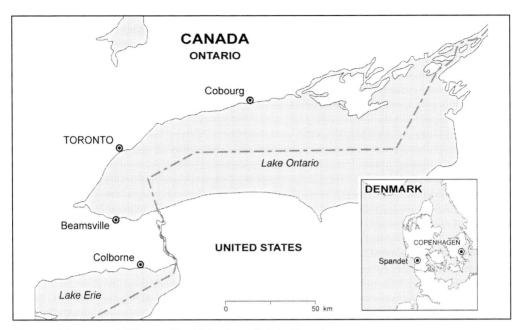

Figure 11.2 The new and old homes of Danish Immigrant Christian Bennedsen.
Map by Andrée Héroux.

that bound him to work for one year for a Canadian farmer. Later in the month, he boarded the SS *Oslofjorden* and sailed to New York. The fare to Canada via New York cost him 1500 *kroner* (approximately CAN $200). The day before his departure, he wrote to his parents and told them that he would spend six days at sea before landing at New York; after clearing American customs and immigration, he would take the train to Toronto where he and his travelling companions would be met by a CNR agent at their office in Union Station.[2]

Upon arrival in Toronto in early December, Bennedsen was met by a CNR agent, who directed him to a train bound for Beamsville, Ontario, in the Niagara Peninsula, where a farmer was to provide him with his first job. However, he stayed there just one night—in the barn—because, it seems, he was not the right Dane: The farmer's wife had been expecting the arrival of her brother! The next day, she drove Bennedsen to the train station and he headed back to Toronto. It was Saturday and the CNR offices were closed. While still in Union Station, a stranger who just wanted to chat spoke to him in English. Bennedsen, who spoke no English, could only respond in Danish. To his great surprise, the stranger switched immediately to Danish: He was a Danish-American bricklayer employed temporarily in Toronto. This Good Samaritan took Bennedsen under his wing until Monday morning. CNR found the young Dane another employer—the Rutherfords—who operated a farm near Colborne, east of Toronto. Bennedsen moved there on December 10, 1951, where he lived for almost a year. In November 1952, he moved to the neighbouring city of Cobourg where he held a series of jobs.

On Labour Day, 1954, Bennedsen decided to move to Toronto, where Eric Skov was already living. With his help, he was hired on in the sheet metal industry and decided to take a night course to learn this trade. After gaining experience with various employers, he eventually became a supervisor on large construction projects in Toronto and throughout Central and Southern Ontario. In 1956, Bennedsen met Concetta (Connie) Colangelo, a second generation Italian-Canadian, whom he married three years later. In 1960, the couple moved into Connie's parents' home in one of the city's Little Italy neighbourhoods where they lived until the mid-1990s. Far from his own family, Bennedsen developed a strong bond with his in-laws, especially his mother-in-law, Carmela. In the 1970s, through the Colangelos, he began to take part in the activities of the Order Sons of Italy of Ontario (OSIO), the oldest and most important Italian-Canadian mutual aid society. In 1991, he became president of the Order, the only non-Italian ever to hold this position. Bennedsen played a central role in transforming the OSIO into a Canada-wide organization, of which he was the first national president in 1994–95. Little by little, he had become part of Toronto's Italian community.

Bennedsen wrote his first letter to his family before he left Denmark. At Mackenzie Rutherford's farm, he became a fervent letter writer. In March 1952, just three months after his arrival in Ontario, he wrote home: "This is letter 51 I have written since I came and I have received 38 total so I am happy to hear from everybody in the neighborhood and from you."[3] Eight months later, he added:

> I have a lot of trouble trying to keep up with my writing now but I still manage all right. I received 11 letters last week and I think that is the most I have received in one week since my arrival. I have just counted all my letters and I have received 119 and they are all safe in my drawer here but I am still ahead in my writing. This letter is number 123 that I have written since I left home.[4]

In less than a year, Bennedsen had become the centre of a network of 20 correspondents, who altogether produced 242 letters. The network included his immediate family, his relatives, former neighbours and friends from Spandet and elsewhere, and farmers for whom he had worked in Denmark.

Danish Immigration to North America

At first glance, Bennedsen's migration experience and his epistolary activity are not extraordinary in and of themselves. He was one of tens of millions of European migrants who left the continent between the end of the nineteenth century and the 1970s. The reasons behind this massive migration are complex, but can be summarized in three interdependent phenomena: demographic transition; the commercialization of agriculture, which, in many areas, created a surplus of farm labourers; and, the industrialization of certain regions, which often led to the de-industrialization of other regions. The repercussions of these phenomena were felt internationally, nationally, regionally and locally, and by families and individuals.[5]

Denmark participated in this large migration movement, with half a million Danes seeking their fortunes elsewhere between the late 1860s and the 1970s. The majority (70 per cent) settled in the United States; 15 per cent chose Canada. They began migrating to Canada at the dawn of the twentieth century when land became scarce south of the border.[6] A second wave of Danish immigrants arrived in Canada after the First World War: 19,000 Danes settled here between 1919 and 1930. These men—for they were mostly men—settled in the Prairie Provinces and, in smaller numbers, in British Columbia and Southern Ontario. The stock market crash of 1929 put an end to this migration and incited some migrants to move back to Denmark.

Bennedsen was part of the third wave of Danish immigration that began in 1945. The publicity campaigns by the federal government and the CNR, as well as the difficult living conditions in Europe after the Second World War, convinced 42,000 Danes to try their luck in Canada. In addition, after a half century of Danish immigration to Canada, the country had captured the imagination of a large number of Danes and, for many young people, the Farm Workers Program seemed to be a relatively easy route by which one could emigrate.[7]

Like Bennedsen, the Danes who migrated to North America from the middle of the nineteenth century onward tended to be young, single, male farmhands who were lured to the New World by emigration agents or the propaganda of railroads, land companies, and governments describing the United States and Canada in roseate terms. And, because they were a small minority group in almost every North American community where they settled, and, owing to the sex imbalance, male Danish immigrants married outside of their groups, usually German, Swedish, or Norwegian women. Originating in a very homogeneous country where mostly everyone spoke the same language and practiced the Lutheran religion, they chose spouses culturally close to them rather than Eastern and Southern Europeans against whom they were prejudiced. Falling in love and marrying an Italian-Canadian represented quite a cultural departure for young Christian Bennedsen.[8]

Historians and Immigrant Letters

Bennedsen's voluminous correspondence was not exceptional either. Both the letter writers themselves and contemporary observers were highly conscious of the role of correspondence in developing chains of migration.[9] In the same vein, authors of the first works on immigration to the United States took note of the immigrant correspondence. The classic, *The Polish Peasant in Europe and America* by sociologists William Thomas and Florian Znaniecki (published in five volumes between 1918 and 1920), was based in part on correspondence.[10] As well, three Scandinavian-American historians—George Stephenson, Marcus Lee Hansen, and Theodore Blegen—trod a promising new path using the immigrant letter to create a more democratic social history they hoped would replace elitist political history. These scholars wanted to create an epic tradition that would give the lead role to their parents' generation, which had been neglected by the Anglo-Saxon historians who dominated the field. In 1935, Hansen wrote, "If an epic is the tale of a heroic soul struggling valiantly against hostile forces, then fifty million epics were lived."[11]

On this basis, a tradition of using letters as a significant source of information for the study of immigrants developed. Correspondence was used both to construct historiographic arguments and to recount the immigrant experience. This is why historians of immigration to the United States chose to publish series of correspondence. Over the years, a great deal of effort went into ensuring the authenticity and representation of selected letters. Special care was also taken to contextualize the letters by conducting exhaustive research on the authors. This was accomplished through the use of local and family history methodologies.[12] At the same time, to pique the reader's interest, the letters were presented in fragments; sometimes only the passages considered most "typical" were retained. This was the unfortunate path taken by Arnold Barton:

> Those [Swedish immigrant letters] given here have, moreover, been selected with an eye to variety, interest, and appeal to the reader. Many have been chosen for colourful and exciting episodes, keen observation, sensitive feeling, and the writer's attractive personality. Most immigrant letters have in fact little of interest to relate. They are often filled with clichés, concerned with mundane matters and local news from the old home parish. Many consist largely of religious platitudes, hearsay information, accounts culled from newspapers, comments on the weather, reports on wages and the price of commodities, news of family affairs and greetings to long lists of relatives and friends at home.[13]

In Canada, although immigrants also produced a considerable amount of correspondence, there are few scholarly publications of these letters; studies on this subject are rare. In general, historians are interested in letters only as a reflection of immigrant realities or as tools of propaganda.[14] Within this context, three books and three articles represent the rare exception. The study conducted by Cecil J. Houston and William J. Smyth on nineteenth-century Irish-Protestant immigration rests in part on series of correspondence, three of which are published. Houston and Smyth demonstrate the central place of the letter at each step of the journey and life cycle of Anglo-Protestant immigrants. In addition, the collection of Daisy Philipps's letters, edited by Cole Harris, illustrates the role of the letter in the conservation of British identity among English immigrants. Philipps believed she was participating in Britain's imperial dream and, through her postal exchange with the motherland, recreated a "little England" in Windermere Valley in southwest British Columbia. In his introduction, Harris exaggerates, perhaps, the role of the letter as a tool for cultural continuity. Yet, he opens a potentially fruitful debate on correspondence and mail as part of the structure of immigrant identity. This issue is also at the heart of Jean Le Bihan's articles on a Breton family in Saskatchewan during the first two decades of the twentieth century. Relying almost exclusively on letters sent and received on both sides of the Atlantic, the author shows how immigrant correspondence allows family ties to remain strong. At the same time, it accentuates the cultural distance between the correspondents by making the immigrants and their Breton relatives aware of their widening difference "jusqu' à ce que la distance fit place à l' étrangeté." Folklorist Robert Klymasz studies the issue of identity in his article on the relationship between Ukrainian-Canadian folklore and correspondence at the turn of the twentieth century.

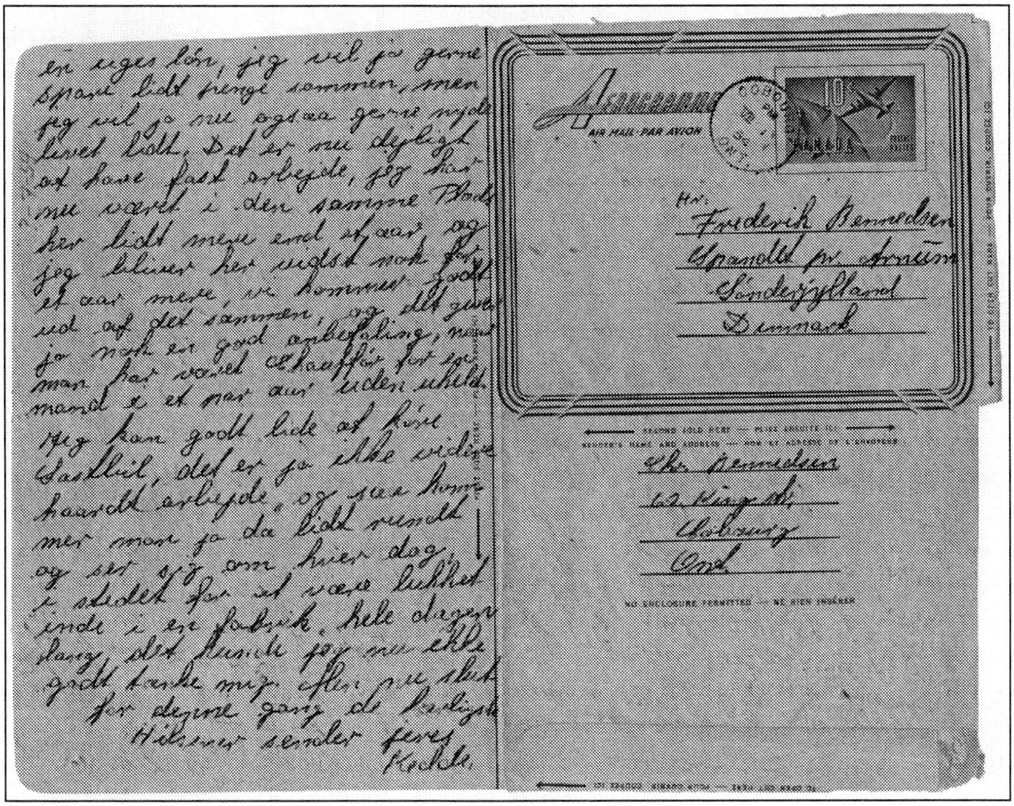

Figure 11.3 An aerogramme destined for Denmark, July 1, 1954.

Christian Bennedsen Collection, Correspondence Series, 16th Group, P29-3-16.19A, Canadian Postal Museum/ Canadian Museum of Civilization Archives.

Ukrainian immigrants relied on well-established cultural symbols when writing their letters. These symbols, however, took on new meaning in their adopted country.[15]

Recently, a milestone was reached with the publication of a superb collection of English immigrant letters to Upper Canada in the 1830s. *English Immigrant Voices* is the first collection of this scope. By putting in context the letters and their authors, by submitting the letters to the canons of historical criticism, especially with regard to the published nature of their material, and by allowing letter writers to speak with little interference, Wendy Cameron, Sheila Haines, and Mary McDougall Maude have set the standard for many years to come.[16]

Christian Bennedsen: Letter Writer

If only because of its sheer volume, a systematic examination of the Christian Bennedsen collection would make a significant contribution to the issue of the role of letters and mail in the construction of cultural spaces and immigrant identities. Begun in 1951, Bennedsen's correspondence ended almost a half century later in 1998 and includes more than 700 documents. The vast majority of them date back to his first five years in Ontario. As well, during a trip to Denmark, Bennedsen collected a large portion of the letters he had sent there over the years. The course of his family correspondence can thus be examined from both sides, a rare occurrence in the historiography of immigrant letters.[17]

Our contribution is also unique, since we are able to compare Bennedsen's correspondence with information obtained in a series of interviews we conducted with him. We will, therefore, be able to shed new light on the use of the immigrant letter as a documentary source for the study of migratory phenomena. We can already caution other researchers about the difficulties of using immigrant correspondence. Bennedsen's letters and interviews present different and often contradictory versions of his migration experience: In his first letter, written in Copenhagen, Bennedsen simply gives his family the details of his next-day departure for New York. Yet, the interviews reveal a terrified young man who, because he was among the first of his generation to leave Spandet, did not want to lose face and therefore hid his apprehension. His difficult first encounter with an Ontario family is also described in two different ways: He wrote to his family that the farmer's wife drove him back to Toronto but, in the interviews, he said that he was only driven to a nearby train station. His letters are filled with an enthusiasm for his life in Canada, as in the following passage: "I get the impression that Canada is a wonderful, free country. One can come and go as one pleases without signing in at least 117 different places."[18] Is it the "love at first sight" that Bennedsen felt toward his adopted country that prevented him from mentioning the fact that he spent the first month at the Rutherfords in bed with a fever? Or, is it because he does not want to worry his mother? Or, perhaps, a combination of both?[19]

Certainly, the interviews with Bennedsen must be regarded with the same critical eye as his letters. There is no doubt that the passage of time led him to reconstruct unconsciously the events of the 1950s; like so many other immigrants, he may have been prone to exaggerating the difficulties he had to overcome. Ideally, the dialogue initiated by the letters and interviews should give way to a three- or four-way conversation, which would include other written and visual material. Twenty years ago, Tamara Hareven and Randolph Langenbach charted this course by relating interviews with former Amoskeag textile workers in Manchester, New Hampshire, to individual employee files maintained by the company and to both old and new photographs. Such a conversation of sources is also possible in Christian Bennedsen's case because his collection contains, in addition to letters, more than 3000 photographs, hundreds of records (LPs, 45s, and 78s), many postcards, videos taken during trips to Denmark, and work related notebooks and notepads, etc.[20]

Bennedsen, first a lone Dane in rural Ontario, then a resident of Toronto's Little Italy, was an immigrant who wanted to tell his friends and family about the new world he was discovering. With this in mind, he wrote and read letters that also kept him in close contact with his family and with Spandet. In this way, Bennedsen could continue to feel close to his mother, a woman whom he admired and who was his main correspondent, even though, out of respect, he always addressed his letters to his father with whom he had a much more difficult relationship. While he was bedridden at the Rutherford farm, Bennedsen could still mentally participate in the daily life and special events of his family thousands of kilometres away. His parents, his brother Sigvard, and his sister Ella continued to celebrate his birthday, even in his absence. Not infrequently, they marked the occasion by writing to the "Dear son" in Canada. In these letters, each person wrote his or her own piece. In return, Bennedsen almost always began his letters with *Kare alles* ("Dear everyone"). "Père et mère d' une part, soeurs et frères d' autre part, mêlent leurs écritures, exposent le partage de leur affection sur le papier comme dans les cœurs," wrote Cécile Dauphin and her collaborators about French family correspondence in the nineteenth century. Writing and reading letters is a family affair.[21]

It is important to keep in mind that the largest part of the correspondence dates from the years before Bennesden met Connie in 1956. From that moment, his letters become more sporadic as he was integrated into his future bride's family. Eventually, his brother and sister wrote to him on their own, no longer content to write just a few words on the letters sent by their mother. To practise their English and, later, to better communicate with their sister-in-law Connie, Bennedsen's siblings introduced English into their correspondence. When Sigvard married, his wife Birgit became a significant correspondent in Bennedsen's letter writing network. She too made the effort to write in English, for Connie's sake. Later, Sigvard and Birgit's children penned a few words at the end of their mother's letters, eventually becoming correspondents with Christian Bennedsen in their own right. After Anna died in 1976, Frederick, Christian's father, wrote more often, attaching newspaper clippings and letters he received from his grandchildren.[22]

Bennedsen's epistolary space thus includes his parents, wife, brother, sister, sister-in-law, nephews and nieces, and several others from Spandet. It also includes other individuals with whom Anna, Christian's mother, shared her letters. By sharing her son's letters with friends and acquaintances in Spandet, Anna Bennedsen participated in a tradition going back to the 1820s in Scandinavia, and longer still elsewhere.[23] Conscious of the semi-public nature of his correspondence, Bennedsen could not confide in his mother as much as he would have liked to, nor could he provide her with moral support in her difficult relationship with her husband Frederick. The degree of intimacy was thus restricted, something that must be taken into account by historians of immigrant letters. It would be wrong, therefore, to make too severe a distinction between published and private letters.[24]

Like countless immigrants before him, Bennedsen sent money home to help his mother and to contribute to the education of Sigvard and Ella. Sending his letters by aerogramme, he inserted the cash or money order in an envelope, along with a note. Bennedsen himself never received money but he did get parcels on his birthday and for Christmas. His family also sent him newspapers and magazines. During his first months in Canada, Bennedsen memorized the content of these publications in order to feel closer to the home he had left behind. Later, however, as he was integrating into Canadian life, through his work and his association with Connie's Italian-Canadian family, he did not give them as much attention.[25]

Upon his arrival in Ontario, Bennedsen had the chance to live with a family that understood the importance of mail in his life. Mackenzie Rutherford, himself a British immigrant, was an essential link in Bennedsen's letter writing network. He bought aerograms in bundles of six for his hired hand. He was also the one who brought

Bennedsen's letters to the post office in Colborne in the morning on his way to work. In the evening, he collected the mail at a rural post office box about five kilometres from the farm. Rutherford was very interested in Bennedsen's correspondence and waited for mail from Denmark almost as impatiently as Bennedsen himself, who usually received a letter about every 10 days. On the other side of the Atlantic, Anna Bennedsen bought her aerograms from a letter carrier who came to the house twice a day. Occasionally, the supply ran out, however, as Anna told her son: "I couldn't get the aerograms from the postman. He says they have such a demand for them they can't keep enough at the Post Office. But I got quite a supply."[26] Except for this problem, the postal connection between the Danish countryside and central Ontario was very effective: Only one letter was lost in 50 years.

Conclusion

The evolution in communications is thus intimately linked with the creation of Christian Bennedsen's epistolary space as well as that of the millions of immigrants who put pen to paper and later used typewriters and computers to stay in touch with their families, friends, and acquaintances in their countries of birth and elsewhere. In this respect, the epistolary space created by North American immigrants and their correspondents beginning in the eighteenth century contributed to the advent of McLuhan's famous global village. It should be remembered that this global village was at first a postal village, where old allegiances changed and out of which arose new and shared identities, sometimes over thousands of kilometres. The study of the correspondence of Christian Bennedsen and other immigrants facilitates a better understanding of these changes.[27] This task, which is just beginning, is all the more urgent since Bennedsen's generation, which immigrated in the postwar period, is disappearing. The letters of these men and women and their oral accounts are central to an understanding of the history of the postal village in an era of air transportation, telephone, and email.

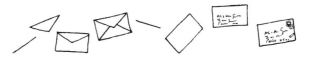

Notes

1. The authors would like to thank Carol Anderson, Andrée Courtemanche, David Gerber, Martin Pâquet, Matteo Sanfilippo, and Judit Szapor who read and criticized earlier versions of this article. They would also like to express their gratitude to the late Christian and Connie Bennedsen, who opened their home and personal archives.
2. The biographical information contained in this article is taken from a series of interviews conducted by Gabriele Scardellato for the Canadian Postal Museum with Christian Bennedsen from January to June 1999. These interviews can be found in the Christian Bennedsen Collection (hereafter, CBC) in the Canadian Museum of Civilization Archives, Correspondence series P 2001–O008.
3. CBC, Christian Bennedsen to Frederick Bennedsen, March 2, 1952.
4. CBC, Christian Bennedsen to Frederick Bennedsen, October 7, 1952.

5. European emigration to America is the subject of a great deal of literature. One of the best summaries is available in John Bodnar's book, *The Transplanted: A History of Immigrants in Urban America* (Bloomington: Indiana University Press, 1985). See also Dirk Hoerder, *People on the Move: Migration, Acculturation, and Ethnic Interaction in Europe and North America* (Providence and Oxford: Berg, 1993), and Walter Nugent, *Crossings: The Great Transatlantic Migration, 1870–1914* (Bloomington: Indiana University Press, 1992). On European de-industrialization, see Sidney Pollard, *Peaceful Conquest: The Industrialization of Europe 1760–1970* (Toronto: Oxford University Press, 1981), pp. 30–31.

6. Among the Danish immigrants is the Feilberg family from which we have published letters: Henning Frederick Feilberg, ed., *Hejemliv Paa Praerien De Derovre: En Raekke Breve Fra Canada* (Copenhagen: Gyldendalske Boghandel –, Nordisk Forlag, 1927). An excerpt has been published in English by Jorgen Dahlie, "Letters Home from a Danish Family on the Prairies," *Canadian Ethnic Studies* 8, no. 2 (1976): 94–95.

7. On Danish migrations, see Kristian Hvidt's classic, *Flight to America: The Social Background of 300,000 Danish Immigrants* (New York: Academic Press, 1975). On Danes in Canada, see Christopher S. Hale, "Danes," in *Encyclopaedia of Canada's Peoples*, ed. Paul Robert Magocsi (Toronto: University of Toronto Press, 1999), pp. 406–413. Advertising to recruit "desirable" immigrants has a long history in Canada: See Donald Avery, *Reluctant Host: Canada's Response to Immigrant Workers, 1896–1994* (Toronto: McClelland & Stewart, 1995). For agricultural immigration policies after the Second World War, see Milda Danys, *DP: Lithuanian Immigration to Canada after the Second World War* (Toronto: Multicultural History Society of Canada, 1986), pp. 161–181.

8. Frederick Hale, ed., Danes in North America (Seattle: University of Washington Press, 1984), pp. xi–xx, 131.

9. On these issues, see Ingrid Semingsen, "Emigration and the Image of America in Europe," in Immigration in *American History: Essays in Honor of Theodore C. Blegen*, ed. Henry Steele Commager (Minneapolis: University of Minnesota Press, 1961), pp. 26–37, 47–48; Kendall Birr and Merle Curti, "The Immigrant and the American Image in Europe, 1860–1914," *Mississippi Valley Historical Review* 37, no. 2 (September 1950): 212–14, 216–18; Marcus Lee Hansen, *The Atlantic Migration, 1607–1860* (Cambridge, Mass.: Harvard University Press, 1940), pp. 81–82, 151–54, 156–58.

10. William I. Thomas and Florian Znaniecki, *The Polish Peasant in Europe and America* (Urbana: University of Illinois Press, 1984), especially pp. 98–188.

11. Marcus Lee Hansen, "Migrations: Old and New," in *The Immigrant in American History*, ed. Marcus Lee Hansen (Cambridge: Harvard University Press, 1940), pp. 12–13. See also, by the same author, "The History of Immigration as a Field of Research," *American Historical Review* 32, no. 3 (April 1927): 500–18; George Stephenson, ed., "'Typical' America Letters," in *Swedish Historical Society Yearbook*, vol. 7 (1921); George Stephenson, "The Background of the Beginnings of Swedish Immigration," *American Historical Review* 31, no. 4 (July 1926): 708–31, and, by the same author, "When America Was the Land of Canaan," *Minnesota History* 10, no. 3 (September 1929): 237–60. See also Theodore Blegen, "Early American Letters," in *Norwegian Migration to America, 1825–1860*, ed. Theodore Blegen (Northfield: Norwegian–American Historical Association, 1931), pp. 196–213, and *Land of Their Choice: The Immigrants Write Home*, ed. Theodore Blegen (Minneapolis: University of Minnesota Press, 1955); Theodore Blegen and Pauline Farseth eds, *Frontier Mother: The Letters of Gro Svendsen* (Northfield: Norwegian–American Historical Association, 1950). On these historians, see O. Fritliof Ander, "Four Historians of Immigration," in *In the Trek of the Immigrants: Essays Presented to Carl Wittke*, ed. O. Fritliof Ander (Rock Island, Illinois: Augustana College Library, 1964), pp. 17–32; Moses Rischin, "Marcus Lee Hansen: America's First Transethnic Historian," in *Uprooted Americans: Essays to Honor Oscar Handlin*, eds Richard Bushman et

al. (Boston: Little Brown, 1979), pp. 319–47. On the treatment of immigrants by American historians, see Edward N. Saveth, *American Historians and the European Immigrants* (New York: Columbia University Press, 1948).

12. These observations are based on a review of a considerable amount of published correspondence. It is not possible to present an exhaustive bibliography. The reader is referred to David A. Gerber's excellent article, "The Immigrant Letter between Positivism and Populism: The Uses of Immigrant Personal Correspondence in Twentieth-century American Scholarship," *Journal of American Ethnic History* 16, no. 4 (Summer 1997): 3–34. As well, the following three works are representative of the evolution of the historiography: Alan Conway, ed., *The Welsh in America: Letters from the Immigrants* (Minneapolis: University of Minnesota Press, 1961); Charlotte Erickson, *Invisible Immigrants: The Adaptation of English and Scottish Immigrants in Nineteenth-century America* (Ithaca: Cornell University Press, 1990); Walter Kamphoefner et al., eds., *News from the Land of Freedom: German Immigrants Write Home* (Ithaca: Cornell University Press, 1991). David Fitzpatrick critiques the methodological practices of historians of immigrant letters in *Oceans of Consolation: Personal Accounts of Irish Migration to Australia* (Ithaca: Cornell University Press, 1994), pp. 19–30. For two examples of studies that use correspondence to support a thesis, see Kerby A. Miller, *Emigrants and Exiles: Ireland and the Irish Exodus to North America* (New York: Oxford University Press, 1985), and Stephen Fender, *Sea Changes: British Emigration and American Literature* (Cambridge: Cambridge University Press, 1992). Miller's book is part of the debate on the nature of Irish immigration. His use of correspondence is critiqued by Donald Akenson, "Reading the Texts of Rural Emigrants: Letters from the Irish in Australia, New Zealand and North America," *Canadian Papers in Rural History*, vol. 7 (Gananoque, Ontario: Langdale Press, 1990), pp. 397–406. Recently Miller and two co-editors have published a voluminous selection of Irish immigrant letters to the United States before 1815: *Irish Immigrants in the Land of Canaan: Letters and Memoirs from Colonial and Revolutionary America, 1675–1815* (New York, Oxford University Press, 2003).

13. H. Arnold Barton, *Letters from the Promised Land: Swedes in America, 1840–1914* (Minneapolis: University of Minnesota Press, 1975), pp. 4–5.

14. Dirk Hoerder makes exhaustive use of published Canadian immigrant letters in *Creating Societies: Immigrant Lives in Canada* (Montréal and Kingston: McGill-Queen's University Press, 1999). Herman Ganzevoort published a book that represents the worst in immigrant correspondence studies. Using letters published in Holland by Dutch immigrants to recreate their lives in Canada and their opinions of their adopted land, he selected letters according to their "historical accuracy" and "literary value": *The Last Illusion: Letters from Dutch Immigrants in the Land of Opportunity, 1924–1930* (Calgary, University of Calgary Press, 1999).

15. Cecil J. Houston and William J. Smyth, *Irish Emigration and Canadian Settlement: Patterns, Links, and Letters* (Toronto: University of Toronto Press, 1990), especially pp. 241–333; R. Cole Harris and E. Philipps, eds, *Letters from Windermere, 1912–1914* (Vancouver: University of British Columbia Press, 1984); Jean Le Bihan, "Enquête sur une famille bretonne émigrée au Canada (1903–1920)," *Prairie Forum* 22, no. 1 (Spring 1997): 73–101 (citation on p. 98); Jean Le Bihan, "L'émigration vers le Canada au début du 20ᵉ siècle: Le témoignage d'une jeune Scaeroise," *Bulletin de la Société archéologique du Finistère* 127 (1998): 351–60; Robert B. Klymasz, "The Letter in Canadian Ukrainian Folklore," *Journal of the Folklore Institute* 6, no. 1 (June 1969): 39–49.

16. Wendy Cameron et al., eds., *English Immigrant Voices: Labourers' Letters from Upper Canada in the 1830s* (Montréal and Kingston: McGill Queen's University Press, 2000). The collection is a companion to the monograph, *Assisting Emigration to Upper Canada: The Petworth Project 1832–1837* (Montréal and Kingston: McGill-Queen's University Press, 2000). On a similar subject, see the work of Terry McDonald, notably "'Come to Canada while You Have a

Chance': A Cautionary Tale of English Emigrant Letters in Upper Canada," *Ontario History* 91, no. 2 (Autumn 1999): 111–130.

17. Two notable exceptions: Fitzpatrick, *Oceans of Consolation*, and Samuel L. Baily and Franco Ramella, eds., *One Family, Two Worlds: An Italian Family's Correspondence across the Atlantic, 1901–1922* (New Brunswick, NJ: Rutgers University Press, 1988).

18. CBC, Christian Bennedsen to Frederick Bennedsen, January 7, 1952.

19. CBC, Christian Bennedsen to Frederick Bennedsen, November 27 and December 10, 1951. Silences and omissions in immigrant letters are analysed in David A. Gerber, "Accounting for Silences and Untruth in Immigrant Letters," paper delivered at the "Reading the Emigrant Letter" Conference, Carleton University, August 2003.

20. Bennedsen returned to Denmark six times. The Amoskeag project methodology is presented in Tamara Hareven and Randolph Langenbach, *Amoskeag: Life and Work in an American Factory City* (New York: Pantheon Books, 1978), pp. 29–33.

21. Cécile Dauphin et al., "Une correspondance familiale au XIXe siècle," en *La lettre à la croisée de l'individuel et du social*, dir. Mireille Bossis (Paris: Éditions Kiné, 1994), p. 134. See also Karl A. Peter and Peter Franziska, "The Kurtenbach Letters: An Autobiographical Description of Pioneer Life in Saskatchewan around the Turn of the Century," *Canadian Ethnic Studies* 11, no. 2 (1979): 89–96.

22. CBC, Frederick Bennedsen to Christian Bennedsen, February 16, March 15, June 16, and December 9, 1977. On the practice of letters written by several individuals, see Dauphin, "Une correspondence familiale," p. 134.

23. Fender, *Sea Changes*, pp. 17–20; Orm Overland, "Learning to Read Immigrant Letters: Reflections Towards a Textual Theory," in *Norwegian–American Essays*, ed. Oyvind Gulliksen (Oslo: Norwegian Emigrant Museum, 1996), pp. 211–12.

24. The semi-public nature of Bennedsen's letters is documented in the interviews. Cameron (*English Immigrant Voices*, p. xxx) characterizes correspondence as "conversation(s) around the kitchen table rather than an intimate discussion or private gossiping session between two people." Immigrant correspondence is in contradistinction to literary correspondence, which is often a way for authors to express ideas that they dare not in their novels and essays. See David Gerber's reflections in "Epistolary Ethics: Personal Correspondence and the Culture of Emigration in the Nineteenth Century," *Journal of American Ethnic History* 19, no. 4 (Summer 2000): 10.

25. CBC, Christian Bennedsen to Anna Bennedsen, January 7, and April 6, 1952; Anna Bennedsen to Christian Bennedsen, October 23 and November 29, 1955. The importance of money in immigrant postal transactions is discussed in John Willis, "The Immigrant, the Post and the Letter" (Unpublished report; Gatineau: Canadian Postal Museum, 1999), pp. 18–21.

26. CBC, Anna Bennedsen to Christian Bennedsen, March 12, 1952. In 1948, generalized (not universal) airmail was introduced throughout Canada. It took some time to extend the system to war-torn Europe, although it is clear that by the time Bennedsen arrived in Canada in 1951 or shortly after, he did have access to direct airmail service between Canada and Denmark. Denmark did not appear among the list of countries doing airmail business with Canada in the 1947 official postal guide, but, according to the 1952–53 version of the guide, it was probably accessible by airmail. The report of the postmaster general for 1950–1951 states: "International mail operations have now reached a normal level and services—air and surface—are in some cases operating on a higher frequency and at greater speed than formerly." The same source was confident that airmail had become a "permanent and integral part" of Canada's overseas postal relations (*Annual Report of the Postmaster General*, 1950–1951, p. 10). Aerograms were available in all Canadian post offices and franked at 10 or 15 cents each. Correspondents were instructed not to enclose anything else in the aerogramme (photos and the like), and they

were not to stick any labels on the cover as in both cases that would add to the weight. See *Guide officiel du service postal canadien, 1952–1953*, partie 1, p. 119.

27. For a similar argument, see David A. Gerber, "Theories and Lives: Transnationalism and the Conceptualization of International Migrations to the United States," pp. 44–52. However, we do not share Gerber's enthusiasm for modernity theories in explaining the creation of an epistolary transatlantic space.

LA VIE FAMILIALE D'UN ADMINISTRATEUR COLONIAL : HERMAN WITSIUS RYLAND[1]

12

Lorraine Gadoury, Bibliothèque et Archives Canada

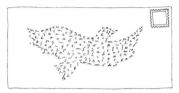

Résumé

Herman Witsius Ryland est né en Angleterre, en 1759 ou en 1760. Il est le fils de John Collett Ryland, ministre baptiste et instituteur, et d'Elizabeth Frith. En 1793, Guy Carleton (lord Dorchester) devient gouverneur du Bas-Canada et le choisit comme secrétaire civil. Les deux se rendent à Québec. C'est là que Ryland épouse, en décembre 1794, Charlotte Warwick, une Anglaise dont il était le fiancé depuis plusieurs années. Après son arrivée dans le Bas-Canada débute, pour Ryland, une longue carrière de fonctionnaire dans l'administration coloniale. Il joue aussi un rôle politique en tant que membre du Conseil législatif jusqu'à sa mort, en 1838. Dans cet article, nous voulons présenter les relations familiales d'Herman Witsius Ryland à partir de sa correspondance. Ryland et sa fiancée correspondent assidûment avant leur mariage et la jeune fille lui soumet des plans et des projets pour leur futur établissement. Après son arrivée dans la colonie, Ryland se plaint souvent qu'il ne gagne pas suffisamment d'argent pour assurer la vie de sa famille et la sécurité de ses enfants. Sa femme et lui tentent de cultiver leurs relations, surtout celles qui pourraient améliorer leur condition familiale et permettre de « placer » leurs fils. À la fin de sa vie, Ryland commence à laisser paraître dans ses lettres son inquiétude face à la vieillesse et à la mort. La pauvreté de sa femme et de ses filles l'inquiète aussi beaucoup. Les lettres de Ryland et celles de ses proches nous révèlent plusieurs facettes de la vie familiale d'un administrateur britannique qui a joué un rôle important dans le Bas-Canada.

Abstract

Herman Witsius Ryland was born in England in 1759 or 1760—the son of Baptist Minister and teacher John Collett Ryland and Elizabeth Frith. In 1793, Sir Guy Carleton, Lord Dorchester, became Governor of Lower Canada (Quebec) and chose Ryland as his secretary. The two went together to Québec, and it was there that, in December 1794, Ryland married Charlotte Warwick: an Englishwoman to whom he had been engaged for several years. Following his arrival in Lower Canada, Ryland's long career as a civil servant in the colonial administration began. He also played a political role as a member of the Legislative Council until his death in 1838.

This article examines Ryland's family relationships, using his correspondence as a starting point. Ryland and his fiancée corresponded assiduously before their marriage, with the young woman expressing her hopes and dreams for their future life together. Following his arrival in the colony, Ryland often complained that he didn't earn enough money to properly support his family and ensure his children's security. He and his wife attempted to cultivate their relations and acquaintances—particularly those who could improve their family's financial status and provide a "place" for their son. Towards the end of his life, Ryland began to let worries about old age and death appear in his letters. The poverty of his wife and daughters also worried him greatly. Ryland's letters and those of his nearest relations reveal several facets of family life for a British administrator who would play an important role in Lower Canada.

Introduction

Le 9 mars 1998, à l'Hôtel des Encans de Montréal, étaient mis en vente 46 lots de lettres et de documents concernant la famille Ryland. Vu l'importance de Herman Witsius, la figure principale de cette famille, et parce que la collection était vaste et riche en informations sur la vie politique, sociale et économique canadienne du XIXᵉ siècle, les Archives nationales du Canada[2] ont décidé de participer aux enchères. Ce soir-là, trois archivistes de la Division des manuscrits ont donc travaillé de concert pour finalement faire l'acquisition de la majeure partie des documents, qui sont maintenant mis à la disposition des historiens, des chercheurs et du public. C'est plus de 550 lettres originales et une cinquantaine de documents divers datant de 1791 à 1906 qui ont été ajoutés fonds Herman Witsius Ryland et famille, MG24-B3, vol. 14-18. Celui-ci comprenait déjà de la correspondance d'ordre politique (vol. 1-5, 1769-1838, surtout des copies et des transcriptions), sept volumes reliés, contenant des copies de documents concernant les colonies d'Amérique du Nord, de 1685 à 1718, pour l'usage du Board of Trade (vol. 6-12), et de la correspondance du fils de Herman Witsius, George Herman Ryland – vol. 13, 1824-1877. Le fonds comprend aussi quatre ambrotypes montrant des membres de la famille Ryland et deux aquarelles de J. Lloyd illustrant les armoiries de la famille Ryland et celles de la famille Collett, acquises à la même vente aux enchères que la correspondance.

Une liste chronologique de la correspondance acquise en 1998 a été préparée : elle précise la date des lettres, les noms des correspondants, les lieux de provenance et de destination des missives. De plus, une liste alphabétique présente tous les correspondants et un index illustre les réseaux d'échange des lettres. Cet instrument de recherche (MSS0256) est accessible en ligne, par le biais du moteur de recherche ArchiviaNet, sur le site de Bibliothèque et Archives Canada[3].

Herman Witsius Ryland est un personnage controversé. Francis J. Audet, qui parsème son article d'extraits de lettres, dit de lui qu'il était « foncièrement imbu de l'idée de la supériorité anglo-saxonne sur le reste de l'univers » et qu'il a eu une « influence néfaste »[4].

Figure 12.1 Portrait de Herman Witsius Ryland par Charles William Jefferys, sans date.
Bibliothèque et Archives Canada, C-069942.

Dans son *Dictionnaire général du Canada*, Louis Le Jeune le décrit comme « un fanatique et un irréconciliable adversaire des Canadiens »[5]. Il cite, pour appuyer son jugement, certains extraits de lettres où Ryland insulte les « papistes » et le clergé catholique. James H. Lambert, dans sa notice rédigée pour le *Dictionnaire biographique du Canada*, utilise également la correspondance de Ryland pour illustrer le point de vue du personnage sur la religion et la politique. Il le décrit comme un homme passionné, persévérant, très honnête, qui se méfie de la démocratie[6]. Dans notre texte, afin d'illustrer la richesse de la correspondance, nous allons plutôt aborder certains aspects intimes de sa vie, comme sa relation avec sa fiancée, l'éducation que lui et sa femme ont voulu donner à leurs enfants et l'inquiétude qu'il a ressentie quant à leur avenir, les difficultés qu'il a lui-même vécues à cause de son éloignement de l'Angleterre et de son isolement de l'élite locale et, enfin, l'anxiété ressentie à la fin de ses jours face à la vieillesse et à l'approche de la mort.

Ces dernières années, la correspondance a été la source de plusieurs études historiques qui ont servi à mieux comprendre la vie familiale et la société canadienne des 18e et 19e siècles. Mentionnons l'étude de Peter Ward sur le mariage dans le Canada anglais au 19e siècle[7], celle de Katherine McKenna sur une épistolière de l'élite torontoise et sa famille[8], le portrait qu'a dressé l'auteure de ce texte sur l'élite coloniale du 18e siècle[9] et, plus récemment encore, l'étude de Françoise Noël sur la famille et la sociabilité entre 1780 et 1870, dans le Haut et le Bas-Canada, qui utilise des journaux personnels en plus de la correspondance[10]. Pour sa part, Jane E. Harrison s'est plutôt intéressée aux communications postales pour les années 1640-1830 ainsi qu'au format général des lettres[11]. Les historiens s'entendent pour dire que, même si elles obéissent à certaines formes, les lettres en révèlent beaucoup sur l'intimité vécue par les membres des familles, l'importance des liens au sein de la famille, au sens large, ainsi que le rôle des hommes et des femmes dans la société. De plus, l'histoire de l'intimité demeure un sujet de recherche prisé, car elle tente de répondre à des questions inscrites au cœur des préoccupations de chaque être humain.

Herman Witsius Ryland est né en 1759 ou en 1760 en Angleterre; il est le fils de John Collett Ryland, ministre baptiste et instituteur, et d'Elizabeth Frith. Il entre dans l'armée britannique à titre de trésorier-payeur-général adjoint (*assistant deputy paymaster general*) des troupes en Amérique du Nord et est affecté dans les colonies américaines en 1781. De retour en Angleterre, avec le commandant en chef Guy Carleton, en décembre 1783, on ne lui connaît pas de fonctions pendant la dizaine d'années qui suit. En 1793, Carleton, devenu lord Dorchester et gouverneur du Bas-Canada, le choisit comme secrétaire civil et les deux se rendent ensemble à Québec. Après son arrivée dans le Bas-Canada débute pour Ryland une longue carrière de fonctionnaire dans l'administration coloniale. Il est en effet tour à tour secrétaire civil de Carleton de 1793 à 1796; de son successeur, Robert Prescott, de 1796 à 1798; du lieutenant gouverneur Robert Milnes, entre 1799 et 1807; de James Craig, de 1807 à 1811, et de George Prevost, de 1811 à 1813. Le poste de secrétaire civil consiste à s'occuper de la correspondance du gouverneur ainsi qu'à préparer et à contrôler la distribution des documents officiels de la colonie. Ryland cumule aussi d'autres fonctions officielles puisqu'il occupe le poste de greffier du Conseil exécutif, de 1796 à 1798 et de 1799 à sa mort (enregistrant les procès-verbaux, donnant des copies des décrets du conseil et vérifiant les comptes publics), celui de greffier de la couronne en chancellerie, de 1802 à 1826 (responsable des élections), et enfin celui de trésorier et de secrétaire de la Commission des biens des Jésuites, de 1811 à 1826. Il joue aussi un rôle politique en tant que membre du Conseil législatif, de 1811 à sa mort.

Peu après son installation à Québec, Ryland y fait venir Charlotte Warwick, une Anglaise à laquelle il est fiancé depuis plusieurs années et les deux se marient dans cette ville en décembre 1794. Pour un jeune homme de cette classe sociale, il était nécessaire, à l'époque, d'avoir une situation stable avant d'épouser sa fiancée et c'est la raison de leur longue attente. Le couple a neuf enfants, dont cinq vont mourir avant leur père. La famille vit d'abord à Québec, puis emménage à Beauport, dans un domaine acquis en 1805 et agrandi en 1813. Selon James Lambert, « ce domaine, qui était à la fois une retraite estivale et une ferme expérimentale, devint progressivement la résidence permanente de Ryland à compter de 1817 »[12]; ce choix montre bien l'attrait de l'élite pour la vie à la campagne. Pensons à John Neilson et à Louis-Joseph Papineau, qui s'installent également sur leurs terres dans la première moitié du XIXe siècle. Ryland meurt le 20 juillet 1838 dans son domaine. Sa femme semble lui avoir survécu quelques années et être retournée en Angleterre. Le fils George Herman suit les traces de son père au Canada en lui succédant comme greffier du Conseil exécutif à partir de 1838. Il est aussi registraire de la ville de Québec à partir de 1840 et de celle de Montréal entre 1845 et 1882. Un autre fils, William Deane, devient pasteur en Angleterre. Nous ne savons pas ce qu'il est advenu des filles.

Herman Witsius Ryland et sa fiancée avaient correspondu assidûment avant leur mariage pendant qu'ils étaient en Angleterre. Ainsi, parmi les documents acquis par Bibliothèque et Archives Canada se trouvent 27 lettres écrites par Charlotte à Ryland entre le 5 février et le 31 août 1792. Par ces lettres, nous apprenons que Ryland était alors à la recherche d'une situation en Angleterre. Charlotte l'encourage dans son entreprise, lui donne des conseils sur les rencontres qu'il devrait faire, les lettres qu'il devrait écrire, les vêtements qu'il devrait porter, lui fait des commentaires sur la vie politique anglaise et lui soumet même des plans et des projets pour leur futur établissement – lettres des 5, 11 et 16 février, par exemple. La jeune fille semble donc jouer une part très active dans cette phase de la vie de Ryland. Ses lettres révèlent aussi, mais de façon pudique, son attachement à son fiancé et l'espoir qu'ils pourront se revoir prochainement.

> I make no doubt but you will do me the Justice to believe that I have never parted from you without extreme reluctance, but I think I never felt so much as this last time, and I believe you were equally affected. But we will not talk of it now, I believe it will do neither of us any good; let us hope that we shall not long be separated.
>
> (5 février 1792)

Les deux fiancés se querellent aussi à quelques reprises et Charlotte exprime sa rancœur à l'égard de Witsius : « I am extremely hurt, and displeased at your last… » (11 mars); « … all I request of you is, never to repeat those words, or anything of this kind again… » (18 mars); « … never tell me again that you are unwilling to give me pain, for I firmly believe that there is not anything in which you take so much delight… » (29 mars). Le 13 juin 1792, après un court voyage avec sa sœur, Charlotte transcrit à l'intention de son amoureux quelques vers du poème *The Traveller*, de Oliver Goldsmith, y précisant

Figure 12.2 Armoiries de George H. Ryland, aquarelle et gouache sur papier par J. Lloyd, vers 1866. Bibliothèque et Archives Canada, R-1427-6.

toutefois ceci : « I know you do not love Rhyme, and I do not often make quotations, but these lines came so often into my Mind during my Journey that I cannot help transcribing them. » Ces extraits dénotent une grande intimité entre les deux épistolaires.

La correspondance écrite par Ryland après sa venue dans le Bas-Canada, en 1793, est remplie de commentaires sur la vie politique de la colonie. Il juge les dirigeants et leur façon de mener leurs affaires de façon souvent très critique. Pour ce qui est de sa famille, Ryland se plaint souvent qu'il ne gagne pas suffisamment d'argent pour assurer son confort et la sécurité de ses enfants :

> I was led to expect that my permanent appointments here would be rendered not only adequate to the support of my Family but sufficient to ensure some small provision for them in case of my decease.
>
> (Lettre au duc de Portland, 6 janvier 1803)

Ryland et sa femme tentent de cultiver leurs relations, surtout celles qui leur permettraient d'améliorer leur sort. Le patronage est, à cette époque, au centre de la vie publique, et le meilleur moyen d'obtenir une place intéressante et avantageuse est de connaître les bonnes personnes qui feront les recommandations nécessaires[13]. Les femmes sont souvent impliquées dans ce réseau de relations et, pour Ryland et son épouse, l'espoir de retourner un jour en Angleterre fait que leurs contacts dans la mère patrie sont au centre de leurs espoirs.

En 1806, leur amie Charlotte Milnes écrit d'Angleterre à madame Ryland : « Mr Smith tells me He [lord Spencer, homme politique très en vue de la haute société anglaise] has often mentioned Mr Ryland's name and I have no doubt will think of him nor will Sir Robert [Milnes, son mari] loose any occasion of mentioning Mr Ryland to Lord Spencer when they meet. » (2 février 1806)

Les liens de la famille Ryland avec l'Angleterre ne sont pas importants que sur le plan des échanges épistolaires. En effet, les deux fils Ryland sont envoyés assez tôt dans la métropole pour qu'ils puissent y parfaire leur éducation. Ce sont des amis de la famille, les Dalton, qui prennent le plus grand soin d'eux. En parlant de William, madame Dalton écrit :

> … and again assuring you that any little attentions we have and in our power to show your dear Boy are more then a thousand times repaid by the sincere interest we have in his future welfare and the warm hold he has taken in our hearths.
>
> (16 juillet 1809)

Les parents espèrent ainsi que la place qu'ils pourront se faire dans la société, que ce soit au Canada ou en Angleterre, sera meilleure. Nous trouvons, dans la correspondance échangée entre 1807 et 1811, quelques très jolies lettres écrites par William (né vers 1796) et George (né en 1801) à leurs parents – voir les lettres du 31 décembre 1807, 27 août et 29 octobre 1808. Dans sa lettre du 25 mai 1811, le père livre à son fils George, âgé alors de 10 ans, une certaine conception de l'éducation, sévère mais quand même pas trop rigide :

> I hope you will continue to be a very good Boy and apply yourself with all diligence to your learning. I have no doubt you will there [in School] meet with several boys not older than yourself, but who are much further advanced in their education, and I hope you will have sufficient spirit to endeavour to get before them. [...] Learn as much as you can in School hours, and play as much as you please out of them.

Charlotte, pour sa part, met l'accent sur l'affection et la tendresse dans cette lettre à son fils George : « Pray do not forget your poor Mama, and love her always as much as she loves you, which will be very much indeed, and be sure to do everything that your Papa bids you for he loves you very dearly, and will never ask you to do anything but what is right and proper for you to do. » (Sans date)[14]

Il arrive à Herman Witsius et à Charlotte de retourner en Angleterre. C'est ainsi que le couple y séjourne de 1810 à 1812. Leur amie Charlotte Milnes écrit, en son nom et en celui de son mari : « … we congratulate you both most sincerely on the happiness of finding yourselves once more together in Dear Old England. » (6 août 1810) Après son retour dans le Bas-Canada, Ryland est de plus en plus déçu de l'administration et de la vie politique. Il s'installe dans son domaine de Beauport, nommé Mount Lilac, et s'occupe de jardinage – voir les lettres du 13 avril 1817 et du 19 mai 1822. Il s'inquiète aussi beaucoup du sort qui attend ses deux fils.

William est d'abord resté en Angleterre sous la protection, entre autres, de George Pownall[15], à qui H. W. Ryland écrit, en janvier 1816 : « … you prove to me in the most flattering manner that you have not forgotten me by your great Kindness to the poor Boy I have left in England, who never fails to mention you in every letter, and I have not words to express how sensibly his Mother and I feel these marks of your Regard. » Par la suite, William revient dans la colonie et assiste son père dans la tâche de greffier du conseil. Ce dernier ne manque pas de le louanger dans sa correspondance avec diverses personnes. Il écrit par exemple :

> I am sure it will give you pleasure if I so far indulge the feelings of a Parent as to declare to you that I do not think there is a youth of more perfect Integrity, of more upright and honorable Principles, nor many of better Talents in the Province.
> (Lettre à son ami James Kempt[16], 26 juin 1817)

D'autres louanges s'adressent également à son fils George : « You will excuse the partiality of a Parent if I add that in point of Person he is one of the handsomest young Men in the Province, that he has not formed one improper acquaintance or acquired a single habit that can be called vicious. » (H. W. Ryland, à George Pownall, 14 juillet 1819)

Son inquiétude quant au sort de ses deux fils transparaît cependant dans un grand nombre de lettres écrites par Ryland. Ce sentiment est lié au fait qu'en avançant en âge

Ryland a de moins en moins d'amis assez puissants pour donner à ses fils (qui ont alors entre 18 et 20 ans) une place d'importance dans l'administration coloniale. Or, pour eux, comme cela l'était pour lui, le patronage est le seul moyen d'obtenir quelque avantage :

> To say the truth I am sadly at a loss how to dispose of my Boys and have not yet been able to determine on any fixed Plan for them. All my old Friends and acquaintances in this Country are dropping off and a new Generation is coming into office with whom I have no connexion.
>
> (Lettre à son ami Robert Milnes[17], 18 septembre 1817)

> I despair of forming new Connexions like those which have passed away, and upon the very few which remain to me the hopes of my Children must rest till they shall be able to acquire Friends for themselves.
>
> (Lettre à James Kempt, 15 octobre 1819)

Finalement, le gouverneur Dalhousie refuse un poste dans l'administration provinciale à William et Herman Witsius cède au désir de son fils de retourner en Angleterre pour y étudier et peut-être s'y installer – voir lettres du 21 mars et du 30 mai 1821. Dans sa correspondance subséquente, Ryland tente encore d'aider son fils à se placer et il exprime également sa fierté devant le succès de ce dernier. William devient finalement pasteur et reste en Angleterre.

À partir des années 1820, alors qu'il est âgé de 60 ans, H. W. Ryland commence à laisser transparaître dans ses lettres son inquiétude face à la vieillesse et à la mort. Ce qui le trouble, c'est d'abord le fait de vieillir dans un pays étranger, car il se considère toujours comme un citoyen de l'Angleterre : « I daily and bitterly lament our being cut off from the old Parent's State but such being our lot we must bring ourselves to submit to it as well as we can. » (Lettre au major général Wilson, en Angleterre, 13 avril 1817) Il regrette aussi le départ de plusieurs amis :

> It has been my misfortune to see almost every friendship I have formed here broken up in this way, and I feel it the more because I am getting too far advanced in life to form new ones, and I expect to end my days here among strangers, or at least among persons with whom it will be impossible for me to form an intimacy.
>
> (Lettre au colonel Ready, 31 mai 1823)

C'est la crainte de la pauvreté pour sa femme et ses filles qui inquiète aussi beaucoup Ryland à la fin de sa vie. Son fils George, qui l'assiste dans ses tâches, n'a pas d'emploi stable et Ryland tente plusieurs fois d'obtenir qu'il lui succède officiellement ou qu'on lui donne un autre poste d'importance pour faire vivre sa famille – lettres des 13 octobre 1830, 20 janvier 1833, 19 avril 1833 et 1er novembre 1835, entre autres. La naissance d'un petit-fils lui fait plaisir : « In the midst of all this worry & difficulty I was on Thursday last made a Grandfather by the addition of a fine boy to my family who with his mother are doing surprisingly well. » (Lettre à George Pownall, 17 mars 1834)

Cependant, les derniers jours de Ryland s'avèrent sombres. Le 27 novembre 1833, à l'âge d'environ 74 ans, il écrit à son ami Pownall : « My heart continues to be as good as I can expect it to be at my advanced age, but the depression of my spirits and the anxiety of my mind allow of little mitigation either day or night and I often feel as though I should sink under them. » Trois ans plus tard, la situation ne s'est pas améliorée puisqu'il se plaint à Steven Walcott, secrétaire civil de 1835 à 1838, que, malgré 43 ans de loyaux services pour le gouvernement, celui-ci lui doit tellement d'argent qu'il se retrouve dans un état de profond désarroi : « I am [...] to a state of pecuniary distress and embarrassment which I must soon sink under if not relieved, and I have before me, at 77 years of age, the prospect of utter ruin to my family whenever it shall please God to remove me from them. » (28 novembre 1836)

La correspondance d'Herman Witsius Ryland est très riche à plusieurs égards. Elle nous permet de découvrir les opinions de cet homme public qui a côtoyé les gouvernants du Bas-Canada pendant une longue période et de prendre connaissance de sa vision de l'administration que l'Angleterre applique à la colonie. À plusieurs reprises, après 1812, Ryland insiste sur les mauvais choix de la métropole et son trop grand laxisme envers les Canadiens : « This may justly be called *le siècle d'or des Canadiens* and as such they manifest every disposition to take advantage of it, which the English part of the community retire into insignificance. » (Lettre au lieutenant-colonel Thornton, 11 juin 1812) Il écrit encore : « I view the affairs of this Country in so despairing a light, and I consider the two last Governors as having given so strong a Revolutionary Impulse to them, that I could wish to banish them entirely from my mind. » (Lettre à Charlotte Milnes, 15 janvier 1819) Il est intéressant de lire que déjà, en 1822, Ryland vante les mérites de l'union du Haut et du Bas-Canada : « I cannot but think that the measure would be attended with infinite advantage if carried into effect with due consideration, and with the necessary information and judgment. » (Lettre à James Kempt, 3 mars 1822) Resté foncièrement britannique, Ryland ne s'est jamais beaucoup rapproché de l'élite francophone et a continué, jusqu'à sa mort, de correspondre avec d'autres Britanniques, déracinés comme lui, ou avec des compatriotes restés dans la mère-patrie.

Ce que nous avons pu découvrir également dans la correspondance de Ryland, c'est que les réseaux de patronage ont une grande importance, autant pour parfaire l'éducation des jeunes hommes que pour obtenir une place au sein de l'administration publique. La majorité des membres de l'élite de l'époque utilisaient cette méthode pour « placer » leurs enfants et d'autres membres de leur famille, et les lettres permettent de mieux comprendre cette façon de faire : il faut cultiver ses « relations » pendant plusieurs années avant d'arriver à un résultat concret. Les femmes jouent naturellement un rôle actif dans le maintien des relations importantes, que ce soit par des visites ou des échanges épistolaires et les lettres écrites et reçues par Ryland nous permettent de constater que celui-ci ainsi que sa femme Charlotte ont entrepris beaucoup de démarches pour aider leurs enfants à s'établir.

Conclusion

Enfin, les missives de Herman Witsius Ryland lèvent le voile sur l'être humain derrière le personnage public et sa déception devant son destin, son aigreur face à la vie, sont des traits de caractère qui peuvent nous le rendre plus attachant. Une lecture plus approfondie de la correspondance de H. W. Ryland aux siens permettrait d'en apprendre plus sur le rôle des femmes dans la société ainsi que sur la place des enfants et de la famille étendue dans la nébuleuse familiale.

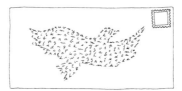

Notes

1. Nous aimerions remercier John Willis, Patricia Kennedy et Normand Fortier de leurs commentaires judicieux et constructifs.
2. Devenues, en 2002, Bibliothèque et Archives Canada, à la suite de la réunion de la Bibliothèque nationale du Canada et des Archives nationales du Canada.
3. http://www.collectionscanada.ca/index-f.html. Mentionnons que d'autres institutions d'archives possèdent des documents créés par Herman Witsius et George H. Ryland, entre autres, le Service des livres rares et des collections spéciales de l'Université de Montréal, Collection Louis-Melzack (http://www.bib.umontreal.ca/CS/ryland.htm); le Service des archives de l'Université McGill (http://www.archives.mcgill.ca/resources/guide/vol2_3/gen07.htm); ainsi que le Séminaire Saint-Joseph, de Trois-Rivières, (http://site.rdaq.qc.ca/seminairedeTrois-Rivieres/).
4. Francis J. Audet. « Herman-Witsius Ryland », *Mémoires de la Société royale du Canada*, troisième série - 1929, volume XXIII, Ottawa, 1929, p. 49.
5. Louis Le Jeune. *Dictionnaire général du Canada*, « RYLAND (Herman Witsius) », Ottawa, Université d'Ottawa, 1931, vol. 2, p. 555.
6. James H. Lambert, « Ryland, Herman Witsius », *Dictionnaire biographique du Canada*, édition en ligne à l'adresse www.biographi.ca.
7. Peter Ward. *Courtship, Love, and Marriage in Nineteenth-Century English Canada*, Montréal / Toronto, McGill / Queen's University Press, 1990.
8. Katherine M. J. McKenna. *A Life of Propriety : Anne Murray Powell and Her Family, 1755-1849*, Montréal / Toronto, McGill / Queen's University Press, 1994.
9. Lorraine Gadoury. *La famille dans son intimité. Échanges épistolaires au sein de l'élite canadienne au XVIIIᵉ siècle, Montréal*, Hurtubise HMH, Cahiers du Québec, Collection « Histoire », 1998.
10. Françoise Noël. *Family Life and Sociability in Upper and Lower Canada, 1780-1870*, Montréal / Toronto, McGill / Queen's University Press, 2003.
11. Jane E. Harrison. *Adieu pour cette année. La correspondance au Canada, 1640-1830 / Until Next Year : Letter Writing and the Mails in the Canadas, 1640-1830*, Hull, Musée canadien des civilisations / Montréal, XYZ éditeur – Hull, Canadian Museum of Civilization / Waterloo, Wilfrid Laurier University Press, 1997.
12. *Dictionnaire biographique du Canada*.
13. Voir, entre autres, Gilles Paquet et Jean-Pierre Wallot. *Patronage et pouvoir dans le Bas-Canada, 1794-1812*, Montréal, Les Presses de l'Université du Québec, 1973, où se trouvent plusieurs mentions de H. W. Ryland.
14. Cette division des tâches entre le père, qui cherche à inculquer des principes, et la mère, qui donne plus d'affection, a déjà été relevée dans mon étude sur la correspondance de l'élite

canadienne grâce à des exemples tirés de lettres de la fin du XVIIIe siècle; voir Lorraine Gadoury, *op. cit.*, pp. 120-122.

15. Comme Ryland, George Pownall est un Britannique qui fut fonctionnaire et homme politique dans le Bas-Canada. Présent dans la colonie de 1775 à 1803, il se retire en Angleterre après cette date.

16. James Kempt est un officier militaire britannique éminent qui deviendra, en 1819, lieutenant-gouverneur de la Nouvelle-Écosse. Il est nommé, en 1828, gouverneur de l'Amérique du Nord britannique, poste qu'il conserve uniquement pendant deux ans alors qu'il rentre en Angleterre.

17. Robert Shore Milnes est nommé lieutenant-gouverneur du Bas-Canada en 1797; il retourne en Angleterre en 1805.

LIAISONS ÉPISTOLAIRES ILLÉGITIMES ENTRE L'ABBÉ CASGRAIN ET L'IRLANDAISE KATE E. GODLEY[1]

13

Manon Brunet, Professeur titulaire à l'Université du Québec à Trois-Rivières

Résumé

Au XIXe siècle, le réseau de l'écrivain canadien Henri-Raymond Casgrain (1831-1904) est extrêmement vaste et diversifié, comme l'attestent la variété des activités et la diversité des origines socioculturelles de ses 850 correspondants issus des cinq continents. De 1850 à 1904, l'abbé anime le projet ambitieux de créer une véritable littérature nationale canadienne-française et de la faire connaître à l'étranger. Casgrain rencontre Charles Stanley Monck, gouverneur général de l'Amérique du Nord britannique, durant le séjour de ce dernier, de 1861 à 1867, consacré à la défense du projet confédératif canadien. Au même moment, il entretient une liaison au statut ambigu avec Mrs Kate E. Godley, épouse de Denis Godley, le secrétaire civil de Monck. Une fois les fragments épistolaires recollés et décryptés, les lettres échangées en secret, de 1867 à 1874, entre l'abbé et l'Irlandaise révèlent l'ouverture d'esprit remarquable pour leur époque de cet homme et de cette femme dont les destins ont frôlé le scandale politique et religieux, et ont failli faire basculer l'histoire canadienne.

Abstract

During the nineteenth century, Canadian writer Henri-Raymond Casgrain's literary circle was large and varied, as suggested by the range of activities and sociocultural origins of some 850 correspondents on five continents. From 1850 to 1904, Abbé Casgrain was the driving force behind an ambitious initiative aimed at both creating a truly national French-Canadian literature, and promoting it outside the country. Casgrain met Charles Stanley Monck, Governor General of British North America, during the latter's term of office from 1861 to 1867, which was devoted to the support of Canadian confederation.

Figure 13.1 Lady Kate E. Godley, Montréal (Québec), 1864. I-12023.1.
Archives photographiques Notman. Musée McCord d'histoire canadienne, Montréal.

At the same time, Casgrain began a somewhat ambiguous liaison with Mrs. Kate E. Godley, wife of Monck's secretary, Denis Godley. Patched together and decoded, the literary fragments and secret letters they exchanged between 1867 and 1874 reveal a remarkable candour for the period between a man and women whose relationship not only flirted with political and religious scandal, but also could have affected the course of Canadian history.

Introduction

Il y a, parmi les 4 000 lettres envoyées à Henri-Raymond Casgrain (1831-1904), historien et chef du réseau littéraire du Canada français au XIX⁰ siècle qui correspond avec 850 intellectuels des cinq continents durant un demi-siècle, soit de 1850 à 1904, année de sa mort, un échange épistolaire des plus singulier entre cet abbé catholique influent et une certaine Mʳˢ Kate E. Godley, Irlandaise protestante, dont on ne savait presque rien[2]. Cet échange épistolaire, entretenu de 1867 à 1874, n'avait sûrement pas comme but d'être connu par l'histoire littéraire, religieuse ou politique du Canada ni de l'Irlande. Il a toutefois l'avantage exceptionnel d'éclairer des pans, plus ou moins intimes et publics, de toutes ces histoires sociales interculturelles.

L'abbé Casgrain a tenté de brouiller toutes les pistes partant de lui à cette femme et de cette femme à lui. Sauf rares exceptions, l'historien méticuleux classe sa propre correspondance reçue dans des volumes de cuir noir qui relient les lettres suivant un ordre chronologique. Or, celles de Mʳˢ Kate E. Godley sont non seulement éparpillées dans quatre tomes distants (tomes 2, 4, 5 et 7[3]), mais les feuillets d'une même lettre sont eux-mêmes dispersés. Nul doute que ce classement indique une mise en scène créée pour confondre tout lecteur non autorisé. S'ajoutent à ces fragments de lettres disséminés deux brouillons de Casgrain, télégraphiques, très raturés et d'une écriture miniaturisée, très pâle, adressés à une anonyme « Madame » et écartelés entre le tome 5 et le tome 7. Pour compléter ce corpus archivistique inédit, on découvre enfin un commentaire très intime de Casgrain, tout aussi difficilement déchiffrable, sur une page laissée blanche d'un feuillet de ce que l'on considère aujourd'hui comme la première lettre conservée de cette correspondance particulière, celle de Kate E. Godley à l'abbé, du 9 septembre 1867[4].

Cet échange épistolaire bilingue – l'Irlandaise écrit en anglais; le Canadien, en français – comprenait encore une difficulté de taille, même une fois tous les morceaux du puzzle réunis, soit celle de la datation. Seulement une lettre sur les quatorze (douze étant de Kate E. Godley; deux, les brouillons des lettres de Casgrain sûrement envoyées, car la correspondante y répond) était marquée de son millésime : le brouillon sibyllin de l'abbé, daté du jeudi 26 septembre 1867[5]. Autrement, les seuls indices temporels étaient bien minces, « Monday », « Thursday », « Eve of Sᵗ. Michael », ou au mieux des dates incomplètes, telles « October 12ᵗʰ », December 3ʳᵈ », « January 26ᵗʰ ».

La reconstitution fidèle de la chronologie et finale du contenu a pu en définitive s'établir en recourant à une analyse sociolittéraire des textes très serrée. Des pistes suivaient l'évocation d'événements internationaux connus, comme la guerre franco-prussienne de 1870-1871. D'autres, plus intimes, ramenaient au début de la correspondance, sept ans auparavant, grâce à une nostalgie soufflée en post-scriptum à la toute fin de l'échange en

1874. Ou encore des croisements pouvaient être faits entre les différentes étapes révélées du lent mais sinueux parcours de la conversion religieuse que Kate E. Godley entreprendra sous la protection amicale, voire très ou trop affectueuse de l'abbé Casgrain. Finalement, des pistes extérieures à la correspondance furent d'un grand secours, telles des lettres de tiers ou la connaissance des événements politiques qui menèrent rien de moins qu'à la création de la Confédération canadienne, en 1867[6], et auxquels le mari, Denis Godley[7], fut étroitement lié, comme conseiller privé très influent auprès du gouverneur général Charles Stanley Monck. Godley était en fait le secrétaire chargé de toute la correspondance civile du gouverneur. Ces informations extérieures confirmaient en tout point le parcours géographique et temporel des lettres écrites par Mrs Godley, depuis Québec (1867), ensuite de Newtown House[8] (1867), à Waterford, enfin d'Ashbury[9] (1870-1871, 1873-1874), à Bray [nom exact à l'époque], dans le comté de Wicklow, en Irlande. Du même coup, voilà résumés le contexte général, les enjeux et l'atmosphère de cette correspondance.

Cet exemple épistolaire est inattendu dans le cadre des sérieuses activités littéraires de Casgrain. Il représente certes un épisode biographique intéressant qui vient corriger la vision par trop conservatrice que l'historiographie littéraire a réservée au père de la littérature nationale Henri-Raymond Casgrain[10]. L'histoire religieuse hésite encore à caractériser les différentes positions idéologiques au sein du clergé québécois avec la même terminologie qui lui sert pour distinguer les clans politiques du XIXe siècle, libéral et conservateur. Nous voudrions montrer que la correspondance a peut-être plus de force idéologique ou amoureuse que la parole ou que tout autre écrit, parce justement elle a intrinsèquement la capacité d'être littéraire, *malgré elle*. Garder le contact avec l'autre à distance exige une intention et une attention stylistiques. L'abbé Casgrain aurait-il pu réussir à convertir l'Irlandaise protestante Mrs Kate E. Godley, si celle-ci était demeurée à Québec, au lieu de rentrer définitivement en Irlande après son séjour de six ans (23 octobre 1861 − 28 septembre 1867) ? À distance, les arguments de l'abbé devront être formulés de manière extrêmement prudente et délicate car, lus, sans l'intermédiaire des gestes du corps, du lieu et du moment ambiants, sur la lettre toute nue, ils apparaissent noir sur blanc. La littérarité s'impose alors comme une prudence doublée d'une audace, rendue inévitable par le truchement de la lettre, parole compensatrice de la distance imposée par le destin.

De même, Kate E. Godley aurait-elle développé des sentiments aussi affectueux envers l'abbé Casgrain si elle n'avait pas eu l'occasion d'exprimer à répétition, dans une correspondance, son grand désir de revoir celui qu'elle soupçonnait ne plus jamais revoir ? Malgré elle, ses salutations finales, trop bien (dé)tournées, trahiront son désir illégitime. Illégitime comme femme mariée, comme protestante, s'adressant à un homme religieux, rien de moins que catholique, et au moment où l'avenir de deux pays est sérieusement en cause : l'indépendance du Canada et de l'Irlande face à la Grande-Bretagne... Les sentiments semblent bien réciproques car, malgré le peu de lettres retrouvées de l'abbé, celui-ci ne ménage ni ses paroles doucereuses et bienveillantes, ni sa persévérance, ni même l'expression tourmentée de son désir de la revoir : « Si jamais je retourne en Ang[leterre], je ne manquerai pas d'aller vous rendre visite [...][11]. » Les lettres de Kate répètent inlassablement les mêmes joies, les mêmes attentes vis-à-vis de cet échange épistolaire sans nom, en s'ouvrant et se fermant de la même façon : « I was so glad to get your kind letter today. […] I shall be so glad to hear from you[12]. » Dans un cas, comme dans l'autre, la distance assumée par la correspondance a obligé les protagonistes, cachés ainsi du public, du mari, des institutions, à se révéler l'un l'autre, l'un à l'autre, plus qu'ils ne l'auraient fait en personne, avec plus de littérarité, c'est-à-dire en usant davantage de circonvolutions et de circonspection dans le discours. L'intimité ainsi créée surcharge d'émotions mal contenues chaque lettre. Sinon, pourquoi l'épouse Godley aurait-elle relu tant de fois et avec autant d'affection les mots de l'abbé : « I have so often read the letters you wrote to me seven years ago & they helped me much in my trouble[13] » ? Sinon, pourquoi Casgrain se serait-t-il donné tant de peine pour conserver les lettres de Kate E. Godley dont lui seul, ou presque, pouvait en reconstituer l'ordre, la trame ?

Lui rappelant de trop intenses et heureux souvenirs, ces lettres ne pouvaient être détruites. Ses souvenirs interdits l'ont forcé à éparpiller ce qui aura occupé sûrement une grande partie de sa conscience pendant au moins sept ans. Brouiller les pistes au lieu de les effacer, n'est-ce pas perpétuer le désir qu'un interdit soit enfin, un jour, levé ? Cet entretien méthodique de la vérité cachée exige héroïquement de sceller, jusqu'à la mort, les lettres et les silences qui les séparent cruellement. Or, malgré cela, Casgrain a pris le risque d'accumuler ces lettres. Des lettres qui témoignent littérairement, parce qu'elles arrivent à sous-entendre ce qui d'abord n'aurait jamais pu être vécu autrement et, ensuite, ce qui n'aurait jamais dû survivre aux mémoires intimes des correspondants. Au-delà de sa mort, l'homme a voulu laisser une trace publique de l'intensité de ce moment trop illicite pour avoir été si bon et si vrai. Cependant, parfois dans l'intimité aussi, il faut pouvoir relire, même des brouillons, pour croire que les choses ont vraiment été telles que sa mémoire les a mille fois recréées. La lettre conservée permet tout cela. Ainsi, Casgrain a souhaité, semble-t-il, que l'histoire littéraire décryptât l'écriture et la lecture de mots qui ne sont jamais assez clairs ou bien choisis, peu importe en définitive la liberté qu'on a d'y avoir accès, quand on veut dire qu'on aime ou croire qu'on est aimé.

La correspondance conservée se divise dans le temps en trois parties. La première partie comprend les six lettres de 1867[14], très rapprochées, soit celles du 9 septembre au 23 octobre 1867, dont cinq écrites de Québec avant le retour définitif en Irlande de Kate E. Godley, le 28 septembre 1867, et une lettre de Waterford. C'est seulement dans cette partie que l'on trouve des lettres de Casgrain, soit deux brouillons. La deuxième partie regroupe, elle aussi, un ensemble concentré de six lettres, de Kate E. Godley uniquement, écrites du 12 octobre 1870 au 26 janvier 1871[15]. Bien que nous n'ayons aucune lettre conservée de Casgrain pour cette période, la correspondance atteste à différents moments de la réception de lettres envoyées par « My dear Mr Casgrain[16] ». Finalement, deux lettres, une de décembre 1873, l'autre de janvier 1874, entrecoupées d'une lettre attestée de Casgrain[17], viennent clore le corpus conservé de la liaison entre le Canadien et l'Irlandaise. Cette division chronologique en trois temps n'est cependant pas représentative des sujets abordés dans la correspondance qui, eux, se limitent à deux : pour les périodes de 1867 et de 1873-1874, les doutes de Kate E. Godley quant à son allégeance religieuse constituent la préoccupation essentielle, alors que, durant les années 1870 et 1871, l'Irlandaise et

Figure 13.2 Le Villa Bagatelle, sise en marge de Spencer Wood. Thérèse Moisan, aquarelliste, 2000.
Collection privée.

Casgrain unissent leurs efforts pour venir en aide aux veuves et aux orphelins français réfugiés à Londres et en Irlande à cause de la guerre franco-prussienne.

La rencontre et la séparation troublantes

Kate E. Godley était arrivée au Canada le 23 octobre 1861[18], avec son mari Denis Godley, secrétaire civil et principal conseiller du gouverneur général du Canada-Uni, Monck[19]. Celui-ci, envoyé par l'Angleterre, débarquait avec sa suite dans le but de régler la question politique canadienne qui était très tendue depuis l'imposition, vingt ans plus tôt, de l'union du Bas-Canada (Québec) et du Haut-Canada (Ontario), à la suite des recommandations du controversé *Rapport Durham* de 1839.

Quand Kate E. Godley arrive au Canada, les Irlandais forment près du tiers de la population de Québec, capitale de la province du Canada de manière intermittente depuis 1852. Les Godley habitent dans sa banlieue proche jusqu'à leur départ, le 28 septembre 1867. Plus précisément, ils demeureront, à compter de 1863, dans la Villa Bagatelle, cottage situé dans le parc de Spencer Wood[20], également le lieu de la résidence officielle du gouverneur général jusqu'à la Confédération. Ces propriétés sont louées par l'épouse de James MacPherson Le Moine, ami intime de Casgrain, qui occupe la partie libre du grand parc. Par conséquent, il n'est pas interdit de penser que Casgrain et Kate se soient fréquentés dans l'une ou l'autre des résidences de Spencer Wood.

La mission de Monck et de Denis Godley, son secrétaire civil, consiste à convaincre les Canadiens de garder un lien avec la mère patrie britannique tout en respectant leur volonté d'indépendance vis-à-vis d'elle et leur désir de réparer les inégalités créées par le Canada-Uni. Le projet confédératif sera adopté, entre autres, grâce à l'habileté du mari de Kate E. Godley, Denis Godley, surnommé le « Tout-Puissant »[21]. Les Godley et les Monck sont très à l'écoute des populations locales canadiennes, religieuses, laïques et politiques, et fréquentent autant les Canadiens français catholiques que les Canadiens anglais protestants. Kate E. Godley se fera des amis au Séminaire de Québec, à l'archevêché, comme le grand vicaire Charles-Félix Cazeau[22], chez les ursulines[23], dansera avec George-Étienne Cartier[24], partagera souvent la même table que Madame la juge en chef Duval[25], que Mlle Henriette de Beaujeu[26], fille de l'écrivain Aubert de Gaspé père, tous des connaissances proches de Casgrain. Peut-être est-ce au contact répété, et trop chaleureux, de cette élite canadienne-française catholique que Mrs Godley songe à remettre en question son identité protestante.

L'évocation de ce contexte politique était incontournable pour saisir combien les échanges épistolaires entre Mrs Godley, dont on ne sait rien de plus sur le plan biographique que ce qui justifiait sa présence au Canada aux côtés de son mari, étaient risqués au point de vue politique et religieux. De son côté, Casgrain est connu dans les années 1860 et 1870 comme le leader d'un réseau littéraire très dynamique, d'un côté comme de l'autre de l'Atlantique, qui fait la promotion d'une littérature proprement canadienne, affranchie des modèles français ou anglais. En septembre 1872, l'abbé Casgrain, affecté d'une ophtalmie devenue chronique, doit abandonner définitivement ses charges ecclésiastiques. Ce qui ne l'empêchera pas de conserver son titre religieux, de voyager régulièrement à compter de 1867, de travailler dans les archives françaises durant de longs mois, de publier des centaines d'articles de critique historique et littéraire[27], d'être l'écrivain canadien le plus édité et le plus lu à l'étranger[28] et de voir, en 1888, l'Académie française couronner son ouvrage *Un pèlerinage au pays d'Évangéline*[29]. Quand il rencontre Kate E. Godley, en septembre 1867, il a 36 ans et demeure au presbytère de la cathédrale de Québec, située dans la haute ville. Il est déjà fort en vue, assez pour que Lady Monck, l'épouse du Gouverneur général, lui envoie une lettre tout à fait personnelle pour le remercier des prières que les ursulines et les religieuses de l'Hôtel-Dieu de Québec ont bien voulu prononcer, grâce à Casgrain, pour souligner le décès de sa fille[30]. N'oublions pas que les Monck sont protestants ! La Confédération est un fait accompli et Casgrain connaît donc parfaitement les idées politiques de Kate E. Godley, de même que son allégeance religieuse, car il y a maintenant six ans que les Godley sont très connus à Québec.

Le 9 septembre 1867, Kate E. Godley répond à une lettre que Casgrain lui aurait écrite. C'est donc l'abbé qui a ouvert les portes de l'échange épistolaire. Dix-neuf jours seulement avant son retour définitif en Irlande, elle ressent l'urgence de revoir Casgrain, qu'elle a rencontré d'abord on ne sait où ni quand exactement : « Dear Mr Casgrain, Thank you so much for your kind letter. I hope to come and see you some afternoon before I go, and bring back your books. [...] I shall never forget your kindness[31]. » Or, c'est sur une page laissée blanche du feuillet que l'abbé a griffonné cette note si intime, qui trahit l'intensité de l'émotion causée par la rencontre toute récente de cette femme : « Elle est venue le mardi rapporter les livres, et m'a fait dire qu'elle viendrait le lendemain. En effet à 4 h. elle m'a fait demander à la porte n'ayant pas le temps d'entrer. Le lendemain, je lui adressai ma 2e lettre, et le m[ême] jour elle vint et prétexta la maladie du Capitaine Walwyn. Conférence intime q[ue] je n'oublierai jamais[32]. » Il est clair que Kate E. Godley utilise toutes sortes de prétextes pour se trouver seule, face à face avec Casgrain : livres à rapporter, maladie de son garde du corps, réponse à donner en personne à une lettre tout juste reçue de lui. L'abbé n'est pas dupe et comprend qu'il a affaire à une rencontre pas ordinaire, du genre de celle que l'on n'oublie effectivement jamais.

Les rencontres et les lettres se succèdent jusqu'au moment redouté du départ. Les livres prêtés par Casgrain n'ont pas l'air empruntés à la poésie, au roman ou à l'histoire nationale auxquels l'animateur littéraire et ses émules s'adonnent à ce moment-là. Les préoccupations quotidiennes de l'abbé sont alors bien loin des considérations religieuses, qu'il délaisse de plus en plus par manque d'intérêt réel pour une vocation qui ne lui avait pas été d'emblée naturelle d'épouser en 1856, après ses études de médecine. La lettre suivante de Kate, du 19 septembre 1867, précise et le genre de livres et le prétexte ultime utilisé, vraiment ou faussement, pour maintenir, voire étirer, la conversation avec Henri-Raymond et multiplier leurs rencontres jusqu'en Irlande : « I must tell you how delighted I am with your book which I have just finished reading. I have been very deeply interested in it & I am so much obliged to you for having given it to me. I am sorry not to see you again before we leave Canada. If you come again to England, I hope to see you, & I hope you will let me know when you are coming[33]. » Elle le supplie de prier pour elle, car elle n'est pas très en paix avec elle-même, ne se décidant pas à quitter l'« English Church ». L'autre jour, elle et lui ont parlé du bréviaire quand ils se sont vus. Casgrain ne pourrait-il pas le lui prêter jusqu'à son départ ? Et après, comment poursuivre l'échange ? « I can read & understand French very well [...] & I shall be very glad to hear from you. May I ask for your prayers ? [...] Will you pray for me [...] ? [...] could you lend me one [bréviaire] to look at [...][34] ? » Kate assure à Casgrain que la langue ne sera pas un obstacle, mais un obstacle à quoi au juste ? La lecture en français d'ouvrages pieux ou la lecture tout court des mots d'un homme qui l'a charmée par sa personnalité si attachante ? Le mode interrogatif de la lettre provoque une insistance qui peut faire douter du bien-fondé des prérogatives religieuses énoncées par l'épistolière. Kate ne désire-t-elle pas maintenir le contact à tout prix, même s'il faut pour cela se convertir ? Néanmoins, l'épistolière se montre consciente du danger qu'elle court en jouant avec le feu de la conver(sa)sion. Ainsi, en parlant du bréviaire : « If you will send it to my husband's office, it will be quite safe.[35] » La relation entretenue entre Kate et Casgrain est donc bel et bien secrète.

Les deux lettres suivantes, qui sont des réponses de Casgrain, sont extrêmement touchantes et pas du tout dans le ton qu'il adopte généralement avec ses correspondants. Le seul fait que Casgrain en a conservé les brouillons est déjà une marque de leur caractère exceptionnel. Ce sont les seules traces tangibles que nous ayons de l'épistolier. Comme leur salutation initiale se résume à un « Madame » et que ces brouillons sont dissimulés dans les tomes 5 et 7 qui regroupent la correspondance reçue de Casgrain d'années bien postérieures, il n'était pas évident de faire le rapprochement avec les lettres envoyées par Kate.

D'abord, l'abbé la rassure : « Mais soyez sûre que je ne cesserai jamais de prier Dieu [...] de vous accorder le calme jusqu'à ce que j'apprenne de v[ous-] même que v[ous] en jouissez pleinement. Continuez de prier avec ferveur, et Dieu, n'en doutez pas, vous guidera lui-même par la main, et vous donnera cette paix [...][36]. » Ensuite, l'homme confirme qu'il tient autant qu'elle à ce qu'ils se revoient en chair et en os « Si jamais je retourne en Ang[leterre], je ne manquerai pas d'aller vous rendre visite; en attendant, si avant votre départ v[ous] désirez me voir, je suis toujours visible, surtout dans l'après-midi. Je demeure, non à l'archevêché mais au presbytère de la cathédrale [...][37]. » Et il précise : « Vous regrettez, dites-v[ous] de ne pas me voir avant v[otre] départ. Il me semble que j[e] pourrais v[ous] donner quelques bons conseils : les bornes d'une lettre sont trop étroites pour cela[38]. » Les répétitions de cette idée de revoir l'Autre, de même que les ratures, témoignent d'un désir profond, difficilement qualifiable pour nous, mais qui dépasse la simple amitié coutumière. Pas moins de six ratures se cachent sous ces dernières phrases dont n'a été retenue que la version la moins révélatrice d'une attraction. Par exemple, la « visite vers deux ou trois heures » est devenue, plus vaguement, une visite « surtout dans l'après-midi ». D'autres ratures[39] ont subi le même sort afin de camoufler une sensibilité trop sollicitée de toute évidence, car « si *je v[ous] entretenais* pend[ant] q[uel]q[ues] instants » ou « c'est ce qui me fait *désirer* de *vous entretenir* pend[ant] q[uel]q[ues] instants » ou un « Je regrette q[ue] les bornes d'une lettre soient si étroites : c'est ce qui me fait *désirer* que » ou « [me] donne la pensée [que] » dévoilent trop crûment le désir d'entretenir corps à corps la femme qui ne laisse guère Casgrain indifférent. L'abbé bégayerait-il autant dans le cas d'une vague conversion possible d'une femme qu'il connaîtrait depuis si peu et qu'il saurait ne plus jamais revoir dans quelques jours ? Ses hésitations nous laissent croire que ses sentiments soudains ne sont pas seulement de nature religieuse ou politique, et que le coup de foudre est partagé.

La deuxième et dernière lettre conservée que Casgrain envoie à Kate frappe par son caractère vraiment dramatique : « Il y a peu [de] jours v[ous] m'étiez absolument étrangère; je ne v[ous] ai vu[*sic*] q[ue] q[uel]q[ues] instants, et très-probablement je ne v[ous] reverrai plus jamais sur la terre. N[ous] ne n[ous] retrouverons que devant Dieu[40]. » Suivent trois conseils qui guideront l'âme et le cœur de Kate pendant sept ans : « 1° Priez, priez avec humilité; priez avec ferveur. 2° Soyez généreuse envers D[ieu]. Sondez bien votre cœur, et veillez avec soin à ce qu'*aucune considération honteuse* ne mette obstacle à ses desseins sur vous. 3° Soyez bien résolue d'embrasser la Vérité, *à tout prix* dès qu'elle v[ous] sera montrée[41]. » Que voulait dire Casgrain par *considération honteuse,* qu'il souligne ? On sent que ces conseils sont très réfléchis et appuyés, le « *à tout prix* » est aussi souligné de deux gros traits de crayon de plomb. Cette lettre est capitale pour la suite des choses. Elle est franchement et fortement spirituelle mais, étant donné la manière dramatique dont elle s'ouvre, on la croit plus utile pour exprimer l'indicible avec force auprès d'une femme aimée que l'on veut protéger de tous les dangers de la vie alors qu'on en sera définitivement éloigné.

La dernière lettre canadienne de Kate, écrite sur le bateau, le jour de son départ, le 28 septembre 1867, n'est pas moins étonnante. Elle révèle que Casgrain est monté à bord du bateau, le matin, sans qu'ils n'aient pu se croiser. Le navire s'étant déjà mis en marche, Casgrain est retourné à terre, mais elle continue à écrire, à lui parler comme s'il était là, malgré les conditions d'écriture difficiles : « The ship shakes so I cannot write[42]. » Elle a lu ses conseils : « I keep your letter of good advise & hope to try to follow it, but it is in many ways very very hard[43]. » Elle ose lui communiquer, pour la première fois, son adresse exacte en Irlande : « Mrs Godley, Newtown House, Waterford, Ireland[44] ». Elle insiste encore pour avoir de ses nouvelles : « I shall be so glad to hear from you », en usant encore du prétexte de livres à lui donner à lire : « Is there any book you could advise me to get[45] ? » L'interrogation force, en principe, son correspondant à répondre. Elle ne voudrait pas rompre l'amarre de leur échange. Or, répète-t-elle, « I cannot write anymore[46] », le bateau tangue. En post-scriptum, à son tour de faire une recommandation impérieuse à Casgrain, lequel prendra livraison de la lettre par la goélette qui suit le bateau, juste pour pouvoir ramener au port les lettres écrites par les passagers à la dernière minute : « Lady Monck will very likely go to see you some day she spoke of doing so, but I am sure you will not speak of anything I have said to you, as she has not an idea of what my real feelings are on these subjects[47]. »

Les Monck, eux, quitteront le Canada dans un an seulement (14 novembre 1868), Kate a donc raison de craindre les indiscrétions du réseau fort populaire de Casgrain, mais à quel sujet précisément ? Religieux, uniquement? Politique, uniquement ? Casgrain et Kate se seraient-ils écrit ces deux lettres aussi dramatiques et littéraires s'ils avaient été sûrs de se revoir ? La distance, qui déjà se transformait en un manque, favorisa le choix de mots chargés de sens et d'affects, de tournures stylistiques, telle la répétition, les phrases-chocs courtes, si propres à traduire, chez l'un comme chez l'autre, la profondeur réelle d'une idée, d'un sentiment. L'interrogation, elle, trahit plus la peur de perdre l'Autre. L'Autre qui pourrait ne plus répondre.

Le rapprochement et l'éloignement épistolaires

Rentrée en Irlande depuis moins d'un mois, Kate se hâte de répondre, le 23 octobre 1867, à son ami qui lui a envoyé « [a] very kind and beautiful letter », qu'elle a relue « many times » : « I feel all your kindness more than I can say[48] », lui avoue-t-elle. On apprend que c'est Casgrain qui l'a soumise à la question afin de poursuivre le contact avec cette femme si mystérieuse pour lui : « You ask me to tell you what are my doubts[49]. » Et voilà la protestante qui proteste, car elle ne comprend pas la place que devrait occuper la Vierge Marie dans ses nouvelles croyances religieuses catholiques si elle les adoptait. La femme cultivée a poursuivi ses lectures; elle fraie maintenant avec les œuvres monumentales des Pères de l'Église, qu'elle dissèque avec grande acuité car, selon elle, ni saint Augustin, ni saint Thomas d'Aquin, ni saint Bonaventure n'accordent d'importance à l'Immaculée Conception. D'ailleurs, pourquoi le feraient-ils ? Dieu, pas plus que les hommes, n'a besoin d'une vierge comme intermédiaire entre le Ciel et la terre : « And our Blessed

Lord said Himself " Come unto *Me* " & " I will give you rest[50] ". And He told us " Ask in My Name ". »

Cette phrase apparemment innocente inspire toutefois une consonance érotique, surtout lorsqu'on connaît le contexte dans lequel elle a été mûrie depuis la rencontre de Kate avec Casgrain. Sur le manuscrit, le « Me » dans « " Come unto *Me* " » est souligné. Il suffit de changer le nom de « Lord » par « Kate », et la première personne du pluriel par la deuxième, désignant alors le destinataire, pour entendre autrement : « And your Blessed Kate said herself " Come unto Me " & " I will give you the rest ". And she told you " Ask in My Name. " » La fin de la lettre trahit un malaise; Kate se cache-t-elle pour écrire à Casgrain : « I cannot write any more now. I am called away[51]. » ? Le « now » assure Casgrain qu'elle ne s'ennuie pas à lui écrire et qu'elle ne l'abandonnera pas, malgré les contraintes qui se présentent dans son environnement familial irlandais.

Les archives sont ensuite complètement silencieuses pendant trois ans, jusqu'au 12 octobre 1870. Pourtant la lettre de cette journée atteste que Casgrain a écrit à sa protégée au moins une fois pour lui parler de son ophtalmie, laquelle sera la raison officielle de son abandon prochain de la pratique de son ministère : « I have very often wished to hear of you [;] the last time I heard from you, you said that you are suffering from your eyes[52]. » Depuis 1869, l'abbé est très affecté par sa maladie qui le confine dans une chambre noire du manoir familial, à Rivière-Ouelle. Il cesse alors presque toute activité d'écriture; ce qui expliquerait son relatif silence dont se plaint Mrs Godley. Durant ses crises, ce sont des parents ou des amis qui lui servent de secrétaires pour sa correspondance. Pourrait-il alors se trouver une main assez discrète pour couvrir ses échanges si particuliers avec Mrs Godley ? Il est difficile de le croire. Peu importe, une distance, souhaitée ou non, s'est installée entre l'homme et la femme. Kate insiste pour le revoir, mais en employant le « we » plutôt que le « I », contrairement à son habitude dans ses lettres des 19 et 28 septembre 1867 : « If you come over to this country you must be sure to come and see us here; we should be so glad[53]. » Depuis son voyage du printemps–été 1867, Casgrain n'a pas quitté le Canada et ne le fera pour ses recherches historiques qu'en 1873. Ensuite, Mrs Godley aborde le sujet principal de sa correspondance : venir en aide financièrement aux pauvres veuves et orphelins français réfugiés à Londres à cause de la guerre franco-prussienne. Elle se présente comme l'intermédiaire entre lui et la marquise Cécile de Lothian, qui est la présidente d'un comité de dames anglaises et irlandaises chargé de recueillir bénévolement des souscriptions[54]. Il est très intéressant ici d'observer que Mrs Godley a été désignée ou s'est elle-même proposée pour réactiver son réseau canadien-français des années 1860, dont Casgrain est toujours le chef de file. Ce réseau ne devrait-il pas être très sensible aux malheurs des Français, leurs cousins ? Plus que Lady Monck donc, Mrs Godley s'était intégrée à la société canadienne-française. Était-ce dû à sa relation privilégiée avec Casgrain ? Kate demande à Casgrain de remettre une lettre à Mlle de Beaujeu, l'informant qu'elle écrira au grand vicaire Charles-Félix Cazeau, et l'invite à lui suggérer le nom de gens qu'il connaît et qui pourraient leur venir en aide. Le ton, plutôt distant et distingué, est différent des lettres de 1867, à une exception près : la salutation d'ouverture de la lettre est amplifiée. Depuis qu'elle est séparée visuellement de Casgrain, Mrs Godley a bonifié sa salutation initiale, passant du simple « Dear Mr Casgrain » de ses lettres de Québec, au « My dear Mʳ Casgrain » depuis sa lettre du 23 octobre 1867. Cette pratique sera maintenue jusqu'à la clôture de la correspondance, en 1874.

Les cinq autres lettres de Kate E. Godley de cette période de 1870-1871 reprennent la même cause, mais elles redeviennent de plus en plus intimes, même s'il n'est plus question de conversion religieuse. Au fur et à mesure que Casgrain se démène au Québec pour activer les membres tant féminins que masculins de son réseau très étendu, les comités de bénévoles se multiplient et les souscriptions s'accumulent pour répondre à l'appel du chef dont l'esprit critique veille toujours en dépit des circonstances atténuantes : « Malgré les torts que la France a eus envers nous, Canadiens français, nous n'avons jamais oublié qu'elle est la patrie de nos pères, et que c'est toujours le sang de la France qui coule dans nos veines. [...] Oui, nous aimons la France, et ses malheurs nous la rendent plus chère.[55] » Le dynamisme du secrétaire du Comité des dames de Québec, Casgrain, imité au sein de son réseau, permet de récolter 821,95 $, somme extraordinaire pour l'époque[56]. Kate Godley en est complètement éblouie : « It is most kind of you and I am very grateful for all you have done. The good and kind Quebec people have done more than we could have possibly expected[57]. » Le « I » revient en lieu et place du « we », qui renvoyait au couple Godley plutôt qu'à Kate seulement : « [...] how grateful I was to you for having taken up this work of Charity[58]. » Elle insiste pour le remercier plus que tous les autres : « I feel that it is you we have to thank for it all and I do thank you with all my heart[59]. » Kate s'intéresse soudain encore plus aux yeux de l'homme fascinant qu'elle retrouve dans son rôle de mentor influent : « I often thought of you and felt so grieved to hear how you were suffering from your eyes. I can never forget your kindness to me[60]. »

À compter de cette lettre du 3 décembre 1870, la salutation finale de Kate Godley devient très affectueuse, plus encore qu'à l'époque du « most sincerely[61] » : « I am always, dear Mʳ Casgrain, yours affectionately, Kate E. Godley[62]. » Les lettres de 1870 et de 1871 ont donc permis au couple d'amis Kate et Henri-Raymond de se retrouver, de raviver leur réseau commun et de se redire leur admiration mutuelle. Celle du 26 janvier 1871 crée un rebondissement inattendu. Alors que Casgrain a terminé son œuvre de charité, et n'a donc légitimement plus aucune raison de correspondre avec cette femme, Kate lui tend la perche religieuse que son correspondant avait lui-même utilisée en 1867 pour éviter de perdre contact avec elle : « I hope if you have time that you will sometimes write to us and I may ask for your prayers. I have just been read with great interest the Life of Sʳ. Ignatius [...] which seems to me to be really inspiring [...]. Always yours affectionately, Kate E. Godley[63]. »

Cette perche, qui les ramène à leurs anciennes amours, si l'on peut dire, Casgrain saura sûrement la saisir, même si nous n'en avons pas de preuves tangibles autres que l'attestation, presque trois ans plus tard, d'une conversion accomplie grâce aux prières et aux bons conseils de l'abbé : « [...] I have been received at last into the Catholic Church. I am sure your prayers have helped me very much and I have never forgotten all your advice in your letters to me on this subject[64]. » Il est le premier à qui elle l'annonce et Casgrain lui répond très rapidement car, dès le 9 janvier 1874, elle lui confirme réception de sa lettre : « I was so glad to get your kind letter today. [...] I feel every day more and more happy to have done, and I at times feel a peace of mind while I never could have imagined before to be possible in this world. After such along struggle (for years I may say) the calm and rest seem[s] at times almost too much. [...] Like a ship that has long been tossed about by the waves and storms finding herself at last in the safe haven where she would be[65]. »

Mrs Godley accueille cette paix si précieuse que Casgrain lui avait promise en 1867 : « Du premier coup d'œil, j'ai compris votre âme; j'ai vu les troubles qui l'agitent, les saintes aspirations qui vous émeuvent; cette soif de justice et de la vérité que Dieu promet de rassasier. Car, Madame, l'œil du Juste qui a continué à regarder au fond des consciences pour diriger les âmes, a bien vite vu ce qui se passe dans un cœur. Le vôtre m'est connu. Et je peux vous le dire avec certitude : réjouissez-vous, *Dieu vous aime* [...] vous trouverez infailliblement ce repos après lequel vous soupirez. *Vous me comprenez*[66]. » Casgrain avait souligné fortement, au crayon noir, deux passages : « *Dieu vous aime* » et « *Vous comprenez* ».

Ce sont ces phrases, ces tournures plus littéraires, créées par l'exigence de la correspondance, qui eurent le plus raison de cet échange à la fois trop amical et trop spirituel, pour n'avoir été que cela. Les lettres révèlent une intimité inavouable pour l'époque, en osant plus qu'il ne pouvait être dit de la part d'un religieux à une femme pendant sept ans, plus qu'il ne pouvait être fait de la part de l'épouse protestante du secrétaire civil du gouverneur général du Canada, au beau milieu des discussions sur le projet confédératif qui aurait pu avorter si la chose s'était sue... À ce que l'on sache, les épistoliers illégitimes ne se reverront jamais.

Notes

1. Cet article constitue une version considérablement révisée d'une conférence prononcée à Queen's University, à Belfast, en Irlande, le 5 avril 2002.
2. Malgré des recherches approfondies, menées tant en Irlande qu'au Canada, nous possédons très peu de renseignements biographiques sur Mrs Godley. Son nom de jeune fille est mentionné seulement dans l'autobiographie de son neveu : «[...] at Stillorgan, near Dublin, Uncle Denis and Aunt Kate's house was always open to me. [...] Aunt Kate (*née* Barron), who was my godmother, was a very remarkable and delightful character, and was adored by all her nephews and nieces. » (Sir Alexander Godley. *Life of an Irish Soldier*. London : John Murray, 1939, p. 6) Son mari, Denis Godley, fut le secrétaire civil particulier du gouverneur général du Canada, Lord Charles Stanley Monck. Au Canada, elle était surnommée « Nimble » par Lady Elizabeth Louise Mary Monck Monck [*sic*], cousine et épouse du gouverneur (William Lewis Morton, ed. *Monck Letters and Journals, 1863-1868 : Canada from Government House at Confederation*. Toronto : McClelland & Stewart, 1970, pp. 323-324) Pour les activités de Mrs Godley durant son séjour canadien, voir aussi Frances Elizabeth Owen Cole Monck. *My Canadian Leaves : An Account of a Visit to Canada in 1864-1865*. London : Richard Bentley & Son, 1891.

3. Musée de la Civilisation de Québec, Musée de l'Amérique française, Fonds Casgrain (P14), *Lettres diverses*, tome 2, O449; tome 4, O451; tome 5, O452; tome 7, O454. Toutes les lettres citées provenant du même fonds, nous indiquerons seulement la référence à la tomaison.

4. Lettre de Kate E. Godley à [Henri-Raymond] Casgrain, [Quebec], Monday [September 9th 1867], tome 2, O449, n° 115.

5. Lettre de H[enri-]R[aymond] C[asgrain] à « Madame » [Kate E. Godley], Québec, jeudi 26 sept[embre] 1867, tome 7, O454, n° 15. Brouillon.

6. William Lewis Morton. *The Critical Years : The Union of British North America, 1857-1873*. Toronto : McClelland & Stewart, 1964.

7. Le prénom de l'époux de Kate E. Godley a été découvert sur un reçu annexé à la lettre de C[écile] de Lothian à [Kate E.] Godley, Refugee Benevolent Fund, Ladies' Committee, [London], 3rd Jan[uary] [18]71, tome 4, O451, n° 67. Ce reçu porte la même date que la lettre et est ainsi libellé : « *Received of* the Ladies Committee Quebec, par Mrs Denis Godley *the Sum of* Sixty three Pounds 2/10 *on Account of the Refugee Benevolent Fund, Ladies' Committee*, C. Lothian ». (La partie imprimée est indiquée ici en italique.)

8. [Unknown]. *Handbook for Waterford and Vicinity*. Waterford : N. Harvey, 1891, p. 3.

9. Ashbury, tout comme Newtown House, désigne un nom de villa (Arthur L. Doran. *Bray and Environs*. Bray : Arthur L. Doran Publisher, 1903; cartes, entre pp. 44-45). Aujourd'hui, à Bray, on trouve le « Ashbury Park » (K. M. Davies. *Bray*. Dublin : Royal Irish Academy, Irish Historical Towns Atlas, n° 9, 1998).

10. Manon Brunet. « Henri-Raymond Casgrain et la paternité d'une littérature nationale », *Voix et Images*, LXV, hiver 1997, p. 205-224.

11. Lettre de [Henri-Raymond Casgrain] à « Madame » [Kate E. Godley], [Québec], [entre le 19 et le 26 septembre 1867], tome 5, O452, n° 36. Brouillon.

12. Lettre de Kate E. Godley à [Henri-Raymond] Casgrain, [Ashbury, Bray, Wicklow], Ireland, Jan[ua]ry 9th [1874], tome 5, O452, n° 3. Lettre attestée de Casgrain perdue. Dernière lettre conservée de l'échange.

13. Post-scriptum de la même lettre.

14. Lettre de Kate E. Godley à [Henri-Raymond] Casgrain, [Quebec], Monday [September 9th 1867], tome 2, O449, n° 115; *idem*, Thursday [September 19th 1867], tome 2, O449, n° 116; lettre de [Henri-Raymond Casgrain] à « Madame » [Kate E. Godley], [Québec], [entre le 19 et le 26 septembre 1867], tome 5, O452, n° 36. Brouillon; lettre de H[enri-]R[aymond] C[asgrain] à « Madame » [Kate E. Godley], Québec, jeudi 26 sept[embre] 1867, tome 7, O454, n° 15. Brouillon signé; lettre de Kate E. Godley à [Henri-Raymond] Casgrain, [Quebec], Eve of S^t. Michael [September 28th 1867], tome 2, O449, n° 116 [*sic*]; *idem*, Newtown House, Waterford, [Ireland], October 23th [1867], tome 2, O449, n° 120 et 116. Toutes les dates sont partiellement ou entièrement restituées, sauf pour le dernier brouillon de Casgrain qui, lui, est clairement daté. Seules les lettres de 1867 de Mrs Godley affichent le monogramme « KEG », lequel ne nous fournit pas de piste pour connaître le patronyme d'origine de l'épistolière, Barron.

15. Lettre de Kate E. Godley à [Henri-Raymond] Casgrain, Ashbury, Bray, [Wicklow], Ireland, October 12th [1870], tome 4, O451, n° 65; *idem*, [Ashbury, Bray, Wicklow], Ireland, December 3rd [1870], tome 4, O451, n° 63; *idem*, Ashbury, Bray, [Wicklow], Ireland, [entre le 3 et le 22 décembre 1870], tome 4, O451, n° 61; *idem*, [Wicklow, Ireland], Dec[ember] 22th [1870], tome 4, O451, n° 46; *idem*, [Wicklow], Ireland, Jan[ua]ry 5th [1871], tome 4, O451, n° 69; *idem*, [Wicklow, Ireland], Jan[ua]ry 26th [1871], tome 4, O451, n° 71.

16. Salutation initiale qui sera invariablement adoptée par Mrs Godley dans toute sa correspondance adressée depuis l'Irlande.

17. Lettre de Kate E. Godley à [Henri-Raymond] Casgrain, [Ashbury, Bray, Wicklow], Ireland, Dec[em]ber 5[th] [1873], tome 5, O452, n° 34; *idem*, Jan[ua]ry 9[th] [1874], tome 5, O452, n° 3. Lettre attestée de Casgrain, perdue.

18. William Lewis Morton, ed., *op. cit.*, p. x.

19. Jacques Monet. « Charles Stanley Monck », *Dictionnaire biographique du Canada,* vol. XII, *1891-1900.* Québec : Presses de l'Université Laval, 1990, pp. 816-818. Voir aussi, sur le couple Monck : Elizabeth Batt. *The Moncks and Charleville House.* Dublin : Blackwater, 1979.

20. Frédéric Smith. « La ville Bagatelle : brève histoire d'un site enchanteur ». Québec : Fondation Bagatelle, 2000, « http://www.cataraqui.qc.ca/Site-internet-Bagatelle/Histoire.html » (page consultée le 24 novembre 2004); James MacPherson Le Moine. *Picturesque Quebec : A Sequel to Quebec Past and Present.* Montreal : Dawson, 1882 , p. 340. Les Godley avait aussi un pied-à-terre à Montréal, au « 68 McGill College Ave[nue] » (*Mackay's Montreal Directory for 1867-1868.* Montreal : John Lovell, 1868, p. 160).

21. « [...] Monck était grandement influencé par son secrétaire et confident Denis Godley, réformateur colonial britannique et fonctionnaire consciencieux, que les Canadiens surnommaient " le Tout-Puissant " et dont les vues sur l'Union et l'indépendance en Amérique du Nord britannique l'encouragèrent dans bien des initiatives politiques » (Jacques Monet, *op. cit.,* p. 816). Monet orthographie « Dennis », le prénom de Godley. Or, toute la correspondance rédigée par le secrétaire civil est signée « Denis », telle que reproduite dans la version anglaise autant que dans la française des *Journaux de l'Assemblée législative de la province du Canada* de 1863 à 1867. Sur Denis Godley, voir aussi Frederic Boase. *Modern English Biography,* vol. I, *A-H.* London : Frank Cass., 1965.

22. Lettre de Kate E. Godley à [Charles-Félix] Cazeau, Ashbury, Bray, [Wicklow], October 7th 1870, tome 4, O451, n° 36 et 36b. Voir aussi Frances Elizabeth Owen Cole Monck, *op. cit.,* p. 199.

23. Grâce à l'abbé Casgrain, Lady Monck et Kate E. Godley auront leurs entrées chez les ursulines de Québec : « [...] Lady Monck et ses Dlles. dont les bienveillantes visites, tant à l'intérieur que dans nos parloirs, les gracieux messages [...] seront toujours d'un si doux parfum [...]. C'est dans ces occasions que nous avons eu l'avantage de faire connaissance avec Madame Godley qui nous a fait part de tant de détails intimes sur nos chères sœurs de Waterford. » ([Anonyme], *Les Ursulines de Québec, depuis leur établissement jusqu'à nos jours,* vol. IV. Québec : C. Darveau, 1866, p. 501). Mère Saint-Charles, en particulier, gardera le contact avec les deux étrangères (Frances Elizabeth Owen Cole Monck, *op. cit.* : 175). Le jour de son départ, Kate reçoit un souvenir de son amie ursuline : « I got from la Mère S[t]. Charles a Chapelet du Précieux Sang [...] and I Hope it will help me to pray more and better. » (Lettre de Kate E. Godley à Casgrain, 28 septembre 1867, *op. cit.*)

24. Frances Elizabeth Owen Cole Monck, *op. cit.*, p. 175.

25. Son mari était le juge Jean-François-Joseph Duval. Elle est connue pour tenir un salon très couru par l'élite intellectuelle et politique de la Côte-du-Sud, région natale de Casgrain : « Inutile de dire que Madame Duval a sa cour à Kamouraska comme à Québec; on comprend en la voyant l'influence que les femmes exercent sur la société [...]. Sa réputation n'est pas surfaite; elle la mérite [...] » (Laurent-Olivier David. « Correspondances », *L'Opinion publique,* 4 août 1870, p. 246). En 1870, madame Duval est membre du Comité des dames qui recueillent des fonds en faveur des veuves et des orphelins français réfugiés à Londres durant la guerre franco-prussienne. Par l'entremise de Casgrain, ce comité est lié à celui de Londres dont font partie Kate E. Godley ainsi que la marquise Cécile de Lothian (Henri-Raymond Casgrain. « Le Canada et la France », *Le Courrier du Canada,* 9 décembre 1870, p. 2-3). Elle est mentionnée dans les lettres de Mrs Godley à Casgrain : celle d'entre le 3 et le 22 décembre 1870; celle du 5 janvier 1871.

26. Le jour de son départ du Canada, Kate E. Godley écrit à Casgrain : « I hope to make acquaintance with your friends M. et Mlle de Beaujeu. » (Lettre du 28 septembre 1867, *op. cit.*) Voir aussi lettre de Henriette de Beaujeu à Révérend [Henri-Raymond] Casgrain, Québec, 20 d[écem]bre 1871, tome 6, O453, n° 39. Mademoiselle de Beaujeu est souvent citée dans la correspondance de Mrs Godley à Casgrain : 28 septembre 1867; 23 octobre 1867; 12 octobre 1870.

27. Manon Brunet. « Travestissement littéraire et trajectoire intellectuelle de Henri-Raymond Casgrain », *Voix et Images*, LXXXVIII, automne 2004, p. 47-66.

28. *Idem.* « Prolégomènes pour une méthodologie d'analyse des réseaux littéraires : le cas de la correspondance de Henri-Raymond Casgrain », *Voix et images*, LXXX, hiver 2002, p. 216-237.

29. Henri-Raymond Casgrain. *Un pèlerinage au pays d'Évangéline.* Québec : L.-J. Demers, 1887.

30. Lettre de E[lizabeth] L[ouise] M[ary] [Monck] Monck à H[enri-Raymond] Casgrain, Spencer Wood, Sep[tember] 30th [entre 1863 et août 1866], tome 3, O450, n° 55.

31. Lettre de Kate E. Godley à Casgrain, 9 septembre 1867.

32. Note de Casgrain, *ibid.*

33. Lettre de Kate E. Godley à Casgrain, 19 septembre 1867.

34. Ibid.

35. Ibid.

36. Lettre de Casgrain à Kate E. Godley, entre le 19 et le 26 septembre 1867.

37. Ibid.

38. Ibid.

39. Ibid. C'est nous qui soulignons.

40. Lettre de Casgrain à Kate E. Godley, 26 septembre 1867.

41. Ibid. Casgrain souligne.

42. Lettre de Kate E. Godley à Casgrain, 28 septembre 1867.

43. Ibid.

44. Ibid.

45. Ibid.

46. Ibid.

47. Ibid.

48. Lettre de Kate E. Godley à Casgrain, 23 octobre 1867.

49. Ibid.

50. Ibid.

51. Ibid.

52. Lettre de Kate E. Godley à Casgrain, 12 octobre 1870, *op. cit.* Lettre attestée de Casgrain, perdue.

53. Lettre de Kate E. Godley à Casgrain, 12 octobre 1870, *op. cit.* Nous soulignons.

54. Lettre de C[écile] de Lothian à [Kate E.] Godley, Refugee Benevolent Fund, Ladies' Committee, [London], 3rd Jan[uary] [18]71, *op. cit.*

55. Henri-Raymond Casgrain, « Le Canada et la France », *op. cit.*

56. Dans ses mémoires, Casgrain parle plutôt d'une somme de 50 000 francs : « Les premiers citoyens organisèrent un comité qui se mit activement à l'œuvre. En qualité de secrétaire de ce comité, je pus bientôt annoncer à la marquise de Lothian l'envoi d'une somme de cinquante mille francs. » (Musée de la civilisation, de Québec, Musée de l'Amérique française, Fonds Casgrain (P14), Henri-Raymond Casgrain. *Souvenances canadiennes*, [s. d.], tome 4, O446, p. 49) Or, puisque Casgrain écrit ses mémoires à la toute fin du XIXe siècle, il s'agit sûrement du montant actualisé du total des dons de 1870. Cette année-là, le montant s'élève à 821,95 $ et est « expédié à Madame Godley pour le Comité de Londres », d'après le rapport de la trésorière du Comité des dames de Québec, Adèle K. Tessier, intitulé « Souscriptions

recueillies en faveur des veuves et des orphelins français réfugiés à Londres » ([1871], 1 feuille imprimée, collée dans Musée de la civilisation, de Québec, Musée de l'Amérique française, Fonds Casgrain (P14), Henri-Raymond Casgrain. *Album*, [s. d.], O425, p. 64).

57. Lettre de Kate E. Godley à Casgrain, 3 décembre 1870.
58. Lettre de Kate E. Godley à Casgrain, entre le 3 et le 22 décembre 1870.
59. Lettre de Kate E. Godley à Casgrain, 3 décembre 1870.
60. *Ibid*.
61. Lettre de Kate E. Godley à Casgrain, 12 octobre 1870.
62. Lettre de Kate E. Godley à Casgrain, 3 décembre 1870.
63. Lettre de Kate E. Godley à Casgrain, 26 janvier 1871.
64. Lettre de Kate E. Godley à Casgrain, 5 décembre 1873.
65. Lettre de Kate E. Godley à Casgrain, 9 janvier 1874.
66. Lettre de Casgrain à Kate E. Godley, 26 septembre 1867. L'auteur souligne.

CORRESPONDANCE D'UN IMMIGRANT FRANÇAIS AU CANADA AU DÉBUT DU XXᴱ SIÈCLE

14

Marguerite Sauriol

Résumé

En 1905, Pierre Gilibert, originaire du Sud-Est de la France, immigre au Canada dans l'espoir de s'enrichir par l'exploitation d'une terre en Alberta. Plusieurs lettres envoyées à ses proches en Europe nous font prendre conscience du rôle que la correspondance a pu jouer dans la vie d'un jeune immigrant venu s'installer dans une région alors en plein développement.

Les lettres de Gilibert se révèlent en effet une source abondante d'informations sur l'histoire de l'immigration française au Canada. Elles nous permettent d'abord de connaître l'itinéraire du voyageur : son départ de France, son passage en Angleterre, son arrivée à Montréal et, finalement, son établissement sur sa terre, en Alberta. Les fréquentes observations de Gilibert, reliées à l'évolution rapide du chemin ferroviaire et à l'état du système postal dans la région, nous renseignent sur une partie de l'histoire du développement de l'Ouest du pays. La correspondance dévoile l'expérience personnelle de l'immigrant dans son nouvel environnement, son adaptation à son nouveau mode de vie sur son établissement agricole, ses découvertes, ses impressions et sa façon de composer avec les évènements. Elle présente aussi l'aspect social de l'aventure, la rencontre avec des habitants de la région, et dresse ainsi un portrait de la vie du milieu rural de cette province, au début du vingtième siècle.

La correspondance expose une autre dimension. C'est grâce au courrier que Gilibert a pu maintenir des liens avec les membres de sa famille et ses amis vivant de l'autre côté de l'océan. Par l'entremise de ses missives, il a fait des confidences sur les gens qui l'entouraient et partagé ses expériences et les épreuves auxquelles il a été confronté. Il y a exprimé ses sentiments à l'égard de ses proches, de ses amis et des situations qu'il a vécues. Cette correspondance nous fait ainsi découvrir l'aspect émotionnel de l'aventure de l'immigrant au Canada.

Abstract

In 1905, Pierre Gilibert, who came from southeastern France, immigrated to Canada, hoping to get rich by developing a plot of land in Alberta. Several letters sent to his relations in Europe demonstrate the role that correspondence could play in the life of a young immigrant who had recently settled in a region whose development was then in full bloom.

Gilibert's letters are a valuable source of information on the history of French immigration to Canada. They reveal, first of all, the traveller's itinerary: his departure from France, his passage to England, his arrival in Montréal and, finally, his settlement in Alberta. Gilibert's frequent observations, related to the rapid evolution of the railways and the state of the postal system in the region, give us information on particular aspects of the history of the development of the Canadian West. His correspondence also reveals the personal experiences of an immigrant in a new environment, his adaptation to a new way of life on his agricultural concession, his many new discoveries, and his impressions of, and ways of dealing with, a wide range of events. In addition, his letters present the social aspects of his adventure and his encounters with the inhabitants of the region, thus providing us with a portrait of life in this province's rural milieu at the beginning of the twentieth century.

Introduction

Au cours de la seconde moitié du XIXe siècle, les Prairies canadiennes s'ouvrent à la colonisation, en partie grâce au prolongement du réseau ferroviaire vers l'Ouest. Dans les années 1870, et jusqu'en 1914, le gouvernement canadien met en œuvre un mouvement en ce sens. Au moyen de dépliants, de brochures et d'affiches, il fait la promotion de l'immigration vers la « Terre promise[1] » en y offrant des terres. Il fait donc paraître des annonces dans la presse périodique et, après 1896, des représentants se rendent même en Europe pour y promouvoir l'Ouest canadien[2]. C'est particulièrement durant les années 1890 que des immigrants francophones viendront de France, de Belgique et de Suisse et s'y installeront. L'Église catholique est l'un des principaux promoteurs de l'établissement de ces groupes dans les Prairies[3]. En arrivant au Canada, les immigrants reçoivent, à la condition de remplir certains critères, une terre qu'ils doivent défricher et cultiver. Certains y voient la chance de bâtir une entreprise; d'autres, une façon de s'enrichir et de retourner ensuite dans leur pays d'origine.

Pour l'immigrant, l'adaptation en sol étranger est une expérience éprouvante sur le plan personnel et affectif. Ceux et celles qui quittent leur pays sont en effet séparés de leur famille et de leurs amis. La correspondance devient alors le seul moyen de maintenir un rapport avec les proches vivant outre-mer. Elle s'avère par ailleurs une source importante qui permet de découvrir le phénomène de l'immigration par l'intermédiaire de ceux qui l'ont vécue. La correspondance dévoile la façon dont l'immigrant a composé avec

Figure 14.1 Brochure de promotion de l'Ouest canadien, en 1900.

Archives du Musée Glenbow (Calgary), 971.2 C212o Pam.

cette entreprise audacieuse, son aspect émotionnel, ainsi que le type de relations qu'il a maintenues.

Nous avons eu accès à une série de lettres d'un immigrant français, Pierre Gilibert, qui nous ont permis d'examiner ces questions[4]. Originaire de Salaise-sur-Sanne, dans l'Isère, dans le Sud-Est de la France, Gilibert a 24 ans lorsqu'il arrive au Canada, en 1905. Il s'établit sur une terre qui lui a été concédée près de Red Deer et de Lacombe, en Alberta. Le motif de ce voyage est la mise sur pied d'une association de colons français qui exploiteraient des terres offertes gratuitement par le gouvernement canadien. Les colons doivent y demeurer trois ans. Au terme de cette période, ils en deviennent les propriétaires s'ils le désirent. Attiré par cette opportunité d'investissement, Gilibert décide de tenter l'aventure avec d'autres Français. Il prévoit s'installer quelques années sur une de ces terres, la revendre à un bon prix, puis revenir en France.

Lors de son séjour au Canada, Gilibert a entretenu une correspondance avec sa famille en France, sa mère en particulier, et avec ses amis. Cette correspondance s'avère une source riche d'informations sur l'immigration française au pays, au début du XXᵉ siècle. L'étude des lettres permet de retracer l'itinéraire emprunté par le voyageur pour se rendre en Amérique, d'apprendre la façon dont il a vécu l'expérience et de comprendre l'adaptation à sa nouvelle vie. De plus, les nombreuses observations sur son environnement font découvrir, en partie, l'histoire du développement de la colonisation de l'Ouest du pays. Les lettres de Gilibert révèlent aussi l'aspect émotif de l'aventure, ses sentiments, ses impressions, ses préoccupations, ses réactions face aux différentes situations et, finalement, la nature de sa relation avec ses proches en France et ses compagnons de voyage.

Nous nous proposons ici de raconter l'expérience que cet homme a vécue au Canada, au début du XXᵉ siècle, à travers l'analyse de sa correspondance. L'article présentera uniquement la perspective de l'immigrant. Il s'agit d'une étude, parmi d'autres, portant sur l'immigration francophone au Canada[5].

Au total, nous disposions de huit lettres de Gilibert : deux adressées à ses amis; les autres expédiés à ses proches, dont trois à sa mère. Trois sont de 1905; trois, de 1906, et deux, de 1912. L'une d'elles, datée de 1912, est cosignée par une certaine « Berry ». Il s'agit en fait d'Anne-Marie Spigre, que Gilibert avait épousée lors d'un séjour en France, au printemps 1910.

Le voyage

Le départ de la France

Le samedi 15 avril 1905 marque le début d'une grande aventure pour Pierre Gilibert. Il quitte Dijon et se rend à Paris en train, en compagnie de son beau-frère Henry et de son cousin, l'abbé François Guigue. Les voyageurs parviennent à la Ville Lumière et y séjournent plusieurs jours avant de se rendre à la gare Saint-Lazare, où ils retrouvent leurs compagnons de colonisation. Leur association comprend une quinzaine de personnes et se compose d'un prêtre, François Guigue, de deux familles, celle de Jean Henry et celle de Plantier, de Salaise, d'un couple, les Revol, et finalement de Gilibert[6]. Ces gens montent à bord d'un train de nuit, qui arrive à Dieppe aux petites heures du matin. À cet endroit, ils embarquent sur un vapeur qui les amène à Newhaven, en Angleterre, et, de là, prennent un train pour Londres.

Gilibert livre les sentiments qu'il ressent face à Londres, dont il trouve le décor plutôt déprimant et en rien comparable avec celui de la France : « Le plouie toujours le plouie ! …Voici Londres. » Henry quitte les membres du groupe avant que ceux-ci montent à bord du train qui les amènera à Liverpool. Avant de se dire adieu, Gilibert et son beau-frère se paient « une bonne tranche de rigolade à la figure de ces braves anglais, qui faisaient tous les frais de [leur] hilarité[7] ». Il n'apprécie guère plus son séjour à Liverpool en raison des conditions « absolument infectes » de l'hôtel où la compagnie Dominion Line leur a réservé des chambres. D'autres personnes, environ une douzaine, venues de France par d'autres voies, devaient aussi y séjourner mais, tout comme Gilibert et ses compagnons, elles refusent d'y passer la nuit. Étant le seul à se débrouiller en anglais, Gilibert sert de traducteur non seulement pour ses compagnons mais aussi pour ces étrangers. Ils parcourent tous ensemble la ville, jusque tard dans la nuit, « éreintés », avant de finalement trouver un endroit convenable pour souper et dormir.

Le jeudi 20 avril, à trois heures de l'après-midi, la sirène se fait entendre : c'est le grand départ. Avant d'embarquer à bord du *Dominion*, le navire qui les amènera à Montréal, Gilibert a une pensée pour ses proches : « […] nous prions pour eux et nous nous endormons à la pensée qu'ils prient pour que rien ne nous arrive de fâcheux[8]. » Il se sent soulagé, une fois arrivé à sa cabine, et en profite pour écrire une lettre qu'il mettra à la poste dès son arrivée. Il pense être tranquille pendant les huit jours que devrait durer la traversée, mais il n'en est rien. Il raconte le trajet en mer, l'agitation des vagues, qui leur a donné la frousse à certains moments, la tempête et, finalement, les icebergs venant du Nord, qui les ont retardés. La traversée prendra finalement quinze jours.

L'arrivée au Canada

Le navire arrive à Montréal le 5 mai. Gilibert trouve l'atmosphère de la ville chaleureuse et l'accent de ses habitants, pittoresque : « La ville est très gentille, nous y tombons dans un bon hôtel où l'on parle canadien français c'est-à-dire le langage français du XVIIème siècle qui n'a pas fait de progrès depuis ce temps-là. C'est très bizarre d'entendre parler ainsi[9]. »

À Montréal, Gilibert et ses compagnons de voyage prennent le train pour se rendre à Red Deer, un périple qu'il mettra cinq jours à parcourir les 3 800 kilomètres séparant les deux villes. Le 30 mai 1905, il est rempli d'espoir quand il décrit le paysage : la forêt qui s'étend continuellement entre Montréal et Winnipeg, les grandes plaines du Manitoba, puis l'immense prairie de l'Alberta. Il parle du Canada comme étant un « [p]ays riche d'avenir qui se peuple avec une rapidité effrayante[10] ». Pourtant, un mois plus tard, dans une lettre à sa mère, il en présente une toute autre image :

> […] il n'y a rien de bien extraordinaire, des bois bornent la vue presque continuel-lement…Et puis, on n'a pas, non plus, le cœur gai pour voir ces choses sous leur meilleur jour, on est malgré tout lassé par le voyage, interminable, puis on songe que toutes ces choses qui fuient si rapidement sous nos yeux, nous éloignent encore de tous ceux qu'on aime. Et puis on pense encore que si c'est tout cela que le Canada

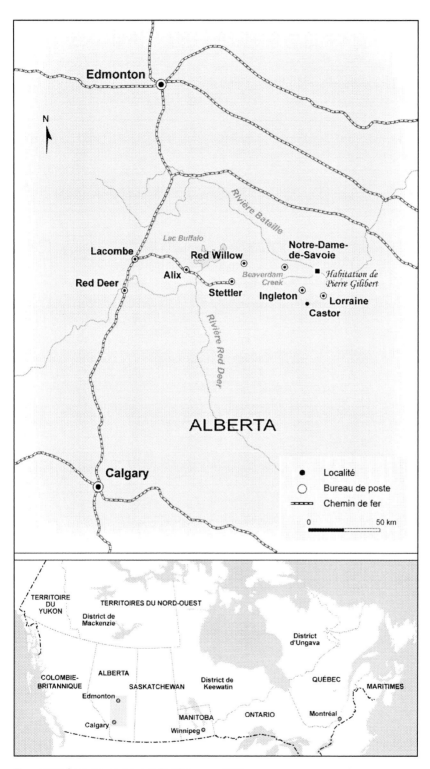

Figure 14.2 Carte des environs de Red Deer, vers 1909.

Carte d'Andrée Héroux.

nous réserve, on a bien tort d'y être venu. [...] toujours du bois, rien que la nature sauvage, qui évoque un peu le souvenir des anciens habitants du pays, Huron et autres, si au moins on en voyait quelques uns, mais zut, sale Canada va ![11]

Le voyageur ressent néanmoins une certaine gaieté à la vue des toits et des cheminées des maisons de Winnipeg, et surtout de l'animation qui règne dans cet endroit qu'il croyait « perdu ». Après un bref arrêt dans cette localité, qu'il décrit d'ailleurs comme une ville très commerciale et la porte de l'Ouest canadien, il remonte à bord du train « avec un peu plus d'espoir dans l'avenir[12] ».

L'installation sur les terres

Gilibert et les futurs membres de l'association parviennent finalement à Red Deer, le 10 mai. Ils y rencontrent le représentant de l'abbé Jean Gaire[13], qui les installe dans une maison pour une quinzaine de jours. Les femmes y demeureront pendant que les hommes iront choisir leur terre. On s'occupe donc d'aller chercher des provisions et un poêle, que Plantier et Jean Henry « charrient sur leur dos », ne se souciant guère des regards étonnés des habitants locaux. Gilibert précise, dans une lettre, que lui et ses compagnons ont bien l'intention de goûter à ce « fameux gibier » tant vanté dans les brochures sur le Canada. Ils se procurent deux chevaux de prairie, une charrette et une tente, puis prennent la route.

Le représentant, installé depuis peu dans la région, ne peut servir de guide au groupe et recommande à ses membres de s'adresser plutôt à l'abbé Jean-François Féroux.[14] Ce prêtre, qui avait correspondu avec Gaire, pourra leur donner des indications sur les terres disponibles. Toutefois, d'après le représentant, la région à l'est de Red Deer semble être la plus prometteuse. Les terres y trouvent preneurs rapidement, en raison de la construction du chemin de fer.

Gilibert part donc avec les hommes du groupe vers le 15 mai afin de se rendre chez Féroux. Les explications fournies pour y arriver s'avèrent cependant imprécises, comme le signale notre voyageur : « ... les routes ou plutôt les chemins sont comme ils étaient en France il y a 3 ou 400 ans; par endroit ils sont marqués quelque peu sur le terrain, puis ils s'écartent sur l'herbe dans la prairie et il est alors impossible de se diriger sans boussole[15]. » Cinq jours plus tard, l'équipe arrive enfin chez Féroux, où elle est accueillie par le neveu de l'abbé qui leur indique les terres disponibles. Les futurs colons les parcourent pendant encore plusieurs jours, remarquant le charme de « ces longues chevauchées (en voiture) à travers des sites pittoresques[16] », puis ils font leur choix.

Les terres que le groupe choisit finalement sont situées dans la plaine, à 100 miles (150 kilomètres) à l'est de Red Deer, près de la rivière Bataille (Battle River)[17]. Le groupe obtient en tout 260 hectares (environ 640 acres), soit un lot de colonisation de 65 hectares (160 acres) accordé à chacun. Ils pourront de plus profiter des 1000 hectares de terres avoisinantes jusqu'au moment où celles-ci seront vendues. Gilibert et ses coéquipiers retournent ensuite à Red Deer pour y remplir les formalités exigées par le gouvernement canadien. Le départ définitif pour les terres se fait le 1er juin. Chacun va construire sa maison sur son « homestead » (propriété familiale rurale) respectif et l'ensemble formera un village. La famille Plantier est demeurée cependant à Red Deer, car la femme attend l'arrivée d'un bébé. Au cours du trajet, le groupe achète deux vaches ainsi que leurs veaux et profite d'un arrêt à Red Willow pour faire des provisions, mais ne peut trouver ni pommes de terre, ni viande, mis à part le gibier.

Au 24 juin, la famille de Jean Henry, Gilibert et son cousin sont installés sur leurs terres. Ils parcourent jusqu'à 150 kilomètres pour se procurer certains matériaux, puis ils commencent la construction des maisons. D'un commun accord, ils conviennent, d'entreprendre, en premier lieu, la construction de la maison de la famille Henry, laquelle sera érigée en troncs de sapin. Le groupe loge sous une tente jusqu'au moment où la maison est terminée, au mois d'août, et y aménage ensuite temporairement. Puis les travaux des champs débutent. La famille Plantier rejoint le groupe à la mi-septembre et s'installe aussi chez les Henry. Plantier se met à son tour à la construction de sa maison, en mottes de gazon, avec l'aide de Guigue, et la termine en 15 jours. Finalement, c'est en novembre que Gilibert entreprend, en compagnie de son cousin, la construction d'une cambuse qui les abritera pour l'hiver. Ils seront donc les derniers à se pourvoir d'un abri propre à eux.

Le développement de l'Ouest

Le chemin de fer

Gilibert est confiant en l'avenir au Canada et c'est ce que laissent entrevoir ses écrits. C'est un endroit qu'il avait d'abord considéré comme « perdu », mais il affirme aussitôt qu'« il n'en n'est rien… ». « [C]e n'est pas un pays perdu, ajoute-t-il, bien au contraire, nous ne sommes qu'au commencement (…) de l'avenir il y en a ici, pas immédiatement mais sans trop tarder. Et puis ! Nous sommes en Amérique et ici, tout va relativement vite[18]. »

Il est impressionné par la rapidité des installations et des constructions avoisinantes, notamment la progression de la voie ferrée qui passera bientôt près de sa terre. Les observations au sujet de l'évolution de son environnement sont d'ailleurs fréquentes et attestent bien l'effervescence et l'essor de la région. Il estime, en parlant du prolongement de la voie ferrée, qu'« en France on mettrait 10 ans pour faire cela, et mettre les projets à exécution. Ici, il n'en est pas de même, à peine les plans sont-ils tracés qu'on met en chantier[19]. »

La gare la plus près de la terre de Gilibert se trouve à Lacombe, à 150 kilomètres, à quatre jours de voyage. Toutefois une nouvelle ligne, en construction entre Lacombe et la rivière Bataille (Battle River)[20], devrait conduire le trafic ferroviaire à environ huit kilomètres des terres concédées au cours des deux années suivantes. La proximité de la voie ferrée était d'ailleurs l'un des critères retenus par le groupe dans le choix des terres, d'autant plus que leur valeur s'en trouverait accrue.

La Canadian Pacific Railway, qui a le mandat de construire le chemin de fer, a reçu des terrains du gouvernement canadien afin d'encourager la colonisation. L'installation d'une voie ferrée incite les colons à venir s'établir à proximité et Gilibert ne manque pas d'en percevoir les nombreux avantages. La CPR procure non seulement la commodité du transport et l'usage du télégraphe, mais offre aussi aux colons la possibilité de vendre leur blé et d'expédier et de recevoir du courrier. La construction de la voie ferrée engendre le peuplement, stimule la construction de maisons, qui « poussent comme des champignons », et l'aménagement de chemins. Gilibert écrit : « [...] maintenant que nos affaires nous appellent à Lacombe nous sommes étonnés du changement survenu sur notre route; ainsi Alix[21] qui n'était (il y deux mois) un ensemble de 3 ou 4 maisons, en compte maintenant plus de 100[22]. » Un an plus tard, il mentionne qu'« il ne reste plus de terres gratuites à prendre dans [sa] région et les terrains qui sont mis en vente par les Compagnies ont des prix très élevés, et encore on se les dispute[23] ». Les observations du colon témoignent donc des changements et de la vitesse à laquelle se développe la région.

Le service postal

L'état du système postal dans cette région nous est également révélé dans les lettres de Gilibert. Celui-ci en déplore la lenteur. Aussi demande-t-il à ses amis de ne pas se fâcher si ses lettres se font attendre, car le bureau de poste le plus près de sa terre se trouve à Red Willow, à 40 kilomètres. Le 24 juin 1905, il mentionne à sa mère que sa lettre lui parviendra tardivement puisqu'il la portera au bureau de poste de Red Willow seulement quand il aura l'occasion de s'y rendre. À la fin de la lettre, il ajoute qu'au moment où il s'apprêtait à la sceller un voisin lui apportait, du bureau de poste, « trois bonnes lettres » de la famille. Deux mois plus tard, à la fin d'août, dans une autre adressée aux membres de sa famille, il s'étonne d'avoir à peine reçu leurs lettres datées du 22 juillet et du 1er août, alors qu'eux n'avaient encore pas encore reçu les siennes, pourtant expédiées au début de juillet. Il répond ainsi aux reproches qu'on lui fait :

> [...] il ne faut pas être exigeant pour la correspondance. Aussi vos reproches me sont-ils très à cœur. Au moment où on a le plus de travail, et où on a tant besoin de réconfort on reçoit des reproches qui vous découragent. Car ce n'est pas de ma faute si vous n'avez pas reçu ma lettre en son temps. Mettez-vous donc je vous en prie, une fois pour tout dans l'esprit que je ne suis pas en France, et que je n'ai pas qu'à traverser la rue pour mettre une lettre ou une carte à la boîte[24].

Il leur suggère de ne pas avoir « la naïveté » de lui écrire toutes les semaines, mais seulement une fois par mois afin d'éviter l'accumulation des lettres au bureau de poste, « car ici il n'y a pas de facteur ». Lui-même compte leur en envoyer une par mois mais, en raison des « hivers rigoureux », il se peut qu'il ne puisse respecter cette fréquence.

Déjà, le 30 mai 1905, Gilibert prévoit que l'année suivante, « à la façon dont vont les choses ici », un bureau de poste sera établi dans une communauté voisine, Notre-Dame-de-Valfleury[25]. Un an plus tard, dans sa lettre du 1er juin 1906, il annonce que le bureau de poste le plus près est maintenant situé à 12 kilomètres de ses terres et que la correspondance doit lui être acheminée à celui d'Ingleton via Stettler. Il ajoute que d'autres bureaux seront bientôt établis à proximité en raison des progrès rapides des travaux du chemin de fer qui desservira la région[26].

Les écrits de Gilibert confirment que le système postal est en plein essor, mais aussi que l'emplacement des bureaux de poste est déterminé en grande partie par la proximité de la voie ferrée.[27]

La vie dans l'Ouest

L'adaptation au pays

À travers les renseignements sur les activités de l'installation agricole et les gens qui l'entourent, Gilibert dévoile la façon dont il s'est adapté à son nouveau milieu. Par ses multiples comparaisons avec son pays natal et ses commentaires sur son nouvel environnement, il offre une perspective sur la vie d'un immigrant dans l'Ouest canadien de l'époque.

Lorsque qu'il achète des chevaux, Gilibert apprend que ce sont des « chevaux de prairie » qui ont passé l'hiver à l'extérieur, « comme cela se pratique ici », et que le colon doit s'en procurer deux, et non un seul, comme en France, en raison de la longueur des trajets à parcourir. Les nouveaux arrivants sont évidemment confrontés aux conditions difficiles du pays, notamment lors de la construction d'une maison. La disponibilité des matériaux et la nature accidentée des chemins rendent le transport laborieux et dangereux, et déterminent des types de construction particuliers. La maison de Jean Henry, par exemple, est bâtie en troncs de sapin, selon la coutume de la région. Celle de Plantier est construite en mottes de gazon, une matière facile à obtenir et à transporter.

Gilibert s'est bien acclimaté au pays et il manifeste ouvertement son optimisme. Il découvre et apprécie la nature du pays, où « l'air est pur et sain, embaumé par les vapeurs des sapins[28] ». Trois mois après son arrivée, il confirme aussi son adaptation au travail : « […] c'est curieux comme on s'américanise, écrit-il, et je me fais fort bien aux travaux qui m'incombent. Je suis sûr que si vous me voyiez maintenant vous me trouveriez bien changé au physique. C'est moi qui ai tout fauché pour les foins, pas loin de 40 hectares.[29] » Il insiste sur le fait que le pays est « sain et excellent » et que « les récoltes s'y font merveilleuses ». Un an plus tard, il fait cette confidence à sa mère : « […] la vie que nous menons ici, toute de travail, m'a quelque peu changé, je me sens plus fort, et l'avenir me paraît souriant[30]. » Il commente aussi la température hivernale qui peut atteindre, au réveil, les –35° C à l'extérieur, –18° C à l'intérieur de la cambuse. En journée, elle grimpe à –15° et à –10° C à l'extérieur. Toutefois, ces froids intenses ne sauraient empêcher les nouveaux habitants de vaquer à leurs occupations quotidiennes. Ils apprennent avec l'expérience. Ils adoptent les mocassins, qui isolent du froid, et partent régulièrement couper du bois pour la construction des clôtures, des maisons et des étables.

La présence d'animaux sauvages, tels les nombreux loups ou chiens sauvages, les coyotes et les ours, est inhabituelle pour Gilibert. Il ne sort d'ailleurs jamais l'hiver sans son fusil. Comme « le Canada est le pays des fourrures », certains animaux sont très recherchés, entre autres, le lynx, l'hermine, le castor, le rat musqué, le vison et le « renard bleu », dont la peau peut valoir, semble-t-il, entre 700 et 800 dollars. Gilibert ne chasse, pour l'instant, que pour assurer sa subsistance : lapins, poules de prairie, coqs de bruyère, canards sauvages, perdrix, blaireaux, et les porcs-épics qui, finalement, ne sont « pas très fameux ». Il se charge de la chasse tandis que son cousin, François Guigue, s'occupe de faire la cuisine.

Certains passages de ses lettres ne manquent pas d'un certain humour, notamment lorsqu'il parle de leur « petite installation hygiénique », à l'intérieur de la cambuse, située « à la cave !...au milieu des provisions !!!! c'est notre seul moyen de ne pas nous geler quelque part ! ce qui serait très mauvais[31] ». Dans une autre lettre, il raconte qu'il est monté sur un de ses chevaux, sans selle, et qu'il a réussi à ne pas « dégringoler ».

C'est donc avec enthousiasme, et parfois un peu d'humour, que Gilibert raconte ses découvertes et les événements qui le marquent, ce qui semble indiquer qu'il s'est bien accoutumé au pays.

Les habitants : Américains et Canadiens

Gilibert a aussi eu l'occasion de rencontrer des habitants locaux et s'est forgé une opinion précise à leur sujet, entre autres, à l'égard des Américains et des Canadiens. En décembre 1905, à sa première année au Canada, il se rend compte que le foin va manquer pendant l'hiver. Il décide donc de se rendre chez un voisin norvégien qui lui conseille d'aller chez un Américain habitant à quelques kilomètres plus loin. Celui-ci lui vend du foin, lui prête un cheval et offre de l'aider, au printemps, à préparer la terre et à l'ensemencer, moyennant un prix raisonnable. Gilibert est enchanté d'avoir fait la connaissance de ce « brave homme » et en conclut que les Américains « sont d'autres hommes que les paysans français ». Plus tard, il mentionne qu'ils ne doivent pas être confondus avec les Canadiens : « [...] l'Américain est plus pratique que tous, plus honnête et plus rond en affaires. Ces gens-là sont à fréquenter, ils s'y entendent pour les grandes opérations[32] »; ils « sont instruits, et s'y connaissent bien en culture[33]. »

L'épouse de Gilibert, Anne-Marie (Berry), quant à elle, exprime clairement son opinion à l'égard des Canadiens. « [Les] gens d'ici, soutient-elle, ne sont guère plus pressés qu'en France ! » Un peu plus loin, elle ajoute qu'ils ont eu l'aide d'un Canadien français pour les travaux des champs, mais que celui-ci n'est resté que onze jours, n'ayant pu s'habituer à la vie de ferme. Elle se montre plutôt critique à l'égard des Canadiens français, surtout leur cuisine :

> Je n'avais jamais vu de Canadien de si près, mais s'ils sont tous comme celui-là il ne me plait guère : sale et blagueur comme il n'y en a pas. Il parlait un français tout extraordinaire parfois si Minny avait été là elle lui aurait ri au nez. Moi même j'avais toutes les peines du monde à me retenir. Il était cuisinier de métier !... Vous voyez de là ! C'est lui qui avait fait les tartes de la fête de Pierre. Mais je les fais mieux que lui (sans me flatter et mes babas et mes autres gâteaux étaient bien meilleurs que les siens).[34]

Les lettres nous renseignent sur la vie en milieu rural albertain du point de vue de leurs auteurs. Elles nous permettent également de comprendre certaines émotions vécues par ces immigrants.

Le rôle de la correspondance

La relation avec les proches

La correspondance révèle les sentiments et les confidences de l'immigrant, ainsi que la nature de ses rapports avec sa famille et ses amis. Ainsi, Gilibert est très près de sa mère. Les marques d'affection à son endroit et envers les autres membres de sa famille sont d'ailleurs évidentes et fréquentes. Il confie ainsi à ses amis le sentiment de déchirement qu'il a ressenti en quittant sa mère et sa sœur, sur le quai de la gare, alors qu'il prenait le train pour Paris :

> Vous dire que le trajet de Dijon à Paris s'est effectué dans l'anéantissement le plus complet est inutile, je puis vous assurer que m'étant tenu cependant continuellement à la portière j'ignore complètement tout des paysages et des villes que nous avons traversés. Toutes mes pensées se trouvaient vers ceux que je laissais…[35]

C'est par la formule « Ma très cher petite maman » que Gilibert commence généralement ses lettres. Il lui confie son sentiment de solitude et s'informe de sa « petite Anne-Marie ». Il semble d'ailleurs prendre en considération le jugement de sa mère à l'égard de sa fiancée puisqu'il lui demande de lui parler de « sa future[36] », de lui donner son opinion sur elle. À un autre moment, il écrit à son auditoire familial[37]: « ma chère maman et tous là-bas, croyez que je ne vous oublie pas, et sachez que je n'entreprends rien sans que ma pensée soit au milieu de vous », puis il conclut la lettre par « Bons baisers, Maman chérie, et ne fais donc pas de vilains rêves, car nous prenons mille précautions pour que rien n'arrive et que tout se passe bien. Ton fils qui te chérit[38]. »

Gilibert anticipe avec espoir son retour en France et laisse percevoir, à plusieurs reprises, sa nostalgie. En juin 1906, il précise sa pensée sur ce projet : « […] plus tôt j'aurais mis ma terre en valeur, plus tôt j'aurais des bénéfices et plus tôt je rentrerais en France[39]. » Deux mois plus tard, il réitère cette déclaration :

> […] dès que mes affaires prendront bonne tournure, je me retournerai vite vers toi; et aussi vers ma petite amie Anne-Marie car vraiment, maintenant que je vois les choses de près et que je comprends mieux tous ces petits détails de la vie qui ne semblent rien et qui cependant présentent mille difficultés, je trouve que la vie est peu agréable pour celui qui est seul…[40]

Environ deux années après son arrivée au Canada, Anne-Marie exprime aussi ce sentiment d'isolement qu'elle partage avec son époux : « 'Comme ce serait gai si nous étions tous en famille'. C'est ce qui fait que l'on ne s'attache pas au Canada; car la France a gardé le meilleur de notre cœur puisque tous ceux que nous aimons y sont[41]! »

La lettre joue donc un rôle important par le réconfort qu'elle apporte à l'être éloigné, à « l'exilé ». Cette importance prend ici tout son sens : « […] tes chères lignes m'ont causé la plus grande joie et c'est avec un vif plaisir que j'ai lu tous les détails qu'elles contenaient[42]. » Dans une longue missive envoyée à ses amis, en juin 1906, Gilibert fait allusion au retard qu'il a mis à répondre aux lettres reçues, qu'il relit régulièrement. Il évoque ainsi le bonheur de recevoir une lettre :

> […] vos lettres me font un plaisir que je ne puis vous exprimer. Ce n'est pas une fois que je les lis mais dix, vingt fois, et toujours elles me paraissent nouvelles (…) vous ne pouvez pas vous faire une idée de tout le bonheur qu'une lettre apporte avec elle lorsque, ayant parcouru des lieues, et des lieues, traversé les océans, les montagnes, et les forêts immenses, elle arrive saine et sauve à son destinataire perdu au milieu d'une plaine sans borne, et qui n'a pour reposer sa vue, que la voûte du ciel qui le protège, et que la glèbe, d'où lui viennent ses misères[43].

Plus loin, il conclut : « […] mes biens chers amis, je termine cette épître, dont la longueur vous aura peut-être lassé, mais aussi, pour me punir, vous m'en enverrez, bien souvent des biens longues, elles me font toujours bien plaisir, et beaucoup de bien. Il me semblera aussi être un peu mieux au milieu de vous que par la simple pensée[44]! »

Gilibert n'aura pas attendu non plus son arrivée au Canada pour écrire à ses proches. Déjà, de Dijon et de Liverpool, il écrit à ses amis pour les mettre au courant du début de son voyage. Moins d'un mois après son arrivée en Alberta, il mentionne, dans une lettre à sa mère, qu'il lui en a déjà fait parvenir une de Montréal, dans laquelle il lui racontait la traversée à bord du bateau. Le colon attend aussi avec impatience l'arrivée du courrier : « […] j'espère qu'en portant cette lettre à la poste, je trouverai la tienne », écrit-il, et plus loin, en s'adressant à la famille, ajoute : « Écrivez-moi vite mes biens chers afin de ne pas me laisser dans l'inquiétude à votre sujet. Je pense que je dois avoir de vos nouvelles en route et que je ne tarderai pas à les recevoir[45]. »

La correspondance de Gilibert indique le rythme des échanges épistolaires en faisant référence aux lettres reçues ou expédiées. La longueur de la lettre détermine aussi le temps que le correspondant a consacré à sa rédaction[46]. Le colon communique avec ses amis outre-mer et il leur fait des confidences, mais les lettres à leur intention sont sans doute moins fréquentes que celles adressées à la famille. Ainsi la lettre datée du 1er janvier 1906 et envoyée à ses amis est d'une longueur exceptionnelle[47]. Elle débute par des excuses pour le long silence, l'absence de nouvelles et représente en somme un bilan des événements qui se sont déroulés depuis son arrivée au Canada jusqu'au début de la nouvelle année. La longueur de la lettre semble compenser pour le retard mis à leur répondre.

Quitter sa famille peut se révéler une épreuve difficile pour l'émigrant qui abandonne tout pour se rendre dans un pays étranger. Les sentiments de solitude et d'isolement sont plus intenses à certains moments. La missive permet alors de maintenir et de resserrer une relation, basée sur l'écrit, avec un proche, apportant ainsi un soutien moral essentiel à celui qui décide d'émigrer.

La relation avec les compagnons de voyage

La correspondance de Gilibert permet de connaître non seulement la nature des relations qu'il entretient avec ses proches en France, mais aussi, grâce à ses confidences, celles qui caractérisent ses rapports avec ses compagnons de voyages au Canada.

Au moment où le groupe en était à choisir les terres, Gilibert et son cousin ont pu découvrir le caractère de leurs compagnons. Dans une lettre adressée à ses amis, Gilibert leur fait des confidences à ce sujet. Il est stupéfait d'apprendre qu'une querelle a éclaté entre les dames Plantier et Henry pendant qu'il était parti, avec les autres hommes, choisir des lots. Cette querelle de femmes, dont l'origine demeure inconnue, entraîne inévitablement celle des maris. Une nouvelle brouille survint, cette fois, entre Gilibert et les Henry. Ce dernier réglait les comptes pour les provisions, quand il constata « certains abus » de la part des Henry. Il décida alors d'exiger le règlement de la note, ce qui causa un certain froid. Ce n'est finalement qu'en la seule compagnie de Guigue qu'il entreprendra la construction de leur cambuse[48]. Gilibert confirme que l'animosité est toujours présente dans le groupe, même durant le temps des fêtes de Noël et du jour de l'An. Dans une lettre à sa mère, il confie que sa relation avec son cousin s'est aussi un peu dégradée. L'association se révèle finalement un échec, chacun gérant sa terre comme il l'entend.

Les épreuves traversées

La même lettre qui évoquait la nature des relations entre Gilibert et ses compagnons nous apprend les drames vécus par le groupe. C'est avec émotion, par exemple, qu'est raconté l'incendie qui, en octobre 1905, a ravagé leurs terres :

> De quel côté qu'on se tourne-t-on ne voyait que de la fumée. La nuit qui suivit fut effrayante. Tout le ciel était embrasé. De tous les côtés on voyait poindre les flammes. Mon cousin avait toutes les peines à rassurer son monde. Que faire ? Isolés au milieu de cette prairie en feu ? Et les maris absents. Je vous ai dit qu'au Canada, certains couchers de soleil ressemblaient à des incendies du ciel. Eh ! bien, dans la noirceur de la nuit ce feu de prairie avait toute l'immensité, et toute la splendeur d'un coucher de soleil. Le vent, au lieu de s'apaiser prenait à chaque instant une violence extraordinaire.[49]

Un autre incident survint quelques jours plus tard. Il s'agit de la perte de la jument de Gilibert, qu'il trouva, un beau matin, morte d'épuisement. Un peu plus loin, nous apprenons que le couple Revol a retardé son arrivée en raison de la naissance prématurée d'un bébé qui malheureusement n'aura pas survécu. La mère fut atteinte de la fièvre typhoïde après l'accouchement, mais elle s'était finalement rétablie.

Bonnes ou mauvaises, les nouvelles sont transmises par l'intermédiaire des lettres. Celles-ci permettent de maintenir, malgré la distance, des rapports avec la famille et les amis, au moyen de confidences et de témoignages d'affection.

Conclusion

La correspondance de Pierre Gilibert représente non seulement le modeste témoignage d'un immigrant français au Canada, mais aussi une page de l'histoire rurale de l'Alberta, au début du XXᵉ siècle. Bien qu'il s'agisse d'un point de vue personnel, Gilibert demeure un témoin oculaire valable et les nombreuses informations qu'il rapporte au sujet de son environnement et de son expérience illustrent le développement de l'Ouest du pays. Il nous livre en effet de nombreux détails reliés à la colonisation de cette région et nous raconte la vie de tous les jours d'un habitant de France.

L'étude de cette correspondance permet, par ailleurs, de saisir l'aspect émotionnel de l'immigration. Elle dévoile certaines facettes de la personnalité de cet immigrant. De toute évidence, Gilibert a reçu une certaine éducation, perceptible à sa façon de s'exprimer dans ses lettres. L'introduction de celle qu'il expédie le 1er janvier 1906, et dans laquelle il présente avec éloquence des excuses à ses amis, en est un bon exemple : « L'affection que vous me portez et qui ressort d'une façon si évidente de toutes les bonnes missives que j'ai reçues de vous tous me permet de juger de la désolation dans laquelle vous devez vous trouver d'être restés aussi longtemps sans avoir de mes nouvelles[50]. » Gilibert se présente comme une personne optimiste, confiante en l'avenir du Canada. Il parle avec fierté de ses nombreux projets d'agriculture : il entend faire de l'élevage et entreprendre la construction de bâtiments pour son établissement agricole.

Même s'ils devaient s'y connaître en matière d'agriculture, ces nouveaux colons commençaient à partir de rien en arrivant au Canada. Ils devaient se familiariser avec leur nouvel environnement, construire des habitations et mettre en culture des champs pour pouvoir survivre. Ils faisaient ainsi preuve de débrouillardise, de détermination et d'audace.

L'aventure de Pierre Gilibert au Canada lui a permis de maintenir et de renforcer des relations avec ses proches demeurés en France par l'entremise de la correspondance. Il a su rester impliqué dans les affaires personnelles et financières de sa famille, tout comme il a utilisé la poste pour manifester son attachement profond à sa mère, à sa famille et à ses amis.

Gilibert devait parcourir des dizaines de kilomètres afin de cueillir son courrier ou de mettre ses lettres à la poste. Cette correspondance lui a en quelque sorte permis d'apprivoiser le vide et peut apparaître comme un exutoire[51]. Elle resserrait les liens entre les correspondants et demeurait l'unique moyen de communication entre des proches séparés par la distance. Elle a joué ainsi un rôle fondamental dans la vie de l'immigrant qui tentait sa chance loin de son pays.

Épilogue

Pierre Gilibert est certainement demeuré au Canada plus longtemps qu'il avait prévu le faire, ses objectifs d'investissements s'étant modifiés en cours de route. En 1929, miné par la maladie, il retourne définitivement en France pour s'installer, semble-t-il, dans son village natal, Salaise-sur-Sanne. Il meurt deux ans plus tard, à l'âge de 50 ans. Quant à François Guigue, il vend sa terre vers 1910 et retourne lui aussi en Europe.

Le couple Gilibert a eu trois enfants, deux garçons et une fille. L'aîné, né en janvier 1914, est le père de Colette Dumarchez, celle qui a précieusement conservé les lettres de son grand-père qui ont fait l'objet de notre étude. C'est elle qui s'est présentée à la porte de la demeure de John Willis, historien au Musée canadien de la poste, un soir d'été 2002, près d'un siècle après que son grand-père eut mis le pied au Canada pour la première fois. Elle avait justement sur elle une transcription des missives sur disquette.

Notes

1. Appellation tirée du texte d'une exposition commanditée par le ministère de la Main-d'œuvre et de l'Immigration, « L'immigration dans les Prairies canadiennes, 1870-1914 », Ottawa, Information Canada, 1972, p. 3. Voir aussi John Willis. « The Immigrant, the Post and the Letter », Gatineau, Musée canadien de la poste – Musée canadien des civilisations, manuscrit inédit, décembre 2001, 32 f.; Jean Bruce. *The Last Best West*, Toronto / Montréal / Winnipeg / Vancouver, Fitzhenry & Whiteside, 1976, 178 p.

2. Robert Painchaud. « Le peuplement francophone dans les prairies de l'Ouest 1870-1920 », dans *Histoire du Canada en images*, [Ottawa], Musée national de l'Homme / Musées nationaux du Canada / Office national du film du Canada, 1974, p. 4.

3. *Ibid.*, p. 2.

4. Au cours des années 1980, des descendants de Pierre Gilibert, dont sa petite-fille, Colette Dumarchez, séjournent au Canada. En 2002, cette dernière vient au pays et se rend en Alberta à la recherche de ses racines. Elle était également venue visiter sa fille, alors étudiante à l'Université de Sherbrooke. Or, cette dernière était la colocataire de la fille de John Willis, historien au Musée canadien de la poste / Musée canadien des civilisations, à Gatineau. C'est à cette occasion que madame Dumarchez et son mari aboutirent dans la demeure des Willis. Au cours de la conversation, l'historien apprend l'existence de lettres d'un immigrant français, Pierre Gilibert, venu en Alberta, au début du 20ᵉ siècle. Le soir même, madame Dumarchez lui remettait une copie électronique de la transcription des lettres de son grand-père. C'est le résultat de l'étude de cette correspondance que nous présentons ici. Aussi aimerions-nous remercier Colette Dumarchez pour sa collaboration et exprimer notre reconnaissance envers John Willis, pour ses judicieux conseils, ainsi qu'Isabelle Charron, conservatrice adjointe au Musée canadien des civilisations, qui a bien accepté de relire cet article et de nous faire part de ses suggestions.

5. Voir Audrey Pyée. « 'Mon Révérend Père, … Je m'inquiète pour mon fils'. Relations familiales transnationales et épistolaires », dans le collectif de Yves Frenette, Marcel Martel et John Willis, *Lettres et correspondances en Amérique française,* Québec, Presses de l'Université Laval, 2006; pp. 201-226. Bernard Pénisson. « Louise d'Hellencourt et Christine de La Salmonière : deux Françaises au Manitoba », *Cahiers franco-canadiens de l'Ouest*, vol. 12, nᵒ 2, 2000, p. 153-179; Marcel Martel, « Conflicting Visions of Society : The Case of Francophone Communities in the Prairies (1860-1920) », communication prononcée au colloque sur l'empire britannique, Calgary, juillet 2003 – York University, manuscrit inédit, 26 f.

6. Le beau-frère Henry ne fait pas partie de l'expédition. Le recensement des provinces du Nord-Ouest de 1906 indique les noms de François Guigue, Pierre Gilibert, Jean Plantier et son épouse Marie-Louise, leurs quatre fils et leur fille, ainsi que Jean Henry et son épouse Eugénie et leurs deux filles. Bibliothèque et Archives Canada, www.archivianet.ca, Recensement des provinces du Nord-Ouest (1906).

7. Red Deer, Pierre Gilibert, à des amis, 30 mai 1905. À noter que l'orthographe et la ponctuation de Gilibert ont été systématiquement respectées.

8. Ibid.

9. Ibid.

10. Ibid.

11. Red Willow, Gilibert, à sa mère, 24 juin 1905.

12. Ibid.

13. Jean Gaire (1853-1925), prêtre originaire de la Lorraine, est un des « ouvriers du mouvement migratoire » qui s'est impliqué dans la colonisation française des Prairies, particulièrement au Manitoba. Il est arrivé au Canada en 1888, à l'âge de 34 ans, et a effectué plusieurs tournées de propagande en France, en Belgique et au Luxembourg. Donatien Frémont. *Les Français dans l'Ouest canadien*, Winnipeg, Les Éditions de la liberté, 1959, p. 75. Gaire est l'auteur de *Dix années de missions au grand Nord-Ouest canadien*, Lille, Imprimerie de l'orphelinat Dom Bosco, 1898.

14. Originaire de la Savoie, l'abbé Jean-François Féroux (Ferroux) arrive au Canada vers 1903 ou 1904, avec une trentaine de familles. Certaines s'installent au Manitoba; d'autres, qu'accompagne Féroux, vont en Alberta et fondent Notre-Dame-de-Savoie ainsi que d'autres missions. Frémont. *Op. cit.*, p. 131.

15. Red Willow, Gilibert à sa mère, 24 juin 1905.

16. Ibid.

17. Selon le recensement des provinces du Nord-Ouest de 1906, leurs terres sont situées dans le district de Strathcona n° 21, dans la section 6, townships 39, rang 12 à l'ouest du 4ᵉ méridien. Gilibert donne ces informations dans ses lettres du 24 juin 1905 et du 1ᵉʳ janvier 1906. Il ajoute que leurs terres sont à la jonction de la rivière Bataille (Battle River) et de Beaver Dam (Beaverdam Creek).

18. Red Willow, Gilibert, à sa mère, 24 juin 1905.

19. Ibid.

20. Une publication gouvernementale confirme que la Canadian Pacific Railway s'affaire à la construction du tronçon du chemin ferroviaire à partir de Lacombe pour rejoindre les terres à l'est de cette localité. Canada Department of the Interior (*Twentieth Century Canada and Atlas of Western Canada 1906 for the Guidance of Intending Settlers – Its Resources and Development, with maps of the Dominion of Canada, Provinces of Manitoba, Saskatchewan, Alberta, Ontario, Quebec, The Maritime Provinces, British Columbia and North America*, 1906, p. 31).

21. Le bureau de poste d'Alix ouvre le 1ᵉʳ juin 1905. Bibliothèque et Archives Canada, www.archives.ca, « Bureaux et maîtres de poste ».

22. Red Willow, Gilibert, à sa mère, 24 juin 1905.

23. Ingleton via Stettler, Gilibert, 1ᵉʳ juin 1906.

24. Red Willow, Gilibert, à sa mère, Rosette et Henry, 30 août 1905. (Rosette est le surnom de Marie-Rose, la sœur de Pierre, et Henry, son époux, donc le beau-frère de Pierre qui se trouvait avec le groupe lors du séjour en Angleterre.)

25. Le lieu de Notre-Dame-de-Valfleury, indiqué dans la lettre du 30 mai 1905, ne figure pas sur les cartes. Nous pensons qu'il s'agit du bureau de poste de Notre-Dame-de-Savoie, situé à l'est de Red Willow, qui a ouvert ses portes le 1ᵉʳ décembre 1905.

26. Il est intéressant de noter les noms des endroits d'expéditions qui figurent au début des lettres de Gilibert et qui correspondent aux différents bureaux de postes qui ont ouvert au fur et à mesure que la région se développait : 30 mai 1905, de Red Deer (bureau de poste inauguré le 15 août 1903); 24 juin et 30 août 1905, de Red Willow (15 août 1903); 1ᵉʳ janvier 1906, de Notre-Dame-de-Valfleury, via Red Willow; 1ᵉʳ juin 1906, de Ingleton (1ᵉʳ avril 1906), via Stettler (1ᵉʳ février 1905); 1ᵉʳ août 1906, de Ingleton; 7 juillet 1912, de Lorraine (1ᵉʳ septembre 1907); 28 juillet 1912, de Lorraine via Castor (1ᵉʳ janvier 1910). Le bureau de poste rural est le complément inévitable de la colonisation. Bibliothèque et Archives Canada, www.archivianet.ca, « Bureaux et maîtres de poste ». En examinant la carte illustrant la région en 1909, nous pouvons constater que certains de ces bureaux sont desservis par le chemin de fer.

27. Chantal Amyot et John Willis. *Le courrier est arrivé ! La poste rurale au Canada, de 1880 à 1945*, Gatineau, Musée canadien des civilisations, 2003, p. 46.

28. Red Willow, Gilibert, à sa mère, 24 juin 1905. Bien que l'habitation de Gilibert soit située dans une région de prairie, il doit y avoir à proximité certains boisés.

29. Red-Willow, Gilibert, à sa mère, à Rosette et à Henry, 30 août 1905.

30. Ingleton via Stettler, Gilibert, à sa mère, 1er juin 1906.

31. Notre-Dame-de-Valfleury, par Red Willow, Gilibert, à ses amis, 1er janvier 1906.

32. Ibid.

33. Ingleton via Stettler, Gilibert à sa mère, 1er juin 1906. De nombreux Américains viennent s'établir sur des terres concédées au Canada. Au tournant du siècle, la quantité de terres à bon marché aux États-Unis s'amenuise. Beaucoup d'entre eux profitent de l'opportunité d'obtenir des terres gratuites au Canada.

34. Lorraine, Berry et Gilibert, aux parents, 7 juillet 1912.

35. Red Deer, Gilibert à ses amis, 30 mai 1905.

36. Précisons qu'au moment de la rédaction de cette lettre, en août 1906, Anne-Marie demeure toujours en France et n'est donc pas encore mariée à Pierre Gilibert.

37. Les lettres étaient généralement destinées à être lues par l'entourage.

38. Red-Willow, Gilibert, à sa mère, à Rosette et à Henry, 30 août 1905.

39. Ingleton via Stettler, Gilibert, à sa mère, 1er juin 1906.

40. Ingleton, Gilibert, à sa mère, 1er août 1906.

41. Lorraine, Berry et de Pierre Gilibert, aux parents, 7 juillet 1912.

42. Ingleton, Gilibert, à sa mère, 1er août 1906.

43. Notre-Dame-de-Valfleury, via Red Willow, Gilibert, à ses amis, 1er janvier 1906.

44. Ibid.

45. Red Willow, Gilibert, à sa mère, 24 juin 1905.

46. Françoise Noël, *Family Life and Sociability, in Upper and Lower Canada, 1780-1870*, Montreal / Kingston, McGill-Queen's University Press, 2003, p. 8.

47. La lettre du 1er janvier 1906 compte près de 10 000 mots tandis qu'une autre en compte moins de 4 300 et les six autres, moins de 3 000.

48. Notre-Dame-de-Valfleury, via Red Willow, Gilibert, à ses amis, 1er janvier 1906. Gilibert précise que la cambuse est une installation provisoire puisque le gouvernement les oblige à construire une maison sur chaque terre concédée.

49. Ibid.

50. Ibid.

51. Cécile Dauphin, Pierrette Lebrun-Pézérat, Danièle Poublan. *Ces bonnes lettres. Une correspondance familiale au XIXe siècle,* Paris, Albin Michel, 1995, p. 135.

WARTIME CORRESPONDENCE

15

Living, Loving, and Leaving through Letters During the Two World Wars

Liz Turcotte, Research Consultant

Abstract

For many Canadians stationed overseas, the two world wars meant prolonged separation from family and friends. Consequently, the military postal service played a key role connecting fighting soldiers with their families and loved ones at home. Wartime mail was a lifeline between correspondents in Canada and the Western Front and prisoner-of-war camps. Based on archival records at Library and Archives Canada and the Canadian War Museum Archives in Ottawa, this paper examines several themes woven through the correspondence. Concern for family welfare on both sides of the ocean was a predominant theme: Soldiers asked often about the well-being of their families, while those in Canada anxiously awaited letters from husbands, brothers, and fathers stating that they were still alive and well. Conversely, the mail brought terrible news of death, sometimes in official government language; at other times, a trench buddy or commanding officer eloquently and poignantly discussed the deceased's life, friendships, and final days in battle overseas. The exchanges of mail illustrate how female-headed families in Canada coped financially and emotionally, in the absence of the patriarch or productive male household members, through paid work or volunteer work for businesses and organizations supporting the war effort. Although peoples' lives were disrupted in many ways during the war years, they remained connected through regular correspondence, sharing their experiences and offering assurances, acknowledging or dismissing fears, and remaining optimistic that families would be reunited in the future.[1]

Résumé

Pour de nombreux Canadiens en poste outre-mer, les deux guerres mondiales ont signifié une séparation prolongée d'avec leur famille et leurs amis. Par conséquent, le service postal militaire a été essentiel pour permettre aux combattants, à leurs familles et à leurs proches restés au pays de garder le contact. Le courrier en temps de guerre a constitué

Figure 15.1 Kenneth Edgard Clayton-Kennedy, who served in the RCAF during the First World War, finds a quiet spot and a few minutes to write a letter to loved ones at home in Canada.

Canadian War Museum, 19900346-32.

un lien vital entre les correspondants au Canada et le front occidental et les camps de prisonniers de guerre. À partir d'archives conservées à Bibliothèque et Archives Canada et au Musée canadien de la guerre, à Ottawa, le présent article étudie plusieurs thèmes qu'on retrouve dans la correspondance. Un thème prédominant était le souci de bien-être de la famille des deux côtés de l'océan : les soldats s'enquerraient souvent du bien-être de leur famille, alors que ceux qui étaient restés au Canada attendaient anxieusement des lettres d'un mari, d'un frère, ou d'un père les assurant qu'ils étaient encore en vie et en bonne santé. Inversement, le courrier apportait la terrible nouvelle de la mort, parfois dans un langage gouvernemental officiel; d'autres fois, un camarade des tranchées ou un officier supérieur racontait avec éloquence et de façon poignante la vie et les amitiés du défunt et ses derniers jours au combat outre-mer. La correspondance décrit comment les familles dirigées par des femmes au Canada se débrouillaient financièrement et émotivement en l'absence du père ou de membres masculins productifs, en travaillant contre rémunération ou bénévolement pour des entreprises et des organisations soutenant l'effort de guerre. Même si la vie des gens a été perturbée de bien des façons pendant les années de guerre, ils maintenaient des liens grâce à une correspondance régulière dans laquelle ils faisaient part de leurs expériences, rassuraient, admettaient leurs peurs ou les niaient, et gardaient l'espoir que les familles seraient un jour à nouveau réunies.

Introduction

In the Second World War movie epic, *Saving Private Ryan*, there is a subtle exchange between soldiers at different times throughout their mission.[2] A letter home—found in the pocket of a dying soldier—is picked up by another soldier who comforts the dying man. Later, the volunteer courier is killed and the letter is passed on to another soldier. In turn, the soldier who takes the letter to mail is also killed, but the letter becomes so important that it is passed on, as one soldier dies and another takes up the quest to ensure the last letter makes its way to its original destination. This is not just a representation of director Stephen Spielberg's imagination, for the "letter" played a key role in connecting soldiers with their families and loved ones at home. Similarly, for most Canadian military personnel, the two world wars meant prolonged separation from family and friends. Wartime mail became the lifeline between two continents and the means by which people separated by space and time could be reassured of the safety of those serving and the well-being of family and friends across the Atlantic Ocean. The research in this article is part of a careful reading of selected Canadian wartime correspondence to examine a few of the themes that frequently arise out of the pages of the missives exchanged between soldiers fighting in Europe and their kin and companion networks in Canada.

Context

Letters written by soldiers and service people in Europe to people back in Canada, frequently have a tone and tenor relative to the different stages of experience gained during a serviceman's engagement in the war. For example, letters written from Canadian training camps in 1914 were jovial and full of the anticipated adventure of war. Letters written while stationed in England waiting to be posted to active combat service were full of impatience and boredom, as the young men became anxious to relieve the tediousness of mundane drilling and rainy English weather so they could experience fighting the enemy and performing their patriotic duty. Simultaneously, as they watched the wounded return from France and heard first-hand stories of trench warfare, tiny dents in their construction of war as a glorious adventure start to appear. Despite censorship, these letters demonstrate how servicemen and women resolved notions of duty and honour with the reality of the brutality of war. For prisoners of war, letters from home had even greater significance. Out of active combat and under heavy censorship, their memories of home and family dominated the thoughts they were able to express.

While much of what is written in letters is constrained by immediate experience and expressed in a complex variety of thoughts and details, there are many themes common to these letters. First and foremost, a letter or a package of goodies from home was always an important event and source of good cheer to be shared by companions. Most often, letters travelling the opposite way across the Atlantic carried reassuring news that the soldier was still alive. Sometimes it carried the most dreaded news of a loved one killed or missing in action. Letters from Canada frequently charted the economic maturity of womenfolk who were left behind in a world void of men and encouraged to enter the workforce and to take over management of households. Soldiers' letters often demonstrate a maturity and cynicism beyond the normal development of the young men who left home expecting an adventure and who were introduced to unimaginable horrors and harsh living conditions on the front lines. Sometimes their candid comments passed the censor and revealed lurid details of wounds and cavalier killing of the enemy. For those who were lucky enough to get leave away from the fighting, a brief sojourn in Scotland or England provided the opportunity to keep Canadian kin up-to-date on Old Country relatives, or to provide pages of vicarious travel or entertainment reading.

The Importance of Letters

There is no doubt the exchange of letters played a key role during the wars. Every correspondent emphasized the importance of the letter from home or the letter received from the battle lines. Communication and connection with loved ones was always on their minds, and, when they felt they had nothing to talk about, they could always talk about the letter that had not arrived, or might arrive, or wonder about the reason for its delay, or relate a tale of how the letter eventually arrived in their hands. Letters from "Dear Old Canada are the best we can get over here,"[3] but the process of censorship and mail delivery frequently created chaos at the front lines as letters bounced around the battle lines following companies of men whose movements had to remain secret for strategic reasons. During the Great War, one correspondent wrote from France in October 1918:

> I received your long looked for letter tonight and was very glad to get it. I knew you must have written long ago so was not so surprised when I got a big envelope from the Canadian record office with four letters in it. They had been all over France and were marked up so bad they were almost unrecognizable. Then, the envelope which came from the record office was all torn open. So I expect there were several other letters that were lost entirely… Some mail service eh![4]

By the Second World War, mail services did not seem to improve much for some recipients. In February 1945, Flight Officer Don Quinn, a native of Montréal, told a friend in his home town: "I don't know if this is a record or not but one of the letters crossed the Atlantic three times before it caught up with me. When I got it the envelope was so covered with cancelled addresses that the colour of it was obliterated. I intended to save it as a memento but the rot of extreme old age finally made this out of the question."[5]

Despite the trials and tribulations of getting the mail across oceans and channels patrolled by German submarines and across miles of front-line trenches, every soldier appreciated the letter from home, and was disappointed when none arrived. Lieutenant Claude Vivian Williams of Hamilton, a second-year medical student at the University of Toronto, joined the 13th Royal Regiment of Canadian Militia as a commissioned officer but served most of his duty with the Canadian Machine Gun Corps. He wrote to his father in November 1916: "You can't understand how much mail does mean to us over here unless you actually see it yourself. If you only saw the rush the fellows make for the ration man as he comes in every night, and the disappointed looks in their faces when some of them receive nothing. I think it would make some people at home write much more frequently if they only knew how much it meant."[6]

During World War Two, RCAF Sergeant-Pilot E .H. (Harry) McConnell-Taylor also commented on the soldier's sentiment surrounding the delivery of a letter from home:

> [N]o matter in what order your letters come, it's a treat to read them. I don't think people at home realize some times how important mail & news from home is to us. You know, you never appreciate home till you're far away from it and many a time when you have a few moments to yourself your thoughts go racing across the ocean to places and people you love and the good times you had—a million years ago. And letters do keep you in touch…[7]

Sharing Information

Often, letters served as vehicles for passing on information about other soldiers to people in Canada, who presumably passed on the information to the friends and relatives of those mentioned in the letters.

As a prisoner of war in Germany, Jack Powerful Griss and another prisoner of war buddy, Jimmy, urged their wives, both living in Montréal, to spend time together. They mentioned each other in their letters. Griss frequently included a message about Jimmy, presumably so Olga could forward the news to Lillian. The information was important as it concerned Jimmy's whereabouts, for example: "I see Jimmy every day, he still keeps his chin up" (October 1, 1943); "Well dear Jimmy is leaving this Stalag on Wen with four hundred Canadians. I may go later on" (January 23, 1944); "Tell Lillian Mc not to worry about Jimmy he is fine and [as] full of beans when he went from her." (February 6, 1944); "Did I tell you that I saw Jimmy last week? He came into camp for some Red Cross supplies. He looks very well I am still in camp" (May 3, 1944); "Have not seen Jimmy for a week but he expects to come into the Stalag for a trip next week" (May 30, 1944); "A chap came in from Jimmy's party yesterday, reports Jimmy OK on the plough" (June 25, 1944).

Soldiers routinely read each other's letters and shared the contents of welcome parcels from home; civilians on the home front shared letters too. Betty Scott, a Canadian Volunteer Ambulance Driver in France during the Second World War, asked her sister in Ottawa to "be an angel and pass this on to Mary or Rita when you've read it as I won't have time to write again for several days."[8]

Final Thoughts

Sometimes the letter became the vehicle for conveying what a soldier believed were his last thoughts to family at home. In June 1916, Frank Maheux, a former Québec logger who joined the 21st Battalion, wrote that he might be called to the front lines at any time to engage in heavy fighting: "Dear wife and kids if anything happened to me, that means if God calls me than dear wife we will be separated until in the new world that we will see each other than dear wife I am tellin [sic] you this I always love you from the first time I saw you …" He asked her to have one high mass said for him and hoped they would never have to send the letter. On the envelope below his wife's address, he wrote: "This letter it is only in case that God calls me, so sent it please to the address mention."[9]

Maheux's comment on the envelope is reminiscent of the movie *Saving Private Ryan*, since clearly he believed that whoever found his body would see the note and send the letter on to his wife. Maheux, who was awarded the Military Cross in October of 1916, did not die during the war, but on other occasions carried a similar last letter with him when he expected the worst from going "over the top" of the trench. He returned home to his family in Maniwaki on the Ottawa River in summer 1919. An interesting aspect of Maheux's letters was his writing style, described by one historian as "the rough transliteration of his speech … as rough a tool as his logger's axe or peavey, and often as sharp …. He spelled phonetically and imaginatively. Maheux's prose flowed without the constraints of paragraphs, capitals or punctuation."[10]

Unlike Maheux's, the last letter a family member received may not have been planned as such. Sergeant E. O. (Ted) Wordon, a Canadian soldier with the Regina Rifles, wrote his last letter to his wife while on board ship waiting to land at Normandy for the D-Day assault on the morning of June 6, 1944:

> We are going in tomorrow morning as I write this we are out on the water, so the big day has come. I often had wondered how I would feel but I don't feel any difference, as I ever did before, thanks to you. I know I can truthful [sic] say if it was not for you I would feel different, but it is the love and trust I have for you and that will help me over many a rough spot …. So promise darling you will not worry for I'll be alright [sic] and home before you know it. Just you and mum look after each other and time will pass swiftly…[11]

Despite Wordon's positive tone and optimism, he did not survive the D-Day assault, but his letter made it back home to Canada. Perhaps his last words of love were some comfort to the grieving widow.

Sometimes military buddies had pre-arrangements to ensure next of kin were notified should any of them be killed or go missing. For example, Air Force Flight Officer Frederick Scythes's wife of seven months learned of her husband's disappearance in May 1943 from several of his buddies. First, Squadron Leader Roy Campbell wrote to Scythes's wife to tell her that her husband, acting as second pilot, went missing in action during a mission to Germany. In the letter, he explained the pact the men had made to forward the pilot's log book containing a record of each airman's missions. "We made a bargain if either went missing the other would see that his log book was sent home. I have his book which he wanted you to have and will forward it or bring it down when I come on leave," Campbell wrote.[12] At the same time, the chaplain wrote to her to express his sympathy and forwarded a separate letter that had been discovered among the pilot's personal affects, adding, "I thought it should be sent to you directly."[13] A couple of weeks later, she received a third letter from another friend who had assumed the responsibility of forwarding Scythes's logbook. This airman explained that Campbell "is now missing on ops. I have [Scythes's] log book in my locker and the briefcase and photo album in my room, and I will see to it that they are sent to you right away."[14] Scythes eventually turned up in a prisoner-of-war camp in Germany. During his incarceration, he kept a journal in which he drew many sketches of daily life and commented on what he considered the humorous contents of other prisoner's letters. For example, one man's girlfriend wrote, "Don't worry about me. I am being well looked after by your roommate." Another's father wrote, "We had a small party when we knew you were safe. I opened a bottle of whiskey and we had quite a time. Grandfather said he wished you were shot down more often." The wife of one prisoner of war wrote, "I'm so glad I married you darling. How much back pay do you have now."[15]

Sometimes the letter with the news of a death of a loved one was written by a family member or close friend and expressed eloquent expressions of sympathy and patriotism. In spring 1917, three farm boys from rural Ontario—Roy 26, Arthur 24, and John 20—were all serving with the 1st Battalion, Canadian Expeditionary Force, in France; all had seen active duty. Arthur, an infantryman who was convalescing in England after being wounded in April prior to the assault on Vimy Ridge, wrote to his parents in May to tell them that their youngest son John had been reported missing in action and presumed dead. The letter covers a lot of territory. Initially, it attempts to soften the emotional blow of the official government notification of their youngest son's death and acknowledges that John had hardly begun the fight before he succumbed to enemy fire. Yet, Arthur also raises the flag of family pride and honour and associates it with John's death. He acknowledges that his parents let all three sons sign up voluntarily to fight, despite the costs, including the possibility that all three boys could pay the ultimate price.

> The news that I have to bear this time will be very disheartening for you, though you will have heard it long before this as they will probably wire you, that John is missing … this will be a terrible shock for you … as you will hardly have heard that he was in France before you would get the word … But if he has gone now it was because he didn't hang back any, and I know that you would sooner hear the "killed in action" than to ever hear that a Macfie hung back. So that makes it easier for me to write, as you will have counted the costs even though you let us go without complaining. And if we all get us[ed] up in this war you may think that we were called on to do more than our share as a family, but if we are fighting for honour and righteousness, who should pay the price but those that lay claim on such…[16]

Most letters conveying notification of a death reinforced similar notions of honour, valour, and duty to their country. Seventy years after the First World War, Muriel Macfie, who had written to her three brothers and many others throughout the Great War, told a nephew that "there was a very patriotic climate for the First World War that doesn't exist today in the nuclear age."[17] But, it was not just in death that soldiers called on such ideas. In February 1917, after recovering from a wound and being sent back to France, Ronald MacKinnon told his father:

You often speak of the hard fighting to come … I am in the first "wave." I do not like to talk about it to make your worry, but Dad when I think of the Lusitania, Zepp raids and some of the things I have seen, I hate Germans like you would a blight on your grain, and I'll go "over the top" with the set purpose of doing my little bit. I often wonder if I'll come thru, and worry about my children, but I can only trust in god to bring me thru. If I don't you can rest assured that I done my duty as a Scotch Canadian.[18]

A soldier with Princess Patricia's Canadian Light Infantry, Ronald MacKinnon was subsequently killed at Vimy Ridge in April 1917.

Harry McConnell-Taylor wrote to his friends in June 1942 that he had walked along the white cliffs of Dover and looked across the channel:

It gave me a queer feeling to stand on the cliffs and look towards France. I couldn't help thinking that here in England was freedom of thought & word, a free people fighting for a free world, and there across the Channel, a scant 22 miles away was tyranny & slavery. Everything that is rotten too. And because it's rotten, it will collapse. And sooner than we think too. I felt good all over knowing I was going to have a chance to get my nickel's worth in and help cause it to crumble.[19]

Wartime letters frequently included philosophical comments on life, war, and patriotism. Despite the belief, widely held among many soldiers, that it was an honour and their patriotic duty to fight for their country and for freedom from tyranny, some soldiers also expressed the sentiment that some people were called on to do more than their fair share and that the responsibility to defend should be shouldered by all, not just a few. When men began to wish for peace rather than a continued adventure of war, they always pointed out they had not lost their nerve. For example, Roy Macfie, in a candid letter to his father only a year into his active service in 1916, wrote about the toll on his fellow fighting men and tried hard to explain that their behaviour was not due to fear:

What few are left of the first cont. [contingent] have been through so many bombardments, and have seen so much slaughter, and bloodshed, that they dread the thoughts of the trenches. Fellows that feared nothing when they came out here are so nervous now that they can't stand anything. The sound of shells will almost set some of them crazy, and it is not because they are afraid, they can't help it is a shame to keep them at it, any that have come through everything since we came out here should be taken home and let some that have such soft jobs, back at the bases and [higher ranking] officers in England, come and take their places, they have done a good deal more than their bit.[20]

And, even though he had only seen a year's service in France, Claude Williams wrote in mid-May 1917:

[I]t seems as if I [have] been born out here and have never known anything but everlasting mud and perpetual shell fire. Now all of us feel ready for peace at the right time: the fire-eaters who before experiencing heavy action only wanted to "get a poke" at Fritz have already simmered down and cannot "get their time" soon enough. I think it is only natural. None of us has lost our nerve but the novelty has worn off and we have seen too much of the shady side of fighting to love it for the mere sake of adventure. When called upon we are cheerfully ready to do anything we are told but do not feel the same wild enthusiasm as formerly. We are all steadied and sobered up, I think … these are just my impressions and very local at that—perhaps they are not true generally.[21]

Such sentiments and musings about the clash of patriotism with the loss of enthusiasm caused by horrific battles, bloodshed, and exhaustion frequently made their way onto the pages of letters from soldiers to their families. Indeed, gruesome details of daily life during the First World War made their way into letters to be read by family and likely chipped away at the formidable propaganda of the Canadian government censors, who sought to maintain a patriotic view of the war.[22]

Censorship

Censorship—both self-imposed and official—often constrained the ability of correspondents to write freely about their situations. Soldiers were not allowed to provide any details about their location or their technology, or any information that might compromise battle security. Answering a letter from his sister in February 1918, Roy Macfie wrote, "[S]o the censor was taking liberties with one of my letters eh? I guess I will have to be careful or I'll find myself in a bad fix. I can't remember what it could be that offended him so I guess you'll never know what that part of it was."[23]

The possibility of their words being edited frequently led soldiers to comment in their letters that there was not much they were allowed to talk about. Yet, many letters from soldiers—especially during the First World War—did contain bitter details of life in the trenches and the dehumanizing elements of battlefield experience. For example, Lieutenant Claude Vivian Williams, who had two years of medical school before he joined the service and was the censor for the men under his command, wrote to his mother in 1917 that it was hard to step anywhere without stepping on a pile of English or German bones:

You know how seemingly morbid I am about "stiffs" etc., well, I used to go searching about every where for good specimens of bone for my collection. I now have nearly a whole skeleton rigged up under my bed, the worst of it is, he is a composite of a French and a Hun. I don't know whether that will agree or not, I will have to put a little English in to temper it down. It is funny how hardened and accustomed you do become to these things though, the sight is so familiar that you never think twice about it, but I must stop, I must write something that the rest will appreciate.[24]

One wonders what Williams's mother thought upon reading that spine-shivering passage and what she might have responded.

Tour Guides for Home

Soldiers often acted as tour guides[25] in their letters home describing the main attractions in, for example, England and Scotland during the First World War and in Asian countries during the Second World War, as though they were seeing parts of the world their families would never see and were trying to convey as much about the lives of the people in other countries as possible. One young soldier apologized to his parents for travelling around Scotland, instead of visiting his uncle. He describes how he and some friends went to Edinburgh Castle, Hollyrood Palace, the Forth Bridge, and other attractions. In addition to geographical and touristic descriptions of what they had seen on leave, some soldiers tried to describe the cultural differences that stood out for them. For example, Lieutenant Peter Lewis MacDougall of the Royal Rifles of Canada, was captured in the Far East and detained in a prisoner of war camp in Hong Kong during the Second World War, tells former co-workers in Montréal of the social and class differences he witnessed:

> We are in Barracks that are in a class by themselves, all kept spotlessly clean by Coolies incidentally there is only one thing cheaper than Coolie labour and that's his wife, it's amazing to see some of the loads the little _____ carry on their yokes ....
> To walk around the native quarter is an education in its self ... it's just a seething mass of humanity with the clip clop of the sandals, the din from the thousand and one little businesses and on top of that the sing song language of theirs. You see everything on the streets from childbirth to death; the poverty and filth is awful.[26]

Harry McConnell-Taylor provided minute details of some of his cultural experiences in England during the Second World War, such as going to a movie and a dance:

> The theatres are divided into front circles, centre stalls & back circles both up & down stairs .... The ushers all love to flash their lights in your face. They'd never get away with it home [sic]. And all through the movie, gals go up & down the aisles selling ice cream & cigarettes. You smoke, of course, in theatres here and can order tea & sandwiches if you want to. Most of the big theatres have restaurants in the foyer. And they usually are smart. But drinking tea in a movie ... I've been dancing a bit, but the style here is very different from ours .... Orchestras are good, but swing bands as we know them don't exist.[27]

The amount of detail in these travelogue letters allows each reader a vicarious experience of the sights and cultures of foreign lands.

Home Life Abroad

Concern for family welfare was another predominant theme as husbands asked often about the financial security of their families, older brothers worried about who would

Figure 15.2 Sketch based on a photograph of Margaret Edith Alston Rutherford Scythes from a scrapbook kept by Freddie Scythes. The scrapbook allowed Scythes to gather snapshots and sketches—some quite humorous—and to track mail and parcel delivery. Scythes was imprisoned at Stalag Luft III (Sagan) in Germany during the Second World War.
Canadian War Museum 1986-0290-070.

look after the crops in their absence, and fathers admonished errant children to behave themselves. In this way, letters helped to ground soldiers in the routine activities of their family lives and keep them connected to a life other than the one that immersed them in the horrors of war. Home matters must have imparted a sense of psychological balance to their harsh lives. For example, John Robert Osborn of the Winnipeg Grenadiers wrote to his son from Hong Kong in April of 1941 to admonish him for behaviour that his wife must have told him about in an earlier letter. The scolding is sandwiched between positive comments:

> Hello Old Man: Very pleased to hear from you again, and sorry I couldn't answer before, no I didn't like those kisses from the cat, but a smell of that Rabbit cooking would be very nice. So you are quite a swell [sic] with your Air Force suit, what's the matter with you all have you gone Air Force crazy, Say Listen Son, Your Mother tells me you have been a bad boy, what's the matter with you, you know you promised me that you would be Good and look after Mother for me but it doesn't look as if you

are, you had better buck up or I'll be coming home and use my stick again. Gee you and John sure must have grown a lot. Fancy weighing all that much, John sure will be a big man now he has so many Ties won't he Well Old Fellow I guess this about [sic] all for this time. So will close Hoping to hear that you are a good boy Again. From your Old Dad and Pal, Jack.[28]

Osborne received the Victoria Cross for several acts of bravery during a daylong battle at Hong Kong on December 19, 1941. He was killed instantly when he threw himself on top of a live grenade that exploded but he saved the lives of many others.[29]

Letters also kept soldiers informed about how the females in their families in Canada coped during their absence. As one mother wrote to her son in a prisoner–of–war camp in Japan in June 1943: "What a change a few years make. All the family are well and it seems odd, Yat is alone, also me, Verna and Jen with no men."[30] A prisoner of war in Germany wrote to his wife in July 1943 that, "I have just come in from Church, where we all said our Prayers for our loved ones. Knowing what a brave part our women folk are playing in this show, we are very proud of you all."[31] Many letters reveal women had to assume the chores normally done by the boys, took on paid or volunteer work, and made decisions without consulting their men folk.

Muriel Macfie was a teenager living in rural Ontario, inland from Georgian Bay, when her three older brothers and the young men from her community went overseas in 1917.[32] Throughout the period, she and her two sisters, Gladys and Jessie, wrote continuously to her brothers and friends. The response to her letters shows how she matured during this time and the impact on her life of the men's absence. Her friend Private Joe Payette wrote in July 1917: "Say, I gess [sic] you will have to start haying and finish it this year and do more than you did last hear ha ha I gess[sic] fellows are pretty scarce around Dunchurch this summer."[33] Roy Macfie told Muriel in July 1915 that he had received a letter from a female friend who wrote: "[W]hen I went back there not to be surprised if I saw her running a taxi, and her mother a ticket collector and so on, I don't think I could help being surprised, but just the same the women are doing a lot of work there."[34] He also wrote to Muriel in January 1918: "So I have a sister a munitions worker eh? That sounds fine, (in a way) but I wish ever body in the world would stop making munitions altogether. If I thought you had a hand in making the noise that we had to go through in the last place we were in, I would give you a talking to when I get home …"[35]

Letters sent to friends often found their way into newspapers and served to make sure attention was directed unofficially where no official recognition was forthcoming. For example, Captain Donald B. Martyn communicated his thoughts on the heroism of female ambulance driver, Grace MacPherson, after a devastating air raid on Étaples on May 19, 1918, wounded many and killed 66, including three nursing sisters. Martyn's letter was published in a Vancouver newspaper:

Grace … is deserving of many medals for her bravery and pluck and undoubtedly is a very gritty woman. The night of the raid she was first on the scene with her machine [ambulance] and she worked all night without a quiver and let me say there were not a few men panic stricken that awful night of horror. It seems to be too bad that such unexampled bravery as hers is not officially recognized, owing to the fact of her affiliation with a more or less freelance organization.[36]

Conclusion

Wartime correspondence demonstrates the key role that the post played in keeping lines of communication open between the home front and the battlefront. Although people's lives were disrupted in many ways for as long as four or five years, they remained connected through regular correspondence, sharing aspects of their day-to-day lives with each other. Perhaps the exchange of letters helped to humanize the soldier on the ground in the trenches, at sea, or in the air. Missives sent back home to Canada may have had a dual impact. On the one hand, the letters probably helped fuel patriotic support for the Canadian war effort. In turn, the support of husbands, sons, and brothers may have been experienced and interpreted as being synonymous with supporting the war effort. On the other hand, the increasingly candid letters from the front lines expressing horror, fatigue, and a waning enthusiasm for war, likely diminished—for some recipients—the glory and fervour that had accompanied a loved one's sendoff to Europe. In short, the wars kept soldiers and their families apart, letters kept them connected.

Notes

1. This article evolved out of research undertaken for the Canadian Postal Museum in 1998, involving some 600 letters written primarily by soldiers to their families and friends in Canada and held at Library and Archives Canada and at the Canadian War Museum Archives in Ottawa. This research was previously presented as a paper at the Canadian Historical Association Annual Meeting at Sherbrooke, Quebec, in 1999. Special thanks to Carol Reid at the Canadian War Museum Archives for her enthusiastic support and unwavering patience in finding and recommending relevant archival material.
2. *Saving Private Ryan* (DreamWorks SKG & Paramount Pictures Corporation © Amblin Entertainment, Inc., 1998), film.
3. Library and Archives Canada, MG 30 E 427, Macfie Family Collection, vol. 1, file 1-23 (1917,1919], Joe Payette to Muriel Macfie Correspondence: Joe Payette to Muriel Macfie, September 25, 1917.
4. Library and Archives Canada, MG 30 E 427, Macfie Family Collection, vol. 1, file 1-21 [1917-19], Herman Dobson to Muriel Macfie Correspondence: Herman Dobson to Muriel Macfie, October 30, 1918.
5. Canadian War Museum Archives, Ottawa, file 219-58A 183.15: F/O Don Quinn to J. M. C. Duckworth, Montreal, February 25, 1945.
6. Library and Archives Canada, MG 30 E400, file Line Service, France, October 31, 1916, to August 14, 1917: Claude Vivian Williams to his father, November 6, 1916.
7. Canadian War Museum Archives, Ottawa, file IL/997022–001 to 003, E. H. McConnell-Taylor, WW II [air]: E. H. (Harry) McConnell-Taylor to a friend in Saint John, New Brunswick, September 27, 1942.

8. Canadian War Museum Archives, Ottawa, file 58A 1 28.5, Betty Scott: Betty Scott to her sister Jean, March 7, 1940.

9. Library and Archives Canada, MG 30 E 427, file 6, Maheux Correspondence, January to June 1916: Frank Maheux to his wife, June 10, 1916.

10. Desmond Morton, "A Canadian Soldier in the Great War: The Experiences of Frank Maheux," *Canadian Military History* 1 (Autumn 1992): 80.

11. Canadian War Museum Archives, file 219-58A 1 83.12, E. O. Worden: Ted Worden to his wife, written on boat while awaiting Normandy "D-Day" assault the morning of June 6, 1944.

12. Canadian War Museum Archives, file 58 A1 24.2, F. S. Scythes: Squadron Leader Roy Campbell to Scythes's wife Margaret, May 9, 1943.

13. Ibid., Flight Lieutenant R. D. Binning; Chaplain to Scythes's wife Margaret, May 10, 1943.

14. Ibid., Dave Young to Margaret Scythes, May 27, 1943.

15. Ibid., Scythes's War Diary,"Extracts from letters from Home (not mine)," p. 126.

16. Library and Archives Canada, MG 30 E 427, Macfie Family Collection, vol. 1, file 1-12 [1917], Arthur Macfie Correspondence: Arthur Macfie to his parents, May 21, 1917.

17. Library and Archives Canada, MG 30 E 427, Macfie Family Collection, vol. 1, file 1-24 (1984): Muriel Macfie to John Macfie, February 3, 1984.

18. Library and Archives Canada, MG 30, E 547, file 6, Ronald and Archie Mackinnon: Ronald Mackinnon to his father, 1916–1917.

19. Canadian War Museum Archives, IL/997022–001 to 003; E. H. McConnell-Taylor: McConnell-Taylor to his father, June 7, 1942.

20. Library and Archives Canada, MG 30 E 427, Macfie Family Collection, vol. 1, file 1-1 (1916) Roy Macfie Correspondence: Roy Macfie to his father, January 3, 1916.

21. Library and Archives Canada, MG 30 E400, file Line Service France, October 31, 1916 to August 14, 1917: Claude Williams to his family, May 16, 1917.

22. See, for example, Jeffrey A. Keshen, *Propaganda and Censorship during Canada's Great War* (Calgary: University of Alberta Press, 1996) for a discussion of the role of Canada's Chief Censor during this period.

23. Library and Archives Canada, MG 30 E 427, Macfie Family Collection, vol. 1, file 1-6 [1918], Roy Macfie Correspondence: Roy Macfie to his sister Muriel, February 15, 1918.

24. Ibid., Williams to his family, November 18, 1916.

25. See, for example, Richard White, "The Soldier as Tourist: The Australian Experience of the Great War," *War & Society* 5, no. 1 (1987): 63–77.

26. Canadian War Museum Archives, file 58 A 1 29.6, Peter Lewis MacDougall: Lieutenant Peter Lewis MacDougall, Royal Rifles of Canada, to his former office buddies, November 26, 1941.

27. Canadian War Museum Archives, IL/997022–001 to 003: E. H. McConnell-Taylor to a friend in Saint John, New Brunswick, June 7, 1942.

28. Canadian War Museum Archives, file 219-58A 1 112.3, John Robert Osborn, VC, Second World War: John Robert Osborn to his children, April 9, 1941.

29. Ibid., *London Gazette*, April 2, 1946. This brief article notes "Company Sergeant–Major Osborn was an inspiring example to all throughout the defence, which he assisted so magnificently in maintaining against an overwhelming enemy force for over eight and a half hours, and in his death he displayed the highest qualities of heroism and self-sacrifice."

30. Canadian War Museum Archives, file 58A 1 6.8, Francis Denis Martyn: Martyn's mother to Martyn, June 28, 1943.

31. Canadian War Museum Archives, file 219-58A 133.7, Jack Powerful Griss: Griss to his wife Olga in Montréal, July 18, 1943.

32. Her brother John was killed in action and Arthur was wounded twice and sent home with a disability. Her friends also sustained serious injuries. Only her eldest brother Roy served continuously overseas until the end of the war without serious injury and returned home to the family farm.

33. Library and Archives Canada, MG 30 E 427, Macfie Family Collection, vol. 1, file 1-23 (1917, 1919] Joe Payette to Muriel Macfie Correspondence: Joe Payette to Muriel Macfie, July 18, 1917.

34. Library and Archives Canada, MG 30 E 427 Macfie Family Collection, vol. 1, file 1-2 [1915], Roy Macfie Correspondence: Roy Macfie to his sister Muriel, July 7, 1915.

35. Library and Archives Canada, MG 30 E 427 Macfie Family Collection, vol. 1, file 1-6 (1918) Roy Macfie Correspondence: Roy Macfie to his sister Muriel, January 8, 1918.

36. Canadian War Museum Archives, file 58A 1 21.12, Grace Evelyn MacPherson: Captain Donald B. Martyn about MacPherson's heroism to a Vancouver newspaper, n.d.

A TIMELESS EXPERIENCE?

Perceptions of Two Educated German Immigrants to the United States, 1863 to 1996

16

Susanne C. Knoblauch, German Studies, University of New Mexico

Abstract

This article examines the amazingly similar experiences of two German immigrants to the United States—140 years apart. Both share common biographical aspects: They are relatives—great-great uncle and great-great niece (the author) in direct line—and are well educated. The main source of the historical research is a collection of 58 letters written between 1863 and 1867 by Carl Eduard Knoblauch, the author's great-great uncle, who emigrated from Berlin, Germany, to New York City in 1863. The second source is the author's immigrant experience 140 years later. The author immigrated to Albuquerque, New Mexico, from Stuttgart, Germany, in 1996 and read the letters in 1999. The fact that a strong personal background has been incorporated into this research opens the door to "all the insight we can garner from the past, so that we may yet have a future,"[1] and thus to an interdisciplinary approach in the wider sense. After examining where Carl Knoblauch came from and where he found himself in the New World, the article focuses on the key question: What made Carl's experience so similar to that of his great-great niece who came to America 140 years later? Is it typical for any immigrant, is it typical only for a German immigrant, or is it "just" a unique personal phenomenon involving two relatives three generations apart?

Résumé

Cet article porte sur l'expérience étonnamment similaire de deux immigrants allemands établis aux États-Unis – à 140 ans de distance. Leurs antécédents biographiques sont comparables : ils ont un lien de parenté – l'un est l'arrière-grand-oncle et l'autre (l'auteur), l'arrière-petite-fille en ligne directe – et tous deux ont un niveau élevé d'instruction. La source principale de documentation pour cette recherche historique est une collection de 58 lettres rédigées entre 1863 et 1867 par Carl Eduard Knoblauch, l'arrière-grand-oncle de l'auteur, qui a émigré de Berlin, en Allemagne, à New York en 1863. La deuxième source est l'expérience de l'auteure elle-même en tant qu'immigrante 140 ans plus tard. L'auteure a quitté Stuttgart, en Allemagne, pour s'installer à Albuquerque (Nouveau-Mexique) en 1996, et elle a lu les lettres en 1999. Le fait que beaucoup de données personnelles aient été intégrées à cette recherche ouvre la porte à « tout ce que peut nous apprendre le passé, afin que nous puissions avoir un avenir »[2], et par conséquent à une approche multidisciplinaire dans son sens le plus large. Après avoir indiqué d'où Carl Knoblauch était originaire et où il s'est fixé dans le Nouveau-Monde, l'article essaie de répondre à cette question importante : qu'est-ce qui rend l'expérience de Carl si semblable à celle de son arrière-petite nièce, qui a immigré en Amérique 140 ans plus tard ? Est-elle commune à tous les immigrants, ou seulement aux immigrants allemands, ou n'est-ce là qu'un phénomène personnel ne concernant que deux parents à trois générations de distance ?

> Deshalb sind Briefe so viel wert, weil sie das Unmittelbare des Daseins aufbewahren.
> Letters are of such high value because they conserve the immediacy of existence.
> —Johann Wolfgang Goethe

The Letters: A Brief Quantitative Analysis

This article analyzes the letters and their contents, Knoblauch's intentions for writing the letters, and his biographical background. It provides the foundation for a better understanding of the general context of the letters and offers a wider interdisciplinary approach to the interpretation of their meaning.

The primary source of this article is a collection of 58 letters written between July 1863 and April 1867 by Carl Eduard Knoblauch. In 1863, Knoblauch immigrated to New York City and wrote to family and friends in several German cities and to his friends in London, England. He kept copies of the letters, which are in excellent condition and still in the family's possession. Knoblauch's handwriting is that of a highly educated man accustomed to writing and, as such, is easy to read. The letters are written in the old German handwriting Sütterlin. I transcribed and then translated the letters into English and, for three letters written in English, from English into German, so that readers of either native tongue can read and understand them.

About one third (21) of the letters were written as "round" letters (letters passed from one member of the family to another) to the entire family in Germany, who were scattered between Berlin, Stuttgart, Frankfurt, and Dortmund; another third (19) were addressed to single family members, mostly to his siblings; and five were sent to a cousin who helped with the family business. The final 18 letters were written to Knoblauch's friends in Berlin (10) and London (8). Three of the letters posted to London were written in English.

The content of the letters varies from descriptions of New York City and its inhabitants—architecture, road conditions, vehicles, fashion, American eating habits, cultural events such as the Metropolitan Fair, theatre, and horseback riding—to two reports of Knoblauch's daily business life, his travels, and political news about events such as the Civil War, Prussian foreign and domestic politics, Lincoln's funeral, the abolition of slavery, and reconstruction issues. Last and most interesting, Knoblauch offers a detailed view into his private life, his personal acquaintances, and his thoughts about world events. In every letter, Knoblauch reminds the reader that he is concerned about his family and friends back home, about the problems and pleasures of their everyday lives, and their worries and hopes.

To determine the issues of greatest importance to Knoblauch, the contents of the letters were organized into three main categories with two or more sub-groups within each category. The number of times that Knoblauch wrote about the same issue was recorded, but the introduction and farewell phrases of all letters were omitted; an issue was only counted when it was in the main body of a letter. The numbers in parentheses after each subject indicate the number of times Knoblauch discussed the issue:

I.   Connection between the new and the old life (62):
    a. Personal contact (43)
    b. Personal business affairs (19)
II. Life in the New World (43):
    a. Pleasure (32)
    b. Work (5)
    c. Travel (6)
III. Politics and economics (27):
    a. America (14)
    b. Europe (13)

Of the 132 results, almost 50 per cent fall into category I: the connection between the new life and the old life. There are a relatively large number of letters regarding personal business affairs. This is due to the death of Knoblauch's father in 1865, which increased the number of personal business affairs letters from 11 to 19. When these 8 letters are excluded, however, category I still has the highest number with 54 mentions.

"Often," states David Gerber, "the continuing desire to maintain relationships and to negotiate and renegotiate their terms amidst changing circumstances characterizes immigrant letters."[3] One could say as much about Knoblauch's letters. He not only urges his family to write to him, he offers a plan to make it easier for them:

> I want to look at the post office one of these days, to see whether there is a letter for me which is incorrectly addressed; however, should there be nothing yet, or is still on its way, let it be an urgent request to all of you to send me a few lines soon. You can imagine how much I look for them. If one of you writes to me one week, then the week after another writes, then a third writes after another week, then no one has to write too often and I would be helped."
>   (Letter No. 13, to the family, New York, September 24/27, 1863[4])

In addition, Knoblauch provides his family members with information about the best postal connections:

> Regarding the mailing of the letters which Gustav wants to influence, I mention the following: Between Europe and here there are three lines: Hamburger, Bremer, and

the English steamers.[5] The latter are the fastest and safest and depart every Saturday from Liverpool. The letters must be sent by you so that they arrive in Liverpool by Friday evening. therefore, for example, the letters must be taken to the Berlin post office on Wednesday evening. Please address the letters to Mr. C. K. c/o Mr. Henry F. Verhuven, 43 Exchange Place.[6]"

(Letter No. 21, to the family, New York, December 8/9, 1863)

He certainly leaves no doubt about his desire to maintain a close relationship with his family abroad.

The second largest number of results falls into category II: life in the New World. As much as Knoblauch needed to connect his new life with the old one with information from the Old World, he also sought to tell his family and friends in the Old World about his new experiences. He wanted them to know and understand his new life. At the same time, he wished to assure them that he was still the same person: "You see, I am still not so Americanized that I don't pursue European issues with eagerness." (Letter No. 31, to the family, New York, February 23/24, 1864) In these letters, the reader finds extended reports about American cultural life such as theatre visits and musical events, travelling, popular behavior, and, eating and swimming habits. He tells the reader about his nightlife at a German club and a custom he experienced when he visited with a young woman, Miss Vanderpool:

Miss Vanderpool is a highly pleasant young girl, who converses with lots of spirit and humour. I didn't get to know much about the rest of her family; the American custom allows, yes demands, that the daughter receives visits where one (whether one is an old or a young person) sees and welcomes only her."

(Letter No. 21, to the family, New York, December 8/9, 1863)

He also describes his travels and his business life: "I do not think there is a place in the world where business is as exciting as here." (Letter No. 17, to friends in London,[7] English original, New York, October 26, 1863)

Political and economic issues make up about twenty-five per cent of all the issues mentioned in the letters. Knoblauch's choice of issues depended on the interests and expectations of the recipients. The family rarely received letters about politics and economics because they seem to have been of less importance to him. Letters to friends in London, however, almost always dealt with politics, economics and/or working conditions in the New World because Knoblauch met these people through business. In addition, he worked as a stockbroker, a profession in which it was impossible to succeed without being aware of political and economic issues:

America is the land of the extremes. If the weather is fine it is exceedingly so, if it is warm it is frightfully hot, if it is cold you get frozen to death almost (so they say) if it rains it pours down in torrents. So it is with the people, with business. One day all is sunshine prices go down some 5-10 pct;[8] next day people get frightened by some unimportant news prices rush up at the same rate.

(Letter No. 17, to friends in London, English original, New York, October 26, 1863)

According to our analysis, Knoblauch's main purpose was to keep in close contact with his family and to assure himself and the family members that he was still part of their lives. He was a man of many interests and horizons, yet, as a newly arrived immigrant, his roots were strong and pulled him back home. Most of the letters were written during the first year of his stay abroad. Between July 1863 and July 1864, Knoblauch penned twenty-three letters; during the second year (July 1864 through July 1865) sixteen letters; during the third year (July 1865 through July 1866) eleven letters; and, by the first half of the fourth year, only eight letters.

The language in the letters can be described as lively, humorous, and extremely warm-hearted. Knoblauch addressed each recipient in an intimate manner and always showed an interest in their personal affairs before going on to other subjects. The beginning of each letter is dedicated to the recipient's life and shows that he cared deeply about the people he wrote to. His style is clear and very descriptive when it comes to his American life. Scenes such as an American dinner, an excerpt of which appears below, are full of humour and make the reader smile or even laugh. His travel descriptions are almost poetic and the expression of his feelings over his father's death is heartbreaking.

Who was Carl Eduard Knoblauch?

Carl Eduard Knoblauch, known as Carl, was born on December 3, 1837, the fourth of six children, to Julie Knoblauch (nee Verhuven) and Carl Heinrich Eduard Knoblauch, called Eduard. Eduard Knoblauch was my great-great-grandfather. The Knoblauch family belonged to the Berliner Bildungsbürgertum[9] and had been engaged in various aspects of the city's community life since the 18th century. Well-known Berliners such as Friedrich Heinrich Alexander von Humboldt, Friedrich Ernst Daniel Schleiermacher, Ludwig Tieck, Christian Daniel Rauch, and Karl Begas were guests in the Knoblauch residence in Berlin. In 1988, the former East German government converted the first family home in the Berliner Nicolai Quarter into a museum to commemorate the family's participation in the city's social and political life.[10]

Carl's mother Julie belonged to a family of Frankfurt bankers. Her brother Heinrich Verhuven, known as Henry, was a stockbroker and a member of the New York Stock Exchange. He was the main reason Carl Knoblauch decided to immigrate to the U.S. Henry introduced Carl Knoblauch to Carl Schurz, the famous 1848 German revolutionary and later a Civil War General under President Lincoln. Knoblauch and Schurz became intimate friends. Schurz wrote Carl Knoblauch's eulogy.

Carl's father, Eduard, was one of the founders of the Berliner Architektenverein (Berlin Association of Architects) and the first freelance architect in Berlin. His architectural style stems directly from his idol, the famous Berliner architect Karl Friedrich Schinkel.[11]

Family in New York City
- Henry Verhuven (uncle on mother's side)
- Hinsdale Jessie Chittenden (second wife)
- Walter (brother of brother –in-law)

Friends in New York City
- Carl Schurz
- Miss Vanderpool

Family in Germany
- Julie Knoblauch, nee Verhuven (mother)
- Carl Heinrich Eduard Knoblauch (father)
- Johanna Caroline (sister)
- Gustav Heinrich (brother)
- Marie Bertha (sister)
- Helene Marie (sister)
- Julie Helene (sister)
- Friedrich Koeppen (brother-in-law)
- Carl Walter (brother-in-law)

Friends in Berlin
- Friedrich Alexander Humboldt
- Friedrich Ernst Daniel Schleiermacher
- Ludwig Tieck
- Christian Daniel Rauch
- Karl Degas
- Wilhelm ?

Carl Eduard Knoblauch
(1837-1886)

Figure 16.1 Diagram of family and friends corresponding with Carl or mentioned in his letters.
Illustration by Mathieu Saint-Amour.

Eduard's work includes numerous castles, factories, and private residences in and around Berlin. His most well-known building was the New Synagogue in Berlin.[12]

Carl's oldest sister, Joanna Caroline (1831–1862), died the year before Carl came to New York. His oldest brother, Gustav (1833–1916), eventually followed in his father's footsteps and became an architect. Gustav took over his father's architectural business and helped finish the synagogue after his father fell ill. He built numerous houses and banks, as well as the city's first hospital in Charlottenburg.[13] Carl had another older sister, Marie Bertha (1835–1914), called Bertha, and two younger sisters, Helene Marie (1840–1924), called Marie, and Julie Helene (1846–1910), called Lenel. Bertha lived in Dortmund with her husband Friedrich Köppen, the head of a publisher's bookstore. Marie lived with her husband Carl Walter, a professor at the Technical University in Stuttgart. Carl Walter's brother had already immigrated to Hoboken, New Jersey, where Carl later joined a riding club.

Carl arrived in New York City in 1863. In 1869, he married a Berliner, Gertraud Wiebe, called Traudel. They had seven children, of whom only four reached adulthood. Traudel died in 1880 after giving birth to the seventh child. Five years later, Carl married Hinsdale Jessie Chittenden, with whom he had another child. In 1886, after only one year of marriage, Carl died of appendicitis.

Carl did not choose to leave Germany for economic or personal reasons. His relationship with his family was extremely close and warm-hearted. His sole purpose in immigrating to the U.S. was to support his aging uncle, the stockbroker Henry Verhuven. Carl had learned banking at the Deutsche Bank in Berlin and had worked for the London bank, Hambro & Sons, before immigrating to New York when he was 26 years old. After Henry's death, Carl inherited his uncle's membership in the New York Stock Exchange.

Coming from a Prussian bourgeois family, Carl found himself in the upper middle class of New York, the same class he had left behind in Berlin. His perceptions of Civil War America were naturally different from that of the general population, whether German or American.[14] What did he perceive about his new homeland? What did he see or not see?

Carl's New Home: Kleindeutschland or Little Germany

The German community was virtually independent of the rest of New York. Little Germany or Kleindeutschland can be seen as a quasi-autonomous city functioning within the larger city of New York, with its own language, culture, and social life. Carl wrote:

> Sometimes it seems a mistake to call New York an American city, since there is such a lot of the German element here. With its 100,000 German inhabitants, it ranks among the largest German cities. The whole time, I hear almost only German. There are long streets without any sign that don't carry German names. Countless tobacco shops are operated by Germans."[15]
>
> (Letter No. 10 to the family, New York, August 1863)

The German immigrants of New York formed a much more cohesive community than many other groups of immigrants. There were several German quarters, of which the largest was in East Manhattan and called Kleindeutschland or Little Germany. By the 1840s, Kleindeutschland was already "the largest residential centre for the German-born population of the City."[16] Kleindeutschland was the first of several large pockets of foreign speaking nationalities and became the prototype for the later ones.

Little Germany was, like the rest of New York City, divided into wards numbers 10, 11, 13, etc. The individual wards differed in their characteristics, both within their entities and in comparison with other wards. Factories as well as slaughterhouses characterized the 11th ward, which had "some of the world's leading shipyards, birthplaces of many magnificent clipper ships (including the famous American clipper, *Flying Cloud*)."[17] To the west, 10th ward was rather commercial in character. Its Grand Street was a major shopping emporium with many drygoods shops and department stores. The small factories concentrated mostly on clothes and furniture. The farther east one went, the more industrial the ward became. Poorer people lived here. Those who could afford to moved to quieter and cleaner wards. Tenements located in the 11th and 13th wards were, as described in 1856 by the tenement committee of New York,[17] in "dirty conditions without ventilation and without room sufficient for civilized existence." One building had 96 rooms and housed 146 families with 577 individuals.

The atmosphere of the 17th ward was congenial. The houses were brick and set back slightly from the street. First and Second Avenues were wide. Tompkins Square, a big public park the Germans called the "Weiße Garten" (White Garden), contributed in a major way to the friendly atmosphere of the ward. Of course, the richer Germans lived there.

Germany did not become a unified nation-state until 1871. And, even following unification, the Germans could not be described as a homogeneous people in terms of culture, religion, and political leanings, not to mention history. The same can be said about the Germans in Kleindeutschland, who also identified more with their regional origins than with the nascent German nation. People from different parts of Germany mostly lived apart from each other in their own blocks. The Prussians, representing twenty per cent of German immigrants in New York in 1860, occupied a third of the 10th ward. By late 1880, when a third of the German immigrants were Prussian, this group occupied half of the 10th ward. In 1860, the Bavarians were the largest group among German immigrants. Their numbers were large in all wards except the Prussian 10th ward and "at all times ... they would be found wherever the Prussians were fewest."[19] It seemed that the Bavarians and the Prussians preferred to avoid one another.

The best indicator of regional divisions among the German immigrants was their marital behaviour. The Prussians, in particular, chose their marital partners very carefully from among their own group. Carl was a Prussian and brought his wife from Berlin. Most Germans lived in traditional family groups as they did in the Old World. In 1850, 80 per cent of German immigrants were living in family units;[20] by 1860, this number had increased to 91 per cent. The number of New-York-born German-American children increased rapidly. In 1850, 37 per cent were American born and, by 1860, this number rose to 64 per cent.

Aside from work and domestic family life, there was a lot of entertainment in Kleindeutschland, but, according to Karl Heinzen, "in New York no adequate German theater can maintain itself, in New York no German opera can prosper, in New York no lecture series can be successful, in New York no worthwhile German newspaper can establish itself; but there is a German beer hall in New York that cost $120,000 to build. There you have German New York."[21] Harsh words, but certainly, in part, correct. Carl was not thrilled by German cultural life in New York. The Bildungsbürger from Berlin missed high class culture:

> Of the local theatres I have only seen a few as yet. In the Americans [sic] the house is mostly the best, the actors are in our eyes very mediocre; nevertheless there is a very good French one here. The German [theatre house] is wretched.[22]
>
> (Letter No. 21, to the family, New York, December 8/9, 1863)

For the majority of people, however, it was the beer halls that made life in New York bearable. According to one historian: "Here an immigrant could meet his friends and relax, away from the dark and crowded tenements."[23] There were thousands of beer halls in New York that offered not only drink but music and dance as well. Most of the beer halls were in the Bowery and did not have very good reputations. Yet, there were also very well furnished ones, such as the Atlantic Gardens, where the wealthy, including Carl, went with or without their families on a Sunday. The music was of high quality, the orchestra members mainly German.

One phenomenon of the German community was the innumerable "Vereine" or clubs for everybody and everything. Even if "Vereinsmeierei" (club mania) may have appeared somewhat strange to the outsider, every "Verein" had its function. In some "Vereinen," such as the "Turnverein" (gymnastics club) or the "Schützenverein" (shooting club), people from all classes and professions met. There were "Vereine" that had purely charitable functions such as the "Unterstützungsverein" (support club), which focused, as the name indicates, on poor members who were ill, and when they died paid about $15 for their funeral expenses. Because of these advantages, the "Unterstützungsvereine" were the most frequented "Vereine" and had on average 100 to 150 members.[24] Carl joined the New Yorker "Gesangsvereine" (singing club), but his expectations were not fulfilled: "There are indeed German Gesangsvereine here; however, the company does not suit me." (Letter No. 20, to family, March 13, 1865) However, he was pleased with the membership in the German Club where he spent many evenings reading German newspapers, playing billiards or cards, and enjoying many special events such as New Year's Eve and birthday parties.

A wide variety of German newspapers were published in New York City covering almost every aspect of the cultural and political scene. The most popular paper was the *New Yorker Staats-Zeitung*, which supported the Douglas Democrats.[25] Other newspapers, like the *Allgemeine Zeitung* represented the Whigs. The *Democrat* and the *Abendzeitung* supported the New Republican Party of Abraham Lincoln.

When Carl Knoblauch arrived in New York in 1863, the political developments that had led to the Civil War were still in progress. The war against slavery, ostensibly the primary issue of the confrontation with the South, seemed to be a threat to the workers because they feared the black freemen would take their jobs; this fear led to anti-draught riots, such as the one in July 1863. Trade also suffered major declines: "The total value of goods carried in U.S. vessels sank from $570 million in 1860 to $185 million in 1864."[26] Public opinion shifted with the alternating southern and northern victories: for or against war, for or against abolition. Over time, the war made the rich richer and the poor poorer. The majority of workers suffered from ever worsening living conditions. The German immigrants were not exempt from all this but, due to their tight community, life was at least bearable.

Carl was not representative of the majority of German immigrants living in New York. As a rich man, he experienced no economic loss due to the war. Carl belonged to neither the group of immigrants who left their country for economic reasons nor the group that had to escape into political exile, like his friend Carl Schurz. As Carl Knoblauch's letters show, he agreed politically with the 1848 revolutionaries and the American Civil War Republicans.

Immigration: A Timeless Experience?

I now bring the reader directly into the current year, 2005. I recount almost exactly the same perceptions of a German immigrant in 1863 and in 1996 by using my own experience and perspective as an immigrant to the United States. I avoid seeking the objective and shamelessly merge Carl's experience into my own, thus following the motto: "Thinking backwards in order to think forwards."[26]

Carl's letters caught my attention by certain personal and implicitly emotional ties. First, Carl wrote his letters between 1863 and 1867 during his first four years in the U.S. I discovered and read them in 1999 after I had been in the U.S. for three years. Carl suffered from being apart from his old friends and family; so did I. Second, his mother died the year before he emigrated, his father during his second year in the U.S. Both of my parents died during the first year of my stay in the U.S. The combination of grieving one's lost parents and feeling homesick produced an acute mixture of feelings, and Carl's words comforted me as only literature can. Third, the fact that Carl is my great-great uncle probably made me feel closer to him, even before I began to read his letters. I recall that I was worried he would turn out to be a person I wouldn't like!

In such a highly charged atmosphere of emotions and expectations, it seemed difficult to analyze Carl's observations critically. How could I connect the past with the present when, in fact, I severed the two by interpreting the past as if I were not part of it, as if Carl's perceptions of the past didn't have anything to do with my present? The answer is perception. Human senses react to external attractions. While we read, we create our own pictures, visual images with our inner eye—a quasi movie. Why limit the meaning of the letters by forcing them to remain in the past when we can easily connect the past and the present by allowing our own perceptions to run loose and by trusting our own associations, when we can "combine acts of memory and imagination"[28]? This redirection of objectivity into a creative subjectivity that is evoked by images from the past and based on perceptions from the present, merges the writer's and the reader's subjectivity, and thus connects the perceptions of writer and reader, building a bridge between past and present.

David Gerber argues that "by finding unities in the experiences of old and new Americans, we may enrich the teaching of American history."[29] Gerber refers to the political and economic aspects of these unities, these links between past and present. Here is an example from Carl's letters:

My dear Wilhelm,
… the reconstruction of the Southern states and the Congress coming together during the next weeks will be of greatest interest. I believe I am certain about one thing: Slavery will be abolished, but the black man, too. The black man will be wrecked, driven out of white society and, after fifty years, he will lead an existence like the Indians do now. In the slave states, the black man was not even regarded as a human being, but at most, as a valuable animal. The same people, who have looked at the black man up to now with the greatest disdain, should now put up with him as an equal fellow man? It seems to me that this is impossible for the hot blooded Southerners; yes, I am convinced that the former disdain will be turned into irreconcilable hate, even more so because now, out of his undefined feeling of freedom, the black man expresses an indolence towards his former master, which fans the flames even more. How does it happen that the black man is so much melted

down? Wherever a Southerner finds the opportunity, he shoots a black man down, nobody cares two hoots about it.

(Letter No. 51, to his friend Wilhelm,[30] New York, December 1865)

Figure 16.2 *Racism*, collage by Gauri Vengurlekar, Architect, Santa Fe, New Mexico.

In retrospect, we know that the so-called Reconstruction period is still with us and that Carl was right in his warning.[31] As I write today, in the U.S., the first association with the term "war" is the war in Iraq. We know that the comparison with the Civil War is not completely justified. Once again, the U.S. behaves as a missionary bringing freedom and justice to misled and suppressed people. Once again, the U.S. creates a disaster that has enormous consequences for generations to come, and once again, the ones who should be freed lose their loved ones in battle, lose their houses and their work. They suffer from hunger and are deprived of human rights; there is not and never was a plan to solve these problems. Carl's assessment remains: There will never be an end to human arrogance and hunger for power.

For Carl and for me, as first generation immigrants, there is another political issue in the country to which we immigrated. Both my great-great uncle Carl and I chose our new country for positive reasons: "I have never seen a more common and earnest mourning than that at Lincoln's death." (Letter No. 51, to his friend Wilhelm, New York, December 1865) As neither of us was forced to leave our native country because of hunger or political repression, we need to explain every political move of our chosen country to others and to ourselves to reassure ourselves that our decision to immigrate was the right one. Every crisis in the chosen country is a personal crisis. As Carl writes, for us, the decisions of the U.S. Congress are of the highest interest. We cannot believe that there is no hope for the country that historically began as the last refuge for many Europeans. As much as we are the critical observers of our new home, we are also its defenders and admirers and thus, at the same time, the defender of our own actions.

We are split inside: We chose our new home, but our hearts are still where the old home is. This excerpt from Carl's letter to his sister illustrates the point:

> My dear sister,
> That I happily received your splendid letter for my birthday you will learn from the attached letter. I thank you heartily for it because it was again a sincere joy for my heart. All the news from the little Dortmunder nest I always welcome as a special event. My heart hangs too much on the dear little party and their mother. I wish we had had them—Max, Julchen and little Bertha—here for Christmas. Everything was complete, only the shiny eyes of the little rascals were missing, and uncle cried over and over again: "What a pity that we don't have children here."
> (Letter No. 44, to Carl's sister Bertha in Dortmund, New York, January 16/17, 1865)

With such familiar rituals as Christmas we can safely assume that the associations of those who grew up with this tradition today are very similar to those of the 19th century. The reader can identify easily with Carl's description because it matches the common view of Christmas as a family event. Even if different readers import individual variations and even if every one of us has different perceptions, we all create a very specific image reading the words. Everyone can **imagine** the pain, but anyone who has immigrated can **feel** the pain of being far away from their beloved family on Christmas:

… instead of being gathered around the table, which the best parents had loaded with presents, every single one is now looking in his circle to replace what is not available to him. Through their love and kindness, Christmas Eve became one of the happiest

Figure 16.3 *Fast Food*, collage by Gauri Vengurlekar, Architect, Santa Fe, New Mexico.

days of the year; they are taken from us and with them the centre around which we gathered. But, as the memory of them is unforgotten, so will—if God so desires—the one everlasting gift, which all of us owe them, that is, mutual love and devotion. Even if not united in reality, all of us are conscious that the others remember him with love wherever he might be.

(Letter No. 21, "round" letter to the family in Germany
(Berlin, Stuttgart, Frankfurt, Dortmund), New York, December 8/9, 1863)

Gathering with family and friends is the most common custom, which includes traditional rituals as well as habits specific to the inner circle of the family or special group. To know an ethnic group, one has to know their eating habits. Carl's description of American eating habits is most amusing and could be applied to the twenty-first century as well:

I believe I will like it here rather well, and that I will reach my goal. Last Sunday was a cold rainy day and I decided to stay at home to see a real American dinner. People have no idea about a comfortable meal. That business people eat in a big hurry, one can explain, but why the same rush at Sunday dinner when one has plenty of time? A roast appears as well as poultry and vegetables of every kind and shape. The gentleman of the house offers me a plateful of beautiful roast, potatoes etc.; I hardly begin working when madam asks if I would like some poultry. I hold out the prospect that I would be inclined to have some later, but such is not the rule. Before I know it, a heap of poultry is placed in front of me. Who can enjoy his meal with two heavily loaded plates in front of him and the constant admonishment to take a sweet potato (things like children's heads) or mashed potatoes, or tomatoes (a peculiar, very good fruit, which appears in all forms), or cucumbers, or this or that. One has hardly eliminated those trifles when instantly a dessert is served, (perhaps others have only finished their first half bite of dinner). He who has enjoyed his share of every course, gets up and lets the others continue to work; a highly uncomfortable way of eating, which, of course, is <u>not</u> to be found among Germans here.

(Letter No. 13, "round" letter to family in Germany
(Berlin, Stuttgart, Frankfurt, Dortmund), New York, September 24/27, 1863)

Table manners and eating habits have always been a central part of any culture. They usually reflect more general attitudes. After a month, Carl discovers that some things are different and not to his liking. The reader has no problem imagining the scene and seeing Carl sweating through this difficult challenge. We enjoy reading it and laughing about it because we can identify with his perception of American eating habits and feel his uneasiness and disgust. The American way of dining seems to be an attack on Carl's very person; he wants the reader to understand that he is, in this case, not an objective observer but an angry participant: The past and the present merge. Some Westerners today might not feel the same way but understand that the quickly eaten dinner of the 19th century has turned into an immense health problem for all Western society. In his letter did Carl not already observe and/or anticipate the modern problem of fast-food and overeating?

Conclusion

As an immigrant myself, I have no difficulty understanding and enjoying Carl's observations. It is an amazing experience for me that the perception of a family member who immigrated to the same country 140 years ago can seem so familiar. I agree in almost every respect with what Carl is writing about and could not put it in better words myself. But more so, being a first generation immigrant and coming from the same background, I am also able to read behind the words and between the lines, and, more importantly, appreciate the immense sadness and emotional turmoil of being neither a part of the old life nor a part of the new one. I am not the only one who can identify with Carl's descriptions. There are many other interpretations possible, especially for other immigrants. Depending on individual experiences, an interpretation will be more or less emotional but nevertheless accurate in its own way. If the current fashion of more synchronic studies in history departments is to be brought a step further, it will necessarily involve a new approach that includes the personal relationship between the historical individual and historian–individual today.

Endnotes

1. R. H. Popkin, *The High Road to Pyrrhonism* (San Diego: CA, 1980), p. 29.
2. Ibid.
3. David Gerber, "Epistolary Ethics: Personal Correspondence and the Culture of Emigration in the Nineteenth Century," *Journal of American Ethnic History* 19, no. 4 (2000): 3.
4. All letters written to family are "round" letters passed from one family member to the next, from Berlin to Dortmund, and on to Frankfurt and Stuttgart. The translations are by me and my husband, Charles Edward Knoblauch.
5. The majority of immigrants "crossed the ocean with sailing ships" (Robert Ernst, *Immigrant Life in New York City, 1825–1863* (New York: Columbia University Press, 1949), p. 12), and only the wealthy among them could afford the fast and comfortable steamers. For impoverished immigrants, the crossing often became a traumatic experience. The ships were "often torture chambers for the poor creatures who had taken passage in them …. The emigrants are not only deprived of proper food and air, but the men are robbed, the women debauched and frequently beaten by scoundrels from whom no penalty is ever exacted" (Junius H. Browne, *The Great Metropolis: A Mirror of New York, 1866* (New York: Arno, 1975), p. 64).
6. This is the address of Heinrich Verhuven's office, located on a street that crossed Wall Street, in the heart of the business district.
7. Before Carl immigrated to New York, he worked for the London Bank Hambro & Sons. He sent letters to his former colleagues and friends, sometimes to a Mr. Briggs, sometimes as a round letter.
8. Per cent.
9. Franz J. Bauer *Bürgerwege und Bürgerwelten: Familienbiographische Untersuchungen zum deutschen Bürgertum im 19. Jahrhundert* (Göttingen: Vandenhoeck & Ruprecht, 1991).
10. Märkisches Museum Berlin, ed., *Knoblauch-Haus* (Berlin: Märkisches Museum Berlin, 1989).

11. Karl Friedrich Schinkel was born on March 13, 1781, in Neuruppin, Prussia, and died in Berlin on October 9, 1841. He designed famous classical buildings in Berlin, such as the "Neue Wache" Unter den Linden, the "Schauspielhaus" on the Gendarmenmarkt, the "Alte Museum" in the Lustgarten, the "Prinz-Wilhelm-Palais" Unter den Linden, and many other buildings not only in Prussia, (Michael Snodin, *Karl Friedrich Schinkel: A Universal Man* (New Haven: University Press, 1991).

12. Hermann Simon and Hg. Jochen Boberg, *"Tuet auf die Pforte." Die Neue Synagoge 1866-1995* (Berlin: Druckerei Vogt, 1995).

13. Märkisches Museum Berlin, Hg. Katalog zur Sonderausstellung vom 9. September 1993 bis 2 Januar 1994 im Museum Knoblauchhaus. *Drei Architekten in Berlin. Eduard Knoblauch 1801–1865. Gustav Knoblauch 1833–1916. Arnold Knoblauch 1879–1963.* (Berlin: Druckerei Graetz, 1993).

14. Sven Beckert, *The Monied Metropolis: New York City and the Consolidation of American Bourgeoisie, 1850–1996* (Cambridge: Cambridge University Press, 2001*)*.

15. In 1863, Kleindeutschland was the third largest German speaking city after Vienna and Berlin. In 1855, 154,000 Germans lived in New York; an additional 30,000 lived in Brooklyn and Williamsburg. In 1855, Vienna had 477,856 inhabitants, Berlin 441,931, and Hamburg 148,754 (Stanley Nadel, *Little Germany: Ethnicity, Religion, and Class in New York City, 1845–80* (Urbana: University of Illinois Press, ca 1990), p. 143). In 1865, 107,267 first generation German immigrants lived in New York representing 14.77 per cent of all New York residents (Junius H. Browne, *The Great Metropolis*, p. 544). Most of the tobacco dealers were Germans; 50 per cent in 1850 and 6 per cent in 1855 (Nadel, *Little Germany*, p. 63).

16. Nadel, *Little Germany*, p. 31.

17. Nadel, *Little Germany*, p. 32.

18. Nadel, *Little Germany*, p. 34.

19. Nadel, *Little Germany*, p. 37.

20. Nadel, *Little Germany*, p. 46.

21. Karl Heinzen, *Pionier*, January 4, 1857.

22. The German theatre, called "Stadttheater," opened in 1854 and offered performances of popular melodramatic and comic pieces. The acting was mediocre. The program was designed to appeal to the taste of the common people, who wanted to be entertained after a hard day's work. New York theatre life during the Civil War seems to have been quite entertaining in general and in the Grand Opera house "the playboy-showgirl nexus was as prevalent in Manhattan as it was in Paris." This provoked hefty reactions from the church people (Edwin G. Burrows and Mike Wallace, *Gotham: A History of New York City to 1898* (Oxford: Oxford University Press, 1999), p. 957).

23. Nadel, *Little Germany*, p. 104.

24. Nadel, *Little Germany*, p. 110.

25. Stephen A. Douglas (1813–1864) was the best known Democrat in the North. During the election campaign for Congress in 1858, Douglas ran against Abraham Lincoln. Lincoln challenged him to a debate, the well-known "Lincoln-Douglas-Debate," whereby they discussed the question of sovereignty of the states regarding slavery.

26. Burrows and Wallace, Gotham, p. 876.

27. Annabel Patterson, *Early Modern Liberalism* (Cambridge: Cambridge University Press, 1997), p. 215.

28. Ibid.

29. David Gerber, "Forming a Transnational Narrative: New Perspectives on European Migrations to the United States," *History Teacher 35* (January 2001): 63.

30. Carl's friend is Carl Wilhelm Magnum, who was living in Berlin at that time.

31. Eric Foner, *Reconstruction: America's Unfinished Revolution, 1863–1877* (New York: Harper & Row Publishers, 1988).

PART FOUR: COMMUNICATION AND TRANSPORT

QUATRIÈME PARTIE : COMMUNICATIONS ET MOYENS DE TRANSPORT

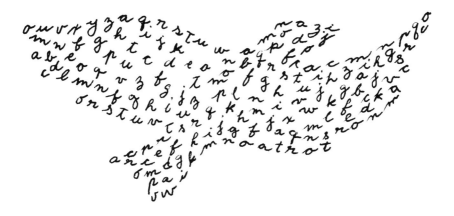

INSTRUCTIONS FROM TERRA NOVA

17

Aspects of Communication in the Sixteenth-Century Fishery

Brad Loewen, Professor of Archaeology, Université de Montréal

Abstract

The sixteenth century remains a distinctive, difficult period of Canadian history, but the myth of isolation and secret that clings to the fishery is not entirely accurate. News gathering and sharing in the Terra Nova havens did not depend only on chance meetings with other crews, but was facilitated by itinerant traders and Native mariners who were attracted to the fishing stations. Formal, written communication was based on the need for sound record keeping and on the Basque tradition of customary law, as well as on planned communication with procurers, insurers, and business partners back home. The staggered timetables of cod and whale fishermen allowed transatlantic communication during the fishing season. Ultimately, however, all depended on the pilots and their experience. When the fisheries are examined from a communications standpoint, sixteenth-century sources gain a new meaning. Despite the fishermen's lengthy absences, they were not isolated and they remained embedded in a network of communication possibilities.

Résumé

Le XVIᵉ siècle demeure une période particulière et difficile de l'histoire du Canada, mais le mythe de l'isolement et du mystère qui entoure la pêche à cette époque n'est pas totalement vrai. À Terre-Neuve, on n'était pas uniquement dépendant de rencontres aléatoires avec d'autres équipages pour apprendre les nouvelles et les diffuser, mais on pouvait également compter sur des commerçants itinérants et des marins autochtones qui étaient attirés par les campements de pêche. Les communications écrites formelles se faisaient pour tenir des registres exacts et pour respecter la tradition basque du droit coutumier, ainsi que pour s'adresser aux fournisseurs, aux assureurs et aux partenaires commerciaux au pays. Les calendriers décalés des pêcheurs de morue et de baleine permettaient les communications transatlantiques pendant la saison de pêche. En bout de ligne, cependant, tout dépendait des pilotes et de leur expérience. Lorsque les pêches sont examinées du point de vue des communications, les sources du XVIe siècle acquièrent une nouvelle signification. Malgré les longues absences des pêcheurs, ils n'étaient pas isolés et disposaient de tout un réseau de possibilités de communication.

Introduction

Despite the great strides of historians working on Canada's sixteenth century, understanding of transatlantic communication during this period remains anchored in a fairly simple paradigm. A large number of notarial acts and related documents describe briefly how fishing captains intended to set sail from the port where their vessels were outfitted and pass "in a direct route" (*en droite route*) to Terra Nova (Newfoundland), where they fished for several months before returning directly to their point of departure. Each year in March and April, notaries' offices were crowded with merchants offering credit to captains in exchange for a share of the catch, at rates up to twenty per cent, causing the volume of notarial acts to swell during these months. After this seasonal bulge in the notarial registers, the ships seem to disappear into the mist of the Atlantic Ocean and historians only catch sight of them again in September and October, when cod redistribution contracts and equipment purchases created a second, much smaller, wave of notarial activity. In the large departmental archives at Bordeaux, France, the visibility of the transatlantic fishery has a particularly sharp seasonal pattern.[1] The annual register of a typical commercial notary held hundreds of acts relating to the Terra Nova fisheries in March and April, often none at all from May through August, up to a dozen in September and October, then perhaps one per month over the winter, until the new season began again. The fishermen seem to be "out of sight, out of mind,"[2] especially in summer between the spring departure and the autumn return.

The fishermen's seasonal absence has given rise to a perception of a ruptured social fabric. European ports are seen to be bereft of a good part of their masculine population and Terra Nova fishing stations seen as resembling today's Northern construction camps in their hard driving work pace and hard drinking off hours. Alain Cabantous has shown that masculine absence slowed human reproduction and, when doubled with winter absences due to coastal shipping, led to a demographic downturn. After a generation or two of intense participation, many small ports dropped out of the transatlantic fishery as a result of demographic exhaustion.[3] By the end of the 1570s, the Basque coast had reaped many of the short-term benefits of the Terra Nova cod and whale fisheries and began to feel the social effects of transatlantic fishery. Judicial records contain depositions by many captains, tradesmen, and ordinary seamen who based their knowledge on twenty years or more of experience on the Terra Nova coast.[4] For example, in 1596, one fisherman had been on more than 50 whaling and cod fishing voyages over an unspecified number of years. The record for longevity as a participant belongs to a 64-year-old whaler who claimed 40 years of experience in 1570; another recalled in 1575 the first Labrador whaling outfit of 1543.[5] These skilled tradesmen and their families were at the core of the transatlantic fishing experience.

Prolonged absences were the lot of a core migratory work force although not of all participants in the fisheries. Tradesmen such as coopers, for instance, tended to ship out two or three times before using their savings to purchase a house and shop and set up a business in one of several cooperage branches. The community of port coopers in Bordeaux during the 1560s numbered at least sixty tradesmen, the vast majority of whom had gone to Terra Nova on whaling voyages as young men, even though fewer than fifteen of them were absent in any given year. Port coopers were principally stevedores, and their daily contact with captains, ships, and small boats made them natural candidates for the whale fishery, even though very few were sufficiently literate to sign their names. In Bordeaux, these *arrimeurs* ran all port loading and unloading operations using their own lighters and heaving gear, signed off bills of lading, arranged meetings among foreign captains, local merchants, and port notaries, and, in general, exercised functions that readily translated into middle officer status on Terra Nova whaling and fishing voyages. Coopers were also accustomed to commanding men since they formed the core of the town watch, a useful quality in times of international tension on the whaling grounds.

In contrast to the port coopers, very few of the 250 or more Bordeaux general coopers who specialized in cask construction or in wine cooperage ever went to Terra Nova.[6] As with the coopers, few Basque whaling captains repeated the Labrador route year after year. The majority of captains were employed on the Seville, Channel, and West Indies routes, and their forays into Terra Nova reflected their status as on-board representatives of the ship's ownership cartel rather than any specific whaling expertise.[7] A good proportion of crewmen were also attracted to the transatlantic fishery only temporarily. Core crews of experienced men were augmented each year by young men from inland towns and agrarian or artisanal families, who, after a couple of fishing seasons, re-established themselves in their original socio-economic context.[8] For these young men, the profits to be made in a couple of fishing seasons were a means of achieving a "middling" status in both rural and urban socio-economic hierarchies.[9] Only the sons of fishermen and coastal mariners became lifelong Terreneuvas. Their "villages" were most affected by seasonal absences and the social disruption of the Terra Nova fishery, to the point of a regular lack of manpower in the 1570s. Thus, captains and outfitters resorted to recruiting crewmen from other socio-economic backgrounds.

It is a telling aspect of the transatlantic fishery that the fishing "villages" where the core participants were recruited did not grow demographically at the same rate as the number of crewmen in Terra Nova. Absence and isolation during the summer and fall months were keenly felt by mariners, their families, and their business associates. A thirst for information and a need for correspondence led to communication strategies that focussed on key actors and instruments, whose role appears in many references. As well, the annual timetable of the fisheries was not as monolithic as it might seem at first, resulting in opportunities for transatlantic communication during the fishing season. This article argues that the functional intricacy and sophistication of this trade made recourse to communication strategies, including written ones, necessary or fruitful, as appears in aspects of information gathering, recording, and transmission.

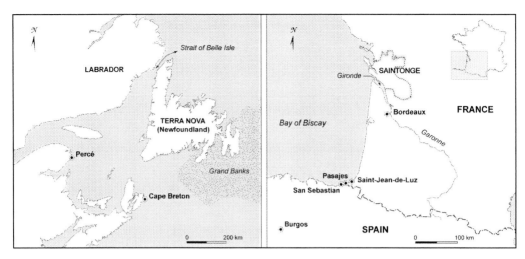

Figure 17.1 The transatlantic fishery in the 16th century: Western and eastern terminal points of a common system of economy and communication.

Map by Andrée Héroux.

Traders

Long-term participants in the sixteenth-century fishery developed ways of attenuating the socio-economic effects of long and repeated absences. In most cases, these strategies are mentioned indirectly and in a tone that suggests their habitual nature. Their supporting role in the fishing effort appears to have relegated them to relative invisibility in sixteenth-century archives, where only essential information was recorded. For example, Jean Alfonce wrote that the Portuguese colony founded on Cape Breton Island in 1524 was occasionally visited by Basque "traders," who sold goods to the colonists. A couple of years later, these traders reported that the colony had been wiped out and suggested that Indigenous peoples had killed the settlers.[10]

Who were these traders? Jean Alfonce emphasizes their role as news bearers, but in the most offhanded way. We may deduce that they offered European goods for sale, probably in exchange for fish, furs, and oil. As traders, they must have passed from one fishing haven to the next, selling their stores and taking on local produce. Similar traders are well documented in the seventeenth century. The emergence of a small, independent category of transatlantic traders has direct parallels in European coastal outfitting practices. In the Bay of Biscay, the practice of peddling stores and equipment to fishing captains on credit in their home ports was common. During the winter outfitting season, and, increasingly as the spring departure approached, Bordeaux merchants would send small ships loaded with cordage, cask, dried fish, beans, biscuits, wine, and other stores to Basque ports, without any prior purchase agreement. The captains, generally from a Saintonge port on the Gironde, were instructed to tie up in Saint-Jean-de-Luz, Pasajes, or San Sebastian for two weeks and hawk the cargo to fishing and whaling captains busily outfitting for Terra Nova. If the merchant was particularly lucky, the captain would return to Bordeaux with a cargo of fish, whale oil, or Mediterranean produce, such as fruit or olive oil that transited the Biscayan ports in winter. If not, the voyage was considered profitable if the Bordeaux products had been sold on credit, with debts to be repaid with interest in the fall. Selling credit in exchange for high-quality provisions was by far the Bordeaux merchant's most profitable way of capitalizing on the Terra Nova fishery.[11] Debts owed by fishermen to merchants were renewed every year with new offers of provisions. Similarly, Basque outfitters in San Sebastian sold credit and provisions to local ship owning cartels, although their proximity to the whalers made their commerce archivally less visible.[12]

While coastal trade from the Basque ports to Bordeaux was shared by both Gironde and Basque mariners, only vessels from the Gironde ports could carry Bordeaux merchandise south to the Basque ports. This coastal trade of fishing provisions continued from October through May, but disappeared in summer when the transatlantic fleet was in Terra Nova.[13] A part of the Saintonge coastal fleet may have continued to ply their trade in support of the transatlantic fishery by following the fleets to Terra Nova.

A study of annual shipping rhythms turns up other anomalies that are best explained by the presence of a secondary transatlantic trade, which filled an economic niche created by the long absence of the fishing fleets. On September 8, 1565, a 30-ton ship loaded with whale oil arrived in Dartmouth directly from Terra Nova.[14] The vessel's small size, its English home-port, and early return are anomalous in sixteenth-century whaling practice. On the other hand, English traders were adept at penetrating the Terra Nova fishery by peddling credit during the fishing season, thanks in part to the relative proximity of their home ports to New World fishing grounds. The arrival in Dartmouth of whale oil fits into this pattern of a secondary trade.[15] In doing so, English merchants were following practices that their competitors in Rouen, Nantes, Bordeaux, and San Sebastian had perfected on a regional scale, that is, providing fishing captains with dependable, "trademark" provisions and establishing ongoing credit relationships with them. One of the key archaeological "markers" of such sustained credit dependency is the provenance of ceramics found at fishing stations. On Basque sites, the dominance of coarse earthenware from pottery centres along the Garonne Valley marks the Bordeaux practice of selling credit for provisions. Competition from the Rouen and Bayonne merchants is illustrated by the archaeological presence of stoneware from the hinterlands of these cities. These stoneware containers, which were used to transport condiments such as butter, lard, meat conserves, and fruit, identify the trade and credit strategy of cities targeting Terra Nova fishermen.[16] Some cities succeeded in establishing permanent financial relationships with fishermen, but other cities dropped out as competition toughened. For example, in the mid-sixteenth century, merchants from Nantes built a fishing industry that is "marked"' archaeologically by Breton pottery, before fading out in the second half of the century.[17]

Avid merchants did not send fishermen to the isolation of the New World, but rather sought them out in their furthest transatlantic confines. Thus, seasonal shipping rhythms and fierce competition for selling credit and provisions formed the context for the emergence of a category of itinerant "traders" mentioned by Jean Alfonce. These traders carved a niche by easing the rigidity of the fishery's dominant fiscal timetable and improved communication between merchants in Europe and captains in Terra Nova, as well as among fishing crews stationed at various havens.

Natives

Itinerant traders were not the only external source of news in Terra Nova. Since the time of Jacques Cartier, groups of Natives voyaged along the coast from as far west as Gaspé to interact with the fishing crews. Although the exact nature of these early contacts is not documented, in August 1534, Cartier met a crew of men returning from the Strait of Belle-Isle; they were fully at ease in boarding the explorer's ship.[18] The men related that the cod fishermen had already sailed for Europe. This incident is remarkable in that it shows the long-distance voyaging abilities of Native navigators, as well as their familiarity with European technology and fishing schedules.

Evidence from the early colonial period indicates the ease with which Native navigators adopted European boats. The most notable case is that of the fishing shallop, called a *xalupa* by the Basques and a *chaloupe* by the French. These craft, about eight or nine metres long, were propelled by oars or sails and held six to eight people.[19] They were prefabricated in Europe and shipped as a disassembled kit to Terra Nova, where the ship's carpenter finished the construction. Once assembled, the shallops could not be returned to Europe and were left over winter in the fishing ports in Terra Nova. To protect the shallops from the weight of snow and the dry winter air, fishermen and harpooners sank them in shallow waters. Hundreds of shallops passed the winter this way. In one Mutriku (Gipuzkoa) contract, a Basque fishing captain sold ten shallops to another captain in 1606 and left instructions as to where to find them and how to recognize them. The craft lay behind the Trepassey barrachoix, to the left, and each was identified by two nails in the side and in the stem post.[20]

For some fishermen, it was more practical to leave the shallops in the hands of a trusted Native employee. A sales document of fishing shallops at Le Havre names two Natives, Rougefort and Jouanis, who had possession of the craft at Percé and were to point out the crafts' identifying marks indicated in the notarial act.[21] The Biscayan shallops were remarkably popular among Gulf and Atlantic Natives before the arrival of the first colonists. In 1607, English settlers on the way to Maine were met off the coast of Nova Scotia by Natives in a shallop; they spoke to them in French and wished to trade with them.[22] In spring 1605, while Marc Lescarbot and the Port-Royal colonists waited for supplies, their spirits rose whenever they espied a sail on the horizon but, each time, the mariners were Natives in shallops. Lescarbot also mentioned Natives sailing alongside French fishermen from St. Malo; the Natives had painted the symbol of a moose on their sail.[23] European craft brought power to those who possessed these boats. In 1607, the Micmac chief, Membertou, assembled a fleet of sixty shallops manned by 500 warriors for a raid on his neighbour.[24] Early colonists left many other surprising accounts of Micmac navigators in European shallops in the first decade of the seventeenth century.[25]

This wholesale adoption of European sailing technology was already underway in Cartier's time. It was a largely peaceable transfer, despite a dry remark by Nicolas Denys that Natives felt free to take these boats when they found them.[26] The cultural history of the sixteenth-century shallop indicates that relationships between fishermen and Natives were frequent and trusting. Fishermen arriving at their stations in spring could count on news from far inland and along the coast as soon as the Native custodians of their shallops hove into view. Coupled with the itinerant traders, Native news bearers kept fishermen abreast of events along the coast as they carried out their daily routines.

Barbers

Writing had a constant, broad based function in Basque fishing and whaling stations. It flourished as a collaborative business custom, which appears to have disappeared in the seventeenth century, when ships and crew were autonomous from spring through the fall so that captains could compete for choice fishing rooms on the Terra Nova shore.[27] When the sixteenth-century fishery is examined from a communications perspective, one gains the impression of a great degree of resource pooling, catch redistribution, and record keeping of the numerous financial transactions undertaken during the fishing season. Part of the need for record keeping stemmed from the system of shares in which crew members were shareholders in the voyage, receiving credit with each hogshead of whale oil stowed on the ship. Detailed record keeping was also needed because of the complex associations formed by Basque whalers and fishermen in Terra Nova, which gave rise to a large body of customary law known as the "Terra Nova customs" (*us y costumbres de Terra Nova*). A hint of the legitimacy of this summer haven customary law is contained in Anthony Parkhurst's 1578 observation that Basques were the "lords" of the ports in which they fished.[28] Their role has been seen as a precursor to seventeenth-century English custom, according to which the "admiral" of a haven was the captain of the first ship to arrive in spring. The English fishing admiral's duties included the administration of customary law among the captains, traders, and crewmen who populated the haven during the summer months.[29]

In many ways, the roles of sixteenth-century Basque lords and seventeenth-century English admirals were similar. However, unique features emerge when Basque commercial and judicial customs in Terra Nova are examined in the archives of the maritime court at Tolosa. The legal roles of ship owners, outfitters, and the crew (including officers) were precisely defined, the role of writing is great, and evidence gathering according to the Spanish inquest system had a broad demographic base. Ordinary seamen were seen as shareholders, not as employees or servants. When fault was alleged or discovered, the tendency was not to impugn the individual but rather to discover which contractual party in the whaling expedition would bear the financial loss created by the fault.[30] Arbitrary power was greatly restricted and customary sharing agreements undertaken in good faith in the summer havens were given the force of law. Ordinary witnesses frequently based their view of events on the so-called Terra Nova customs as they had taken shape since the 1540s.[31]

Joint strategies among Basque whaling expeditions within a given port typically included a sequence of ownership (agreed upon in advance) for whales brought into port by the harpooners, a system for progressively downsizing crews and releasing some ships for an early return as winter approached and navigation became more hazardous, and, above all, joint bookkeeping by the port barber. Repairs by carpenters and coopers, redistribution of material when a ship ran out of supplies or found itself with a surplus, storage of unused supplies, and, especially, crediting the various shareholders in the expedition with whale-oil barrels as they were safely stowed, required a trusted bookkeeper who knew the Terra Nova customs.[32]

Barbers, in addition to their primary functions as doctors and surgeons, fulfilled the role of port bookkeeper according to Basque practice. They also functioned as scribes who were mostly occupied by preferred employers, but they also acted as public scribes when matters of an individual nature arose. For example, the barber could take down a sailor's last will and testament, which could be transmitted to his beneficiaries. One of the earliest surviving documents to have been written in Canada is such a personal testament, dating to Christmas Day, 1572.[33] In a society where illiteracy was not a criterion for distinguishing social categories, the barber was sought after by captains and crewmen alike.[34]

Although surviving examples of writing in Terra Nova fishing stations are rare, the presence of writing in everyday fishing life is well attested, a result of a customary commercial structure that combined elements of Spanish judicial and notarial practices, Atlantic maritime law, and, especially, the Terra Nova customs. Perhaps Basque captains became the "lords" of the ports where they fished, as Anthony Parkhurst phrased it, because of the sophistication and legitimacy of their commercial practices and customary law based on the Spanish tradition of writing, rather than by arbitrary power or some competitive edge.

Procurers

Barbers may have originated the written word in Terra Nova, but standard business communication among captains and merchants relied on procurers. These bearers of instructions are well documented in period archives; an analysis of their periods of activity shows that they were accustomed to communicating business instructions while captains were in Terra Nova. While cod fishing vessels typically set sail in March or April and returned in September or October, whaling ships bound for southern Labrador left in June, after the ice left the Strait of Belle-Isle, and returned around Christmas. The Labrador context provides some of the most interesting examples of transatlantic communication during the fishing season. These examples concern the practice of insuring ships and cargo for the return voyage to the Basque Country, as revealed in the archives of the Merchants' Guild in Burgos.[35]

In the cod fishing industry of Bordeaux and Saint-Jean-de-Luz, merchants distributed the risks of spoilage, ship wreckage, and piracy by lending small amounts to the captains of many ships. Whaling voyages, on the other hand, involved much larger ships and a greater potential for loss, so they were insured like the expensive cargo. Basque merchants did not insure themselves for loss coverage, preferring the Merchants' Guild at Burgos, about 120 kilometres inland.[36] Since the Middle Ages, Burgos had been the seat of the Castillean wool trade and its merchants turned to maritime insurance as a way of participating in Spain's sixteenth-century acquisition of colonial wealth. The city was linked to ports by way of the Deba Valley, a well established communication route through the coastal mountains. In late May, the Basque merchants sent word to procurers in Burgos to purchase insurance on specific ships and their cargo with the amount of insurance required.

Various types of insurance were purchased. In some cases, only the ship was insured and in others, only the cargo, reflecting the division between shipowners and outfitters. Interestingly, the time period covered by the insurance also varied. Some policies covered the entire round trip, including short voyages from port to port in Terra Nova. For the outward voyage, outfitters insured "biscuit, wine, cider, ham, shaken hogsheads, and other tools, and all the food needed for the voyage and the fishery." On the homeward voyage, they insured the remaining equipment and food for the voyage home as well as the whale oil and other products obtained in Terra Nova.[37] The rate for round trip insurance was eight per cent of the value. Even though the insurance was purchased in May, payment was sometimes due in October, in advance of the whalers' return.[38] Significantly, some policies covered only the homeward voyage and included the whale oil and remaining outfit at a lower rate of five and a half per cent and were dated in November.[39] This economic saving was significant but, more importantly, it appears that precise insurance needs for the homeward journey were calculated on the basis of the ship's true cargo and the success of its fishery.

Sometime in October, the shipowners and outfitters on the Basque coast sent word to the Burgos procurer of the level of insurance needed for the return voyage from Terra Nova. The timing of the requests coincided with the return of the cod fishing fleet in October and suggests that whaling captains in Labrador arranged to send messages home to their business partners. Many factors affected the amount of insurance required: The progress of the hunt, the number of whales in the Strait, the activity of rival fishermen, tensions between international crews, and the health of the men all affected the rate of work and determined the number of hogsheads to be insured for the return voyage. By early September, when the cod ships hurried back to the European markets, the general outcome of the season could be announced. Rather than buying unnecessary insurance in spring, the Burgos procurer purchased the appropriate policy in October. Whaling ships arriving in June or July at Terra Nova could depend on the cod fishermen departing in August to carry instructions to the Basque Country. By this time, the state of shore installations, the degree of whaling competition, and the number of whales in the strait were known. These factors greatly affected the whale catch, as ships returned with loads varying from a quarter to full capacity with an average of about 75 per cent capacity.[40] As a result, the amount of insurance required also varied, making communication with business partners back in the Basque Country a priority.

Pilots

Traders, Natives, barbers, procurers, and staggered sailing schedules all contributed in unique ways to communications in the sixteenth-century fishery. The most critical role, however, belonged to the pilots who directed ships across the Atlantic with precision and largely without loss of life or material. Whalers leaving from the deepwater port of Pasajes would make their way slowly westward, stopping at the ports that studded the rocky coast, while the captain went ashore to sign on sailors and tradesmen. Once this coastal procession was completed, the pilot pushed away from the coast, keeping it at a safe distance until he recognized the coast of Asturias:

When leaving this coast, they take a bearing from 15 leagues [85 kilometres] at sea on the Cape de las Penas, which is in Asturias and two leagues from Gijon. From here, they go west-north-west until fifty-two degrees and a half where the Grande Baie (the entrance to the Gulf of St. Lawrence) is found, touching neither land nor isle, for the whole distance of eight hundred leagues is an abyss.[41]

Pilots knew they were within forty leagues of the Grand Banks when they began to notice large flocks of birds called *faulquetz* and *marmyons*, a small bird. These birds, according to Jean Cordier of Rouen, would convoy the pilot to the edge of the banks, and, as soon as they disappeared, the pilot could begin sounding to find the soil of the Banks.[42]

A reliance on seamarks, landmarks, and the compass was part of the Atlantic pilot's lore since the Middle Ages. As well, the constant use of soundings distinguished the Atlantic pilot from his Mediterranean counterpart. Atlantic pilots found their way by "treading" along the ocean bottom, sending down a lead sound to measure the depth and then bringing up a sample of the bottom using a lump of wax. Sand, marl, silt, or any combination, mentally cross-referenced to depth, told the pilot his location. His second tool was the compass, which he used to set his bearings and as a timepiece to indicate when the tide would turn by measuring the angle of the moon in the sky. In foggy conditions, the Atlantic pilot would not hesitate as long as he knew open water lay ahead, since his art only depended on celestial sightings to verify his latitude every few days. When coasting, he pushed away from southern shores to avoid the offshore wind and the inevitable shoals and hugged the rockier, windward northern coasts. These coasting principles that guided him safely through the English Channel were also applied when traversing the Strait of Belle-Isle or penetrating the Gulf of St. Lawrence.[43]

Ultimately, communications in the sixteenth-century fishery depended on the pilot's art and on his mental template of the North Atlantic. News gathering in Terra Nova, the recording of essential information, and the transmittal of written instructions to Europe were a sophisticated superstructure that relied on oral skills, in turn, founded on pure experience. In this respect, the historian's traditional paradigm of transatlantic communication remains hard to challenge.

Conclusion

The sixteenth century remains a distinctive, difficult period in Canadian history, but the myth of isolation and secret that clings to the fishery is not entirely accurate. News gathering and sharing in the Terra Nova havens depended not only on chance meetings with other crews, but was facilitated by itinerant traders and Native mariners who were attracted to the fishing stations. Formal, written communication was based on the need for sound record keeping and on the Basque tradition of customary law, as well as on planned communication with procurers, insurers, and business partners back home. The staggered timetables of cod and whale fishing allowed transatlantic communication during the fishing season. In the end, however, all depended on the pilots and their experience. When the fisheries are examined from a communications standpoint, sixteenth-century sources gain a new meaning. While absence had deep social effects, isolation was not a matter of course for fishermen and they remained embedded in a network of communication possibilities, even in Terra Nova.

Notes

1. Archives départementales de Gironde (Bordeaux) (hereafter ADG), series 3E (especially notaries Berthet, Brigot, Cazamajour, Duprat, Faure, Payron, and Soteau for the 1560s).
2. Laurier Turgeon, "Bordeaux and the Newfoundland Trade during the Sixteenth Century," *International Journal of Maritime History* 9, no. 2 (1997): 1–28.
3. Alain Cabantous, *Les citoyens du large: Les identités maritimes en France (XVIIᵉ–XIXᵉ siècle)* (Paris: Aubier, 1995), pp. 120–131.
4. Archivo General de Gupuzkoa (Tolosa), hereafter AGG.
5. Archivo de la Real Chancelleria (Zaragosa) (hereafter ARCh), Pleitos civiles, Perez Alonso fenecidos 455-1, n.f. (1570; the witness is 64 years old and claims 40 years of whaling experience in Terra Nova); Pleitos civiles, Rodriguez fenecidos 54, caja 312-1, fo. 26v-27r (1575; the witness claims 35 years of whaling experience in Terra Nova); ibid., fo. 60v (1575; the witness recalls that the Terra Nova whale fishery began in 1543); ibid., fo. 125v (1575; the witness has 25 years of experience). See also AGG, Civiles Lecuona, legajo 9, expediente 219, fo. 48v (1596; the witness has been on about 20 whaling voyages); ibid., fo. 51v (1596; the witness claims more than 50 years of whaling and cod fishing voyages); ibid., fo. 134v (1596; the witness has 35 years of experience on whaling and fishing voyages); AGG, Civiles Mandiola, legajo 369, fo. 46v (1587; the witness has 22 years of experience as a harpooner and captain-outfitter); ibid., legajo 424, fo. 34r (1591; the witness has about 20 years of experience as a cooper). See Henry Harrisse, *Découverte et évolution cartographique de Terre-Neuve* (Paris: Welter, 1900), p. lix: In 1561, a witness aged 70 declared that the Terra Nova whale hunt is 17 to 20 years old.
6. ADG, series 3E. See Brad Loewen, "Les barriques de Red Bay et l'espace atlantique septentional, vers 1565," (Ph.D. dissertation, Québec: Université Laval, 1999), pp. 182–195.
7. Selma (Huxley) Barkham, "Guipuzcoan Shipping in 1571 with Particular Reference to the Decline of the Transatlantic Fishing Industry," in *Anglo-American Contributions to Basque Studies: Essays in Honor of Jon Bilbao*, 3 (Reno: Desert Research Institute, 1977), pp. 1–9.
8. Loewen, "Les barriques de Red Bay," pp. 182–195.
9. See Matthew Johnson, *An Archaeology of Capitalism* (Oxford: Blackwell, 1996).
10. Jean Alfonce, *Les voyages aventureux* (Poitiers: Pélican, 1559), pp. 23v–28v. See Jean Alfonce, "Le routier," in *Voyages de découverte au Canada entre les années 1534 et 1542* (Québec: Cowan, 1843).
11. Loewen, "Les barriques de Red Bay," pp. 83–91.
12. Selma (Huxley) Barkham, "Los Vascos y las pescerias transatlanticas, 1517–1713," in *Itsasoa 3. Los Vascos en en marco Atlantico Norte. Siglos XVI y XVII*, eds, E. Ayerbe and S. (Huxley) Barkham (San Sebastian: ETOR, 1988), pp. 26–164 and appendices. See Jean-Pierre Proulx, *Les Basques et la pêche à la baleine au Labrador au XVIᵉ siècle* (Ottawa: Parks Canada, 1993).
13. Jacques Bernard, writing of seasonal shipping rhythms in the French Atlantic, has suggested that the summer season was devoted to repairs, ahead of the busy fall and winter season of hauling Aquitainian products to the Channel countries, and returning with textiles, cereals, shaken cask, tar, and linseed oil, in *Navires et gens de mer à Bordeaux, 1400–1500*, 3 vols (Paris:

SEVPEN, 1968), tables in volume 3. The Atlantic rhythm of a summer low season and a winter high season contrasts with that of the Mediterranean at the same period: "L'hivernage est ... la règle normale, une si bonne règle que longtemps les villes et les États soucieux d'ordre interdisent purement et simplement les voyages hivernaux. Encore en 1569, à Venise, ils étaient prohibés 'su'l cuor dell'invernata', du 15 novembre au 20 janvier. De leur côté, les Levantins ne naviguaient que de la Saint-Georges à la Saint-Dimitri (5 mai–26 octobre, selon les dates du calendrier grec)." Fernand Braudel, "La mer," in *La Méditerranée: L'espace et l'histoire*, ed. F. Braudel (Paris: Flammarion, 1985), p. 64.

14. Public Records Office (Kew) (hereafter PRO), Port Books, E190-925-5, fo. 12. For other 1565 whale oil arrivals, some very early in the season, see PRO, E190-925-3, fo. 1 (Ilfracombe, May 7, 1565); E190-925-10, s.f. (Barnstaple, May 27, 1565); E190-587-2 (Ipswich, July 13 and August 24, 1565); E190-587-4, n.f. (Ipswich, November 19, 1565).

15. Peter E. Pope, *Fish into Wine: The Newfoundland Plantation in the Seventeenth Century* (Chapel Hill: University of North Carolina Press, 2004), pp. 98–116 (on trading "sack ships"), and Peter E. Pope, "The European Occupation of Southeast Newfoundland: Archaeological Perspectives on Competition for Fishing Rooms, 1530–1680," in *Mer et Monde: Questions d'archéologie maritime*, eds C. Roy et al. (Québec: Association des archéologues du Québec, 2003), pp. 122–133.

16. Brad Loewen, "Céramiques françaises et réseaux de commerce transatlantiques aux XVIe et XVIIe siècles," in *Champlain ou les portes du Nouveau Monde: Cinq siècles d'échanges entre le Centre-Ouest français et l'Amérique du Nord*, eds M. Augeron and D. Guillemet (La Crèche: Geste, 2004), pp. 217–221.

17. Pope, "The European Occupation of Southeast Newfoundland."

18. Jacques Cartier, *Voyages au Canada* (Paris: La Découverte, 1992), p. 154 (Natashquan, August 5, 1534): "... vinrent deux barques, environ douze hommes, qui vinrent aussi franchement à bord de nos navires que s'ils eussent été français. Ils nous firent comprendre qu'ils venaient de la Grande Baie, et qu'ils appartenaient au capitaine Thiennot, lequel était sur le cap, nous faisant signe qu'ils s'en retournaient dans leur pays, vers là d'où nous venions; et que les navires avaient appareillé de la dite baie, tous chargés de poisson. Nous nommâmes le dit cap le cap Thiennot."

19. An archaeological example is displayed at Red Bay, Labrador.

20. Archivo Historico Provincial de Gipuzkoa (Onati) (hereafter AHPG), partido de Vergara, legajo 2598, reg. 3, fo. 50 (Mutriku, April 13, 1606), reproduced in Selma (Huxley) Barkham, "Los Vascos y las pescerias transatlanticas, 1517–1713," p. 185, doc. 78: "... recibir tomar y sacar en el puerto del Trespas en la Provincia de Terranoba en alaguna que en el dicho puerto se aze yendo por el fundamen adelante el grao llamado Varrachoa, y se aze dicha alaguna a mano yzquierda como vamos al dicho Barrachoa diez chalupas que dexe bebaxo de agua el ano passado de seisceintos y cinco ... y tienen por senas las dichas chalupas a dos aguxeros con varreno del costado en el branque de proa y en la amara y en el say por partes de dentro, ye estan como dicho es en la dicha alaguna por la mano izquierdo y por la otra parte se aze la mar ..."

21. Archives départementales de Seine-Maritime (Rouen), 2E 70/119 (notary Martin Frequet, Le Havre 1608). Thanks to Bernard Allaire for bringing this reference to my attention.

22. "This illand standeth in the lattitude of 44 d[egrees] and 1/2 and hear we had not ben att an anker past to howers beffore we espyed a Bisken shallop cominge towards us, havinge in her eyght Sallvages and a Lyttell salvage boye," Anonymous English colonist, "Relation of a Voyage to Sagadohoc, 1607," in Ruth Holmes Whitehead, *The Old Man Told Us: Excerpts from Micmac History, 1500–1800* (Halifax : Nimbus, 1991), pp. 28–29.

23. Marc Lescarbot, *Histoire de la Nouvelle France* (Paris: chez Jean Milo, 1609), p. 628: "[Les colons] prenaient bien souvent les chaloupes sauvages ... pour les chaloupes Françoises," and

p. 577: "deux chaloupes, l'une chargée de Sauvages, qui avoient un Ellan peint à leur voile; l'autre François Maloins, qui faisoient leur pecherie au port de Campseau."

24. Ruth Holmes Whitehead, "Navigation des Micmacs le long de la côte de l'Atlantique," in *Les Micmacs et la Mer*, ed. Charles A. Martin (Montréal: Recherches amérindiennes au Québec, 1986), pp. 227–232.

25. Whitehead, *The Old Man Told Us*, pp. 20–30.

26. Nicolas Denys, *Description géographique et historique des costes de l'Amérique septentionale avec l'Histoire naturelle du païs*, 2 vols (Paris: Claude Barbin, 1672), p. 180: "Il est bon de remarquer que les Sauvages de la côte ne se servent de canots que pour les rivières & ont tous des chalouppes pour la mer, qu'ils acheptent quelques fois des Capitaines qui sont sur leur départ, après avoir achevé leur pesche, mais la plupart les prennent où les Capitaines les ont fait cacher à la côte ou dans les étans pour s'en servir en un autre voyage."

27. Pope, "The European Occupation of Southeast Newfoundland."

28. Anthony Parkhurst, November 13, 1578, in Richard Hakluyt, *The Principall Navigations* (London: 1599), I, pp. 132–134.

29. Pope, *Fish into Wine*, p. 257.

30. AGG, Civiles Mandiola, 424 (1591), fo. 41v–42v.

31. Loewen, "Les barriques de Red Bay," pp. 235–241.

32. Among many examples, see AGG, Civiles Elorza, legajo 65 (1565).

33. Selma (Huxley) Barkham, "Two documents written in Labrador, 1572 and 1577," *Canadian Historical Review* 57, no. 2 (1976): 235–238. On scribes, see Christine Métayer, *Au tombeau des secrets: Les écrivains publics du Paris populaire: Cimetière des Saints-Innocents, XVIᵉ-XVIIIᵉ siècle* (Paris: Albin Michel, 2000).

34. Brad Loewen, "Les 'signatures graphiques' de Red Bay et l'extension du capitalisme en Atlantique, vers 1565" *Archéologiques* 11–12 (1997–1998): 213–222.

35. Archivo de la Diputacion de Burgos (hereafter ADB).

36. Selma (Huxley) Barkham, "Burgos Insurance for Basque Ships: Maritime Policies from Spain, 1547–1592," *Archivaria* 11 (1980–1981): 53–95.

37. ADB, 95, fo. 20r (May 29, 1565): "sobre pan bino sidra toçino barricas abatidas y otros qualquier pertrechos y armaçon neçessarios para su biaje y pesca, y a la vuelta sobre lo dicho y sobre grasas y otras qualquier mercaderias."

38. ADB, 95, fo. 13 (May 24, 1567): "sobre armaçon y todo el bastimens y pertrechos nesçesarios para el byaje y pesca de dichas ballenas, y de estada en dicha Terrannoba y puertos della y en un puerto a otro, y de buelta a Portugalete sobre el armaçon y pesca pertenesçientes al dicho Jhoan Martinez de Mendia a catorze por çiento a pagar en otubre de 1567."

39. ADB, 95, fo. 135r, n.d. (November 1565): "sobre la pesca de grasas y pesca de ballenas y sobra la armaçon, pertrechos y bituallas nescessarias para su biaje y pesca."

40. Proulx, *Les Basques et la pêche à la baleine*.

41. Archivo general de Simancas, GA 75/24 (Cristobal de Barros, 1571). Cited in Barkham, "Los Vascos y las pescerias transatlanticas, 1517–1713," p. 58, note 10 : "Quando parten de esta costa recononcen las penas de Goçon como a XV leguas la mar adentro, que es en Asturias a dos leguas de Jijon, y de alli ban al osnorueste hasta çinquenta y dos grados y medio donde esta la Gran Baya sin topar tierra ni ysla, sino todo es un golfo de ocho zientas leguas."

42. Cited in Michel Mollat, *La vie quotidienne des gens de mer en Atlantique, IXᵉ au XVIᵉ siècle* (Paris: Hachette, 1983), p. 191.

43. Albrecht Sauer, Das 'Seebuch': *Das älteste erhaltene Seehandbuch und die spätmittelalterliche Navigation in Nordwesteuropa* (Bremen: Kagel, 1996).

LA FILIÈRE MORUTIÈRE NORMANO-BRETONNE

18

Capitaines et habitants pêcheurs de l'île Scatarie (1714-1754)

Jean-Pierre Chrestien, conservateur, Musée canadien des civilisations

Remerciements Je suis très reconnaissant à Nelson Cazeils et à John Willis d'avoir accepté de lire cet article en fin de rédaction. Je les remercie de leurs suggestions, de leurs commentaires toujours pertinents et de leurs encouragements amicaux.

JPC

Résumé

Au lendemain de la signature du traité d'Utrecht, les résidants français de Terre-Neuve sont rapatriés à l'île du Cap-Breton. Simultanément à l'établissement de Louisbourg, des concessions sont accordées dans plusieurs îles et baies environnantes. L'île Scatarie est réservée aux capitaines de France pour la pêche d'été. Cependant, les officiers et les pêcheurs qui ne peuvent trouver un emplacement dans le havre de Louisbourg, obtiennent une concession sur l'île. Scatarie connaît un peuplement prometteur. Bientôt, 22 familles de pêcheurs y sont établies. Des navires viennent, de Saint-Malo, de Granville et de Bayonne, pêcher et approvisionner les insulaires. Mais après quelques années, la population décroît. Le nombre de chaloupes de pêche diminue. Des bateaux sont armés pour la pêche sur les bancs éloignés. Les campagnes de pêche des navires de France sont moins nombreuses et plus irrégulières. Leurs capitaines viennent échanger du sel, des vivres et du gréement contre des morues sèches pêchées et conditionnées par les insulaires. Ils transportent des passagers et des engagés pour les habitants pêcheurs. Leurs allées et venues sporadiques laissent l'île ouverte aux navires « américains » en dépit des interdictions. Les rapports des capitaines marchands et des officiers français de passage brossent un tableau de l'île, de sa population et de leurs relations avec les insulaires. Les témoignages des officiers du navire *Le Saint-Jean*, de Saint-Malo, sont particulièrement révélateurs de la vie quotidienne à Scatarie, du pouvoir des capitaines, des conflits entre officiers et des difficultés de communication à partir d'une île située aux confins de l'Amérique.

Abstract

Following the signing of the Treaty of Utrecht, the French residents of Newfoundland were repatriated to the island of Cape Breton. At the same time Louisbourg was being established, land concessions were being handed out on several nearby islands and bays. Île Scatarie was reserved for French naval captains for the summer fishing season. In addition, naval officers and fishermen who could not find a berth in Louisbourg harbour were also given concessions on the island.

At first, population growth at Scatarie was promising, with twenty-two fishermen and their families quickly settling there. Ships came from Saint-Malo, Granville, and Bayonne, fishing off the coast and provisioning the islanders. After several years, however, the population began to decrease. The number of fishing sloops diminished. Boats were now being equipped for fishing on the more distant Grand Banks. Fishing expeditions by French ships were fewer and less frequent. They still, however, came to trade salt, provisions and rigging for the salt cod which had been caught and treated by the islanders. The ships also transported passengers and workers for the fishermen-settlers. These sporadic comings and goings left the island open to "American" ships, despite existing bans. Reports by merchant captains and passing French officers paint a picture of the island, its people and the writers' relations with the islanders. Firsthand accounts from the officers of the ship *Saint-Jean*, out of Saint-Malo, are particularly revealing of daily life at Scatarie, as well as of the power of ship captains, conflicts between officers, and the communication difficulties for an island situated on the outermost fringes of North America.

Introduction

Pendant quarante ans, entre 1714 et 1754, des capitaines marchands, des officiers coloniaux, des navigateurs et hydrographes français ont visité l'île Scatarie dans le cadre de leurs activités. Au cours de leurs séjours, ils entrent en contact avec les habitants pêcheurs[1], ils identifient les gens présents, témoignent des évènements, dépeignent le milieu et divers aspects de la vie quotidienne des insulaires.

Nous connaissons les opérations de la pêche et du conditionnement de la morue grâce au traité de Duhamel du Monceau[2]. Les ouvrages de Balcom[3] et de Clark[4] ont situé Scatarie dans l'économie de l'île Royale. Préalablement à des recherches archéologiques sur l'île Scatarie, nous avons profité de dépouillements dans les archives de l'amirauté de Saint-Malo et les archives coloniales françaises pour nous approcher des habitants pêcheurs qui ont vécu sur cette île entre 1714 et 1758. Les recensements[5] et les archives notariales[6] nous ont offert des rencontres avec les insulaires et les capitaines marchands qui venaient partager leurs pêches et les approvisionner. Leurs rapports, les contrats et les requêtes nous révèlent des bribes de l'histoire de ces gens souvent originaires des environs du golfe de Saint-Malo. Ils nous font entrevoir les allées et venues des navires de commerce et les liens qui unissent ces insulaires à un réseau d'échanges privilégiés entre Scatarie, Louisbourg, Saint-Malo (Bretagne), Granville (Normandie) et parfois les colonies de la Nouvelle-Angleterre. Nous explorerons quelques évènements révélateurs des tensions sociales françaises et des conflits opposant marins français et anglais. En bref, nous tenterons de mettre en évidence quelques signes de changements sur cette petite île tout comme en France.

Une visite tumultueuse et révélatrice

Le 6 août 1732, dans le havre de l'île Scatarie, des capitaines marchands et quelques insulaires s'apprêtent à dîner à bord d'un vaisseau « américain »[7]. Soudain un matelot du navire *Le Saint-Jean*, de Saint-Malo, mouillé à portée de voix, perturbe la célébration par ses cris au capitaine Moysan de La Marette, un des convives. Moysan a déjà assez bu et il a du mal à reconnaître René Marie[8], qui vient annoncer une mauvaise nouvelle. Le pilote, second officier, Pierre Le Buffe de Vaujoyeux est mourant. Moysan renonce avec regret au repas et se rend sur son navire accompagné par quelques officiers malouins et le chirurgien de Scatarie, Sollet Le Cluzeau[9].

Le Buffe de Vaujoyeux, un jeune noble breton, est tombé de faiblesse à bord du *Saint-Jean* et a perdu conscience. Il ne parvient plus à respirer. Sollet lui enlève sa cravate et lui pratique une incision à la base du cou (trachéotomie) pour rétablir le passage de l'air. Vaujoyeux rend du sang coagulé et revient à la vie. Pendant ce temps, Moysan qui a obtenu la clé du coffre de Vaujoyeux en retire une belle chemise de batiste pour lui faire des bandages et des compresses. On descend le jeune homme à terre et on le porte chez le chirurgien, qui vit avec son épouse, trois enfants et un domestique, près de l'*anse Darambourg*[10] Sollet prendra soin de Vaujoyeux pendant 15 jours de convalescence, il lui procurera les médicaments et les aliments nécessaires.

Une fois sur pied, Vaujoyeux se rend à bord du navire, y prend sa veste et redescend à terre. Certaines personnes ont rapporté qu'il vagabonde, chasse et boit avec les engagés, qu'il vit de rapines en libertin, vendant aux habitants de l'île des rubans et autres menus articles dérobés sur *Le Saint-Jean*. Moysan affirme qu'il lui avait volé 244 hameçons.

Le 3 septembre, le capitaine Moysan, furieux de l'absence prolongée de Vaujoyeux, réunit quelques capitaines et des habitants de Scatarie. Il fait rédiger un procès-verbal dans lequel il accuse Vaujoyeux de sédition et de mutinerie. Il proteste contre la désertion de son second, tombé malade « par son dérangement et malversation », qui passe son temps à courir et à boire avec les engagés des insulaires. Plusieurs personnes signent le procès verbal : François-Louis Merven de la Rivière, capitaine du navire *Le Henry,* de Saint-Malo[11], Martico DiBaignette, capitaine de *L'Aigle*[12], de Bayonne, Élie Thesson Laflourie, propriétaire pêcheur prospère, de Scatarie, Pierre Henry Le Paumier, commis de Laflourie et François Michel Lebreton, originaire de Granville, habitant pêcheur agissant comme notaire sur l'île.

Quelques jours plus tard, son document en main, le capitaine Moysan se rend à Louisbourg porter plainte auprès de Monsieur Le Vasseur, lieutenant général de l'amirauté, contre Vaujoyeux qui s'est « dérangé de son devoir » pendant toute la traversée. Moysan exige le retour à bord de son second, il explique que l'absence de l'officier l'empêche de vaquer à ses affaires et qu'il lui est impossible de laisser son navire aux matelots pendant qu'il va négocier et acheter sa cargaison de morue. Il réclame la permission d'engager un autre officier si Vaujoyeux ne regagne son poste. Une mise en demeure est présentée à Vaujoyeux, le 15 septembre, devant témoins à Scatarie. On lui intime l'ordre de revenir sur le navire dans les 24 heures. Vaujoyeux obtempère. Il demeura à bord trois jours. Mais le 18, entre 10 et 11 heures du soir, il s'embarque dans la chaloupe qui ramène les matelots qui sont allés dîner chez un habitant de l'île; il ne reviendra pas. Désirant aller à Louisbourg, Vaujoyeux demande passage à un compatriote, Pierre Chamelin, maître de chaloupe. L'engagé lui répond qu'il n'est pas son maître et qu'il faut demander à sa maîtresse. Madame Laflourie (Simone Million) aimerait bien l'aider, mais elle craint de se brouiller avec le capitaine Moysan[13] !

Le troisième capitaine du vaisseau *Le Henry* de Saint-Malo, François Lefebvre[14], a déposé sous serment que, lorsqu'il était à Scatarie, il a vu Vaujoyeux malade. Ce dernier lui a affirmé avoir été maltraité par son capitaine, ce que le chirurgien a confirmé. Un jour, alors que Lefebvre réparait son navire, Vaujoyeux ayant appris qu'il devait se rendre à Louisbourg, lui demande passage pour aller porter plainte contre Moysan. Il souhaite également obtenir six mois de vivres en échange d'eau-de-vie de la cargaison du *Saint-Jean*. Lefebvre lui répond qu'il ne le transportera pas sans un congé du capitaine Moysan. Sur ce refus, Vaujoyeux lui remet une lettre à porter au Sieur Desmarest, greffier de l'Amirauté de Louisbourg[15]. Mais la lettre est mouillée pendant l'embarquement de Lefebvre qui la laisse à sécher dans sa chambre. À son retour à Scatarie, il la confiera au chirurgien en le priant de bien vouloir la transmettre à Desmarest. La plainte de Vaujoyeux est revenue à son point de départ.

L'automne s'annonçait orageux. Le 14 octobre, vers 3 heures de l'après-midi, Martico DiBaignette est à faire peser et embarquer de la morue sur la grave[16] de Thesson Laflourie avec deux autres habitants, les frères Louis et Charles Lebon. Soudain de la fumée noire commence à s'échapper de la poupe du navire de 110 tonneaux, *L'Aigle,* de Bayonne. Le capitaine DiBaignette, son équipage et tous les gens présents courent et rament jusqu'au navire. Le feu s'est déclaré dans la soute et fait rage avec tant de violence que l'on est forcé d'abattre le gaillard et de percer des ouvertures dans le plat-bord pour porter de l'eau jusqu'au brasier. On parvient enfin à maîtriser l'incendie. Pendant la nuit, le vent soufflera avec tant de violence que tous les navires présents dans le havre seront chassés sur leurs ancres[17]. DiBaignette sera obligé de quitter l'île pour faire réparer son navire, car le havre de Scatarie n'est pas convenable pour ces travaux. De plus, le bois manque toujours sur l'île et il faut aller le chercher dans la baie de Miré ou à Niganiche[18].

Le 20 octobre, Vaujoyeux est toujours absent. Moysan proteste. Certains affirment qu'il est « en maraude », « buvant avec des *trente-six mois* »[19], « battant la côte » ou courant les bois selon Louis Chenu du Clos et Joseph Châtel, officiers du navire *Le George,* de Saint-Malo[20].

Une île méconnue

Situons tout d'abord cette île confondue au *cap Breton*. À la fin du XVIIe siècle, les cartes montrant Scatarie présentent une île de forme superficielle et erronée. Le cartographe, encore ignorant de sa topographie, la dessine selon ce qu'il veut mettre en évidence. Scatarie s'avance au sud-est de l'île du Cap-Breton juste avant l'entrée du golfe du Saint-Laurent. Une carte de Nicolas Sanson, datée de 1656, identifie l'île *Scatori*[21]. (Figure 18.1 et 18.2) L'origine de ce toponyme variable, *Scatori, Scatari, Scatarie* ou *Scatary,* est

Figure 18.1 *Le Canada, ou Nouvelle France*, par Nicolas Sanson d'Abbeville, 1656.
Bibliothèque et Archives Canada, NMC-21100.

Figure 18.2 Détail montrant l'île *Scatori* avec le Cap-Breton, Terre-Neuve et le golfe Saint-Laurent.
Bibliothèque et Archives Canada, NMC-21100.

incertaine. Provient-il du portugais, du basque ou est-ce tout simplement la déformation de *S.CATARI*, signifiant Sainte-Catherine[22], patronne des marins basques, normands, rochellais, ou de la chapelle de Scatarie ? Dès 1714, les cartes montrent le havre de Scatarie à la pointe sud-est de l'île. Vers 1725, l'île voisine appelée *La Tremblade* borde ce havre qui sera identifié formellement en 1732. La forme de l'île Scatarie est encore très imparfaite, mais sa pointe sud est déjà nommée Laflourie, du nom de son occupant. En 1735, deux havres, le petit et le grand, dominent la partie est de l'île qui prend la forme d'une main ou d'une faucille[23]. Cette année-là, à la suite du naufrage du vaisseau *Le Chameau*, le pilote Latour Cruchon, à bord du *Diligent*, avec Morpain, capitaine de port de l'île Royale, a été envoyé à la découverte des hauts fonds entourant Scatarie. Une carte anonyme, datée de la même année, est peut-être le fruit de leur relevé[24].

Il faut attendre le rapport de voyage de Monsieur de Chabert pour découvrir enfin une île qui s'approche de la réalité géographique. Selon Chabert, l'île Scatarie, située à la pointe sud-est de l'île Royale, « est le lieu de l'*atterrage* ordinaire de tous les vaisseaux qui viennent à Louisbourg ». Peu élevée, comme toutes les côtes méridionales de l'île Royale, on la découvre depuis six à sept lieues (30 à 35 km) de distance et on la reconnaît facilement par sa situation, avec ses collines en partie couvertes d'arbres rabougris. Son côté nord-est est bas, dénudé, et l'on aperçoit deux îlots noirs au bout de sa pointe, *les Cormorandières*[25].

Les 27 et 28 octobre 1750, par gros vents et la mer fort agitée, Chabert se rend sur l'île Scatarie en chaloupe de pêche pour observer et mesurer la latitude de la pointe nord-est par rapport à Louisbourg. Il décrit brièvement l'île de « figure à peu près triangulaire » qui fait environ dix kilomètres de longueur est-ouest par moins de cinq. Il la représentera sur une de ses cartes particulières.

Scatarie est séparée de l'île Royale par un bras de mer de deux kilomètres qu'on appelle le passage de *Menadou*. Selon Chabert : « … la petite île de la Tremblade… », située du côté sud-est de Scatarie, forme « … un petit port où il ne peut tenir qu'un ou deux bâtiments de 100 tonneaux au plus, l'entrée en est même périlleuse, il y a … quelques anses autour de l'isle où les habitants sont établis pour la pêche, mais ils y trouvent à peine un abri pour leurs chaloupes lorsqu'il fait mauvais temps. » Les habitants de Scatarie appellent « *islots de la gueule d'enfer…* » les rochers noirs des *Cormorandières* situés à l'est de la pointe du nord-est, car le petit intervalle qui les sépare de la pointe permet le passage des chaloupes. « Le sol de l'isle de *Scatari* est couvert de mousse encore plus légère que dans aucun autre endroit de ce pays, on y enfonce, presque partout … on y trouve un grand ruisseau, plusieurs petits, & des barachois, surtout dans la partie orientale[26]. »

Pendant son séjour, Chabert loge dans la cabane d'un habitant, sans doute construite en piquets de bois comme le sont souvent les bâtisses des pêcheurs français à Terre-Neuve et à l'île Royale[27]. Cette cabane est trop basse pour permettre à l'hydrographe d'y installer son quart de cercle et mesurer le méridien. Les insulaires construisent ces cabanes basses pour éviter de faire obstacle aux vents violents de la mer. Ceux-ci emporteront la tente de Chabert, tandis que la mer crèvera sa chaloupe, perturbant tous ses plans.

Cette année-là (1750), la gelée et la neige ont commencé dès le 2 novembre[28]. Quelques jours plus tard, Chabert doit rentrer à Louisbourg en profitant de la chaloupe d'un habitant de Scatarie. Les insulaires vont souvent à Louisbourg pour leurs affaires, pour passer un contrat devant le notaire et pour obtenir justice. La capitale de l'île Royale n'est qu'à 25 kilomètres. Chabert y passera l'hiver et découvrira la poudrerie et les rigueurs du froid hivernal. Puis vers la fin de février, il sera étonné de voir l'envahissement des glaces descendues du golfe Saint-Laurent qui couvrent la mer à perte de vue « s'entrechoquant en se brisant sur le rivage[29] ». On peut imaginer l'isolement des habitants de Scatarie pendant ce temps de l'année !

Le peuplement de Scatarie

Trente-cinq ans avant la visite de M. de Chabert, un plan de la grave de l'île Scatarie a été dessiné par Dupont de Teillene[30]. S'agit-il de ce plan anonyme (Figure 18.3) et sans date, intitulé « Thoisé de la grave de lisle Ponchartrain » ? Ce dernier montre les concessions accordées sur l'île. Il situe les chafauds, les habitations, les emplacements occupés ainsi qu'une chapelle[31].

En 1714, les autorités de l'île Royale ont attribué des concessions aux habitants rapatriés de Terre-Neuve, mais plusieurs n'ont pu trouver place autour du havre de Louisbourg. Le gouverneur, De Costebelle, et le commissaire-ordonnateur, Soubras, ont distribué des graves au sud-est de l'île Scatarie, appelée *île Pontchartrain* en l'honneur du ministre. Le lieutenant du roi, St-Ovide de Brouillan, s'est réservé la pointe est de la *Grande Grave*. Il est entouré de quelques capitaines marchands, officiers, fonctionnaires ou amis. D'est en ouest, on trouve la concession de Vincent Desmarais qui partage sa grave avec le capitaine Olivier Orange de Bellesève, commandant du navire *Le Maure*, de Granville, armé par François Baillon de Blanc-Pignon[32]. St-Ovide accapare deux emplacements stratégiques qui donnent sur le havre. Suivent les concessions de Comer dit Lachapelle, de « De Carré[33] » et celle de Benjamin Le Manquet[34]. À l'ouest de la chapelle, on aperçoit la grave du sieur Laussois, suivi de celles de Jean Durant, de Julien Durant, de Jean Michel et enfin celle de Clos Petit. Les capitaines « Du Parque »[35] et « Lenage »[36] ont dû s'accommoder d'anses isolées beaucoup plus loin au sud-ouest de l'île.[37] En 1718, les brevets de concessions nous apprennent que l'île de la Tremblade, bordant le havre, a été partagée entre Jean Million, François Lénée[38] et Jean Spart[39].

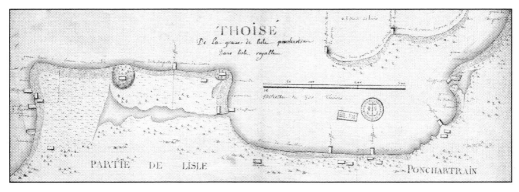

Figure 18.3 Plan ou toisé de la grave de l'île Pontchartrain, vers 1714.
Cliché Bibliothèque nationale de France, Paris, GE SH18E PF 131 DIV.

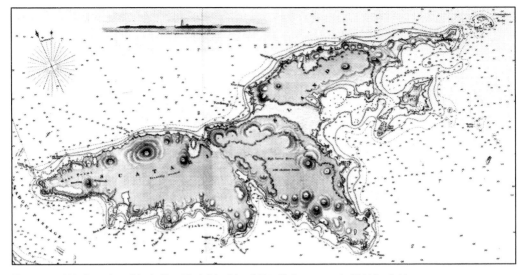

Figure 18.4 L'île Scatarie et l'île *La Tremblade* (Hay Island) Détail d'une carte de H.W. Bayfield, Amirauté de Grande-Bretagne, 1850.

Bibliothèque et Archives Canada, NMC-104395.

Lors de la remise des brevets, le roi réprimande le nouveau gouverneur de Louisbourg pour l'accaparement des graves. St-Ovide est étonné d'apprendre que l'on ne peut continuer à profiter des avantages de sa fonction comme d'autres l'ont toujours fait à Plaisance. Il se résignera à vendre « sa concession ».

Dès 1714, Françoise Patard, originaire de Granville en Normandie, veuve du sieur Onfroy du Bourg de Saint-Malo, a demandé au ministre de la Marine une concession à l'île Royale. Elle a fait valoir que la famille de son défunt mari a été une des premières à envoyer ses navires pêcher à l'île Royale[40] – à cette époque on confond encore souvent Terre-Neuve et Cap-Breton – et que le succès de leurs pêches a incité d'autres négociants de Bretagne et de Normandie à les suivre[41]. Le ministre transmet sa requête et demande s'il convient de lui accorder un privilège[42]. Elle ne recevra pas directement une concession, mais St-Ovide profitera de l'occasion pour vendre son habitation de Scatarie au sieur Jacques La Salle du Bournay, capitaine du navire marchand *Le Saint-Joseph*, un bourgeois de Saint-Malo lié à l'armement de la veuve Onfroy[43]. La même année, St-Ovide fera appel à Du Bournay pour transporter 250 hommes de troupes à Québec[44].

Vers 1720, une seconde génération d'habitants succède aux premiers concessionnaires. Les Thesson Laflourie, Borny, Charpentier, Raux, Tréguy, et Villedieu s'installent sur les graves libres. Puis suivent les Bérichon, Lebon, Legrand, Jourdan et Philipot[45], qui prennent la relève d'anciens propriétaires autour du havre et à proximité de la chapelle. La plupart ont épousé la fille d'un concessionnaire en titre. En 1724, les Anquetil, Lebreton et Philibert occupent l'anse *Darambourg*, du côté nord-ouest de l'île, à proximité du lopin de terre du chirurgien Sollet Le Cluzeau. Pendant la guerre de succession d'Autriche (1745-1748), alors que Louisbourg est occupé par les troupes de Pepperell, Pierre Leberteau, Jean Barbier et Nicolas de Malvilain demeurent sur l'île tandis que les Grandville, Sabot, Le Maréchal et Lafond se sont réfugiés en ville. Ils reviendront en 1749.

En principe, les graves de Scatarie[46] sont réservées aux équipages des navires venant de France pour la pêche d'été. Cependant, plusieurs capitaines malouins et granvillais prennent avantage de la présence des habitants pêcheurs. D'abord ils louent leurs installations : des graves et des chafauds déjà aménagés, des bâtiments et des espaces surveillés pour ranger les équipements et les chaloupes pendant l'hiver. Au fil des ans, ils viendront avec des équipages réduits pour troquer des marchandises contre la morue déjà salée et séchée par les engagés des habitants[47].

L'origine de la population de Scatarie

Un véritable réseau d'approvisionnement et d'embauche relie Scatarie à Saint-Malo et à Granville. Les navires amènent la main-d'œuvre recherchée par les habitants de l'île. Les capitaines recrutent dans les villages des évêchés riverains de la baie de Saint-Malo, en Bretagne et en Normandie. Au retour, ils ramènent les morues achetées ainsi que les surplus à livrer vers les marchés. Ce réseau n'est pas exclusif. Il existe également avec Bayonne, Bordeaux ou La Rochelle. Mais Saint-Malo est le plus grand port français de la pêche à la morue séchée et des liens privilégiés lient les habitants de Scatarie à la Bretagne et à la Normandie. Plusieurs habitants sont originaires de Saint-Malo, de Granville ou des villages des évêchés avoisinants : Dinan, Coutances ou Avranches. Des 55 individus identifiés dans les recensements, 13 sont originaires de Bretagne, 10 de Normandie, tandis que 16 sont natifs de Terre-Neuve. La plupart de ces derniers sont nés de parents bretons ou normands.

Dès 1716, appuyées par des capitaines et des armateurs métropolitains, les vingt-deux familles résidentes (Figure 18.5) constituent une petite communauté avec leurs engagés

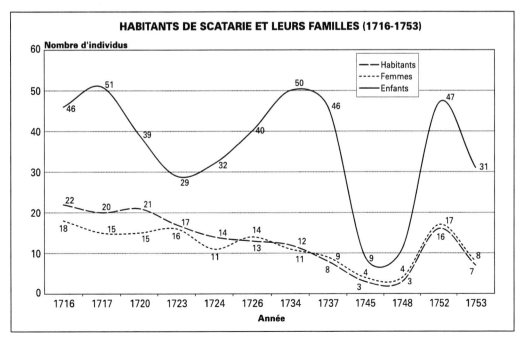

Figure 18.5 Les habitants de l'île Scatarie et leurs familles (1716-1753).

souvent issus des régions d'origines de leur patron. Vers 1720, la population de l'île représente plus de 16% de la population de l'île Royale (Tableau 18.1)[48]. Ce pourcentage décroîtra jusqu'à 5% en 1734 et 2% en 1752. La population de l'île Royale s'accroît tandis que celle de Scatarie diminue. Les habitants les plus prospères quittent l'île pour aller vivre à Louisbourg, tandis que ceux qui ne parviennent pas à tirer parti de leur concession vont s'établir en d'autres lieux, par exemple dans la baie de Miré, où l'on exploite la forêt, ou à Petit Bras d'Or, où l'on fait « dégrat »[49]. En 1735, Thesson La Flourie et Michel-François Lebreton sont devenus propriétaires à Louisbourg; tandis que Madame Bérichon est maintenant au Petit Bras d'Or avec une partie de la famille Borny.

Tableau 18.1 Comparaison des populations de l'île Royale, Louisbourg et l'île Scatarie

Année	Île Royale	Louisbourg	Île Scatarie	% par rapport à l'île Royale
1719/1720	2 012	853	329	16,35
1726	3 528	1 296	220	6,24
1734	3 955	1 616	200	5,06
1752	5 845	4 174	144	2,46

En 1723, l'aumônier de la chapelle de Scatarie dénonce un capitaine granvillais, qui désire entreprendre une expédition au Cap-de-Ray (Terre-Neuve) pour rapatrier des pêcheurs normands à l'emploi d'un propriétaire anglais[50]. À l'automne de l'année suivante, Rousseau de Souvigny, officier de la garnison de Louisbourg, est détaché à Scatarie pour transmettre une ordonnance interdisant aux insulaires d'envoyer leurs bateaux au Cap-de-Ray[51]. En dépit des restrictions, le recensement de La Roque (1752-53) identifie plusieurs résidants venus du Cap-de-Ray : Antoine Sabot[52] a épousé Jeanne Legrand, née à Scatarie, fille de Pierre Legrand et de Madeleine Diars. Par son entremise, deux pêcheurs, Louis Grandville et Sabasse Lafond, épouseront les sœurs d'Antoine : Michelle et Guillemette Sabot. On compte également d'autres transfuges du Cap-de-Ray comme Jean Rabié, au service de Thomas Porée et de Marie Vincent Desmarais.

Les femmes de Scatarie

On ignore trop souvent le rôle des femmes dans le commerce maritime, l'armement des navires et la pêche. Pourtant les armatrices étaient nombreuses à Granville et à Saint-Malo. À Scatarie, plusieurs épouses, mères, sœurs et filles de pêcheurs dirigent l'établissement familial. En 1720, l'épouse de feu Benjamin Le Manquet occupe une grave située au centre du havre. Quatre ans plus tard, elle a pour voisine la veuve Marie Comer Lachapelle et ses trois fils. En 1726, cette dernière emploie huit engagés, tandis que la veuve Borny, Anne Vincent Desmarais et sa fille, en occupent dix. Sa sœur Barbe, veuve de Louis Lebon, mère de 4 fils et de 5 filles, emploie 41 engagés en 1734. Elle est le second employeur de l'île après Thesson Laflourie. En 1754, Gillette Le Manquet, veuve de Charles Lebon, exploite l'une des graves les plus vastes de l'île avec ses 5 fils, ses 3 filles et 5 engagés.

Les épouses des habitants pêcheurs de Scatarie ont toute autorité en l'absence de leur mari. On les rencontre au greffe de l'amirauté, comme Barbe Vincent, affrontant les réclamations d'un voisin et d'un capitaine fournisseur[53]. Elles sont appelées « maîtresses » par les domestiques et les « trente-six mois », lesquels demandent directives et permissions[54]. Si la plupart d'entre elles semblent confinées à l'île et ses environs, La Roque nous apprend que Julienne Bassin, âgée de 35 ans, épouse de Jean Philipot, originaire de Saint-Michel-des-Loups, près d'Avranches en Normandie, est en voyage en France avec deux de ses enfants[55].

Les femmes ou les filles des pêcheurs sont domestiques chez les propriétaires prospères. Comme les épouses des habitants modestes, elles prennent soin des enfants, de la maison et des vêtements. Elles travaillent sur la grave ou dans le jardin. Elles s'occupent des poules, de quelques brebis ou chèvres et parfois d'une vache.

Chez les mieux nantis, des jeunes gens voyagent. En 1734, le rôle d'équipage du navire *Le Saint-Laurent*, de Saint-Malo, mentionne le retour de Gillette Grandin (14 ans)[56]. Citons aussi l'exemple de Madeleine Thesson Laflourie, qui épousera, à 15 ans, le second capitaine du navire *Le Saint-Antoine*, Michel Auguste Le Desdet, 28 ans, fils de François Le Desdet Du Désert, notaire royal à Saint-Malo[57]. Cependant la plupart des jeunes filles se marient avec le fils d'un habitant ou avec un engagé de son père, comme la mère de Madeleine, Simone Jeanne Million[58]. Isabelle, fille de Magdeleine Durant et de Jean Nicolas de Malvilain, épousera Guillaume Faucheux, le fils d'un habitant de Miré, qui approvisionne en bois les insulaires[59]. Cas d'exception, deux femmes sont les épouses des chirurgiens de l'île : Marie Le Manquet, fille de Jean et de Barbe Vincent, est mariée à Sollet Le Cluzeau[60], originaire de Saint-Bertrand-de-Comminges (Gascogne); Françoise Fayé, née à Bordeaux, est venue habiter à Scatarie, vers 1750, avec son époux Sylvain Jean Sémidon Gatiou, originaire de Saint-Servan, paroisse de Saint-Malo[61].

Tableau 18.2 Recensements des habitants de l'île Scatarie (1716-1754)

Année	Habitants	Femmes	Enfants	Domestiques ou engagés	Pêcheurs et graviers	Nombre de personnes	Chaloupes de pêche	Bateaux de pêche
1716	22	18	46	—	319	405	54	4
1717	20	15	51	—	341	347	70	4
1718	—	—	—	—	—	—	117	—
1720	21	15	39		323	398	90	9
1723	17	16	29		325	387	65	16
1724	14	11	32	10	137	204	27	10
1726	13	14	40	8	148	223	27	10
1734	12	11	50	10	198	281	18	11
1737	8	9	46	11	160	234	32	2
1745-48	3	4	9	—	3	19	10	1
1752	16	17	47	22	35	137	18	1
1753-54*	7	8	31	—	69	115	20/10*	1

Selon les recensements, trente familles ont moins de cinq enfants, mais ces dénombrements ne permettent pas un décompte précis de la marmaille de chaque ménage. Au total on mentionne 83 garçons et 83 filles ! Quatorze familles ont moins de dix enfants. Mais celle de Nicolas de Malvilain en compte onze : sept garçons et quatre filles. Les Thesson Laflourie ont eu 8 filles et un seul garçon. Ces nombreuses jeunes femmes permettront à la famille Thesson d'étendre sa parentèle à d'autres familles de Scatarie, de Louisbourg et de Saint-Malo, ville d'origine des Thesson Laflourie[62].

Pêcheurs, chaloupes et bateaux de pêche

Le nombre de pêcheurs, graviers ou engagés présents sur l'île Scatarie témoigne des fluctuations des activités. (Figure 18.6) Les premières années augurent bien. Dès 1716, deux ans après la distribution des concessions, on compte 319 travailleurs. Mais en 1724, la main-d'œuvre chute de 325 à 137. Elle remontera légèrement entre 1726 et 1734 avant de connaître un nouveau déclin de 1734 à 1745. L'exploitation de la pêche ne retrouvera pas sa vigueur par la suite.

Dès le début, la pêche est pratiquée par des équipages de trois pêcheurs en chaloupe. Mais en 1717, le recensement mentionne quatre bateaux. On en comptera seize en 1723, puis une dizaine seront maintenus jusqu'en 1734. Les pêcheurs font « dégras », ils vont pêcher loin de l'île en bateau ou en goélette monté par six à dix hommes. Ces voyages nécessitent des marins plus expérimentés. Les dénombrements nous offrent des regards sporadiques sur les embarcations en activité. Les chaloupes sont nombreuses avant 1723.

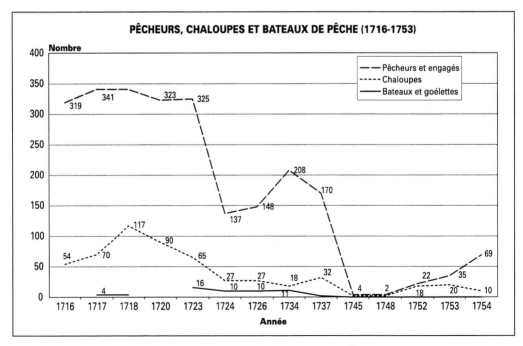

Figure 18.6 Pêcheurs, chaloupes et bateaux de pêche à l'île Scatarie (1716-1753).

Leur nombre diminue après le sommet de 1718 (117 chaloupes). Ce pic exceptionnel est peut-être dû à la présence de plusieurs chaloupes appartenant aux navires de France. Si l'on compte en moyenne 3 chaloupes par famille, on en obtient 66, ce qui constitue la flotte de pêche rapprochée des insulaires.

À partir de 1717, les recenseurs commencent à dénombrer des embarcations de plus fort tonnage. La pratique de la pêche change. Après avoir transposé l'ancienne méthode de pêche en chaloupe de Terre-Neuve à l'île Scatarie, les habitants les plus fortunés adoptent le bateau ou la goélette. Ces embarcations de 30 à 60 tonneaux permettent d'atteindre les bancs éloignés à l'est ou au sud du Cap-Breton. En 1724, Bernard Vincent Desmarest, Louis-Pierre Durocher et Pierre Legrand possèdent chacun un bateau; Duclos Gernot et Thesson Laflourie en ont deux, tandis que Louis Lebon en compte trois. Les documents d'archives révèlent de plus en plus des transactions de bateaux.

L'autre versant de Scatarie

Le recensement de 1724 révèle un nouveau phénomène observable qui se précisera dans les dénombrements suivants. Des habitants se sont installés dans l'anse Nord-Ouest, généralement appelée *Darrambourg*, située de l'autre côté de l'île, (Figure 18.4) face à la côte du Cap-Breton. Les liens avec la terre ferme y sont plus directs. On y retrouve les services, les syndics[63] : François Michel Lebreton (1724) et Thomas Porée (1752); ainsi que les médecins : Sollet Le Cluzeau (1734) et Sémidon Gatiou (1752). Ces derniers défrichent un coin de terre et possèdent un jardin indispensable pour la culture des plantes médicinales et des légumes. Quelques familles de pêcheurs vivent dans les bois environnants. Ils ne possèdent pas de grave et constituent la main-d'œuvre disponible sur l'île.

Les navires forains

Nous connaissons peu de navires venus de France pour pêcher à Scatarie, comme le capitaine du navire *Le Maure*, de Granville, Olivier Orange de Bellesève[64]. La destination inscrite sur le rôle d'équipage ou le congé est généralement l'île Royale ou le Cap-Breton. Pourtant, ils longent tous l'île de Scatarie avant de se rendre à Louisbourg, mais les documents mentionnent rarement ceux qui y font escale, y établissent leur station de pêche ou leur base de traite, comme Moysan, en 1732. Nous les découvrons dans les rapports des capitaines lorsqu'il y a eu une querelle, une avarie, un naufrage ou un échouement, comme celui du brigantin *Le Jeune-Alexandre*, de Blaye, propriété de Jean-Joseph Taillasson, sous le commandement de Daniel Meige, en 1733[65]. Les officiers mentionnent rarement un simple arrêt à Scatarie, avant leur retour, comme Michel de la Juganière de Jugon, capitaine du navire de 100 tonneaux, *Le Comte d'Évreux*, rentré à Saint-Malo via La Rochelle et Saint-Martin-de-Ré la même année[66]. C'est pourquoi les évènements survenus à Scatarie, en 1732, sont importants et dépassent leurs circonstances anecdotiques. Ils nous permettent de confirmer la présence de cinq navires mouillés dans le havre de la petite île (Tableau 18.3 Figure 18.7). Les rôles d'équipage nous apprennent que plusieurs d'entre eux étaient venus à l'île Royale l'année précédente[67], mais s'étaient-ils arrêtés à Scatarie ?

Tableau 18.3 Navires forains de pêche ou de commerce à Scatarie (1716-1753)

Année	1716	1718	1723	1727	1731	1732	1734	1735	1739	1745	1749	1753
Nombre de navires	4	6	2	2	3	5	4	4	0	0	0	2

L'augmentation du nombre de goélettes est peut-être un indice de la modification des activités des navires malouins et granvillais. (Figure 18.6) Ils ne viennent plus avec un équipage nombreux pour pêcher en chaloupe à partir de l'île. Ce sont des navires de commerce de 50 à 100 tonneaux, montés par dix à vingt marins, qui amènent des marchandises de troc et quelques engagés pour les habitants de l'île. Ils rapporteront, en échange, de la morue pêchée et séchée par les habitants de l'île.

Les habitants de Scatarie, tout comme ceux de l'île Royale, sont dépendants de ces navires de commerce. Ils profitent parfois de leur départ pour effectuer un voyage en France, à l'occasion d'une succession, ou simplement pour revoir des parents. En l'absence de ces fournisseurs, il faut trouver ailleurs les marchandises de consommation courante : farine, beurre, viande salée, animaux vivants, vin et eau-de-vie, chaussures, textiles et autres accessoires ou équipements pour la pêche, des hameçons jusqu'aux pièces de gréement et la toile pour les voiles des embarcations.

Si les navires ne viennent pas jusqu'à Scatarie, il faut transporter la morue à Louisbourg pour l'embarquer sur un vaisseau en partance et faire ses achats par l'intermédiaire des marchands locaux. Entre 1719 et 1731, les navires semblent peu nombreux et les insulaires

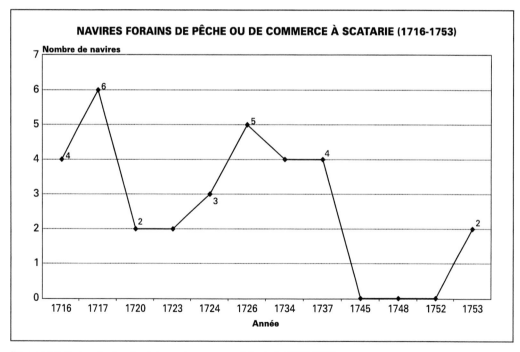

Figure 18.7 Navires forains de pêche ou de commerce à Scatarie (1716-1753).

D'après les chiffres de B.A. Balcom, *The Cod Fishery of Isle Royale, 1713-58*, Tableau 12, Annual distribution of the migrant fishing vessels in Isle Royale for selected years 1718-53, p. 53, avec mise à jour de J.-P. Chrestien.

doivent se déplacer; d'où la nécessité d'avoir un charroi, un bateau ou une goélette pour transporter les marchandises. On peut parfois compter sur la venue d'une goélette « américaine » qui, en dépit des règlements prohibitifs, s'aventure dans un havre de l'île Royale ou de Scatarie. On possède peu d'informations sur leur va-et-vient, mais on en découvre quelques-unes, mentionnées dans des contrats de vente de bateau ou à l'occasion dans le rapport d'un capitaine marchand de France. Les rencontres ne sont pas toujours cordiales.

En 1734, Pierre de La Rue, capitaine du navire le *Saint-Laurent*[68], de Saint-Malo, porteur d'une commission en guerre et marchandises, saisit deux goélettes de Nouvelle-Angleterre présentes dans le havre de Scatarie : *La Jeanne-Elizabeth* du capitaine Andres King et *La Contente* d'Abraham Mors. La confiscation des goélettes anglaises sera approuvée par le ministre de la Marine, en dépit des protestations du gouverneur de Louisbourg qui justifie leur présence par la disette de vivres à l'île Royale[69]. La prise est justifiée par la prohibition du commerce étranger. En principe, tout navire étranger aperçu à moins d'une lieue d'une île française peut être saisi[70]. Le *Saint-Laurent*, jaugeant 160 tonneaux, armé par Potier de Boisouze et monté par un équipage de 24 hommes, ramenait deux jeunes gens à Scatarie : Louis Lebon (13 ans), fils de Charles, et Gillette Grandin (14 ans), fille de Julien Grandin, maître de chaloupe marié en second noce à la veuve de Charles Lebon, Gillette Le Manquet[71].

Le dénouement de l'affaire Vaujoyeux contre Moysan de La Marette

Ces saisies n'étaient peut-être pas le fruit du hasard. Si les habitants de l'île connaissaient bien les allées et venues des navires anglais à Scatarie, l'affaire Vaujoyeux contre Moysan de La Marette avait confirmé leur présence aux Malouins qui se plaignaient depuis 1728 de leur commerce illicite[72].

L'année 1732 avait été mémorable aussi pour les habitants de Scatarie : célébrations sur ce navire « américain », incendie de *L'Aigle*, de Bayonne, achat d'un navire anglais par Thesson Laflourie, puis l'incident et la désertion de Vaujoyeux avaient dû causer bien des bavardages dans les cabanes de l'île. Le 5 août, le navire *Le Saint-Jean*, de 60 tonneaux, appartenant à l'armateur Philippe Lemeigre et associés, de Saint-Malo, avec ses 10 hommes d'équipage, avait sans doute été remarqué dès son entrée dans le petit havre de Scatarie, si l'on en croit le capitaine Moysan, qui protestait contre l'incapacité et l'ignorance de son second officier[73].

En novembre, Moysan s'apprête à quitter l'île Scatarie avec l'assistance d'un nouveau pilote, Michel Legoupil, et un chargement de 500 quintaux de morue sèche. De son côté, Vaujoyeux tente de s'embarquer sur un navire en partance vers la France, mais tous les capitaines refusent de le prendre à bord. C'est à la suite de l'intervention de l'aumônier de Scatarie et du chirurgien, Sollet, que les autorités de Louisbourg obligent Moysan à prendre Vaujoyeux comme passager !

Le *Saint-Jean* quitte l'île Scatarie le 28 novembre[74]. La sortie du havre est difficile. La traversée de l'Atlantique par gros temps conduit Moysan et son navire au sud de la Bretagne, à Belle-Île-en-Mer, puis à la Roche-Bernard, le 7 janvier 1733[75]. Vaujoyeux demande son congé, mais Moysan le lui refuse, alléguant qu'il a déserté. Vaujoyeux rentrera à Saint-

Malo par la route tandis que Moysan se rend au Croisic. Arrivé à Saint-Malo bien avant *Le Saint-Jean*, le jeune noble se fait examiner par les médecins et chirurgiens du roi, et il exige un rapport de son état de santé avec l'inventaire de ses blessures et cicatrices. Puis il dépose une plainte à l'amirauté pour mauvais traitements, injures, coups et blessures, ce qui déclenche la procédure.

Tous les membres d'équipage et les capitaines malouins, présents à Scatarie l'année précédente, sont appelés à témoigner par Jacques Gouin, sieur de Beauchesne, lieutenant général civil et criminel. La plupart des matelots confirment que dès, le départ du *Saint-Jean*, le 28 mars 1732, Moysan n'a cessé d'injurier Vaujoyeux, le traitant de « vauchien, vaubougres, vaumalheureux … », et bientôt en est venu aux coups : soufflets provoquant la perte de sang, coups de pied, coups d'arbalestrille, de porte-voix et coups de marteaux. Vaujoyeux a été traîné par les cheveux sur le pont devant l'équipage. Son capitaine lui a même lancé le plat à viande au visage lors d'un repas. Un coup d'anspect[76], assené par Moysan au moment où le pilote faisait une fausse manœuvre, pendant le mouillage du navire dans le havre de Scatarie, a provoqué la défaillance et l'évanouissement de Vaujoyeux. Il était presque mourant à l'arrivée du chirurgien.

La plupart des témoins s'accordaient sur l'incompétence de Vaujoyeux, surtout ceux de Saint-Servan, qui soutenaient davantage leur capitaine habitant la même paroisse. Les Malouins et ceux des campagnes environnantes étaient plus favorables à Vaujoyeux. Mais la méchanceté de Moysan devenait évidente.

L'instruction s'est prolongée jusqu'à l'été 1733. À la fin de mai, Vaujoyeux a fait une rechute et on a craint pour sa vie. Son procureur a présenté une seconde expertise des médecins qui affirmaient que la santé de Vaujoyeux était irrémédiablement handicapée. Il réclamait plus de 6 000 livres de dommages et intérêts, le remboursement du salaire, la valeur des marchandises et effets personnels saisis dans ses coffres, l'obligation de réparer publiquement son honneur et une pension de 500 livres pour défrayer les frais et les médicaments que requerrait son état de santé[77].

Le procureur de l'amirauté investi des pouvoirs civil et criminel a rendu son verdict le 16 juin. Moysan a été condamné à 300 livres de réparation, dommages et intérêts, à 10 livres d'amende avec défense de recommencer, n'y de médire de Vaujoyeux. L'offensé pouvait réclamer son salaire et la restitution de ses coffres. Moysan devait payer 110 livres, 15 sols et deux deniers de dépens ainsi que les épices de la procédure. C'était bien peu en comparaison des réclamations de l'accusation et, la même année, on retrouve Moysan, second du capitaine Jacques Chenu, en route pour Marseille sur le navire *L'Heureuse Union*[78].

L'ignorance, l'incapacité et l'incompétence de Vaujoyeux ont été prises en compte par l'amirauté comme par la plupart des officiers présents à Scatarie l'année précédente. La connivence de Vaujoyeux avec les matelots de son équipage et ses relations avec les engagés des habitants de Scatarie ont été perçues comme un manquement à son rang d'officier. Le commandement d'un navire n'était pas héréditaire, mais la bourgeoisie maritime acceptait tout de même le principe d'un seul maître après Dieu à bord, même s'il était roturier. Qu'est-ce qui avait conduit Moysan à autant d'excès ? Les coups et blessures n'étaient pas rares à bord des navires malouins. Plusieurs capitaines et de nombreux marins étaient connus pour leur brutalité dans ce port comme ailleurs[79]. Mais on a du mal à comprendre que toutes ces injures, tous ces coups n'aient été provoqués que par l'incapacité du second. Il est vrai que la conduite d'un voilier et d'un équipage est une rude besogne qui exige du caractère et l'attention de tous les instants, le jour comme la nuit. La maîtrise de la navigation est souvent une question de vie ou de mort lorsque l'on affronte la fureur de l'océan. Cependant la fatigue, l'abus d'alcool, la promiscuité et l'incompatibilité de caractère constituaient des éléments explosifs à bord d'un navire.

Deux mentions très brèves ont attiré mon attention à la lecture du témoignage de Moysan, car elles surgissent d'une manière si inattendue. Moysan affirme qu'il n'avait aucune raison d'injurier Vaujoyeux puisqu'il était l'époux de sa cousine au second degré et que ces injures seraient retombées sur elle et sur sa famille, c'est-à-dire sur Moysan et sa propre famille. Cette cousine, était-elle la véritable raison de la haine que Moysan éprouvait contre Vaujoyeux ?

Revenons aux habitants de Scatarie avant de terminer. La vie quotidienne de ces insulaires était-elle particulière ou semblable à celle de tous les pêcheurs des hameaux côtiers de l'île Royale? Louisbourg n'était pas le seul lieu habité du Cap-Breton. En 1732, plus de 2 000 personnes vivaient éparpillés le long de ses côtes. L'île Scatarie est-elle un microcosme représentatif du monde maritime de la Nouvelle-France ou du nord-est américain ? Seule la multiplication d'études semblables permettra de répondre à ces questions.

Notes

1. Le terme « habitant » désigne le propriétaire ou concessionnaire résidant d'une habitation.
2. H.-L. Duhamel du Monceau. *Traité général des pesches…*, Paris, Saillant & Nyon, et Veuve Desaint, 1772, vol. 2.
3. B.A. Balcom. *The Cod Fishery of Isle Royale, 1713-58*, Ottawa, Parks Canada, 1984, 94 p.
4. Andrew Hill Clark. *Acadia. The Geography of Early Nova Scotia to 1760,* Chapitre 7, *"Cape Breton Island to 1758"*, Madison, University of Wisconsin Press, 1968, p. 262-329.
5. Archives de la France d'Outre-Mer, Colonies, Série G[1] et G[2].
6. Archives départementales de la Charente-Maritime; La Rochelle, Amirauté de Louisbourg, Audiences et jugements civils, Série B, vol. 268, 1731-1734; vol. 278, 1737-1738.
7. Les témoins interrogés mentionnent un vaisseau américain : « Le sieur Desmarettes ayant passé à bord d'un vaisseau américain où il se divertit un peu plus qu'il ne connenoit son équipage… » (Archives départementales de l'Ille-et-Vilaine, Sous série, 9 B, Archives de l'Amirauté de Saint-Malo, Minutes du greffe, liasse 284, 5 février 1733).
8. Services historiques de la Marine, Brest. *Rôle d'équipage du navire « Le St Jean, à l'armement, »*, 1732, n° 72, département de Saint-Malo.
9. Loc.cit., 9 B, liasse 284, 1732-1733.
10. L'anse *Darambourg* ou *Darrambourg*, appelée aussi anse Nord-Ouest, tient peut-être son nom de Dominique de Lerembourg, armateur et bourgeois de Libourne, près de Bordeaux. Ses navires de pêche ont sans doute occupé cette grave pendant quelques pêches d'été. Il était

parfois représenté par le capitaine Dominique Daguerre (G3, vol. 2056, section 2, pièces 17-18, 9 oct. 1716; 2058, section 3, no 16, 6 juin 1725).

11. *Le Henri*, 1728-1736 : 120 tonneaux, 10 canons, 32 hommes, armé par Jallobert, cité dans Martin-Desgrèves et Thomas-Cadiou, *Navires de Saint Malo (17ᵉ-18ᵉ siècles)*, n° 2169.

12. Navire incendié à l'île Scatarie en octobre 1732 (Archives départementales de la Charente Maritime, Archives de l'Amirauté de Louisbourg, Série B, vol. 274, 16 oct. 1732; 24-26 nov. 1732).

13. Archives de l'Amirauté de Saint-Malo, 9 B, liasse 284, 1732-1733, 2 mars 1733.

14. *Ibid.*, 12 fév. 1733.

15. Claude-Joseph Le Roy Desmarest, greffier au siège de l'Amirauté de Louisbourg; confirmation de sa charge de notaire royal en 1730 (Correspondance générale; Île Royale, Série C11B. vol. 11, fol. 109-110, Louisbourg, 1730/12/05).

16. *Grave* : « Nom que les pêcheurs de Terre-Neuve donnent à la place choisie près de leur échafaud pour y faire sécher la morue sortie du sel. La grave est un sol ferme près d'un rivage qui s'étend en pente douce vers la mer; …bien exposée au soleil. » (V.-A. Willaumez, *Dictionnaire de marine, 1820-1831*, Douarnenez, La Chasse-marée Armen, 1998, p. 320.)

17. *Chasser* : « Un bâtiment mouillé qui, par l'effort d'un grand vent et d'une grosse mer, entraîne ses ancres, leur fait labourer le fond, chasse; ce qui s'appelle chasser sur ses ancres, leur fait labourer le fond … » (V.-A. Willaumez, *op. cit.*, p. 146).

18. Les capitaines Jacques Chenu du Chenot et Guillaume Duval, commandant et second du navire marchand *L'Heureuse-Union* (100 tonneaux, 19 hommes), de Saint-Malo, furent témoins de ces événements comme plusieurs insulaires : Élie Thesson Laflourie, son commis Le Paumier et Charles Lebon (Procès-verbal rédigé et enregistré les 1ᵉʳ et 3 nov. 1732. Amirauté de Louisbourg, Billets, lettres de change, engagements, factures, quittances, Série B, vol. 274, fol. 133.

19. Les « trente-six mois » : hommes engagés pour trois ans.

20. Archives de l'Amirauté de Saint-Malo, 9 B, liasse 284, 1732-1733, 1733/02/09.

21. *LE CANADA, ou NOUVELLE FRANCE, &c. Ce qui est le plus advance vers le Septentrion est tiré de diverses Relations des Anglois, Danois, &c. Vers le Midy les Costes de Virginie, Nouᵘˡˡᵉ Suede, Nouveau Pays Bas, et Nouvelle Angleterre Sont tirée de celles des Anglois, Hollandois, &c. LA GRANDE RIVIERE DE CANADA ou de ST LAURENS, et tous les environs sont suivant les Relations des Francois. Par N. SANSON d'Abbeville Geographe ordinaire du Roy. A PARIS. Chez Pierre Mariette Rue S. Jacque a l'Esperance Avecq. Privilege du Roy, pour vingt Ans. 1656* (Bibliothèque et Archives du Canada: NMC 21100 H3/900/1656).

22. Sainte Catherine d'Alexandrie, parfois représentée avec une roue de gouvernail, est la patronne des mariniers de plusieurs ports de France : Honfleur, La Rochelle, etc.

23. Cette forme est-elle à l'origine du nom du passage et de la baie voisine : *Main-à-Dieu* ou *Menadou* ?

24. Dans son rapport, Latour appelle l'île de la Tremblade l'île *aux Cocus* et c'est bien le nom qui apparaît sur ce plan (« Journal du Sʳ. de Latour pour la découverte des battures de Scatary, 1735, pour le dépôt des cartes et plans », France. Archives de la Marine, Série C7, Personnel individuel, vol. 221, n° 2, 42 pages).

25. M. de Chabert. *Voyage fait par ordre du Roi en 1750 et 1751, dans l'Amérique septentrionale septentrionale* … Paris, Imprimerie Royale, 1753, p. 41.

26. *Ibid.*, p. 83-85.

27. Peter N. Moogk. *Building a house in New France*, Toronto, McClelland and Stewart, 1977, p. 30-31.

28. M. de Chabert, *op. cit.*, p. 93.

29. *Ibid.*, p. 111. Le port de Louisbourg était également bloqué pendant cette période de l'année.

30. Son dessin a été reçu le 12 février 1715 (Archives coloniales, Série B, vol. 37, Lettres envoyées, fol. 29, 12 fév. 1715) par Jérôme Phélippeaux, comte de Pontchartrain (1674–†1747), ministre de la Marine de 1699 à 1715 (Michel Mourre, *Dictionnaire encyclopédique d'Histoire*, Paris, Bordas, 1986, vol. 6, p. 3746).

31. La carte de 1751 de M. de Chabert indique la chapelle par une croix à l'est de la grande grave, contrairement au « Thoisé… » (vers 1714), qui la situe à l'ouest.

32. François Baillon, sieur de Blancpignon (1669-1746), chevalier à partir de 1725. Né à Granville en 1669, capitaine et armateur terre-neuviers à ses débuts, il maria ses filles à la meilleure noblesse militaire dont Lévis (André Lespagnol *Messieurs de Saint-Malo. Une élite négociante au temps de Louis XIV*, Saint-Malo, Éditions l'Ancre de Marine, 1990, p. 845).

33. Peut-être Daccarrette.

34. Parfois écrit « Le Marquet ».

35. Probablement Couray du Parc de Granville.

36. Peut-être Lemage ou Legage Macé de Saint-Malo.

37. « Brevet de confirmation des concessions faites aux habitants de l'Isle de Scatarie adjacente à l'Isle Royale », Série C^{11}G, vol. 12, fol. [50] 17, 23 juin 1718.

38. Peut-être Million l'aîné.

39. « Brevet… », Série C^{11}G, vol. 12, fol. [51] 18, 23 juin 1718.

40. *Le Pierre-Auguste* (150 tonneaux), de Granville, semble le premier navire armé pour l'île Royale par la Veuve Onfroy du Bourg. Sous le commandement de François Levirais, avec 49 hommes d'équipage, il séjourne à l'île du 15 mai au 22 septembre 1714 et en ramène 130 milliers de morues, 26 barils d'huiles et trois tonneaux de charbon de terre (9 B registre 481, fol. 33, 17 octobre 1714).

41. J. S. McLennan. *Louisbourg from its Foundation to its Fall 1713-1758*, London, MacMillan and Co., 1918, p. 20, 220.

42. Archives coloniales, Série B, Lettres envoyées, 21 nov. 1714, vol. 36, f°. 465v–466.

43. *Contrat de vente d'une habitation située à Scatary, par M. de St-Ovide de Brouillan, gouverneur, au sieur La Salle du Bournay, bourgeois de St-Malo* (Archives de la France d'Outre-Mer, Colonies, G^3, registre 2056-4, fol. 40, 10 décembre 1718).

44. *Ibid.*, 20 août 1718. Le navire de La Salle du Bournay a rapporté des vivres; voir « État des vivres tirés des magasins du roi à Québec et chargés sur la flûte nommée LE SAINT-JOSEPH …pour porter et remettre au port de Louisbourg aux ordres de M. de Soubras commissaire ordonnateur ». Signé Bégon (Série C^{11}A, vol. 38, fol. 193-194v. Québec, 5 nov. 1718).

45. Jean Philipot, ou Phélipot, était en relation avec l'armateur granvillais Du Parc Couraye. Cet armateur a expédié une lettre, en 1775, demandant une subvention pour la famille de Philipot (Archives départementales du Calvados, Caen, Série A 15, vol. 1020, Granville, 12 déc. 1775).

46. Lettre de Pontchartrain « Aux Bayles et Jurats de St. Jean du Luz et Siboure » (Série B, vol. 36, fol. 47, 1er février 1714).

47. Charles de La Morandière. *Histoire de la pêche française de la morue dans l'Amérique septentrionale*, Tome II, Paris, G.-P. Maisonneuve et Larose, 1962, p. 670.

48. B. A. Balcom, *op. cit.*, p. 8.

49. Dégrat : Lieu où l'on envoie les embarcations pêcher à la recherche de la morue (E. Paris et P. de Bonnefoux. *Dictionnaire de la marine à voiles*, Paris, Layeur, 1999).

50. Lettre de Mézy au Ministre, Louisbourg, 22 novembre 1724 (Série C^{11}B, vol. 7, fol. 68-74, cité par Balcom, *ibid.*, p. 68).

51. Rousseau de Souvigny, Louisbourg, 22 septembre 1724 (*ibid.*, fol. 72).

52. B. A. Balcom, *op. cit.*, p. 67-68.

53. Joseph Pitrel du Morier, capitaine du navire *Le Saint-Germain*, de Saint-Malo (Amirauté de Louisbourg, Audiences et jugements civils, Série B, vol. 268, 1731-1734, fol. 174v-175v. 24

juillet 1734). Nicolas Boitié Bérichon (Amirauté de Louisbourg, Série B, vol. 278, 1737-1738, fol. 3, 1737/11/09).

54.   Amirauté de Saint-Malo, 9 B, liasse 284, 1732-1733, lundi, 2 mars 1733.

55.   Archives de la France d'Outre-Mer, Colonie, Série G¹, 466, pièce n° 81, « Voyage fait par le Sr De La Roque … cinq février 1752 », p. 100.

56.   Services historiques de la Marine, Brest *Rôle d'équipage du navire « Le St Laurent, à l'armement »*, 1734, département de Saint-Malo.

57.   *Ibid.*, Série G³, Dépôt des papiers publics des colonies; notariat, vol. 2046, 26 sept. 1739.

58.   *Ibid.*, G³, vol. 2056, section 1, fol. 25, 5 nov. 1714.

59.   *Ibid.*, G³, vol. 2045, pièce 98, 6 juin 1758.

60.   Série B, vol. 278, Louisbourg, 9 nov. 1737, fol. 3.

61.   Série G¹, 466, pièce n° 81, « Voyage fait par le Sr De La Roque… cinq février 1752 », p. 101.

62.   La Flourie était un quartier de la ville de Saint-Malo.

63.   Mandataire désigné par les autorités de Louisbourg pour enregistrer les procès-verbaux et les contrats d'engagements en l'absence d'un notaire sur l'île de Scatarie.

64.   Exceptionnellement, le capitaine de Bellesève est mentionné tout comme Du Parc Couraye, aussi de Granville, et Legage Macé, de Saint-Malo, sur le *thoisé de la grave de l'île Pontchartrain* (Bibliothèque et Archives nationales du Canada: NMC-F/201/[1730]146).

65.   Soumissions de capitaine de navire, 14 mars 1732, Fonds des Archives départementales de la Gironde, Bordeaux, Série de l'Amirauté de Guyenne. Attributions administratives, 6 B, vol. 94, fol. 22v. Procès-verbal signé par Daniel Meige touchant l'échouement du brigantin *L'Alexandre*, appartenant à Gareche et Labire, 1732/10/02. Enregistrement des ordres donnés par Jean-Joseph Taillasson, propriétaire du navire *Le Jeune-Alexandre*, de Blaye, à Daniel Meige, capitaine du bâtiment, qui aurait fait naufrage au havre de Scatarie, 1732/03/19 (Amirauté de Louisbourg, Billets, lettres de change, engagements, factures, quittances, 1730-1735, vol. 274, fol. 102-107).

66.   Gérard Hélias, « Le commerce maritime de Saint-Malo en 1733 », Mémoire de diplôme d'études supérieures d'histoire à l'Université de Rennes, 1964, p. 101.

67.   Services historiques de la Marine, Brest, *Rôles d'équipage de l'année 1731*, département de Saint-Malo.

68.   Amirauté de Louisbourg, Audiences et jugements civils, 1731-1734, Série B, vol. 268, fol. 188-191. *Le Saint-Laurent*, 1729-1730, 1732, 1734-1735, cité dans Martin-Desgrèves et Thomas-Cadiou, *op. cit.*, 1992, p. 132, no 4692.

69.   Amirauté de Louisbourg, Correspondance générale, B 6110, fol. 18, 19 avril 1735.

70.   Lettres patentes d'avril 1717, EO, I : 362, cité dans Jacques Mathieu. *Le commerce entre la Nouvelle-France et les Antilles au XVIIIᵉ siècle*, Montréal, Fides, 1981, p. 43-44; et dans James Pritchard. *In search of empire : the French in the Americas, 1670-1730*, New York, Cambridge University Press, 2004, p. 190-193.

71.   Services historiques de la Marine, Brest, *Rôle d'équipage du navire « Le St Laurent, à l'armement »*, 1734, département de Saint-Malo.

72.   « Requête adressée à Maurepas par Cotterel, armateur de Saint-Malo; plaintes portées contre Saint-Ovide, qui favorise le commerce anglais à l'île Royale » (B³, vol. 327, fol. 313-313v. 1728). « Lettre du président du conseil de marine à M. le comte de Toulouze. Au sujet des mauvais traitements que le Sieur Cotterel, de Saint-Malo, prétend avoir reçus de M. de St-Ovide à Louisbourg » (B, vol. 51, fol. 62, 3 août 1728). « Lettre du président du conseil de marine à M. de St-Ovide affirmant que le seul moyen de se justifier des plaintes portées contre lui pour le commerce étranger est de tenir la main à l'exécution de l'ordonnance de 1727 à cet effet. Les excuses qu'il donne sur les plaintes portées contre lui par les pêcheurs et négociants ne le disculpent pas. N'approuve pas les mauvais traitements qu'il a fait subir au Sieur Cotterel, de Saint-Malo et à Baptiste Guyon. » (B, vol. 53, fol. 590. 22 mai 1729).

73. Archives de l'Amirauté de Saint-Malo, 9 B, liasse 284, 3 sept. 1732 ; 22-27 avril 1733.

74. Le 21 novembre selon une autre déclaration de Moysan, ibid., 22-27 avril 1733.

75. Extrait du Registre de comparution au greffe du Greffe de l'amirauté établi à La Roche-Bernard, évêché de Nantes, daté du 12 janvier 1733, selon 9 B 284, 28 fév. 1733.

76. ANSPECT, du néerlandais : *handspike*. Levier en bois de chêne servant à la manœuvre des pièces d'artillerie (Paris et de Bonnefoux, *Dictionnaire de la marine à voiles, op cit.*, cd-rom).

77. *Ibid.*, 3 juin 1733.

78. Le capitaine Chenu était à Scatarie avec le même navire en 1732. Son témoignage a été plutôt défavorable à Vaujoyeux (Services historiques de la Marine, Brest, *Rôle d'équipage du navire « L'Heureuse Union, allant à Marseille …à l'armement »*, 1733, département de Saint-Malo).

79. L'armateur de Roscoff, Prigent de la Porte-Noire, écrivait à De Parcq Cauray, de Granville, qu'on avait beau recommander de n'engager « que des gens doux et paisibles », on avaient du mal à y parvenir (Cité par Olivier Zeller, « La côte et l'océan vus de Roscoff : la correspondance de l'armateur Prigent de la Porte-Noire (1721-1725) », dans *Les activités littorales*, CTHS, 2002, p. 54).

A DISTANT SHORE

Steamer Mail to and from Gold-Rush California

19

Marianne Babal, Historian, Wells Fargo & Company, San Francisco

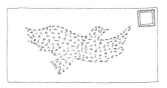

Abstract

Even though the discovery of gold in California in 1848 touched off a great migratory rush westward, the West Coast of North America remained isolated in terms of communication and commerce for more than a decade afterward. Arrival of a steamship bearing mails from the East was an occasion of great celebration in gold-rush San Francisco. Incoming mail steamers brought the latest news from the "States" and longed-for letters from loved ones. Letters typically took nearly a month to reach California from the eastern seaboard, travelling first by Atlantic steamer to Panama, then across the Isthmus by mule and canoe before being loaded aboard steamers of the Pacific Mail Steamship Company from Panama to San Francisco. Outbound mails departed twice monthly and, prior to each "Steamer Day," San Franciscans engaged in an orgy of letter writing home to family and friends. Meanwhile, local merchants frantically settled accounts, made remittances to East Coast creditors, and took stock of business affairs. Steamships and the mail they carried were a lifeline of communication for early Californians until inauguration of mail service overland by stagecoach beginning in 1858, and mounted mail delivery via the Pony Express in 1860.

Résumé

Même si la découverte d'or en Californie en 1848 a provoqué un énorme flux migratoire vers l'Ouest, la côte ouest de l'Amérique du Nord est demeurée isolée, pour ce qui est des communications et du commerce, pendant plus d'une décennie après. L'arrivée d'un vapeur apportant le courrier en provenance de l'Est était l'occasion de grandes festivités dans le San Francisco de la ruée vers l'or. Les paquebots-poste apportaient les dernières nouvelles des « États » et des lettres très attendues des proches. En général, les lettres mettaient un mois à faire le trajet entre la côte est et la Californie. Elles étaient d'abord acheminées jusqu'à Panama à bord d'un vapeur, puis traversaient l'isthme à dos de mule et en canot avant d'être chargées à bord de vapeurs de la Pacific Mail Steamship Company, qui faisaient le trajet entre Panama et la Californie. Le courrier quittait la Californie deux fois par mois et, avant chaque « jour de bateau », les gens de San Francisco rédigeaient des montagnes de lettres pour leur famille et leurs amis. Pendant ce temps, les marchands locaux se hâtaient fiévreusement de régler leurs comptes et de préparer les paiements pour leurs créanciers de l'Est, et faisaient le point sur leurs affaires. Les bateaux à vapeur et le courrier qu'ils transportaient furent vitaux pour les premiers Californiens jusqu'à l'instauration du service postal par voie de terre en diligence, en 1858, et ensuite par courrier à cheval assuré par le Pony Express, en 1860.

Introduction

In the first half of the nineteenth century, the West Coast of North America remained isolated in terms of communication and commerce from the rest of the continent. A small population engaged in raising cattle and trapping and trading furs did not warrant regular mail service. In 1836, the Hudson Bay Company steamship *Beaver* began sailing the Western Coast collecting furs and connecting the company's far flung outposts.[1] Farther south, English investors financed the Pacific Steam Navigation Company in 1840 to transport mail to the Pacific Coast of South America under contract with the British government.[2] Beyond these early endeavors, communication up and down the Pacific Coast remained limited to occasional passing ships flying English or American flags.

In the 1840s, the movement of thousands of settlers westward, along the Oregon Trail into territory disputed by England and the United States, increased demand for mail service. The Oregon Boundary Treaty settled the international boundary along the 49th parallel and made Oregon an American Territory in 1846. That same year, the United States declared war on Mexico and soon occupied Alta California and the small hamlet of Yerba Buena on San Francisco Bay.

In 1847, the U.S. Congress authorized the secretary of the navy and postmaster general to accept bids for the establishment of regular mail service between Eastern states and new Pacific territories by steamer via the Isthmus of Panama. The winning bidders, A. G. Sloo and Arthur Harris, promptly assigned their mail contracts to other better capitalized entrepreneurs, George Law and partners in the East, and William H. Aspinwall and his partners in the West. These gentlemen, in turn, founded two transportation companies: the United States Mail Steamship Company that took charge of the Atlantic route from New York to Chagres, and the Pacific Mail Steamship Company on the West Coast from Panama City to Astoria, Oregon.

The U.S. government subsidized these two steamship operators in return for regular mail service and contract provisions for conversion of mail steamers to auxiliary warships as necessary. Mail subsidies for the Atlantic segment between New York and the Isthmus of Panama amounted to $240,000 per year. The Pacific Mail Steamship Company initially received a government subsidy of $150,000, an amount that more than doubled as volume of mail increased to accommodate demand from gold seekers who flooded into California after gold was discovered there on January 24, 1848.[3]

New York merchant William Henry Aspinwall incorporated the Pacific Mail Steamship Company on April 12, 1848, several months before news of California gold

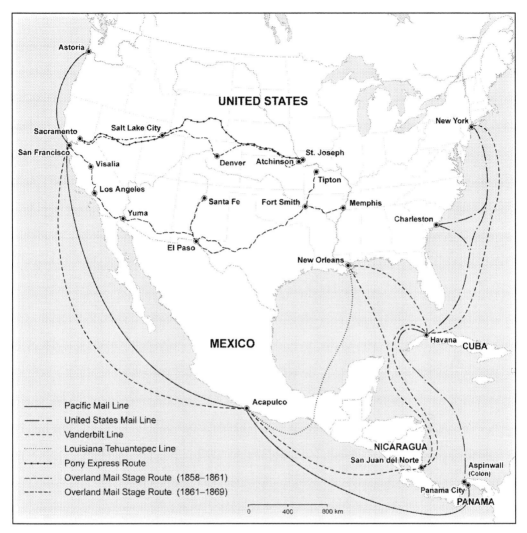

Figure 19.1 Early communications routes to the Pacific prior to 1869.
Map by Andrée Héroux.

reached the eastern seaboard. Over the next 75 years, his company came to dominate Pacific coastal steamer business and trans–Pacific mail service.[4]

The first Pacific Mail steamer, *California*, departed New York for San Francisco on October 6, 1848. The new 1,057-ton [1074-tonne] side-wheel steamer boasted accommodation for 60 salon and 150 steerage passengers, but, on its maiden voyage around Cape Horn, carried only half a dozen. While the *California* lumbered south around Cape Horn, heavily laden with coal and a complete set of replacement parts for its engines, word of fantastic gold discoveries in California began to spread. When *California* dropped anchor in Panama City on January 17, 1849, the vessel was besieged by hundreds of eager Argonauts newly arrived in Panama and clamouring for immediate passage to San Francisco. The *California* departed Panama on February 1 with 365 passengers and

36 crew wedged into every available space and reached San Francisco four weeks later on February 28. When the vessel dropped anchor in San Francisco Bay, the ship's crew deserted and joined the frenzied hordes headed for the diggings.[5] One of the *California*'s passengers, William Van Voorhies, had been appointed special agent of the postmaster general charged with inaugurating government postal service in California.[6] Upon arrival, he found the post office in San Francisco had already opened on November 9, 1848, but did not receive any mail to distribute until the arrival of the steamer three months later.[7]

Steamer Day in San Francisco

Until inauguration of scheduled overland stagecoach service in 1858, coast-to-coast telegraph service in 1861, and completion of the transcontinental railroad in 1869, steamers remained the main transportation and communication link between California and the eastern seaboard. Arrival of a steamship bearing mails from the East was an occasion of great celebration in gold rush San Francisco, as arriving steamers delivered the latest news from the "States" and longed-for letters from loved ones. When an incoming mail steamer was sighted approaching the Bay entrance from the headlands surrounding the Golden Gate, the news was relayed by semaphore telegraph thence to the city station atop

Figure 19.2 "Arrival of a Steamship," from *The Annals of San Francisco*, published in 1855.
Wells Fargo Archives.

Telegraph Hill. By the time the steamer had fired its gun and docked, a crowd gathered to greet the vessel, listening eagerly for news and curiously inspecting arriving passengers as they stepped ashore.

Mail taken off the steamer was carted to the post office to be sorted. San Francisco's postal clerks sometimes found it necessary to barricade themselves inside the office as an impatient crowd lined up outside, some of whom had been waiting days for mail to be distributed. Once the mail was in hand at the San Francisco post office, clerks sorted letters and newspapers for distribution to other Pacific Coast destinations. Letters to coastal Southern California, Washington, Oregon, and British Columbia were forwarded on steamers twice monthly, while mail bound for other California cities such as Stockton, Sacramento, and San Jose travelled daily by river steamboat or stagecoach. For destinations further inland, mail was carried overland on a more irregular basis or delivered by private express.[8]

All western mail flowed through the San Francisco post office. Even new arrivals fresh off the boat headed straight for the post office from the docks. Forty-niner Enos Christman was luckier than most:

> I proceeded immediately to the post office, very anxious to hear something of the objects nearest my heart and I was gratified to the fullest extent. Letter after letter and paper after paper were handed out until the postage amounted to six dollars out of my scanty purse of twenty-seven, but had they cost the whole sum ... I should have willingly paid it.[9]

Letters from home proved more precious than gold to homesick San Franciscans and miners searching for gold in remote camps in the Sierra foothills. Miner Lucius Fairchild described his delight at receiving a letter from family left behind in Wisconsin, January 1, 1850:

> If you could have seen us when we received our letters, you would have laughed and perhaps called us fools, such hurrahing, jumping, yelling and screaming—my hat fell into the water pail but I could not stop to pick it out until I had read my letter all through. So you will take good care and write often when I tell you that I live upon your letters—with a small sprinkling of pork and bread.[10]

The imminent departure of an Atlantic-bound steamer on Steamer Day precipitated frenetic activity among San Francisco's business community as merchants settled accounts and prepared orders for East Coast suppliers. Henry Wells, co-founder of Wells, Fargo & Co., wrote from his company's banking and express office in San Francisco on February 14, 1853, just before Steamer Day: "All are at work & will be until 12 as tonight & tomorrow night all night not a man sleeps the night before the steamer leaves, and two thirds of all our drafts are drawn after lamps are lit on the last night."[11]

On April 12, 1849, the steamer *Oregon* carried the first eastbound mail from San Francisco.[12] The post office kept mailbags open until thirty minutes before the Atlantic-bound steamer's departure.[13]

Opposition Lines

Initially, government contract mail steamers departed San Francisco once a month. The local postmaster was forced by both volume and popular demand to ship outgoing mail twice a month beginning in October 1850. In addition, they placed supplementary mail shipments aboard steamers of competing opposition lines, which soon began capitalizing on the lucrative trade in passengers, goods, and treasure travelling between California and Panama.[14]

Panama remained the main land bridge between the Atlantic and Pacific Oceans, but soon a competing route through Nicaragua gained favour. Although two-and-a-half times the distance at 265 kilometres [165 miles] across, passage via the Nicaragua route eliminated 1600 kilometres [1,000 miles] of sea travel. Service on the Nicaragua route, funded by New York shipping magnate Cornelius Vanderbilt, began in summer 1851.[15] Vanderbilt's Nicaragua line provided spirited competition for passengers, but all but disintegrated in 1856 in the chaos of ongoing civil war in that Central American state.[16] A later, alternate mail route from New Orleans to San Francisco via Tehuantepec in Mexico was abandoned in 1859 after short-lived and unsatisfactory service.[17]

A Letter's Journey

Steamers made the sailing between New York and San Francisco in three-to-four weeks' time, averaging 23 to 29 days at sea, thus delivering their cargo of mail in an average 25 days' time.[18] In contrast, passage around Cape Horn averaged five to six months under sail, or 116 to 125 days aboard swift Clipper ships built in the early 1850s for the California gold-rush trade.[19] Because of their relative speed and reliability, steamships carried the bulk of passengers and mail and most of the gold from California. Most vessels were wooden side-wheel steamers, built in the Atlantic states or Europe and adapted for the Pacific coastal trade.

Letters posted in San Francisco went by steamship to Panama City. From there, mail and cargo crossed the Isthmus of Panama by mule and riverboat, to Aspinwall (now Colon) a five-day journey. After January 28, 1855, mail and goods transited the Isthmus by rail in under four hours across 75 kilometres [47 miles] of the Panama Railroad Company's track.[20]

In the early days of the gold rush, postal rates were 40 cents per half ounce [14 grams] for steamer mail between the Atlantic and Pacific Coasts, and "one bit" or 12 ½ cents for postage within California.[21] In 1851, these rates were reduced to six cents for steamer mail, or ten cents if sent collect. From 1855 to 1863, the cost for prepaid letters per half-ounce was three cents if sent under 5000 kilometres [3,000 miles], and ten cents for distances over 5000 kilometres [3,000 miles]. In 1858, half-ounce [14-gram] letters to Canada and the rest of British North America were 15 cents and letters to Europe were from 26 to 46 cents, depending upon final destination. Newspapers were one cent to any part of the U.S.[22] Private letter express carriers such as Wells Fargo charged 20 cents for mail sent by steamer in the 1850s.

Although the price remained dear, the volume of mail rose apace with the pitch of gold fever. Consider the following statistics regarding the volume of mail transiting between California and the Atlantic states: In January 1849, the first steamer departing New York carried 6,000 letters and a large shipment of newspapers. By November, letter shipments per sailing had increased to 30,000 pieces, according to reports by the postmaster general.[23] On July 20, 1851, the steamer *Tennessee* was carrying eight tonnes [eight tons] of mail in 45-kilogram [100-pound] sacks when it docked in San Francisco.[24] By autumn 1854, San Francisco post office staff were overwhelmed by the amount of mail, when each arriving steamer delivered nearly 300 bags of mail. Eastbound mail accounted for about a third as much volume during that same period.[25]

Despite the U.S. government's mail contract with the Pacific Mail Steamship Company, no prohibitions prevented individuals from carrying mail aboard company steamers in "letter bags" held by couriers. These postal entrepreneurs typically collected letters in San Francisco for a fee, bagged them, and sent them East on competition steamers in care of responsible couriers or agents. Letters sent on Vanderbilt's competitor line of steamers often carried provocative stamps boasting phrases such as "Via Nicaragua in Advance of the Mails." Competitor lines also carried letters for free, mailing them in the regular post upon arrival in New York, as explained by this notice for the July 1, 1852, sailing of the

Figure 19.3 This letter was addressed to Major General Ethan Allen Hitchcock in New York and left San Francisco on the steamer *St. Louis* destined for Panama on February 21, 1863. The cover, delivered by Wells Fargo, bears both a mandated ten cents of U.S. Postage and Wells Fargo & Co.'s distinctive red frank. The missive arrived in New York on March 19, 1863.

Wiltsee Stamp and Cover Collection, Wells Fargo Archives.

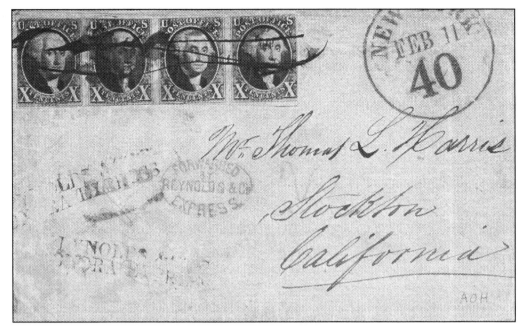

Figure 19.4 This letter left New York by steamer on February 11, 1850, and was delivered to Stockton California by Reynolds & Co.'s Express. The cover bears a strip of four ten-cent postage stamps, the first issued by the U.S. Post Office.[26]

Wiltsee Stamp and Cover Collection, Wells Fargo Archives.

competition steamer *Sierra Nevada*: "The mail bag will close 15 minutes before the sailing of the ship. Letters not over one-half ounce [14 grams] FREE, provided they are covered by postage stamps in accordance with the United States Postal regulations, C.K. Garrison, agent."[27]

Letters by Express

Few in the government in Washington, D.C., anticipated the sudden and long-lasting surge of demand for mail service brought about by the gold rush. Not surprisingly, the establishment of government post offices in California was delayed by bureaucratic inefficiency. As a result, in the first decade after the gold discovery, the bulk of mail in California was delivered by privately-owned express companies.

In 1854, in response to the carriage of letters by private parties and express companies, the U.S. postmaster general ordered all letters handled by others to carry full government postal rates in addition to express charges.[28] As of 1855, there was still no local mail delivery in San Francisco by the post office, perpetuating the long lines at the post office after each steamer arrival.[29] Private expresses, in contrast, delivered letters throughout the city for a small charge, a practice that the postmaster sought to curtail, prompting more than one scathing editorial by local press. The editor of the *Alta California* wrote on July 13, 1855:

The Post Office system, so far as California is concerned, is a humbug and a nuisance. It does not facilitate intercourse between different parts of the State, but it impedes it. It subjects correspondents to an onerous tax if they select a speedier and sure conveyance for their letters than the mail, and it benefits no one save office holders and contractors. … And yet our business men generally prefer to pay the double postage and send their letters by the Expresses, to waiting for the slow coach of Uncle Sam.[30]

In the hinterlands, enterprising express operators collected mail and newspapers at the San Francisco and Sacramento city post offices for delivery to miners in distant diggings, who had previously recorded their names on a list authorizing mail pickup on their behalf. Early expressmen like Alexander Todd and Samuel Langton typically charged $1 to $2 per item delivered and 50 cents for letters taken to the post office for mailing. Several express companies soon dominated letter delivery in gold rush California. The earliest enterprise, Adams and Company, opened in San Francisco on December 1, 1849. With connections to existing Adams offices in the East, Adams soon became the industry leader, competing with half a dozen smaller express companies on the West Coast. These express companies also entered the banking business, buying gold dust, forwarding gold, taking deposits, and selling drafts drawn on Eastern states. Express companies shipped millions of dollars of California gold to the East and delivered shipments of minted coins West. When the steamer *Northerner* left San Francisco on March 2, 1852, Adams and Berford & Company express messengers aboard guarded $1.4 million in gold.[31]

In 1852, another express player entered the California scene. On July 13, Wells, Fargo & Company opened its first offices in San Francisco and Sacramento and soon expanded to Portland, Oregon, and mining towns and camps throughout California. In October, 1852, John Q. Jackson, Wells Fargo's agent in Auburn, California, described his duties buying gold dust, forwarding and receiving packages, filling out bank drafts and cheques, and, of course, delivering mail: "I have just come from the Post Office, from which I have got 100 letters to be forwarded to the different parts of the country to which they are ordered by Express. On these I make $25, as my charge on each is 25 cents."[32]

In 1855, a financial panic nearly destroyed Wells Fargo along with other California express and banking firms. On February 17, the steamer *Oregon* arrived with news that drafts of the private banking house of Page, Bacon & Co. in St. Louis had been refused by New York banks for non-payment a month earlier, and the St. Louis bank had suspended operations. This dire news caused a run on that firm's office in San Francisco and other local banking houses and express companies.[33] Page, Bacon closed their doors in San Francisco on February 22, 1855, while Adams and Wells Fargo suspended business the following day. Panic rippled across the state as express offices closed throughout the hinterlands. Wells Fargo called in coin from its gold country offices and managed to reopen three days later, emerging from the crisis as the dominant surviving Western express company.

Delivery of mail, in fact, comprised a large and profitable portion of Wells Fargo's business. In 1858, the post office in San Francisco sold 120,000 three-cent stamped envelopes. Wells Fargo accounted for 100,000 of them.[34] The company added its own frank to the envelopes, thus adhering to government regulations, but then sold the covers for ten cents; there was no shortage of willing customers. Wells Fargo maintained its letter express service until 1895.

How, exactly, did express companies handle mail aboard steamers? An 1855 letter from headquarters gave very explicit instructions to W. B. Latham, Wells Fargo's messenger aboard the northbound steamer *Northern Light*:

> You will have charge of our express matter this day for San Francisco by Nicaragua route .... In no case nor under any consideration whatever, let any package, or letter or letters which we have put under your *immediate charge* go out of your care until you deliver the same to persons connected with our San Francisco office as after herein directed.

> While on way up on Pacific side, prepare a careful alphabetical list of all San Francisco (City) letters in your bag .... Get the Purser's Report and put it and your letter list in Letter Bag, and when nearing San Francisco our News Boat (with flag and Capt Martin on board) will come off—then throw bag of letters and bag of newspapers to him. Be ready for him so as not to misfire .... PS: *Be sure* to have *all the bags of news-papers on deck* ready for *immediate deliver*y on arrival in the Bay of San Francisco.[35]

This last directive—to deliver newspapers and dispatches as quickly as possible—enabled express companies to fulfill the voracious demand for news by isolated citizens of California and earn favourable mentions from editors of local papers. Express companies competed for the honor of delivering "the latest" to local news editors and prided themselves on quick delivery. To earn these bragging rights, small craft from competing express companies swarmed about each inbound steamer, with employees on board ready to catch the sacks of letters and papers thrown overboard by the steamer messenger. On shore, express riders or wagons stood ready at the dock to receive the bags and race through the streets to deliver their precious cargo to news offices and the express office. "It would have been a sight pleasing to the gods to have seen the young gentlemen of Adams & Co.'s and Wells, Fargo & Co.'s expresses, making tracks for the *Journal of Commerce* office on the morning of the arrival of the *Columbia*," reported Portland's newspaper editor in 1853.[36]

The End of Steamer Day

Steamer Day continued to mark the rhythm of commerce and communication along the Pacific Coast for over a decade after the bonanza days of 1849. Mail by steamer remained the only option for Californians until the advent of semi-weekly overland stagecoach and mail service between St. Louis and San Francisco in 1858. By 1860, overland stagecoaches carried more mail than steamers.[37] Between April 1860 and October 1861, thousands of letters crossed the continent tucked into the leather *mochilla* saddle of Pony Express riders, whose mounts covered the distance between Missouri and California in just ten days. When pony service began, the cost per half-ounce letter was five dollars, reduced to a dollar by the time the pony service was put out of business by the advent of the transcontinental telegraph wire.

Neither swift ponies nor six-horse stagecoach teams completely replaced the steamship and its seaborne mail delivery. Wells Fargo continued to send most of its Letter Express by semi-monthly steamer unless otherwise designated "overland" by the customer.[38] After completion of the transcontinental railroad in 1869, however, mail travelled by train and the glorious mail steamships sailed into the sunset of history.

Days of Gold

The great gold rush remains the defining moment in California history. The mass movement of people westward to California beginning in 1849 created cities, society, and political identity almost overnight. So sudden and profound was the impact of the gold rush in the region that California became the nation's thirty-first state on September 9, 1850, without ever having achieved territorial status. The news of statehood travelled to California by steamer, of course.

In the turbulent decade that preceded the Civil War, the Golden State remained separated from the rest of the nation by 1600 kilometres [1,000 miles] of unsettled frontier territory. Mail—and the steamers, stagecoaches, pony riders, and express messengers who carried it—became California's tenuous link to the outside world that extended West throughout the Pacific and East to the Atlantic seaboard and beyond. Letters kept Californians in touch, politically regarding world and national events and personally for thousands of Californians, who had left everything and everyone they held dear to search for fortune in the new El Dorado.

In this modern day of live broadcasts and instant messaging, it is hard to imagine the anxiety and anticipation that pioneer Californians felt regarding postal service, or the elation when letters found their way to homesick miners working remote diggings in California's mountains. Thankfully, many of their letters survived to tell the human story of the great California gold rush.

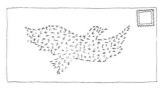

Notes

1. Carlos A. Schwantes, *Long Day's Journey: The Steamboat & Stagecoach Era in the Northern West* (Seattle & London: University of Washington Press, 1999), p. 48.
2. John Haskell Kemble, *The Panama Route 1848–1869* (Berkeley and Los Angeles: University of California Press, 1943), p. 3.
3. Ernest A. Wiltsee, *Gold Rush Steamers of the Pacific* (San Francisco: Grabhorn Press, 1938), pp. 6, 21.
4. John Haskell Kemble, *A Hundred Years of the Pacific Mail* (1950; reprint, Newport News, Virginia: The Mariners' Museum, 1950), p. 5.

5. Oscar Lewis, *Sea Routes to the Gold Fields: The Migration by Water to California in 1849–1852* (New York: Alfred A. Knopf, 1949), pp. 225–228.

6. Wiltsee, *Gold Rush Steamers*, p. 14.

7. Alvin F. Harlow, *Old Waybills: The Romance of the Express Companies* (New York: Arno Press, 1976), p. 96.

8. "The History of a Letter," *Hutchings' California Magazine* 2, no. 7 (1858): 31–34.

9. Enos Christman, *One Man's Gold* (New York: Whittlesey House, 1930) as quoted in Lewis, *Sea Routes to the Gold Fields*, pp. 274–275. Prepayment of postage did not become compulsory until April 1, 1855.

10. Lucius Fairchild to J. C. Fairchild and family, January 1, 1850. In *California Letters of Lucius Fairchild*, ed. Joseph Schafer (Madison: State Historical Society of Wisconsin, 1931), p. 59.

11. Henry Wells to Messrs Wells Fargo & Co. New York, February 14, 1853, in *Truly Yours Henry Wells* (Aurora, NY: Wells College Press, 1945), p. 12.

12. Henry C. Needham and Victor M. Berthold, "Ahead of the Mails: A Brief Story of the Transportation of the U.S. Mail by Sea, 1848–1860," *The Collectors Club Philatelist* 7, no. 2 (1928): 6.

13. *Hutchings'*, p. 34.

14. Kemble, *A Hundred Years*, p. 11.

15. Lewis, *Sea Routes*, p. 201.

16. In 1855, American mercenary William Walker led an armed expedition to Nicaragua and installed himself as dictator of that Central American nation until deposed in 1857.

17. Kemble, *The Panama Route*, p. 80.

18. *Hutchings'*, p. 30.

19. Wiltsee, *Gold Rush Steamers*, p. 2; and James P. Delgado, *To California By Sea: A Maritime History of the California Gold Rush* (Columbia: University of South Carolina Press, 1990), p. 44.

20. Lewis, *Sea Routes*, pp. 186–188.

21. Harlow, *Old Waybills*, p. 106.

22. *Hutchings'*, pp. 32, 33.

23. Needham and Berthold, "Ahead of the Mails," p. 7.

24. Delgado, *To California by Sea*, p. 68.

25. *Hutchings'*, pp. 30, 32.

26. In 1847, the U.S. postal service issued its first five- and ten-cent postage stamps. Inexplicably, these stamps were not distributed to California post offices, requiring Pacific postmasters to hand stamp "40 cents Paid" on each prepaid cover. "Stampless" California covers prior to July 1, 1851, are highly prized by collectors. Rarer still is stamped mail originating in California during that era, of which only a few examples are known. The Ernest A. Wiltsee Collection, shown in Wells Fargo's San Francisco museum since 1941, is the premier collection of California gold-rush postal and express covers on public display.

27. Wiltsee, *Gold Rush Steamers*, p. 324.

28. Harlow, *Old Waybills*, p. 152.

29. In 1855, the population of San Francisco was generally estimated at 55,000 residents, according to figures compiled by Dorothy H. Huggins from contemporary magazines and newspapers and published in the *Continuation of the Annals of San Francisco,* Part I, June 1, 1854 to December 31, 1855 (San Francisco: California Historical Society, 1939), p. 77. This number is difficult to verify from official sources due to the transient nature of much of the city's populace.

30. [San Francisco] *Alta California,* July 13, 1855, in Harlow, *Old Waybills*, p. 153.

31. Harlow, *Old Waybills*, p. 134. At the time, gold was valued at $20.67 per troy ounce [31 grams].

32. John Quincy Jackson to brother, October 23, 1852, Wells Fargo Archives.

33. Mail and passengers on the *Oregon* had departed New York twenty-eight days previously. The California banking crisis inspired one French Canadian rancher to take extreme measures to save his fortune. Louis Remme had just finished driving a herd of cattle to Sacramento and had deposited $12,500 in gold with Adams & Company Express there. Unable to redeem his certificate of deposit when the panic began, he set off on horseback for Oregon, racing the next northbound Pacific Mail steamer *Columbia* to Portland. An exhausted Remme arrived in Portland shortly ahead of the steamer and received his gold, less a commission fee of 1½ per cent. This story is told in *Gold in the Woodpile: An Informal History of Banking in Oregon* (Eugene: University of Oregon Press, 1967), pp. 27–39.

34. *Hutchings'*, p. 33.

35. Jesse Payne, Wells Fargo & Company, New York, to W. B. Latham, steamer messenger, April 27, 1855. Copy in Wells Fargo Archives.

36. Harlow, *Old Waybills*, p. 149.

37. Robert J. Chandler, "Steamer Days!" *Western Express* 52, no. 1 (2002): 20.

38. Ibid.

"A LIVING, MOVING PAGEANT"

The CBC's Coverage of the Royal Tour of 1939

20

Mary Vipond, History Department, Concordia University, Montréal

Abstract

This chapter discusses the role of radio in Canadian society in the late 1930s by focusing on the CBC's broadcasts of the Royal Tour of 1939. It argues that the publicly owned broadcaster's continuous and costly coverage of the Tour served to legitimize the authority of the Canadian state, the Commonwealth, and the monarchy, and to promote the bonds of amity between Great Britain and North America at a time of looming international crisis. The Tour broadcasts also served to legitimize the CBC itself. The CBC presented itself to the Canadian people as efficient, authoritative, and technologically up-to-date, capable of performing nation-building duties beyond the capacity of its competitors, the privately owned stations. By acting as the liaison for the Tour coverage of the BBC and the American networks, the CBC also established its international credentials as the principal Canadian broadcasting authority.

Résumé

Ce chapitre porte sur le rôle de la radio dans la société canadienne à la fin des années 1930, et plus particulièrement sur les émissions diffusées par Radio-Canada sur la visite royale de 1939. L'auteur y soutient que la couverture, continue et coûteuse, de la visite par le radiodiffuseur public a servi à légitimer l'autorité de l'État canadien, du Commonwealth et de la monarchie, et à promouvoir les liens d'amitié entre la Grande-Bretagne et l'Amérique du Nord à une époque où une crise internationale était imminente. Les émissions sur la visite ont également servi à légitimer la Société Radio-Canada elle-même. Celle-ci s'est présentée à la population canadienne comme étant efficace, faisant autorité et étant à la fine pointe de la technologie, capable de s'acquitter de tâches d'édification de la nation bien au-delà de ce que pouvaient faire ses concurrentes, les stations privées. En faisant office d'intermédiaire pour la présentation de la visite par la BBC et les réseaux américains, Radio-Canada s'est aussi acquis la réputation d'être le principal radiodiffuseur canadien.

Figure 20.1 Eaton's Catalogue, Fall/Winter 1927–1928, cover. Radio was a common denominator of the Canadian cultural imagination.

Sears Canada Inc.

Introduction

In recent years, historians have become increasingly interested in cultural history, defined broadly to mean historical "ways of life" and, more narrowly, to focus on cultural institutions and products such as art, books, music, and so on. This process has occurred parallel to another that has led scholars to examine the past "from the bottom up," in other words, to study the life experiences of ordinary people. One consequence of the development of these new lines of inquiry has been a turn to the analysis of popular forms of culture, including the mass media. Considerable scholarly attention has been devoted to the history of film, for example, and television. For a variety of reasons, however, radio, the first of the electronic mass media, has been relatively neglected,[1] even though, between approximately 1920 and 1950, radio was an extremely influential medium of expression, locally, nationally, and internationally. It provided not only mass entertainment but because of its intimacy, immediacy, and ubiquity, it served important functions in building national consensus in many countries. In its heyday, radio was a primary site of social and political power and discourse. However difficult it may be to accomplish, therefore, radio's cultural impact must be studied. This chapter discusses one specific Canadian radio institution, the publicly owned Canadian Broadcasting Corporation (CBC), at a particular moment in its history. It situates the CBC within a broader Anglo-American world by focusing on the role played by the CBC in broadcasting the events of the Royal Tour of Canada and the United States in May and June of 1939. The emphasis is on how an organization like the CBC strove to enhance its authority and legitimacy with national listeners by positioning itself as the vehicle for conveying significant symbolic moments in the nation's life.

The late 1930s was a very sensitive period in the Anglo-American geo-political relationship. As war in Europe loomed, a significant portion of the American public and political elite maintained an isolationist (or anti-interventionist) stance.[2] In Britain, those who believed that war was almost inevitable calculated how to win over American opinion to once again provide full support for the Allies, but they were also very conscious that the propaganda efforts of the First World War had aroused much cynicism in America and could not be repeated.[3] Canada also had a strong isolationist element (mainly but by no means entirely in French-speaking Canada) as well as a significant population of pro-imperial, English-speaking Canadians who were willing to rush to Britain's (and the Empire's) side instantly if needed.[4] The leaders of these three countries manoeuvred through various trade and arms agreements in the late 1930s but did not reach a clear resolution of the issue before the war began at the beginning of September 1939. Canada declared war on September 9, a week after Britain did. The United States moved towards various forms of arms supply and mutual defence arrangements but did not enter until after the attack on Pearl Harbor in December 1941. Nevertheless, the tasks of the two North American leaders, William Lyon Mackenzie King and Franklin Delano Roosevelt, were parallel: to build consensus toward support for the war through careful cultivation, indeed manipulation, of both political and public opinion.

There is a very large historiography about the Anglo-American relationship in this period.[5] For the purposes of this chapter, it is useful to focus very briefly on popular attitudes in the United States toward Britain. Those attitudes were very mixed. On the negative side were factors such as the residue of anti-British feeling inherent in the constant celebration of the origins of the American Revolution; the dislike of Britain's imperialism; the aversion to the class system; the hostile feelings of the substantial Irish population; the suspicion of manipulation; and the unpaid debt from the First World War. There were, however, positives as well. British popular culture was well known and appreciated, especially by movie audiences; it was recognized that both countries shared a common belief in democracy and liberty. Indeed, there was even rhetoric (on both sides) about the common destiny of the "English-speaking race."[6]

Canadians believed that they fit into this story in a very special way. Canada was, after all, according to its constitution, British North America. It had a close (and ever closer) relationship to the United States on the North American continent, but it also retained its British ties and was the senior Dominion in the Commonwealth. Canadians too talked of the "English-speaking race" of which they were a part; just as often, they talked about how Canada was the "linchpin" of the English-speaking world, the keystone in the arch of unity stretching across the North Atlantic.[7] In the late 1930s, as has already been suggested, Canada was at least as riven as its neighbour to the south by the tensions between North-American-style isolationism and gung-ho "Ready-Aye-Ready" imperialist enthusiasm for helping Britain out in any time of need. Of special concern in Canada was the issue of conscription. During the First World War, the country had split badly over the imposition of conscription for overseas service, which was opposed by the vast majority of French Canadians as well as certain elements of the English-speaking population. The fear was that another war would destroy the precious national unity Mackenzie King had worked to reconstruct in the interwar period.

The invention of radio broadcasting was the most important mass cultural innovation between the two World Wars. Initially growing out of amateur and experimental uses of point-to-point radio communication that began in the early twentieth century, and bolstered by military use during the First World War, radio developed in the early 1920s into a medium for simultaneous communication (literally, broad-casting) to large groups of people. From the beginning, entertainment was a principal function of radio, but the medium was also seen to have significant educational possibilities, and even more important, the capacity to facilitate communication over vast distances such as the modern nation state. In Canada, the awareness of the potential uses of radio for fostering national unity and identity (and the concomitant fear of the "Americanization" of the medium) led, after an experimental ten-year period of private broadcasting, to the creation of a public broadcasting organization, the Canadian Radio Broadcasting Commission (CRBC) in 1932. Charged with regulating all of Canadian radio (including the private stations that continued to exist), the CRBC also immediately set to work creating a national radio network of stations (both its own and many private stations from which it purchased time) strung together by telegraph lines from coast to coast. The CRBC lasted only four years. It was administratively awkward, politically distrusted, and under attack from some listeners, who disliked paying for a service they thought was better provided by the private sector, especially by the American networks whose programs they had access to either directly or through affiliated Canadian stations.[8]

When the federal government changed hands in 1935, the Liberals under Mackenzie King were determined to abolish the CRBC. They continued to appreciate, however, the utility of having a national network to weld Canadians together and knew that such a scheme could only be realized with government subsidy. They then reorganized the public broadcasting organization into the CBC, and ensured that it had more funding and more competent leadership.

The CBC was only three years old when the war began. It had not had time to achieve all its reconstruction goals, and it continued to be viewed with suspicion by some of the private broadcasters and some segments of the public. It desperately needed a project to demonstrate its utility to the Canadian state and to enhance its credibility in the eyes of Canadian citizens. In late 1938, the opportunity arrived with the announcement that the King and Queen would be touring Canada the following year. The CBC's executives immediately seized on the opportunity the Tour offered to take the lead in representing and publicizing the monarchy, the Canadian state, and the royal couple not only to the Canadian public but to the people of Britain and the United States through the BBC and the American networks.

It will be argued here that the Royal Tour and the radio coverage of the Tour played a role in what one might call the "softening up" of North American public opinion about Britain in this crucial period. As diplomatic historian Benjamin Rhodes put it, it "strengthened the hand" of President Roosevelt in his battle with the anti-interventionists in Congress by demonstrating that many Americans thought of Britain fairly fondly, if not to the point of going to war.[9] It had a similar effect in Canada, where the enthusiastic reception of the royal couple by both French and English Canadians was seen to suggest a common loyalty.[10] It would be a great exaggeration to claim that the Tour represented an essential turning point in the march toward full Allied participation in the war in Europe. But, the personal experiences of the leaders and other participants, the publicity in the mass media, and the contacts among the broadcasting organizations engendered by the coverage of the Tour did contribute to the smoother functioning of the North Atlantic "team," and especially its broadcasters, once the war began.

This, then, is an examination of an incident in the cultural, or more properly perhaps, the symbolic, relationship among the three countries, as made manifest through the major new mass medium of the day. Indeed, one may perhaps go further to argue that the Tour became a "media event" in the sense used by Daniel Dayan and Elihu Katz in their influential book *Media Events: The Live Broadcasting of History*.[11] While Dayan and Katz study only television, their conclusion that the event and its impact are transformed by being made widely available simultaneously to the whole community (and perhaps the whole world) applies to radio as well. Moreover, electronic transmission enables the event to penetrate the homes of the nation. The home thus becomes a "political space," as broadcasters expound on the event's significance in ways that integrate the society, evoke a renewal of loyalty, and reinforce the legitimacy of authority.[12] In the case being studied here, not only the authority of the nation and the Empire but that of the public broadcaster itself was being legitimated.

Mackenzie King first proposed the Tour to the King at the time of the Coronation in May 1937. Although the initial response to the invitation to come to Canada was favourable, the situation in Europe discouraged immediate action on it. The governor-general of Canada, Lord Tweedsmuir (John Buchan), continued to press the issue and finally the invitation was accepted in the summer of 1938.[13] In the meantime, Mackenzie King had also informally told President Roosevelt that the Tour was in the offing, and Roosevelt had hastened to address a personal invitation to the King to include the United States in the trip to North America.[14] Although the three leaders said little about the clouds of war overhead, they did frame the visit from the beginning as an opportunity to demonstrate the friendship among their nations, and as an opportunity to get to know one another personally.[15]

By 1939, King and Roosevelt were on a first-name basis. Of course, one did not get on first-name terms with the King and Queen, but there were, nevertheless, many moments of observation, informality, and chat among the leaders over the course of the Tour that facilitated the personalization of the three-way relationship.[16] Several observers were convinced that a genuine friendship arose between the royal couple and the Roosevelts.[17] Even more important, from the point of view of this chapter at any rate, was that through the intensive publicity provided by, among others, the radio broadcasters who accompanied the tour, the monarchs were personalized—quite deliberately on their part—for the North American public.[18] It was on this visit, for example, that the Queen initiated the first royal "walkabout," chatting with spectators after she laid the cornerstone for Canada's new Supreme Court Building. Much publicity was given as well to the royal couple's consumption of hot dogs at an American picnic. Moreover, again from the focus here, another significance of the Tour lay in the personal relationships that were formed or strengthened among broadcasting executives and practitioners from the three countries, relationships that were to become tighter once the war began. To cite one example, the work of Ernest Bushnell, the CBC's programme director, who was one of the principal organizers of the CBC Tour coverage, so impressed British public broadcasting officials that, early in the war, they requested he be seconded to the BBC for six months as North American programme organizer—in other words, to help the BBC develop programs that would be more appealing to Canadian and American audiences. Similarly, the already close liaison with the American networks was even more tightly coordinated during the War for security reasons, especially during the period before the U.S. became a combatant.[19]

Before going further, it is necessary to fill in some background about the previous use of radio for events surrounding the British monarchy. The most significant fact is that in the 1930s the broadcasters at the CBC (and at its predecessor, the CRBC) had much closer ties to the American networks than they did to the BBC. Although the CBC aired, and sometimes participated in, important BBC monarchical and imperial programs such as the King's Christmas broadcasts and the Empire Day programs beginning in the early 1930s, regular program interchange across the Atlantic was minimal due to the vagaries of time zones, inadequate short-wave facilities at the Canadian end, inflexible schedules, and cultural differences.[20] The Canadian broadcaster's links with the American networks (NBC, CBS, and Mutual) were, on the other hand, close and cordial. Not only had Canadian audiences been accustomed to listening directly or via private station affiliates to American radio since broadcasting began, but the CBC was actually an NBC network affiliate, and picked up numerous commercial and non-commercial programs (including some popular ones like "Fibber McGee and Molly") from all three U.S. networks. Regular telephone lines between Montréal and New York had long been established and were utilized many times each day. For the BBC's part, after the Empire Service was developed in the early 1930s, increasing attention was paid to sending programs to Canada and other parts of the Empire, but when BBC officials realized that they were getting even more response to their programs from Americans than Canadians, they began to focus on the potential of pleasing the large American audience. In 1935, the BBC appointed a North American representative, Felix Greene; significantly, he was headquartered in New York. Greene frequently travelled to Ottawa, Montréal, and Toronto to meet with CBC personnel, but his contacts with the American network executives based in New York were simpler and more regular. Indeed, his office was in Rockefeller Center, NBC's headquarters.[21]

The same year, the BBC also hired American journalist and broadcaster Raymond Gram Swing to give regular talks about America, something it never did for Canada.[22] The BBC's assumption was that radio could both take advantage of and facilitate the interest of the British in the United States and vice versa. Both the BBC and the CBC, however, were more ambivalent about establishing a close working arrangement between the "Mother Country" and the Dominion. At the British end, there was some antipathy to the kind of overly patriotic programming involved in the Empire Service as well as some irritation about Canadian demands; in Ottawa there seems to have been some resentment of the "superior" attitude of the BBC.[23] The relationship was fostered to some extent, however, by the fact that the first general manager of the CBC, Canadian-born Rhodes Scholar Gladstone Murray, had worked for the BBC for a number of years. Although he harboured some bitterness toward the Corporation because of his lack of promotion, he knew personally all the key BBC personnel with whom the CBC had to deal in the late 1930s and early 1940s.

On May 17, 1939, Their Majesties arrived in Canada at Québec. Their tour of Canada on a special train progressed to Ottawa and Toronto and then to points West, all the way to Victoria, before returning via the Rocky Mountains to southern Ontario. In Winnipeg, on Empire Day, May 24, the King sent a broadcast message over the airwaves of the CBC, BBC, and the American networks, one of five radio addresses he gave during the Tour; the Queen also gave two.[24] On June 7, the Royal Train crossed into the United States at Niagara Falls. Two days were spent in Washington, a day in New York at the World's Fair, and then two days at the Roosevelts' summer place at Hyde Park, New York, before Their Majesties returned to Canada to visit various Maritime centres and to depart from Halifax on June 15. It was a most ambitious, exhausting trip, one which drew large enthusiastic crowds at almost every venue, and which was marked by a nuanced mix

Figure 20.2 King George VI delivers a radio broadcast to the Empire on Empire Day, May 24, 1939.
National Film Board of Canada, Library and Archives Canada, PA-122957.

of ceremonious pomp and friendly cordiality. As the King's biographer put it, "Within a week of their arrival the King and Queen had completely won the heart of the whole North American continent."[25] George VI was now "The North American King."[26]

As soon as news of a Royal Tour had surfaced in 1938, the CBC had spotted its opportunity. Anomalous as a public broadcaster in the commercially oriented North American radio market, the Corporation constantly sought opportunities to legitimize itself by performing its authoritative role as the Canada's national—and international—broadcaster. Here, then, was the "biggest publicity opportunity" the Corporation had ever had.[27] Quickly ensuring that it was placed in charge of the Canadian part of the journey, the organization swung into action. New equipment was ordered, a phalanx of announcers was hired and trained, and complicated scheduling details were worked out. All in all, the CBC put a huge amount of time, energy, and money into what it confidently declared was "the biggest sustained job of actuality broadcasting ever undertaken."[28] For the thirty days of the Tour, two teams of CBC announcers travelled leapfrog ahead of the Royal Train, taking turns organizing local radio coverage of the main events at each stop. All the broadcasts went out live to the CBC's national network and were also recorded at the Toronto studios to provide a fifteen-minute re-broadcast of highlights each evening.

The project cost the CBC over $50,000 of its own funds on top of the $50,000 allotted by the government for the special occasion. For the first time, the CBC was able to demonstrate convincingly that it could offer what Canadian private broadcasters could not—a well coordinated cultural project, technically up-to-the-minute, and available simultaneously to Canadians from coast to coast.

From the outset, the CBC was also conscious of interest from British and American broadcasters, and it positioned itself as the liaison for this task.[29] Charles Jennings, the CBC's senior announcer, was put in charge of distribution of programs outside the country. The CBC's files reveal the extent to which its managers were preoccupied with protecting and enhancing the Corporation's status by exerting control over all aspects of the broadcasts. The three U.S. networks and the BBC were informed early on that they were welcome to free feeds of the CBC's Tour programming (including live coverage of virtually all events and the evening re-cap), but that it would not be possible for them to cover the story live (except for the U.S. portion of the Tour, which was left to the U.S. networks). Eventually the CBC facilitated some U.S. "observers" at events in Québec, Ottawa, Niagara Falls, and Halifax, and U.S. representatives did ride on the pilot train that ran half an hour before the Royal Train, but they did not do direct broadcasts; they only reported in by telephone to their home stations, which used the material for news items.[30] Thus, most of the live coverage carried by the U.S. networks was a CBC feed.

Although the Canadians initially wanted to make the same arrangements with the BBC, they were eventually persuaded to let a BBC broadcaster, Richard Dimbleby, use their facilities to send five-minute nightly summaries of events to London.[31] In fact, the CBC managers exhibited considerable deference toward the BBC's superior knowledge of covering royal events, borrowing sample recordings and even requesting that a BBC official be sent to help out (although this did not happen in the end).[32] The main drafting of the script for the central event of the Empire Day program that preceded the King's address from Winnipeg was left to Felix Greene in New York, although he did consult with CBC program planners. Generally, the British and American networks picked up only the most important events—the arrival, the ceremonies in Ottawa, the Empire Day speech, and the departure. The BBC, undoubtedly surfeited with royal appearances, took almost nothing but the Empire Day program and Dimbleby's five minutes per day. In the U.S., the smaller Mutual network took by far the most coverage; the more established U.S. networks used only the most ceremonial moments of the Canadian part of the visit and a few other short bits that could be squeezed in around commercial programs.[33] It should be noted that sending the programs to the United States cost almost nothing; the material for the BBC, however, had to go out over the costly commercial Marconi beam at Drummondville, Quebec.

There is no doubt that through these broadcasting arrangements (as well, of course, as newspaper stories), a significant part of the American public was informed, entertained, and enthused about the royal couple. The Canadian coverage "primed" popular opinion in the United States for the American part of the Tour well before the King and Queen actually arrived. As historian Nicholas Cull put it, the United States was already "charmed and ready for conquest" the day the royal train crossed the border; the huge and enthusiastic crowds in Washington and New York (an estimated three-and-a-half million lined the streets of New York, for example) are the evidence.[34] The June 3 edition of the *New Yorker* carried a poem by Anne Forbes about the broadcast of the monarchs' arrival in Québec. The first stanza set up the particular power of radio to personalize events because of its penetration into the daily life of the home:

> Boom go the guns! The flags fly free
> Canada welcomes royalty.
> The morning coat is pressed, the topper dusted
> And we, with radio adjusted,
> Going about our household labors,
> Can listen in upon our neighbors.[35]

But, I repeat the caution mentioned earlier. Although the Tour produced an emotional and psychological high, it did not transform American public opinion. A poll by *Fortune* in September 1939, after the war had started, revealed that 65 per cent of respondents got a "favourable" impression of the King and Queen during the Tour, but 31 per cent remained "neutral" and a few (3 per cent) reacted unfavourably.[36] When asked what they thought had motivated the visit to the United States, almost a quarter believed that it had grown out of a desire "to influence [the U.S.] to go to war to defend England." A Gallup poll later that fall showed that 68 per cent of Americans still thought it had been a mistake for their country to enter the First World War, and that a plurality (34 per cent) believed that it had done so because it had been "the victim of propaganda and selfish interests."[37]

My main purpose here, however, is not to attempt to answer the unanswerable question of the effect of the Royal Tour on public opinion in North America, but rather to draw attention to the concrete ways in which mass media organizations like the CBC operate to enhance their own credibility by "performing" symbolic moments. In an article about the BBC and the Empire, John MacKenzie argues that the BBC's first director-general, Sir John Reith, saw the projection of Empire in ritual-laden programming as "a route to respectability for the Corporation, a means of demonstrating that it could through national and patriotic symbols be a consensual and not a divisive body."[38] While employed by the BBC in publicity and public relations, Gladstone Murray had been one of the most enthusiastic proponents of that goal, and this was exactly the model developed at the CBC under his direction for the Royal Tour coverage. Within Canada, the CBC's Tour programming was comprehensive. From coast to coast, all major and minor events were provided in English and French, an unprecedented action for the CBC. Moreover, the CBC quite consciously positioned itself as the voice of Canada internationally, presenting the country to audiences in Britain and the U.S. as prosperous, diverse, interesting, and, above all, loyal. Not only was Canada the "linchpin" of the trilateral relationship; the CBC was, for this moment at least, the linchpin of North Atlantic broadcasting. The CBC summed up its own role as follows:

We are charged with the task of making the Royal Visit a living, moving pageant, first of all, in every home in Canada within range of a radio signal .... Secondly, we are charged with the responsibility of conveying to the United Kingdom and other parts of the Empire a continuous, realistic account of the progress of the Tour and particularly of the many-sided aspects of the Canadian scene as revealed by the Tour. Thirdly, and by no means the least important, we are charged with the responsibility of giving to the great multitude of radio listeners in the United States a vividly interesting impression.[39]

Special attention should be drawn to the use of the word "pageant" here. In the book mentioned previously, communications scholars Daniel Dayan and Elihu Katz argue that media organizations (in their study, specifically television producers) adopt what they call a "priestly" role in conveying moments of current history to audiences. The media do not act as objective observers but as guides and mentors to their listeners and viewers, providing them with solemn and reverent access to great ceremonial events.[40] While Dayan and Katz studied this process by which journalists in commercial news organization become part of the event rather than observers of it, it is even more likely that a public broadcaster will play this role and act in this way. In the case of a public broadcaster in a country like Canada, only a generation away from colonial status and faced with the presentation of the two main living symbols of the Empire, the tendency to hushed reverence, to participation rather than observation, was exacerbated even further. The CBC's Tour announcers were drilled for weeks on how to maintain the proper tone of voice, on the various formalities of titles and behaviour of the British upper classes, on what to do in the case of a delay or disturbance, and so on. After listening to some rehearsals, Gladstone Murray advised his staff to take a "psychological approach" of "quiet confidence," and concluded: "I was impressed this morning by your balance. In attitude there is reserve and a sense of poise, which are important. This avoids, on the one hand, the torrential manner which disfigures the work of some American commentators, and, on the other hand, the awkward silences and the casual leisureliness which is a weakness of some British commentators."[41]

After the Tour broadcasts ended with an emotional farewell in Halifax, the CBC received many letters of congratulations for its coverage from listeners in Canada, the United States, and even from a man in Iraq. A number of those correspondents picked up on the tone used by the CBC commentators in painting what the Corporation liked to call "word pictures" of the various events. One Brantford, Ontario man, for example, called the descriptions "awe-inspiring," and then added: "I use the word awe-inspiring because of the utter grandeur and pageantry coupled with the earnest sincerity of the commentators."[42] Even more explicitly a woman from West Vancouver wrote: "They [the announcers] 'put over' the thrill so successfully, and I like to think that it was because their own response to the occasion was warm and genuine."[43] An Ottawa woman added: "It seemed to me that the announcers had also come under the spell of the kindliness of Their Majesties .... Without the radio, the Royal Visit could not have come to us as such a personal experience."[44] And, an American man from New York state perceptively wrote: "You sure handled every detail in a way that anyone can call truly patriotic to the Crown."[45] The CBC did not cover the Tour to provide an objective outside viewpoint on it. Its employees embraced an event that apparently had the same meaning for them as it did for thousands of other Canadians in troubled times. But, they also embraced it as an opportunity to improve their skills, to have an exciting if tiring break from routine, and most importantly, to enhance the status of their employer as a public institution. They must have been delighted to read an editorial in a Winnipeg farm and grain market paper, the *Weekly Market News*, two days after the King and Queen sailed from the colony of Newfoundland, their last North American stop:

> Without doubt, and without minimizing the part which our newspapers played, it can safely be said that much of the unparalleled acclaim which greeted Their Majesties in the United States found its origins in the fact that long before our neighbors had seen the King and Queen, they had learned to know and admire them—via the daily broadcasts of the Canadian Broadcasting Corporation. In this respect therefore the Corporation has rendered a valuable service to the British Commonwealth of Nations and to the United States, in paving the way for a visit which is destined to lead to a greater understanding between these two Democracies, with far reaching and beneficial effects on the world situation.[46]

Radio was an important tool for building national and international bonds in the crucial interwar years, but that did not occur by happenstance. The CBC, desirous of enhancing its own legitimacy in a continental commercial radio marketplace, deliberately allocated a large proportion of its technical, financial, and personnel resources in the early summer of 1939 to show Canadians—as well as their American and British cousins—that all were part of a common democratic, liberal and English-speaking "race." By doing so, the CBC positioned itself as the authoritative Canadian broadcaster and the voice of Canada abroad.

Notes

1. According to American radio historian Michele Hilmes, these reasons include early scholarly disdain because of radio's lowbrow appeal to mass audiences and the medium's eclipse and cannibalization by the more "modern" network television in the 1950s. In Canada, the lack of preserved audio sources has also been a major handicap. See Michele Hilmes, "Rethinking Radio," in *The Radio Reader*, eds M. Hilmes and J. Loviglio (New York: Routledge, 2002), pp. 1–19.
2. See, among others, William L. Langer and S. Everett Gleason, *The Challenge to Isolation: The World Crisis of 1937–1940 and American Foreign Policy* (New York: Harper and Row, 1952).

3. Nicholas Cull, *Selling War: The British Propaganda Campaign against American "Neutrality" in World War II* (New York: Oxford University Press, 1993), p. 3. On the various indirect means of propaganda the British adopted between the wars see Philip M. Taylor, *The Projection of Britain: British Overseas Publicity and Propaganda, 1919–1939* (Cambridge: Cambridge University Press, 1981), pp. 68–77.

4. The standard text on Canadian foreign policy in the period is James Eayrs, *In Defence of Canada: Appeasement and Rearmament* (Toronto: University of Toronto Press, 1965). See also J. L. Granatstein, *Canada's War: The Politics of the Mackenzie King Government, 1939–1945* (Toronto: Oxford University Press, 1975), Chapter 1, and James Eayrs, "'A Low Dishonest Decade': Aspects of Canadian External Policy, 1931–1939," in *The Growth of Canadian Policies in External Affairs,* eds H. L. Keenleyside *et al.* (Durham, NC: Duke University Press, 1960), pp. 59–79.

5. A good survey of the historiography is Justus D. Doenecke, "U.S. Policy and the European War, 1939–1941," *Diplomatic History* 19 (1995): 660–98.

6. Cull, *Selling War*, p. 6.

7. The most famous usage of the term "linchpin" occurred in a speech by Winston Churchill as he welcomed Mackenzie King to London in September 1941. The concept was an old one, however, and as early as the 1880s Canadian Imperial Federationists were talking of their country as the "living link" between the United States and Great Britain. See Carl Berger, *The Sense of Power: Studies in the Ideas of Canadian Imperialism, 1867–1914* (Toronto: University of Toronto Press, 1970), pp. 171–72.

8. Annual licence fees paid by radio owners provided the principal income for the Canadian public broadcaster until 1953. By the end of the 1920s, the overwhelmingly private American radio industry had coalesced into two major networks, NBC and CBS. Four Canadian stations, two each in Montréal and Toronto, were affiliated to the U.S. networks. The Mutual network was set up in 1934.

9. The Tour *per se* has received very little scholarly attention in the United States. Benjamin D. Rhodes, "The British Royal Visit of 1939 and the 'Psychological Approach' to the United States," *Diplomatic History* 2, no. 2 (1978): 197–211, focuses on the visit from the point of view of Sir Ronald Lindsay, Britain's ambassador to the U.S. (quotation on p. 198). David Reynolds, "FDR's Foreign Policy and the British Royal Visit to the U.S.A., 1939," *The Historian* 45, 4 (1983): 461–472, highlights the official American viewpoint. The latest addition to this sparse literature, Fred Leventhal's "Essential Democracy: The 1939 Royal Visit to the United States," in *Singular Continuities: Tradition, Nostalgia, and Identity in Modern British Culture,* eds G. K. Behlmer and F. M. Leventhal (Stanford: Stanford University Press, 2000), pp. 163–77, stresses the effectiveness of the Tour in presenting the King and Queen as, within limits, "approachable, even ordinary, mortals with familiar concerns and domestic responsibilities," (p. 170). All these American works more or less ignore the Canadian part of the visit, although they make use of Prime Minister Mackenzie King's observations about his experiences touring the United States, when he accompanied Their Majesties as their minister-in-attendance (Lord Halifax, the British foreign secretary, having bowed out for fear of alarming the American public by politicizing the event). There are also some popular accounts of the visit, some of which are footnoted below.

10. There are no scholarly Canadian studies of the Tour. Popular accounts include R. B. Fleming, *The Royal Tour of Canada: The 1939 Visit of King George VI and Queen Elizabeth* (Toronto: Lynx Images, 2002), Tom MacDonnell, *Daylight upon Magic: The Royal Tour of Canada—1939* (Toronto: Macmillan, 1989), and Elinor Kyte Senior, "They Came, They Saw, They Conquered," *Monarchy Canada,* March 1980, pp. 11–13, 22–23, as well as others footnoted below. A contemporaneous account by a journalist is R. K. Carnegie, *And the People Cheered* (Ottawa: self-published, 1939). Carnegie's chapter on the radio coverage of the Tour was

actually written by CBC personnel. The official history of the Tour was written by national archivist Gustave Lanctot at the time, but published only in an abbreviated version years later. See Gustave Lanctot, *The Royal Tour of King George VI and Queen Elizabeth in Canada and the United States of America 1939* (Toronto: E. P. Taylor Foundation, 1964).

11. Daniel Dayan and Elihu Katz, *Media Events: The Live Broadcasting of History* (Cambridge: Harvard University Press, 1992).

12. Ibid., pp. 23, 9.

13. For more on Tweedsmuir's role, see J. William Galbraith, "Fiftieth Anniversary of the 1939 Royal Visit," *Canadian Parliamentary Review* 12, no. 3 (1989): 7–11.

14. As Dayan and Katz point out, the naming of the event is important. Most Canadians called this one a Royal Tour (capitalized and implying that a monarch was viewing his realm), while the usual American usage was royal visit (often uncapitalized and suggesting a relationship between two different states). Dayan and Katz, *Media Events*, pp. 30–31.

15. See the correspondence reproduced in John W. Wheeler-Bennett, *King George VI: His Life and Reign* (New York: St. Martin's Press, 1958), pp. 372–73, 382.

16. Canadians find it amusing that although Mackenzie King celebrated the fact that he and FDR were "Franklin and Mackenzie," in fact he never worked up the nerve to tell Roosevelt that his real friends called him "Rex." See J. H. Thompson and S. J. Randall, *Canada and the United States: Ambivalent Allies* (Montréal and Kingston: McGill-Queen's University Press, 1994), p. 146. A small example of the intimacy established is the tale of the night at Hyde Park when Roosevelt, King, and the King stayed up late talking about the affairs of the world, until the president tapped the King on the knee and told him: "Young man, it's time for you to go to bed." P. T. Cantelon, "Greetin's Cousin George," *American Heritage* 19, no. 1 (1967): 110.

17. See, for example, G. Gordon Young, *Voyage of State* (London: Hodder and Stoughton, 1939), p. 225.

18. Wheeler–Bennett, *King George VI*, p. 393.

19. See Peter Stursberg, *Mr. Broadcasting: The Ernie Bushnell Story* (Toronto: Peter Martin Associates, 1971), pp. 81–95.

20. For exchanges on these problems in the pre-war period, see Library and Archives Canada, RG 41, CBC Collection, (hereafter cited as CBC Collection), vol. 378, file 20-3-5, part 2: Felix Greene to W. E. G. Murray, June 2, 1938; ibid., Charles Jennings memo to Murray, July 6, 1939; ibid., J. C. S. Macgregor to E. Bushnell, July 26, 1939. On British Empire broadcasting generally, see John M. MacKenzie, "'In Touch with the Infinite': The BBC and the Empire, 1923–53," in *Imperialism and Popular Culture,* ed. John M. MacKenzie (Manchester: Manchester University Press, 1985), pp. 165–91, and Siân Nicholas, "'Brushing up Your Empire': Dominion and Colonial Propaganda on the BBC's Home Services, 1939–45," in *The British World: Diaspora, Culture and Identity,* eds C. Bridge and K. Fedorowich (London: Frank Cass, 2003), pp. 207–30.

21. A fact that seems to have been rather resented at the CBC. See BBC Written Archives Centre [hereafter cited as WAC], R49/692/1 Staff Policy: North American Representative, J. B. Clark memo "Duties of North American Representative," August 11, 1939.

22. See R. G. Swing, *"Good Evening!": A Professional Memoir by Raymond Gram Swing* (New York: Harcourt, Brace & World, 1964), Chapter 26.

23. WAC, E1/528/1, Countries: Canada: Felix Greene: Reports, 1935-6, [Felix Greene], "2. Canada," December 27, 1935, p. 8. On the debate within the BBC about the pros and cons of pro-imperial programming, see Gerard Mansell, *Let the Truth Be Told: 50 Years of BBC External Broadcasting* (London: Weidenfeld and Nicolson, 1982), p. 11.

24. On the Empire Day broadcast, see Mary Vipond, "The Mass Media in Canadian History: The Empire Day Broadcast of 1939," *Journal of the Canadian Historical Association*, New Series 14 (2003): 1–21.

25. Wheeler-Bennett, *King George VI*, p. 379.

26. This is the title of the chapter on the U.S. part of the visit in one popular history. See A. Bousfield and G. Toffoli, *Royal Spring: The Royal Tour of 1939 and the Queen Mother in Canada* (Toronto: Dundurn Press, 1989), Chapter 4. Every account of the Tour describes the large numbers of people who turned out, cheering and waving flags, for parades through city streets, brief stops at train stations, and even at stations where the Royal Train simply whistled on through. An estimated one million people lined the streets of Montréal on May 18, for example, while 4,000 francophone school children gathered at the Montreal Stadium. In Edmonton, there were 200,000; in Windsor half a million, the majority of them apparently Americans from across the river. See Lanctot, *Royal Tour*, pp. 10–11, 64, 76. The *New York Times* estimated that six million of Canada's eleven million people had "personally glimpsed" the monarchs (June 4, 1939, p. E1). On the positive press coverage in the United States, see Rhodes, "British Royal Visit," p. 205.

27. CBC Collection, vol. 749, file 18-16-2-32, part 5: E. A. Pickering to C. W. Gilchrist, telegram, ca July 11, 1939.

28. CBC Collection, vol. 242, file 11-37-14, part 1: "The Royal Tour," press release, [early April 1939].

29. See CBC Collection, vol. 748, file 18-16-2-32, part 1: Gladstone Murray to E. H. Coleman, November 14, 1938. Extensive correspondence between CBC, BBC, and American officials is scattered throughout volumes 242 and 243 especially.

30. See CBC Collection, vol. 242, file 11-37-14-2, part 1: E. Bushnell to C. Jennings, January 9, 1939.

31. Dimbleby also rode on the pilot train. On BBC unhappiness with the CBC's stonewalling on this issue, see WAC, R47/768/1, Relays: Royal Visit to Canada, file 1a, Felix Greene to [J. B. Clark?], March 7, 1939, and ibid., Greene memo to Lindsay Wellington, "King's Visit," March 10, 1939. The BBC argued that it was more appropriate to have the story told to a British audience by a British voice. For more on Dimbleby, who went on to a distinguished radio and television career announcing royal broadcasts, see Jonathan Dimbleby, *Richard Dimbleby: A Biography* (London: Hodder and Stoughton, 1975).

32. See CBC Collection, vol. 242, file 11-37-14-2, part 1: R. Bowman to Murray, November 18, 1938 and ibid., B. Nicholls cable to Murray, January 7, 1939. For the BBC's version of what happened, see WAC, R47/768/1, file 1a: Felix Greene to Lindsay Wellington, February 27, 1939, personal. Regarding the records of royal ceremonial broadcasts that the BBC lent to the CBC, see CBC Collection, vol. 242, file 11-37-14-2, part 1: J. C. S. Macgregor to R. Bowman, April 18, 1939.

33. CBS had more extensive coverage on its shortwave service.

34. Cull, *Selling War*, p. 28.

35. Anne Forbes, "Wednesday the Seventeenth," copy in CBC Collection, vol. 243, file 11-37-14-2, part 6.

36. *Public Opinion Quarterly* 4 (March 1940): 96–97.

37. *Public Opinion Quarterly* 4 (March 1940): 102.

38. MacKenzie, "'In Touch with the Infinite,'" p. 172.

39. CBC Collection, vol. 748, file 18-16-2-32, part 2, Parliamentary Committee on Radio: Notes for Evidence on Friday, March 24, 1939, "The Royal Tour," p. 1.

40. Dayan and Katz, *Media Events*, especially Chapters 1 and 2. The Tour coverage most closely corresponds to what Dayan and Katz call "Coronation" events, but it also had some characteristics, especially in the Quebec and American parts, of a "Conquest."

41. CBC Collection, vol. 748, file 18-16-2-32, part 3: Meeting of Commentators: Synopsis of Remarks of the General Manager, May 11, 1939.

42. CBC Collection, vol. 749, file 18-16-2-32, part 5: Extracts from Letters of Listeners, July 3, 1939, p. 3.

43. Ibid., p. 10.

44. Ibid., p. 12.

45. Ibid., p. 21.

46. CBC Collection, vol. 748, file 18-16-2-32, part 4: Editorial, "Congratulations to the CBC," from *Weekly Market News*, June 22, 1939.

TRANSPORTER LE CANADA À L'ÉTRANGER

21

Les militaires canadiens à travers le monde, de 1945 à 1975

Jean Martin, Direction de l'histoire et du patrimoine, ministère de la Défense nationale, Ottawa

Résumé

Depuis son engagement au service du maintien de la paix, au lendemain de la Seconde Guerre mondiale, le Canada a envoyé au-delà de 100 000 de ses citoyens dans tous les coins du monde pour participer à des opérations militaires diverses. En transportant ces Canadiens et ces Canadiennes à l'étranger, c'est un peu aussi le Canada qu'il fallait transporter avec eux pour que leur exil temporaire reste supportable et qu'ils ne se sentent pas abandonnés par les leurs. Il était donc nécessaire d'établir, sur place, une sorte d'extension des réseaux de communication canadiens. Ces réseaux s'élaboraient autour des services de transport, de courrier et de communications électroniques mis à la disposition des troupes déployées à l'étranger, pendant les premières opérations d'envergure que le Canada a menées en Corée (1951-1953), en Europe (OTAN, 1951-1993), en Égypte (FUNU 1, 1956-1967), au Congo (ONUC, 1960-1964), à Chypre (UNFICYP, 1964-1993) et ailleurs.

Abstract

Since it began engaging in peacekeeping activities following the Second World War, Canada has sent more than 100,000 of its men and women to participate in military operations in all corners of the world. As these Canadians travel to other countries, they try to take a bit of Canada along with them, helping to ensure that their temporary exile remains bearable, and that they don't feel completely cut off from their loved ones. To assist in this process, it became necessary to establish an extension of Canadian communications networks in these foreign locations. These networks grew up around existing transportation, mail, and electronic communications services. They were then placed at the disposal of troops deployed overseas during major peacekeeping operations, which have taken Canadians

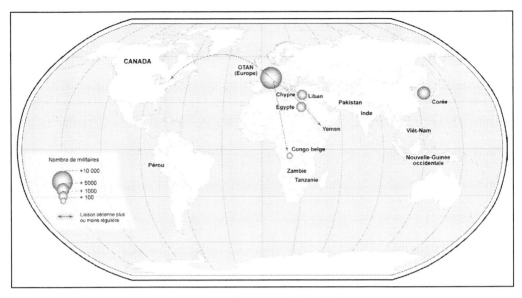

Figure 21.1 Les grands déploiements militaires canadiens entre 1950 et 1970.
Carte d'Andrée Héroux.

to Korea (NATO 1951–1953), Europe (1951–1993), Egypt (FUNU 1, 1956–1967), the Congo (ONUC, 1960–1964), Cyprus (UNFICYP, 1964–1993) and elsewhere.

Introduction

Les problèmes liés au déploiement de contingents militaires loin de leur pays d'origine sont nombreux. Il faut, bien sûr, les transporter sur place avec tout leur équipement, les loger et assurer leur ravitaillement, des obligations qui exigent la mise en place d'un réseau de transport complexe, mais il faut faire davantage encore. Les militaires canadiens qui s'engagent au service de leur pays le font sur la base d'un engagement réciproque de la part de leur gouvernement, qui devra déployer les efforts nécessaires pour atténuer le plus possible les effets de l'éloignement. On s'efforcera donc de recréer, sur les lieux du déploiement, un environnement qui s'approche le plus possible de celui auquel les militaires sont habitués au pays, un petit morceau de Canada à l'étranger.

L'importance de cet effort se reflète dans la proportion du personnel de soutien affecté aux armées, qui est aujourd'hui beaucoup plus nombreux que les troupes combattantes. Toutes ces unités de soutien ne sont pas employées au transport ou aux communications, mais ces fonctions occupent une forte proportion du personnel et des efforts militaires. On peut répartir le déploiement d'une force militaire à l'étranger en quatre étapes : 1- son recrutement (ou sa sélection) et son entraînement; 2- son transport vers la zone d'opération; 3- son équipement et son déploiement sur le terrain; 4- son approvisionnement et le maintien de ses communications internes et externes. Ce sont les trois dernières étapes qui seront plus particulièrement examinées dans les pages qui suivent.

Le transport vers le théâtre d'opération exige des moyens particulièrement importants qui doivent souvent être trouvés à l'extérieur des ressources militaires normales et même parfois à l'extérieur du pays. La nécessité de réagir rapidement aux crises qui éclatent fait en sorte qu'on aura de plus en plus recours à l'avion après la Seconde Guerre mondiale, mais les pièces d'équipement les plus lourds devront encore souvent être expédiées par voie maritime. Assurer l'approvisionnement et maintenir des communications régulières avec la force, après son déploiement, supposent qu'on pourra ensuite compter sur un réseau d'équipements, de personnel et de relais qui s'étendra souvent dans plusieurs pays et parfois même sur plus d'un continent. Le Canada a dû mettre en place et maintenir de tels réseaux au cours des soixante dernières années, en collaboration avec ses alliés et les autres participants des grandes opérations internationales. L'organisation actuelle est l'héritière directe des mesures qui ont été prises au sortir de la Seconde Guerre mondiale alors que le Canada commençait à définir son rôle sur le nouvel échiquier mondial.

La situation au sortir de la Seconde Guerre mondiale

Le Canada a transporté 368 000 de ses citoyens vers les théâtres d'opération européens et asiatiques, entre 1939 et 1945.[1] Pendant quatre ans, il a dû maintenir d'importantes bases en Grande-Bretagne avant de pouvoir transporter ses troupes sur le continent, avec tout le matériel et l'équipement nécessaires pour l'établissement de bases mobiles en Italie, en France, en Hollande et en Allemagne. Pour ce faire, le Canada avait dû s'équiper de navires, d'avions, d'armes et de matériel de toutes sortes. Les forces armées du Canada, qui comptaient à peine 5 000 membres permanents en 1939, disposaient, à la fin du conflit, en plus d'une armée de 250 000 hommes et d'une puissante aviation, de la quatrième marine de guerre du monde.[2] La Marine royale du Canada avait même fait l'acquisition, en 1946, de son premier porte-avions, le NCSM *Magnificent*.[3]

C'est sur des navires qu'on fit traverser l'Atlantique aux hommes et au matériel pendant la Seconde Guerre mondiale, des paquebots surtout, une soixantaine, de toutes les tailles. Naviguant souvent en convois, ces transports ont effectué quelque 300 traversées entre le 4 novembre 1939 et le 8 mai 1945, partant la plupart du temps de Halifax pour accoster dans l'un des ports de la Clyde, en Écosse, ou encore à Liverpool. Les soldats canadiens durent aussi parfois se rendre à New York pour embarquer sur les mêmes navires que leurs collègues américains, à partir de 1942, et effectuer ensuite la traversée sans escorte navale. La chance a cependant voulu qu'un seul transport de troupes canadien soit coulé par l'ennemi, durant toute la guerre, le petit *Nerissa*, torpillé au large de l'Irlande, au mois d'avril 1941, entraînant la mort de 73 militaires canadiens. On notera au passage que, malgré des pertes totalisant 44 000 morts, pendant le conflit, le Canada rapatria, après la guerre, un plus grand nombre de citoyens qu'il n'en avait expédié à l'étranger. En raison des nombreux mariages contractés par les militaires canadiens outre-mer, surtout en Grande-Bretagne, un phénomène qu'on ne retrouvera plus dans les engagements qui suivront, plus de 40 000 épouses et 20 000 enfants furent ramenés au Canada entre 1942 et 1948.[4]

Pendant quatre ans, les militaires canadiens s'étaient entassés dans leurs bases anglaises en attendant de pouvoir entrer en action.[5] Les bases canadiennes à l'étranger étaient déjà, dans la mesure du possible, des petits morceaux de Canada, mais les communications n'étaient pas ce qu'elles seront quinze ou vingt ans plus tard, au moment des opérations d'Égypte et de Chypre, et la priorité allait au transport des approvisionnements essentiels.

Le Quartier général militaire à Londres avait mis sur pied, en Angleterre, tous les services habituels de santé, de communications, de transport et de logistique pour soutenir les activités de ses unités. Les grandes organisations bénévoles avaient été mises à contribution dès le début de la guerre pour aider à meubler les loisirs et veiller au bien-être de la troupe.[6] On organisait des cours, on présentait des causeries, des films et des spectacles; les sports étaient toujours populaires et les Chevaliers de Colomb se faisaient hôteliers pour accueillir les soldats en permission dans les grandes villes. On ne vivait tout de même pas en vase clos dans les camps canadiens et les contacts avec la population civile britannique compensaient pour les communications difficiles avec le Canada.

Les choses changèrent brusquement, une fois la paix rétablie. Le Canada maintint pendant quelques mois une petite force d'occupation en Allemagne, mais l'armée canadienne comptait très peu de militaires de carrière et la grande majorité des soldats n'aspiraient qu'à rendre l'uniforme pour retourner le plus rapidement possible à la vie civile. Les navires et les avions furent envoyés par centaines à la ferraille, les forces d'occupation rentrèrent au pays et le Canada se prépara à revenir à une modeste force militaire de temps de paix. Pas pour longtemps. La guerre froide avait commencé à établir ses règles avant même que les combats ne prennent fin et la crainte d'un nouveau conflit ouvert augmenta dès la fin des années 1940. Les puissances occidentales se regroupèrent en 1949 à l'intérieur de l'Organisation du Traité de l'Atlantique Nord (OTAN) pour faire face au bloc communiste et le Canada décida de s'y engager fermement. L'Organisation des Nations Unies avait été créée en 1945 pour « préserver les générations futures du fléau de la guerre qui, deux fois en l'espace d'une vie humaine, a infligé à l'humanité d'indicibles souffrances » et « créer les conditions nécessaires au maintien de la justice et du respect des obligations nées des traités et autres sources du droit international[7] », mais son fonctionnement avait tout de suite été handicapé par l'opposition entre les deux blocs. Soumis au veto des grandes puissances, son Conseil de sécurité n'arrivait pas à jouer le rôle qui aurait dû être le sien. N'empêche, l'ONU allait lancer, au cours des années 1950, une série d'opérations qui allaient définir et affirmer l'idée du maintien de la paix international.

Le passage à l'armée de métier

Les cendres étaient retombées depuis à peine cinq ans sur Nagasaki et Hiroshima que le Canada repartait faire la guerre en Extrême-Orient. Déclenchée comme une « opération de police » autorisée par l'ONU, la guerre de Corée allait faire rage de juillet 1950 à juillet 1953. Le Canada allait y engager, en plus de plusieurs bâtiments de guerre, une brigade dont les dernières unités ne reviendraient au pays qu'au début de l'été 1957. Plus de 20 000 Canadiens allaient servir en Corée ou au Japon, la base arrière principale, pendant cette période.[8] La force spéciale de 5 000 hommes mise sur pied par le gouvernement canadien, au mois d'août 1950, était constituée de vétérans de la Seconde Guerre mondiale, de réservistes et de recrues sans expérience militaire. L'opération de Corée avait été placée sous la direction des États-Unis et c'est à partir des États-Unis, sur des transports américains, que les troupes canadiennes allaient effectuer leur traversée du Pacifique.

Figure 21.2 L'avion long-courrier Yukon, construit spécialement pour les Forces canadiennes et dont les douze unités transportèrent le courrier, les militaires, leurs familles et leur équipement partout à travers le monde pendant les années 1960.

Photo, MDN, Direction de l'histoire et du patrimoine, dossier Yukon.

Regroupées à Fort Lewis, dans l'État de Washington, elles s'embarquèrent sur de vieux Liberty Ships, dans le port de Seattle, pour une traversée d'une vingtaine de jours.[9]

La guerre froide ne se menait cependant pas que sur un seul front et, en même temps que le Canada se trouvait entraîné dans la lutte contre les communistes coréens, les engagements qu'il avait pris en tant que membre de la nouvelle Organisation du Traité de l'Atlantique Nord l'amenaient à renvoyer des troupes en Europe, à peine quatre ans après son retrait des forces d'occupation de l'Allemagne. La 27e Brigade canadienne d'infanterie établit ses quartiers dans la région de Hambourg, à la fin de 1951, pendant que la 1re Division aérienne de l'Aviation royale du Canada (ARC) installait ses huit escadrilles de chasse dans les bases françaises de Marville et de Grostenquin, et dans celles de Zweibrücken et Baden-Soellingen, en Allemagne. Au début des années 1950, le Canada avait environ 20 000 militaires déployés à l'étranger, incluant les quelque 5 000 qui se trouvaient en Corée; c'était quatre fois plus que l'ensemble des forces permanentes du pays à la veille de la Seconde Guerre mondiale.

Contrairement aux centaines de milliers de Canadiens qui avaient été envoyés au front entre 1939 et 1945, ces 20 000 expatriés étaient, pour la grande majorité d'entre eux, des militaires de carrière. Alors que les soldats de 1940 étaient surtout des civils qui avaient accepté de porter l'uniforme, le temps d'une guerre, et qui n'aspiraient qu'à retrouver la vie civile, une fois cette guerre gagnée, les membres de la 27e Brigade d'infanterie et de la 1re Division aérienne s'étaient enrôlés pour faire carrière dans les Forces canadiennes et leur engagement à long terme supposait qu'on leur fournisse des services sur une base plus permanente. Les bases européennes n'étaient plus de simples camps de cantonnement, c'étaient de véritables communautés possédant leurs écoles, leurs magasins et des services de toutes sortes. On ne pouvait pas demander aux familles qui étaient allées rejoindre les militaires en Europe de vivre dans les conditions qu'on impose généralement aux soldats en campagne ou en garnison. Ces familles devaient pouvoir communiquer avec leurs parents et leurs amis restés au pays; ils devaient aussi pouvoir voyager régulièrement entre le Canada et leur milieu de vie temporaire.

Le Corps postal canadien, qui avait été dissous après la guerre, fut réactivé à la fin de 1950 et le Bureau de poste numéro 1 fut aussitôt ouvert à la base de Jericho Beach, à Vancouver, pour s'occuper de l'expédition de tout le courrier à destination de l'Extrême-Orient.[10] De l'autre côté du Pacifique, un bureau de poste central fut d'abord établi à Pusan, en Corée, avant d'être déplacé vers Kure, dans le Sud du Japon. En Europe, le Corps postal canadien établit d'abord le centre de ses activités à Londres, avec des bureaux de poste dans toutes les bases allemandes et françaises qui accueillaient des Canadiens. Le courrier arrivait du bureau de poste central pour l'Est du Canada, qui se trouvait à l'aéroport de Dorval, à Montréal. Les terminus européen et canadien furent ensuite transférés respectivement à Marville, pour l'Europe, et à Trenton, en Ontario.

Le courrier, comme les passagers, était dorénavant acheminé par avion, dans les North Star de l'ARC. Le trafic prit une telle ampleur que les Forces canadiennes inaugurèrent, en 1962, des vols réguliers, à raison de six par semaine, entre Trenton et Marville, avec leurs nouveaux appareils Yukon CC-106, capables de transporter 135 passagers et construits spécialement pour elles par Canadair. Les douze Yukon furent remplacés en 1970 par cinq Boeing 707 (CC-137, dans les Forces canadiennes) de 170 places, qui devaient rester en service jusqu'à l'arrivée des actuels Polaris CC-150 (Airbus A-310), au milieu des années 1990. Les Forces canadiennes ont maintenu, avec ces appareils, des services équivalents à ceux d'une compagnie aérienne internationale pour soutenir leurs nombreux déploiements à travers le monde pendant toutes ces années.

Les premières opérations de maintien de la paix

Lorsque l'ONU créa, au mois de novembre 1956, sa première Force d'urgence des Nations Unies (FUNU) pour répondre à la crise engendrée par l'invasion combinée de l'Égypte par les forces israéliennes et franco-britanniques, le Canada, comme les neuf autres pays qui contribuèrent à la force, se trouvait devant un nouveau type de déploiement.[11] Composé de membres des forces régulières, comme pour les unités stationnées en Europe dans le cadre de l'OTAN, le contingent canadien de la FUNU se trouvait cependant engagé dans une mission d'urgence dont la durée restait indéterminée. Son déploiement devait se faire rapidement, mais son casernement et l'organisation de sa vie sur place devaient avoir un certain caractère de permanence que n'avaient pas ceux des troupes cantonnées en Grande-Bretagne pendant la guerre, en attente de traverser pour engager le combat sur le continent. Il y avait déjà eu des militaires canadiens envoyés, en nombre beaucoup plus restreint, vers d'autres parties du monde, dans le cadre de missions de l'ONU, mais la FUNU, par ses objectifs et son ampleur, était la première mission dont la logistique et le cadre d'opération en faisaient une sorte d'hybride entre l'armée envoyée combattre outre-mer pendant la Seconde Guerre mondiale et les troupes installées en garnison pour l'OTAN en Europe depuis quelques années.

Le transport du millier de soldats canadiens qui allaient faire partie de la force posa quelques difficultés. L'urgence exigeait qu'on achemine le personnel le plus rapidement possible par la voie des airs, mais la masse de l'équipement ne pouvait pas être transportée par avion et on fit appel au porte-avions NCSM *Magnificent,* qu'on adapta rapidement pour le transport des troupes et du matériel. Le personnel d'état-major et de soutien s'envola vers l'Italie à partir du 12 novembre 1956, une semaine seulement après la création de la FUNU et l'engagement du Canada d'en faire partie, mais il dut attendre jusqu'au 24 avant d'être transporté vers Abu Suweir, en Égypte. Le *Magnificent* se trouvait au port de Halifax, prêt à prendre la mer dès le 18 novembre avec, à son bord, le 1er Bataillon des Queen's Own Rifles of Canada, choisi afin de composer le gros des troupes canadiennes sur le terrain. Les autorités égyptiennes refusèrent toutefois cette partie de la contribution canadienne et les QORs, qui avaient voyagé de Calgary à Halifax pour embarquer sur le *Magnificent,* durent s'en retourner chez eux pour laisser la place à un escadron de reconnaissance qui ne put finalement s'embarquer qu'au début de 1957.[12]

La FUNU obtint la permission d'utiliser la base de Capodichino, près de Naples, où une unité de transport de l'ARC vint s'installer, le 22 novembre, avec cinq North Star et quatre Boxcar CC-119, pour instaurer un pont aérien et assurer les liaisons entre l'Égypte et le Canada.[13] Le vol transatlantique allait de Dorval à Gander, puis aux Açores et à Gibraltar, pour aboutir finalement à Capodichino, une affaire d'une trentaine d'heures. Le transport de l'Italie vers l'Égypte se fit rapidement à partir du 24 novembre, de sorte que 300 Canadiens se trouvaient déjà en Égypte le 7 décembre. Lorsque le *Magnificent* fit son entrée à Port-Saïd, le 11 janvier 1957, transportant 406 soldats, 233 véhicules, quatre avions Otter, deux hélicoptères et quelques centaines de tonnes de matériel divers, le Canada avait déjà quelque 800 soldats en Égypte, auxquels il fallait ajouter 275 membres de l'ARC. L'arrivée du 56e Escadron de reconnaissance, au début de mars, porta le total à quelque 1 200 militaires. Même si le Canada n'était plus engagé dans une guerre depuis la fin des combats en Corée, en 1953, plus de 13 600 militaires canadiens se trouvaient toujours déployés à l'étranger au printemps 1957.

Dans une situation d'urgence comme celle de l'Égypte, en 1956, les troupes ne sont pas encore tout à fait installées qu'il faut déjà planifier leur rapatriement en cas de besoin. Le ministère de la Défense nationale commença à élaborer des plans en ce sens dès le début de 1957, mais le commandant canadien de la FUNU, le lieutenant-général E. L. M. Burns, refusa de prendre en compte tout plan de retrait parce qu'il « considered that discussion of plans for withdrawal would seriously prejudice the position of the force vis-à-vis Egypt or Israel ». Les planificateurs canadiens durent par conséquent s'activer pour élaborer un plan d'évacuation dès que le général Burns eut cédé sa place au général indien P. S. Gyani, à la fin de 1959[14]. Le plan prévoyait, entre autres, qu'on utiliserait les avions de l'ARC basés dans la région pour évacuer le contingent canadien en cas de « désintégration » de la FUNU, l'île de Chypre pouvant être utilisée comme base de repli.

Lorsque la crise éclata au Congo belge, à l'été 1960, l'ONU y dépêcha sa plus importante force de maintien de la paix, qui atteignit un sommet de 20 000 soldats provenant de 35 pays, dont le Canada[15]. L'engagement du Canada se manifesta justement surtout dans le domaine des transports et des communications. Les deux avions CC-119, fournis pour aider au transport à l'intérieur du pays, ont convoyé quelque 170 tonnes de marchandises, en plus d'une centaine de passagers, pendant la deuxième moitié de 1960.[16] L'ARC effectua aussi des vols réguliers avec ses longs-courriers North Star, puis ses Yukon, entre la base italienne de Pise et Léopoldville, au Congo : 2 000 tonnes de marchandises et 12 000 passagers sur près de 400 vols en quatre ans. Au sol, le 57e Escadron des communications canadien fournissait l'essentiel des communications électroniques aux forces de l'ONU : lignes téléphoniques, stations radio à travers tout le pays, etc.

Le Canada s'engagea à nouveau massivement dans une opération de l'ONU en 1964, pour une période qui, croyait-on, n'allait pas dépasser trois mois, mais qui s'est finalement étirée sur près de 30 ans. La participation canadienne à la Force des Nations Unies à Chypre prit la forme d'un bataillon d'infanterie chargé de s'interposer entre les forces grecques et turques dans le but de faire respecter le fragile cessez-le-feu intervenu entre les deux parties. Les 1 100 militaires canadiens furent rapidement transportés par avion jusqu'à Nicosie, le matériel lourd les rejoignant deux semaines plus tard, à bord du porte-avions NCSM *Bonaventure*, qui avait remplacé le *Magnificent* en 1957. Pendant ce déploiement initial, les avions Hercule et Yukon de l'ARC effectuèrent 28 vols en un peu plus d'une semaine entre Trenton et Chypre, transportant 400 tonnes d'équipement, en plus des 1 100 soldats du contingent canadien.

Presque au même moment, le Canada expédiait un avion Caribou au Pakistan pour soutenir l'effort que l'ONU y menait depuis plusieurs années dans le but d'empêcher le déclenchement d'une guerre entre ce pays et l'Inde (Groupe d'observateurs militaires des Nations Unies dans l'Inde et le Pakistan – UNMOGIP). Lorsqu'une nouvelle mission (Mission d'observation des Nations Unies pour l'Inde et le Pakistan – UNIPOM) fut mise sur pied pour surveiller le cessez-le-feu intervenu après les combats de septembre 1965, trois Otter et deux autres Caribou allèrent rejoindre le premier appareil pour constituer la 117e Unité de transport aérien. Pendant les six mois que dura l'UNIPOM, les six avions canadiens totalisèrent plus de 1 600 heures de vol au-dessus de la zone frontalière entre l'Inde et le Pakistan.

Plus de 25 000 Canadiens sont passés à Chypre depuis le déploiement initial, en mars 1964, jusqu'à la dernière rotation, à l'été 1993. Ce sont donc 59 rotations de six mois chacune, au terme desquelles il fallait transporter entre 600 et 1 000 nouveaux soldats vers l'île de la Méditerranée et ramener au Canada ceux qui y terminaient leur service, sans compter les vols de soutien réguliers. Dorval, près de Montréal, était le centre de tout ce trafic aérien vers l'Europe, le Proche-Orient, l'Extrême-Orient et l'Afrique, jusqu'à ce que le Commandement des transports aériens (CTA) soit transféré à la base de Trenton, où il se trouve toujours[17]. En 1966, par exemple, le CTA avait des unités basées à Marville, en France, à Düsseldorf, en Allemagne, à Srinagar et à Rawalpindi, au Pakistan, et à El Arish, en Égypte[18]. Ses 197 appareils avaient totalisé plus de 100 000 heures de vol et fait régulièrement escale dans des aéroports aussi éloignés que Gatwick (Angleterre), Beyrouth (Liban), Nicosie (Chypre) ou Pise (Italie). Pendant les années 1960 et 1970, d'autres opérations, plus ou moins longues, furent lancées vers le Congo, la Zambie, le Pérou, le Vietnam et la Nouvelle-Guinée occidentale.

Les risques étaient souvent élevés pendant ces missions et les tragédies ne pouvaient pas toujours être évitées. La pire s'est sans doute produite le 9 août 1974, lorsqu'un avion Buffalo de la 116e Unité de transport aérien, installée depuis quelques mois seulement dans la zone du canal de Suez, fut abattu par un tir de missile pendant un vol de routine entre Beyrouth, au Liban, et Damas, en Syrie. Les neuf militaires canadiens qui se trouvaient à bord furent tués. Les unités de transport aérien basées au Proche-Orient entre 1957 et la fin des années 1970, la 114e, la 115e, la 116e et la 134e, agissaient comme une véritable ligne aérienne entre les diverses zones d'opération des nombreuses missions auxquelles le Canada participait dans la région : l'Égypte, pour les FUNU 1 et 2; Chypre, pour l'UNFYCIP; le Yemen, pour l'UNYOM; le Liban, pour l'UNOGIL, et la Syrie, pour l'UNDOF, avec Israël qui se trouvait associé à plusieurs de ces opérations.

Maintenir le contact

Pendant toute cette période, c'est la poste qui restait le moyen privilégié pour permettre aux militaires canadiens de demeurer en contact avec leurs proches restés au pays. Pendant la Seconde Guerre mondiale, la poste était pratiquement le seul moyen disponible pour les communications transatlantiques, et les statistiques de la censure, qui devait inspecter chaque envoi, donnent une bonne idée de sa popularité auprès des troupes : Claude Beauregard évalue à 70 000 lettres par semaine le volume du courrier expédié par les soldats canadiens stationnés en Grande-Bretagne au milieu de la guerre[19]. Sur le front, chaque unité avait son bureau de poste de campagne qui apportait le courrier deux fois par jour aux soldats, en même temps que les rations.

La situation n'avait guère changé pendant la guerre de Corée, mais les communications électroniques prirent de plus en plus d'importance avec l'installation des forces de garnison en Europe et les opérations de maintien de la paix au cours des années 1960 et 1970. Les lignes téléphoniques installées par les unités des communications canadiennes en Égypte ou à Chypre ne permettaient pas aux soldats de communiquer directement avec le Canada, mais on s'assurait à tout le moins que les nouvelles du pays parviendraient rapidement aux soldats en poste dans ces régions éloignées. Les films d'information voyageaient à bord des vols réguliers du Canada à destination de l'Europe, puis du Proche-Orient. À l'aide de la radio à ondes courtes, on pouvait même suivre le match de la coupe Grey ou la finale de la coupe Stanley. Des lignes de communication étaient naturellement établies entre le quartier général de la mission et celui de l'ONU, à New York, tout comme entre les contingents nationaux et leur capitale nationale, mais elles étaient réservées aux opérations militaires et ne pouvaient pas servir à contacter les familles. Pour les communications personnelles, le contingent canadien de la FUNU obtint des autorités égyptiennes l'autorisation d'établir une station de radio à ondes courtes intégrée au réseau canadien[20]. Par l'intermédiaire d'une autre station située au Canada, on pouvait ainsi se mettre en contact avec le réseau téléphonique canadien et effectuer des appels à travers tout le pays.

Des arrangements postaux furent pris dès les premiers jours de la FUNU. Le service postal devait être assuré par une unité du Corps postal royal canadien, censé offrir aux militaires l'expédition gratuite des lettres, une mesure qui se répétera dans la plupart des opérations de maintien de la paix qui suivront. Le bureau de poste principal pour la

FUNU fut d'abord installé à Naples, en Italie, puis on en établit un nouveau à Rafah, dans la bande de Gaza, en avril 1957. Le bureau de poste central de Naples fut transféré à Beyrouth, en mars 1958, afin de servir de point de transfert pour le courrier de toutes les missions de la région : la FUNU, l'Organisme des Nations Unies chargé de la surveillance de la trêve (ONUST) et bientôt le Groupe d'observation des Nations Unies au Liban (GONUL). Les déploiements se multipliant, le Corps postal royal canadien se retrouva, à la fin de 1964, avec 125 de ses membres servant à l'étranger dans des bureaux de poste militaires[21]. Un service postal régulier restera toujours l'un des éléments essentiels de l'organisation de tout déploiement à l'étranger.

L'autre élément essentiel, pour transporter les troupes, mais aussi leur ravitaillement, les films, les journaux, les revues et les informations de toutes sortes qui les gardaient en contact avec le pays, tout autant que les sacs de courriers, c'était un service de transport aérien efficace. Il fallait des avions, mais aussi des aéroports qui puissent servir d'escales, et du personnel pour former les unités qui devaient s'établir dans chacun de ces aéroports. Entre sa mise en alerte pour servir d'appui aux opérations de Corée, en juillet 1950, et son retour à Dorval, au début de juin 1953, les avions de l'Escadrille de transport 426 effectuèrent 599 traversées du Pacifique[22]. Au cours des deux décennies suivantes, les appareils de l'ARC, puis ceux des Forces canadiennes, furent engagés dans des déploiements de troupes et de matériels vers l'Égypte, le Congo, Chypre, la Nouvelle-Guinée et le Vietnam, en plus d'assurer les liaisons régulières entre le Canada et les quelque 14 000 militaires déployés chaque année en moyenne à travers le monde.

Conclusion

Il n'y a plus aujourd'hui (2005) que 1 400 militaires canadiens à l'extérieur du pays, quatorze fois moins qu'en 1954, mais la logistique des opérations est devenue de plus en plus complexe et il faut toujours déployer d'importants efforts pour transporter les militaires et maintenir les contacts pendant les missions. Les progrès de l'électronique ont permis au téléphone et à Internet de prendre le dessus sur le courrier conventionnel, qui continue malgré tout de jouer un rôle essentiel dans les communications des militaires canadiens[23]. Les North Star, Yukon, Boeing, Boxcar et Caribou du passé ont cédé la place au Polaris et au Hercule, mais les diverses unités de la 8ᵉ Escadre aérienne de Trenton maintiennent toujours le lien vital entre le Canada et le personnel militaire en poste à l'étranger.

Le militaire qui part aujourd'hui rejoindre l'Opération Athéna monte à bord de l'un des cinq Polaris CC-150 de l'Escadron 437 pour un vol transatlantique, dont le confort se compare à celui des grandes lignes aériennes internationales. Une fois à Kaboul, les communications satellites lui permettront de regarder en direct, en tenant compte du décalage de huit heures et demie avec l'Est du Canada, les émissions de Radio-Canada ou du Réseau des Sports. Dans ses temps libres, il pourra utiliser l'un des postes Internet ou des appareils téléphoniques mis à sa disposition pour communiquer avec les membres de sa famille ou ses amis. Le soir du 23 juin 2004, on a pu voir les soldats québécois du Royal 22ᵉ Régiment célébrer la Saint-Jean-Baptiste dans l'un des mess du Camp Julien, la principale base canadienne à Kaboul : le Canada transporté au cœur de l'Afghanistan.

Ce même militaire avait cependant dû quitter le confort du Polaris pour effectuer la dernière partie du trajet vers Kaboul à bord d'un Hercule CC-130, se faire secouer pendant quatre heures et demie, attaché aux sangles qui font office de sièges, des bouchons enfoncés dans les oreilles afin de se protéger un peu du bruit assourdissant des moteurs, le casque sur la tête et la lourde veste anti-fragmentation sur le dos; et il lui avait en plus fallu avoir l'estomac solide pour résister aux brusques décrochages, aux virages serrés et aux ascensions rapides imposés par l'atterrissage tactique sur l'aéroport de Kaboul[24]. Bien sûr, il pourra profiter de ses temps libres pour contacter ses proches via Internet pendant son séjour à Kaboul, à condition de s'assurer de bien refermer derrière lui la porte de la salle des ordinateurs pour ne pas y laisser pénétrer la fine poussière qui s'infiltre partout. C'est vrai aussi qu'il pourra célébrer la Saint-Jean-Baptiste ou la Fête du Canada avec ses camarades en buvant une ou deux Molson Export ou Labatt Bleue, mais il lui sera formellement interdit d'en prendre une troisième, et il ne saurait être question, pour lui ni de lancer des feux d'artifice ni d'allumer un feu de joie[25]. Les célébrations devront se faire derrière des portes closes et à des milliers de kilomètres de la plupart des gens qu'il aime.

Notes

1. C. P. Stacey. *Six années de guerre. L'armée au Canada, en Grande-Bretagne et dans le Pacifique*, Ottawa, ministère de la Défense nationale, 1966, pp. 195-196.
2. Après le désarmement de l'Allemagne et du Japon, en 1945, la puissance navale du monde se trouvait majoritairement concentrée dans les forces des États-Unis, de la Grande-Bretagne, de l'Union soviétique et du Canada.
3. La Marine royale du Canada avait déjà utilisé le HMS *Nabob* et le HMS *Punch,* deux porte-avions de la Royal Navy britannique, pendant la guerre.
4. C. P. Stacey, *op.cit.*, p. 442.
5. À l'exception des expéditions malheureuses de Dieppe et de Hong Kong, et de quelques autres actions mineures, les soldats canadiens n'ont guère eu à combattre avant l'invasion de l'Italie, à l'été de 1943.
6. Le gouvernement avait mobilisé, dès le mois de novembre 1939, l'Armée du Salut, les Chevaliers de Colomb, le YMCA et la Légion canadienne.
7. Préambule de la Charte de l'ONU.
8. Voir *Le Canada et la guerre de Corée*, Montréal, Art Global, et Ottawa, Direction de l'histoire et du patrimoine du ministère de la Défense nationale, 2002.
9. Les États-Unis construisirent plus de 2 500 Liberty Ships pendant la Seconde Guerre mondiale. Assemblés à partir d'éléments préfabriqués pour répondre à la situation d'urgence, les Liberty Ships pouvaient être complétés en environ deux mois.
10. W. J. Bailey et E. R. Toop. *The Canadian Military Posts* Vol. 3: *Operations in NATO, United Nations and Canada, 1947-1989,* [s. l.], Edward B. Proud, 1990, pp. 21-30.
11. Les autres pays qui se sont engagés aux côtés du Canada pour faire partie de la FUNU étaient le Brésil, la Colombie, le Danemark, la Finlande, l'Inde, l'Indonésie, la Norvège, la Suède et la Yougoslavie.

12. Les Égyptiens refusèrent la première offre de contribution du Canada en faisant valoir que le nom, les uniformes et tous les symboles associés aux Queen's Own Rifles étaient beaucoup trop similaires à ceux des troupes britanniques, qui venaient tout juste de les attaquer, et que la population aurait, pour cette raison, bien des difficultés à accepter les soldats canadiens comme des observateurs neutres. Le général E. L. M. Burns, commandant de la FUNU, proposa que le Canada fournisse plutôt des unités de soutien, moins visibles mais tout à fait essentielles au bon fonctionnement de la force.

13. Une fois le déploiement complété, la 114e Unité de transport aérien conserva quatre Boxcar à Capodichino, tandis que la 115e UTA se trouvait basée à El Arish, dans la bande de Gaza, avec trois Dakota (DC 3) et les quatre Otter, transportés par le *Magnificent*. Les Caribou CC-108 viendront s'ajouter dans les années 1960.

14. Document de discussion présenté par le chef d'état-major de l'armée, le lieutenant-général S. F. Clark, au Conseil des chefs d'état-major canadiens, le 2 février 1960, p. 3. DHP, 112.3M2.009 (D251).

15. La crise dans l'ancienne colonie belge du Congo éclata en 1960. Venant tout juste d'accéder sans préparation à l'indépendance, le nouveau pouvoir congolais connut rapidement de graves dissensions qui fournirent le prétexte d'une intervention des forces belges. La force d'urgence de l'Organisation des Nations Unies au Congo (ONUC) fut mise sur pied pour voir au retrait des forces belges et aider à restaurer l'ordre à l'intérieur du pays. Les casques bleus durent cependant faire face à une guerre civile provoquée par la sécession de la province du Katanga et la situation de l'ONUC se compliqua rapidement.

16. Voir, à ce sujet, Larry Miberry, dir., *Sixty Years : The RCAF and CF Air Command, 1924-1984,* Toronto, CANAV Books, pp. 327-328.

17. Le Commandement des transports aériens, transféré de Dorval à Trenton en 1959, est devenu le Groupe des transports aériens en 1975.

18. Statistiques tirées de la « Air Transport Command Commanders Annual Review 1966 » (23-02-1967), DHP, 75/501.

19. Claude Beauregard, « Guerre et censure au Canada : l'expérience des journaux, des militaires et de la population pendant la Deuxième Guerre mondiale », Québec, Université Laval, thèse de doctorat (histoire), 1995, f. 156.

20. En utilisant les lettres d'appel VE assignées aux stations canadiennes.

21. Les bureaux de postes de la FUNU, par exemple, comptaient douze membres au moment de leur formation, à la fin de 1956. Le titre « royal » fut octroyé au Corps postal à l'occasion de son cinquantenaire, en 1961. Voir Directorate of Forces Postal Services, « A History of the Royal Canadian Postal Corps », texte dactylographié, 1965, 4 f.

22. L. Milberry, *op. cit.,* p. 470.

23. Encore récemment, des militaires canadiens ayant servi outre-mer expliquaient pourquoi ils apprécient de pouvoir tirer de leur poche une lettre qu'ils peuvent relire à loisir, ce qui est impossible pour un appel téléphonique. Voir, entre autres, l'entrevue de John Willis avec Al Williams, du Corps postal royal canadien, Musée canadien de la poste, 4 avril 1995.

24. Pour ne pas offrir une cible trop facile aux éventuels tirs de roquettes ou de missiles, les avions qui atterrissent à Kaboul ou qui en décollent effectuent des manœuvres compliquées qui mettent l'estomac des passagers à rude épreuve.

25. Les militaires canadiens sont soumis à un strict rationnement quotidien de deux consommations alcoolisées lorsqu'ils sont en mission à l'étranger.

EPILOGUE

Meg Ausman, Chief Historian, United States Postal Service

Writings on North American postal history have evolved from the sweeping panoramas of McReynolds, Smith, and Scheele (who took on the world) to the more specific, richly toned and vibrantly painted historical sketches in *More than Words: Readings in Transport, Communication and the History of Postal Communication.*[1] The subject matter is so vast that thousands of pointillists dabbing away could only begin to cover the canvas. In this book, the essays encourage a new vision of other canvases, those of social, archaeological, business, and technological history, and they stimulate questions that could frame future research.

For centuries, postal administrations have transmitted the tactile—papers, pictures, packages, films, and tapes holding messages—like gentle behemoths, collecting and distributing hundreds of millions of individual items a day. In the United States, survey after survey shows that people *trust* the Postal Service. Both Canada Post and the U.S. Postal Service have linked migrant pioneers to their families back East or in the Old Country. They have connected service men and women in perilous times with those they loved and who loved them, and have delivered intergenerational greetings on birthdays, sympathy in times of trial, and sought-after information about the lives of family and friends. They also are big businesses that serve businesses, government, and people as individuals or as "the public." They have subsidized and/or relied upon all forms of transportation, the legs of the messenger. And, of course, the messages themselves give purpose to these efforts; all other activities are in service to assure the secure and quick passage of communications and goods.

Messages in the post, their transport, and their content offer layer upon layer of subjects for study and a range of study as wide as the imagination. The essays in this book have expended the depth and scope of communications research, taking it into new areas and generating new ideas for future study.

In "Instructions from Terra Nova," Brad Loewen looks at 16th-century fisheries through a different lens of communications that not so much stretches a point as it leaps to a new peak from which to view this fascinating subject. He describes the bookkeeping records and notary registers used to clarify business operations among European merchants, Terra Nova captains, and fishermen stationed at various havens—clearly a form of communication. These demonstrate the early commercial needs that triggered later postal developments: In the case of the neighbouring colony of New France, business and governmental needs constituted the bulk of postal communications. His reference to Basque captains' sophistication in commercial practices, based on the Spanish tradition of writing, brings to mind the need for further research on Spanish communications in North America, particularly in what is now the western and southwestern United States.

The challenges he may have faced in interpreting 16th-century records might have a parallel with 26th-century historians looking back 500 years. Constantly morphing technology may drown communications historians and make access to resources a challenge. Will media limit the message and further complicate the task of future historians?

Not to fear. According to Archivist Margaret Adams of the National Archives and Records Administration in Washington, D.C., the Digital Age has been here since, at least, the punch cards of the Second World War era.[2] Cautioning that electronic records should not be lumped together any more than gilded manuscripts, scripted ledgers, and printed manuals, Ms. Adams offers the comforting knowledge that the American Standard Coding II system can store coding schemes independent of software or hardware and will make data available for centuries to come.

Richard Kielbowicz's paper on postal enterprise and the free-market economy in the United States remarks that postal savings, parcel post, and a wired communication system deserve attention by more than postal historians. How true! Despite the many government documents existing and accessible on these subjects, the number of books is surprisingly minimal, given the huge amount of money spent on the post. In 2005, the U.S. Postal Service was a nearly $70 billion enterprise, and the mailing industry, a $9-billion one. In the United States, direct mail advertisers spend $52 billion a year and they generate an estimated $13 in sales for every dollar spent.[3] Yet advertising mail is a no-show in the indexes of virtually every book on the history of advertising. Business historians can take note.

They also might want to look at early and mid-19th-century postal innovations in administrative structures and centralizing resources, which may have predated, by several decades, similar practices by big business in North America.[4] There is ample room for research in this area, which has been surprisingly overlooked given the enormous "ripples" of related postal enterprises, not to mention the mail itself, on business and social life.

B. Allaire's study and description of the work of 18th-century crown officers charged with ensuring that mail was placed on ships sailing between Canada and France helps trace the growth of this cadre of specialized officials. His work creates further interest in the evolution of the quasi-postal civil servant, an official responsible for the flow of mail during this period. This French semi-official postal cadre was succeeded by an entirely new class of postal officials serving national governments. Further studies of the postal civil service in North America, beginning in the colonial era and featuring comparisons between the various services, would be of considerable interest.

Contrary to the stereotype of bureaucracy as slow and set in its ways, postal administrations have actively sought new technologies and embraced them to move mail more rapidly while holding costs down. The detail and thoroughness in Krista Cooke's paper on the development of automated mail processing systems in Canada offers a fine basis for further study on the impact of technology on the work force, international cooperation in developing and adapting postal technology, productivity models, and governmental experimentation.

Marianne Babal's essay on steamer mail to and from California during the Gold Rush, an interesting study of the challenge of handling communications during a migratory rush, conveys the drama and delight in getting letters from home. Using letters and histories rather than legislative or regulatory records, she presents another view of the synergy between government subsidies and private enterprise in promoting transportation, the same synergy that has furthered developments in science, technology, agriculture, and waterways in North American history.

For centuries, the federal governments of Canada and the U.S. have used the postal service to promote other national and public interests, e.g., subsidizing the transportation infrastructure, such as stagecoach lines and airlines; promoting public awareness of health issues; honouring heroes and leaders on stamps; and testing federal authority in the "race problem," as when President Theodore Roosevelt put federal force behind the reappointment of an African-American woman as postmaster of Indianola, Mississippi, 1902, despite some local objections.[5] Postal buildings themselves represent the national government, as Cooke points out.[6]

Stacey's portrait of the demonstration by unemployed, desperate men in the Vancouver Post Office and their eviction shows the reverse side of the coin: a national government unwilling to listen to their concerns. The demonstrators succeeded in garnering attention but not, unfortunately, the aid they sought in 1938.

During the 1930s and early 1940s, murals and sculptures depicting the histories and lives of "the people of this country by their own kind" were placed in U.S. post offices and other federal buildings, some with fairly pointed themes—a magician using a ticker tape to lure money from working people, for instance.[7] What do the behaviors and images of people permitted in federal buildings say about the federal-personal relationship? How has that relationship changed over the decades in terms of congressional or legislative mediation, union activity, and consumer expectations?

In contrast to events in 1938, the next year saw use of a public medium, the Canadian Broadcasting Corporation, to promote a national and international agenda, British-Canadian-U.S. amity and the authority of the Commonwealth. The CBC's personal strategy helped carry the charm and dignity of the King and Queen into private homes across North America.

Besides bringing the oft-neglected study of radio to the scholarly forefront, Mary Vipond describes different cultural paths to a common goal, unity in the face of an emerging enemy, Nazi Germany. The citation of Gladstone Murray's entertaining reference to the "torrential manner" of American commentators and the "awkward silences" of the British engenders a desire for even further study on communication styles.

The impacts of technology and the Digital Age on these styles have been examined but deserve more study.

Nancy Pope and John Willis show us how integral, affecting, and reflective a post office is to the life of a community—Willis through his comprehensive study of the post office-railroad-community *gestalt* on Prince Edward Island, and Pope through her moving self-examination of the sensitivities of preserving postal relics following the September 11, 2001, destruction of the World Trade Center in New York City and the nearby Church Street Station, which served the buildings. While neither may have read the Maori proverb, "Unless the heart sees, the mind will never see," both go to the heart of communities through postal research.

On Prince Edward Island, postal records help document the economic life of the community but also the point at which residents felt they not only needed a post office but the respectability one conferred. Further study of petitions for postal services, such as money orders, can trace social and economic growth. For instance, 19th-century U.S. postmasters received compensation based on a complicated formula involving stamp sales, lockbox rentals, and newspapers delivered—all indicators of business activity.

Other times, a postal artifact depicts more strongly than a thousand words the sense of community—locally, nationally, and perhaps internationally—especially in the case of items collected from the postal station that served the World Trade Center. The everyday becomes sacred and treasured, and the ordinary becomes heroic or tragic, or both.

Pope carefully depicts not only the very real physical dangers of collecting possibly contaminated artifacts but considers the feelings, ethics, and morality of presenting their history. This deeply felt essay triggers a greater awareness of the sensitivities that may be involved when using artifacts or, for other researchers, personal correspondence, for research in communications. Yet, these communications can enlighten people centuries after they were created and both humanize and immortalize their authors. They offer insights into material culture, military history, and immigrants' lives during the lifespan of the exchange of mail.

Secret codes and correspondence would pique the interest of just about anyone, but the findings and highly original work in N. Castéran's paper, "Sous le sceau du secret," must delight even the jaded. Castéran has unearthed valuable documents that shed light on the self-consciously strategic nature of the battle between France and Britain for supremacy, *inter alia*, in North America. French generals and officials were concerned with the possibility that the British might intercept their confidential military and ministerial messages, hence, their recourse to coding important messages destined for transatlantic exchange. The strategies of interception and duplicity would not surprise a reader of John Le Carré. Castéran's discoveries should encourage other researchers to explore the world of intelligence and disinformation, a practice that is still very much with us.

The essay by Ceceile Dauphin-Memteau and Daniele Poublan examines the physical act and art of writing. Songs and illustrations become texts worthy of historical exploration. While not "objective" sources, they can be primary ones. The endurance of popular songs and illustrations suggests their strength and influence upon a society. In 2005, the U.S. Postal Service issued a stamp to honor Yip Harburg, whose name might not be widely recognized but whose lyrics in "Over the Rainbow" have remained widely known and sung since 1939. The post itself has "starred" or been represented in songs, books, and films, such as, *The Postman Always Rings Twice* written by James M. Cain in 1934 and later a 1946 film noir classic, remade in 1981; "Return to Sender," sung by Elvis Presley: "P.S. I Love You" by John Lennon and Paul McCartney; and, "Please, Mr. Postman," performed by the Marvelettes in 1961 and written by a postal employee, Freddie Gorman.

Sheila McIntyre's look at handwriting as a representation of gentrified self should stimulate further study of the form of writing and letter writing during and long after the colonial period. When did individualism become accepted or prized in penmanship and expression? What do handwriting and letter writing tell us about the personality of the author?

Manon Brunet shines a bright, hot light on the activities of the l'abbé Casgrain through his correspondence with a married Irishwoman, Kate E. Godley, revealing the passion beneath intellect—a new look at the abbot whose enthusiasms were not restricted by the clerical cloak and collar. Susanne Knoblauch's approach to the correspondence of two educated German immigrants, an interdisciplinary approach using quantitative analysis and personal experience, demonstrates that new combinations of approaches can enhance studies of correspondence.

Lorraine Gadoury and Liz Turcotte searched through public archives and brought to light more evidence of the importance of letters when they added new dimensions to the life of a high-ranking civil servant (Heman Witsius Ryland through Gadoury) and the importance of mail to correspondents on the battlefield (Turcotte). Letters from the battlefield tell the story of war in a way more eloquent than any fiction writer could imagine.[8] Marguerite Sauriol uses correspondence to present a very personal biography of a dispirited Frenchman who came to conquer the Canadian West at the beginning of the 20th century. He came, he farmed, he turned around and headed back home. How many sojourners passed through the gates of Ellis Island, only to leave the island and America behind, choosing to return home, wherever home was.

Bianca Gendreau's paper on the harvesting of geese for their feathers demonstrates the need for further work on the material culture of the post. The feathers were gathered and subsequently carried to London where they were sold as writing quills in an upscale market. The traffic was a sideline to the commercial ventures of the venerable Hudson Bay Company, but it was part of the writing life nonetheless, an important tool of communications. Twenty-first century calligraphers still value the strength and clarity of quill pens.

Jean-Pierre Chrestien sheds new light on mid-18th-century transportation and the role of women in running fisheries. Jean Martin brings home the fears and challenges in transporting communications for peace-keeping expeditions in the 20th century—essential for morale. In the early 21st century, despite access to the Internet and telephone services, U.S. troops in Iraq flock to mail call, described as the "highlight of the day" by one veteran of service in Iraq. The mail brings messages and homemade snacks, all representations of love, to men and women in a perilous situation.[9]

Figure 1 Stamp commemorating Mercury, winged messenger of the gods, issued by the Canadian Post Office Department, December 4, 1930.
Library and Archives Canada, POS-000968.

Taken together, the studies in *More than Words* bring life to the histories of post, transport, and communications. They hopefully will stimulate further research and put existing historical knowledge into new perspectives. The objective of *More than Words* is to allow history and historians to come to terms with a huge topic and a grand, if often ignored, actor on the historical scene.

The path of winged Mercury, that puissant symbol of communication, can be unpredictable and global. He can alight upon any surface of the globe. His flight is swift, shrewd, adaptable, independent in spirit, and multifarious with respect to means. This adaptive figure represents the energy and power of communications, a mainstay of the human condition:

"For the mail was like the tide with a mind and momentum of its own."[10]

Notes

1. Ross Allan McReynolds, *History of the United States Post Office, 1607–1931* (Chicago, IL: University of Chicago, 1935); William Smith, *The History of the Post Office in British North American, 1639–1870* (Cambridge, England: University Press, 1920); and Carl H. Scheele, *A Short History of the Mail Service* (Washington, DC: Smithsonian Institution Press, 1970).

2. Telephone interview with Margaret O'Neill Adams, reference program manager, Custodial Electronic Records Program, Office of Electronic and Special Media Records Services Division, National Archives and Records Administration, College Park, Maryland, May 5, 2005. Adams is the author of "Three Decades of Description and Reference Services," in *30 Years of Electronic Records*, ed. Bruice I. Ambacher (Lanham Maryland and Oxford, England: Scarecrow Press, 2003), pp. 63–89.

3. Conversation with George T. Hurst, manager, Direct Mail, United States Postal Service, July 25, 2005. $22.4 billion of the $52 billion spent by direct mail advertisers annually is for postage, the reminder, for list work, paper, printing, etc.

4. Conversation with Richard John, author of *Spreading the News: The American Postal System from Franklin to Morse* (Cambridge, Massachusetts: Harvard University Press, 1995) on July 25, 2005. John cites the Railway Mail Service as an example.

5. *The New York Times*, January 3, 1903, front page.

6. For a Canadian perspective on postal geography and architecture, see: C. Amyot and J. Willis, *Country Post: Rural Postal Service in Canada, 1880–1945*, CPM Mercury no. 1 (Gatineau: Canadian Museum of Civilization, 2003), chapter two.

7. "Belief in Magic," one of twenty panels in "The Search for Truth" murals by Maurice H. Sterne in the Library of the U.S. Department of Justice, 950 Pennsylvania Avenue, N.W., Washington, D.C. The murals were completed in 1939 and installed in 1941 under a contract awarded by the Section of Fine Arts, Federal Works Agency, Public Buildings Administration, Washington, D.C.

8. United States Postal Service, *Letters from the Sand: The Letters of Desert Storm and Other Wars* (Washington, D.C.: United States Postal Service), p. viii.

9. Conversation with Jennifer Wolf, CW3, U.S. Army, July 4, 2005.

10. John Willis, "The History and Geography of the Post Office on Prince Edward Island, 1870–1914, *More than Words: Readings in Transport, Communication and the History of Postal Communication*, p. 105.

The author would like to thank Timothy Carr, former librarian, National Postal Museum, Smithsonian Institution, for his contributions.